HIGHER EDUCATION IN TRANSITION

HIGHER EDUCATION IN TRANSITION

A HISTORY OF AMERICAN COLLEGES
AND UNIVERSITIES, 1636–1976

John S. Brubacher

UNIVERSITY OF MICHIGAN

Willis Rudy

FAIRLEIGH DICKINSON UNIVERSITY

THIRD EDITION, REVISED AND ENLARGED

HARPER & ROW, PUBLISHERS
New York, Hagerstown, San Francisco, London

1817

To Our National Bicentennial

HIGHER EDUCATION IN TRANSITION (Third Edition, Revised and Enlarged). Copyright © 1958, 1968, 1976 by Harper & Row, Publishers, Inc. All rights reserved. Printed in the United States of America. No part of this book may be used or reproduced in any manner whatsoever without written permission except in the case of brief quotations embodied in critical articles and reviews. For information address Harper & Row, Publishers, Inc., 10 East 53rd Street, New York, N.Y. 10022. Published simultaneously in Canada by Fitzhenry & Whiteside Limited, Toronto.

Library of Congress Cataloging in Publication Data

Brubacher, John Seiler, 1898–
  Higher education in transition.
  Bibliography: p.
  Includes index.
  1. Education, Higher—United States—History.
2. Universities and colleges—United States—
History.   I. Rudy, Solomon Willis, 1920–   joint
author.   II. Title.
LA226.B75   1976   378.73   75–6331
ISBN 0–06–010548–8

   77 78 79 10 9 8 7 6 5 4 3 2

Contents

v

PART IV

HIGHER EDUCATION
IN THE TWENTIETH CENTURY

PART V

IN PERSPECTIVE

Preface

The authors of this book undertook its first edition because they thought historical perspective necessary for coping with the great boom in higher education expected in the second half of the twentieth century succeeding World War II. The boom did occur and lasted two decades. Then there was an arrest. In the late sixties student protest challenged much of the conventional wisdom of higher education and then in the seventies financial inflation and recession clipped the wings of expansion. As the resulting slowdown coincides with the advent of our national bicentennial, the present seems an appropriate occasion to take time for incorporating the events of the recent past into our evolving historical perspective. Hence this third edition of *Higher Education in Transition*.

It may be said that the events of the decades just past are still too near us to afford a true perspective. No doubt the passage of time will improve our perspective but there is also something to be said for capturing the freshness of impression which recency affords. As we go into the third century of our national existence and as we try to diagnose and prescribe therapies for new problems in higher education, it is always well to keep the latter's clinical record up to date.

J. S. B.
W. R.

PART I

THE COLONIAL COLLEGE

1

Beginnings

Higher education in the United States has been molded and influenced by a variety of historical forces. On one hand, there are the patterns and traditions of higher learning which have been brought over from Western Europe. On the other, we find the native American conditions which have affected and modified the development of these transplanted institutions. Out of the interaction of these two essential elements and, most important, out of the growth of democracy in every area of American life, has developed a truly unique system of higher education.

English Influences

Oxford and Cambridge furnished the original model which the colonial colleges sought to copy. The prototype for the first English-American college was Emmanuel College, Cambridge University.[1] As we read the explicit statements left by Harvard's founders, we find that the earliest Harvard College statutes were taken directly from the Elizabethan statutes of the University of Cambridge; that the phrase *pro modo Academiarum in Anglia* ("according to the manner of universities in England") is to be found in the first Harvard degree formula; that early Harvard, like Elizabethan Cambridge, welcomed "fellow commoners" as well as serious degree students, "gentlemen" who paid double tuition for the privilege of residing in the college and dining with the Fellows; that even the names of the four college classes—freshmen, sophomore, junior sophister, and senior sophister—were borrowed directly from England.[2] In other points involving student discipline, curriculum, administrative regulations, and degree requirements, Harvard followed English college precedents as closely and faithfully as she could; and Harvard, in turn, became the great prototype for all the later colleges of English America.

As late as the middle of the eighteenth century, President Clap of Yale prepared himself for his administrative duties by borrowing histories of Oxford and Cambridge and seeking information from Americans who had secured En-

3

glish college degrees. When Clap waged his campaign of 1745 to secure a new Yale charter, he based it on a careful and detailed study of administrative practices at Oxford and Cambridge.[3]

Even at William and Mary, English influence soon challenged an earlier Scottish trend. From 1729 to 1757, eight of thirteen faculty members were Oxford men, and of these eight, seven had been in one way or another connected with a single college there, Queens College. After 1757, a battle raged almost continuously between this Oxford-bred faculty and the native Virginian Board of Visitors. By 1766 the Visitors "had rid the college of the last of that band of able Oxford graduates, ministers all of them, whose chief fault had been that their ties with England were too close, that they looked too blindly to their homeland."[4]

In almost every case, however, the English colonists eventually found that the unique conditions of the American physical and social environment produced unexpected changes and modifications in their academic institutions. Some of these were destined to be of great importance for the later development of higher education in the United States.

It was soon discovered that it would be impossible to erect in English-America any great university collection of colleges such as existed at Oxford or Cambridge. For one thing, it was doubtful that the Crown would ever grant the required royal charter for such an American university. Besides, the land was too vast and the people too poor. The narrow fringe of British settlements which faced the broad Atlantic on one side and the trackless forests on the other represented what for that time was the far western frontier of English civilization. All that could be done under these circumstances was to establish a number of scattered, widely separated degree-granting colleges, thus diffusing educational effort.

After a time, still another colonial divergence from the English norm made an appearance. Because of the heterogeneity of the American population, collegiate boards of control were established which were interdenominational in make-up and at least one of which was completely secular. Nothing like this had yet been seen in the home country, although the University of Leyden in the Netherlands already followed this pattern.

Other modifications were due mainly to Scottish influence. The post-Reformation Scottish universities, unlike Oxford or Cambridge, were nonresidential, professionally oriented, and under the control, not of the faculty, but of prominent lay representatives of the community. At the College of William and Mary some of these Scottish ideas seem to have been influential from the very founding. Commissary James Blair, founder and first president, was a graduate of both Marischal College, Aberdeen, and the University of Edinburgh. Reverend William Smith, graduate of Aberdeen, exercised a great influence, as we shall see, over the curricular planning of both King's College in New York, later Columbia, and the College of Philadelphia. John Witherspoon, Scotch theologian who came to the New World in 1768 to become president of the College of New Jersey, later Princeton, exerted an important influence over American higher education.

Although even Harvard was not immune to Scottish university influence,[5] it was at William and Mary that it was felt most directly. The charter Blair obtained for the Virginia school resembled that of a Scottish "unicollege" institution. Like Aberdeen, Glasgow, King's, and Marischal, it incorporated both a university and a degree-granting college by a single letter-patent. At the same time, a governing board was created, made up of members of the nonacademic community; this was, in characteristic Scottish fashion, to have real administrative authority over the college. Even William and Mary's architecture reflected Scottish influence, as did Blair's early plans for a course of study.[6]

As an afterthought on how different the development of higher education in the United States might have been if Continental rather than English precedents had been dominant, we might well look for a moment at the institutions of higher learning founded by the Spanish and French in America. Originally, the English and Continental European universities had a somewhat similar type of organization. Nevertheless, Oxford and Cambridge very early began to follow a largely independent line of development. By the time of the Renaissance, these English universities were changing into loosely federated associations of residential colleges.[7] The Continental universities, on the other hand, were becoming nonresident graduate schools providing specific types of postbaccalaureate training.

The French and Spanish universities in America represented the later Continental type of university. When Charles V of Spain in 1551 founded "the Royal and Pontifical University" of Mexico and the University of San Marcos in Lima, Peru, he accorded them all "the privileges, exemptions, and limitations of the University of Salamanca." This meant that they were definitely to follow the Continental model, because Salamanca was essentially a collection of graduate faculties in arts, theology, law, and medicine. Besides Mexico and Lima, eight other universities were chartered and opened for instruction before a single college appeared in English America. In all, the Spanish-Americans established twenty-three such institutions.[8]

In contrast, higher education in New France developed more slowly. It was not until the 1660s that Bishop Laval developed at Quebec a "great seminary" for advanced theological training. Although modern Laval University developed from this nucleus, in colonial times the Quebec institution never covered as broad a field as had the Spanish-American universities.[9]

Educational Aims

In each part of the New World, the European settlers sought to create as close an approximation as they could to the culture with which they had been familiar back home. The English-Americans, for example, were determined that their children should preserve those aspects of Old World civilization which their fathers held to be all important. In achieving this aim of the transmission and preservation of intellectual culture, higher education was the most valuable tool that lay at hand.

In this connection, the early Puritans in New England conceived of themselves as helping to bring about a *translatio studii*—i.e., a transfer of the higher learning from its ancient seats in the Old World to the wilderness of America. The founders of Harvard took for granted the essential continuity of Western learning—the direct link between the colonial American college and earlier institutions, such as the schools of Hebrew prophets, the Academy of Athens, the Palace School of Charlemagne, the medieval universities, and the Reformation academies. The precious *veritas,* for which the world was indebted to the Hebrews and the Hellenes, had been handed down from generation to generation, and now the settlers of the "Holy Commonwealth" must take up this torch of learning and carry it along.[10]

To be more specific, the desire of important religious denominations (such as the Anglican and Calvinist) for a literate, college-trained clergy was probably the most important single factor explaining the founding of the colonial colleges. This was the central element in the transfer of learning and intellectual culture as seventeenth-century Englishmen saw it. The Christian tradition was the foundation stone of the whole intellectual structure which was brought to the New World. It is equally important, however, to keep in mind that the early colleges were not set up solely to train ministers; their charters make it amply clear that from the very beginning it was intended that they also educate professional men in fields other than the ministry and public officials of various kinds. The civil society would thus get educated orthodox laymen as its leaders; the church would get educated orthodox clergymen as its ministers. This was the ideal which colonial higher education hoped to attain.

Under these circumstances, it is useless to argue whether the colonial colleges were intended to be theological seminaries or schools of higher culture for laymen. They were clearly designed to perform both functions, although in a strictly technical sense special vocational training for the ministry in distinct professional institutions did not develop in the United States until the nineteenth century.

A historian of the College of New Jersey, writing in 1764, expresses the colonial point of view when he explains why that institution was founded at Princeton. The middle colonies, he says, labored under a disadvantage in not possessing a college of their own. The British universities, and even the colleges of New England and Virginia, were too far away. He then adds:

As the colonies increased, the exigencies of affairs, both of an ecclesiastical and political nature, became more and more urgent. Religious societies were annually formed, in various places; and had they long continued vacant, or been supplied with an ignorant illiterate clergy, Christianity itself, in a course of years, might have become extinct among them. Affairs of state also became more embarrassed for want of proper direction, and a competent number of men of letters, to fill the various political offices. The bench, the bar, and seats of legislation, required such accomplishments, as are seldom the spontaneous growth of nature, unimproved by education.[11]

The view that the advancement and preservation of learning was one and the same thing as the training of literate ministers came easily to the New England

Puritans; together with Presbyterians, Anglicans, and Lutherans, they accepted and carried on the traditions of the medieval Schoolmen. Like the Scholastics, they took for granted the fact that piety could not be separated from intellect; that religious faith should be rationalized. The Grace of God was indispensable, but not enough; philosophy and reason were also important, while knowledge of the arts and sciences was very useful.[12]

Perry Miller has cautioned us that this commitment to higher learning on the part of the founders of Harvard does not necessarily mean that they were motivated by "a disinterested dedication to the pursuit of learning in the abstract." As a matter of fact, much of the early Puritan concern with higher learning has to be understood in the context of the attacks which were then being made on it from Antinomian and Pietistic quarters. Advocates of undisciplined religious enthusiasm and of a nonliterate ministry like William Dell and John Webster were demanding that religion be taken out of the monopolistic control of universities. Orthodox Calvinists were obliged to respond to this attack by upholding more firmly than ever the importance of formal curriculums, academic degrees, and syllogistic interpretation of the Scriptures. And in this defense of the higher learning, "Puritan divines stood shoulder to shoulder with Anglican priests."[13]

All of this represented the continuance of the medieval university tradition in a New World Protestant setting. The medieval mind had conceived of the whole of human society as unified in Christ in terms of his royal, priestly, and prophetic roles. This threefold authority was seen as being embodied in three co-ordinate earthly institutions: the State, based on Law; the Church, founded on Revelation; and the University, upheld by Reason. To this day, this concept is preserved in the symbolism of the Western world by the gowns worn by justices in court, ministers in church, and professors and graduates at commencement.

The Puritan founders of the first colonial college derived this doctrine from Calvin and the writings of English divines like William Ames and John Henry Alsted. To the early Harvard scholars, the university man was in direct line of succession to the original prophets and apostles. The college was a local encampment of the universal "militia" of Christ. To be sure, the fundamental truth had been lost in Paradise, by Adam's disobedient grasp for knowledge of good and evil. But all was not lost. Schools of the prophets, corporate bodies of disciplined and dedicated teachers, devoted to Christ, could at least in part rectify the primal error and safeguard knowledge, human and divine, from being further fragmented or perverted.[14]

The role of organized Christianity was important in the founding of eight of the nine pre-Revolutionary colleges. Only the College of Philadelphia was not at first specifically under church control, and it soon came under the dominance of Anglicans. In addition, the purpose of training students for the Christian ministry is specified in all colonial college charters with the single exception, again, of the College of Philadelphia. The Quakers, having no specially trained clergy, did not feel a great need for a college in colonial Pennsylvania. As a result, none was established in that province until the College of Philadelphia was chartered in 1755. Indeed, Philadelphia Quakers very quickly became hostile to the new institution when they discerned in it a threat to their own political dominance.[15]

The earliest printed rules of Harvard announced as the chief aim of that institution that "Every one shall consider the Mayne End of his life & studyes, to know God & Jesus Christ, which is Eternall life."[16] William and Mary, according to the pronouncements of its founders, was established in order to furnish the Church with a piously educated youth of good letters and manners, and also to propagate Christian faith among the Indians.[17] Yale's purposes paralleled Harvard's. In 1701 it was declared to be a place "wherein youth may be instructed in the arts and sciences, who through the blessings of Almighty God, may be fitted for public employment, both in church and civil State." In 1754, the president of Yale stated that "Colleges are Societies of Ministers, for training up persons for the Work of the Ministry."[18]

The College of New Jersey, founded during the Great Awakening controversy between "old lights" and "new lights" within the Calvinist movement, was primarily designed to produce ministers with a "new light" point of view, although political considerations peculiar to the Province of New Jersey seem also to have figured in the picture.[19] King's College, in New York City, was only chartered after a bitter fight between the Anglican and Presbyterian elements, "a politico-religious battle of inter-colonial and even imperial importance." Eleazar Wheelock's purpose in founding Dartmouth was principally that of Christianizing the Indians; and, to achieve this end, preparation for the ministry was of course all important. In similar fashion, the College of Rhode Island was instituted in 1764 to raise the educational level of Baptist ministers, who had been, up to that time, the butt of criticism because of their lack of formal training. And, lastly, the Dutch Reformed Church in 1770 founded Queen's College in New Brunswick, New Jersey, "for the education of youth in the learned languages, liberal and useful arts and sciences, and especially in divinity, preparing them for the ministry and other good offices."[20]

Thus it is clear that the clergy were the leading force in the founding of the colonial colleges and in the formulation of the original purposes of these institutions. The vast majority of faculty members were clergymen, and they represented, on the whole, the leading intellectual class of their time throughout the colonies. Despite this clear-cut sectarian dominance, it should be kept in mind that none of the English-American colleges, desperate as they were to attract tuition-paying students and local patrons, ever prescribed specific doctrinal tests in religion for admission or for the granting of degrees. In this way they were very different from the Oxford and Cambridge of their homeland, which retained such tests as late as 1870.

In the earlier colonial period, this unusual situation seems to have been as much due to the fact of a homogeneous community as to anything else. Thus at early Harvard and Yale the enforcement of tests or oaths was not necessary because the supporting community was almost uniformly Puritan.

In the middle of the eighteenth century, the growth of religious diversity in many of the colonies made some form of denominational coexistence necessary for prosperity and progress. The founders of all the later colleges had to reckon with this situation, and it is reflected in their plans and statements of aims. In order to found their institutions, they had to allay the hostility of other denominations by granting them at least minority representation on governing boards. In order to attract more students in the face of stiffened competition from other colleges, and to enlarge the basis of their financial support, these colleges had to stress in their public pronouncements interdenominational policies and practices. Here again, this was very different from the situation confronting the English universities.

In this new and more relaxed atmosphere, Quakers and Jews were exempted from religious requirements at some of the colonial colleges. The Rhode Island College charter, remarkable for its time, not only prohibited the establishment of any religious tests but specifically forbade the injection of religious bias into teaching: ". . . sectarian differences of opinions shall not make any part of the public and classical instruction: although all religious controversies may be studied freely, examined, and explained."[21] Although it did not go as far as this, the King's College charter forbade the faculty or trustees to "exclude any Person of any religious Denomination whatever, from equal Liberty and Advantage of Education." In similar vein, the Presbyterian founders of the College of New Jersey provided that "those of every religious Denomination may have free and equal Liberty and Advantage of Education in the said College."[22]

Many of the college founders after 1750 came to reflect this changing orientation. Some of them, for the first time, were prominent laymen, rather than clergymen; many of the former were connected with town library companies and the establishment of popular lecture courses for mechanics. Benjamin Franklin is the best known of this later group of college promoters, but other men of his type were active in the founding of the colleges of King's, Rhode Island, and Philadelphia, and in abortive efforts to establish colleges at Newport and Charleston. In its most extreme form, their program envisioned a completely secular college, training students for service to the commonwealth and encouraging free inquiry and independent thinking. The usual situation, however, was one in which clerical leaders interested in the advancement of a particular sect retained control. They were nevertheless now obliged to promise toleration and minority representation to all Protestant Trinitarian sects.[23]

One of the best indications of the different intellectual climate which was developing is provided by the decreasing emphasis on training for the ministry. At Harvard, as far back as the mid-seventeenth century, we find President Dunster trying to obtain books in law and medicine so that the school might train for those professions. The Massachusetts General Court, which gave Harvard financial support throughout the colonial period, expected it to "fit for the magistracie."[24] This secularistic trend was accelerated after 1727, when primary influence on the Harvard governing board passed to wealthy Boston men of affairs. An increasingly large proportion of the students during the remainder of the colonial period came from the homes of merchants and magistrates. What was true of Harvard came to be true of most of the other colonial colleges.

The whole pattern of occupational specialization in the colleges tended to show an ever smaller percentage of students going into the ministry as the colonial period wore on. The percentage of college graduates going into the ministry was 50 during the first half of the eighteenth century. By 1761, however, this had fallen to 37 per cent, and by 1801 to 22 per cent. Revivalism brought the figure back to 30 per cent by 1836, but then a steady decline set in, and it was 20 per cent in 1861, 11 per cent in 1881, and 6.5 per cent in 1900.[25]

Even under Thomas Clap's administration, in which the primary emphasis was on ministerial training, Yale undertook an ambitious program of preparation for the secular professions. President Clap personally gave this course, lecturing on such subjects as "The nature of civil government," "The various kinds of Courts," "Statute, Common, Civil, Canon, Military and Maritime Laws," "Agriculture, Commerce, Navigation, with some general Sketches upon Physick, Anatomy, Heraldry and Gunnery."[26] In eighteenth-century William and Mary College the stress was similarly not only on the training of Anglican ministers but also on the preparation of prospective lawyers and physicians. Thus the college's faculty issued a statement in 1770 declaring that its aim was to train young men for the three traditional professions referred to above and also "to become Gentlemen," which was evidently regarded by the aristocratic Virginia society of the time as being equivalent to a fourth profession.[27]

The theory of higher learning which prevailed at this time was definitely hierarchical, just as it was in contemporary Europe and had been ever since ancient Greek times. Outside of colonial New England the college outran primary and secondary education in development. The university-trained clergymen and magistrates who dominated colonial legislatures took steps to establish colleges long before they attempted to do anything on a colony-wide basis for primary or secondary education. The tendency in colonies like Virginia was "to put the capstone on the educational structure before the foundations were well laid." The prevailing colonial theory conceived of education, higher and lower, as being based on a hierarchy of functions. The school was thought of as an instrument for preserving, not reconstructing, the established society.

This identification of the interests of class with the cause of cultivating higher learning and maintaining a learned ministry was nowhere more frankly avowed than by one speaker at a colonial Harvard commencement. He declared that had the first Puritan settlers not founded the College, "the ruling class would have been subjected to mechanics, cobblers, and tailors, the gentry would have been overwhelmed by lewd fellows of the baser sort, the sewage of Rome, the dregs of an illiterate plebs which judgeth much from emotion, little from truth."[28] To this point of view the Antinomian exiles in Rhode Island responded with satiric verse such as this:

They vilify the Spirit of God,
　　and count School Learning Best.
If that a boy hath learned his Trade,
　　and can the Spirit disgrace,
Then he is lifted up on high
　　and needs must have a Place.[29]

At the same time, we must not overlook the fact that in seventeenth-century New England the proportion of the total population which had a chance for at least some secondary or college schooling was much higher than in the other colonies, in the England of the same period, or in early nineteenth-century New England. Poor boys did go to seventeenth-century Harvard on what we would today call "scholarships."[30]

Entrance Requirements

Apart from the Latin grammar schools, which were particularly good in New England,[31] the only way to secure college preparatory training through most of the colonial period was by means of private tutoring or instruction by a local minister. During the eighteenth century, for example, prospective students of Yale very often prepared for college by going into residence with a minister for an indeterminate length of time. When the latter felt that his charge was "ready," the student was sent off to be examined before the president and faculty of the college.[32]

Admissions procedures tended to follow a more or less uniform pattern at the various colonial colleges. The entrance examinations were usually oral, although Harvard required, in addition, that an essay be written in Latin. They were customarily held in the spring so that the entering student could begin his course the following autumn. It was always possible, however, to be examined during term time or just before the opening of college in the fall. If successful, the candidate secured a copy of the college laws and had the president inscribe an *admittatur* thereon. This served as evidence of matriculation. At Yale, it was also necessary for the candidate to furnish satisfactory evidence of good moral character and to have his father or guardian post a bond sufficient to cover his quarterly bills.[33]

The formal statements of entrance requirements published by the colonial colleges make abundantly clear how strong was the influence of the traditional classical concept of a liberal education. As we read the original laws of Harvard College (1642–50), we find that their requirements for admission amounted very simply to a knowledge of Latin and Greek:

I. When any Schollar is able to read Tully or such like classicall Latine Authour ex temporare, and make and speake true Latin verse and prose *Suo (ut aiunt) Marte,* and decline perfectly the paradigmes of Nounes and verbes in the Greeke tounge, then may hee bee admitted into the Colledge, nor shall any claim admission before such qualifications. . . .[34]

The first stated entrance requirements of other colonial colleges—Yale, William and Mary, New Jersey, and King's, among others—followed almost exactly the original Harvard requirements. In turn, American grammar school masters all through the seventeenth century and far into the eighteenth drilled their students in Latin and Greek and little more, because they realized these were the subjects the boys required for college admission.[35] Even though the colonial entrance requirements admittedly covered a narrow field, they were intensive in their approach to the subjects required. These standards presupposed a really high order of linguistic ability. They would undoubtedly put to the test, in these specific areas, most modern college students.

As secondary education expanded in colonial America, with the founding of more Latin grammar schools and the beginnings of the academy movement, a tendency developed to broaden the scope of college entrance requirements and to differentiate them as much as factors of academic supply and demand and the financial conditions of the colleges would permit. The first new subject which was formally added to the original stated list of entrance requirements was arithmetic. Yale decided to require it in 1745, and the College of New Jersey and King's College followed her in this step. During the first half of the nineteenth century the list of required college entrance subjects was expanded still further. By 1870, to the original Latin, Greek, and arithmetic (now enlarged into mathematics) three other subject-matter fields had been added: history, geography, and English.[36]

The whole tendency of the colleges was to move on to work of a higher grade by dropping some subjects down into the secondary school. Thus, in 1720, when Jonathan Edwards was in his senior year at Yale, his class studied Euclidean geometry. In 1743, President Clap refers to geometry as a study of the sophomore year. In 1825, the same subject was dropped to the third term of the freshman year. Thirty years later geometry had become a requirement for admission to Yale.[37]

This trend included more than just geometry. In 1822, the Yale catalogue listed arithmetic, geography, algebra, and English grammar as freshman studies. By 1834–35 all these subjects, with the exception of algebra, had disappeared from the college curriculum. By mid-century, algebra, too, had become a subject for entrance examination.[38]

A survey of the entrance requirements of twenty-two institutions, ranging in location from Maine to Tennessee, was made in 1829 by the *Quarterly Register* of the American Education Society. This study revealed that the pattern just described was fairly uniform throughout the country.[39] The expansion of secondary education had made possible the slow but steady broadening in scope of college entrance requirements. Of course, as these, in turn, were expanded and differentiated, the secondary schools themselves had to find a place in their programs for the new required subjects.

Curriculum

When Henry Dunster set up the first course of study of the first English-American college, he described it as follows: "Primus annus Rhetoricam docebit, secundus et tertius Dialecticam, quartus adiungat Philosophiam."[40] This was an attempt to establish in the New World the academic program of Dunster's alma mater, Cambridge, as it existed in the early seventeenth century. This, in turn, went straight back to the hallowed trivium and quadrivium of classical antiquity.

The central core of this kind of curriculum was the classical languages and literatures. In addition, such subjects as Aramaic, Syriac, Hebrew, ethics, politics, physics, mathematics, botany, and divinity were to be studied. The Harvard curriculum of 1723, nearly one hundred years later, was much the same, except that more Latin was stressed in the freshman year, metaphysics had been added and botany dropped, and subjects were listed in conjunction with the name and author of the textbook assigned.[41] The other colonial colleges followed substantially the same kind of curriculum, stressing, as did Harvard, the traditional language arts and philosophy.[42]

This course, which was the only one leading to a bachelor's degree, was rigidly prescribed for all. There was no concept that the varying interests or professional plans of the individual student should be taken into account in constructing a curriculum. It was felt that there was a fixed and known body of knowledge—the "liberal arts" as they had come down from antiquity via the Middle Ages, Renaissance, and Reformation. This constituted absolute and immutable truth, and it was important that it be absorbed—not criticized or questioned—by every student.[43]

About the only way in which the studies in the early colonial colleges differed from those in contemporary Oxford or Cambridge lay in the greater prominence accorded in the New World to the learning of Hebrew. Many colonial scholars regarded that language as being of divine origin and one which would be spoken by the saints in heaven. President Ezra Stiles at Yale, for example, sought earnestly to make all freshmen study Hebrew. When, in 1790, this requirement was abandoned, he tried to reconcile himself to giving Hebrew instruction only to volunteers. Stiles sought to increase interest in the course by informing the students that one of the Psalms he taught them would be the first they should hear sung in heaven; he would be ashamed that any of *his* pupils on that occasion should be ignorant of the holy language.[44]

There was, of course, general agreement in colonial America on the necessity for existing faculty prescriptions of Greek and Latin. The utility of a knowledge of the classics for the practice of the professions of law, medicine, and theology was taken for granted by all in the seventeenth and eighteenth centuries, and with reason. Also, many in the colonies, as in Europe, considered classical learning to be a badge of gentility, a sign of class status. Finally, it was thought that this literature was a depository of all ancient wisdom and, as such, would definitely help in the training of leaders and in preparation for service to the community.[45]

Even the most advanced critics of the established academic order in this period, men like Jefferson and Franklin, were convinced of the value of the classics. Jefferson wished, however, to supplement the classical curriculum with more modern subjects, such as history, government, science, and modern languages; and Franklin wished to establish a parallel utilitarian curriculum for those who would not profit from studying Latin and Greek.

In its early stages of development this colonial curriculum represented the transplanting, not only of the contemporary English university course, but of the traditions of the medieval higher learning. Thus, the seventeenth-century Cambridge curriculum reflected a pattern of scholasticism, Aristotelian categories and all; it was not until 1700 that the pressures of the new Newtonian science, Cartesianism, and Neoplatonism began to produce basic changes.[46] It was this essentially scholastic curriculum, as modified by the logical system of the Protestant philosopher Petrus Ramus, which was brought over by the first generation of American Puritans to serve as the pattern for early Harvard and Yale. This Ramist system was the central unifying principle linking together all the subjects of the seventeenth-century curriculum. Ramism held that the various human arts in the curriculum reflected an archetypal divine order, and that their eternal and immutable rules could be discovered by the proper logical method.[47]

The basic type of classical curriculum which we have described remained in effect throughout the colonial period. By 1765, however, certain modifications in the direction of more attention to mathematics, natural science, English language and literature, and modern foreign languages made their appearance. While the fundamental pattern was not in any way transformed, it was visibly affected.

These changes had various causes. Perhaps most important was the fact that the impact of the European Enlightenment was now beginning to be felt full force in the English-American colonies. Important, too, was the example of the curricular developments which were occurring in the English dissenting academies and the Scottish universities.

The intellectual revolution which took place at eighteenth-century Yale may serve as a good illustration of the first point. In 1715 Yale secured from Jeremiah Dummer a collection of 800 books, which included much material on Newtonian science. These books made a profound impression upon the young students of the time. Samuel Johnson, then a Yale tutor, and later the president of King's College, felt "like a person suddenly emerging out of a glimmer of twilight into the full sunshine of open day." Indeed, he and his classmates had been warned, when taking their degrees, against this "new philosophy" of Descartes and Newton, which they were told "would soon bring in a new Divinity and corrupt the pure Religion of the Country." They nevertheless proceeded avidly to read the forbidden books.[48]

The result of this strong infusion of the "new learning" was that the nature of the Yale curriculum was considerably altered by the middle of the eighteenth century, although the old outward structure and terminology remained. Students continued to prepare their theses "Technologia," but the Ramist-type logic was no longer dominant. Side by side with it, Yale students grappled with Aristotelian rhetoric, Berkeleian idealist metaphysics, and the new Newtonian physics. The logical contradictions between these different systems did not bother the faculty. Students were expected not to evaluate them critically and choose between them, but to learn them all without question.[49]

In the spread of the "new science" to American colleges, we must not overlook the role played by the Scottish universities. Unlike Oxford or Cambridge, institutions such as Aberdeen and Edinburgh were deeply influenced by newer tendencies in science and philosophy during the eighteenth century. This influence was transmitted to colonial higher education by the work of such men as William Smith, Francis Alison, and John Witherspoon. Witherspoon, in particular, made Princeton the New World headquarters of the Scottish "common sense" version of the Enlightenment. His "realism" enabled him to harmonize a Newtonian universe founded on empirical method with the Christian religion. His lectures to the students of the College of New Jersey sought to disclose all the "natural laws" of human conduct which had been set up by the Divine Mechanic whose will was revealed in the Scriptures. The great appeal of Scottish "common sense" to the orthodox leaders of the American academic community was that this philosophy was able, according to their mode of presentation, to be at one and the same time moralistic, theistic, and rationalistic.[50] "It was a restatement of Locke against David Hume, and contradicted Hume's scepticism by a blanket assertion that idea and object correspond so faithfully that Americans, intent upon their business, need never give a second thought to so unprofitable a worry."[51] Absolutely dominant in the "Mental and Moral Philosophy" courses of American colleges by the year 1820, Scottish common sense continued its unchallenged reign as late as 1870; and not until 1890 had its influence in academic circles been completely undermined by Darwinism and idealism.

Another factor which must be considered is the possible influence on American higher education of the English dissenting academies. When the Restoration Parliament in 1662 passed the Act of Uniformity, it excluded large numbers of Englishmen from Oxford and Cambridge by making subscription to the doctrines of the Church of England a prerequisite to residence there. English nonconformists thereupon set up their own "dissenting academies," institutions of university grade which soon came to rival Oxford and Cambridge in curriculum as well as in numbers. It has been pointed out that these new institutions "gave not merely an education to Dissenters, but a 'dissenting education.' " Their curriculum was much broader than that of the universities, including, as it did, the newer utilitarian subjects as well as the classical ones. Mathematics, chemistry, physics, English prose and poetry, and elocution could be studied in their classrooms as well as Latin and Greek. The children of middle-class Englishmen flocked to these academies.[52]

It is not entirely clear how great a role in colonial education was played by the dissenting academies. We know that Whitefield opened his own dissenting academy in 1768, and he was an intimate associate of the younger Tennents, who were trustees of Princeton. When William Tennent, Jr., and Samuel Davies went to England on a fund-raising mission for the infant College of New Jersey, they visited many of the English dissenting academies. Then, too, we have evidence that President Burr of Princeton corresponded regularly with Doddridge, the most influential of the English dissenting academicians.[53] Furthermore, Charles Morton, who had been head of one of the best of the dissenting academies, came to Harvard as vice-president in 1697. One student of these developments cautions us that the transatlantic influence of the academies, like that of the Scottish universities, "cannot be assessed without examining the variety of factors, from personal intellectual convictions to the pressures of competing for students, that shaped the context in which Colonial educators made decisions."[54]

Whatever the reasons, a new interest in the teaching of the natural sciences became increasingly manifest in the colonial colleges after 1750. Insofar as colonial science received organized institutional support, this came mainly from the colleges. By the mid-eighteenth century they had assembled enough apparatus to demonstrate to their students experimental methods in astronomy, physics, and chemistry. Some of this, like Rittenhouse's famous orrery at Princeton, served to enhance the reputation of the institution.[55] Then, too, the colonial colleges frequently included technical subjects such as surveying and navigation under the heading of instruction in mathematics, while the founding of medical schools at Philadelphia, King's, and Harvard gave a strong stimulus to the study of botany and chemistry. Indeed, professorships of mathematics and natural philosophy were among the earliest chairs established in the colonial colleges.[56]

At Yale, two eighteenth-century presidents emphasized science. Thomas Clap taught Newton's *Principia* to his classes, built an orrery for his classroom use, and made astronomical observations which attracted the attention of the Royal Society in England.[57] Ezra Stiles was interested in a wide range of scientific fields, but in astronomy most of all. This well-established scientific tradition in New Haven explains President Dwight's interest later on in persuading Benjamin Silliman to become a Yale professor of science. Dwight wished to establish a separate scientific chair, and in order to ensure that it would be conducted under the "proper" orthodox auspices,[58] he appointed young Silliman.

At Harvard, instruction in science (including Copernican astronomy) appeared early. Then, in 1728, the Hollis Professorship of Mathematics and Natural Philosophy was founded. The express duty of the Hollis Professor was to carry on scientific teaching by means of demonstration experiments. The many different scientific instruments owned by Harvard at this time indicate that teaching by experiment played an important part in its colonial curriculum. In addition, original research was not overlooked. During the eighteenth century the holders of the Hollis Professorship, the librarians, the presidents, and other Harvard professors were active in undertaking various types of scientific research and publishing the results in scholarly journals both in America and England.[59]

The favorable position achieved by science in the colonial college was undoubtedly due to the favor with which American theologians looked upon it.

There were clashes between science and religion in the colonial period, as illustrated by the famous quarrel between the Reverend Thomas Prince and Professor Winthrop of Harvard over the cause of earthquakes. But the scientists won this dispute with remarkable ease. Perhaps they were able to do so because Puritan clergymen like Cotton Mather viewed science as complementary, rather than antagonistic, to theology: many clerical college presidents and professors found nothing "godless" in the Newtonian natural philosophy.[60] Any opposition to the existing world view which might lie in independent scientific investigation was as yet unrecognized and, therefore, disregarded.

The most notable illustrations of the new mid-eighteenth-century curricular trends were to be found at King's College, the College of Philadelphia, and William and Mary. One of these projects never got beyond the planning stage, and it is not clear how far the other two were implemented; nevertheless they all demonstrated which way the wind was blowing. The growing importance of an urban merchant class in the colonial seaport towns, and, in the case of William and Mary, the impact of American Revolutionary ideology, were beginning to demand a radical reconstruction of the college curriculum.

In 1754, President Samuel Johnson of King's College publicly advertised a course of study which was remarkably advanced for its time. It seemed to be designed to meet the needs of the practical New York businessman, as well as the student destined for one of the traditional professions. Among the subjects proposed for this curriculum were surveying, navigation, husbandry, mineralogy, geography, commerce, and government "and of everything *useful* for the Comfort, the Convenience and Elegance of Life, in the chief *Manufactures* relating to any of these Things." However, Johnson's ambitious plans were never put into effect. Once established, King's College instituted a rather traditional curriculum in which the new utilitarian studies played little part.[61]

The first noteworthy development of a new type of curriculum in the colonial period came in 1756 at the College of Philadelphia under Provost William Smith. To some extent, Smith's administration of the Philadelphia institution represented the realization of the plans for a broader, more utilitarian training which Benjamin Franklin had suggested seven years before in his *Proposals Relating to the Education of Youth in Pennsylvania.* When in 1753, Smith, newly arrived in America from Scotland, published a pamphlet entitled *A General Idea of the College of Mirania,* Franklin summoned him to take charge of the recently founded institution in Philadelphia.[62]

In his *Mirania* pamphlet, Smith visualized a New World institution of learning where there would be a separate course for all those preparing to follow the "mechanic profession," as well as the traditional classical course. While Latin instruction was not to be slighted, all of the college's proceedings were to be in English. The scheme was comprehensive enough to visualize a higher education for the whole people, both those in the mechanic arts and those destined for the learned professions. Even the proposed classical course was to contain many modern subjects, such as science, surveying, history, agriculture, English writing and speech, concluding "with a view of our colonies in this hemisphere; their state, produce, interests, government, etc., taking some notice as they go along of the French and Spanish settlements that we are chiefly concerned with in trade."[63]

In 1756, Smith drew up a "scheme of Liberal Education," which sought to realize in actual practice the Miranian ideal which he had formulated. The principal divergences from the original plan were the reduction of the classical course from five years to three (American students simply would not spend that long a period on their preprofessional training!) and the failure of the Philadelphia trustees to set up the parallel "mechanic arts" college which Smith had contemplated. However, even in its limited form, the curriculum which was actually adopted represented a great advance for its time. Considerable emphasis was placed on training for government office. One-third of the curriculum continued to be devoted to the traditional Latin and Greek, one-third to mathematics and science (including practical subjects such as agricultural chemistry, surveying, dialing, mechanics, and navigation), and one-third to logic, ethics, and metaphysics (in which group were included subjects such as political science, trade and commerce, and history). There was stress throughout on improving the students' mastery of written and oral English, and the reading of modern English classics was to be encouraged. To this end, detailed recommendations were listed, under the heading of "Private Hours," of supplementary reading "for improving the youth in the various branches." Included here were works such as the *Spectator,* the *Rambler,* Locke, Dryden, Francis Bacon, Newton, Hooker, and Harrington. "Through all the years," it also stated, "the French language may be studied at leisure hours."[64]

During most of this period, the College of Philadelphia remained much smaller than Harvard, Yale, or the College of New Jersey. However, the significance of its secularism and its broadened curriculum should not be judged by the size of its enrollment. It seems fairly certain that Smith's plan had a direct effect, not only upon the development of the University of Pennsylvania, but also upon Washington College and St. John's College in Maryland, both institutions he himself helped to found.[65] It is certainly more than a coincidence that the most comprehensive, and what might be termed encyclopedic, college curriculum of the whole colonial period developed in the city of Philadelphia, then the largest thriving commercial center in English America and the second largest in all the British dominions.[66]

The Philadelphia College, among other things, may have had some influence on Thomas Jefferson in his reform of the curriculum of William and Mary. We have no definite evidence to prove this, however. We do know that Jefferson's interest in his Virginia alma mater was only part of his revolutionary plan for the creation of a "natural aristocracy" of talent and reason. All through the period of 1776–79, Jefferson was active on the Virginia Committee on Revision of the Laws, seeking to hasten the coming of the new era of republicanism by drafting bills on a great variety of subjects. This was the purpose of his bill (No. 79) for the More General Diffusion of Knowledge and his bill (No. 81) for a Public Library (and institute of advanced research).

Part of this comprehensive scheme was represented by Jefferson's bill (No. 80) for Amending the Constitution of William and Mary College. The essence of his plan was to create a state-supported university in Virginia, completely secularized, in accordance with the kind of relationship between Church and State he was seeking to establish with his Statute for Religious Freedom. All preparatory work was to be relegated to lower schools. Subjects like natural history, medicine, chemistry, fine arts, modern languages, and law and political administration were to be added to the curriculum, while the old divinity professorship and the professorship of Oriental languages were to be abolished. Students were to be free to choose the courses they wished to take. This curriculum shares honors with that of Philadelphia as the most remarkable in eighteenth-century English America. The bill, however, was never acted upon by the legislature.[67]

In 1779, shortly after being elected governor, Jefferson became a member of the Board of Visitors of William and Mary. That body now proceeded to introduce many of the changes that had been aimed at in his bill. The nature of the divinity professorship and the professorship of Oriental languages was transformed. Natural philosophy and natural history were combined with mathematics as one professorship; in similar fashion, chemistry was combined with anatomy and medicine. Work in modern foreign languages, politics, law, economics, and practical and applied arts was added to the course of study. There was to be opportunity for electives. The clear purpose was to infuse a strong admixture of the Enlightenment into what had been the traditional classical course of a church-dominated college. Robert P. Thomson observes:

> . . . Its curriculum was secular and pragmatically professional in orientation. The reformed curriculum of the College, even more dramatically than Jefferson's own plan of education, challenged the inviolability of the scholastic sequence in the classical curriculum. That these innovations were intellectual responses to the grinding realities of historic experience does not lessen their force. Rather it identifies them as legitimate efforts to create ideas and values that could give meaning to the uniqueness of American experience. . . . President Madison, Jefferson, the faculty, and the Visitors share credit jointly for that achievement.[68]

Degrees

From the beginning the colonial college granted the two degrees which had by this time been established as the principal academic awards of Oxford and Cambridge—namely, the bachelor of arts and the master of arts. Though not all present-day degrees are descended from the medieval university, the master's degree clearly is.[69] Furthermore, the whole modern machinery for the awarding of academic degrees in the Western world is descended from the medieval *licentia ubique docendi,* conferred by a corporation, or guild, of master teachers under the tacit or explicit authorization of pope, emperor, or king.[70]

As we have noted, the bachelor's degree was based in America upon a four-year course, with the subjects largely prescribed. The earliest formal statement of requirements for this degree was that of Harvard in its laws of 1642–50:

Every scholar that on proofe is found able to read the originall of the old and New testament into the Latin toungue, and to Resolve them Logically withall being of honest life and conversation and at any publicke act hath the approbation of the overseers, and master of the College may bee invested with his first degree.[71]

The baccalaureate requirements of other colonial colleges were similar, although by the mid-eighteenth century they tended to demand that the students show proficiency, not only in the ancient tongues and logic, but in all "the sciences wherein they have been instructed."[72]

The master of arts degree in the colonial period was a three-year degree with no prescribed subjects and no residence requirements. Often the prospective master did little real study but simply waited for his degree to come along automatically "in course" three years after his bachelor's. On the other hand, some master's candidates, usually prospective clergymen, would remain in residence at their college to "read divinity" systematically. At the same time they might also teach a college class or two.[73]

The early Harvard College laws state that the master of arts would be awarded to "Every Scholar that giveth up in writing a Synopsis or summa of Logicke, Naturall and Morall Philosophy, Arithmeticke, Geometry, and Astronomy, and is ready to defend his theses or positions, withall Skilled in the originals as aforesaid and still continues honest and studious." The requirements of other colonial colleges represented no essential change from this basically medieval and scholastic pattern.[74]

Many of the subjects presented by master's candidates at colonial commencements in the form of oral Latin dissertations are of more than passing interest even today. At Harvard, as elsewhere, these commencement "parts" were always listed in the commencement program under the heading *Quaestiones Pro Modulo Discutiendae in Comitiis Publicis a Laureae Magistralis Candidatis.* The treatises were always presented in the traditional medieval disputation form, with the candidate taking either the affirmative or the negative of a controversial question.[75]

As early as 1692 the American colleges began to grant honorary degrees. In that year Harvard awarded Increase Mather an honorary S.T.D., perhaps so that he could impress European "doctors" on his travels abroad. No other honorary doctoral degrees were awarded for three-quarters of a century, although Benjamin Franklin did receive an honorary master's in 1753. In 1773, the first LL.D. was granted to Professor John Winthrop of Harvard. Later General George Washington got this degree from Yale (1778), Pennsylvania (1780), and the College of Rhode Island (1790). Harvard also awarded the honorary LL.D. to Jefferson, John Jay, and Alexander Hamilton.[76] Ezra Stiles of Yale was particularly interested in introducing the more ceremonial and formal procedures of the

European university in making the award of such honorary doctorates.[77]

Although no mention of the power to grant academic degrees is to be found in the Harvard College charter of 1650, the institution conferred nine bachelor of arts degrees as early as 1642. This was a bold action; it amounted to an unauthorized assumption of sovereign powers.[78] In England, Oxford and Cambridge, under exclusive rights granted by the Crown, had long controlled the granting of all university degrees. The English colleges were part of, but subordinate to, one or the other of these universities, and therefore for a college to undertake to grant degrees on its own was a departure from long-established custom. The founders of Harvard therefore preferred to leave out of the 1650 charter all reference to the way in which they were defying tradition and the Crown.[79]

Actually, the colonial colleges had no choice; there was as we have seen no degree-granting university in the American wilderness with which they could affiliate. There were, however, certain precedents for such unusual and independent proceedings. As we have already pointed out, the Scottish colleges, such as Aberdeen, Marischal, and Edinburgh, had been granting degrees on their own authority for many years before the founding of Harvard. Perhaps even more instructive was the establishment in England itself of Durham College. Oliver Cromwell founded this college by letters patent in 1657, and two years later Parliament granted it the power to award degrees the same as if it were one of the original universities. This college went under when the Commonwealth was overthrown, but the whole incident shows that the colonial college founders were not unique in their setting up of independent, degree-granting institutions.

Probably this explains why Old World universities accepted the first colonial degrees as valid. Four of the nine members of Harvard's first graduating class (1642) later received advanced degrees abroad: one at Oxford (M.A.); one at Padua (M.D.); one at Leyden (M.C.); and one at Dublin (B.T.). In addition, James Ward, who received his B.A. degree from Harvard in 1645, was awarded a master's degree by Oxford three years later while serving as a fellow of Magdalen College. Thus he secured his second degree at about the same time he would have received it had he remained at Harvard. At Oxford his Harvard baccalaureate was apparently considered just as legitimate as any he could have received from the university itself.[80]

With the founding of the other colonial colleges, the precedent established by Harvard was followed by each new institution. Each became a law unto itself in granting degrees and in establishing standards for them. Unlike the English system, there was no old-established seat of learning to enforce uniform standards of quality in academic work as represented by certain recognized degrees.

A word about colonial college commencements. The first of which we have record is that described for us in a New England Puritan pamphlet published in England in 1643. Here we learn that Harvard College students who had been trained up in "University-Learning" for four years attended "two solemne Acts for their Commencement, when the Governour, Magistrates, and the Ministers from all parts, with all sorts of Schollars, and others in great numbers were present, and did heare their Exercises; which were Latine and Greeke Orations, and Declamations and Hebrew Analasis Grammaticall, Logicall & Rhetoricall of the Psalms; And their Answers and Disputations in Logicall, Ethicall, Physicall and Metaphysicall Questions! and so were found worthy of the first degree, (commonly called Batchelour) *pro modo Academiarum in Anglia.*"[81]

Without doubt, such a commencement must have been a most imposing occasion, one of the great events of the year in a provincial society that knew few splendid assemblages. As time went on, it came to be quite a festive occasion as well. In addition to the formal program of orations, there seems to have been a good deal of "unofficial" boisterousness which worried the college authorities. In particular, colleges were anxious to prevent the attendant feasting and imbibing by the students, since it was expensive and the celebrants usually ended up drunk.[82] These efforts at regulation, however, were not too successful. A description of one early American college commencement, in this case at the College of New Jersey, gives us the flavor of all of them:

> It was a public holiday and gala occasion not only for the College but for all the country around. Lines of booths and wagons where refreshments were sold made their appearance at that time, and the town took on the aspect of a fair. The "Old Road" was a race-course; there were playing for pennies, and dancing and fiddling, and even bull-baiting.[83]

Main Patterns up to The Yale Report of 1828

These, then, were the main patterns of the colonial colleges. Small institutions every one of them, with meager equipment and scanty funds, they were in the beginning, as Carl Becker pointed out, "rather a promise than a performance."[84] Their entrance requirements at first were narrow, their opportunities for training beyond the baccalaureate level severely limited. Their student enrollments were small. Yale, beginning with only 36 students in 1710, reached a peak of 338 in 1770. Harvard, which had 123 students in 1710, enrolled 413 in 1770.[85] These were tiny provincial schools, often consisting of a president and one or two tutors. During the whole of the seventeenth century less than 600 persons attended Harvard College; of these, only 465 are recorded as having graduated. And these institutions grew slowly.[86]

The important thing, however, was not the dimensions but the permanent significance of the colonial achievement in higher education. This was all out of proportion to the size of student enrollments. Granted the graduating classes of that era were tiny, they nevertheless comprised the intellectual and political elite of English America. The influence of this select group and, through it, of the colonial college itself percolated down to the mass of the population from the legislative assembly, the pulpit, the law court, the mercantile house, and the school.

Important, too, was the fact that the colonial college had been planted and that it had survived. The European heritage of higher learning, going back for more than two thousand years, had not, as some had feared, perished in the American wilderness.

Although many of the early college charters announced their interest in the advancement of knowledge, as well as its transmission, it is noteworthy that the main emphasis was not upon original research. The old-time college was primarily involved in the conserving of existing knowledge rather than the search for new knowledge.[87] We might explain this by saying that these struggling pioneer institutions had enough to do just preserving and transmitting the Western intellectual heritage to the next generation, but this would not be the whole story. Eighteenth-century Oxford and Cambridge, certainly neither poor nor isolated, made few original contributions to learning. Involved here, besides the obvious handicaps of provincial isolation, was a philosophy of higher education which did not consider scholarly or scientific research as such to be the major purpose of an institution of higher education.

The colonial American college was in many ways a blood brother to its English model. Like the latter, it upheld the tradition of a prescribed liberal-arts curriculum, based upon a primarily classical preparatory course; it was more deeply concerned with the forming of character than the fostering of research; it placed great value on a residential pattern of life for students (what Cotton Mather called the "collegiate way of living"); and it was concerned primarily with training a special elite for community leadership. To these fundamental policies it held steadfastly and without essential change for nearly 200 years.

2

Early Patterns of Organization and Administration

In setting up the colonial colleges the founding fathers gave them a legal as well as an educational frame. The governmental structure which this frame took from the exigencies of the seventeenth and eighteenth centuries was fraught with a number of potential strains. Two principal ones developed. One occurred within the power structure of the college itself. The other occurred between the college and public authorities, at first the English Crown, then later the colonial, and still later the state legislatures. But before tracing these strains it will be well to sketch the types of administrative organization by which the colleges came to govern themselves.

The President and Board of Control

From the very beginning of higher education on American shores the principal agencies of administration were a president and a board of control. Neither agency seems to have been an American innovation—as thought in some quarters —much less a copy of the later American business corporation. On the contrary, both were importations from Europe. Yet even Europe had not always had these structures in its administrative organization of higher education. Anciently power seems to have been vested by prescription in an autonomous guild of scholars. Masters and students came together voluntarily to form a corporation *(universitas)* of scholars. Although this university looked to pope or emperor for protection it tried to maintain its independence from both, claiming according to Aquinas to be a *collegium scholasticum* and not a *collegium ecclesiasticum* or a *collegium secularium.*

Conditions were not ripe to transfer this academic tradition to the American colonies of the seventeenth and eighteenth centuries. On the one hand there was an insufficient body of learned men to set up a *collegium scholasticum,* and on the other, even if there had been, there was insufficient wealth to maintain them as an independent guild of scholars. In addition, after the Reformation exception was taken notably by Luther to the autonomous university protected as it was by imperial law and papal privilege. Hence with the proclamation of the principle of *cuius regio eius religio* there was a turn in Protestant countries to the territorial state for the needed funds for higher education and also for a tighter pattern of its organization and control.[1]

As Protestant principalities came to assume some ecclesiastical functions, it was but a short jump from lay control of the church, which is the heart of Congregational polity, to lay control of the college.[2] Beyond that it was but a further short jump from including secular aims of the college along with religious ones as at Yale where students were to prepare for "public employment in church and state." The consequent prototype for the administration of the colonial college can be seen among others in the University of Leyden in Holland. There the university was under the authority of *curatores* appointed by the Estates General. The curators together with the mayor appointed the resident professors who became a *senatus academicus*. The two bodies were not unlike Harvard's later bicameral government by overseers and corporation.

The presidency derives from the English college rather than the English university. The university was ruled by a chancellor, not unlike the rector in continental universities. The office of the chancellor, however, possessed limited powers, held for a short term. In time, indeed, the chancellorship became almost altogether honorary. The college "head" (or "president" as he came to be called in the colonies) on the contrary exercised wide-ranging powers for an indefinite term. It is this circumstance, no doubt, which laid the base for the great strength of this office in the United States.[3]

These European precedents found their way into American practice by varied routes. Harvard, for instance, started with a board of overseers composed of magistrates and clergy on which the only educational representative was the president of the college. Since it was difficult in those early days of transportation for this nonresident board to meet conveniently, the president had to carry much responsibility on his shoulders with correspondingly little authority. Hence, when the administrative arrangements under which Harvard had been operating were formalized in its first charter of 1650, an additional administrative body was set up, the "corporation," consisting of the president, five fellows, and the treasurer. This body provided a resident group in constant and immediate touch with college affairs and one which could choose its own officers, perpetuate its own membership, sue and be sued, and manage the college generally. It seems to have been President Dunster's idea to have the faculty as fellows and to lodge in this body the real control of the institution in the European tradition of autonomy. The charter, nevertheless, retained the board of overseers to review the actions of the corporation. As a result Harvard has come down to the twentieth century as the first and leading exponent of a bicameral form of college and later university administration. The great advantage of this system, as President Eliot was to say two centuries later, lay in having two vigilant bodies each jealous to excel in guarding the welfare of the institution.[4]

The founders of William and Mary kept the European tradition of a self-governing faculty more clearly in view. But at first even their autonomy was eclipsed by a board of trustees since the founding instrument of government temporarily called for a bicameral administrative structure wherein authority was divided between a body consisting of trustees and another of faculty. At the beginning the trustees were empowered to appoint presidents and legislate for the college, but the charter directed that ultimately they were to surrender these powers and the property of the college to the faculty. It was not till 1729 (the college had been founded in 1693) that the trustees reluctantly carried out this part of the founding instrument. Thereafter the trustees receded into the background as a board of visitors, and the faculty till the Revolution became as nearly self-governing in the traditional sense as any American college faculty has ever been.[5]

When Yale came into existence, the tradition of faculty autonomy did not seem even to have been in the minds of the founders as a frame of government for the college. Perturbed at the struggles between the overseers and the corporation at Harvard, the Congregational clergy who sponsored Yale decided to keep tight control of the "collegiate school" in their own hands. To this end they set up a single governing board on which they held all the seats. In fact, fearing the advent of a strong personality, they did not even admit the rector to membership in the Yale Corporation till the charter of 1745. As a result the Yale frame of government was still farther removed from the English tradition than either Harvard or William and Mary. But Timothy Dwight, Yale's president a century later, was confident that the unicameral form of organization was superior to the bicameral.[6] A chief drawback of the latter, he held, was that the reviewing board could negate but not initiate legislation. This could easily lead to indecision and compromise. Then there was always the danger that the second board, especially where composed in part of laymen, might not be fully competent to judge the course of academic affairs. Whatever the merit of these objections, it is notable that the great majority of colleges and universities founded after the first three followed the Yale pattern.

Yale was not the only institution to mistrust the potential power of its principal academic administrator. The University of Pennsylvania also denied this officer representation on its board of control. If Yale and Pennsylvania mistrusted the power of their chief executive it is interesting to note that Thomas Jefferson, in planning for his University of Virginia, provided for no president at all. Rather was it his plan that a rotating chairman of the faculty should exercise the president's duties but never be more than *primus inter pares* among his colleagues.

While in general the control of higher education in America became lodged in a president and a board of governors, there can be little doubt that, as between the two, ultimate control lay with the board. Not only Yale, as already seen, but the University of Pennsylvania, too, attest this fact because both had the power to deny their chief administrative officer a seat on the board. These possibly democratic attempts to reduce the prestige of the chief academic administrator, however, did not work well. Since boards of control only met from time to time they lost touch with the day-to-day state of academic affairs which only the president could give. Even at Harvard, where the president sat with both the overseers and the corporation, it was still found necessary to evolve an executive committee called the "immediate government" which could make on-the-spot interim decisions. Confronted with the same problem Yale in the middle of the eighteenth century solved it by finally making its president the ranking member of the Yale Corporation. Pennsylvania did not arrive at this point till the next century[7] and Virginia did not even adopt the presidential form of administration till the twentieth century.

What about the organization of the college below the president? When colleges were in their infancy there was no organization below him, or rather the president was the whole administration. He did the work which in the nineteenth and twentieth centuries was delegated to such lieutenants as deans, registrars, and librarians. Thus the pioneer college president was not only charged with the general oversight of his college but carried many specific duties as well. Chief among these was a heavy teaching load which was reduced only a little when later he taught just the senior class. But even then all the cases of college discipline came to him as a court of last resort. Ordinarily each day found him presiding at chapel and each Sunday found him occupying the pulpit. In the early days before there were registrars the president usually kept the student records, to say nothing of being the recording secretary of the board of control when it met. Not a few energetic presidents became their own college librarians. As if all these duties were not enough, presidents had to be assiduous fund raisers and find odds and ends of time to execute the business details of the college. Obviously, even when enrollments were small the presidency was an exacting and time-consuming responsibility.

These burdensome duties were much the same whatever the title borne by the college's chief administrative officer. Harvard's first executive, Eaton, bore the title "master" which was the common practice in England at the time. His successor, however, carried the title "president." While most new institutions adopted the same practice, Yale changed to that title only after having started with "rector," a title used later at Georgetown. At the University of Pennsylvania for many years the chief officer was a "provost" and at the early University of Nashville he was a "chancellor," a title reminiscent of a once powerful office in the English university. Dickinson, perhaps, employed the title of least prestige when it called its leader "principal," a title more frequent in secondary schools.

It would be a serious omission to describe the simple machinery of college government without mentioning the kind of men who were at its controls. Probably the outstanding characteristic of these men in colonial times was the fact that they were clergymen. Till the end of the Revolutionary War, college presidents were almost without exception gentlemen of the cloth. Governing boards, too, abounded with clerics, exclusively at Yale and generally in a majority elsewhere. In itself this fact should not occasion surprise, since the clergy were the learned men of their day and therefore not only most interested but also most capable of attending to the purposes of the higher learning. On the whole the men chosen to be presidents were a capable lot, some of them actually achieving distinction beyond the walls of their colleges. President Witherspoon at Princeton, for example, became a signer of the Declaration of Independence.

Faculty Versus Lay Control

Two basic components are discernible in the power structure of the American college. One component was a professional body giving instruction and resident in the college. The other was a governing body, nonresident, and often composed at least in part of laymen. The interests of these two bodies overlapped, and strains were therefore bound to occur in the power structure. Inasmuch as the professional body, the faculty, were most familiar with the problems arising from carrying the main burden of the college, it is understandable that they should wish to determine the educational policies of the institution. But it is equally understandable that the founders, usually represented by the board of control, also had educational policies they wished carried out. The predominant position of the board over the president, however, held for the faculty as well. Yet the faculty did not acquiesce to this balance of power without some continued rumble of dissatisfaction.

From time to time this discontent reached crescendo proportions. Perhaps the most notable, if not most successful, early struggle for faculty power occurred at Harvard. There, it will be remembered, the college was first governed by a nonresident board of overseers composed of clergy and magistrates, later supplemented by a resident corporation composed of the president and fellows or faculty. As mentioned, it had been the hope of Dunster, the first president, that the corporation would inherit the European tradition of autonomy and become the principal governing body of the college. His hopes, however, were not to be fulfilled. The senior body, the overseers, accustomed to power, did not stand idly by but actually tended to dominate the corporation, especially in the appointment of new presidents, a power actually vested in the junior body. Irked at this overreaching of their power, the proponents of a new charter for Harvard at the end of the seventeenth century tried to curtail the importance of the overseers, but they failed when the English Crown disallowed each proposal.

This defeat for the advancement of faculty autonomy, however, was shortly to be followed by the much more serious loss of faculty control of the corporation itself.[8] Early in the eighteenth century three vacancies occurred on the corporation at about the same time. Up to this moment it had been customary to elect tutors as fellows of the corporation after they had served a short period of probation. On this occasion, however, two tutors who were eligible for election were passed over in favor of two Boston clergymen. Now their election was not the first occasion of electing nontutors as fellows, but it was the first time an eligible tutor had not been selected. Strong protests were entered by both the neglected tutors and by the overseers. The protest of the tutors was against further nonresident control of the college, a control which they thought demanded a too compliant attitude on the part of the faculty. The protest of the overseers was complicated by disagreements with the corporation over religious matters.[9] Protests to the contrary notwithstanding, the nonresident lay membership of the corporation continued to grow. Before the century was out both a prominent Boston merchant and a member of the Massachusetts judiciary had been added. With one exception after 1806 no more faculty were chosen.

One last faculty protest was launched about 1825. The moment chosen was marked by dissatisfaction with the administration of collegiate affairs and not just at Harvard, where a serious student rebellion was of recent memory. There was general discontent with the traditional curriculum, as witness the founding of Rensselaer Polytechnic Institute as an alternative or its defense by the Yale Report of 1828.[10] To assert themselves more effectively on the issues at stake a number of the Harvard faculty tried once again to capture seats on the corporation. The argument they advanced was very similar to that of a century earlier and rested on the premise that the government of Harvard was vested in the president and fellows. Since a fellow by ancient usage at Oxford and Cambridge meant a "resident" instructor they claimed a right to representation on the corporation. Committees of both the overseers and the corporation, however, rejected this faculty claim.

In spite of the rejection, when the strife subsided, the faculty could count significant gains. In 1826 the overseers published a new set of statutes for the governance of the college.[11] These seemed to recognize a distinction drawn by one of the overseers, John Lowell, at the height of the controversy. What he did was to distinguish the external from the internal control of the college. External control had to do with the formation of policy and the allocation of financial resources to carry out policy. Internal control concerned the discipline of students and the direction of instruction.[12] Accordingly, the new statutes provided for faculty control over the admission of students, student discipline, and the conduct of instruction. If the faculty had lost the battle for external control, it had won the one for internal control, a victory which has never since been challenged.

Although William and Mary had succeeded better than the other colleges in achieving a span of faculty autonomy, it too finally surrendered to control by a nonresident board of visitors. Down to the Revolution the faculty had been able to maintain its independence by appeal to England for an interpretation of its royal charter. The Revolution, however, foreclosed this recourse. Moreover, when the courts of Virginia, upholding the right of the college to dismiss one of its faculty, denied that a faculty member held a freehold in his chair, the death knell had sounded for faculty autonomy of the old guild variety.[13]

To some it has seemed strange that in the very decades that the colonies were winning their political freedom, the Harvard faculty was losing a large measure of its guild autonomy; that just as the colonies were successfully protesting taxation without representation, the Harvard faculty was unsuccessfully resisting government by a nonresident board without faculty representation.[14] As a matter of fact this paradoxical situation marked not so much a loss as a transition to a reorganization and specialization of functions to suit American conditions. Expanding on these new functions, Francis Wayland, the outstanding president of Brown, seemed to take the new Harvard statutes as his norm.[15]

On the one hand Wayland assigned the management of finances to the board of trustees. European guilds of scholars had owned and managed the sources of their income, and the plan worked fairly well in an old civilization where capital funds were not impossible to come by. In America the financing of higher education was an unremitting anxiety. The Revolutionary War in particular ravished both buildings and endowment. It is small wonder, therefore, that it was about this time that Harvard looked more and more toward laymen for leadership on its corporation. As already noted, by the end of the century it had added both a prominent businessman, James Bowdoin, and a leader of the Massachusetts bar. By contrast the tutors, whom these men replaced, were often very young men, recent graduates of the college, who were teaching just till they might receive a call to some pulpit.

On the other hand Wayland allowed the faculty to retain a modicum of its former autonomy by assigning to its discretion the course of study, the mode of instruction, and the discipline of the students. But even in this province he recognized the authority of the lay board to amend the course of liberal education and the requirements for academic degrees, thus ultimately defining the intellectual aims of the community pretty much as they wished. It was because the college obtained its financial support from the public that Wayland thought laymen should have such authority in academic affairs. If this principle be accepted then too trustees must be made responsible to the public. To this end Wayland recommended that boards should neither be self-perpetuating nor their terms be indefinite. Not every board accepted these strictures but they did long remain the norm to strive for.[16]

Private Versus Public Control

The uneasy equilibrium of power within the frame of the college itself was matched by another one without, one between the college and the public authorities. The strain of this uneasy equilibrium was first felt between the colleges and the English Crown, but latterly between the colleges and the colonial and subsequently the state legislatures. The problem with which the early colleges wrestled was how to incorporate under public statutes and at the same time preserve their academic independence.

According to Blackstone's *Commentaries,* it was the English law of the seventeenth and eighteenth centuries that no corporation could come into existence without the consent of the Crown. Yet, contrary to this prohibition, more than a decade of Harvard's existence had elapsed before it received its first charter in 1650. And even this charter was of dubious authority since it was granted by the colonial legislature without first consulting the British monarch. Yale, too, founded in 1701, did not receive its first charter till 1745. The occasion for such evasions of the law is not far to seek. The founding fathers of these colonial colleges were fearful that if the king's consent were sought it would only be granted with a reservation to the Crown of the right of visitation. The danger in such a reservation was the possibility that the sovereign at some time might interfere with the freedom of the college to teach its preferred religious point of view. This threat was a real possibility inasmuch as many of the originators of these colleges were nonconformists, and nonconformists had suffered discrimination both religiously and educationally in the mother country. During this interim period both these seats of learning seem to have existed as legal trusts like the dissenting academies in England with the right of visitation reserved to the original donors rather than the crown.

Despite the cloud that hung over the legality of Harvard's charter, the college was able to carry on without interference till 1684, when the colonial charter of Massachusetts was revoked. With that revocation even any appearance of legality for Harvard's incorporation vanished too. A new charter, this time sent to England for approval, failed to receive assent from the Privy Council because, as might have been expected, it made no reservation to the king to appoint visitors. Consequently Harvard operated without a charter till 1707. In that year the Massachusetts legislature, standing on the thin ice that the charter of 1650 had never been formally repealed or annulled, directed the college authorities to regulate themselves from time to time according to the provisions of the original document. Astonishingly enough, neither the Crown governor of Massachusetts nor the advisers to the Crown in England took exception to this stricture. So Harvard carried on till the Revolution without interference from the Crown.

While Harvard was going through the latter stages of this episode, Yale was passing through the initial stages of its legalization. In the light of Harvard's experience, the founders in New Haven were in a quandary what to do. To seek a Crown charter risked royal or episcopal interference. To seek a colonial charter risked indirect revocation should Connecticut's charter be recalled as Massachusetts' had been. Of the two the latter seemed like the lesser risk. To decrease the risk further, founders and legislators connived to draw up an instrument which ambiguously referred to the founders as "trustees, partners, or undertakers," to the president as a "rector," and to the college itself as the "collegiate school." Though the language was modest, there can be little doubt the intention was bold. In any event this subterfuge, plus British indifference to or downright ignorance of colonial affairs, they hoped, would render Yale's inception inconspicuous and assure her freedom from unfriendly interference.

By no means all the colonial colleges had such trouble with their initial incorporation. William and Mary, for one, took a royal charter, but then the fear of visitation on religious grounds did not present such an obstacle in a colony where the Church of England was dominant. Moreover, the charter intended a close connection between the college and the government because it included the old English custom of permitting the faculty to name two members of the Virginia

House of Burgesses. At another point, however, the charter made the government rest more lightly on the shoulders of the faculty and students of William and Mary than it did on other citizens. It extended to the former the ancient medieval university custom of exemption from taxes. At Harvard and Brown this privilege extended even further to exemption from military service, guard duty, warding against fires, and service on juries.[17] The College of New Jersey came to terms with the public authorities by admitting some of them to representation on its board of control but without yielding control to them. Perhaps this concession was easier to make in the second half of the eighteenth century, when there was an abatement of the fires of sectarian zeal. King's College and Brown did not even fear the prospect of visitation because they took charters opening their doors to all confessions.

Colleges, on the contrary, which continued to reflect a narrow sectarian or even single political control ran a protracted struggle with public authorities which did not terminate till the Dartmouth College Case. An early skirmish leading up to that famous adjudication occurred at Yale. If the religious interest in the "collegiate school" there succeeded in escaping the notice of the Crown, it was less fortunate in avoiding the critical gaze of its own colonial legislature. In 1763 an appeal was made to that body by the sectarian enemies of President Clap to appoint visitors to make Yale more responsive to other interests in the colony. The appellants proposed this public invasion of the college because, in accepting financial subsidies from the legislature, it had made itself a public institution. President Clap contended that the legislature had no right to appoint visitors. The moment was critical. In an argument which even Justice Story later called masterful, Clap expressed gratitude for the financial aid of the colony but insisted that the legislature had no greater control over Yale than it did over other persons and estates. Most telling was his argument that the colonial legislature was not the incorporator of Yale in the first instance because, as already seen, the college had the status of a trust before it received its first legal recognition from the legislature.[18] Consequently the only proper visitors, if any, must be the original founders or their successors. For the legislature to appoint other visitors to visit the original visitors would lead to an absurd regression. In the end Clap's argument carried the day. But that was only the first round. The second round, after the Revolutionary War, went to the state. In financial straits following hostilities, Yale had to go to the new legislature to beg funds. To win them and avoid the threat of starting another college serving interests not represented on the Yale Corporation,[19] Yale had finally to yield some of its long-cherished autonomy by admitting the governor and other dignitaries of the state government to ex officio membership in the corporation. Ezra Stiles, then president, expressed deep relief in his diary that the "civilians," holding the whip hand, acquiesced to being a minority.[20]

Well he might, for there were strong forces abroad in the land which wanted the state governments to go much farther in asserting control over their institutions of higher education. At the founding of King's College, William Livingstone agitated for an institution under public auspices, and even while the Revolution was in progress Jefferson was promoting a bill in the Virginia legislature to exert greater control over William and Mary, which he regarded as a public corporation. Neither was entirely successful, but it is worthy of note that Jefferson's frustration led him to transfer his affections from his alma mater to the founding of the University of Virginia, which would be indisputably under public control. But the most dramatic attempt by men of Livingston's and Jefferson's point of view to assert state control over one of the old foundations occurred at Dartmouth.[21]

The train of circumstances which led from Dartmouth College in New Hampshire to the Supreme Court of the United States in Washington originated in so local a dispute that no one would have ever expected it to swell later into such national significance. Unlike Harvard and Yale, Dartmouth begged and won a royal charter from the English Crown. This deed of trust provided not only for a self-perpetuating board of trustees but for the president to appoint his own successor. When Eleazar Wheelock, the original founder, died, he indicated that his son John was to succeed him. John, however, was a military man rather than a cleric and consequently possessed neither the theological scholarship nor the solemnity of manner usually associated with a college president. In the course of time he became involved in a sectarian quarrel in the local Congregational church, which went against him. This same sectarian division later caused him to lose control of the Dartmouth faculty as well. In both instances the president's diminution of prestige basically reflected vexation of the trustees with the presidential dynasty. Eleazar had ruled the college much as he pleased in the eighteenth century, but now in the nineteenth the trustees were beginning to assert themselves.

Disappointed and frustrated, John Wheelock tried to regain ground by an appeal to the New Hampshire legislature through an anonymous diatribe against the trustees of the college. Exasperated in turn, the trustees voted the president's dismissal. Jeffersonian Republicans, out of office at the time, sought to make political capital of the controversy. Referring to the "venerable and learned" Wheelock, they professed anxiety for the "literary progress" of the people of the state. In 1816 the people hearkened and returned the Republicans to office, who made it a matter of early business to press through legislation reorganizing Dartmouth College as Dartmouth University. To achieve this end the legislature had to amend the college charter. To make any amendment effective it had to capture the board of trustees. This it attempted by enlarging its number to a point where a majority favored Wheelock and his adherents. The new board so constituted met and elected Wheelock president, but he died soon after and was succeeded by his son-in-law. In the meantime the original trustees of the college refused to obey the law, so that for a while Dartmouth College and Dartmouth University operated side by side under different administrations. The festering conflict came to a legal head in the question of which administration was entitled to the seal and records of the institution. The secretary-treasurer of the college, a Wheelock man, refused to surrender these critical items to the original trustees. Consequently they sued to recover them.

Obviously the case turned on the point which had been gnawing at the vitals of college authorities ever since Harvard and Yale had flown in the face of Blackstone's dictum by incorporating without the public assent of the Crown. Were these incorporated institutions of higher learning public corporations? Yale, Harvard, and Princeton had avoided coping with this issue frontally by admitting public officials to their boards of control. At Dartmouth forces seemed to move inexorably toward meeting the issue head on. However other colleges had faced the problem, it was clear that their fate as well as Dartmouth's now hung in the judicial balance. Conscious of this common jeopardy, Dartmouth begged financial help from them to see the case through the courts, but none was forthcoming in spite of friendly interest expressed in the outcome. In fact some colleges, fearing an adverse decision, would have been just as happy if the case had never been brought to the attention of the courts in the first place.

Of course the case was first heard in the courts of New Hampshire. There a court of Republican complexion upheld the view that Dartmouth was a public corporation and therefore its charter was subject to amendment by the legislature. If Dartmouth lay beyond the reach of the public will, the court was ready to take alarm at the possibility that the trustees of the college might forget the public trust reposed in them and might exercise their powers to promote narrow sectarian or even political views. Here the court was slapping at the establishment or "standing order," as it was then known, which had been dominated by a clerical-political alliance of Congregationalism and Federalism since the college's founding. The antidote for such imbalance was public control. The prosperity of the college, the court continued, depends on the public esteem in which it is held. If this esteem is impaired by public distrust of the motives of private trustees, it will avail the college nothing to maintain at law successfully that the public will was wrong.[22]

This reasoning had the backing of none other than Thomas Jefferson. Writing to Governor Plummer of New Hampshire he vigorously contended that "the idea that institutions established for the use of the Nation can not be touched or modified even to make them answer their end, because of rights gratuitously supposed in those employed to manage them in trust for the public, may, perhaps, be a salutary provision against the abuses of a monarch, but it is most absurd against the Nation itself."[23]

Daniel Webster, who had undertaken the brief for his alma mater, did not expect to win in the state court. Rather his hope lay in an appeal to the United States Supreme Court, where he could argue the added point that the Dartmouth charter was a contract and that the attempt of New Hampshire to amend it was unilateral impairment of the obligation of contract in direct contravention of the federal constitution. While such unilateral action would not have impeded the English Parliament in legislating for Oxford and Cambridge, it was a real stumbling block in the new federal constitution. Apart from this technical argument Webster also returned to the question of public control. On this point he reasoned to the court that the college would lead a precarious existence if it were to be subject to the fluctuation of public opinion or the rise and fall of political parties. Then private benefactors would turn away, uncertain of the purposes to which their bounty might be put, and learned men would be wary of devoting their lives to teaching, unsure of the title to their freeholds or professorships. Chief Justice Marshall, himself a Federalist, sided with Webster and carried a majority of the court with him on both the point of contract and the point of holding the college a private rather than a public corporation.[24]

The decision in the Dartmouth College Case was a momentous one. Chancellor Kent, great commentator on American law, declared that it gave "solidity and inviolability to the literary . . . institutions of our country."[25] While this has been the general view of posterity, the immediate effect was undoubtedly a victory for conservative forces. This decision together with the Yale Report[26] a decade later proved effective barriers against advancing democratic forces pressing for control of higher education and alteration of conventional curriculum policies. Neither barrier endeared the colleges to the populace. Gathering forces soon to find expression in Jacksonian democracy registered their misgivings by greatly reducing legislative subsidies to colleges, especially denying any notable share to them in the distribution of the surplus federal revenue returned to the states in 1837. Not only that, but, put on guard by this decision, state legislatures amended their laws of incorporation so as to limit the amount of property colleges might hold and also to reserve to the states the right of visitation in the newly established colleges.

Finance

This account of the early organization and administration of the colonial college would be incomplete without some attention to its financial structure. As might be expected, basically this structure reflected the private character of the institutions founded. The public subsidies which some early colleges received, regularly at first but later more and more sporadically, have misled some in the nineteenth and twentieth centuries to regard the colonial college as the state university of its day.[27] From the long history leading up to and ending in the Dartmouth College Case it must be clear that the colonial colleges considered themselves private foundations. They accepted public grants, to be sure, but never surrendered control over policy formation, not even when the state gained ex officio representation on some boards of control. As this critical point became more and more clear, it must be said, the grants became more and more sporadic. But they did not cease. Massachusetts made a last grant from the public treasury to Amherst as late as 1848. Even Dartmouth, undaunted by the judicial rebuff administered to the state of New Hampshire, had the temerity later on to ask its legislature for further public moneys.

Public subsidies took various forms. In addition to outright legislative grants Massachusetts early assigned to Harvard the income from the ferry across the

Charles River and later on the tolls when a bridge replaced the ferry. William and Mary, starting with a royal grant of £2,000, later received from Virginia the duties levied on skins and furs and still later a tax levied on tobacco. Connecticut turned over to Yale the proceeds from a French prize of war brought into the port of New London. Much later Massachusetts divided bank taxes among Harvard, Bowdoin, and Williams. All of which is to say nothing of the tax exemption enjoyed by seats of learning in these states. The total largesse of Massachusetts to Harvard during the colonial period amounted to $115,797.73.[28] Indirectly almost every colony aided the struggling colleges within its borders by granting them the right to run one or more lotteries. All these were successful in spite of grossing only 10 to 15 per cent of the take. Thus eighteen lotteries before the Revolution produced a total revenue of £12,000.[29]

Public subsidies, however, were never enough to meet the limited budgets of even colonial days. Consequently the colleges were constantly seeking subscriptions. The most handsome of these, of course, came from England. The famous *New England's First Fruits,* from which so much is learned of early colonial life, was really intended as a promotion pamphlet to solicit funds from the mother country. On one occasion, when agents of King's College and the University of Pennsylvania discovered that they were soliciting in England at the same time, they joined forces and divided the ultimate proceeds. In addition to political ties sectarian sympathies also prompted gifts. The English Bishop Berkeley's benevolence to Yale, however, was an interesting instance of an Anglican aiding an offshoot of dissenters. English benevolences, it is noteworthy, dropped off sharply after the Revolution. Yet, even without the Revolution it is likely that these funds would have ceased, since the English were beginning to suspect the integrity of American agents who often did not publish lists of givers as they had promised.

American gifts, while steady, were seldom large, the largest being £15,555 to King's College. Some benefactors gave what was most plenteous in this country, land, but values were low and rents difficult to manage if lands were distant from the beneficiary. While colleges tapped support from the lower middle class through lotteries they tried to tap the upper middle class and above by subscription lists after the middle of the eighteenth century. By the Revolution such lists had yielded £20,000. Yet capital endowment accumulated very slowly. Harvard's endowment, for instance, a century after its founding was only £11,500.[30]

A sizable portion of the college budget was met by tuition fees. But even with the higher purchasing power of money in colonial times this income was never great. As late as 1779, Dartmouth's tuition was only $13, with an additional dollar for incidentals. But student expenses were constantly rising from earliest times. Board, room, and tuition which came to 15 pounds, 12 shillings at Yale in 1720, came to 16 pounds, 17 shillings eight years later and to 19 pounds, 9 shillings in 1737.[31] With currency inflation caused by the war, Harvard was only charging $20 in 1807. Not all colonial tuitions were paid in currency; they were frequently paid in kind—grain, cotton, sheep, pewter, and the like. There is a record of the Harvard treasurer's having sold a pair of shoes which had been given in lieu of cash. Sometimes colleges were not even paid in kind but in promissory notes. Only six of Dartmouth's graduating class of thirty-nine in 1806 had squared their financial accounts with the college. The rest owed a combined account of $1,222.18, to say nothing of $2,317.47 owed by the other three classes.[32] This amounted perforce to a student loan fund long before the day of such formally recognized funds.

The principal current expense of the colonial college was faculty salaries. As usual they were distressingly low. Indeed, tutors were paid so little that except by remaining celibate during their tutorship they could not have made ends meet. William and Mary paid its faculty a minimum salary together with such fees as they might collect from the students. This system was expected to prick the energy of the faculty and reward initiative. But the chances are that the poverty of the institution had a part to play in it. However earned, salaries were still discouragingly low in the early part of the nineteenth century. At that time Francis Wayland, the president of Brown, noted that college salaries were far below those of other professionals. Not only that but a man's salary on entering a college career was likely to remain practically unchanged throughout his incumbency and that with very little expectancy of supplementing it on the side. Indeed it was not difficult to argue that early higher education in America was financed in part by the exploitation of the professor.[33] Consequently it came as no surprise that it was difficult to recruit capable young men for college teaching.[34]

The colonial charter of Brown provided an indirect subsidy to its faculty by exempting them from taxes. While Brown seems to have been the only American college enjoying this privilege, the custom was more widespread in Europe, deriving as it did from the medieval university which perpetuated the custom from the times of the Roman emperors. This privilege, however, proved invidious and odious to the citizens of Rhode Island and early steps were taken before the Revolutionary War to curtail or terminate it. No success attended these efforts till nearly a century later, at the time of the Civil War, when there was a clamor that its taxes be borne more evenly by the population. The issue was compromised in 1863 by an act of the state legislature and approved by the college to limit the tax exemption to a maximum of $10,000 of real estate. Obviously without the approval of the college the law would have been unconstitutional according to the Dartmouth College Case. This vestige of privilege disappeared altogether when after World War II the college itself voluntarily petitioned the legislature to end it.[35]

Obviously, with income and outgo never better than precariously balanced, early college administrators had to make a little go a long way. As most of the college income had to be spent for current expenses, little at first accrued in the form of permanent endowment. Consequently the "dead hand" did not lie so heavily on American institutions of higher learning as it did on European ones. Probably for the same reason America did not develop a theory of endowments in the eighteenth century as Turgot had done in France and Adam Smith in England.

Unfortunately what permanent funds accumulated were not always managed to the best advantage. Princeton's early funds are an example. There permanent funds were sometimes applied to current deficits; sometimes they were not all fully invested; and on still other occasions they were loaned out on mere personal security.[36] Among the examples of better management was the way in which Harvard pulled through the currency depreciation of the Revolutionary period with a minimum impairment of its resources. This was due not only to the excellent discretion of the treasurer but also, as claimed earlier, to the transformation of the corporation from an educational to a lay membership.[37]

3

Early Student Life

The history of higher education, especially in the English-speaking world, pertains to more than college charters, courses of study, administrative systems, and degree requirements, important as all of these may be. It also must take into account the student—his characteristics, his attitudes, his organizational activities.

The history of college life in America before the twentieth century breaks down into two distinct periods, with a clear-cut dividing line coming about 1850. During the first of these eras, religious influences were important, a strict system of moralistic discipline prevailed, literary societies played a dominant role on the campus, and student rebellions peppered the annals of every college in America. In the second period, ebullient student energies found new outlets in intercollegiate athletics and the varied activities of Greek-letter fraternities. It is with the first of these periods that we deal in this chapter.

Social Origins and Personal Finances

Even in the colonial period the American college man by no means represented an exclusive caste. In the atmosphere of growing democracy which the opportunities of a pioneer society made possible, there was no special elite which could, as in still basically feudal Europe, maintain a monopoly of the higher learning. In early America there were always chances for a poor and ambitious youth to go to college and thus elevate himself into the professional classes.

A survey of the social status of parents of Harvard College students during the later seventeenth century (1677–1703) bears this out. Of 300 fathers listed, the largest number (79) were ministers. These were followed by "merchants, shopkeepers, master mariners" (45), "magistrates and lawyers" (34) and "wealthy farmers, militia officers, etc." (28). However, there were also 31 Harvard parents listed as "artisans, seamen, and servants" and 11 who were "ordinary farmers."[1] In the eighteenth century, however, students at Yale and Harvard were ranked arbitrarily for purposes of recitation and academic procession and were listed in the Triennial Catalogue on the basis of the "supposed Dignity of the Families" to which they belonged. The first 10 per cent of each class was made up of the sons of magistrates, the next 20 per cent was composed of children of graduates of the college, and the final 70 per cent included sons of merchants, farmers, and artisans arranged, according to one authority, "in an order which cannot be explained by wealth or social position."[2]

By the late eighteenth and early nineteenth centuries, however, the yearly expenses at older colleges like Harvard, Yale, and Pennsylvania had become high in terms of the available cash income of most American families of the time. These high fees tended increasingly to restrict such institutions to the well-to-do and to give them a fundamentally "patrician" character. In this period, expenses of college life at Harvard averaged from $300 to $400 a year. Although the average charge at Princeton was somewhat lower, well-to-do students there often spent $100 to $200 in excess of the minimum, and a few even had from $500 to $1,500 to spend. These "bloods" and "sports" brought stables of saddle horses and packs of hunting dogs with them. The Princeton faculty was finally obliged to prohibit the keeping of horses, dogs, or sporting arms by students, and to make participation in a duel a cause for instant dismissal.[3]

The high cost of a college education worried some educators, and they tried to overcome it. Harvard ever since colonial times had maintained a number of petty positions for poorer students, whose services were compensated by assessments on the paying students. Princeton in 1831 introduced the experiment of two tables for board, one at $82 and the other at $61 a year.[4] President Day of Yale about this time tried to raise a fund to aid needy students.[5]

Many impecunious young men "worked their way" through college during the early period. A favorite way of doing this was by means of part-time school teaching. The long college winter vacations were often arranged in such a way that by granting students a couple of weeks extra leave they were enabled to teach a "district school" for the entire winter term.[6]

Even more important for the would-be college student of limited means was the founding of new "hilltop" colleges which made a definite appeal to this kind of clientele. Such, for example, were Williams and Amherst, strict denominational colleges where poor but deserving lads could prepare for the orthodox ministry uncontaminated by contact with the profligate rich. In these ascetic communities could be found the poor but pious sons of local farmers, stirred to pursue higher education by the eloquence of their local parsons.[7] At Williams College, Nathaniel Hawthorne took careful note of the type: "Country graduates —rough, brown featured, schoolmaster-looking, half-bumpkin, half-scholar, in black, ill-cut broadcloth. . . . A rough-hewn, heavy set of fellows from the hills and woods in this neighborhood."[8]

Most of the colleges founded in every part of the union in the first half of the nineteenth century were just such denominational "hilltop" colleges. This movement was multiplying opportunities for a higher education. At many of these schools young men intending to become ministers could obtain financial aid from the denomination to pay for their education. In addition, there were special scholarships at some of them, such as the ten prize Eliphalet Nott scholarships at Union College.[9] Also, some of the colleges extended credit to their students.[10]

It was with these denominational schools in mind that the Reverend John Todd, in an appeal on behalf of the Society for the Promotion of Collegiate and Theological Education at the West, declared in 1847: "Our Colleges are *chiefly* and *mainly* institutions designed for the poor and those in moderate circumstances, and not for the rich. . . . We have no institutions in the land more truly *republican* than our Colleges."[11]

Dormitories: The "Collegiate Way of Life"

English concepts of the proper housing of college students were planted in America by the colonial college. These may be summed up simply by the phrase the "collegiate way of life." Unlike the Continental university, which was not concerned with the student outside the lecture hall, Oxford and Cambridge had made the residential colleges the heart of their educational procedures. These institutions were more than dormitory houses. They were designed to bring the faculty and students together in a common life which was both intellectual and moral.

The colonial colleges tried to follow this pattern, but it was not long before they were obliged to diverge from it. No group of coordinate colleges clustering around one university center was built up in the New World. In addition, the poverty of American resources prevented the construction of elaborate quadrangular structures; the spareness of the resultant barrackslike dormitories was not designed to foster the characteristic close and well-knit social life of the English college. Indeed, the first coherent architectural plan for an American college did not make an appearance until 1814, when Joseph Jacques Ramée, aristocratic French *émigré*, drew one up for Union College at the request of President Nott.[12]

From the first there were American critics of the "collegiate way of living." Increase Mather, president of Harvard toward the end of the seventeenth century, advised the organizers of Yale to follow the example of the Continental universities, whose students boarded in town. In 1800, the Reverend Manasseh Cutler advised against the erection of elaborate residence halls for a contemplated university in Ohio. In Cutler's view, such halls were too often "the secret nurseries of every vice and the cages of unclean birds." President Wayland of Brown wrote in 1842 that the elaborate residential colleges of Oxford and Cambridge were an inadvisable financial extravagance. Far better, he argued, to have used the money to erect twenty universities to elevate the mass of the people. One of Wayland's principal worries was that dormitories presented a menace to the maintenance of the system of paternalistic discipline and close supervision of student life which he felt to be essential. "It matters really but little," he wrote, "whether an Institution be situated in a town or in the country. Place it where you will, in a few years, there will cluster around it all the opportunities of idle and vicious expenditure. Under such circumstances, it is obvious that no physical means can be devised which shall furnish such supervision as will present an impassable barrier to unlawful inclination."[13]

Occasional criticisms of this nature did not turn the early American college against the dormitory. Nevertheless, the pressure of American circumstances tended to make it difficult to apply the English system here as it was meant to function. The colleges of Oxford and Cambridge had become by the nineteenth century important educational agencies, while American dormitories of the same period were little more than places for students to sleep, eat, and study. Why this difference? The absence of self-contained quadrangles in America undoubtedly played a part in it as did the fact that American professors were usually married men, residing at some distance from the college. (English dons were compelled to remain unmarried and to live in the college.) Also, in America the common table came to be occupied frequently by students alone, while in England it remained "common" because the whole college, students and faculty alike, ate there regularly.

Most important, in America, the problem of student discipline came to inter- fere with the development of a coherent college life. During the eighteenth century, the responsibility for disciplinary problems at Oxford and Cambridge fell into the hands of special officials known as deans, proctors, and beadles. This freed the dons from the necessity of enforcing petty administrative regulations. Students and their teachers were thus enabled to become close intellectual, and sometimes personal, friends. In this setting, the English colleges found it easy to liberalize their instructional procedures by developing the individual tutorial system.

The contrary came to be true in America. Faculty members remained saddled with the responsibility of enforcing all disciplinary regulations. They thus ap- peared in the guise of the students' natural enemies. Instead of separating the teaching and proctoring functions, American colleges, with their compulsory class and chapel attendance, disciplinary regulations, and daily recitations, made it practically impossible for students and professors to develop close and amicable relations.[14]

Religion in College Life: Moral Supervision

In the early colonial period religion dominated student life. All the colleges prescribed regular prayer, church attendance on the Sabbath, and theological study. Even with the liberalization of many of these institutions along inter- denominational lines, these prescriptions remained. Student conduct was closely supervised according to the moral precepts of the Christian religion.

The impact of the American and French revolutions proved unsettling to this system of intellectual control.[15] Entering William and Mary College in 1805, Winfield Scott, later a famous military commander, found that "the spring tide of infidelity had been reached."[16] Williams College, founded in 1793, was swept by much the same influence. Few church members enrolled there at first, and ridicule was heaped upon students who showed signs of Christian orthodoxy. And so it went at college after college. It was now the fashion for students to scoff at formal religion as superstition, to form rationalist clubs, to salute each other with nicknames like "Volney," "Voltaire," and "Rousseau." A president of Harvard found himself obliged to deny publicly as a vicious lie the charge which had appeared in a Boston newspaper that professors at his institution were poisoning the minds of the students with Gibbon's *Decline and Fall of the Roman Empire.*[17]

When the pendulum of student opinion had swung so far to the left, it was almost inevitable that it would some day swing almost as far in the opposite direction. Indeed, this is what came to pass in the early nineteenth century. Colleges now came to be agitated by fervent religious revivals, and numerous Christian associations were formed. This change in the academic atmosphere definitely reflected the influence of the powerful conservative attack upon the Enlightenment which was going forward in the United States at this time. What Dixon Ryan Fox has denominated the "Protestant Counter-Reformation" was regaining much lost ground for orthodoxy. Conservative clergymen were fastening the label of "infidelity" on all domestic sympathizers with the Enlightenment or with the French Revolution.[18] As late as the 1860s the following rule was in effect at Yale: "If any Student shall profess or endeavor to propagate a disbelief in the divine authority of the Holy Scriptures, and shall persist therein after admonition, he shall no longer be a member of the College."[19]

This outburst of orthodox religiosity was signalized on college campuses by the development of evangelistic "revivals." As early as 1801 Williams experienced such a movement, and soon other institutions were similarly affected.[20] A good example of the workings of the revivalistic spirit is afforded by Amherst College. Here the faculty made the most energetic efforts to "save" the souls of each succeeding crop of freshmen. A desperate "now or never" attitude toward conversion prevailed. The professors, nearly all of whom were evangelistic clergymen, felt this was the last chance to convert the "unsaved" among the students to Christian truth and to steer into the clerical profession as many among the "saved" as could be interested.

It was considered a calamity if a class passed through its whole four years at Amherst without going through at least one revival. Therefore every possible occasion was used to impress upon the students their need of salvation. The atmosphere was emotional, subjective, romanticist—a far cry from the rational temper of seventeenth-century Puritan Christianity.[21]

The diary of William Otis Carr, a student at Amherst during the 1850s, gives us a vivid picture of one of these revivals. In March, 1855, he tells us, the president's preaching started the movement going, and a visiting evangelist stirred it up further.

One young man, who gloried in his wicked ways and seemed the first in any forbidden scheme, was stopped in his maddened course and, blessed be to God, made a new creature. And what a change! . . . His first act was to banish from his room the servants of sin. He threw into the fire his cards. To the same flame he consigned his immense cane so carefully prepared to row the Freshmen, and upon this he poured the contents of his brandy bottle. . . . Many are giving up their foul feasts on tobacco, and instead of the curse, from almost every room may now be heard the voice of prayer. It is wonderful to perceive the holy calm that reigns around us.[22]

Of course, if a student happened to be a nonconformist who was not impressed by these emotional crusades, life at an evangelistic college could become unpleasant. All the weight of the college administration was thrown behind participation. President Heman Humphrey of Amherst kept a "little list" where he noted down the numbers in each class who were "hopefully pious" and those who were not![23] Even more serious were the pressures brought by one's own fellow classmates. Just as in the late eighteenth century the herd instinct of students made life uncomfortable for those who did not choose to emulate Voltaire and Rousseau, so now the same adolescent mob psychology harassed those who did not "see the light" of evangelistic religion. Rutherford B. Hayes, nineteenth United States President, found this to be true when a student at Kenyon College, Ohio, in 1839. A revival had become the all-engrossing subject, and only ten students had not as yet "changed." He was one of the ten. "Every single one of my best friends are 'gone,' as it is called," he wrote home. "I have but little hope I shall be among them. If I am not, I fear I can never spend as happy a time in Kenyon as I have."[24]

Closely involved in sponsoring revivals were the many student religious associations, or "societies of inquiry," which now sprang up, mushroomlike, throughout the land. A typical example was the Yale Moral Society, organized in 1797. This group required its members to pledge themselves to conduct their lives according to the precepts of the Bible, to abstain from profanity, to refrain from card playing and gambling, and to suppress all vice or immorality at college. It was particularly active in helping to bring about the Yale revivals of 1802 and 1812.[25]

One survey of the student religious societies found that over ninety of them were established between 1810 and 1850. During this period, their principal emphasis, originally set in motion by the so-called Haystack Group at Williams College, was focused upon the problem of worldwide evangelism. Thus it was a result of this student movement that the first American Foreign Missionary Sending Society was organized in 1810.[26]

In the early American college, one of the principal instruments for moral supervision and religious indoctrination was compulsory chapel. This usually took the form of prayers held twice every day and prescribed services on the Sabbath. With the coming of religious toleration for all denominations of Protestants, students were permitted to attend churches of their own choice on Sundays, but sometimes this freedom was more nominal than real.[27]

The pattern is to be found in one college after another in the early and mid-nineteenth century. One historian has given us a vivid picture of how it went at early Union College:

. . . it is easy to picture the College in President Maxcy's time, when the ringing of the Chapel bell called sleepy boys to "repair in a decent and orderly manner" without running violently in the entries or down the stairs, to prayers that were to open the day. We can see the college butler on a cold pitch-black winter morning at his post beside the pulpit stairs, when the officers file in, holding his candle high so that the president may safely mount to read the scripture lesson from the sacred desk, to petition the Almighty on behalf of the little academic group, and to address to his charges such admonition as in his judgment they require,—sure of each lad's attention, on penalty of a four-cent fine. . . . All this was repeated in evening prayers each day.[28]

In the ante-bellum South, at Oglethorpe University in Georgia, much the same state of affairs prevailed. Everybody had to be in chapel for morning prayers at 6:30 A.M. At 5 P.M., when classes were finished, all students returned to the chapel to hear one of the professors pray for forgiveness for the sins committed since sunrise. All lesson assignments over the weekend were made from the Bible or some theological work, so that the students would be concerned with proper subjects over the Sabbath. On Sunday, students attended two religious services —a long one in the morning, and a shorter one at 5 P.M.[29]

What did students of the time think of these requirements? Some confided to their diaries a distaste for compulsory chapel, but in many cases this seems to have been inspired more by laziness than by profound convictions that intellectual freedom was being violated.[30] William G. Hammond, a student at Amherst in the 1840s, had thought seriously about the problem, however. He noted in his diary his reasons for disliking chapel: "I do really think these public prayers do more harm than good to the religious feeling of a majority of students: they are regarded as an idle bore, and only tend to do away with that feeling of reverence with which everyone naturally regards an address to the Deity."[31]

The author of an article on college chapel in Barnard's *Journal* for 1857 did not agree with young Hammond. Professor F. D. Huntington argued here that attendance at chapel should be universal, should be required, and "decorous deportment should be positively enforced under strict sanctions." Why? The student should understand that he must come to chapel because of "the combined dictate of revelation, of history, of human want and welfare, and of the ripest judgment of the best men." What if a student should plead that his heart was not in the service; that outside compliance would be an insincerity? He should be told that the rule exists to aid his deficiency and facilitate his interested participation. Huntington concluded by asserting that a college which wholly renounced compulsory chapel would soon lose the confidence of the community.[32]

Fagging, Hazing, and the Class System

The development of the class system is a unique feature of American college life. From earliest days all students who entered at the same time were considered members of a single class and continued so for instructional and administrative purposes throughout their college course. The common dormitory life for four years built a social bond among members of the same class which came to last throughout life.

From England came the tradition of listing each class in strict order of seniority.[33] Along with this was imported the English school custom of "fagging," whereby lower-class members had to run errands and serve as unpaid servants for upperclassmen.

Oliver Wolcott, who served at one time as governor of Connecticut, has left us a priceless description of the fagging system as he saw it when he applied for admission to Yale in 1773. He observed men in black robes, white wigs, and high cocked hats; young men in black silk gowns, some with bands and others without; and young men in camlet gowns. He was told that the first were professors; the second either tutors or resident graduates, to whom the title of Sir was to be accorded; and the third, students. He also noted a group in the College Yard who wore no gowns and who walked, but did not dare to run or jump. They either appeared to be much in awe of the young men in gowns or gave them surly looks. In turn, the young "gownsmen" treated these young fellows with what Wolcott thought was hardness and indignity. "Nevill," one would say, "go to my room, middle story of the old College, No. ———, and take from it a pitcher, fill it from the pump, place it in my room, and stay there till I return." The answer would vary, depending on the circumstances. It might go like this, "I have been sent on an errand." "Who sent you?" "Tutor H." Or the mandate might be submitted to, "pleasantly with a smile, or contemptuously with a sneer." Wolcott was told that the domineering young men in gowns were sophomores and those without hats or gowns freshmen who "out of the Hours of Study, were waiters or servants to the Authority, President, Professors, Tutors, and Undergraduates."[34]

Conditions had not changed appreciably when Lyman Beecher enrolled at Yale in the 1790s. He was soon "sent for to a room so full of tobacco-smoke you could not see across it. There I was asked all manner of questions, in English and Latin, and received all manner of solemn advice. Then Forbes, a big fellow, took me as his fag."[35]

G. Stanley Hall once compared fagging in schools to the primitive initiation rites of savage peoples, a form of predatory adolescent aggression.[36] Certainly there were some educators in colonial times who considered the practice undesirable and sought to suppress it. As early as 1667 the Harvard Board of Overseers imposed penalties on all found guilty of participating in it. The system was not easily overturned, however. Some college presidents resisted change in this respect. Ezra Stiles of Yale liked the old English system so much that when freshmen came to him complaining of oppression by the sophomores, they were sent away. His successor, Timothy Dwight, had a different attitude: He secured the official abolition of all fagging at Yale. Gradually, the coming in of a more democratic social philosophy after the American Revolution doomed fagging in all the colleges where it had existed.[37]

As fagging faded out, "hazing" came in as a new method of initiating and disciplining freshmen. This new practice soon had college administrations just as worried as they had been by the old. Often hazing came to be institutionalized in the form of a "rush"—an organized struggle between the freshman and sophomore classes. This ranged all the way from rough-and-tumble fighting to organized wrestling matches. Sometimes "townies," such as lumbermen at Bowdoin and sailors at Yale, would pitch in enthusiastically during the more violent rushes. If the freshmen won, they had to be accorded some privilege, such as the right to carry canes.[38]

The Literary Society

A wide range of undergraduate activities developed in the early American college, but among them all, the literary society enjoyed undisputed pre-eminence until well after the middle of the nineteenth century. The literary society was essentially a debating club. Its primary concern was with public speaking of various kinds—oratorical display, criticism, debate, or disputation. Since the nineteenth-century college's methodology, except for the lingering place of the forensic (English) disputation, was dominated by the recitation, there was little opportunity for free and unreserved expression. The literary societies provided an outlet where student discussion could develop without restraint. Moreover, public speaking played a prominent part in the various professional pursuits for which the students were preparing. Political oratory, sermonizing, pleading a case in court, and teaching were all activities which might play a vital role in the later lives of these youths, and they needed all the oratorical practice they could get. Not all society proceedings were decorous, however, nor were all the questions debated solemn and serious. Minutes of early literary societies indicate that horseplay and frivolity sometimes spiced their sessions.[39]

As time went on, these societies came to be the center of interest on the campus. "A new order of champions and hero worship developed." At most colleges, at least two rival literary societies appeared, and sometimes three. Between them the most heated rivalry existed. It was expressed in competition over the building of the societies' libraries, in the electing of honorary members, and in the recruiting of new student members. Rivalry was especially hot in debates between representatives of the contending societies and in the selection of student speakers for commencement or for the public displays of oratorical prowess which were referred to at that time as college "exhibitions." The literary societies commanded the kind of passionate student loyalty which was later accorded to fraternities and athletic teams. This is why such hectic efforts were made to raise money for the society libraries and for the furnishing of clubrooms.[40] It also explains why such frantic electioneering went on during the campaigns for offices in the societies. The question of status and rank within the society interested many students far more than the formal curriculum. President Hitchcock of Amherst found the literary society elections were "often as hotly contested as those for the various offices in our State and National governments." The importance of this kind of activity as a training ground for a political career is obvious.[41]

As the nineteenth century progressed, college administrations became increasingly aware of the significance of the role played by the literary societies. The result was that faculties provided for more careful supervision of the activities of these organizations; in some cases, colleges contributed to their support. The societies were correctly recognized as being more than a mere extracurricular phenomenon. They came to be the center of interest on the campus, a powerful student-financed and student-controlled educational enterprise paralleling (some feared even threatening) the narrow and traditional classical program of the old-time college.[42]

The history of literary societies at Princeton may serve to illustrate the general development of these student organizations. Here the famous American Whig Society and the Cliosophic Society had got started as early as 1770 as the two great centers of student life. They soon acquired impressive halls of their own and large private libraries, financed by subscriptions from graduate members and those still in college. Strictest secrecy was enjoined on all members in regard to laws, usages, and transactions. On public occasions, however, the students wore a badge, blue for Whig and pink for Clio, to indicate their affiliation.

A high spirit of competition developed between the two societies, involving the question of the division of college and commencement honors (such as salutatorian and valedictorian) between their members. Furthermore, the two halls made strenuous efforts to "hoax" or "hux" members of each incoming class and secure them for members of their society. Students were approached before they even came to Princeton or were waylaid at the railroad station. When debates were held between the two halls they attracted as much student interest as football was later to do. In fact, the student body was so divided into opposing camps that it was not practicable for friends to continue amicable relations if they belonged to different halls. It was unheard of, for example, for a Whig to room with a Clio.[43]

In the years following the Civil War, the literary societies gradually declined in importance. A student of this phenomenon explains the decline as an inevitable reaction to the rise of competing student organizations, the increasing importance of intercollegiate athletics, the improvement of the college libraries, and the broadening of the curriculum to include subjects which were once the special domain of the literary societies (notably public speaking, modern literature, political science, and history).[44] While this explanation for the demise of the societies sounds plausible, there may well have been a number of other factors involved, some developing on campus and others coming from beyond the college gates.

Other Student Activities

As the eighteenth century wore on, many different kinds of student clubs came to be formed in American colleges. Harvard had them as early as 1719, when groups of pious youth got together, partly as a form of self-defense against the "rakes" and "blades" of the time. The boys met at one another's rooms, read poems, held learned conversation, and enjoyed some tobacco and beer. Later in the century came the Porcellian Club, which catered to the "bloods" and had as its motto *Dum vivimus vivamus.* Soon afterward the Hasty Pudding Institute was established, aiming at a combination of literary activity with conviviality.[45]

In the early nineteenth century, there continued to be an active extracurricular life in addition to that provided by the regular literary societies. Taking Amherst as an example, we find there a number of "quaint" or convivial student organizations, which usually went to great lengths to keep their proceedings secret. Such was the Concatenation Society, which possessed a ghostly room in the "Old South" College, from which its members sallied forth to "tongue" the bell or discipline freshmen. More convivial was the H.E.O.T.T. Society, whose motto was popularly interpreted as meaning "Ho! Every One That Thirsteth."[46]

Students in these times also indulged in amateur dramatics. Early in the history of William and Mary College, its students produced a play. Student acting could also be found at Princeton as early as 1754 and at Harvard by 1758. Then, too, one of the main activities of the early Amherst literary societies, "to break the monotony of the regular exercises," was the performance of comedies which were composed and acted by the members. Thus, although some still regarded the regular theater as the haunt of Satan, this did not prevent college students from enjoying amateur theatricals.[47]

Music, too, where not banned from the campus, had charms for the student of this period. There was a small student orchestra at Princeton in 1791, and Harvard students had a singing club by 1793 and a student orchestra by 1808. Music served as a diversion for many of the students at the early University of Virginia. At Dartmouth College, the Handel Society, which was even older than the famous Handel and Haydn Society of Boston, sang both at chapel services and at special concerts for the people of the community.[48]

Dancing was not welcomed as warmly at all colleges. Jefferson permitted dancing lessons at the University of Virginia, and many balls were held within the "precincts" of that institution. There were many colleges, however, which maintained definite rules against such "Satanic" goings on.[49]

Students in these early days had few opportunities for physical exercise in the form of play or sports. As time went on, college authorities became more and more concerned about the effects of lack of exercise upon student health. Many felt that something had to be done to stave off "the hectic glow of consumption's hidden fire," which was beginning to be seen on far too many student countenances. Moreover, it was thought that an active physical training program would be an excellent means of discipline to keep the boys busy and prevent undergraduate rebellions.[50]

It was largely for this last reason that the Harvard faculty in 1826 decided to try to "work the devil out of the students" by authorizing the new German instructor, Carl Follen, to establish a college gymnasium. Elaborate rules of exercise were drawn up in accordance with the best contemporary German principles. Although Harvard students soon tired of gymnastics, finding the drillmaster element in them disagreeable, the movement spread rapidly from college to college. After 1840, a number of college gymnasium buildings were constructed. This is the closest that the pre-Civil War college came to official sponsorship of athletic activities.[51]

Rowdies, Riots, and Rebellions

G. Stanley Hall saw the history of early student life as one of the richest possible sources for the illustration of parallelism and recapitulation in human cultural development. Here was an authentic counterpart of the savage life studied by the anthropologist. Here the rigors of overwork and excessive restraint, unrelieved by a vent for superabounding animal spirits in athleticism, led to exorbitant license, rioting, dissipation, vandalism, and even personal assaults. Here were illustrations of all phases of subcivilized existence, complete even to the secret associations so characteristic of savagery: the elaborate initiations, the abuses perpetrated on newcomers, and the personal encounters.[52]

Anyone who studies the history of American undergraduate life from the first colonial colleges to the Civil War will find ample evidence to justify Hall's generalizations. This was a period when constant warfare raged between faculty and students, when college government at best was nothing but a paternal despotism, when the most outrageous pranks and disturbances were provoked by undisciplined and incredibly bold young men. It was pre-eminently a period of rowdies, riots, and rebellions.

Many contemporary observers agreed that one reason for this state of affairs was the almost total lack of friendly relations between student and professor. Outside the classroom it was not "good form" for the two to be good friends. If a student went unsummoned to a professor's room, he almost always went at night. If he entered a classroom before the bell or remained after class to ask the instructor a question, he ran the risk of being considered an outcast by his fellows, a "blue," a "blue skin," or a "fisher."[53] Some college presidents publicly deplored the situation, but even these refused to face the fact that the main reason for this long-standing feud was the parental system of petty discipline which prevailed in every American college.[54]

In this country, the instructional officers were also saddled with sole responsibility for maintaining discipline. The hapless clergymen-professors of this era had to do more than teach; they were also required to be "detectives, sheriffs, and prosecuting attorneys." Most of the time at faculty meetings was taken up with discipline cases. In the case of general student disturbances, which under this system were endemic, the entire faculty would go on the chase for offenders![55]

Published college records and laws of this period make quite clear that American college "government" then meant rigorous control of student conduct both in and out of the classroom. The atmosphere resembled that of a low-grade boys' boarding school straight out of the pages of Dickens. It was adapted more to restless and unruly boys than to responsible young college men, and, indeed, most of the students of this time resembled the former far more than they did the latter.

The Harvard College Laws of 1642 set the pattern, and they in turn were borrowed from seventeenth-century English Latin school and residential college regulations. Subsequent American colleges followed this example and erected a veritable strait jacket of petty rules in which to confine their young charges. Every possible aspect of student life was regulated—promptness, attendance at classes and prayers, dressing, idling, fishing, gunning, dancing, drinking, gambling, fighting, gaming, swearing, and so on ad infinitum. The nineteenth-century disciplinary regime was by no means limited to colleges which were Protestant or severely Calvinistic in outlook; it could be found in similarly rigid form in the early Roman Catholic institutions.[56]

The attitude of President Wayland of Brown was typical. The students must be protected from the moral dangers of the city of Providence. The control of "impulsive and thoughtless young men" was necessarily different from the government of adults. It must be "conciliatory, kind, persuasive, or, in a word, parental." Wayland's philosophy of discipline was summed up in his address to his first senior class. "But a few men fail for want of intellect," he declared. "There are two sources of failure in the world, first moral deviation, second indolence."[57]

The source of this rigorous paternalistic regimen was obviously to be found in the sternly pietist and religious matrix of the "old-time" college. Noah Porter of Yale expressed its philosophy very well when he said: "To hold the student to minute fidelity in little things is an enforcement of one of the most significant maxims of the Gospel." Laurence Veysey hits the nail on the head when he observes that "college disciplinarians essentially desired a controlled environment for the production of the morally and religiously upright."[58]

Elaborate punishments were devised for offenses against these rules. Although corporal punishment for college students had gone out of fashion by the early eighteenth century, various types of fines continued to be imposed by faculties, some of them quite stiff. In addition, seniority rights and other privileges were taken away at times, or students were excluded from classes, suspended from college, or even permanently expelled. The last-named was the ultimate disciplinary weapon at the disposal of college administrations.

One of the leading sources of discontent among students of this period was the food served in college commons. The earliest recorded rebellion at Harvard occurred in 1766 over bad butter at the commons. Numerous others followed, for similar reasons, both there and elsewhere.[59]

Another disciplinary problem which gave the authorities trouble was student drinking. In the colonial period, alcoholic sociability was a regular and accepted part of social relations, not just at college but in every circle of society. Colleges put restrictions on the use of "hard" liquors, but had none whatsoever on ale, beer, or wine. In fact, for a long time beer was furnished at commons, and a regular provision of wine was given out to students at commencement. In the early nineteenth century, many colleges, perhaps under the influence of the temperance movement, undertook to ban all drinking by students. Some even tried to extend this ban to all use of tobacco and all cardplaying. It does not seem that these official restrictions cut down appreciably on college imbibing.[60]

The early American colleges were apparently not bothered with too many problems arising from student relations with the opposite sex. There are occasional reports of wenching, as when complaints were made at Harvard that students were meeting ladies of easy virtue at a tavern in Somerville, just over the line from Cambridge. However, faculty minutes of the period never specify problems of illicit sex relations. Either the topic was not mentioned in polite company or there was a high degree of student chastity.[61]

In dealing with problems of student discipline, there were a few scattered efforts before the Civil War to bring about a more democratic system of college government, but not much was accomplished. In 1828, the Amherst undergraduates organized what was known as a "House of Students"; this early experiment with student self-government functioned for only a few months. A few years later, the students at the Hamilton Literary and Theological Institute (Colgate) formed a students' association which was permitted by the faculty to take over many of the functions of policing the institution. About the same time, Kenyon College in Ohio introduced a system of individual faculty advisers for each student. In addition, there was a tendency under presidents Dwight of Yale, Nott of Union, Hopkins of Williams, and Wayland of Brown to moderate somewhat the severity of college discipline and to appeal to the manly self-respect of students. Nevertheless, in most colleges the traditional authoritarian system, buttressed by religious concepts, remained the rule.[62]

The most notable of the early experiments with student self-government was that at the University of Virginia. Thomas Jefferson firmly believed in the ability of students to govern themselves. He wished to do away with the employment of fear in discipline and preferred instead to substitute appeals to pride and ambition. For this reason, in addition to elective courses, he advocated the enforcement of university ordinances by a board of student censors selected by the faculty. Following the example of European universities, there was also to be a proctor to look after discipline, and this official was to have the powers of a justice of the peace. A university court, made up of student representatives, was to consider all disciplinary cases, with the professor of law serving as presiding judge. This court was to have coordinate jurisdiction with other regular state courts and was to have the power to summon a grand jury.

The plan did not work out well in practice for a number of reasons. First of all, the Virginia legislature twice refused to establish the proposed court (with its own university jail) and also was unwilling to make the proctor a justice of the peace. Then, too, the majority of the first students at Charlottesville proved to be younger boys of an unruly disposition rather than the mature, serious type of student which Jefferson had in mind originally. Finally, the students were bound by a strong code of "honor" which prevented even the censors from informing on wrongdoers. Since there was no other compulsion but a moral one, students would not give evidence against each other. The result was that the university authorities found themselves practically helpless during the 1830s when serious rioting broke out on the campus.[63]

The most dramatic response of the pre-Civil War college student to the disciplinary system which ruled him was violent and open rebellion. Nearly every college experienced student rebellions or riots, some more serious than others. In certain cases, they eventuated in broken windows or cracked furniture; in others, they resulted in deaths. All involved some kind of collective action, either of a class or of a whole student body. These outbursts could be found in all sections of the country, at state universities and denominational colleges, at "godless" Harvard and Virginia and at pious Yale and Princeton. Everywhere the atmosphere was like that of a revolutionary brawl or a violent modern strike.

These rebellions posed perplexing problems for college authorities. Whatever their cause, the outbreaks were bound to damage the reputation of an institution. They might even bring about its financial ruin. They would occasion severe criticism of the faculty by parents, trustees, and the public in general. And how many students could most small and struggling colleges afford to expel without having to go out of business?

The most serious rebellions were those which either occurred in Southern colleges or took place in Northern institutions with large contingents of Southern students. Southern youth of this period simply did not take kindly to the rigorous discipline of the old paternalistic college system. These sons of the planter aristocracy hated college rules as fit only for slaves and were highly sensitive about anything that might compromise their "honor" as "gentlemen." Of course, New England clergymen had a different explanation for this situation. In their view, it was all due to the vogue of infidelity, Jeffersonianism, and rationalistic philosophy in the Southern states.[64]

In any event, some of the worst rioting came at the University of Virginia, where Jefferson had hoped to enshrine the principles of individual liberty and student self-government. These disturbances began while the founder was still alive, giving him some painful moments during this last period of his life. They reached a crescendo of violence during the 1830s and 1840s, and before they died down a professor had been killed and armed constables had to be brought to the campus by the local sheriff to restore order.[65]

Next to the Virginia riots, the worst seem to have occurred at Princeton. Here, too, could be found a large contingent of Southern students. Presbyterian faculty and trustees charged these youths with Deism, irreligion, and false notions of liberty, while the students responded with equal fervor, charging that their "natural rights" were being suppressed. More than half of the student body was suspended after a particularly violent rebellion in 1807. A new wave of disturbances began in 1814, during the presidency of Ashbel Green. The Reverend Dr. Green's diary gives us a plaintive picture of these rebellions, as seen from the faculty's point of view:

April 5, 1814. There were crackers in the institution today, and the evening was a most painful one to me. We met in faculty in a room of one of the tutors, and determined to dismiss two or three of the students. . . .

April 6, 1814. The faculty met in the evening, and a pistol was fired at the door of one of the tutors. I ought to be very thankful to God for his support this day.

January 19, 1817. A very serious riot commenced, with the manifest intention of preventing the usual religious exercises of that sacred day. . . . A great deal of glass was broken; an attempt was made to burn the out buildings, and the bell was rung incessantly.[66]

We should by no means assume, however, that all was peace and quiet on campuses in more northern latitudes. Student rioting at Yale, which had begun in the 1760s, reached a climax in the renowned "Bread and Butter Rebellion" of 1828 and the "Conic Section Rebellion" of 1830.[67] At the same time, town-and-gown riots in New Haven grew ever more serious. In 1841, in the "First Firemen's Riot," Yale students bested the local fire laddies in a general street fight and destroyed their equipment. In 1854, a fight between New Haven "townies" and the Yale boys resulted in the death of a local bartender. Four years later, a "Second Firemen's Riot" occurred, in the course of which a student shot and killed one of the firemen.[68]

Historian William H. Prescott, while a student at Harvard, lost the sight of one eye as the result of a brawl in the Harvard Commons. On another occasion a riot at a Harvard commencement blocked the way of President Everett and the British ambassador. One Harvard tutor of this period went through the rest of his life with a limp after an encounter with a group of student rioters. On another occasion, the college expelled forty-three of a class of seventy-three seniors on the eve of commencement, one of them the son of John Quincy Adams. By 1849, Harvard Commons had become so troublesome that President Jared Sparks ordered it abolished.[69]

Andrew Dickson White, recalling his own student days at Hobart and Yale in the 1850s, wrote: "I had, during my college life, known sundry college tutors seriously injured while thus doing police duty; I have seen a professor driven out of a room, through the panel of a door, with books, boots, and bootjacks hurled at his head; and even the respected president of a college, a doctor of divinity, while patrolling buildings with the janitors, subjected to outrageous indignity."[70]

In order to tighten their control of student unrest, many of the leading colleges formed a "gentleman's agreement" not to admit to their institutions students expelled from other schools. The weak point in this college combination against insubordination was Union College under President Eliphalet Nott. Justifiably or not, other Eastern college officials thought of Union as a kind of academic "Botany Bay" where students suffering under penal disabilities elsewhere could find an easy refuge. It was charged that this was the way Union built up its large enrollment of the time. Nott always vigorously denied these charges, although at the same time he refused to take part in the college combination against expellees.[71]

One reason that most American colleges were helpless in the face of these disturbances was that they lacked the legal power of the European universities to secure testimony and administer punishment. As we have seen, the University of Virginia was unable to secure such authority. When President Quincy, in 1834, called for grand jury action after a bad riot at Harvard, nothing was accomplished. It seemed to go against the American grain to take judicial measures against student disorder.[72]

How can we explain all this turbulence and trouble? Benjamin Silliman of Yale stated in a confidential memorandum that the cause was American democracy itself. It was all due to "the inflammable materials that are accumulated here, partaking too much—as regards a considerable portion of our youth—of the factious, insubordinate, and ambitious spirit which is so strongly manifested in our public affairs. . . . This country is literally swayed by a democracy of greater extent and power than ever existed on earth, and its spirit infests our seminaries of learning."[73]

Andrew D. White, another contemporary observer of this time, disagreed with Silliman's diagnosis. The difficulty arose, he felt, because students were not treated as responsible citizens and because members of college faculties were forced to perform the duties of policemen.[74] Some college presidents felt it to be their bounden duty to shield their students from political agitation and reform activities. Thus Francis Wayland of Brown was much annoyed when in 1836 the Rhode Island Anti-Slavery Convention assembled in Providence with a number of students from the college conspicuously participating. Ten years later other Brunonians barged into an abolitionist assembly and heckled Wendell Phillips. After this episode Wayland forbade his students to attend future meetings of this kind and even cracked down on those who wished to deliver temperance addresses or attend the Mechanics Association lecture series at which the president's controversial friend Charles Sumner was scheduled to speak.[75]

Undoubtedly, the phenomenon of student rebelliousness reflected, at least in part, the whole social fabric of America at this time. In this exuberant young nation, there was an inner conflict between an over-repressive, Calvinistic morality and a frontier pattern of heavy drinking and brutal fighting. Violence was general throughout nineteenth-century American society. These conditions found their counterpart on the campus in student revolutions. A modern historian attributes much of this unrest to the new spirit of liberty let loose by the American Revolution. This was heady wine for the younger generation. Tact and thoughtful guidance by the administrative authorities, together with more student self-government, would, in this view, have avoided the worst of the trouble.[76]

Perhaps so. One thing is sure—during the post-Civil War years there were fewer student rebellions. Why? First, there were important changes in the curriculum that helped to create a new attitude on the campus. Secondly, many colleges were doing away with their excessively rigorous systems of college discipline and were beginning to treat their students as young adults. Thirdly, coeducation in many institutions was coming to exercise a moderating and pacifying influence on the conduct of male students. Fourthly, the rise of intercollegiate athletic sports and the fraternity system was tending to absorb much of the superabundant youthful energies which in earlier times had gone into fomenting rebellions. Finally, many institutions had now ceased to require police duties of tutors, and had hired a special force of men to police their grounds and buildings.[77]

PART II

NINETEENTH-CENTURY INNOVATIONS

IN THE COLONIAL COLLEGE

4

Multiplication and Variation of Colleges

American higher education has never been forced to conform to any one uniform pattern of organization, administration, or support. In the United States, there has been neither a national ministry of government nor a state church to impose norms of university procedure and control. The vast size of the country and the heterogeneous make-up of its population have made it difficult to establish uniformity in higher learning.[1]

The Dartmouth College Case of 1819 furthered this pluralistic trend by legalizing the existence of a great private sector in American higher education, immune from governmental interference. As might be expected, there followed during the remainder of the nineteenth century the founding of the most diverse types of colleges in every part of the land and a vast multiplication in the numbers of such institutions. This multiplication and diversification of colleges, seen in perspective, was but part of a larger movement for diffusion of knowledge to the people. American democracy in the nineteenth century was also building popular academies, establishing common schools and public high schools, developing a "penny press," enlarging its public libraries, and flocking to local lyceums and Chautauquas.[2]

By the coming of the Civil War, scores of colleges had been founded in the United States.[3] The trend was all in the direction of a scattering of educational effort. Many weak institutions were set up without the resources necessary for permanent survival. Undoubtedly this overexpansion was fostered by the conditions characteristic of the laissez-faire, individualistic society of the time. Americans were able to enjoy the luxury of unrestrained individualism because of the unique military security which they then enjoyed.[4] Then, too, the country was one of vast distances, and roads were still very poor. The national government was federal in nature, and the states, retaining degree-granting powers in their own hands, were usually liberal in issuing college charters. Religious diversity was a permanent reality. In such an environment, educational localism was sure to run riot, and it did.[5]

Neither fear of Indian attacks, lack of proper secondary-school facilities, severity of climate, sparseness of population, nor poverty of local resources slowed down the college-founding movement. The building of the main "trunk" railway systems after the middle of the century proved to be a tremendous stimulus to it. One can plot on a map the early "college belt," running from east to west across the United States, and find that it coincides to a remarkable degree with the "railway belt" which was laid out at this time.[6]

The movement was further stimulated by the fierce rivalries which raged between the newer American communities and their competing groups of real estate speculators in seeking to attract settlers. Colleges were considered an asset in this competition, besides satisfying local pride and meeting the need for adequate educational facilities close at hand. This phenomenon, which has been described by one observer as that of "the Booster College," illustrated the close connections which had developed between college and community in America. When public support of higher education developed, rival communities fought bitter battles to secure projected new institutions such as normal schools, technical institutes, agricultural colleges, and state universities. Often these were distributed, along with insane asylums, prisons, and reformatories, as political plums to satisfy the demands of powerful local groups. Sometimes an educational institution would be awarded as a consolation prize to a community that had been unsuccessful in securing the insane asylum or the penitentiary![7]

Many observers have questioned whether this unplanned, helter-skelter multiplication of colleges did not go too far. Yale, which helped to found at least sixteen new colleges in various sections of the country before the Civil War, "became a Mother of Colleges a century before it could accumulate the substance of a university."[8] In 1881, sixteen New England colleges possessed approximately the same combined endowment as all 123 existing Southern colleges and universities.[9] Writing about 1900, President Harper of the University of Chicago estimated that at least one-quarter of the colleges then chartered in the United States were doing work of a character little different from that of a high school or academy.[10]

There were some, however, who argued that the multiplicity of small colleges in America might actually be a good thing. Thus, President Noah Porter of Yale wrote that it was not so much a case of too many colleges, as of too many poorly located colleges. He saw a congestion of colleges in some parts of the country and a serious scarcity of them in other regions. The abuse of excessive competition, in his view, could be overcome by following the English plan of affiliating colleges with a common university organization, which would then serve as an examining and degree-granting body for them.[11]

Another commentator, writing in 1883, asserted that in this new kind of country it was infinitely more important to have a college for every hundred square miles, where local impecunious boys could be "tolerably well educated," than to have a limited number of institutions where a select few could be trained for the highest forms of scholarship. This would diffuse "the greatest possible amount of learning and intelligence" through the entire mass of the citizenship.[12]

Rise of Technical Institutes

Not only did the sheer numbers of American colleges increase markedly during the nineteenth century, but many new types of colleges, dedicated to special purposes, made their appearance. Among these none was more closely attuned to the utilitarian spirit of the booming republic than the technological college or institute. The development of such an institution on this side of the Atlantic was stimulated by, and paralleled in many ways, the earlier emergence of similar schools in the more highly industrialized portions of Europe.[13]

Although instruction was given in what may be termed "technical education" in the later colonial colleges and in the United States Military Academy (founded in 1802), it was not until 1824 that the first distinct and separate technical school was set up in the United States.[14] In that year, Rensselaer Polytechnic Institute was founded by the largess of an upstate New York patroon. Stephen Van Rensselaer wished his "School of Theoretical and Practical Science" to prepare teachers who would instruct the sons and daughters of local farmers and mechanics in the art of applying science to husbandry, manufactures, and domestic economy.[15]

In addition, the first head of Rensselaer, Amos Eaton, pioneered in the laboratory method of instruction and in what might be described as "university extension" work through evening classes and branch schools. In 1835, he added courses in civil engineering to the curriculum, which up to that time had emphasized agriculture. Soon a class of eight graduates attained the degree of C.E., the first to be granted in the United States.[16]

In 1849, Rensselaer underwent a further reorganization, following a study of certain notable European technical schools by B. Franklin Greene, and became a general polytechnic institute. Its new and broader curriculum was now "designed for the education of Architects, Civil, Mining, and Topographical Engineers, upon an enlarged basis, and with a liberal development of Mental and Physical Culture." Through its classrooms passed many who were destined to be among America's leading technologists in the nineteenth century.[17]

With engineering and technology beginning to emerge from the curriculum as an independent discipline, it behooved the older liberal arts colleges to take serious note of what was happening. They responded by organizing separate departments or schools of engineering on their campuses. For example, the utilitarian-minded president of Union College, Eliphalet Nott, founded in 1845 a department of civil engineering.[18] Then, in 1847, Harvard "thrust out another of those organs of learning in the evolution from the arts-college amoeba to the university primate," and the Lawrence Scientific School was founded.[19] In the same year Yale instituted a new department which was later to become known as the Sheffield Scientific School. In 1852, Dartmouth founded the Chandler Scientific School and Brown organized a department of practical science. Three years later the University of Pennsylvania created a department of mines, arts, and manufacturers.[20]

Once the technical movement got under way, it rapidly gained momentum. An important stimulus was provided by the opening of the Massachusetts Institute of Technology in 1865. Under the energetic and far-seeing leadership of William Barton Rogers, this institution provided a full course of scientific instruction and laboratory investigation for prospective engineers and technicians. In addition, it required basic courses in general education for all degrees, and it provided evening lectures for the general public. Aside from Rensselaer, the M.I.T. system, combining as it did original research in applied science with the diffusion of popular knowledge, was probably the most important determinant in setting the pattern for the mushrooming American technological schools of the later nineteenth century.[21]

The Morrill Act of 1862 also played an important part in stimulating the growth of technological education.[22] By 1900, there were 42 technological institutes in the United States. Fifty years later, the country possessed more than 160 engineering colleges.[23] By this time training in technical disciplines important to the modern age of technology had become a fundamental part of the American system of higher education.

The Land-Grant Colleges

In 1859, the very year that President Buchanan vetoed the original Morrill bill providing for land-grant colleges, Charles Darwin's epoch-making book, *The Origin of Species*, appeared. It was becoming increasingly clear that the Western world was about to enter a new era of free inquiry, of more extensive scientific research. The movement for land-grant colleges represented the American phase of this new emphasis on the role of science in human affairs.

There was a good deal of dissatisfaction in the second quarter of the nineteenth century with the traditional liberal-arts college in America. President Wayland of Brown asserted in 1850 that the United States had 120 colleges, 47 law schools, 42 theological seminaries, and yet not a single institution "designed to furnish the agriculturist, the manufacturer, the mechanic, or the merchant with the education that will prepare him for the profession to which his life is to be devoted."[24] As late as 1862, there were only six "higher" schools in the whole country purporting to deal with these utilitarian fields.[25]

The individual states did not possess sufficient resources to push forward educational developments of this type on their own. Hence a number of enthusiasts launched a movement for federal support. By the 1840s the so-called farmer's vote in America was becoming increasingly self-conscious politically. There was more grass-roots support for the program of "vote yourself a farm" at this time than for special training in how to till such farms. Nevertheless, some farm organizations came to regard agricultural education as at least a partial cure for the farmer's economic ills. In the 1850s, the agitation of a gradually expanding agricultural press and of various local and national agricultural societies built up a growing body of opinion which demanded the establishment of what were called "democracy's colleges." Such men as Evan Pugh of Pennsylvania and Jonathan B. Turner of Illinois played a prominent role in mobilizing public sentiment in favor of such a project. Turner of Illinois College was an influential advocate in the Middle West of a government-subsidized "industrial university" and he may have been responsible for interesting Abraham Lincoln in the movement. The result was the introduction, in 1857, by Justin Morrill of a bill in Congress calling for federal aid to agricultural and mechanical colleges. Sectional differences prevented final approval until 1862. Then, with the southern delegations absent due to the Civil War, Congress passed the Morrill Act and President Lincoln signed it.[26]

Difficult as the launching of the land-grant colleges had been, it proved to be even more difficult to work out an acceptable program of study for these new institutions. During the first two decades of their existence, they had to face the apathy, or even the hostility, of the great mass of American farmers. Many of the latter wanted little more than a trade school. Even the interpretation of the wording of the Morrill Act was in hot dispute in this connection. The National Grange and the Farmers' Alliance made constant complaint that the new colleges were too theoretical and classical in their curricular offerings and had little to offer the average farmer. Indeed, many of these new foundations did seem to go to great lengths to imitate eastern liberal-arts colleges in order, among other things, to attain what was then considered academic respectability. Ultimately, agitation by Populists produced state legislative investigations of the use of Morrill Act funds in California in 1873 and in Ohio in 1877.[27] In response to political pressures of this kind, many agricultural and mechanical colleges were obliged to establish short courses in various "practical" branches of farming, foreshadowing the later extension movement.[28]

There were also difficulties in finding students adequately prepared to enter. Many of the A. and M. institutions, before the rise of public high schools, had to admit students just out of the common schools.[29]

In addition, the necessary scientific and technical information on which to base the curriculum of the new institutions was simply not available at first. In the early days, one observer recalled, there were not enough textbooks on the subject to enable an American professor of agriculture to operate for thirty days! One contemporary leader of the movement described the first group of A. and M. professors as somewhat like a brass band trying to play without instruments.[30] Andrew D. White, who experienced considerable difficulty in getting the agricultural college at Cornell started, thought that "we seemed to be playing 'Hamlet' with Hamlet left out."[31]

The passage of the Hatch Experiment Station Act of 1887 represented a great stimulus to the A. and M. colleges because it provided a growing body of scientific subject matter which they could teach. The formation, in the late 1880s, of the Association of Land Grant Colleges stimulated support for their work and mobilized forces in Congress to pass favorable legislation. Finally, the passage of the second Morrill Act of 1890, and of subsequent legislation in the twentieth century, greatly increased the amount of federal aid to these institutions.[32]

How shall we summarize the significance of the land-grant colleges? They were among the first institutions of learning in the United States to welcome applied science and the mechanic arts and to give these subjects a recognized place in the college curriculum. They fostered the emancipation of American higher education from a purely classical and formalistic tradition. President Welch of the Iowa State Agricultural College expressed this pragmatic philosophy in 1871 when he asserted "that knowledge should be taught for its uses; that culture is an incidental result." The purpose of Iowa State was defined as being that of promoting "the liberal and practical education of the industrial classes in the several pursuits and professions of life."[33]

Finally, these colleges stood pre-eminently for the principle, increasingly so important in the twentieth century, that every American citizen is entitled to receive some form of higher education. Together with the first state universities and municipal colleges, the early land-grant colleges represented the force of democracy working as a mighty leaven in the world of American higher learning.

Women's Colleges and the Rise of Coeducation

The American impulse toward the diversification and popularization of opportunities for higher education came, in the nineteenth century, to include women as well as men. Ancient barriers due to sex, which had hitherto limited such opportunities to one-half of the population, fell. The result was a new kind of college—the women's college—and a new situation in many existing colleges, namely, the coeducation of young men and young women.

This was all part of a great reform movement begun in the early part of the nineteenth century. Reformers such as Mary Wollstonecraft and others argued that differences in mental ability between the sexes were solely due to the existing social environment. They therefore demanded that women be placed on a plane of equality with men in political affairs, in opportunities for employment, in legal position, in social status, and, of course, in education. In the United States, with its strong democratic spirit, a campaign to achieve these objectives and, especially, to secure opportunities for the higher education of women had begun very early.[34]

A scattering of female "academies" and "seminaries" had made an appearance in the early years of the century, the majority of them modeled on the famous institution that Emma Willard had founded in 1821 at Troy, New York. It is questionable whether these can be characterized as women's "colleges."[35] Rather they seemed to be designed to give woman a specialized kind of instruction which would "fit" her for her established "place in society."[36] Certainly these early seminaries made no attempt to grant baccalaureate degrees.

The first women's colleges arose in the South. In 1836, the Wesleyan Female

College of Macon, Georgia, made history by becoming the first educational institution in the country to confer higher degrees on women. Judson College, a similar institution, was founded in Alabama in 1838 and the Mary Sharp College for Women, now extinct, was established in Tennessee in 1852.[37]

The first chartered college for women in the North was Rockford in Illinois (1849). In Wisconsin, the Female Normal Institute and High School (Milwaukee-Downer) was chartered in 1851 and given the right to confer collegiate degrees. Elmira College in New York was chartered in 1853.[38]

"Female colleges" in ante-bellum days had a hard row to hoe. The age of admission had to be kept low because many girls were unable to obtain an adequate secondary-school education. Standards often had to be sacrificed in order to attract paying students. Material endowments were almost totally lacking.

Even more discouraging was the deep-seated skepticism of the public with respect to the value of higher education for women. It was feared that such training would raise woman above the duties of her "station." A man would not love a learned wife. Better far to teach young ladies to be "correct in their manners, respectable in their families, and agreeable in society."[39]

Furthermore, many feared that advanced training would have an adverse effect on the health of women. They were such delicate creatures, so different in mental as well as physical make-up from men, that they would never be able to survive the prolonged intellectual effort. Dr. Edward H. Clarke, a professor at Harvard, presented arguments of this nature in his *Sex in Education, or a Fair Chance for Girls* (1874) and *Building a Brain* (1880). In turn, feminists like Lucinda H. Stone and Sarah Dix Hamlin made a vigorous rebuttal by arguing for the beneficial physical effects of higher education on girls.[40]

It seems clear that educational leaders such as Henry Philip Tappan were unalterably opposed to college training for women because of a genuine conviction that girls were intellectually inferior and that their admission in large numbers would make it impossible to create true universities in America. To a certain extent these fears seem to have had some justification, since the preparatory training of girls in this period was usually inferior to that offered to college-bound boys. Also, many of the early women's colleges for this and other reasons found it difficult to maintain an intellectual standard which matched that of the men's colleges. As a result, a college or university was taking the very real risk of losing public confidence if it moved too precipitately to admit a large number of women.[41]

Thorstein Veblen speculated that another reason for the deep-seated hostility to women's higher education was that it derived from the thought patterns of a period when learning was the absolute prerogative of a priestly and leisure class which was predominantly male. To admit women, once a subservient caste, to all the privileges of higher learning would have been to take away from the honorific position of the dominant class. Hence the tradition arose that all knowledge of a serious, nondilettante, nonvicarious nature was "unfeminine."[42]

Be that as it may, the first prototype of the American coeducational college made its appearance in Ohio in 1833 when Oberlin opened its doors. Established by deeply religious people who were, among other things, passionately opposed to Negro slavery, this school made it a special point to admit women from the very beginning, just as it admitted members of the colored race.[43] This action was unprecedented in the educational history of the English-speaking world. Even more remarkable was the Oberlin commencement of 1841, when three female graduates joined nine male classmates to receive the degree of bachelor of arts. These were the first American women to earn a regular A.B. degree by completion of a program of studies identical with that required of male candidates for the same degree.[44]

During the three decades following the Civil War, the issue had narrowed down, for the most part, not to the question "Should women receive a college education?" but to one of "What kind?" As the public and parochial school systems of the nation expanded in size a demand was generated for college-trained women to serve them as schoolmistresses. The main cleavage, by this time, had come to be one between proponents of coeducation and advocates of separate women's colleges.[45] Both scored impressive gains in this period.

In the rich, populous northeastern states, the dominant pattern came to be that of the superior, but separate, women's college. This was in accord with the reigning Genteel Tradition and, moreover, it was inevitable since eastern colleges steadfastly refused to admit women. An example was Matthew Vassar's large gift which created the college bearing his name. "It occurred to me," Vassar declared to his trustees, "that woman having received from her Creator the same intellectual constitution as man, has the same right as man to intellectual culture and development." Opening for instruction in 1865, the new college's ample funds made possible high standards of scholarship which at previous women's institutions had been largely a matter of theory. Then, in 1875, Wellesley College began its career with 300 students and the first scientific laboratories that had been opened to women. About the same time, Sophia Smith launched the college in Northampton, Massachusetts, which is named after her.[46] And, lastly, in 1885, Bryn Mawr made its debut and ambitiously sought to offer to young women opportunities for graduate study comparable to the best of Harvard and Johns Hopkins.[47]

Efforts were repeatedly made during these years to secure the admission of women to existing Eastern centers of higher learning, such as Harvard, Columbia, and Johns Hopkins. These were in every case sternly resisted. What was finally worked out was something like the compromise then emerging at the great English universities, namely, coordinate colleges for women affiliated with colleges or universities for men. Such, for example, was the "Annex" for women begun in 1879 on a rather informal basis by individual members of the Harvard faculty. In 1894, the name Radcliffe was adopted for this "women's branch," which now received an official charter as a college.[48] Such, also, was Barnard College established in 1889 as a separate college affiliated with Columbia University.[49] Three years before, a donation of $100,000 to Tulane University set up in New Orleans the H. Sophie Newcomb Memorial College for "white girls and young women."[50] Lastly, in 1891, women were admitted for the first time to Brown University, and soon Pembroke College was organized as a coordinate part of its structure.[51]

Throughout the post-Civil War era, the number of students in American women's colleges showed a slow, but steady, increase. By 1901, the United States Bureau of Education listed in its report a grand total of 119 women's colleges. This figure kept climbing until it reached 154 by the middle of the twentieth century.[52] After 1896, the principle of separation in women's higher education received renewed emphasis due to the entry of Roman Catholic institutions into this field.[53]

In the western states, and in the newer universities of the East, such as Cornell and Boston University, coeducation, rather than separation, came to be the pattern. At least a dozen small western denominational colleges and state universities followed in the footsteps of Oberlin, and established coeducation before 1860. This current swelled to a flood in the postwar years. In the "Old" Northwest, particularly, the Morrill Act was looked upon "as a provision upon which women had the same claim as men." Consequently, women were admitted almost immediately on the same terms as men to the new colleges and universities established by the land grants. Indeed, by the early twentieth century, all state universities admitted women with the exception of three in the South—Virginia, Georgia, and Louisiana.[54]

In the West, particularly, academic traditions were less hidebound and the social influence of women was greater than in the East. Women were organizing lyceums, schools, and lending libraries in the early West. They were active in every movement for "cultural uplift." They were even beginning to assume political responsibilities. Wyoming in 1869 and Utah in 1870 had pioneered by granting women the vote. In this social context, it was impossible to deny them an equal chance with men to receive a higher education.[55]

At the same time, we cannot overlook the practical appeal that coeducation would have to a new region like the West. Along the frontier it was financially impossible to duplicate the expensive educational facilities of the eastern states. There was usually not enough endowment available to maintain one good college, let alone two. Coeducation enabled western institutions to serve a larger number of students without a corresponding increase in expense.

Advocates of coeducation argued further that it would accustom members of the opposite sexes to form intelligent relationships with each other, thus preparing for their role in later life. Perhaps the most telling argument, however, was the assertion that coeducation was necessary so that all persons, irrespective of sex, would have the democratic right to be taught all branches of knowledge. This was particularly effective in the West, where secondary schools, unlike those in the East, were already operating on a basis of complete coeducation. It was claimed that tax-supported public higher education must be freely available to the daughters, as well as the sons, of the taxpayers.[56]

Opponents of coeducation remained unconvinced.[57] All the old arguments about the terrible effects advanced study would have on the health of young women were revived and refurbished. G. Stanley Hall asserted that coeducation would impair the normal physical and psychological development of both boys and girls.[58] Some critics charged that it was bound to lower standards of scholarship because the two sexes would be more interested in each other than in their studies.[59] Lurid tales were spread that coeducation fostered immorality. The Reverend Lyman Beecher warned: "This amalgamation of sexes won't do. If you live in a Powder House you blow up once in a while."[60] Finally, some male students and faculty members at newer institutions such as Cornell opposed coeducation for fear that it would "discredit" their alma mater in the eyes of more ancient and renowned universities.[61]

These arguments notwithstanding, the American tide was running strongly in the direction of coeducation. In 1870, coeducational colleges and universities already outnumbered separate women's institutions twentyfold. By 1900, coeducation had spread to 71.6 per cent of American institutions of higher education. This included fourteen of the largest private universities of the country and thirty state universities.

The same development was to be seen at Catholic colleges and universities, hitherto exclusively and defiantly male. The first feminine inroads were made in these schools in the early twentieth century, and by 1960 twenty-seven of the twenty-eight Jesuit institutions in the United States had accepted coeducation.[62]

If we were to compare this situation with provisions in Europe for women's higher education, we would find America far in the lead. In Europe it was not so much a choice between coeducation or separate education, but a question of whether women were to have any opportunities at all to pursue higher learning.[63] In some countries, they were barred from the universities. In others, the lack of adequate preparatory-school facilities for girls made it difficult for them to qualify themselves for university work.[64]

As time went on, women came to be admitted into the majority of American colleges.[65] Yet despite this, critics charged that the practice of American coeducation belied its professions; that in faculty appointments, curricular offerings, and student activities, "it is permeated not merely with indifference, but with antagonism towards women."[66] With the emergence of the militant "women's lib" movement of the 1960s, strong pressures began to develop to change this situation. The federal government finally responded to these pressures. Title 9 of the Education Amendments bill of June, 1972, prohibited sex bias "under any education program or activity receiving federal financial assistance." Two years later, in June, 1974, the U.S. Department of Health, Education and Welfare announced the rules under which it proposed to implement this legislation. All colleges receiving federal aid after January 1, 1975, were required to satisfy the department that they were maintaining equal opportunities for men and women in their admissions policies, educational programs, hiring and utilization of staff, housing facilities, pension plans, and athletic programs. It was the most sweeping directive with respect to the status of women in higher education since the founding of the Republic.[67]

Basic to much of this discussion was the question: What are the proper objectives of higher education for women? The eighteenth century thought principally of preparing women for home duties and cultivating their grace and gentility. With the emergence of the women's colleges an interest in mental development and preparation for professional competence was joined to the earlier emphasis upon preparation for graceful domesticity.[68] Throughout this period, also, religious objectives were very important.[69]

One marked tendency in certain of the early women's colleges was their proclivity to follow rather slavishly the programs of existing men's colleges. Embattled feminists were anxious above all else to prove that women's minds were identical with men's. This outlook was particularly notable at Bryn Mawr from 1895 to 1910 during the regime of M. Carey Thomas.[70] Even in the nineteenth century, some commentators regretted this trend and believed that the women's colleges should attempt to establish their own distinctive type of higher education.[71] It was not, however, until the twentieth century, with the emergence of experimental programs such as those at Scripps, Bennington, and Sarah Lawrence, that new objectives were proposed for women's higher education. Only then was it suggested that there might be differences in curricular programs without inequality and that women's colleges need not be simply carbon copies of male institutions.[72]

By the 1960s, however, the very concept of a separate women's college was being called into question. Of 300 such institutions which existed in 1960 (the great majority of them private), only 146 still maintained their distinctive identity in 1973. A few had closed their doors, but most of them had become coeducational. This trend was apparent also in the case of all-male colleges, such as Dartmouth. Of 261 men's colleges operating in 1960, only 101 were still in that category in 1973. Again, most of the remaining 160 had gone coeducational; the others were out of business. Kenneth M. Wilson, director of the College Research Center, attributed these developments to "shrinking application pools, tougher competition for students, a general softening of the economy, as well as major shifts in the life styles, preferences, and goals of young people." The result was that separate women's colleges were compelled to "reestablish a distinctive rationale and justification for their mission . . . in a set of circumstances which differs dramatically from that . . . which motivated their founders." Proponents of these institutions now argued more forcefully than ever that separate women's colleges should be continued "as available options for young women who may prefer to attend a sex-segregated rather than a coeducational college."[73]

Denominational Colleges

During much of the nineteenth century, the impulse toward college founding in the United States came largely from the Christian churches. Hundreds of liberal-arts colleges were established by religious denominations and were affiliated in one way or another with a parent church.[74] Many of these "hilltop" colleges began as frontier ventures west of the Alleghenies. In all of them, control and staffing was largely by clergymen of the interested denomination. Support came not only from tuition fees but also from subscriptions by the faithful.[75]

Of the various denominations, the Presbyterians and Congregationalists played the leading role up to 1830. After that date, the Methodists and Baptists began to catch up with them in the college field, while other denominations, such as the Quakers, Lutherans, Episcopalians, Universalists, and Roman Catholics, started to take a more active interest.[76] This denominational movement in higher education continued in full force all through the nineteenth century.[77]

What developments in the young American Republic facilitated the rise of the denominational college? Undoubtedly, one important factor was the provision in the First Amendment to the federal Constitution for the fundamental principle of separation of Church and State. Closely related to this was the assurance resulting from the Dartmouth College decision (1819) that privately organized colleges would be free from governmental interference. With these guarantees, there was a free and secure field for denominational competition, and colleges swiftly multiplied across the face of the land as the frontier pushed westward.

When we ask what was the principal dynamic behind this college-founding movement, the most likely answer is that it was the spark furnished by revivalism, or, in other words, the Christian missionary spirit. The churches wanted to establish vital centers of both Christian education and Christian living. They believed in the moral perfectibility of man and society. In crusading for these goals, they founded colleges in the hope that this would hasten the coming of the new day. This revivalist spirit first began to influence American higher education significantly during the "Great Awakening" of the mid-eighteenth century. In the early nineteenth century, the movement became much more comprehensive and militant.

The founder of Oberlin College, Reverend John H. Shipherd, was said to have come to the Western Reserve to save the people from "rum, brandy, gin and whiskey" and to rescue the church from "Romanists, Atheists, Deists, Universalists, and all classes of God's enemies."[78] The churches also had more specific aims in mind. Colleges would help to meet the need for an educated ministry. They would at the same time provide an educated leadership for the laity of the denomination. They would strengthen denominational loyalty, meet denominational rivalry, and extend denominational influence. They would offset any "secularistic" influences which might emanate from the rising state universities. Finally, they would make the higher learning available to more and more people. In this respect, religious zeal and American frontier democracy combined to emphasize the same goal of equality of educational opportunity.[79]

In addition, there was anxiety in New England, and along the eastern seaboard generally, that the ideals and culture of the older regions would be lost irretrievably by those going into the western wilderness unless a concerted effort was made to prevent this from happening.[80] To remove the threatening "moral darkness" of the trans-Allegheny country, eastern-born preachers and educators roamed everywhere in the western lands. Though not all of these were New Englanders born and bred, a large proportion were. There were aspects of a Protestant crusade about the westward expansion of New England in this period.[81] The "Yale Band," the "Iowa Band," and other organized evangelical groups from Yankeedom were fighting hard to win the soul of the West from the clutches of "atheism, infidelity, the slaveholder, and the Pope."[82] Founding of denominational colleges was but one aspect of this busy crusade: It also resulted in the establishment of the first public-school systems of states such as Ohio, Indiana, Michigan, Iowa, and California; it raised up everywhere New England-type towns with New England-style churches; it even imported New England place names and New England conceptions of literature and politics.[83] It was this same impulse which led to the temperance crusade, the Sunday-school movement, the enterprises of the many Bible and tract societies, and the far-reaching world missionary campaigns.[84]

The success or failure of a particular college often depended on the specific abilities of the individual serving as president. Only a really capable leader would be able to attract effective support from the local community or from denominational headquarters. Presidents who were weak and incompetent could cause the serious decline, and ultimately even the total ruin, of a collegiate institution.[85]

It was soon realized by many denominational leaders that in the domestic college field, as in the foreign missionary field, direct and unrestricted competition would be ruinous to all concerned. Thereupon a rough apportionment of territory was made, as in the famous plan of union between Congregationalists and Presbyterians worked out in the early nineteenth century by the younger Jonathan Edwards, then president of Union College. This was expanded in 1826 into the American Home Missionary Society, and was followed in 1843 by the establishment in New York of the Society for the Promotion of Collegiate and Theological Education at the West. These interdenominational Protestant organizations acted as a restraining influence on excessive competition, created something like a common front in approaching eastern philanthropists for funds, and in general served to stimulate the founding of Christian colleges in the western country.[86]

As time went on, a tendency developed within the various denominations to establish a more centralized supervision and control over the church-affiliated colleges. This did not come until the twentieth century among the Congregationalists, but the Presbyterians created a board of education as early as 1819. In 1868, the Methodist Episcopal Church (North) set up a similar board, which was given more supervisory authority in 1892. Two years later, the Methodist Episcopal Church (South) followed suit. The Baptists created a national educational agency for the first time in 1888, and expanded its authority in 1912. The three main bodies of Lutherans in the United States, each with its own board of education, merged in 1918 and established one new over-all board. These national boards performed yeoman service in helping to prevent the multiplication of unnecessary denominational colleges and raising the standards in those that already existed. Their influence was somewhat circumscribed, however, by the fact that a large degree of autonomy in educational affairs still remained in the hands of local authorities. In many cases, the national board could only suggest, not decree.[87]

What of the attitude toward higher education of non-Protestant religious groups in America? Among the Jews, sporadic efforts were made, going back to 1821, to establish denominational colleges. All of these attempts failed, due to insufficient support and to serious theological divisions within the small American Jewish community of the nineteenth century. Ultimately, theological seminaries rather than denominational colleges were set up, such as Hebrew Union College (1875), representing the Reform Jewish point of view, and the Jewish Theological Seminary of America (1887), representing Conservative Judaism.[88]

In contrast with this, the Roman Catholic effort in American higher education was vigorous and extensive. As early as 1789, Georgetown College was founded. By 1860, 14 permanent Catholic colleges had already been established in the United States. This total grew until it reached 63 by the turn of the century and 126 by 1930, including 49 colleges for women. About three-quarters of the Catholic institutions in existence in 1970 were founded in the present century, more than one hundred of them since 1950.[89]

In the early phase of this movement, Catholic institutions, expanding with the increase of Catholic immigration, often had to contend against deep-seated religious antagonisms. American nationalism had long been identified with Protestantism, and a particularly bitter anti-Catholic agitation expressed itself in the nineteenth century in "nativist" movements such as the Know-Nothing party and the American Protective Association. Evangelistic Protestant groups charged that the Catholic hierarchy was seeking to violate the American principle of separation of Church and State by seeking public support for parochial schools. Due largely to suspicions of this nature, the granting of a charter to Boston College in the middle of the nineteenth century was delayed until a provision was included that no non-Catholic student was to be discriminated against in any way.[90]

The Catholic colleges originally were conducted almost exclusively by members of the clergy. The majority were controlled by various Catholic religious orders, particularly the Society of Jesus. The motives which led to the founding of these institutions seem to have been much the same as those involved in the founding of Protestant denominational colleges and seminaries. Because of the prominence of Jesuits in conducting these institutions, the curriculums of most Catholic colleges tended to follow rather closely the Ratio Studiorum, as compiled in the sixteenth century by the Society of Jesus and modified in 1832.[91]

What was the significance of the denominational college in the life of nineteenth-century America? Alexis de Tocqueville noted, when he visited the United States in the 1830s, that although the country lacked a national church, religion was its foremost institution, more influential than any other. The denominational college was one of the main reasons for this. "By 1830 the nineteenth century pattern of village thought in America had been set" with Deism and "infidelity" in full retreat and the evangelical churches in the ascendancy.[92] It was of incalculable importance for the development of the American mind that in this critical period in the history of the young republic the denominational college appropriated much of the field of higher learning in the West before state universities and other public secular institutions were functioning in an effective manner.[93]

In their social organization, the frontier denominational colleges seemed to bear out the truth of Frederick Jackson Turner's thesis about the transforming effects of the American westward movement. They were more democratic in spirit than contemporary colleges in the East; they showed greater readiness to open their doors to women on an equal footing with men; they snubbed snobbery and excluded exclusiveness. The multiplication of these colleges along a succession of frontiers undoubtedly furthered the broadening and democratization of American higher education, as well as its decentralization and diversification.[94]

If we turn, however, to the ideological patterns of the early denominational college, we find little evidence of anything new or radical. The American liberal arts college by this time was dedicated to the upholding of a carefully articulated view of life, an elaborate synthesis of seventeenth-century religious ideas with those of the Enlightenment which Stow Persons has called "Protestant Scholasticism." It was an appropriate act of symbolism when Allegheny College embedded in its cornerstone a chip of Plymouth Rock and some mortar from Virgil's tomb. These institutions sought to conserve and maintain without change as much as they could of the traditional culture and world view of the eastern centers of learning. In curriculum, pedagogy, philosophy, and theology, their aim was to maintain, not upset, the *status quo*.[95]

Knowledge without religion they considered worse than useless. Thus the Reverend T. M. Post, in a commencement address at Iowa College in 1856, stressed that religion and science belong together because all Truth at base is one. Higher education "pervaded by the general consciousness of religious truth and duty" must be recognized as being just as "practical" as education for commerce, finance, or politics. The amazing growth of the American West, he declared, had developed a vast power potential for either good or evil. Christian faith was urgently needed as an integral part of the educational process, so that this power would be used ultimately for "goodness, safety, and permanent glory."[96]

The popular symbol of social stability for the America of this time was the village church.[97] Recognizing the vital part that the denominational college was playing in shaping this outlook, a student at Andover Seminary in 1825 wrote the following words to a missionary student in Basle, Switzerland:

> There are in the United States 40 or 50 colleges containing perhaps in the whole 4,000 or 5,000 students. . . . A great proportion of these colleges and with two or three exceptions all of the most flourishing *are managed more or less by the pious orthodox clergy who are thus preparing to exert an immense influence on the national character.*[98]

A student of the history of the nineteenth-century college observes:

> Colleges were religious as well as educational institutions. Reflecting the impact of the waves of revivals on the broader culture . . . , the Christian colleges in ante-bellum America were pervaded by religion. . . . Undergirded by evangelistic motives, the Christian colleges

spread throughout the land, extending education, religion, and culture to the expanding population in the West and the hinterlands.[99]

Higher Education of Blacks and Indians

Although a remarkably varied and comprehensive system of higher education was developing in the United States in the course of the nineteenth century, there remained two minority groups for whom opportunities for advanced training were at first severely limited. These were the American blacks, the vast majority of whom were in chattel slavery until 1865, and the various tribes and nations of aboriginal Indians. In time, important progress was made in extending to black Americans fuller opportunities for a college education, but no comparable effort was made in developing higher education for the American Indian.[100]

During the years of slavery, it was a statutory crime in many southern states even to teach a black to read or write. Under these circumstances, it is not surprising that the first black college graduate in America did not receive his degree until 1826.[101] The grand total of such graduates by 1860 was only twenty-eight.[102]

There were a few experiments with black education before the Emancipation Proclamation. In 1849, the Avery "College" for blacks opened in Allegheny City, Pennsylvania. In Washington, D. C., the Miner Academy for black girls opened in 1851. A year later, an institute for "colored youth" began to function in Philadelphia. These were not true colleges. Two denominational institutions that were founded during this period began their work on a somewhat higher level. Wilberforce University in Ohio was founded by the Methodists in 1856 and Lincoln University in Pennsylvania was sponsored by the Presbyterians in 1854.[103]

A period of growth of colleges for blacks occurred during the thirty years following the Civil War. More than 90 per cent of American blacks resided in the South at this time. This was an era dominated by the benevolence, zeal, and humanitarianism of northern Christian churches, especially the Congregationalist, Presbyterian, Methodist, and Baptist churches. These organizations were active in sending "Yankee schoolmarms" down South to staff common schools for the newly emancipated colored people. They also showed a great deal of interest in the higher education of blacks.[104]

An example of this type of organization was the Baptist Home Missionary Society of New York, which in 1867 organized the Augusta Institute, afterward Morehouse College. Still another was the American Missionary Society of New York, which founded Atlanta University in Georgia and Talladega College in Alabama. In fact, prior to 1900, practically all of the faculty members in southern colleges for blacks were idealistic educational missionaries who had been educated in northern colleges.[105]

The problems they faced were enormously difficult. Unlike any other immigrant group in America and most minorities in other countries, the black American brought over with him very little of his indigenous culture. Centuries of slavery tended to suppress much of that which had, somehow, survived the ocean crossing. His civilization therefore tended to include whatever he could borrow from the dominant white man.[106] During the long period of slavery the black had been purposely kept either completely illiterate or, at best, only semiliterate. The northern missionaries faced the herculean task of educating more than three million such people in the whole range of knowledge and skills which had previously been denied to them.

The missionaries were warned by pessimists and opponents of education for blacks that they would soon reach a point beyond which the black's innate mental capacity would be unable to go. Some of the northern idealists, rejecting this counsel of despair, went to the other extreme of seeking to teach the freedmen, without adequate preparation, a full duplicate of the liberal-arts curriculum given in contemporary northern colleges. These attempts, of course, were ludicrous failures.[107] The majority of the educational missionaries were far more realistic, however. Many of them realized that the illiterate former slave would have to be introduced gradually to higher learning. This is why institutions such as Hampton, Fisk, and Talladega were at first primarily concerned with secondary education. They began by establishing primary departments where the three R's could be taught. As soon as a few students were sufficiently advanced, "normal" and theological departments were instituted. The missionaries were convinced that the great and immediate need of the southern black was for a sufficient number of teachers and preachers to lead him to higher attainments. In this stage, too, agricultural and industrial training was given to those who desired it. Only as a final step, then, did the missionary colleges institute a formal New England-style academic course for those who were prepared to absorb an advanced classical training. The dominant policy of the time seems to have been one of groping, testing, and experimenting, rather than stubbornly seeking to impose an artificial stereotype on unprepared students.[108]

In addition to northern church groups, the United States Army and the Freedmen's Bureau were active in helping to get education for blacks started after the Civil War. The Freedmen's Bureau was actually the first federal agency to take a serious interest in the higher education of blacks. In this cause, it worked in close partnership with the northern missionary organizations, coordinating their educational activities and eliminating duplication of effort. When, for example, a group of Congregationalists founded Howard University in Washington, D. C., they proceeded under the authorization of the Freedmen's Bureau. The institution was named for General Oliver O. Howard, head of the bureau and at one time president of the university. In addition, General Clinton B. Fisk, head of the bureau's Western Branch, helped to secure the site at Nashville for the university which was later named after him.[109] Some of America's most distinguished colleges that today have a predominantly black enrollment, such as Meharry Medical College, date from this period. By 1895 there were more than eleven hundred graduates in the United States who had gotten their training at these pioneering schools for blacks.[110]

The early attempts to found colleges for blacks aroused much hostility among southern whites. During the bitter days of Reconstruction feelings ran high. There were cases of incendiarism. In 1870, the president of Talladega was shot and killed by a mob.[111]

The educational program of the Freedmen's Bureau came to an end in 1872. About this time the difficulties of colleges for blacks increased. Newly reorganized "white supremacy" southern legislatures passed laws limiting the political and civil rights of blacks. The North was losing interest in the question. It was at this time that Booker T. Washington, president of Tuskegee Institute, began to champion vocational training for blacks. At the same time that he seemed to sidetrack the demand for equality in liberal-arts education, Washington advocated resignation to the now-dominant policies of separation and segregation. This program conciliated the white South, as legislators who would balk at anything like liberal-arts training for blacks came to approve giving public aid to vocational institutes such as Tuskegee. Northern investors in southern industry, eager to have more efficient manual workers, also proved receptive to appeals for funds by these institutes.[112]

This vocational-training trend in higher education for blacks was further stimulated by the second Morrill Act, which specifically prohibited payments of federal funds to states which discriminated against blacks in admissions to their tax-supported colleges. But the southern states held that the establishment of separate colleges for the two races constituted compliance with this act. Six years later the *Plessy* v. *Ferguson* decision by the nation's highest court gave federal judicial sanction to this concept of "separate but equal." This doctrine was not to be struck down until *Missouri ex rel. Gaines* v. *Canada* in 1938. The result was the founding of a number of black land-grant "colleges."[113] Seventeen southern and southwestern states ultimately set up such institutions. As late as 1917, a report by the Phelps-Stokes Fund revealed that in all seventeen of the land-grant schools for blacks there were only twelve students enrolled in courses that could be classified as college level.[114] This situation was in essence an extension of the principle of segregated "separate-but-unequal" education, which had long existed in these states on the primary school level, to the field of higher education. Southern legislatures and state departments of education were not overly friendly to these institutions. They insisted on keeping them purely as trade schools, and opposed any offering of liberal-arts programs in them. In one state college for blacks the only way that Latin could be smuggled into the curriculum was by offering it under the title of "Agricultural Latin."[115]

The success of lawsuits brought by blacks in the 1930s before the United States Supreme Court to secure the actual establishment of equal, if separate, public educational facilities forced many of the southern states to re-examine their programs for the black A. and M. colleges. They now sought to improve these institutions and increase the liberal-arts offerings there. Nevertheless, North Carolina and Virginia were the only southern states which established publicly supported nonvocational colleges for blacks.[116]

Another source of support for the higher education of blacks was forthcoming from the great philanthropic and educational foundations. Prominent in this field have been the Slater, Rosenwald, and Phelps-Stokes funds, the Carnegie Corporation, and the General Educational Board. Their function has been not so much to help found new colleges for blacks as to support more effectively those which already exist. This aid has been vital to these institutions, which have had to contend with the most grave economic problems in recruiting qualified faculty members and maintaining adequate facilities.[117]

In the early twentieth century, a new, more militant note began to be heard in the colleges for blacks as Dr. W. E. B. Du Bois, Harvard graduate and professor at Atlanta University, led a strong protest against the dominant Tuskegee philosophy of Negro education. Vocational institutes were no longer enough, he asserted. Advanced liberal education must be furnished to all blacks who were ready for it! Here again, the economic question proved to be a serious stumbling block. It was difficult to raise funds to support advanced liberal-arts and professional training for blacks. The bulk of the aid for this ambitious program had to come from the foundations.[118]

As the twentieth century advanced, more and more blacks were attending northern institutions whose student bodies were preponderantly white, but the bulk of black college graduates in America still came from colleges for blacks, most of them in the South.[119] One notable trend was the remarkable growth of colleges for blacks which were supported by public funds. In 1940, such institutions accounted for the majority of black students.[120] Another important development was the improvement of standards in colleges for blacks; they began, by the early 1920s, to receive regional and national accreditation.[121]

Beginning in the 1930s a number of developments combined to produce still broader opportunities for black Americans in the field of higher education. One of the most important factors which accelerated this trend was the vast migration of black people from southern states to northern and western urban centers. By 1970 nearly half of the black population of the United States lived outside the South. Thus, what had been primarily a southern issue had become a national one. This social revolution was accompanied by an increasingly militant black protest movement (especially after World War II), a heightened white sensitivity to black demands for civil rights, and a more liberal and sympathetic attitude on the part of the United States Supreme Court on cases involving racial issues. The NAACP began to have great success in winning decisions from the high court, which reversed *Plessy* v. *Ferguson* and established the constitutional rights of blacks to attend publicly supported institutions of higher education in the South.

The first of the important cases of this nature was *Missouri ex real Gaines* v. *Canada* in 1938. Here the court ruled that the state of Missouri was denying equal educational opportunity to a black by giving him a scholarship to attend a law school in another state. The state, it held, must provide education for all its residents and this should be done within the state. Missouri and other southern states began now to establish separate professional schools for blacks as part of their state university systems.

In *Sweatt* v. *Painter* (1950) the NAACP challenged the constitutionality of the concept of a separate "but equal" professional school for blacks as part of a state university. The state of Texas had created just such a law school for its black citizens. The Supreme Court agreed with the NAACP contention that such a school, though separate, was far from equal. It ruled that blacks had been denied equal protection of the laws by this policy because the law school for blacks could not possibly provide professional training equal in quality to the widely respected University of Texas law school.

In the same year, in *McLaurin* v. *Oklahoma State Regents,* the high court outlawed all efforts to force black students in state universities to use segregated facilities. It ruled that a black graduate student at the University of Oklahoma had been denied equal protection of the laws because he was required to sit in an anteroom adjoining the lecture hall while attending classes, to sit in a special area of the university library, and to take his meals separately from the other students. This hindered the student's effective pursuit of his educational goals, said the justices, because it prevented meaningful intellectual exchange with the other students.[122]

Following these decisions, most southern states quietly opened their universities to blacks. By 1952 only five states—South Carolina, Georgia, Florida, Alabama, and Mississippi—still barred black students from their publicly supported universities. Then, in 1954, the Supreme Court ruled, in the epoch-making decision *Brown* v. *Board of Education of Topeka* that all racial segregation in public education was outlawed. Very soon thereafter the court made it clear that its decision applied to higher education as well as elementary and secondary schooling. Vehement resistance to this ruling continued for a time in such states as Alabama and Mississippi, and ultimately federal authorities had to employ force to secure at least token observance of the court's mandate in the universities of the above-mentioned commonwealths. Desegregation of higher education in these states and others was quickened by a momentous act of Congress, the Civil Rights Act of 1964. A federal court ruling based on this act (*Adam* v. *Richardson,* 1972) ordered the United States government to cut off all federal funds in aid of higher education from ten states where it was felt progress in the direction of desegregation was too slow and unsatisfactory. To avoid such a cut-off, the affected states were ordered to submit plans to the U.S. Office of Education showing how they intended in the immediate future to end all vestiges of a dual, racially segregated system in their publicly supported colleges. In 1974, the Department of Health, Education, and Welfare approved plans for racial desegregation which had been submitted by eight of the states that had been cited. The plan submitted by Mississippi was rejected as incomplete, while the tenth state, Louisiana, which to that point had submitted no plan, was sued for noncompliance.[123]

There were other ways in which the Civil Rights Act of 1964 produced a significant impact on American higher education. The act stated that any business firm, state or local government, college or university doing contract work or receiving grants from the federal government must not practice discrimination based on race, color, sex, or national origin if it wished to continue to receive federal monies. The federal government sought to implement this legislation by demanding that colleges and universities institute "Affirmative Action" programs which would end all forms of racial discrimination in the hiring of staff, admission of students, granting of financial aid, and allocation of dormitory space. Threats to withhold federal funds were made to Columbia, Harvard, Cornell, Michigan, and other institutions which were held to be too slow in implementing these guidelines to satisfy the law. A report, published in 1974 for the Carnegie Commission on Higher Education, pointed out that many colleges and universities were being forced to lower their academic standards and to undermine the quality of their faculties because of the demands flowing from Affirmative Action programs. The author, Richard A. Lester, warned that such programs "fail to take into consideration either the inadequate supply of qualified people among those groups currently under-represented on our faculties or the characteristics of academic employment that distinguish it from employment in industry." The present system was characterized as one "that deals more with the hiring of typists, bricklayers or punch press operators," not scholars.[124]

Another device to increase the enrollment of blacks and members of other nonwhite minority groups in colleges and universities was the "open-admissions" policy. This approach was now adopted by an increasing number of institutions of higher education, especially junior colleges and community colleges, but perhaps the most dramatic example of the implementation of such a program came at the City University of New York. There in 1970 local political pressures forced the Board of Higher Education to abandon the university's historic policy of granting admission solely on the basis of academic excellence and to substitute a policy guaranteeing entrance to some branch of the city's system of higher education to all high school graduates, whatever their scholastic standing. As a result, minority-group enrollment in the City University grew from 18.8 per cent in 1969 (before "open admissions" went into effect) to 35.6 per cent in 1974. Considerable controversy was generated by attempts to evaluate the city's program. This involved questions such as: How well were the new entrants doing in the municipal colleges; indeed, how many of them were actually doing college-level work?[125]

Another controversy was provoked by charges that the new federal programs against discrimination were, in reality, producing "reverse discrimination." It was asserted that the effect of Affirmative Action programs to help more blacks, Puerto Ricans, Mexican-Americans, and other minority groups obtain a college education or secure a faculty position was to establish what amounted to racial quotas in colleges and universities. The federal government was now requiring the colleges to gather data with respect to the racial or ethnic origins of their students and their faculty members. What were the implications of such a data-collecting program? Having assembled such information, how was one to define true "integration"? What proportion of blacks must be hired as faculty or admitted as students before a college could be considered to be nondiscriminatory? If preferential treatment in hiring or admissions for minority-group individuals was demanded in order to remedy past inequities, might not this lead, in specific cases, to a sort of reverse discrimination against those majority-group members who happened to be better qualified?

This dilemma was finally brought to the attention of the United States Supreme Court in the case of *De Funis* v. *Odegaard* (1974). Marco De Funis, Jr., a white student, charged that the University of Washington discriminated against him and violated his rights under the Fourteenth Amendment to equal protection of the laws when it rejected his application for admission to its law school. De Funis noted that the university had admitted to this school thirty-six members of nonwhite minority groups who had lower test scores than his. Indeed, the university admitted that it was utilizing criteria for the minority-group applicants entirely different from the more rigorous ones that were applied to De Funis and other white applicants. De Funis won his case in a lower state court, which ordered him admitted to the law school. The university appealed to the Washington State Supreme Court and there won a reversal of the decision, although De Funis was ordered to be kept on as a student pending the outcome of his appeal to the U.S. Supreme Court.

On April 23, 1974, the Supreme Court ruled by a 5–4 vote that De Funis's case was moot since he was by this time shortly to graduate from law school. The majority thus refused to rule on the merits of the case, arguing that the issue involved was no longer a live one. The minority, Justices Douglas, Brennan, Marshall, and White, maintained on the contrary that the case should have been decided on its merits, that avoiding the issue "clearly disserves the public interest." However, their position was hardly unambiguous. In an ambivalent twenty-nine-page dissent Justice Douglas condemned the use of race as an admissions criterion, pointing out that it was invalid under the Constitution, but he also stated that social and economic criteria for admissions might well be considered along with standard tests. It is difficult to assess the significance of *De Funis* v. *Odegaard*. It might forecast a more definitive opinion on the question by the Court at a later date. Would admissions officers of graduate schools, influenced by the Douglas dissent, exercise more caution in giving preference to persons from minority groups primarily on the basis of race? On this last point opinion among contemporary observers was sharply divided.[126]

Equally significant at this time were the new developments which pertained to blacks in the private sector of American higher education. Previously all-white private colleges in the South admitted blacks for the first time in their history. In the North and West, black enrollment in colleges and universities increased from 45,000 in 1954 to over 95,000 by 1970. Well-known institutions, such as Harvard, Yale, Amherst, Wesleyan, Bowdoin, and Michigan, made strenuous efforts to recruit black students, especially entrants from the urban black ghettoes for whom they set up special counseling and remedial services, reduced course loads, various types of financial aid, and longer permitted periods for graduation.[127] By 1970 blacks constituted 7 per cent of all full-time undergraduates in the United States, but this still fell short of the black percentage of the general population, which was 11 per cent. More discouraging still were the figures for black student enrollment in graduate and professional schools in 1970. In this vital area, blacks constituted only 4.1 per cent of the total full-time enrollment.[128]

As more and more black students appeared on American campuses they began to demand fuller recognition in the college curriculum of what they termed "the black experience in the nation's life." Some militant black student leaders resorted to forceful measures, even violent protest, to achieve such recognition. In some cases campus riots were sponsored by black nationalists or separatists who were opposed to the whole concept of integration. In any event, this agitation made an immediate impression on the nation's colleges. By 1973, it was estimated that some two hundred institutes, or independent programs, of "black studies" were in operation in colleges and universities. In another four hundred institutions various courses in this new field were offered by traditional departments of instruction.

Born in the midst of controversy, these new programs remained highly controversial. A professor of sociology at Portland State University wrote in 1973 that "black studies courses in a number of schools are losing enrollments after peaking a year or two ago. Both black and white students complain that the courses have low intellectual content and tend to be repetitious. They register their dissatisfaction by dropping out. . . . White scholars who objected to the low intellectual level of black studies programs and to their political content found themselves characterized as racists and bigots."[129] A black professor from U.C.L.A., writing in the *New York Times,* commented: "Black students, by and large, are very pragmatic about black studies programs and stay away from them in droves when they don't measure up. . . . Black people in general have had enough experience with inferior education not to want any more of it."[130]

In a few universities efforts were made to teach black studies at a high level and to grade course work stringently. While such examples seem to have been in the minority, scholars in the field were at work to raise standards of achievement in what they insisted should be approached as a valid academic area, not a political indoctrination program or a training school for revolutionists.

What was happening, meanwhile, to the traditional colleges for blacks? In 1973 there were 105 such institutions in the United States, and of this number 85 were four-year colleges granting the bachelor's degree. All but two of these four-year colleges were located in the South, the District of Columbia, and several border states. The continuing importance of these 85 institutions was emphasized by the fact that they granted 70 per cent of all bachelor's degrees earned by American blacks although they enrolled only 42 per cent of the black college students in the country. This situation indicated that as of 1973 there was still a very high attrition rate among the black students who had been admitted to predominantly white colleges.[131]

The colleges for blacks faced a number of critical problems as they entered the 1970s. The movement northward and westward of southern blacks was diminishing the population pool which constituted their principal source of students. The breaking down of the walls of segregation at white institutions and the efforts of some of these institutions to recruit black students and scholars meant that the black colleges might well lose some of their brightest students and ablest professors. The financial burdens for the black schools increased as they were obliged for the first time to compete on a national scale with better-endowed institutions which had previously been all-white. Finally, the Supreme Court's ruling outlawing segregation and the action of Congress in 1964 in passing the Civil Rights Act raised serious questions in the minds of some observers with respect to the wisdom of continuing all-black or predominantly black institutions in the new era that was dawning. Indeed, a number of the publicly supported colleges for blacks faced the real possibility that they might lose their identity through merger with other campuses as part of a unitary state university system or even that they might be abolished outright. As for the privately supported colleges for blacks, they sought to comply as much as they could with the desegregation edicts, even though in the early 1970s nearly 95 per cent of the enrollment in such institutions remained black.[132]

Some educational leaders felt that the formerly all-black institutions still had a vital and unique role to perform in the nation's system of higher education. For this reason they felt that such colleges should not be permitted to go under. Reflecting this viewpoint, the Ford Foundation announced in 1971 that it was granting $100 million to improve the opportunities for members of minority groups in higher education. Half that sum was earmarked for ten of the strongest and best private colleges for blacks and the remainder was designated to help support a fellowship program for deserving black college and university students. In making this grant, the leaders of the Ford Foundation expressed their conviction that there was still a place in America for colleges "under black leadership and with a tradition of service to black students," provided they made a sincere effort to move in the direction of racial integration. Such colleges, the foundation declared, "clearly have an opportunity to play unusual and important roles in preparing black and other youth for a complex, multiracial, multiethnic society, but, in order to serve that purpose effectively, they must put their own houses in order, consolidate and maximize their scarce resources and strive for new levels of excellence."[133]

If we can say, then, that higher education for American blacks has made slow but very real progress in the years since emancipation, we must acknowledge that college training for another minority group, the American Indian, has been practically nonexistent in any special or distinct sense. The Bureau of Indian Affairs, the United States government agency with supreme authority for planning an educational program for the tribes, decided early to terminate the schooling of Indian youths at the secondary-school level. Talented Indian youth were only occasionally sent out to secure further training at established American colleges and universities.[134]

In the later nineteenth century, private philanthropy developed the same kind of interest in building up industrial schools for Indians that had been demonstrated in the institutes for blacks established at Hampton and Tuskegee. It was thought that this type of training would shift the base of Indian culture away from the tribal reservation and in the direction of closer contact with white civilization. To express this new emphasis, the Carlisle Indian School was founded in 1879. Its success led to the founding of a number of other "nonreservation" boarding schools for Indians. This group included Haskell Institute in Lawrence, Kansas; Sherman Institute in Riverside, California; and the Chemawa School near Salem, Oregon.[135]

Although Carlisle's football team occasionally played Harvard, it is important to remember that these institutes were not true colleges. Their standards of training, at best, approximated only those of a good manual-training high school. One specialist on Indian affairs has asked whether this was enough to meet the needs of a people striving to convert in one generation from the way of life of a primitive society to the more complex realities of modern American culture. His feeling was that an institution like Carlisle, which taught no higher than the tenth grade, "failed, despite its many admirable qualities, to equip Indian youths with sufficient education to face American life on equal terms."[136]

5

Early Methods of Instruction

Of all phases of the history of higher education the one that was earliest to take form and perhaps least frequently to be the subject of dramatic change has been the method by which youth have been instructed. The lecture, still very popular in twentieth-century America, can trace its lineage beyond these shores to the medieval university and thence to classical times. So too, the dialogue between professor and student, spreading in recent times as democracy spreads, goes back at least to Socrates. Only the method of the laboratory has been of relatively recent innovation. But, old or new, the method of instruction has long been viewed principally as an art. Consequently on the whole professors have not been notable for examining its theoretic aspects. The historian, however, must not be guilty of repeating this professorial neglect.

The Class Recitation

In tracing the development of methods of instruction in higher learning we should begin with the early way collegiate instruction was organized into classes. A class consisted of all the men who entered college in a given year and expected to graduate together four years later. Such a class not only constituted a social unit which would continue to have cohesive quality long after graduation but it also formed a compact instructional unit as well. In the day before electives, when the curriculum was tightly prescribed, a college generation took the whole four-year curriculum as a single class. Everybody took the same subjects at the same time of day in the same room under the same tutor. After four years of such close association it is small wonder that class solidarity lasted long after college.

It was, furthermore, customary for a single tutor to take a class through the whole curriculum of any given year. If he stayed long enough at his post the tutor might even take a single class through the whole college triennium or later quadrennium. But that did not occur often because frequently tutors were recent graduates who taught only till they received a call to occupy some pulpit. In the early centuries when enrollments were small the president himself might teach all the classes, as did the first presidents of Harvard and Columbia. After classes grew larger so that the president needed tutors to take over some of the instruction, it still long remained the presidential prerogative to teach the senior class. The senior Noah Porter's experience at Yale was typical. After reciting his Latin, Greek, and mathematics during freshman, sophomore, and junior years to Benjamin Silliman, the future scientist, he recited senior year to Timothy Dwight, the president.[1]

Obviously, to teach the whole college curriculum of any one year, let alone the whole quadrennium, made extraordinary demands on a president's or tutor's scholarship. It made even the stoutest intellectually humble. At the time Princeton invited New England's greatest theologian, Jonathan Edwards, to become its third president, he expressed grave misgivings about his qualifications because of deficiencies he sensed in his command of higher mathematics and the Greek classics. In spite of conscientious effort to keep abreast of a curriculum no wider than that of the seventeenth and eighteenth centuries, a strong move set in during the latter century for more specialized teaching. In some instances the tutor confined his preparation to the subjects of one college year. But more important was specialization in subject matter. Yet even with this advent the professor's chair remained an unusually broad one, almost a divan. It would not be at all unusual, for instance, to find the same man teaching mathematics, natural philosophy, astronomy, and geography. Professorial specialization, however, did not result in any similar modification of the class system. Students continued to study in undifferentiated classes till well into the nineteenth century.

The college day in colonial times was a long one, often extending from sunup to sundown. At Dartmouth it began as soon as there was sufficient daylight for the president to read the Bible at morning chapel. In those pious times the college day not only began with chapel but concluded with chapel too. One class period was usually sandwiched in between chapel and breakfast. This first class of the day was usually omitted on Mondays since to prepare for it the day before would have been a violation of the injunction against work on the Sabbath. After breakfast followed more class periods, generally alternated with study ones. Coincident with the noon meal was a brief period for recreation. In the afternoon again study and recitation periods alternated with a longer time for recreation at the end. Evening concluded in a final bout with study. When not attending class or engaged in recreation students were supposed to be in their rooms studying. Indeed tutors made regular rounds to guard against the devil's finding occupations for idle minds.

Classrooms in the colonial colleges were on the whole bare and in the winter ill heated. Sometimes, but not always, the tutor sat upon a chair at a desk which was raised above the floor on a modest dais. On the desk might be a box from which the tutor would draw students' names by chance so that none could predict when it would be his turn to recite. In the early days, of course, there was no such classroom equipment as blackboards. As late as 1803 John C. Calhoun, later to become the leading statesman of the ante-bellum South, was told to bring his slate to a mathematics class at Yale.[2] The idea of a blackboard as an enlarged slate hung on the wall had yet to occur to an instructor at Bowdoin two decades later. With a few exceptions, such as Nassau Hall at Princeton and William and Mary's main building designed by Christopher Wren, the architecture of college buildings made little impression upon the undergraduate generation.

The two most popular methods of instructing during class periods were the recitation and the lecture. Although more popular in the seventeenth and eighteenth centuries, the recitation method gradually yielded ground to the lecture method, especially in the nineteenth century. The heart of the recitation consisted in an exchange between the tutor and the student, the tutor citing and the student *re*citing. The citation was usually an assignment in a textbook, but might just as well be a previous lecture or scientific demonstration. In the recitation the student proved that he had learned his lesson, at least the portion for which he was called on in class. As a matter of fact there was a wide range of performance in the recitation's exchange between tutor and student. It ranged all the way from reproducing the textbook, lecture, or demonstration verbatim to a highly developed Socratic dialogue.

Various merits were claimed for the system. For one, the tutor could tell accurately whether the student was diligent and had studied his lesson. This he could not gauge so well when the student sat passively listening to lectures. Again, since the student could expect to be called on daily, the recitation built a wholesome and steady sense of responsibility in him. Likewise it trained his faculties. This won for it the endorsement of the Yale Faculty Report of 1828 which warmly embraced the recitation as a means of giving the faculties a strenuous workout every day.[3] At its best the recitation trained the student in exactness and analysis, but even at its worst it was still a vigorous exercise of memory. Perhaps these advantages of the recitation method were most appreciated in the first two centuries of collegiate development when many colleges were little better than secondary schools where the disciplinary quality of the recitation suited the preceptorial methods of lower schools.

As the quality of college work rose, however, there was a growing discontent with the recitation's educational results. The principal objection seems to have been its heavy if not exclusive emphasis on rote memory. These complaints were all the more telling because they came, not from idle, listless fellows who probably would have resisted any kind of severe study, but from those who were fond of it. In recollecting his own undergraduate instruction, President James B. Angell of Michigan described how his classmates formed the belief that the faculty, although it had made no public statement of policy to that effect, gave higher credit to students who could glibly repeat their lessons verbatim than to those who gave the substance in their own words.[4] This produced a situation, as a Harvard graduate remembered, wherein the tutor merely "heard" his class instead of "taught" it.[5] John Quincy Adams, sixth President of the United States, confided just this criticism to his student diary at Harvard at the end of the eighteenth century: The good students counted the recitation a complete waste of time because they learned nothing from the tutor which their preparation for the lesson had not already yielded.[6] Brilliant Timothy Dwight, who piloted Yale from the eighteenth into the nineteenth century, took no particular pride in his extraordinary success as an undergraduate because his tutors had only taxed his memory, a faculty in which he chanced to be richly endowed.

Other Yale men than Timothy Dwight found themselves at odds with the recitation system on deeper grounds. In spite of Yale's defense of the system one of its more illustrious graduates, Andrew D. White, subsequently first president of Cornell, retained a sour memory of his experience under it. What a miscarriage of education, he exclaimed, that even good teachers like James Hadley, who would have drawn throngs to lectures in a German university, surrendered to a barren recitation from texts instead of complementing them with his vast learning.[7] So bad was the system that another Yale graduate and later eminent professor of classics, James L. Kingsley, remarked to his class with subtle irony, after a lesson in Tacitus's *Agricola,* that they had been reading "one of the noblest productions of the human mind without knowing it."[8]

But even for the average student the recitation was often a failure because too frequently it degenerated into a contest of wits in which the tutor won if he could catch a student in his ignorance and the student won if he could conceal his ignorance. Sometimes students did succeed in covering up their lack of preparation in Latin and Greek by the use of "ponies." As one wag chronicled, "The keepynge of the same doth tende to produce stable scholarshype." At other times students protected themselves against what they regarded as the unreasonable demands of the recitation system by "bolting" or boycotting class.

Happily not every teacher made a treadmill of the recitation. Here and there gifted men managed to lift it, as already suggested, to the level of inspiring Socratic dialogue. Princeton's sixth president, John Witherspoon, imported from Scotland, was one to succeed in this task just as the eighteenth century was ending. But even more notable in their success were Nott, Wayland, and Hopkins in the first half of the next century. Building on the core of the recitation, Brown's Francis Wayland accustomed his class to extemporaneous illustrations of the material contained in the text. If he disagreed with its author he said so and gave his reasons. Not only did he allow his students to ask him questions but he actively invited them. As a result the study of a text under his leadership covered not only a review of its contents but an animated discussion of related topics as well.[9] For his success Wayland was no doubt deeply indebted to his own teacher, Eliphalet Nott, who held the presidency of Union College some threescore years, indeed the longest tenure of any American college on record. He too began his classes with a recitation from the text but immediately thereafter plunged into the consequences which the lesson might have for individual, social, and political life. No student wanted to miss the stimulation of such vital discussions. In fact boys began to think of themselves as men because, as Wayland tells us, Nott treated them as men by asking them to form their own judgments about the matters in hand.[10]

In the same tradition was Mark Hopkins, the president of Williams and a contemporary of both Wayland and Nott. A gleaner rather than an original scholar, Hopkins was a positive genius in the art of interrogation. His reputation for lively yet gracious interchange of views with his class has been immortalized in the terse description of a well-endowed college, ascribed to President Garfield, as a log with a student on one end and Mark Hopkins on the other.[11]

Some escaped the lean fare of the recitation, not through resort to the Socratic method, but through employment of the prelection of the Jesuits. Although the common method of instruction in Catholic colleges, it seems to have been more rarely used elsewhere. In spite of White's condemnation of Hadley, there is record that he used the method with considerable success at Yale.[12] The prelection was particularly suited to instruction in languages, and was neither quite a recitation nor quite a lecture. In this method the instructor, instead of requesting the conventional student translation of some classic, would himself take half a dozen of the author's lines, which first he carefully read through for accent. If poetry, he scanned the lines for meter. Next he rendered a literal translation of the passage, after which he went back and took up each important word and phrase, giving its syntax, and estimating its rhetorical effect. After that he cited other examples of style or argument either from the same author or from different ones. Here he might also take occasion to comment on historical or mythological references in the lines under study. In a final reading of the passage the instructor would give some polish and even elegance to his translation. The next day commenced with a review by the student of the previous prelection, after which the instructor subjected a new selection to an analysis like that of the day before.[13]

The Lecture Method

Although the recitation was the most popular form of instruction in the seventeenth and eighteenth centuries, it was by no means the exclusive one. There was some lecturing too, if only to supplement the recitation. As a matter of fact, lecturing had an ancient lineage extending back at least to the medieval university. It was customary then to lecture, on account of the scarcity of books. Indeed, as the etymology of the word should suggest, a lecture was a reading. The professor read his book while the students tried to write fast enough to catch not only the thought but even the phraseology of the lecturer. Later the students gathered to compare notes and ensure a complete and correct copy of the reading. Lecturing in the colonial colleges was not unlike the medieval practice. The gift setting up the Hollis Professorship of Mathematics and Natural Philosophy at Harvard in 1726 required its incumbent to "read" his lectures both publicly and privately. An early president of Dickinson, Charles Nisbet, wrote out his lectures and then delivered them so slowly that any student, if a good penman, could copy them down verbatim. But lecturing of this sort was rapidly disappearing as the nineteenth century approached.

While men like Samuel Johnson, the first president of Columbia, and Timothy

Dwight, Yale's capable president at the turn of the century, were successfully keeping alive the great medieval tradition of lecturing on subjects such as moral philosophy, metaphysics, and logic, it was the men lecturing in the rapidly growing field of natural philosophy or science who were building up new popularity for the lecture method. This they did by accompanying their lectures with experimental demonstrations of the phenomena of physics and chemistry with which they were dealing. So ingenious, indeed, were the devices they invented for this purpose that enthusiasm for the experimental lecture overflowed from the college classroom to the public lecture hall. If anything, it was the public which was more enthusiastic; it watched these scientific wonders with the same awe it had formerly bestowed on demonstrations of magic. With the backing of Benjamin Franklin it is no surprise that William Smith, the first provost of the University of Pennsylvania, was a prominent advocate of this type of lecturing there. Isaac Greenwood came back from abroad to introduce the method at Harvard after having studied with Desagulier, who wrote one of the early texts in the field, *A Course of Experimental Philosophy.*[14] And of course none was more brilliantly successful in this field than Benjamin Silliman at Yale.

In logical organization the experimental lecture followed contemporary texts on logic, of which Isaac Watts's *Logic*[15] was one of the more popular in American colleges from the middle of the eighteenth century onward. These texts distinguished between the logic of discovering truth and the logic of explaining it once found; the former proceeded from particular things to general principles while the latter passed from general principles to particular things. Since general principles seemed to logicians like Watts to present knowledge in its clearest, simplest form, these became the proper point of departure for the experimental lecture. Leaning, therefore, on the old pedagogical injunction to proceed from the simple to the complex, the experimental lecture always started with the enunciation of some scientific principle and then proceeded to illustrate it with a concrete demonstration. At least one logician recognized that the logic of discovery or invention was more stimulating, but nonetheless he advised against its use for instructional purposes because the outcome was fraught with too many uncertainties.[16]

A further spread and invigoration of the lecture method occurred as a result of the influx of German university ideas from the second quarter of the nineteenth century onward. Pre-eminent in scholarship, German professors were using the lecture as the means par excellence for informing their students of the latest research, for helping them organize wide ranges of information, for giving them an overview of the domains yet to be conquered, and finally for electrifying them with the professors' enthusiasm for their specialties. As American professors increasingly lighted their candles at German university shrines, they too found the lecture method a more and more congenial method of instruction.

As college instruction seemed to come of age through the use of this more mature method, the recitation with its preceptorial and disciplinary methods by contrast seemed out of place in higher education and more appropriate for secondary and preparatory schools. Yet the lecture method did not reach its nineteenth-century ascendancy without a struggle. For a considerable period there was a lively debate about the respective merits of the recitation and lecture methods. The Yale Faculty Report was willing to concede the challenge which the lecture presented to a professor's best talents, but on the other hand it was concerned for the way a student might "repose on his seat" and fail to come actively to grips with the subject in hand.[17] The student mind must work in order to grow. Some decades later President Noah Porter of Yale, himself a product of the kind of education recommended in the 1828 report, came to its further defense.[18] He did not fail to recognize the advantages the lecture possessed in presenting material not otherwise available in texts, in comprehensively organizing a whole field of knowledge, nor did he overlook the magnetic advantages of oral communication. Nonetheless he missed the disciplining of the faculties provided by the recitation. A lecture remembered was not so effective, Porter thought, as a textbook mastered. Indeed the lecture is best for students who have already mastered books. To the argument that the discipline of the recitation was all right in its place, the secondary school, Porter was quick to point out that the secondary school serving the American college was not nearly so effective as the gymnasium which served the German university.

None of these objections prevented the lecture method from rolling on to dominate American collegiate instruction as it did that of the German university. Yet misgivings continued to dog it well into the twentieth century. Some critics could not forget the origin of the lecture method in the medieval scarcity of books and therefore thought that the continuance of lecturing into the era of the power-driven press, the linotype, and the multigraph was an unwarranted anachronism. To encourage the student to become a note-taking machine and fraternity houses to become archives of last year's lectures when such machines stood at hand did not make sense. Neither did it make sense to have the professor year after year laboriously pump water—even though it was pure water—into the all too frequent sieves that were the student minds. Even in the case of good students the lecture system often had a debilitating effect because they would put great reliance on their notes, not as a guide to mastering a field of knowledge, but as a means of cramming for examinations. Thus the lecture-note-taking method might be a good way to acquire honors but not what honors signify.[19]

The Laboratory Method

The great innovation to occur in collegiate methods of instruction in the nineteenth century came in the introduction of the laboratory method of teaching the sciences. The first step in this direction, of course, was the introduction of the experimental lecture. This kind of lecturing, however, was still a considerable step away from the laboratory method itself. At best students were only able to witness scientific demonstrations performed by the professor himself in the lecture room. This is as far as Benjamin Silliman went at Yale in spite of the fact that he had improvised one of the earliest college laboratories. He welcomed students to his basement room to see what he and his assistants were doing, but much preferred that they would refrain from meddling with his apparatus in any way.

It remained for Amos Eaton, a pupil of Silliman's, to take the notable pedagogical step of having the student himself perform scientific demonstrations. In fact Eaton was influential in having this idea incorporated specifically into the fundamental document by which Stephen Van Rensselaer set up the Rensselaer Polytechnic Institute in 1824. Order No. 7 of that document prescribed that students in chemistry were *not* to be taught by listening to lectures and watching demonstrations but were themselves to lecture and demonstrate under the supervision of the professor. Furthermore the next order, No. 8, directed that the examination of chemistry students should not be in terms of the conventional question and answer but in terms of the facility with which they performed experiments and gave their rationale.[20]

From enlisting students in the performance of scientific demonstrations it was but a step to another innovation which the Rensselaer Polytechnic Institute pioneered. Shortly after its opening it designated well-managed farms and workshops in the vicinity where students could witness and learn the application of scientific principles. The institute even made so bold with its pedagogical innovations as to have the student reverse the logic of Watts and start his lesson not with some clear scientific principle, but with some practical application of it. Thus the student visited a tannery or bleaching factory before he proceeded to the laboratory to analyze the chemical principles involved.[21]

Even with all this advance it still remained for the study of science to win academic respectability and with that academic acceptance the resources to provide laboratories and laboratory equipment commensurate with its expanding techniques. There had to be a transition from college cabinets meagerly filled with "philosophical apparatus"[22] to modern laboratories filled with scientific instruments. After the middle of the nineteenth century, however, the Lawrence and Sheffield Scientific Schools at Harvard and Yale respectively were beginning to give students training in laboratories more like the ones in which professors themselves were doing genuine experimental work. Here the method of instruction was the very method of investigation used by the professor himself in his own research. Accordingly he encouraged the student to probe some unsolved problem. At every step—definition of the problem, collection of data, formulation of a hypothesis, testing—the professor was sympathetic guide and critic.

The Manual-Labor Movement

Before leaving the laboratory method, particularly as Amos Eaton employed it, it may be well to refer to another pedagogical device which enjoyed intermittent popularity from Eaton's day onward but whose similarity to his conceptions was more apparent than real. This was the manual-labor movement which flourished and petered out in the second quarter of the nineteenth century and then had a brief revival when the land-grant colleges were getting under way.[23] The movement was most active on campuses where college buildings were just beginning to rise. In the early stages of all such institutions there was much work to be done, and slender financial resources to accomplish it. There was land to be surveyed and leveled and buildings to be drafted and built. A most fortuitous conjunction of circumstances seemed to provide a way of solving this problem with a minimum of expense and a maximum of educational benefit. Many of the young men who sought to attend these struggling institutions were themselves endowed more richly with brawny arms and willing hearts than with money in their jeans. Why should they not earn their tuition by helping to erect the institution in which they were going to learn? This solution seemed the more plausible because at the time the Swiss philanthropist Phillipp Emanuel von Fellenberg, strongly influenced by Pestalozzian object instruction, was winning many converts to the importance of the educational by-products of work.

The educational advantages of making manual work a regular part of the American college program were several. At the head of the list was the fact that manual work would provide illustration and verification of the principles learned in the classroom. It is at this point, probably, that the manual-labor movement most nearly appeared to approximate the innovations introduced by Eaton at Rensselaer. On closer inspection, however, it must be clear that the educational possibilities of the manual-labor movement were much more circumscribed than those Amos Eaton had in mind. How, indeed, could they be otherwise since they only grew out of the soil of physical need in a growing institution? When the institution got on its feet the opportunities for manual labor usually dried up and educational by-products were forgotten. Besides, the variety of technical skills needed to launch the physical plant of a college were so limited as to render the variety of collateral educational benefits illusory. Since from the student's point of view, too, earning was more important than learning, the manual-labor movement in the end proved educationally abortive.

Secondary by-products claimed for the manual-labor technique of instruction pointed to concomitant moral and social advantages. Manual labor taught habits of industry, orderliness, and dependability, so it was urged. Doubtless it is a tribute to this expectation that parents often sent indolent and shiftless sons to these colleges in the hope that some of these virtues would rub off on them. On the other hand it is a sad commentary to record that there was much complaint of slovenly work done by the students. Ezra Cornell had high hopes for the benefits of manual labor at the institution to bear his name, but it fell so far short of the expectations of Andrew D. White, Cornell's first president, that much of the student work done in laying out the new campus had to be done over by skilled workmen.

Disputations

In addition to recitations and lectures there was one other method of instruction which was probably universal in colonial colleges. That was the syllogistic disputation inherited from the medieval university. At Yale in the eighteenth century a student spent the bulk of his time—twelve to fifteen hours—in recitations. Another five to ten hours he spent at lectures, leaving two to four hours for disputations and another one to three hours for forensics.

In the case of the disputation the tutor would appoint a thesis such as *animae immortalitas patet ex lumine rationis* ("the immortality of the soul is manifest by the light of reason"). The student called upon to respond could choose either to affirm or deny the thesis, but in either event had to do so in Latin. In the first part of his response he explained the terms of the thesis and cleared them of any ambiguity. After making clear the issue he set forth his affirmation or denial in a series of Aristotelian syllogisms. When he finished the other students were allowed to object, but their objections too had to be couched in Latin syllogisms. After the objections had been stated it was the respondent's turn to rebut them in further syllogisms. And so the disputation continued till the respondent or objectors had been silenced. At this point the tutor, who had been acting as moderator, stepped in to summarize the arguments and state his own point of view.

By the middle of the eighteenth century, however, the disputation was beginning to lose its place in the college regimen. In part this may have been due to a changing climate of opinion, as witness the student who elected to defend the thesis that "Syllogisms do not aid in exploring the truth." But this was no more than Cotton Mather had been saying earlier and Francis Bacon before him. At any rate forensic disputations began to displace syllogistic ones at about this time. The forensic disputation differed from the syllogistic in that it was not restricted to syllogisms but permitted ethical and pathetic in addition to logical proof. Forensics were also more popular because they were conducted in English. But even forensics began to lapse into the extracurriculum by the middle of the nineteenth century.[24]

It has already been stated that disputations were carried on in Latin. It would be a mistake to regard this practice as an exceptional part of early methods of instruction. As a matter of fact Latin was not just a subject of instruction in the colonial college but the vehicle or language of instruction as well. Greek by contrast was treated as a dead language and therefore taught through the medium of Latin. To ensure easy and effective command of Latin, colonial colleges had regulations requiring students under penalty to carry on conversation among themselves in Latin. In view of the fact that all learned books were written in Latin and that Latin was the language of savants, these regulations hardly seemed unreasonable to the faculties which enacted them. Nevertheless by the end of the eighteenth century these regulations were rapidly becoming dead letters. As a living language Latin was definitely on the defensive. A Harvard president confirmed this deterioration by offering no better reason for opposing the plea of John Quincy Adams's class for an English oration at commencement than that it might be mistaken for a decline in the intellectual vigor of the college. But the students carried the day. The rising tide of nationalism and republicanism reinforced the trend toward rhetoric and composition along English models.

Marks and Examinations

The principal method of testing student achievement in the early colonial college took the form of a public exhibition. On this occasion the president and tutors, together with the governing board and such gentlemen of liberal education as might be interested, constituted a sort of court or board of examiners. On one such occasion Ezra Stiles of Yale noted as many as twenty taking part.[25] Students were called up singly and each examined orally. This display of learning made quite a public appeal and remained popular till well into the nineteenth century.

But popular as this sort of examination was, it had severe limitations which finally brought about its demise. Not least of these limitations was the fact that it militated against dependable comparisons of the relative ability of the different students. Often by chance good students would make only a mediocre achievement on a difficult question and thereby suffer in comparison with some inferior student who would manage to make a good showing on one of the easier questions. Not only that but in the nineteenth century, long before the era of objective measurement, F. A. P. Barnard of Columbia was pointing out that the marks given by the examiners on a single recitation might vary all the way from two to nine points on a basis of ten.[26] Another limitation of the public exhibition took the form of tutors putting leading or even easy questions to their students. But this practice is understandable. The public exhibition was as much a test of successful teaching as it was of successful learning. The college consequently had a stake in making a good showing.

By the middle of the nineteenth century the public exhibition was rapidly giving way to the practice of written examinations. The obvious advantage which this form held over the oral consisted in having all the examinees react to the same set of questions. The college missed the public advertisement of the exhibition, but in its place it could boast of much greater equity in the results of its testing. But even written examinations were not without their critics. The critics, however, were not so much the advocates of the public exhibition as the defenders of the recitation. The daily recitation with carefully recorded grades was an examination itself, they thought, and, when grades were averaged, more unerring in its results than those given only annually or even semiannually. Proponents of the written, longer term examination pointed out in reply that reliance on the daily recitation caused the student to study subjects piecemeal, thereby losing the over-all grasp of material engendered by the newer examining procedure. President Eliot had a criticism too, but his was constructive and one to be pressed more frequently in the twentieth century. He thought it a mistake to join the teaching and examining function in the same person because, while such a practice might provide a measure of the learning done, it afforded no satisfactory measure of the teaching.[27]

The marking or ranking of students has produced a great diversity of practices in American colleges. One of the earliest ways a student learned of the faculty's estimate of his achievement was through the assignment he received in the class exhibition of sophomore year or the kind of oration he was asked to deliver at commencement in senior year. More honor, for instance, attached to giving an oration in Latin than in English, to delivering a disputation than a dialogue or colloquy. Sometimes these assignments were very unpopular and led to student protests. Thus the great latent oratorical powers of Daniel Webster were silent on his commencement day at Dartmouth because an undergraduate organization to which he belonged thought its members had been discriminated against in the award of commencement honors.[28]

It was only after the colonial period that modern marking systems began to take hold. One of the earliest of these was that used by Ezra Stiles.[29] He divided students into four categories: *optimi,* second *optimi, inferiores* (but nonetheless *boni*), and *peiores*—best, next best, satisfactory, and inferior. William and Mary had four categories too, but more elaborately descriptive: (1) first in their class, orderly and attentive, and making flattering improvement; (2) orderly and attentive and making respectable improvement; (3) making little improvement, probably from want of diligence; and (4) having learned little or nothing, probably on account of escapades and idleness.[30] When F. A. P. Barnard took over as president at Columbia he suggested a simplification to two categories, proficient and deficient.[31]

Numerical marking systems followed not far behind. At some time later than Stiles, Yale was marking on a basis of 4, with decimals later added to show intermediate gradings. Harvard marked at different times on a basis of 8 and of 20. After the middle of the nineteenth century marking on the basis of 100 became increasingly popular. The percentage of 100 that was passing in mid-nineteenth century was low enough, usually being 50 but as low as 40 at Dartmouth till a decade after the Civil War.[32] By the end of the century, however, there were misgivings here and there whether marks could be as precise as the use of cardinal numbers implied. Some colleges, Mount Holyoke among them, employed the first five letters of the alphabet to mark off levels of achievement.

Whatever the system of marking, it bears noting that grades were sometimes subject to discount. Some colleges, favoring the recitation as against the lecture method of instruction, counted the latter only half the value of the former. At a later date some conservative faculties made one of their last stands against the elective curriculum by requiring a higher passing grade in elective as compared to prescribed studies. At Harvard two-fifths of the maximum grade was required for the former and only one-third for the latter.

The rating scale at William and Mary was composed of both a scholastic and a moral component. Although the two components appear more clearly there than elsewhere, the practice was common. The college authorities kept both a scholastic and a moral record for each student, but often combined them when final accounts were rendered. In an individual case, for example, a student's scholastic average might be reduced by the demerits he had accumulated for lapses against the decorum of the college. As a result inferior students not infrequently graduated ahead of their more able classmates. Naturally this resulted in considerable grumbling by students against their tutors. Nor did it cease till colleges began to keep scholastic and moral accounts distinctly separate throughout their academic bookkeeping.

The mixing of scholastic and moral accounts throws an interesting sidelight on earlier notions of motivating studies. Mediocre achievement was pardonable if associated with average intellectual powers but not if due to a lack of diligence. Yet, how to arouse diligence? That was the ever-besetting question. At first there was resort to close supervision of the student's time. Tutors called at his room to be sure he was there and, if there, gainfully occupied. Later the daily recitation with its inevitable daily grade carried the burden of spurring the student's effort. If that was insufficient, demerits were loaded on, as already seen, to increase the discomfort and goad him the more. William and Mary even imposed a "mulct" of three shillings for each failure.[33] Too many mulcts and a student was up for public reprimand or possible dismissal. Many colleges inflicted one penalty short of dismissal, "rustication." To remind high-spirited students of their academic responsibilities they were sometimes sent away from the campus to live and study in some clergyman's home till more sober preference for the intellectual life prevailed. In any event the dominant spirit of motivation was one of discipline, learning to work against the native inclination of the flesh.

While discipline was undoubtedly the goal, there were some who tried to reach it more positively. Although none stated a theory of interest, some practiced one. Mark Hopkins for one was convinced that the main effort of the college instructor should be not so much the transmission of knowledge, as important as that was, but the stimulation of young men to reach out for it. Of course no one was a better exponent of this view than Hopkins himself. George Ticknor at Harvard and F. A. P. Barnard before he went to Columbia believed scholarship could be incited by sectioning the students according to their capabilities.[34] In this fashion the inferior would not operate as a drag on the superior and, if their inferiority was due to lack of application, they might be stimulated to escape from their degradation. Brown's Francis Wayland wished, too, that American undergraduates had the direct and positive motive for excelling at their studies that their cousins had in England, where academic success led to preferment in both Church and State. Disappointed, Wayland in the 1840s tried the extraneous motivation of posting prize money for academic excellence.[35] Bowdoin at the end of the preceding century had employed this device, and Brown was to try it again after the Civil War, but no enduring success attended any of these efforts.

Some college leaders took lofty moral ground on the question of student motivation. Yale's Timothy Dwight was one of them. It was unavoidable, as he saw it, to recognize academic merit by giving oratorical appointments to the more competent students. He denied, however, that the purpose in awarding them was to excite student emulation. On the contrary, he prayed that students would be minded to do their academic best just for the glory of their Creator.[36] Of the same mind as Dwight but going him one better was President Lord of Dartmouth. He outrightly abolished scholastic distinctions to ensure that growth in virtue rather than acquisition of knowledge should stand as the main objective of a college education.[37] But these distinctions returned after his incumbency terminated. Charles William Eliot was more pragmatic. He saw no reason to expect young men to be any more high minded in their motivation than their elders. And how many of them, he asked, perform their daily tasks for the glory of God? "Most people," he noted, "work for bare bread, a few for cake. The college rank-list reinforces higher motives . . . no auxiliaries are to be refused."[38]

Library Facilities

It is natural to associate the higher learning with a library. Consequently it is not surprising that the founding of colleges in colonial America was usually accompanied by the gift of books. In drawing up his last will and testament John Harvard not only set aside money for the founding of the college to bear his name but also bequeathed it his library. The Congregational clergy who assembled to establish Yale each came bearing books from his own personal library. But in spite of the generosity of these and other benefactors college libraries long suffered from stunted growth. Starting with 300 volumes, Harvard had only 12,000 by the conclusion of the Revolutionary War. But even at that its library was far larger than its nearest rival, William and Mary, with 3,000 or Dartmouth with 1,000, the smallest of the then college libraries.[39] This situation reflects a general scarcity of books in the colonies at the time both because there was little money to spend on them and because most purchases had to be made abroad. But an even worse handicap to the accumulation of books took the form of disastrous fires which raided the frame buildings in which college libraries were stored. Nearly every colonial college suffered at least one such disaster.

One of the most active men in building up colonial college libraries was Jeremiah Dummer, who graduated from Harvard in 1699 and then took an advanced degree at Utrecht. Unable to obtain a satisfactory business opportunity on his return to America, he set sail for England, where he spent the rest of his life. As agent for several of the colonies he served two decades, soliciting gifts of books for the struggling colleges in the New World. A good mixer, he made excellent contacts among England's chief political, financial, and literary leaders, many of whom, like Elihu Yale, he persuaded to send books as endowments for these institutions.[40]

As might be expected, books on theology predominated in the early college libraries. More modern authors were in short supply. With limited funds, however, accessions had to be made with great care. Even in the nineteenth century, when Thomas Jefferson was making plans for the University of Virginia, he laid down strict rules for its library. For one thing only books of great reputation and too expensive for purchase by private means were to be bought. Again, he would only tolerate authoritative expositions of science and translations of superior elegance. As disputations gave way to forensics and as forensics occupied themselves more and more with political issues during the gestatory period of the new nation, urgent need arose for works on politics and economics. When the college library did not stock them, the student debating societies did. In the course of time their libraries grew to such considerable proportions that when, on the demise of the societies, they were sometimes incorporated into the college library they made a significant addition.

Rules for the use of college libraries down to the Civil War will strike the reader as quaint indeed. Usually they allowed the library to be open only certain days in the week and for a very limited amount of time even then. In the eighteenth century the Dartmouth Library was open for an hour once every fortnight and only five students were admitted at a time.[41] Freshmen were permitted to withdraw only one book at a time, sophomores and juniors two, and seniors three. Yet it is startling to realize that a century later the rules for the use of the Princeton Library were only slightly more liberal.[42] How many books did undergraduates withdraw annually under such regulations? About 1840, at Union College in Schenectady, students usually withdrew no books at all in their first year but increased their use of the library so that by senior year only six out of a class of seventy-five still were withdrawing none. Those patronizing the library read on the average about five books. One student, a "Phi Bet'," although not an outstanding one, read as many as twenty. If students made only slight demands on the college library, they used their debating-society libraries two to three times as much. Thus these seventy-five seniors drew out only 196 of Union's 5,000 volumes but 486 from the debating-society libraries' 2,000 volumes.[43]

Ordinarily the first librarians were members of the faculty, or even the president himself, who undertook oversight of the books in addition to their regular duties. Perhaps college libraries were so little used because these busy men had little convenient time to spare them. But there is another reason more likely. The predominant recitation method made no demand on the library. Assignments were made in textbooks of which each student had his own. No one thought of the library as a place to study. Dusty, ill lighted, and unheated, it would have been an uninviting place even if it had been open more frequently and regularly.

Attitudes toward the library and its use began to change as the recitation surrendered its sway to the lecture and German research methods. As students began to study subjects rather than textbooks, they had need of a much wider circle of reading. From a marginal or peripheral consideration libraries came to occupy a central importance in the higher learning. The library's unimportance at Harvard and its pre-eminence at Göttingen led Ticknor to suppose that America spent too much on library buildings and not enough on the books put in them.[44] On this latter point George Bancroft, a fellow student abroad with Ticknor, noted the conspicuous absence in American libraries of scientific collections.[45] Later the position of librarian became a full-time job in itself. Instead of hoarding books or treating them as a treasure to be guarded, as had their untrained predecessors, professional librarians exerted every energy to make library resources more and more available to students and faculty. At the same time these resources themselves began to grow phenomenally. With its head start Harvard continued in the van, rising from 122,000 volumes after the Civil War to 373,000 at the turn of the century.[46]

6

The Elective Struggle

As noted earlier, the college in America was, in its origins, "a borrowed instrument."[1] For over two hundred years the American people continued to use this instrument without making fundamental changes in it. Then, in the mid-nineteenth century, they began to refashion the academic structure in a really fundamental way, and it is with this effort that we shall now deal.

The reconstruction of the American college assumed two principal phases. The first sought to extend the duration of higher education, bringing about a vertical expansion in the form of universities such as Johns Hopkins. We shall refer to this trend later when we discuss the rise of graduate schools. The second phase, by way of contrast, was primarily concerned with a horizontal expansion of the college, which was to be achieved by extending the breadth of its course of study. This pertained directly to the remaking of the curriculum on an elective basis.

Indeed the central educational battle of nineteenth-century America was fought over the elective system. This is the question which aroused the greatest amount of controversy in the academic world, inflamed passions as no other educational issue was able to do, and most clearly reflected the impact of modern technology upon the traditional college. Involved in this struggle was a whole cluster of related issues, many of the highest significance. Perhaps the central one was the following: Should the American college remain predominantly religious in orientation, training for Christian piety and a broad liberal culture or should it become essentially secular, serving the interests of utilitarianism, social efficiency, and scholarly research? Other questions were tied closely to this one. Should American higher education follow the ideal of the German university or the English college? What were the values of self-motivation as against external compulsion? Which was valid, the old "faculty psychology" or the new experimental psychology? Was there such a thing as "mental discipline," and could one devise a college curriculum that would develop it? Should higher education be "practical" or "liberal," a means to an end or an end in itself? Were the "new" studies (such as science) more important than the "old" studies (such as the

100

classics)? Should the college aim to be aristocratic, and train the elite, or should it seek to attain a democratic all-inclusiveness? On the answers to these questions depended the future of American higher education; and the struggle over the elective system touched, in one way or another, on every one of them.

Early Movements for Curricular Reform

Long before Charles W. Eliot introduced his elective system at Harvard, prominent Americans had been advocating the granting of a larger element of choice in college studies. Before the end of the eighteenth century, men of the stature of William Smith, Francis Hopkinson, Jonathan Trumbull, and Benjamin Rush were making much the same point which Benjamin Franklin had once stressed, namely, that the existing college curriculum was too heavily classical. The American student, they said, should have a chance to pursue subjects such as English, which would be related more directly to his later business or professional life.[2] Trumbull commented in rhyme on the pointlessness of classical learning:

> How oft the studious gain,
> The dulness of a letter'd brain;
> Despising such low things the while,
> As English grammar, phrase and style;
> Despising ev'ry nicer art,
> That aids the tongue, or mends the heart . . .
> And plodding on in one dull tone,
> Gain ancient tongues and lose their own.[3]

Perhaps the most important of the early advocates of electives was Thomas Jefferson. We have already noted his sweeping reorganization of William and Mary College in 1779.[4] Dissatisfied with the results obtained at Williamsburg, Jefferson concentrated all his energies during his last years on seeking the establishment of a great state university which would more adequately embody his ideas. The Virginia legislature did not concur with Jefferson's proposals for common schools and intermediate academies, but it did finally authorize the establishment of the University of Virginia, which opened on March 7, 1825.[5]

The cornerstone of the Virginia plan was the principle that the student was to have complete freedom of choice in the lectures he chose to attend.[6] However, this Jeffersonian freedom of choice was allowed only *between* the offerings of the university's separate and distinct "schools." There were originally eight such "schools," covering the fields of ancient languages, modern languages, mathematics, natural philosophy, natural history, anatomy and medicine, moral philosophy, and law.[7] Once a student had chosen his field of specialization, no electives were permitted *within* a school; there the course leading to the degree was entirely prescribed. Students not interested in securing a degree, however, were free to take whatever courses they wished.[8] This was, then, essentially a "parallel" course scheme, combined with provision for "partial" courses for special students.

The whole philosophy of the University of Virginia curriculum was based on a confidence in the maturity of the student. He was supposed to have arrived at an age when he knew what he wished to study. There was no annual promotion from class to class. A student completed the course as fast, or as slowly, as he was able. Degrees were awarded only after the passage of a stiff general examination which was both oral and written. What Jefferson and his colleagues had sought to do was to transplant to the New World the system of the early nineteenth-century German university, such as Göttingen or Heidelberg, with its emphasis on specialized training for the mature student. However, Charlottesville could only maintain this level of instruction if American students asked for it and had been properly prepared to receive it. This did not immediately prove to be the case.[9]

The University of Virginia was watched closely by nineteenth-century American pioneers in the reconstruction of the college curriculum.[10] A talented young Boston man of letters, George Ticknor, provided the link between the Virginia experiment and the cause of academic reform in the North. From the time of their first meeting in 1815 until the death of the elderly Jefferson in 1826, a cordial friendship existed between the young New Englander and the sage of Monticello. In organizing his university, the Virginia statesman paid close attention to Ticknor's ideas and made repeated efforts to secure the Bostonian for its first faculty. In turn, Ticknor followed the development of the Virginia institution with close interest, although he chose, after an extended period of European travel and study, to accept a professorship of modern languages at Harvard.[11]

It was not long before Ticknor was energetically agitating for changes in the venerable institution in Cambridge.[12] He wished to sponsor the same kind of academic system at Harvard that Jefferson had developed in Virginia.[13] His unceasing activity, coupled with the dramatic impact of a student rebellion, finally prodded the authorities to action. A new set of college rules, recommended by the Story Committee, was approved by the college corporation and put into effect in 1825.[14] The Harvard faculty was now reorganized into distinct departments of study; upper classmen were permitted a limited number of electives; students were allowed to proceed within a specific division as speedily as they were able; and nonmatriculated specials were accorded the right of taking a "partial" course at Harvard without, however, receiving a degree.[15]

This program was, by and large, a compromise. Ticknor did not get the complete reorganization he desired. There was no free election or complete liberty of choice between "parallel" departmental programs. No earned M.A. degree, as in Charlottesville, was established. Thus Harvard was not remade into either a simple Gymnasium or a German-style university.[16] Nevertheless, the seeds of the elective system had been planted and the foundations for the eventual expansion of Harvard University had been laid.[17]

Ticknor, however, was to find that even this partial victory was a Pyrrhic one. A conservative faculty did not like the new laws and resented the controversial Section 61, which arranged class sections according to proficiency.[18] They were given a fair trial only in Ticknor's own department, for the reformers soon discovered "that a professor's power of passive resistance is immense and unpredictable."[19] President Kirkland was finally obliged to have the system modified so that its application was optional with the different departments.[20]

The Virginia and Harvard experiments of 1825 started a limited chain reaction in American colleges. Popular demands began to be voiced for a democratization and liberalization of the higher learning.[21] A few colleges tried to respond to this agitation with positive action, introducing the device of the "parallel" and "partial" course. Though none of these changes were as thoroughgoing and extensive as Jefferson's and Ticknor's, they were straws in the wind, indicating that an innovating spirit was stirring in academic halls.

In 1826 a group of professors at Amherst College petitioned the board of trustees to establish a more flexible curriculum.[22] The authorities responded favorably to this request and set up a "parallel" course which featured modern languages, English, history, political economy, and the sciences. The new course also included such subjects as architecture; the study of bridges, locks, and aqueducts; and applied chemistry. In addition, there was to be a sort of manual-labor course in theoretical and practical mechanics to keep the college's plant in repair and a course in the science and art of teaching, complete with an in-service teacher-training program for the regular faculty.[23]

After a two-year trial, the Amherst experimental course was abandoned. Lack of funds had much to do with this failure, but there was also strenuous opposition by some members of the faculty, suspicion on the part of the administration that the new system was impairing discipline, and a notable absence of the anticipated popular response on the part of the students.[24] Amherst now retreated to the more secure and economically stable citadel of the traditional classical curriculum.[25]

Other evidences of the stirring of Jeffersonian influence can be seen in the efforts, during the middle and later 1820s, of President Horace Holley to introduce the "parallel" course idea at Transylvania University in Kentucky and of President Philip Lindsley to sponsor a similarly broad program at the University of Nashville in Tennessee. Local circumstances conspired to limit the success of both of these efforts.[26] Also, in 1826, the transcendentalist philosopher, James Perkins Marsh, tried ineffectually to reorganize the curriculum of the University of Vermont in terms of four departments of knowledge. Under his system, the student would elect one, or at the most two, of these departments. This program, however, probably never went into formal operation.[27]

More successful was the "parallel" course introduced at Union College in 1827 by its enterprising president, Eliphalet Nott. This was a "scientific" course, substituting modern subject matter for Latin and Greek during the last three years of the curriculum. Students were permitted to take the new program in place of the established classical course. Nott, as Union's president for the incredible term of sixty-two years, managed to combine the career of active and ingenious inventor with those of minister of the Gospel, educator, and man of affairs.[28] Under his vigorous leadership, the "scientific" course persisted at Union, in one form or another, until modern times. To it was added, in 1845, a program of training in civil engineering and, in 1856, a curriculum in applied chemistry.[29]

However, even Nott, with all his daring, did not at first presume to award a bachelor's degree upon satisfactory completion of the new course. For many years, therefore, only a certificate of proficiency or diploma of work accomplished was granted to the scientific students at Union College. Yet even with these precautions, Nott was roundly criticized by the academic conservatives of his time for having introduced a substandard course and Union College was denounced as a "dumping ground for scholastic derelicts."[30]

Besides the instances which have been mentioned, there were other attempts by ante-bellum American colleges to enlarge their curriculums and introduce an element of choice through "parallel" courses and "partial" courses. Had not financial stringency been so great at this time, there might have been more. Most of the early western state universities established courses of study of this type.[31] In addition, certain northeastern institutions, such as Columbia, New York University, Wesleyan, Trinity, Lafayette, and Hobart, at one time or another experimented with such programs.[32] The University of Rochester, established in 1850, went even farther: it not only set up "parallel" classical and scientific courses but also granted respectively the degrees of B.A. and B.S. for satisfactory completion of the same.[33]

By 1825 a second approach to the reconstruction of the curriculum had made its appearance, namely, the establishment of new and independent schools for the sole purpose of teaching nonclassical subjects. The best illustration of this trend is the founding of the Rensselaer Polytechnic Institute.[34] We should not forget, in this connection, the United States Military Academy at West Point, which, after 1817, placed its main emphasis on the training of engineers.[35] The American Literary, Scientific, and Military Academy, a civilian school for training soldiers and engineers which was founded at Norwich, Vermont, in 1819, was yet another institution of this type.[36]

The Yale Report and After

By September of 1827 the tide of academic reform was lapping at the precincts of Yale College. Demands had been voiced there, as elsewhere, for reforms after the fashion of Virginia and Harvard. The Yale Corporation felt it necessary to appoint a special committee to inquire into the expediency of eliminating the prescription of the "dead languages." The result was the famous Yale Report of 1828, to which we have already referred.[37]

This report was probably the most influential publication in the whole history of American higher education between the Revolution and the Civil War. It marked a real turning point. As a thoroughgoing defense of the traditional American liberal-arts college, it gave heart to academic conservatives everywhere. To be sure, this was but a temporary stemming of the tide; nevertheless, during the ante-bellum period, the Yale pronouncement exercised great sway.[38]

The report declared that a prescribed curriculum, featuring "the thorough study of the ancient languages," was the only proper system for a college. This was, in part, justified on the basis of the "faculty psychology" concept of mental discipline, a theory of learning which went far back in the history of learning. In part, prescription was upheld on the ground that the aim of the college was to lay a general foundation common to all the professions through a course in the liberal learning.[39] The student could then go on from there to secure whatever advanced training he might require. Meanwhile, in college, he had secured that expansion and balance of mental powers, that liberal and comprehensive view of life, which would serve him in good stead no matter what he later decided to do.

Why should all the students in a college be required to tread in the same steps? The Yale faculty answered that this is because every liberally educated man must come to know certain branches of knowledge which "are the common foundation of all high intellectual attainments." These the undergraduate cannot select for himself because he is not mature enough intellectually to realize what they are.

The Yale Report, contrary to some interpretations, did not reject advanced study in various specialized or professional fields. It did, however, insist that all such studies be kept out of the undergraduate college, which was to maintain a unified liberal-arts course as a core around which could be added, as material circumstances warranted, various graduate and professional schools. Collegiate and specialized training were to be kept separate because it was held that their purposes were different. Comparisons of American colleges with German universities were described as misleading, not only because the latter then had greater financial resources, but also because they dealt with a different kind of student body. German university students were far more mature, and much better prepared for advanced work, than American undergraduates. The latter were more comparable to the German Gymnasium (secondary) students. To attempt to introduce the freedom of choice and specialized studies of German universities into American colleges was therefore declared to be "ludicrous." It is clear that this nineteenth-century American concept of mental discipline and a classical curriculum flowed inevitably from the ruling idea of a college that would be unassailably orthodox in its Christianity and primarily concerned with the building of moral character rather than the fostering of intellectual power as an end in itself.[40]

Though the spirit of the Yale Report henceforth ruled the colleges, demands for collegiate reformation were not completely stilled. These became more numerous in the 1840s and 1850s, paralleling the quickening pace of industrialization and westward expansion. It was the era of "manifest destiny" for the United States, a time of cultural nationalism when "young America" was just beginning to sense its power. This new spirit was eloquently articulated in 1837 by Ralph Waldo Emerson in his famous address at Harvard on "The American Scholar." This intellectual manifesto set the keynote for a new wave of academic reform. Emerson made a strong plea for adapting education to the individual, rather than vice versa, and for developing a distinctively American intellectual culture, rather than tamely submitting to a prescribed curriculum derived from other lands and times. "We have listened too long," he said, "to the courtly muses of Europe." The remedy, he suggested, was for "the single man [to] plant himself indomitably on his instinct, and there abide . . ." His conclusion was a clarion call to action: "We will walk on our own feet; we will work with our own hands; we will speak our own minds."[41]

Not long after Emerson's address was delivered, Harvard began to be agitated once again by proposals for changes in its curriculum. By 1839, the faculty had agreed in principle to permit a student, after the freshman year, to substitute subjects such as science, modern languages, and history for required Latin and Greek. In 1841, the Harvard Corporation officially sanctioned this importation of the "parallel" course system into Harvard. President Quincy justified the new departure on the grounds that the arts and sciences had so multiplied that it was impossible in four years to study everything. There must be a selection. Quincy argued that the new system would raise, rather than lower, standards of classical learning by establishing for the first time a searching examination in Latin and Greek after completion of the freshman course, just as in the European universities.[42]

The Quincy reforms produced no more of a fundamental change in the Harvard curriculum than had Ticknor's. The classicist professors continued with their passive resistance, the governing boards found it difficult to finance the teaching of a broadly elective curriculum, and the marking system was such as actually to penalize gifted students desirous of college honors who chose to take the new electives.[43] In 1846, the faculty were polled by the incoming president Everett, and it was found that they were fairly evenly divided in their views on the elective system. Accordingly, in that year the number of electives was reduced to three each in the junior and senior years. The rest of the curriculum remained completely prescribed.

More in tune with the spirit of Emerson's declaration of intellectual independence was Francis Wayland, president of Brown University. In a little book published in 1842 he indicted the American college for its classicist conservatism. Looking at the academic world from the vantage point of fast-industrializing Providence, Rhode Island, he demanded a curriculum broad enough to meet the needs of men who were to manage great instruments of production. "Let it," he wrote, "besides being a preparatory school to the professions, be a Lowell Institute to the region in which it is placed." Failure to meet the needs of farmers, mechanics, and industrialists, he pointed out, was resulting in a dangerous falling off of college enrollments.[44]

In 1850, Wayland used a threat of resignation to force the Brown Corporation to adopt the program he desired. The report which he now wrote to outline these proposals was widely read and discussed from one end of the country to the other. Far more than his book, it served to bring the whole question of the elective system to the public's attention. The report proposed a system under which "Every student might study what he chose, all that he chose, and nothing but what he chose." The offerings in applied science were to be greatly increased. Although a "partial" course, for which no degree was granted, had been established at Brown as early as 1831, such work was now to be expanded. A kind of university extension division was to be set up by means of lyceums taught by Brown professors. Finally, a new degree of Ph.B. was to be established, with the master's degree being granted for the same amount of work previously required for the bachelor's.[45]

To implement this program, the Brown Corporation raised $125,000, but this later proved to be insufficient for such an ambitious design. Enrollment spurted for a few years, but in 1854 it began to fall off once again. In addition, unmistakable evidence began to accumulate that the quality of the student body was deteriorating. The public did not rally with any degree of enthusiasm to Wayland's experiment; in particular, there seems to have been widespread objection to his "lowering of the standards" of the bachelor's degree.[46]

Unable to accomplish his purposes, Francis Wayland resigned in 1855. Brown then returned substantially to the traditional curriculum. Wayland remained unrepentant, however, and continued to call for a fundamental reconstruction of the American college. At the celebration of Eliphalet Nott's fiftieth anniversary as president of Union College, Wayland, his one-time pupil, asked: "In a free country like our own, unembarrassed by precedents, and not yet entangled by the vested rights of bygone ages, ought we not to originate a system of education which shall raise to high intellectual culture the whole mass of our people?"[47]

A different approach to reconstructing the college curriculum was advocated by Henry Philip Tappan, like Wayland a graduate of Union College under the regime of the innovating Eliphalet Nott. Tappan was one of the most searching and incisive critics of American higher education to make an appearance in the nineteenth century. He had gone overseas to attend German institutions, where he became a devotee of the German system of higher learning.[48] He differed from Wayland in that he wished to sponsor, in addition to the elective principle, the vertical, as well as the merely horizontal, expansion of the curriculum. Like Jefferson and Ticknor, he was interested not only in introducing new subjects, but in having all subjects, new and old, taught on a higher and more scholarly level, after the fashion of the great European universities. Where Wayland was primarily concerned with utility, popular influence, and mass culture, Tappan's main emphasis was on the cultivation of originality and genius. For Tappan, education meant "the cultivation and discipline of the spiritual faculties of man." Its highest form was what he called the ideal or philosophical, which concerned itself with the "unfolding of the capacities of the mind." The questions explored in such an approach would be fundamental ones—for example, What is man?[49]

Tappan knew full well that such a philosophical education would not be widely popular and, in its highest form, would serve the needs of only a few. "The commercial spirit of our country," he noted, "and the many avenues to wealth which are opened before enterprise, create a distaste for study deeply inimical to education." And he added:

The manufacturer, the merchant, the gold-digger, will not pause in their career to gain intellectual accomplishments. . . . The political condition of our country, too, is such, that a high education and a high order of talent do not generally form the sure guarantee of success. The tact of the demagogue triumphs over the accomplishments of the scholar and the man of genius.[50]

In Tappan's eyes, most American colleges remained inferior to European Gymnasiums because in their attempts to modernize they had tried to introduce too many new courses without the proper curricular framework to assimilate them. As he saw the situation,

The course of study in our colleges, copying from the English was, at their first institution, fixed at four years. The number of studies then was far more limited than at present, and the scholarship was consequently more thorough and exact. There was less attempted, but what was attempted was more perfectly mastered, and hence afforded a better intellectual discipline. With the vast extension of science, it came to pass that the course of study was vastly enlarged. Instead of erecting Universities, we have only pressed into our four years' course a greater number of studies. The effect has been disastrous. We have destroyed the charm of study by hurry and unnatural pressure, and we have rendered our scholarship, vague and superficial. . . . We have not disciplined the mind by guiding it to a calm and profound activity, but we have stimulated acquisition to preternatural exertions, and have learned as it were, from an encyclopedia the mere names of sciences, without gaining the sciences themselves.[51]

In 1851 Tappan was elected president of the University of Michigan. He now had visions of a sort of New World version of the University of Berlin, devoted to the advancement of learning and specialized research, which would flower under his guidance in the Valley of Democracy. The ideal university would be more than just a "successful institution." Tappan conceived of it as a place of "free and independent study where knowledge is the object, and culture the necessary attendant." It would not be merely a center for successful and useful projects. "A university," he held, "thus, by its nature and provisions, . . . is, evidently, a school where study may be pursued indefinitely." But knowing that he could not attain his ultimate objectives at once, he experimented with certain intermediate measures. In his inaugural address, Tappan stated that the university should have attached to it a school for the fine arts, and a school for the industrial arts which would serve the needs of agriculturists, mechanics, and manufacturers. Such work could be offered by way of special courses. In addition, he worked to set up a "parallel" scientific course as an integral part of the college; and, going beyond Nott, he awarded the bachelor of science degree for its satisfactory completion. Tappan felt that the college student should have such a course available to him because "from the barely useful, he may after a time, go to the ideal and beautiful. But if he abide by the barely useful, let him be well educated for that." He also established an earned master of arts degree, based on real graduate work, a required thesis, and a rigorous examination. Then, in 1855, he introduced the degree of bachelor of civil engineering. Finally, he took the novel step of offering elective courses *within,* as well as between, the different "parallel" courses. These were at first strictly limited, however, to the curriculum of the senior year.[52]

Imperious in personality and forthright in speech, Tappan succeeded in antagonizing important elements in the local democracy of Michigan. Kent Sagendorph writes that Tappan's inaugural address at Ann Arbor on December 21, 1852, "chilled and frightened his audience." Among other things, that address declared:

> In our country we have ever begun at the wrong end. We have erected vast dormitories for the night's sleep, instead of creating libraries and laboratories for the day's work. ... We have had gorgeous shells that seemed like mother of pearl, but there were no pearls within. It were better, like Abelard, to lead our students into the desert, if we could there give them truth and arouse thought.

Tappan added that American colleges and universities were too much involved in teaching rudimentary courses which really belonged in intermediate or even primary schools. These universities were lowering educational standards by admitting poorly prepared students. "And of what avail," he asked, "could the learned professors and preparations of a University be to juvenile students?" From his point of view, "to turn raw, undisciplined youth into Universities to study the Professions, to study the Learned Languages and the Higher Sciences, is a palpable absurdity."[53]

Powerful political and sectarian forces rose in opposition to Tappan. "Ann Arbor is not Berlin," a local newspaper informed him. Unable to carry through his full program, he nevertheless hung on for twelve years, tenaciously battling for his views. In the end, he shared the same fate as his contemporary, Wayland, and was forced out by adverse circumstances: In 1863, a hostile board of regents voted to remove him from office.[54] But his administration had left its mark upon the University of Michigan. A member of his faculty, Andrew D. White, was later to testify to the importance of Tappan's influence on his own thinking about university reform and to make the claim that the beginning of the American university came, not in Cambridge or Baltimore, but in Ann Arbor.[55]

There is one aspect of the movement for reform of the ante-bellum college curriculum about which we have not as yet spoken. This is the founding of "scientific schools" to teach the newer subjects alongside of, and affiliated with, traditional liberal-arts colleges. This trend developed at institutions which had otherwise been cool to demands for an elective system. They favored this approach because they saw in it a way of maintaining the integrity of the classical undergraduate course, while at the same time satisfying public demands for a broader curriculum.

In 1846, both Harvard and Yale inaugurated presidents favorable to moderate reform—Everett in Cambridge and Woolsey in New Haven. They both approved the founding of new departments to teach the rapidly expanding body of subject matter outside of the traditional college curriculum. Harvard's faculty had been planning what amounted to a graduate school of arts and sciences, but when

Abbott Lawrence in 1847 offered the university $50,000 for the support of scientific education, this scheme was abandoned.[56] In its place, there was established the Lawrence Scientific School, exclusively concerned with the natural sciences, and giving instruction solely on a non-graduate level. In fact, its admission requirements only called for the equivalent of a good common-school or elementary-school education.[57] Thus the impression was definitely conveyed that the new scientific course was not to be considered in any way the equivalent of the established Harvard College course.[58] Similarly, at Yale, when a new department of philosophy and the arts was set up in 1847, schools of applied chemistry and engineering soon arose within it which, by the time of the Civil War, combined to form the nucleus of the Sheffield Scientific School. While one branch of the new department, as we shall see, evolved into a real graduate school, granting an earned Ph.D., the scientific-school side of it, like Harvard's, had lower entrance requirements than the regular liberal-arts college. At "Sheff," a non-descript two-year course was ultimately expanded to a three-year course leading to a Ph.B. degree.[59] But both the Harvard and Yale "scientific" courses were for many years considered "lower" in intellectual quality than the traditional arts course, and their students were looked down on by the regular undergraduates.[60]

Amherst tried in the 1850s to set up a nondegree-granting "scientific" department, but this attempt failed for lack of adequate endowment and patronage.[61] Only one other liberal-arts college was successful in erecting an affiliated scientific school before the Civil War. This was Dartmouth, which received $50,000 from Abiel Chandler in 1851 to establish a department of engineering and practical arts. As in the case of the Lawrence and Sheffield establishments, the Chandler School of Science and the Arts admitted students who had completed an education in the "common schools of New England."[62] Later, when Dartmouth granted a B.S. degree to students who had entered under these requirements, protests were made against what was called a "cheap degree."[63]

The net result of the work of the pre-Eliot college reformers was not great. Their efforts, although zealous and energetic, produced no nationwide trend which transformed the curriculum. As late as 1879 G. Stanley Hall estimated that of the more than three hundred colleges then in existence in the United States, all but a score were still under the control of people who believed in mental discipline.[64] Why was this so? One reason was the lack of any overwhelming popular demand for a new kind of higher education. College training as late as 1860 remained a luxury, rather than a necessity. The colleges still attracted, at best, only a tiny minority. These students, who were mainly interested in becoming preachers, lawyers, physicians, or teachers, found a traditional liberal-arts education to be useful for their future plans. In addition, sufficient funds were not as yet available to finance the kind of wholesale expansion that full-fledged adoption of the elective system by the colleges would have necessitated.[65] The time was not yet ripe economically: The ante-bellum industrialists were still too busy making money to have much time to consider giving it away. Then, too, federal funds in large amounts had not as yet been made available to the colleges. This would come only with the Morrill Acts of 1862 and 1890.

Another unfavorable factor was the poor reputation that the new "parallel" courses and scientific programs came to enjoy among the students and the public generally. Because of their separation from the "regular" student body, lower admission standards, and lack of recognition by a bachelor's degree, "scientific" students found that they were not accorded the same social prestige as if they had received a traditional B.A. degree. At institutions like Wesleyan, Lafayette, New York University, and Brown, faculty members hostile to the new programs helped to foster these feelings of inferiority. College presidents like the Reverend James Walker of Harvard managed to combine a middle class economic philosophy with an intellectual outlook of classical traditionalism. Many American academic leaders of the 1850s shared Walker's concept that the liberal-arts college must be a fortress against *both* the social leveling and the utilitarian curricular demands of the Jacksonian period.[66]

Moreover, the level of experimental and original work in newer fields such as science and engineering had not, before 1860, been brought up to such a level of generally recognized achievement that the academic world would be forced, willy-nilly, to accept these subjects as the equals of the respected higher studies of the classical curriculum. Yet this would not be long in coming. At this very time the research laboratories of European universities were helping to bring these fields to just such a high academic stature.

In all of this, the Civil War played a catalytic role. It was such a thoroughgoing social convulsion that it forced American academicians to recognize, once and for all, the professional "respectability" and social indispensability of the engineer, the natural scientist, and the industrial technician. Given this recognition, training for these careers could no longer be denied its equal place in the college curriculum alongside the education of prospective lawyers, physicians, and ministers. This trend was greatly reinforced by the industrial expansion that followed the war.

Eliot's Reforms

The most dramatic development of the elective curriculum in the immediate post-Civil War period came at Harvard. Though this was primarily due to the forceful leadership of President Charles William Eliot, the way had been well prepared by a series of earlier measures and proposals. We have already referred to the programs instituted by Ticknor and Quincy. In the 1860s, under the presidency of Thomas Hill, the elective system was carried still farther in Cambridge. By 1867, the study of subjects such as Latin and Greek in the junior and senior years was made entirely optional with the student.[67] This trend was given public support in 1866 by a prominent Harvard professor, Frederick Henry Hedge.[68]

In 1869, a thirty-five-year-old chemist, Charles W. Eliot, was elected president of Harvard. He chose to announce in his inaugural address his firm commitment to the elective system. In American higher education, he declared, the individual traits of differing minds had not been taken into account sufficiently. The nation must rid itself of the dangerous "conceit that a Yankee can turn his hand to anything." For the individual, the only prudent course was "the highest development of his own peculiar faculty." It was for these reasons that Eliot held to the view that a true university college should give its students three essentials: first, freedom of choice in studies; second, opportunity to win distinction in special lines of study; and, finally, a system of discipline which imposes on the individual himself the main responsibility for guiding his conduct.[69] Underlying all of this was a conviction that all non-vocational college subjects have an equal "cultural" or disciplinary value, provided they are equally well taught and studied. Thus not only election but a vast broadening of the curriculum was justified. As the opening sentences of the inaugural address put it:

> The endless controversies whether language, philosophy, mathematics, or science supplies the best mental training, whether general education should be chiefly literary or chiefly scientific, have no practical lesson for us today. This University recognizes no real antagonism between literature and science, and consents to no such narrow alternatives as mathematics *or* classics, science *or* metaphysics. We would have them all, and at their best.[70]

Eliot proceeded during his long forty-year administration of Harvard affairs to carry out the major features of this plan. This was not done all at once, nor was it achieved by any dictatorial impositions on the faculty. Rather it was accomplished slowly, step by step. Much of this success was due not only to Eliot's determined and strong personality, but to the fortuitous circumstance that he was able to outlive his principal opponents.[71]

By the academic year 1874–75, Eliot was able to announce that all Harvard required courses were now limited to the freshman year, with the exception of rhetoric, philosophy, history, and political science. The only restriction on election was that elementary courses had to be taken before advanced ones. Electives were extended to freshmen in 1883–84, covering three-fifths of their work. In 1895, the remaining required courses for Harvard's freshmen were reduced to two English courses and a modern foreign language. To this were added other curriculum innovations. In 1870–71, courses were listed in the Harvard catalogue for the first time according to department rather than class, and in 1881 year courses were divided for the first time into half-courses.[72]

The Influence of Eliot's Reforms

As might have been expected, Harvard's experiment with the elective system attracted national attention. A determined Old Guard, made up principally of leaders of the smaller denominational colleges, but including presidents of larger institutions as well, fought a vigorous battle in defense of the old order. Clergymen-presidents of an evangelical frame of mind fought hard against Eliot's system as making for impiety, secularism, and excessive scientism. They saw the emerging American university as a menace to all the values they held dear.[73] President Noah Porter of Yale was one such advocate of the traditional liberal-arts college curriculum, with its prescription of a broad, general training.[74] President James McCosh of Princeton, who in 1885 had engaged in a public debate with Eliot over the merits of the elective system, warned that many educational crimes might be committed in the name of liberty.[75] Presidents Franklin Carter of Williams and Alexander Winchell of Syracuse joined in hammering away at Eliot's position. That steadfast classicist, Andrew F. West of Princeton, took up the cudgels in article after article in opposition to Eliot and all his works. West took the statistics which Eliot was using to prove the beneficial results of the elective system and hurled them back in his face, maintaining that all that they proved was premature specialization, scattering of effort, and slighting of important subject-matter fields. West and other advocates of liberal culture maintained that the elective system would in time destroy the essential unity of the college and produce an atomistic intellectual and social life on the campus.[76]

One point which all critics of Eliot's program stressed was the fundamental difference between American college and university education. The former, it was argued, was *general* education, in which elective studies properly had no place, while the latter involved advanced and specialized study. Allied to this was the contention, at least as old as the Yale Report, that the American college was in no way comparable to the German university, where freedom was permitted because the students had already undergone a stiff, high-quality preparatory course. Finally, the point was repeatedly made that there are certain permanent and fundamental studies which must be mastered by any person wishing to call himself educated and that these, therefore, must be required.[77]

The defenders of Eliot's reforms were no less vocal.[78] Adherence to a strictly classical curriculum was pure fetish worship and a poor preparation for life in the modern world.[79] Latin and Greek, taught in a *memoriter* fashion, had no more value for "mental discipline" than any other study.[80] There was a vast difference between the American elective system, even at its most unregulated, and the German university, where there was completely unsystematic study, with no course tests or grades.[81] No body of men could presume to regulate the studies of youth by what they had found "good" for themselves twenty, forty, or sixty years before.[82] The prescribed curriculum had shown itself to be a failure, even in its own chosen field of preserving and extending humanistic values, because it stressed arid and petty studies of grammar rather than true literature.[83] The prescribed study of "dead" languages continued to be advocated mainly because of its "talismanic" value as a voucher of scholastic respectability.[84]

And so the battle of words proceeded. In the thick of the fray, Eliot remained steadfast and serene, as confident of the essential rightness of his ideas when he retired from the Harvard presidency in 1909 as he had been when he first took office in 1869. For him, the prescribed curriculum meant routine learning and routine teaching. It produced only an average product, "a gregarious enthusiasm and a unanimous motive." By way of contrast with this, the elective system awakened individual interest and, in so doing, resulted in harder, better work. Thus the whole burden of motivation was shifted from external to internal compulsion. The student's own moral autonomy was developed. This, in Eliot's view, was the only way the effective leaders of the future could be trained. They could only be produced in an atmosphere of freedom. One further point. Eliot always saw the elective plan as a true "system," not a "wide-open, miscellaneous bazaar." According to him, it presupposed a "well-ordered series of consecutive courses in each large subject of instruction, such as Latin, German, history, or physics." But he shied away from purposefully arranging electives in "groups." This, he felt, would fetter spontaneous diversity of choice. Groups of studies, he wrote, were "like ready-made clothing, cut in regular sizes; they never fit any concrete individual."[85]

Whence came Eliot's ideas? The stress on the crucial role of the individual and on the importance of self-reliance reflected the influence on his mind of Jefferson, of William Ellery Channing's brand of Unitarianism, and of Ralph Waldo Emerson. Certainly Eliot's devotion to democracy was always of the selective Jeffersonian and Emersonian kind, rather than the broad, all-inclusive Jacksonian variety. Eliot called Emerson "the greatest of American thinkers" and constantly quoted from the writings of the Sage of Concord to justify the educational experiments which were going forward at Harvard.[86] In addition, there was a vein of utilitarianism running through Eliot's thought which seems similar to that of Herbert Spencer and his system of Social Darwinism.[87]

In one respect, at least, Eliot's elective system did amount to Social Darwinism transported to an academic setting. Before the days of college departments of guidance and student counseling, his system amounted to "survival" of the intellectually "fittest." By a process of "natural selection" the collegian who was not a member of the "natural aristocracy" was pretty much permitted to go his own way. His collection of "gentleman's C's" and his intercollegiate athletic activities might or might not help to make him a useful citizen, but the system was not primarily concerned with him.[88]

Not only did free electives, consciously or otherwise, foster a Darwinistic struggle between students; they also produced the same kind of competition between broad fields of knowledge, subjects, and even professors. Now that students were free to choose, how would the professors of Greek and Latin make out in competition with the professors of chemistry and physics? And would the "fittest" fields and professors necessarily survive? If so, in what sense were they "fit"?

The heyday of curricular laissez faire in America was from 1870 to 1910. A great number of institutions tried to follow in Eliot's footsteps, some more closely than others. The smaller liberal-arts colleges, together with practically all of the Jesuit colleges, hung back, but after 1890 they began to incorporate in their courses aspects of the elective system.[89] Actually, in many post-Civil War denominational colleges there was a surprisingly favorable milieu for the introduction of such new fields of study as natural science, psychology, history, and sociology, as long as clergymen-presidents and professors were able to harmonize the "exact facts" which such disciplines uncovered with an orthodox interpretation of the meaning of the Word of God.[90] One student of the subject has suggested that, because of the complexity of the situation, we would do better to speak of "elective systems," rather than of *the* elective system.[91] Following this suggestion, we can classify the various elective programs, for purposes of convenience, into four main groups.

First of all, there were those colleges, like Harvard, which had made practically their whole curriculum elective.[92] A second group was made up of colleges whose curriculums had become roughly about one-half prescribed and one-half elective.[93] A third division was composed of institutions following the "major-minor" system. Under this system, the student chose at the beginning of his junior year a field of study to be his "major" and another to be his "minor."[94] Finally, a number of colleges, headed by Johns Hopkins, were following what was called the "group system." This system organized all college studies into certain broad "groups," such as science, philosophy, history, etc. The student was required to take most of his work within one or more of these groups.[95]

There were also certain special variants of the basic archetypes described above. The most important plan was that of President Lowell of Harvard. In 1909 he introduced a system of "concentration and distribution" which was essentially an adaptation to Harvard's curriculum of aspects of the "group" and "major-minor" plans. A number of studies had been made at Harvard from time to time to determine the impact of free electives on the student body.[96] The most influential survey was made by a committee of the faculty in 1903. It was found that students were doing far less work in preparation for class than the presumed average, that courses were being chosen haphazardly with little regard to content, and that "soft" courses or convenient hours seemed to be the chief considerations in choosing courses.[97]

The publication of this report brought strong demands at Harvard for modifications of the elective system. Eliot, while remaining convinced of the wisdom of free electives, permitted each department to do what it wished with its own courses by way of "stiffening" them. The general practice was to require a "concentration" of a half-dozen or more courses in a field, and sometimes also the submission of a thesis and the passing of an oral examination.[98]

When A. Lawrence Lowell took over Harvard's presidency in 1909, he wasted no time in securing the establishment of new course regulations.[99] Under his system of "concentration and distribution" undergraduates were required to "concentrate" six of their sixteen full-year courses in one major field, and to "distribute" six more in three remaining fields.[100] As we shall see, the establishment of this new system led, beginning with the class of 1917, to the giving of general examinations for those "concentrating" in political science and history. Also there later came the related phenomena of the tutorial system and the honors system.[101] One important fact should be noted, however. Harvard had *not* abandoned the elective system. After 1910, she, and those colleges influenced by her example, had definitely given up unrestricted free electives in favor of a system of careful controls over election by the student. But this was still not the old prescribed curriculum of the Yale Report. Indeed, no unified new philosophy had emerged. American higher education remained essentially eclectic. By 1910, "rather than an academic community, there had been several competing definitions of academic community."[102]

In the last analysis, the elective system flourished from 1870 to 1910 because it met the needs of the American culture of that period. A rural society was being transformed into a great industrialized nation. Keynoting the era were optimism, competitiveness, and materialist expansion. Applied science was more important than ever before. In the realm of thought, it was the age of James's "pragmatism," Dewey's "instrumentalism," and Thorndike's "behaviorism." In such a social and economic setting—in such an atmosphere of thought—the "old-time" liberal-arts college, with its predominantly clerical administration, its prescribed course founded on an absolute ethics and a theistic faith, and its recitation system, was on the way out. Eliot's elective system, with all its revolutionary implications, was a logical expression of the spirit of the time.

Expansion of the Curriculum

One of the most significant results of the triumph of the elective principle was that it made possible a tremendous expansion and broadening of the American college curriculum. This will become apparent to anyone who compares, say, the typical college course of 1828 with that of a century later. This expansion had several well-marked aspects. One was the acceptance of a philosophy of the importance of all subjects. Another was the rise of scientific and utilitarian courses to a prominence which had once been enjoyed only by the classics and the humanities. Still another was the speedy development of subject-matter specialization, with the attendant departmentalization of the curriculum. And, finally, there was a seemingly endless proliferation of courses.

The essence of Eliot's position, formulated publicly as early as 1869, was his belief in the equal value of all "liberally taught" subject matter. This would exclude from college such special-skill subjects as welding or surgical technique, but it would open the door wide for all other fields, humanistic or scientific, old or new, which could be characterized as "liberal arts." This reform had been long in the making. The ancient supremacy of the classics could no longer be maintained now that "the ancient tree of learning had become top-heavy with numerous new branches."[103] Modern languages, natural sciences, social sciences, all were clamoring for more room. Eliot's remedy was to upset the venerable hierarchy of the arts and give them all a respected place.

For this reason, Eliot always opposed compulsory requirements, whether of Greek, Latin, or any other subject. As late as 1917, he was categorically opposed to the requirement of Latin, whether for college admission or graduation. This, of course, had an important effect on college preparatory schools. The professions, in Eliot's view, had become much more in the nature of intellectualized callings than ever before. Fields such as finance, architecture, journalism, public health, and engineering were now being systematically taught in universities. Since the practitioners of these new professions could profit in so many directions by other studies, he did not see why in college, or even in secondary school, they should "all indiscriminately . . . be obliged to study Latin."[104] The final result was that the American secondary school was revolutionized just as radically by the elective principle as was the college.

To some degree all who followed Eliot's elective policies were committed to a similar philosophy. Particularly was this the case in the state universities and land-grant colleges. Of all Eliot's contemporaries, none was more outspoken on this question than President Andrew Dickson White of Cornell. In his institution, all students and all studies were supposed to be on a footing of equality.[105]

Since a perfect balance in life is at best difficult to maintain, the result of the overthrow of the old classicist hegemony was, in many cases, to set up a new supremacy, this time of the sciences. Without doubt science had once labored under serious disadvantage in American colleges.[106] In many denominational colleges it had been presented in a spirit which, if not positively antiscientific, was at the very least nonscientific.[107] But all this was changed in the Age of Eliot. The Morrill Acts fostered scientific instruction in land-grant colleges and state universities.[108] Yale and Harvard greatly expanded their scientific schools, and Princeton set up one of its own for the first time.[109] Colleges such as Union enlarged scientific curricula which dated back to ante-bellum days.[110] College catalogues everywhere listed greater numbers of scientific courses than ever before. Texts favorable to Darwinian evolution by Gray, Dana, and LeConte began to be widely used.[111] College presidents like Eliot, White, Gilman, Jordan, and Harper rose to power who, even when not themselves scientists, were strongly in favor of science.[112]

The extraordinary advances which were being made during the later nineteenth century in both pure and applied science gave enormous prestige to experimental and investigative research, especially as it was going forward in Germany. American higher education fell under its spell. Every effort was now made to follow the research methodology of natural science and, if possible, its laboratory techniques. Even humanistic fields like literature, history, and philosophy felt honor-bound to prove that they, too, had their "scientific" side and were based on precise data.[113] Along with this came new conceptions of the needs of college and university plants. Where the old type of small college could depend upon a moderate-sized collection of books as its intellectual storehouse, the modern university's requirements proved far more costly. Not only did it need a much larger library, but it was obliged to accumulate great quantities of scientific equipment—specimens, test tubes, microscopes, and laboratory instruments.[114]

We may sum up the significance of these developments by saying that science had become the guiding star of higher education, as it had of modern civilization.

Some latter-day Baconians hailed this event.[115] Science training would give the mind real discipline, they asserted, not the "safe and elegant imbecility of classical learning." It would replace the arid verbalisms and deductive analysis of an aristocratic, stratified society with the free, inductive inquiry and tangible observations of an advancing, progressive social order.[116]

There were others, however, who looked with a critical eye at the new dispensation. They asked whether the sciences were not now encroaching on the domain of other subjects, and even seeking to dominate the world of learning.[117] As far back as 1864, Ralph Waldo Emerson had expressed misgivings of this sort.[118] And one embattled modern humanist, annoyed at the tendency to stress "practical" rather than "liberal" fields, characterized the educational policy of the Ohio legislature as one of "millions for manure but not one cent for literature."[119]

It has often been suggested that the modern conflict of studies had little to do with the intrinsic values of science and the humanities. William Allen Neilson has pointed out that mankind always has needed *both* science and the humanities. Although their methods might be different, they need not conflict. Antagonisms, he suggested, have grown up only when each side becomes false to its own best insights.[120]

The old-time college professor was a jack-of-all-trades. He was expected to teach practically everything—and usually did! Specialization was neither needed nor desired. In the Eliot period, the college professor tended increasingly to become a subject-matter specialist. The curriculum now was divided into different specialized departments. Boundary lines for areas of scholarly investigation were carried over into the domains of college instruction. In place of the former breadth of the course of study there was now compartmentalization and minute specialization. College faculties were reorganized on the basis of subject-matter departments rather than individual chairs of instruction.

This change was in large part made necessary by the vast expansion of knowledge in modern times. Entirely new fields of study, such as experimental psychology, sociology, anthropology, political science, modern literature, and all the various modern subdivisions of natural science, were pushing their way forward and had to be given recognition in the college curriculum.[121] Their emergence enlarged considerably the intellectual horizons of the American college.

The trend toward specialization was partly stimulated by the returning German-trained professors who came to dominate college faculties by the turn of the century. Many of these scholars sought to carve out a domain for their own fields whereby they could offer the courses which were *sine qua non* for them and concentrate on turning out more specialists like themselves. One observer commented sarcastically that for many college departments "protection" of their academic interests came to be the central concern. Maneuverings for departmental advantage took place which would have done credit to lobbying groups in Washington. There was even a struggle for "high protection," namely, for including the department's offerings on the list of required subjects. Failing this, some departments were willing to settle for "free trade."[122]

Along with this purely academic preoccupation with the proliferation of subject matter, there was another important influence operating in the colleges to foster extreme specialization. This was the increasing preoccupation of students with the utilitarian value of a higher education. To ensure access to expanding opportunities for wealth and economic security, young people were demanding that colleges offer an adequate number of "practical" preprofessional or prevocational courses. The Morrill Acts helped finance public institutions which specialized in offering such courses. As these colleges began to draw ever larger enrollments, financial pressures mounted on the private liberal-arts colleges to offer similar programs. University administrators particularly sensitive to the growing public demand, professors in the increasingly influential applied sciences, and spokesmen for the newly emerging social sciences joined their voices in a powerful campaign for "real life," "democratic," public-service courses. For them, and more and more for the American public, the main yardsticks of value for the college and university came to be utility and "social efficiency."[123]

Sometimes powerful inducements were held out to the hard-pressed colleges by business interests to stimulate the development of training courses. Thus, in 1894 the General Electric Company sponsored the establishment of a strong department of electrical engineering at Union College by offering a sizable endowment for that purpose. Soon courses like "engineering English" and "engineering economics" were being offered at Schenectady, and Capella's bridesmaids to philology had become handmaidens to Vulcan.[124]

College catalogues now became so fat that they began to resemble those put out by mail-order houses, and so many short, patchwork courses were offered that David Starr Jordan suggested that an appropriate degree to award for satisfactory completion of such work would be a B.S., "bachelor of surfaces."[125] These trends, let it be emphasized, were not limited to a special group of colleges prior to the First World War. They were characteristic of most of them, southern as well as northern, women's colleges as well as men's, Catholic institutions as well as secular ones.[126] In every case, there was a great increase in the number of specialized baccalaureate degrees which were offered.[127]

The specialization brought about by the elective system raised many serious questions. President Tucker of Dartmouth felt that, on the whole, the effect of the new subject matter upon the college was invigorating and wholesome, but some conservatives feared that it was breaking down the intellectual unity once possessed by higher education.[128] President Seelye of Amherst felt that the American college should not allow the intrusion of vocational and specialized studies to divert it from its traditional goal of training the "Christian gentleman."[129] And President William DeWitt Hyde of Bowdoin maintained that the proper function of a small liberal-arts college was to provide a good general education, not to multiply many highly specialized electives.[130] As late as the period 1900–30 many of the presidents of the liberal-arts colleges of Ohio, reflecting a deeply rooted Christian and humanistic point of view, agreed most emphatically with Seelye and Hyde.[131]

7

The Period of Fraternities
and Athletics

The period from the Civil War to the First World War witnessed not only a remarkable transformation of the curriculum and organization of the American college; it saw profound changes in the nature of student life. Before 1865 this life was more cohesive. The literary society was the focus of student attention, but its activities were not too remote from the aims of the largely verbalistic course of study. Concern with college honors, primarily involving a display of oratory, reinforced this tendency. Thus we may say that, despite the sporadic warfare which raged between the faculty and the student body, a basic unity existed between the *curriculum* and the *extracurriculum.*[1]

Following the Civil War, a new situation arose. Students came to represent a broader group than heretofore and some of them were lacking in any serious intellectual or preprofessional interest. Others were coming to college mainly as a prelude to an active career in business and finance. This was the era of the emergence of modern America, when strong-willed entrepreneurs were constructing a vast industrial plant and creating the economic basis for a complex urban society. The goals that were being pursued by the ambitious young men of the country were, more than in ante-bellum times, predominantly materialist, tangible, pragmatic ones. The attitude of such young people was very often likely to be one of profound anti-intellectualism. A popular college motto that epitomized the prevailing mood admonished the undergraduate: "Don't Let Your Studies Interfere with Your Education."[2]

It was at this very time that college faculties began to relax their paternalistic grip on undergraduate life and the dormitory system went into decline. This latter development did not mean, however, that a positive program of guidance or counseling was substituted; for a long period of time students were generally allowed to drift aimlessly. As a result, American students now improvised their own pattern of collegiate living. The existing vacuum was filled by a "college life" which was independent of, and frequently in opposition to, formal courses of study. In this new era, strenuous extracurricular activities, by way of clubs, fraternities, intercollegiate athletics, and publications, took the place in student hearts once held by literary societies and oratorical exhibitions.

President Woodrow Wilson of Princeton in 1909 summed up the meaning of the situation when he wrote that, in college life, "the side shows are so numerous, so diverting—so important, if you will—that they have swallowed up the circus."[3] Without question, a wide gap had opened up during this period between two college worlds—that of the curriculum and that of the extracurriculum. It was not clear, on the eve of the First World War, whether the two worlds would drift completely apart or whether, as Wilson feared, the latter would end by completely dominating the former.

Boarding Out Versus Boarding In

We have already noted that the early American colleges followed an imported English pattern which looked upon a residential unit of students and teachers as an essential ingredient in academic life.[4] For two hundred years, the dormitory system remained entrenched in the American college, although it did not follow in important details the same line of evolution as the colleges of Oxford and Cambridge. In the latter half of the nineteenth century, however, the dormitory system came under increasingly heavy fire; college after college began to follow a policy of laissez faire in student housing, much the same as in the case of the course of study.

To be sure, there remained earnest advocates of the "collegiate way of living." President Noah Porter of Yale, for example, felt sure that there were social and educational virtues in the "common life" of a college dormitory that residence in scattered boardinghouses could never supply.[5] It was largely because of the influence of men of his mind that the dormitory system continued to exist in many liberal-arts colleges of the East and Middle West while the tide was running strong against it everywhere else.

Even before the Civil War, dormitories had come in for serious criticism. Some charged that they helped to foster student rebellions. Others asserted that they constituted an outmoded remnant of medievalism. Many critics maintained that dormitory living led to evil habits and disorderly conduct.[6]

Two of the outstanding leaders of ante-bellum higher education, Francis Wayland and Henry P. Tappan, were strongly against dormitories.[7] Their views came to be more widely followed as the influence of German-trained scholars on the American college scene grew apace. Many educators came to feel that America, like Prussia, should spend the bulk of its available funds for university libraries, laboratories, observatories, and eminent professors, not for dormitory buildings, which belonged more properly at a boys' secondary school. College students should be mature enough to provide for their own boarding facilities and social life.[8] Then, too, as new state universities and agricultural colleges struggled to get under way in the West, they found themselves without the funds to provide dormitory facilities for their constantly enlarging enrollment. It was all they could do to find enough money for instruction, salaries, and classroom buildings. Thus the dormitory system fell into disuse for financial as well as ideological reasons.[9]

In this new era of college housing, the students, left to their own devices, resorted to various expedients to provide the board and room they had once been able to secure at the dormitory. The private boardinghouse was one. The transformation of the fraternity and sorority from what had been primarily a social and intellectual group into an organization providing residential facilities on a large scale was another. A third solution, limited principally to Harvard and Yale, was the building for profit by private entrepreneurs of palatial residence halls for the wealthier students. Such was Harvard's "Gold Coast" and Yale's "Hutch."

The last two trends had the effect of dramatically accentuating social distinctions between college students. Perhaps this simply mirrored the increasing stratification which, after the Civil War, came to characterize American society. Whatever the cause, it was clear that two contradictory trends were under way. On one hand, opportunities for a college education were being made available to more people than ever before by state universities, municipal universities, and land-grant colleges. On the other, an ever larger proportion of wealthy students were invading the older, privately endowed colleges of the East. As if to confirm these trends, the cost of obtaining a college education in the private institutions was going up all the time.[10] This was reflected in the realm of student housing. In the new expensive private dormitories, "university counterparts of the vast mansions of the Morgans, Vanderbilts, Fricks, and Carnegies," were concentrated the "prep school" boys from wealthy homes. These socially ambitious students were anxious to attract campus attention with their high scale of living. At these same Eastern institutions, however, one could still find "grinds" and "fruits," struggling hard to work their way through college.[11]

Some college authorities were inspired by this rash of off-campus building to attempt the construction of lavish dormitories of their own. Thus Yale under President Timothy Dwight the younger pulled down most of the old Brick Row and replaced it with neo-Gothic stone dormitories. Soon Princeton was following suit with her own "Gothic Age" dormitories. One observer sees this as symbolic. The Brick Row barracks style of college architecture reflected "the poverty and simple life of the early colleges." The neo-Gothic piles of the late nineteenth and early twentieth centuries, on the other hand, were sophisticated versions of a new "Romantic" period subsidized by vast wealth. Unlike the older buildings, they were related neither to their national heritage nor to the functional values of their own time.[12]

The development of the new luxury residence halls alarmed even Charles W. Eliot, who previously had been inclined to keep hands off the housing of students. Writing at the end of the nineteenth century, he now declared that it was necessary for colleges to build dormitories with "common rooms" and dining halls so that "students of all sorts" could mix together freely. This foreshadowed the policies of Eliot's successor in the Harvard presidency, A. Lawrence Lowell.[13]

The tendency which worried Eliot had already been present before the period under review. The social life of the residence hall had come to be regarded as separate from, and unrelated to, the intellectual life of the classroom and laboratory. Even more was this true of fraternity houses and private off-campus residence halls. The result was to widen the split between the college life of the classroom and the extracurricular life of the campus.[14]

The Government and Discipline of College Students

In the years after 1865 two opposing concepts of college discipline increasingly came into conflict. One, dating back to the colonial colleges, was the traditional paternalistic system, with its elaborate rules for government and control. The other, which came into prominence only after the introduction of the elective system, was patterned after the freedom of the German universities and came to treat the student as a responsible adult.

The old system, deriving from England, regarded college education as far more than a purely intellectual enterprise. In its view, the college was to look after the moral as well as the intellectual development of its students; character training was just as important as mind training. This venerable concept of the "collegiate way of living" stressed the housing of students in closely supervised college dormitories, compulsory attendance at religious exercises, and the enforcement of discipline *in loco parentis*.[15] One consequence, as we have seen, was the ever-threatening student rebellion. Another was the development of a bitter enmity between faculty and students, a "ten-foot-pole" relationship akin to that between an oppressive schoolmaster and a resentful schoolboy.[16] Professor Barrett Wendell of Harvard noted that "many students seem as unable to meet us intellectually as a near-sighted eye to detect a small star, or a color-blind man to read railway signals." President Taylor of Vassar in 1893 explained the faculty's point of view by observing: "One is obliged to suspect, at times, that the student comes to be regarded as a mere disturber of ideal schemes, and as a disquieting element in what, without him, might be a fairly pleasant life."[17] The trouble was that there was a great gulf between the goals and ideals of the two groups. The professors, by and large, had chosen to withdraw from the surrounding world of competitive materialistic activity into an oasis of books and abstract ideas; the students, contrariwise, neither understood nor sympathized with this type of life and visualized for themselves a "practical" future, the kind which made sense to most American businessmen and men of affairs.

President Eliot had called for a new system of college discipline in his 1869 inaugural address, one which would substitute self-discipline and a mature sense of responsibility for the traditional concept. Other reformers of higher education in this period, men like Barnard, White, Jordan, and Harper, worked toward a similar goal.[18] The trend now was more and more toward a concept of college government which William Rainey Harper defined as follows: "The college professor of today is not an officer of the state, but a fellow student. . . . The college community is one made up of older and younger students, all of whom have joined the community in order to make progress in intellectual life."[19]

The new system reflected at least in part the growing influence in many institutions of German-trained or Johns Hopkins-trained scholars who felt it was demeaning to their professorial dignity to serve as petty disciplinarians keeping attendance records and checking up on the conduct of students outside the classroom. The research-oriented scholar was interested in the student only as a fledgling scholar and for the rest preferred to regard him as a self-reliant young adult. For different reasons the same result was brought about at state universities and expanding urban institutions. There the emphasis on utilitarian considerations and the spirit of democracy made the old-time authoritative and paternalistic approach seem increasingly out of place.[20]

How did these new and freer concepts work out in practice? It is difficult to give a categorical answer. Although student rebellions of the violent ante-bellum type no longer occurred, there was no lack of disciplinary problems to be dealt with. As might have been expected, some conservatives charged that these lapses were the fruit of letting in more liberal and easygoing systems of college government. However, problems such as gambling, excessive drinking, violent hazing, and sexual laxity could be found just as frequently on campuses where the old stern discipline was maintained as on those where reformers had brought in the new ideas.[21] Certainly a fundamental relaxation of the old Puritan taboos was under way in America. Also, the excitement produced by "big-time" football undoubtedly proved a fertile breeding ground for many student excesses. Furthermore, some saw a correlation between the growing wealth and luxury of undergraduate life and the incidence of disorder, although President Hadley of Yale vigorously denied this.[22]

The whole situation was complicated by the fact that the American college embodied aspects of both secondary school and university. It took in boys and graduated men. At the great American universities, one could find callow adolescents and mature graduate students on the same campus, sometimes in the same classroom. Under these circumstances, it was a serious question whether any uniform system of discipline could be applied indiscriminately.[23] One observer suggested that the wisest course would be to retain a strict parental system for entering freshmen, while gradually delegating more and more adult responsibilities to upper classmen.[24]

Improving post-bellum faculty-student relations were most graphically illustrated by the widespread development of plans for student self-government and "honor systems." As early as 1825, Jefferson had sought to set up a form of student self-government at the University of Virginia, but it had been abandoned after a year's trial. Trinity and Amherst also experimented with delegating more responsibility to students before the Civil War, but these efforts had no permanent influence.[25]

In the later nineteenth century, the movement for student self-government assumed three principal forms. At Vanderbilt, Pennsylvania, and Chicago, student committees were set up to maintain order in dormitories. At Princeton, Vermont, Virginia, Wesleyan, and Bates, groups of student advisers were formed to consult with the faculty on various matters. From this basic root, by the way, the student-council movement of the twentieth century arose.[26]

The third aspect of this development was also the most thoroughgoing. This involved the actual delegation of responsibility for disciplinary control to bodies of students. Such a plan, modeled on the form of the federal government, was put into effect as early as 1867 at the University of Illinois. The students elected members of an executive, legislative, and judicial branch. These undergraduate officials were given general disciplinary control over student life. In time factionalism and lax enforcement became serious problems, so that in 1883 the students themselves voted to abandon the experiment. President Andrew S. Draper of the University of Illinois declared flatly in 1904: "Student government is a broken reed. If actual, it is capricious, impulsive and unreliable; if not, it is a subterfuge and pretense."[27] When a similar scheme was attempted by the University of Maine in 1873, it was somewhat more successful because the student government showed from the very beginning that "it meant business."[28] On the other hand, student government plans at Iowa State College and the University of Wisconsin came a cropper, largely because of cliquishness, inadequate enforcement, and lack of cooperation from the administration.[29]

One of the most successful of the student government plans of this period was instituted in 1883 at Amherst by President Julius Seelye. In this case, a student senate was given supervision of discipline in place of the faculty. President Seelye retained veto power over its deliberations, but was obliged to utilize it only once in eight years.[30]

The self-government movement also affected the women's colleges, particularly institutions such as Barnard, Bryn Mawr, and Vassar. There were, of course, differences in approach. For example, at Bryn Mawr the students were actually permitted to determine policy, while at Vassar they were allowed only to execute it.[31]

A special form of the new concept of self-discipline and responsibility among American college students was represented by what came to be called the "honor system." Set up with a good deal of moral enthusiasm, this meant, in some institutions, putting students on their honor in taking an examination, without faculty supervision. In other colleges, it extended to student conduct, the preparation of assignments, and other aspects of campus life. The University of Virginia pioneered in this field, and similar codes appeared at West Point in 1871, the University of North Carolina in 1875, and Princeton in 1893.[32]

By 1915, at least 123 American institutions of higher education were employing some variant of the honor system. The plan seems to have taken deeper root in southern universities than in those north of the Mason and Dixon line. The principal difficulty in the way of the effective functioning of the system was the continued vitality of the ancient student tradition that it was not "honorable" to inform on a fellow student. This might not have been so serious if there had not been an increasing number of undergraduates who were not serious, mature students, but had been "sent" to college by their families.[33]

An important aspect of the traditional college life had been compulsory chapel. All the ante-bellum colleges had required daily attendance at morning, and sometimes also evening, prayers. As late as the 1880s, most of the smaller denominational colleges continued this requirement. Indeed, a survey made in 1913 revealed that thirty-two out of sixty "representative" institutions still compelled all students to attend chapel.[34] This group included large private universities like Yale and Princeton, and even state universities such as Georgia.[35] It was just such a system that Stephen Vincent Benét pictured so vividly in his novel of college life at Yale in the early nineteen hundreds. He tells how in the early morning's "dim irreligious light" the "whole sleepy College congregated together."[36]

After the Civil War, both academic control and curriculum were being increasingly secularized; clergymen were losing their predominance in the American higher learning. In this new setting the spirit of evangelistic revivalism, previously so important, began to lose much of its vital force for American students.[37]

All of this led to a powerful movement for the abandonment of compulsory chapel. Cornell was notable for pioneering with the innovation of an interdenominational pulpit made up of guest preachers.[38] Eliot of Harvard, with his deep concern for individual freedom, dropped compulsory chapel in 1885.[39] Other influential institutions, including state universities such as Wisconsin and Ohio State, eliminated chapel services, though not without considerable public controversy.[40]

The disappearance of compulsory chapel in many places by no means signified that religious vitality had fled the American campus. There continued to be an important group of professed believers at every college, and much of the energy that in previous days had gone into prayer meetings and revivalism now was concentrated on the work of the college YMCA's. At institutions like Yale, the "Y" became one of the leading prestige activities on campus at this time. In 1877 an intercollegiate YMCA organization was formed, and the movement soon came to have great influence throughout the American academic world.[41]

Clubs and Secret Societies

One of the most important developments in student life during the later nineteenth century was the rise of the college fraternity. This was indeed *sui generis.* Neither England, where there were many student clubs at Oxford and Cambridge, nor Germany, with its student *Corps* and *Burschenschaften,* had seen anything quite like it.[42] Phi Beta Kappa, founded in 1776, is commonly referred to as the first national Greek-letter fraternity, although in its early years it was essentially a literary society. It came to be marked off from other literary societies of the time by its high degree of selectivity and its secrecy. Indeed, there are clear indications of Masonic influence in the early history of the honor society.[43] As for the social fraternities, their real beginning came with the founding of the so-called Union Triad—Kappa Alpha, in 1825; Sigma Phi, in 1827; and Delta Phi, also in 1827.[44]

The rise of fraternities did not come without strife. On many campuses, both faculty and students were bitterly opposed to them, mainly on the grounds of secrecy. The general climate of public opinion was similarly hostile. It also appears that conservatives in the late eighteenth and early nineteenth centuries identified secret societies with conspiratorial revolutionary organizations, like the Illuminati, who were allegedly plotting the overthrow of organized society and a Reign of Terror on the model of the French Revolution. After the Morgan case in 1826, when it was charged that members of a Masonic organization had murdered a man to prevent him from revealing their secrets, a nationwide campaign got under way against all such groups. College secret societies received some of the backlash of this revulsion of public feeling.

In 1831 a 290-page book was published denouncing Masonry; its author wrote under the pseudonym Avery Allen. Among other things this work charged that Phi Beta Kappa was an infidel society because its initials stood for the Greek words meaning "Philosophy the Guide of Life." Instead, claimed the author, the Bible was the guide of life! Many doubtless agreed with the librarian of Brown University, Reuben A. Guild, who wrote in 1852: "Secret Societies . . . originate with the Devil, all of them." Francis Wayland was disturbed not only by their secrecy, but also by their intercollegiate character. Such groups, he warned in 1846, "fraternizing with other societies in all the colleges of the country and under the veil of secrecy" seemed "very liable to great abuse" and were likely to be made "an instrument of combination [without] limit for any purpose." Moreover, new dangers could arise if these brotherhoods turned to "purposes of secret conviviality." In many places, the fraternity movement was driven underground, but it was by no means extirpated completely. The attempts by college faculties to wipe out fraternities ultimately failed because it was impossible to achieve a common front on this matter. Many small colleges would not cooperate, largely because they could not afford to lose students to other institutions which still tolerated fraternities. It was at this time, though, that Phi Beta Kappa dropped its secrecy requirements, Supreme Court Justice Joseph Story and ex-President John Quincy Adams taking the lead in effecting that change.[45]

After 1865, opposition to fraternities subsided for a time, and they entered an important period of growth and diversification. Already, in the 1850s, the first Greek-letter societies for women had been established. Many new types of fraternities made their appearance, including professional ones servicing fields like law and medicine and honorary ones in specialized subject-matter areas. It was at this time, too, that fraternities and sororities began to provide residential facilities for their members. Thus, by the end of the century, the fraternity had definitely displaced the literary society as the central rallying point in American campus life.[46] The declining literary societies sought to revitalize themselves by becoming debating societies. This was not too successful, however, because eventually student interest in all forms of debating waned.

To collegians, the appeal of fraternities was powerful on several counts. They seemed to satisfy deep emotional needs which did not find sufficient outlet in the cultural activities of existing extracurricular organizations such as the literary and debating societies. The group activities developed by the "frats" for under-graduates would be entirely their own. They furnished centers of sociability and good fellowship. For students at the more rigorous denominational colleges they offered the excitement of release from Puritan austerity. They arranged for parties and dances to which members of the opposite sex would be invited, such as junior "proms." Thus the very existence of these secret student organizations offered an implicit challenge to the college authorities and their rigid rules and pietistic atmosphere. Furthermore, they furnished comfortable housing for students at a time when college authorities were showing less and less interest in providing it. One observer has noted that they "became a breeding ground for conformist expectations such as would make for success in later life." In an age when pecuniary standards of differentiation were becoming increasingly important, their policies of exclusiveness enabled socially ambitious undergraduates to gain recognition as members of a special college caste.[47]

Despite the growing predominance of fraternities after Appomattox, opposi-tion to them had by no means disappeared. Many denominational colleges con-tinued to regard them as irreligious, immoral, and subversive both of good discipline and study. The occasional injury or death of a student during a frater-nity initiation added fuel to the fire. Some college presidents continued in their efforts to stamp out the movement.[48]

The most serious challenge, however, came from the growing Populism of the South and West. Here fraternities and sororities in state universities were attacked as antidemocratic and exclusive. There were definite indications, as a matter of fact, that fraternities, which were not particularly divisive at a New England college such as Amherst where more than three-quarters of the students belonged to them, became much more so in western universities. There they tended to cater to the sons of the new rich and limited their membership to a fifth or a quarter of the undergraduates. It was charged with some justice that they opposed the whole spirit and purpose of public higher education by representing a special clique of the rich and well-born. Members of state legislatures were also told that such groups fostered gambling, drinking, and sex irregularities. When, in the 1890s, the Populist party began to win political power in these sections of the country, laws were enacted to outlaw, or at least to hamstring, fraternity activities at state institutions of higher education. An Indiana Supreme Court decision in 1882 prevented state university trustees from barring students who refused to sign an antifraternity pledge. A number of other important decisions, however, au-thorized the state universities to take all college privileges save that of attending classes from students who refused to sign such a pledge. Finally, in 1913, Missis-sippi's highest court upheld as constitutional a statute outlawing fraternities and sororities at state-supported colleges and universities. This case was appealed to the United States Supreme Court, and the Mississippi decision was upheld.[49]

Thus the fraternities, going into the twentieth century, found themselves on shaky legal ground. Once again, however, they demonstrated a remarkable resiliency and staying power. Whereas in 1865 there had been only 25 national fraternities, by the middle of the twentieth century 77 national fraternities and 45 national sororities were in existence. Even more impressive was the growth in the amount of property these organizations held in custody. By 1920, this amounted to a grand total of $17,468,200 and only seven years later it had soared to $63,582,705.[50]

The rise of fraternities was aided in no small way by the endorsement given to their activities by prominent leaders of higher education, such as Andrew Dickson White of Cornell.[51] Furthermore, the prevailing laissez-faire attitude toward student life helped the fraternities because it made possible the reaching of something like a tacit understanding under which a good deal of the responsibility for student welfare, government, housing, and social relations was thrown on the local chapter house.[52]

Another trend which facilitated the acceptance of fraternities after 1865 was their willingness to abandon secrecy. As alumni began to play a greater role in managing these organizations, the local chapters indulged in less and less *sub rosa* activity. At the same time, the national offices of the fraternities, and the Interfraternity Conference itself, sought to allay the criticism that members placed social life ahead of scholastic life. This they did by working to improve the scholarship of fraternity members and by calling upon them to put college interests first.[53] However, just as these developments were beginning to bring about a more favorable turn of public sentiment toward the fraternities, new criticisms were made of their snobbishness and exclusiveness. To these were added, in the twentieth century, allegations that they practiced racial and religious discrimination. In this respect, they simply reflected the general intolerance of ethnic minorities, such as Jews and Chinese, that prevailed among students in homogeneous or inbred campus communities such as Princeton's.[54]

Not all college secret societies of this era affiliated themselves with a national fraternity. A few developed and flourished on a purely local basis. Perhaps the most famous of these were the senior societies at Yale, which by the end of the nineteenth century totaled six. Yale's Skull and Bones and Scroll and Key were imitated by a number of other local societies, such as Axe and Coffin at Columbia, Owl and Padlock at the University of Michigan, and Skull and Serpent at Wesleyan. For headquarters, these societies maintained mysterious and clandestine "tombs." If anything, they were more secretive about their proceedings and more exclusive in their attitude than many fraternity chapters. For this reason, like the fraternities, they became the subject of acrimonious public controversy.[55]

The Yale senior societies became the strongest of these secret orders. Indeed they came to be such an integral part of undergraduate life at New Haven that they successfully resisted any and all criticism. Stephen Vincent Benét, in *The Beginning of Wisdom,* has left us with a vivid account of them. We are shown the frantic process whereby students, almost from their first days in college, plotted and schemed to climb the undergraduate social ladder so that, at last, they might gain admittance to the hallowed senior societies. "The uncanny ones held hushed converse with the blinds pulled down as to their own and others' chances for Senior Societies two years away." Then came the supreme suspense and tenseness of "Tap Day," when all the juniors congregated nervously and expectantly in the hope of receiving the coveted "tap" for one of the societies.[56]

At other prominent eastern colleges, similar student groups flourished in this period. While neither secret nor affiliated with a national fraternity, they shared the same emphasis on exclusiveness and social differentiation. At Harvard, for example, famous societies like the Porcellian, which recruited most of its members from the wealthy and "eligible" young men of the "Gold Coast," became the goal of all socially ambitious undergraduates. To "make" such clubs, it became increasingly obvious that one must enter from the "right" preparatory school, do the "right thing," avoid originality, and conform to all existing social taboos.[57] Owen Wister's *Philosophy Four* gives us a picture of two jolly and wealthy young Harvardians of this period, not "greasy grinds," students who could well have been charter members of "Pork's" elect circle.[58]

At Princeton, similar student groups achieved social dominance during these years. Since the fraternities had been utterly crushed by McCosh, the undergraduate desire for comradeship, combination, and social exclusiveness was satisfied by another kind of organization, the "eating club." Limited in membership to juniors and seniors, these societies soon came to possess their own clubhouses, libraries, billiard rooms, and residences for students, just like major fraternities. It was soon clear that these were Old Nassau's answer to Yale's senior societies and Harvard's "Gold Coast" clubs. Elections of new members came on a "fatal morning" in March and produced a similarly wild scramble among the ranks of "suddenly neurotic" lower classmen. Then, too, the Princeton clubs were the fulcrum of the same frantic college life, "that breathless social system," as F. Scott Fitzgerald put it, "that worship, seldom named, never really admitted, of the bogey 'Big Man.' "[59]

It was to do away with the undemocratic features of this system that President Woodrow Wilson proposed, in 1907, to reorganize Princeton into a number of residential quadrangles, or colleges, patterned after Oxford and Cambridge. The "eating clubs" would be abolished and the whole student body would be distributed among "quads," where they could live, eat, study, and talk together. Wilson hoped by this reform not only to wipe out cliquish exclusiveness but also to reabsorb the social life of the undergraduates into the fundamental intellectual processes of the college. His effort went down, however, to ignominious defeat. Vested interests, both undergraduate and alumni, successfully blocked it.[60]

Despite the ascendancy of social fraternities and other types of selective student groups, every pre-World War I campus was the scene of vigorous activity by numerous organizations which made no pretensions to exclusiveness. Thus the average undergraduate, if at all interested, could normally find some college club or society which would be glad to welcome him into its membership. These extracurricular organizations tended to be of two main types. On one hand, there was the club concerned with a special academic field, such as history or English, in which faculty members participated along with the students. On the other, there were many clubs run by the students alone. These catered to every conceivable interest. There were, for example, religious clubs, music clubs, drama clubs, glee clubs, debating clubs, mandolin clubs, hobby clubs, and many others. At the same time the growth of a serious student interest in contemporary social problems was reflected on a number of campuses by the organization of units of the Student Christian Movement, sponsored by Walter Rauschenbusch, and the Intercollegiate Socialist Society, organized by Upton Sinclair.[61]

Big-Time Athletics

Sharing a place of eminence with the most famous clubs and fraternities, intercollegiate athletics came, after the Civil War, to provide a stage for the winning of honors as campus "big man." It had not always been so. In the early American college physical exercise was spontaneous, unorganized, and certainly not intercollegiate. Games were planned on an informal basis entirely for recreation and enjoyment. Moreover, there existed at many denominational colleges something like a contempt for mere physical prowess, as detracting from the desired high spiritual atmosphere. As late as the 1890s there were presidents at Miami University and the College of Wooster in Ohio who opposed intercollegiate athletics on the ground that they infringed on the "holy time" which was made available to the college student to prepare for later usefulness in life.[62]

The introduction of physical training and the gymnasium movement in the middle of the nineteenth century helped to dispel some of the coolness to systematic physical activity by undergraduates. In organized team play, however, American colleges lagged behind those in England. The first intercollegiate competitions did not come in the United States until the 1850s, when an upsurge of interest in boat racing occurred.[63] During the Civil War, baseball began to attain a measure of popularity with undergraduates, as well as with the general public. After 1865, "track and field" athletics also became popular and, by 1874, intercollegiate meets were being held.[64]

More important than any of these, as later events would disclose, was the first appearance of American college football. In 1869, the first intercollegiate football game occurred between Rutgers and Princeton. This was not yet the game as known today, but soccer. During the next few years, football was played between various American colleges under a confused rules situation until, in 1876, an intercollegiate conference adopted a modified form of Rugby Union rules. These modifications came to be expanded during future years to such an extent that American football came to be differentiated markedly from English rugby, soccer, or Canadian football.[65]

The influence of the growing British interest in team and school sports may well have played an important part in the rise of American collegiate sport at this time. The "Muscular Christianity" movement in Britain and the immense popularity of the book *Tom Brown's Schooldays* seem to have been factors helping to explain the rush to organize athletic activities at American institutions paralleling the team sports of the English schools.[66]

Howard Savage, in his thorough and illuminating analysis of American college athletics, has suggested that the year 1880 be taken as the dividing line between the earlier, informal period of college sports and the rise of highly organized "big-time" intercollegiate athletics. Before that date, he points out, neither training nor coaching had become specialized. Equipment was simple. Participants in matches away from home customarily paid their own expenses. Management was entirely in the hands of undergraduates. After 1880, all this began to change. Training was intensified and elaborated. Coaching became a paid profession, and a highly technical and specialized one at that. Equipment costs mounted rapidly. Alumni came to play a large role in the management of the teams. "Because it was joyously irrational," notes one observer, "(beneath the convenient façade of its supposed rules) and because it fastened upon practical rather than abstract prowess, football asserted itself as the archetypical expression of the student temperament. . . ."[67]

The new situation was one in which financial demands mounted rapidly. The result was a thoroughgoing commercialization of intercollegiate sport. Money to support the expanded athletic program had to be raised on a scale such as had never been seen before. The principal sources of such financing came to be gifts from wealthy alumni (who were thus enabled to secure a dominating position in the sports program) and receipts from admission charges to football games. Because the latter revenues were so important, a winning football team was considered "good business" by many college administrations. Since the game was becoming increasingly popular with a sports-hungry public, a good team could attract "big money" at the gate. In fact, many colleges took to building vast football stadia, some of them larger than the Colosseum of imperial Rome, in order to increase gate receipts by accommodating tens of thousands of spectators. The temporary grandstands of earlier days, where a handful of spectators had watched the game either free or at nominal cost, were things of the past.[68]

As college sport became a big business, a number of practices arose which were, to say the least, questionable. Many of these were introduced by overzealous alumni, eager for victory and bent upon "booming" their alma mater. The "tramp athlete" and his cousin, "the ringer," made their appearance, as able players canvassed the colleges and enrolled at those institutions willing to award them the most lucrative scholarship. Graduate students, even coaches, played on some teams along with the undergraduates. Many coaches found that retention of their position depended upon winning games, whether by fair means or foul. In addition to all of the foregoing, large-scale betting on college games began to pose serious problems.[69]

Despite these conditions, a number of college presidents were enthusiastic supporters of big-time athletics, largely on the ground that it provided good advertising for their schools. For example, President Charles Kendall Adams of the University of Wisconsin, himself a great football fan, firmly believed that an important factor in the drawing power of any American institution of learning was the prowess of its athletic teams.[70] Of a similar mind was President William Rainey Harper of the University of Chicago. Like Adams, Harper was accustomed to making stirring appeals to the university's team between the halves of football games. Harper made strenuous, and finally successful, efforts to get the famous coach Amos Alonzo Stagg to come to Chicago as athletic director. In one letter, he told Stagg: "I want you to develop teams which we can send around the country and knock out all the colleges. We will give them a palace car and a vacation too."[71] David Starr Jordan of Stanford started out by being an intensely sports-minded college president while Woodrow Wilson at Princeton and Vernon L. Parrington at the University of Oklahoma combined the coaching of football teams with a career of college teaching.

Presidents of small colleges were just as anxious to gain national recognition through intercollegiate athletics as heads of large universities. Thus President Crowell of Trinity College in North Carolina was convinced that the development of a winning football team in the late 1880s was what "carried the record of Trinity's prowess beyond state limits" and enabled the institution to "enter upon a new era of its enviable and honorable career."[72]

There nevertheless remained a few leaders of American higher education who earnestly wished to see reforms in the whole system of intercollegiate sport. Such men as Presidents Eliot of Harvard, Butler of Columbia, and Wilson of Princeton deplored the brutality, overemphasis on winning, commercialism, and false scale of values induced by big-time football. In these criticisms they were joined by a number of periodicals,[73] particularly those of a religious or denominational nature.[74]

Responding to these critics were a do-or-die group of college alumni, ex-players, and pro-football faculty members, who claimed that the existing situation was not as black as it had been painted.[75] In the middle stood moderates like Walter Camp of Yale, who argued for the value of intercollegiate sport but called for the rigorous observance of certain standards of sportsmanship and gentlemanliness.[76]

Although the Harvard faculty promulgated a detailed code regulating all undergraduate sports as early as 1882, most colleges continued to drift and follow a laissez-faire attitude.[77] In 1905, however, the academic world was stirred out of its lethargy by the publication in the Chicago *Tribune* of statistics showing that 18 players had been killed and 159 seriously injured during the football season just past.[78] Immediately, President Theodore Roosevelt, a great lover of football as an expression of his concept of the "strenuous life," summoned athletic representatives of Harvard, Yale, and Princeton to the White House for a conference. There the President called upon them to save the game by helping to eliminate from it all brutality and foul play.[79]

In the wake of the White House conference, action was taken all over the country to reform intercollegiate athletics. Some institutions, like Columbia, abolished football outright, while others, like Northwestern and Union College, suspended it for a year. In many places, shorter schedules were adopted. On the West Coast, the experiment was tried of substituting a modified form of rugby for football. Institution after institution set up special committees, usually representing faculty, students, and alumni, to superintend and control the whole field of intercollegiate athletics. A few schools, such as the University of Missouri and the University of Chicago, raised "physical culture" to the dignity of a full-fledged department of instruction, centralizing authority over both sports and physical training in one professor.[80]

Much of this zeal for reform petered out during the next few years, but one permanent element continued to work for improvement. This was represented by various regional intercollegiate athletic associations and conferences, such as the "Big Ten" of the Middle West. In 1905, this movement reached national proportions when the National Intercollegiate Athletic Association was established.[81]

The fact remains, however, that in 1929, when Howard E. Savage made his comprehensive study of intercollegiate sports for the Carnegie Foundation, he was obliged to report that these expedients had by no means eliminated the old evils of commercialism and overemphasis. Savage recommended that the colleges set up true standards of amateur sportsmanship and more actively go about their proper business of challenging the best intellectual capabilities of undergraduates.[82] These findings corroborated an analysis made by President W. H. P. Faunce of Brown more than twenty years earlier.[83]

More than four decades later, in 1974, a report published for the American Council on Education found that many abuses still existed in intercollegiate sports. The report criticized aspects of the financing of college athletics, ethical abuses in recruitment and subsidization of team members, deleterious effects of competition with professional teams for the entertainment dollar, the pressures resulting from the costs of extensive athletic plants, and a continuing confusion over the educational role, if any, of collegiate sport.[84]

What, then, can we say about the lasting significance of intercollegiate athletics in American higher education? In all fairness, we should note both the bright and dark tones in the picture. On the darker side, we must acknowledge that sports had to some extent diverted the interests of students from the intellectual aims which were supposed to be the principal purpose of higher learning.[85] At Amherst, the famous philosophy teacher Garman noted that the students were demanding for themselves a higher standard of perfection in athletics than in studies.[86] Another observer found that "honors" in football, baseball, and rowing had come to be esteemed at least as highly as academic honors, and soon the letters A.B. in America might come to stand for "bachelor of athletics" rather than bachelor of arts.[87]

We have already spoken of the commercialization of American college sport and of the overemphasis on certain spectacular aspects. In these respects, the situation differed markedly from that at the British universities and public schools, where the amateur spirit reigned. The American emphasis on winning games for their financial or publicity value, the mass enthusiasm of "college spirit," stimulated by bands and cheer leaders, the high degree of professional organization and specialization involved in the really "big-time" athletic contests, were in many ways unique in the world.[88]

It was generally assumed that intercollegiate athletics were a profitable business enterprise for those conducting them, but this conclusion has been challenged by at least one study. An investigator in 1934 found that college football during the 1920s did not "pay off" in helping to raise endowment for a group of average-sized institutions emphasizing it as a promotional technique. A similar group of colleges, which made no effort to emphasize big-time football, definitely outdistanced the others in this respect.[89]

It was claimed by proponents of intercollegiate athletics that the fierce competition of the playing field furnished good training for the "game" of life. This claim was belied by the findings of A. Lawrence Lowell, who made a detailed study of the careers of students who had attended Harvard during the later decades of the nineteenth century. Lowell discovered that there was no correspondence between attainment of the status of college athletic "hero" and distinction in later life.[90] Lowell's study gave documentation for a conclusion reached a little later by George Fitch in his novel *At Good Old Siwash:* "The college athlete may discover that the only use the world has for talented shoulder muscles is for hod-carrying purposes . . . and the fishy-eyed nonentity, who never did anything more glorious in college than pay his class tax, may be doing a brokerage business in skyscrapers within ten years."[91]

On the question of health, there is no clear evidence that intercollegiate athletic competition in any way improved the physical condition of the average undergraduate, or even of the active participant in varsity play. In fact, the Carnegie Foundation discovered in the 1920s that college athletes had no better life expectancy than the general run of the college population, itself a selected group, and definitely not so good a one as college men of high scholarship rank.[92] Then, too, there was the problem of physical injuries, many of them serious, resulting from football games. From 1893 to 1902, a total of 654 known serious injuries occurred among those playing college football in the United States.[93]

Some observers argued that the vogue for intercollegiate athletics helped drain off the excess energy of undergraduates and in so doing brought to a close the era of violent college rebellions.[94] Proponents of intercollegiate sport also made the claim that it helped develop ideals of sportsmanship, of loyalty to a cause, and of team play. In so doing, they asserted, college athletics had contributed important elements to the moral development of America.[95] In this connection, some have noticed a parallel between the role of physical training and athletic contests in the life of ancient Greece and their place in modern America. The cheerleaders, the "majorettes," the rooters, the intersectional "bowls," reminded at least one Briton of the great Panhellenic festivals, which, like the modern American sports spectacles, were religious exercises of a kind and instruments of national unity.[96]

One final point. College sport tended to sound a note of democratic opportunity and individualism in a society that was becoming increasingly stratified and conformist. The accident of origin or wealth meant little on the athletic field. The colleges, and the general public, too, wanted a winner.[97] To quote our British observer again:

> The sons of Czechs and Poles can score there, can break through the barriers that stand in the way of the children of "Bohunks" and "Polacks." And although Harvard may secretly rejoice when it can put a winning team on to Soldier's Field whose names suggest the Mayflower, it would rather put on a team that can beat Yale. . . .[98]

Publications

In a college novel dealing with Harvard life around 1900, two students at one point are gloomily discussing their failure to "get anywhere" in college life. Studies, of course, were just "a detail." They had failed to make the Glee Club; they couldn't play football or any other sport well; they couldn't play the banjo or the mandolin. "What on earth can a person do who hasn't any talent or skill or ability of any kind?" one of them asked, plaintively. "He can always write," the other replied, "and he can always be an editor."[99]

This just about sums up the place of student publications in campus life at the turn of the century. Next to the fraternities and the varsity teams, they had prestige, but certainly of a much lower order. Of course, if a student journalist ever attained to the exalted position of editor, there was always a chance that he might be recognized as one of the college "big men."

In this period, four main types of student publications were produced— literary magazines, newspapers, class annuals, and humorous periodicals. Before 1865, all American college periodicals, modeled on some earlier English examples, took the form of monthly literary magazines. This type went back at least to the first decade of the nineteenth century. There was, however, an abnormally high mortality rate. Few survived their first numbers, whether because of student indifference, poor management, or other reasons.[100]

The oldest college literary magazine to achieve permanence of publication and lasting renown was the *Yale Literary Magazine,* founded in 1836. In approach and content, it reflected in its early years the lofty and somewhat detached attitude characteristic of the literary societies of the time. In the early twentieth century, it became a sort of proving ground for a number of undergraduate writers who were in later years to achieve distinction in the world of letters. The five editors of the *Lit* were elected annually by the whole junior class to function in this capacity during their senior year. Election carried a great deal of prestige, and competition for the honor was keen.[101]

Another important college literary magazine was the Harvard *Advocate,* established in the spring of 1866. Many important writers published their first work in its columns.[102] In addition, there were a number of other important undergraduate literary monthlies, too numerous to mention, which succeeded in establishing themselves on a permanent basis.[103]

After the Civil War, the main emphasis in American college journalism shifted from the literary magazine to the newspaper. On almost every campus a publication was established which modeled its form, contents, organization, and purposes on regular daily newspapers. The *Yale Daily News,* first to be founded, is still in operation. The *Harvard Crimson* began in 1873 as a more newsy rival of the *Advocate.* Ten years later, it merged with a competitor to become a daily. The spread of the college newspaper movement was marked, in 1886, by the formation of an Intercollegiate Press Association, consisting of the *Crimson,* the *Yale News,* and the *Daily Princetonian.* Dozens of other American undergraduate newspapers appeared before the year 1900, a development which had no close parallel in the student publications of Europe. Many of these college periodicals came, in time, to maintain direct wire service from leading news agencies and to serve their local communities just as regular newspapers would do.[104]

Another kind of student journalistic effort was represented by the college annual. Usually produced by the seniors, it preserved a record of that class and customarily contained material about other activities on the campus.

Finally, we should take note of the appearance of a fourth type of campus publication, the college humor magazine. Although some pioneer college "comics" appeared at Princeton as early as 1835, these proved to be ephemeral. The movement really got started in 1876, when the *Harvard Lampoon* was founded. Not only did "Lampy's" success set in motion a nationwide trend toward the founding of similar undergraduate publications; it also had no little influence on the founding of national humor magazines such as *Life.*[105]

College Life

Wilbur Cortez Abbott, in an illuminating analysis which he entitled "The Guild of Students," pointed out that the American college was far more than some physical equipment and a list of courses and faculty names. There was another whole side to it, equally important and real. This was "the undergraduate's university," the educational system he had devised for himself. It was made up of student habitations, teams, clubs, secret fraternities, vocal and instrumental groups—all highly competitive. Its "degrees" and insignias of honor—fraternity pins and varsity letters—were hotly contested for. It had its own traditional and customary laws, a sort of modern American version of the medieval *Codex Studentium.* It appealed to youth on the basis of the romance which was felt to inhere in old taprooms like "Mory's," ivy-covered buildings, nicknames, mascots, venerable student societies like Skull and Bones, chimes and bells, even college colors.[106]

Much of this hectic activity developed originally in the context of the college "class," which continued to be an important bond in the period under review. Distinctions between students of different class years went back to the early

English origins of American colleges. In addition, the annual classes served for a long period of time as teaching units, and this practice helped to heighten the sense of identity which their members came to feel. The characteristic community life of the dormitories and the eating together in commons produced the same effect. The result was a "class spirit," an *esprit de corps,* among those students who were obliged, under this system, to associate closely with a specific group of classmates for four years.[107]

The rise of class spirit led to the development of certain well-marked college customs which involved relations between the classes. "Freshman laws" were evolved. Fagging was taken over from the English public schools, and when it was abolished class rivalry was continued under the guise of hazing, "rushes," "cane sprees," and similar boisterous activities. Class orators, poets, and valedictorians made their appearance. Classbooks and class reunions served to strengthen the ties which had already been developed.[108]

From the American college class a comradeship developed far more diverse than anything produced by the social fraternities. The familiar term "classmate" suggests the very real sentiment which was fostered. Nothing quite like it could be found in the universities of Continental Europe. Even in England, where "college life" traditionally had been considered an integral part of baccalaureate training, nothing like the American concept of class loyalty developed.[109]

The class spirit continued to be important on into the twentieth century, but its relative weight tended to decline. This was due in part to the impact of the elective system, which broke up the classes as teaching units, and in part to the growing size of college enrollments, which made the yearly classes too large for the effective maintenance of close-knit social ties.[110]

Although the unity of undergraduate life was being undermined by growing complexities, it was restored in great measure by the activities of students in sports, social relations, and other fields. Thus the whole diverse realm of college life furnished the unity which had formerly been supplied by class and curriculum. The rise of this *imperium in imperio* was facilitated by important sociological trends. The coming of modern transportation to hitherto isolated college towns, for example, brought the students of those institutions in closer touch with the main currents of life in nearby urban centers.[111] Furthermore, the growing wealth of the country, as Nicholas Murray Butler observed, produced a change in the kind of student going to college. Where formerly the majority had possessed some sort of scholarly or serious professional purpose, now it was becoming "fashionable" to go to college for social and business rather than intellectual reasons. The sons of the new-rich of the "Gilded Age" were sent to college to participate in college life and to learn how to mingle more or less freely among college-bred men.[112]

Life for the American undergraduate under these circumstances was by no means leisurely. The social pressure to engage in some form of extracurricular activity made it highly competitive and active. Henry Seidel Canby described the prevailing pattern as "strenuous idleness."[113] The great goal was to be rated a "success" by one's classmates. Conformism to the mores of the group was the *summum bonum,* not independence of mind. Dean Andrew F. West of Princeton boasted that the result of four years residence at his institution was the elimination of "personal eccentricity, conceit, diffidence, and all that is callow or forward or perverse."[114]

Of course, not all students would, or did, conform. There were always a few rugged individualists, like Sinclair Lewis, who refused even to pretend an interest in athletics or college politics;[115] and there were the "grinds," who William Lyon Phelps thought must be the happiest men in college, because they had the wonderful privilege of undisturbed study.[116] The position of the iconoclastic nonconformist was summed up by the undergraduate radical who told Owen Johnson's fictional Dink Stover of Yale: "I came to Yale for an education. I pay for it—good pay. . . . Work for Yale, go out and slave, give up my leisure and my independence to do what for Yale? To keep turning the wheels of some purely inconsequential machine, or strive like a gladiator. Is that doing anything for Yale, a seat of learning?"[117]

For the majority, however, the demands of the campus proved to be much more persuasive than those of the classroom. Canby has described the typical college of the period as a place where two philosophies of life saluted in passing and sometimes even stopped for a chat.[118] A much harsher judgment was that pronounced by Burges Johnson, who saw the situation as essentially a war of the Campus against the Classroom. The shock troops in this war were the fraternities and intercollegiate athletics, draining the energies of students from their proper concerns, wasting countless hours of potential classroom time which had to be excused so that student teams could make prolonged trips and dramatic clubs could rehearse their performances. The resulting situation created divided loyalties, brought pressure to bear on faculty members to raise the grades of students important in "college life," fostered dishonesty and bribery.[119]

One significant question remains, however. Was the spontaneous demand of American students for a life apart from the classroom in any way legitimate? Increasingly, educators in the twentieth century came to believe so. One interpretation of the growth of the extracurriculum in the period under consideration might be that it originally arose, at least in part, as a protest against the aridity of the old prescribed curriculum. For example, when the regular curriculum emphasized the classics, the students found an outlet for expression in their mother tongue in literary societies and in publications. Then in the era of German-inspired faculty impersonalism, the fraternities and varsity athletes gained ascendancy. Many observers felt that the real trouble was not that certain forces were leading to the evolution of a "students' university," with its own distinctive life, but that American college faculties and administrations were coping with the situation in such a poor, bumbling way. Again to quote Professor Abbott: "As it stands now, this part of our collegiate system is perhaps ill done. But it is now beyond us to end it; it remains to mend."[120]

PART III

THE RISE OF UNIVERSITIES

IN NINETEENTH-CENTURY

AMERICA

8

The American State University

Thus far we have spoken principally of the American college. Brought from England in colonial times, this institution at first was really more akin to a secondary school—what the Germans would call a Gymnasium—than it was to an agency of the higher learning. We turn now to the rise of a more elaborate educational structure in the United States, one which more properly merits the name "university." The origins of this movement can be traced back to the era of the eighteenth-century Enlightenment, although its full realization did not come until after the founding of Johns Hopkins in 1876.

The growth of universities in America was brought about by many factors—the rationalism and empiricism of the Enlightenment, the impact of the American and French revolutions, the influence of the resurgent German universities of the nineteenth century, and the utilitarian need for incorporating new fields of knowledge such as science and modern languages into the curriculum to serve the requirements of an expanding society. When most of the older collegiate foundations failed to respond adequately to these demands, initiative passed into the hands of those who planned to organize, or who were actually organizing, foundations called universities. Although many of these were universities in name only, other new institutions, such as Cornell and Johns Hopkins, began to do really significant work. At the same time, certain private colleges, notably Harvard, under Eliot, reorganized themselves thoroughly so as to assume definite university functions.[1]

In America, the name "university" has sometimes been claimed by institutions whose advanced program of instruction and research has remained little more than a noble aspiration. To be sure, the precise meaning of the word "university" has undergone profound changes in modern times.[2] Nevertheless, it has generally come to connote an educational institution of large size which affords instruction of an advanced nature in all the main branches of learning. As a matter of fact, if one were to hold strictly to the definition which Continental Europe since the nineteenth century has tended to recognize as the only proper one—namely, a graduate institution giving various forms of advanced training—

no American university would qualify, not even Johns Hopkins or Clark. Actually, the American university, though modeled on the European, has evolved its own unique framework. And, in so doing, it has assimilated, rather than destroyed, the pre-existing college.

On this basis, we can say that a number of "university" centers of learning had developed in the United States by the coming of the twentieth century. Although in academic organization they were all basically similar, in systems of support and control they represented two main types. One, representing public action by the democratic community in the realm of higher learning, was dramatically symbolized by the American state university. The other, inspired by private initiative and benevolence, led to the growth of great endowed institutions, centers of advanced learning and research. Both types can be traced back to the plans of the late eighteenth century; both began to expand with true force in the last quarter of the nineteenth century; and both attained a position of world significance in the twentieth century. In this chapter, we speak only of the first phenomenon, the publicly supported university in America. In the next, our emphasis shall be primarily, though by no means exclusively, on the other type, the privately endowed university.

Late-Eighteenth-Century Forms

The American state university can be traced back to the late eighteenth century, but not in the form that we know today. A premonitory stirring can be noted in this early period, the beginnings of a change in traditional English-American notions of higher education. What were the reasons? Unquestionably the impact of the European Enlightenment upon American thought was one.[3] Another was the effect produced by the American and French revolutions. Indeed, this second influence seems to have strengthened the first. For a time liberal ideas were much in vogue, particularly among the planter and merchant aristocrats of the South. Now, precisely how did these circumstances lead to the founding of state universities in the United States? For one thing, a demand was generated for enlargement of the curriculum to include newer subjects, such as the natural sciences, which the philosophers of the Enlightenment considered vital. Some of this had been already seen at the College of Philadelphia and other colonial colleges. Now the campaign for such reforms became louder and more insistent. Echoing Franklin's views, there was a strong vein of utilitarianism in this position. Philosophically it went back at least as far as Francis Bacon, with his insistence that knowledge was power and that it be actively applied for the improvement of human living. Tied in with this was the strong note of humanitarianism characteristic of the Enlightenment. Applied knowledge should be used to relieve human pain and suffering, to reform human institutions. The new, broader education was to be the instrument of man's ultimate perfectibility.

When none of America's established educational foundations responded wholeheartedly to these demands, it became increasingly apparent that it would be necessary to organize new state-sponsored institutions to do the job. This, too, correlated with the dominant thinking of the Enlightenment and Revolutionary periods. A new concept of the functions of government was developing, a belief that by taking proper governmental action social institutions could be remolded to a more just order. The classical tradition in the higher learning was seen, from this point of view, as nothing but a decadent scholasticism. Its narrow scope reflected the old concept of society as embodying a hierarchy of functions. In the new age of American independence and republicanism, education of the highest sort should be broadly disseminated. It must not be limited to a select few in a limited number of "literary" professions. And, Enlightenment thought insisted, it should be free of control by religious sects. The mind of man must be unfettered; it must be free to reason boldly, to create a rational order in which human happiness could be advanced. This was an era in which a powerful drive for the separation of Church and State was under way in many parts of the United States.[4]

The result was an attempt to found state and national universities that would be free of sectarian control and would offer equality of educational opportunity. Attempts were made in Pennsylvania, Virginia, and New York to transform existing private colleges into state institutions, but with no success.[5] Ambitious plans for state-sponsored systems of education and national universities were projected on paper, but these remained very much in the realm of Utopia-building rather than positive action.[6]

What, then, was actually done to implement the state-university idea during the last two decades of the eighteenth century and the first two of the nineteenth? Not very much. It is true that a number of institutions were founded, especially in the South, which called themselves state universities. Indeed, a profitless dispute has ever since proceeded as to which of these was the *first* state university in American history.[7] Although this question may have some importance in relation to local pride, it seems rather meaningless in any larger sense because these early universities lacked many of the characteristics which we would today expect to find in a public institution bearing that name.[8]

Among these early state institutions were the universities of North Carolina, Georgia, Vermont, Ohio, Tennessee, Maryland, and also South Carolina College and Transylvania University in Kentucky. None of them gave instruction which was advanced enough to be characterized as university work. Even more notable, however, was the fact that these first so-called state institutions were more nearly private than public. The idea of public responsibility for education had not yet been widely accepted in America. English tradition conceived of a "public" secondary school or college as an institution established under government charter and supervision, but with direct management delegated to a corporate group. Although throughout colonial times institutions we now regard as private, such as Harvard and Yale, were financed at least in part by public grants, it was nowhere accepted that they should receive all their support from the state and that they should be under public control. In the later nineteenth century, public support without public control dwindled and this tended to accentuate the demarcation line between public and private institutions of learning.[9]

The first "public" universities of the newly independent states reflected in many ways these colonial traditions. Their charters treated them as if they were private incorporations, and the courts backed up this interpretation. Thus, when the University of Vermont was founded in 1791, its charter treated the trustees as if they were private individuals rather than public officials. Not until 1810 did the legislature provide that it would select the trustees, thus placing the university under public control. Similarly, the University of Georgia started in 1789 with a self-perpetuating board of trustees, while university funds derived from private sources were held in the custody of the state. Not until 1876 were the Georgia trustees appointed by the legislature, and not until 1881 did the state make direct appropriations for the support of the institution.

Another case in point occurred at the University of North Carolina with similar results. There, after the state granted escheated lands to the university for its support, a new law was passed requiring that all such lands which remained unsold revert to the state. But the state's highest court declared the latter statute null and void on the interesting ground that the state had alienated the property in the first instance as completely as if it had been granted to a private person and therefore could not take it back without compensation.[10] Other states, like Georgia, limited themselves to endowing their "state" universities and then letting them shift for themselves with little more than an occasional special appropriation or permission to raise money through a lottery.[11] In many of these states, the principle of regular tax support for university work did not become established until after the Civil War.

The so-called University of the State of New York, frequently cited as an early example of strong state control of higher education, appears upon examination to be something different. It is true that at the height of a public controversy in the province of New York in 1753 and 1754, William Livingstone demanded the establishment of a college which would be completely under public control. This plan, however, seems to have been motivated primarily by a Presbyterian desire to head off Anglican control of the proposed King's College.[12]

Next, we find that in 1774 the members of the governing board of King's College came forward with a proposal for a new charter creating the Regents of the University of the Province of New York. On this board of regents were to sit high church officials of various denominations, together with leading New York governmental dignitaries and the trustees of King's College. These regents were apparently to govern various colleges which might later come under their jurisdiction on the plan of Oxford and Cambridge universities. The interesting point here is that, although the American Revolution frustrated this particular plan, the Act of 1784, setting up the University of the State of New York, followed it closely. When this system proved unwieldy, a new plan was enacted by the legislature in 1787. It is significant that this reorganized University of the State of New York followed the ideas of Alexander Hamilton, not those of Ezra

L'Hommedieu (who proposed a much greater degree of centralization). As a result, the "University" was granted power to inspect educational institutions, and to grant charters and degrees, but it was separated from existing incorporations, such as that of Columbia College, which retained all their independent and self-perpetuating rights, as in colonial days.[13] The New York situation, then, is another illustration of the fact that the early tendency toward state control of higher education was weaker than appears on the surface, even though New York did unquestionably go farther than any other state in this period in at least laying the general foundations for central control of higher education.

In addition to the lack of any active backing for direct public support and control of higher education, American advocates of new "revolutionary" state universities faced other obstacles. For one thing, the high tide of the Enlightenment was beginning to recede after 1800 under the impact of the "Protestant Counter Reformation." Revivals were spreading through American colleges; church-related institutions were being founded in every part of the new nation; missionary organizations, Bible societies, and theological seminaries were being enthusiastically established.[14] Orthodox college students now found a more favorable atmosphere in which to organize prayer meetings.[15] The French Revolution in its bloody, extremist phases had succeeded in convincing many of the leaders of American public opinion that the principles of the Enlightenment were synonymous with the most flagrant atheism and murder.[16] The dangers of "Jacobin" infidelity were denounced in sermon after sermon by the predominantly clerical college presidents and professors.[17] The College of William and Mary, now under "Jeffersonian" influences, was pictured in Northern periodicals as a hotbed of irreligion, while any news of student disorder there was quickly set down as proof of the dire effects of "Jacobinism" on youthful morality.[18]

In this new atmosphere it was difficult to secure solid public support for the pioneer state universities. The resurgent evangelicals were quick to denounce these new public foundations as "godless."[19] In most cases, control of these supposedly secular, public institutions was captured by sectarians. Thus Presbyterians very soon dominated the board of trustees of the University of North Carolina. Other Southern "state" universities, such as Georgia and South Carolina, recruited their first presidents in the North, hiring clergymen of a Calvinistic persuasion. Indeed, the Presbyterians of South Carolina were so satisfied with their control of the state university that they made no effort to establish a college of their own in that commonwealth.[20]

The Early "Revolutionary" University: Jefferson and the University of Virginia

The university which Thomas Jefferson established at Charlottesville in Virginia was America's first real state university. It is an authentic example of this type for a number of reasons. First of all, it aimed from the beginning to give more advanced instruction than the existing colleges, to permit students to specialize and to enjoy the privileges of election. Its course of study when it opened for instruction in 1825 was much broader than that which was customary at the time.[21] Secondly, the University of Virginia was by the express intent of its constitution a thoroughly public enterprise, rather than a private or quasi-public one. Finally, its early orientation was distinctly and purposely secular and non-denominational. In all of this, it represented the most thoroughgoing embodiment of the "revolutionary" spirit of the Enlightenment to be found in American higher education during the first decades of the nineteenth century.

If ever an institution of learning could be described as "the lengthened shadow of a man," the University of Virginia is such a one. Jefferson had been planning a university of this kind ever since the later 1770s. Then, as an influential member of the revolutionary Virginia legislature helping to draft the general "revisal" of the laws, he formulated a plan for a system of public education so comprehensive that it would be a powerful engine making for a truly republican society. This project was as dear to his heart as any in which he had ever become engaged. Through it, he hoped, the idea of excellence would be combined with that of popular enlightenment; knowledge would be spread on a wide scale to every citizen, while at the same time the truly gifted would have ample opportunity to be trained for places of leadership as the "natural aristocracy" of the new society.[22]

In 1779, Jefferson attempted to reconstruct the College of William and Mary into the state university which was an essential part of his ambitious educational blueprint. Though important changes were introduced, the college languished. Jefferson then turned to the idea of setting up a completely new university which would be located in the central part of the Old Dominion. When he retired from the Presidency, he gave more and more time to this project and finally, in 1818, succeeded in getting a legislative charter for this institution of his dreams. Referring to it as the "child of his old age," Jefferson took the closest personal interest in setting up his university. Besides leading the fight for the legislation establishing the school, he busied himself with selecting its site, designing its buildings, planning its first course of study, negotiating for the hiring of its first professors, and pressing hard for adequate appropriations. And when the institution finally went into operation, he made, although now in his eighty-third year, almost daily trips on horseback over rough mountain roads to visit its campus. The students of the time remembered the "tall, venerable gentleman in plain but neat attire." Many of them, and many members of the faculty also, had been regularly invited to dine with him at his nearby mountaintop home, Monticello.[23]

What kind of institution of learning was Jefferson seeking to create in early nineteenth-century Virginia? We have already spoken of the exclusively public pattern of administration and control which was written into the university's charter. This, clearly, Jefferson considered basic. From the beginning, the institution was placed in the hands of a board of visitors, directly appointed by the governor, and confirmed by the legislature. In the hands of these visitors were lodged all powers which had been customarily exercised by incorporated boards of trustees. In addition, the state of Virginia made a large investment in the original buildings, library, and equipment of the university, and continued regularly to give it an annual appropriation of money to support its work.[24]

Another basic cornerstone of the university system which Jefferson wished to install was that of freedom from domination by any and all religious sects. He believed it was appropriate for the different denominations to erect centers of worship adjacent to the university grounds, but he was adamant against allowing them to dictate the choice of professors or trustees, as was the case at many other so-called state universities of this period. For the same reason, he was opposed to the establishment of any professorship of theology. As he expected, these policies stirred up a hornet's nest of opposition. Representatives of powerful denominational groups, in particular the Presbyterians, soon made it clear that for them the religious opinions of professorial appointees were very much an issue. They might be willing to accept Episcopalian professors; but Unitarian ones, never![25] Jefferson himself noted at this time that "there are fanatics both in religion and politics, who, without knowing me personally, have been taught to consider me as a raw head and bloody bones."[26] At a crucial point in the legislative campaign for endowment funds, a remark he was alleged to have made, that the orthodox might well "be afraid of the progress of the Unitarians to the South," was quickly spread far and wide. Joseph C. Cabell pointed out to Jefferson: "The Bible Societies are in constant correspondence all over the continent, and a fact is wafted across it in a few weeks. Through these societies the discovery of the religious opinions of Ticknor and Bowditch was made."[27]

To make matters even more difficult, denominational enemies of the university were joined by demagogues who charged that the institution was chiefly of benefit to the rich. To help counter this criticism, friends of the university put through a bill providing that one promising poor student from each senatorial district should be sent free to the university. For a time the state even paid the board bills of these scholarship students. By this policy the Virginia legislature implemented Jefferson's basic concept that a "natural aristocracy" of virtue and talent should be recruited by means of special state scholarships.[28]

Further insight into Jefferson's objectives in setting up the university is furnished by his interesting correspondence with Joseph C. Cabell, his principal legislative agent in the campaign to get the institution approved and endowed. Here we learn, first of all, that Jefferson was aiming at the creation of an institution of higher grade than any of the existing American colleges—a true "university" in the contemporary European sense of the term.[29] Timothy Dwight in 1816 gave it as his opinion that there was not a single such center of advanced learning in the United States. Jefferson wanted to found just such a one:

> The great object of our aim from the beginning has been to make the establishment the most eminent in the United States, in order to draw to it the youth of every State.
> . . . We have proposed, therefore, to call to it characters of the first order of science from Europe, as well as our own country; and, not only by the salaries and the comforts of their

situation, but by the distinguished scale of its structure and preparation, and the promise of future eminence which these would hold up, to induce them to commit their reputation to its future fortunes. . . . It is not a half project which is to fill up the enticement of character from abroad. To stop where we are, is to abandon our high hopes, and become suitors to Yale and Harvard for their secondary characters to become our first. Have we been laboring then merely to get up another Hampden Sidney or Lexington? Yet to this it sinks, if we abandon foreign aid.[30]

The advanced type of institution which Jefferson had in mind for Virginia is made immediately clear when we examine the first curriculum which, under his guidance, was established there. Eight professorships were instituted, covering the fields of ancient languages, modern languages, mathematics, natural philosophy, natural history, anatomy and medicine, moral philosophy, and law.[31] A student had ample opportunity to specialize and do advanced work in any of these fields if he so desired. The elective principle which was introduced permitted him to choose three fields, or "schools," for concentration, in contrast to the conventional college curriculum of the time which was completely prescribed.[32]

In many other portions of Jefferson's correspondence, we see the great store he set upon attracting eminent foreign scholars to the university. The contemplated outlay of money, he thought, would be of little value if the staff were made up only of ordinary American college teachers. At one time or another, he had tried to establish a French-style academy in Richmond which would attract European professors, transplant to the United States the whole faculty of the University of Geneva, and bring to the New World the University of Edinburgh faculty.[33] None of these efforts proved successful, but Jefferson remained profoundly convinced that the type of illustrious scholar he wanted for his university's first faculty was not to be found in the United States.[34] He was aware, however, that there was a strong public opinion which would have none but native professors. As a concession to this, he offered positions in 1820 to Nathaniel Bowditch and George Ticknor. When negotiations for their appointment fell through, he promptly sent an agent to recruit the majority of the faculty overseas, principally in England. At the same time, Jefferson did feel that there were two professorships which could not be safely entrusted to foreign hands—those of ethics and law. These, indeed, were eventually filled by Americans.[35]

Another purpose which stands out in this correspondence is Jefferson's hope that the proposed university would help win for the South and West intellectual independence from the North. That this conception had definite political overtones is made clear when we read Jefferson's repeated assertions that he was receiving letters from "almost every State south of the Potomac, Ohio, and Missouri," all "looking anxiously to the opening of our University as an epoch which is to relieve them from sending to the Northern universities."[36] He warns that the university must get the entire fund asked from the legislature, else Harvard "will still prime it over us, with her twenty professors." He adds bitterly: "How many of our youths she now has, learning the lessons of Anti-Missourianism, I know not; but a gentleman lately from Princeton, told me he saw there the list of the students at that place, and that more than half were Virginians. These will return home, no doubt, deeply impressed with the sacred principles of our holy alliance of Restrictionists."[37]

One final problem arose in connection with the planning of the university: What should its relation be to the other projected branches of Jefferson's original grand design—namely, the primary schools and intermediate academies? When it became clear that legislative appropriations could not be secured for all three levels, Jefferson declared himself in favor of establishing the primary schools and the university first. He was against giving a dollar of public money to established private academies or colleges, such as Hampden-Sidney: "Let this," he argued, "with all the other intermediate academies, be taken up in their turn and provided for systematically and proportionally. To give to that singly, will be a departure from principle, will make the others our enemies, and is not necessary."[38] And in another letter, he declared: "With respect to the claims of the local academies, I will make no compromise. The second grade must not be confounded with the first, nor treated of in the same chapter. The present funds are not sufficient for all the three grades. The first and third are most important to be first brought into action. When they are properly provided for, and the funds sufficiently enlarged, the middle establishment should be taken up systematically." Jefferson was willing in the meantime to leave the intermediate field to private enterprise, "1, because there is a good number of classical schools now existing; and 2, because their students are universally sons of parents who can afford to pay for their education."[39]

With all of Jefferson's devotion to his cherished university project, he remained convinced that public primary education had the higher claim. "Were it necessary," he wrote Cabell, "to give up either the Primaries or the University, I would rather abandon the last, because it is safer to have a whole people respectably enlightened, than a few in a high state of science, and the many in ignorance. This last is the most dangerous state in which a nation can be. The nations and governments of Europe are so many proofs of it."[40] This position is not strange in view of the prominent strain of utilitarianism which Daniel Boorstin and others have shown ran through Jefferson's thinking. The sage of Monticello always sought for "an useful American education." The University of Virginia, he hoped, would become an institution "in which all the branches of science useful *to us,* and *at this day* should be taught in their highest degree" (the emphasis is his). The study of agriculture he highly recommended because "it is the first in utility." The natural sciences, civil history, and law were valued for the same reasons. Even the study of the classics, valuable as it might be, should not be permitted to distract men from the urgent practical tasks of building a prosperous republican society, an empire for liberty.[41]

Although the University of Virginia during the first fifty years of its history "had about it more of the atmosphere of a true university than any other institution in this country,"[42] it did not become all that Jefferson had hoped. Why was this? One reason was the low state of secondary education in Virginia. The university had to rely on whatever training the existing private academies and colleges offered, and this was not advanced enough to prepare students for European-style university work.[43] Many of the constituent elements necessary for a great university—laboratory equipment, collections of antiquities, and libraries—were lacking in early nineteenth-century America and could not be assembled overnight. In this connection, we have already spoken of the difficulty of securing adequately trained professors. Jefferson's correspondence—particularly with the young Bostonian, George Ticknor—tells us how difficult was the search for the books, equipment, and professors needed at Charlottesville.[44] These efforts were not always successful and, in any case, the new American establishment could not hope for some time to match the venerable and wealthy university foundations of Europe.

Despite these difficulties, the University of Virginia from the day of its opening had an important influence, not only on Southern institutions of learning, but "upon higher education in other sections, North and West."[45] Forward-looking educators throughout the length and breadth of the Republic watched Charlottesville closely. The University of North Carolina repeatedly sought information from it. President Thomas Cooper of South Carolina College, a close personal friend of Jefferson, followed its work with great interest and used it as a model in his efforts to build up a liberal-minded and rationalistic center of learning in the Palmetto State.[46] The geological surveys and programs for the advancement of scientific agriculture, so dear to Jefferson's heart and consequently so actively sponsored at his university, were copied widely at many other southern institutions. In similar fashion, the extensive interest of a number of southern state universities in natural science and its applications for human betterment likely derived from this source.[47] Then, too, we should not overlook the close connection between Charlottesville and the university which the Reverend Philip Lindsley was seeking to create at Nashville, Tennessee. Not only was Lindsley constantly quoting Jefferson, he was hoping to build up a postcollegiate institution closely resembling Virginia. He had a vision of a vast system of public education in Tennessee. There would be common schools throughout the state and intermediate academies or "classical schools" to teach languages and science. At the apex would be a greatly expanded University of Nashville, and Lindsley in 1829 proposed that the state government grant to it regular financial support. In this way there would be "sufficient funds to support at least part of their instructors upon condition that the sons of the poor should be enabled to complete their studies free of charge." Limited financial resources and unfavorable local conditions hindered his efforts.[48]

Dr. Horace Holley, president of Transylvania University in Lexington, Kentucky, also strove to introduce many of the characteristics of the Charlottesville system in his institution. "I aim," Holley announced, "to be liberal without indifference, moderate without coldness, rational without skepticism, evangelical without fanaticism, simple without crudeness, natural without licentiousness, and pious without the spirit of exclusion or intolerance." Prominent men of learning such as Constantine Rafinesque and Dr. Daniel Drake served on his faculty. Again, adverse local circumstances proved too difficult to be overcome. A split in the Jeffersonian Republican party in Kentucky and the bitter opposition of local Presbyterians forced the liberal-minded Holley to resign in 1827.[49]

The influence of Jefferson's university was by no means limited to the area south of the Mason and Dixon line, although it does seem to have been strongest there. George Ticknor, as one example, seems to have derived a good deal of inspiration and moral support for his own attempted reforms at Harvard from Jefferson and the Virginia experiment.[50] Francis Wayland made a flying visit to Charlottesville before announcing his own ambitious proposals for curricular changes at Brown.[51] There is, moreover, convincing evidence of a close connection between a former University of Virginia professor and the movement which resulted in the founding of the Massachusetts Institute of Technology.[52] Lastly, it is evident that Judge Augustus B. Woodward, the prime mover in pushing through the first legislation for the "Catholepistemiad," or University of Michigania, of 1817, was deeply influenced in his thinking by discussions he had held with Jefferson.[53]

The "New West" and the State-University Idea

Outside the South, the only part of the United States in which state universities were founded before the Civil War was the West.[54] Some of the great universities of the Middle West originated in this ante-bellum period.[55]

What were the influences which shaped the development of these early western universities? First, as already stated, we must note the influential example set by Jefferson's University of Virginia. This gave a general impetus to western university building and is seen clearly in a state such as Michigan. Then, too, the movement owed much to the leadership exerted by emigrants from New England. In Minnesota, for example, the founding of the state university was largely the result of the work of a notable group of Yankees, led by John S. Pillsbury.[56] In addition, we should not overlook the influence of foreign educational ideas in giving a distinctive cast to early western institutions. At first, the centralized French educational system attracted great interest in the West. By the middle of the nineteenth century, however, the influence of the German university displaced it, most notably in President Tappan's administration of the University of Michigan.[57]

Probably the most important stimulus to the establishment of state universities was the extensive granting of public lands for this purpose by the federal government. This went back to the Confederation period. In 1787, the Reverend Manasseh Cutler included in the set of terms he submitted to the confederation government (on the basis of which the Ohio Company proposed to purchase great tracts of federal land) provisions for the granting of two whole townships for the endowment of a university. At first, Congress caviled at this. The Land Ordinance of 1785 had included federal land grants for primary schools only, not for higher education. When it was proposed that this part of the bargain be dropped, Cutler prepared to leave without concluding the sale. The federal officials finally agreed to meet his terms when he permitted a politically influential group—the Scioto Company—to be included in the deal.[58]

This first federal grant for higher education served as a powerful precedent. Beginning with the state of Ohio, which took over from the company the management of the university endowment in 1804, every new state west of the Appalachians was granted federal lands for a university. To qualify, these states were required by the enabling acts which admitted them to the Union to make definite provisions in their constitutions guaranteeing that these lands would be used only for educational purposes. By 1857, the year the Morrill Act was first introduced in Congress, the federal government had already donated 4,000,000 acres of public land to fifteen states for the endowment of universities.[59]

Perhaps Congress, with its early land grants, was a deciding factor in the founding of state universities in the western country. The federal grants furnished exactly the right measure of encouragement to primitive frontier communities to project ambitious schemes of higher learning.[60] The first constitution of Indiana (1816) was typical in its direction to the legislature "as soon as circumstances will permit" to "provide by law for a general system of education; ascending in regular gradation from township schools to a State University, wherein tuition shall be gratis and equally open to all."[61] Many of the early state universities openly acknowledged their indebtedness to the federal grants. The charter of the University of Alabama, for example, explicitly stated that it "was called into existence by the generosity of Congress."[62] President James B. Angell of the University of Michigan upheld his institution's policy of welcoming students from all parts of the Union on the ground that its "original and chief permanent endowment was the gift of the United States."[63]

Despite their psychological significance as a precedent serving to involve the "New West" in the support of public higher education, these early land grants produced little permanent revenue for the state universities. They got the movement started, but they did not ensure its ultimate success. For this, regular and substantial tax support was necessary and this, in turn, had to be authorized by the state legislatures. It proved difficult, however, to convince the American public of the wisdom of this policy.[64]

Financial woes were not the only obstacles that stood in the path of these first American experiments with public higher education. The jealousy of established private colleges and the suspicions and fears of denominational interests continued to work to inhibit their growth. The sectarian colleges dotting the western frontier did not relish competition from state institutions. As in the early South, a battle royal proceeded between proponents of publicly controlled and nonsectarian higher education, on one hand, and champions of independent church-related colleges on the other.[65]

In Illinois, denominational groups were strong enough to prevent for many years the founding of a state university. In Ohio, clergymen continued to be elected presidents of state institutions and compulsory chapel continued to be required at such schools as late as the 1880s and 1890s.[66] In Michigan, the leading denominations early banded together to assure themselves of what they considered a "proportionate" representation on the board of control of the state university. In Indiana, Presbyterians took over control of Vincennes University, established on the basis of the original federal land grant, and asserted their dominance over the state institution later chartered at Bloomington. This so infuriated the Methodists that they established their own collegiate center at Asbury College, later DePauw University. Resentment ran so high that the legislature, in its act of 1828 regulating the seminary at Bloomington, specified that no sectarian beliefs were ever to be taught therein. The wrangling continued, however, and there was not even a passing mention of the state university in the Indiana constitution of 1850.[67]

Michigan, in the 1850s and early 1860s, became a notable battleground of the state university versus the denominational colleges. Open war broke out when Henry P. Tappan took over control of the university and tried to separate it from all sectarian influence. Tappan was soon campaigning vigorously to monopolize all degree granting in the state for Ann Arbor, while the denominations, in turn, battled to cut off all public support from the state university and limit it to its original land grant.[68]

Bad as it was, denominational hostility was not the only reason for the public antagonism which early state universities encountered. Equally important was an anti-intellectualism which was rife throughout the New West. There was a general unwillingness on the part of these hard-working pioneer people to be taxed for public projects, such as higher education, which did not seem immediately to touch their vital interests. In the frontier country there were not many men like Bayard R. Hall of Indiana, the first "state university professor" in his area, who willingly worked for $200 a year because of the thrill of being "the very first man since the creation of the world to read Greek in the New Purchase."[69] Indeed, public appropriations for higher learning tended to be looked upon with suspicion as helping to build up "great aristocratic establishments, hostile to the interests of the commonalty." Local solons insisted with some heat that such moneys might better be expended upon the common schools.[70] State university proponents, by way of reply, tried earnestly to convince the public that higher learning would not undermine the common schools but, on the contrary, would strengthen them. Given the realities of life in the frontier regions, their task was not easy. In Indiana, for example, friends of the university only repulsed by the narrowest of margins a powerful campaign to divide up the land-grant endowment among the lower schools.[71]

We should not be surprised, then, to find that these early western state "universities" were little more than colleges, with small enrollments, limited staff and equipment, and few, if any, professional schools. The level of instruction seems to have been far below what would have been deemed university work in Europe. As a result of the lack of adequate secondary schools throughout the western country, most of these "universities" were obliged to maintain their own preparatory departments. There were usually more students enrolled in these preparatory departments than in the "regular" college classes.[72] Thus, in the decade 1850 to 1860, only twice did student enrollment at the University of Wisconsin reach a total of 300. And as late as 1865, only 41 out of 331 registered students were in "regular" college classes. The rest were in the preparatory department, the "normal" department, or were classified as "specials."[73]

In these early, unpromising times, nevertheless, an important precedent was being established, that of publicly supported, state-controlled higher education. In the later decades of the century, as we shall see, this would be continued and implemented more successfully. From the first, these state institutions were more representative of the community as a whole than many of the private foundations. They tended to respond to new educational trends more readily than the tradition-bound eastern institutions.[74]

From every point of view, it can be argued that the University of Michigan was the pacemaker among these early state universities of the West, just like the University of Virginia in the ante-bellum South. Indeed, Ann Arbor was the most complete embodiment of the Jeffersonian ideal of higher education in the pioneer West. Under Henry P. Tappan it pursued more ambitious and loftier aims than any of its fellow institutions; it strove mightily to become a university in fact as well as in name. As a result, its influence became as predominant in the West as that of Charlottesville in the South. The Michigan charter of 1837 was copied almost verbatim in the basic document which set up the University of Minnesota in 1851. It also appears to have had an important effect upon the drafting of the charter of the University of Wisconsin, founded in 1848.[75]

How can we explain this early Michigan lead? First, a strong tradition was established in Michigan which favored a centralized, tax-supported state system of education. Second, a succession of able leaders arose to keep the foregoing policy in effect. The result was that denominational and other private collegiate interests were weaker in Michigan than in any other ante-bellum state west of the Alleghenies.

This Michigan concept of centralized public education goes all the way back to Judge Woodward and his "Catholepistemiad" plan of 1817. As we have seen, Woodward was in close touch with Jefferson in drafting this ambitious, if completely unwieldy, scheme. The classical-minded judge seems also to have been deeply influenced by the centralized French system of education established following the Revolution of 1789. In any event, the influence of his plan, though never put into effect, remained strong enough to be reaffirmed in a territorial act of 1821; and following its principles, the Michigan legislature for many years steadfastly refused to grant to denominational foundations the right to award college degrees.[76]

When Isaac E. Crary and John D. Pierce drafted a general educational code for the new state of Michigan in 1837, they furthered this trend. Both of these leaders became deeply interested in copying the centralized educational system of Prussia. They consequently projected an educational pyramid at the apex of which would stand a great state university. Below it were to be "branches" under public control which would give a secondary education and serve as "feeders." And below these, as the foundation of the system, would be a vast network of common schools.

In line with these views, the Michigan legislature not only held out for many years against allowing private institutions to grant higher degrees, but even permitted the University of Michigan, through its "branches," to establish a monopoly of college preparation in the state. Denominational interests fought this policy tooth and nail and finally, in 1855, were able to secure legislation which authorized private collegiate incorporations in Michigan. Yet even this act limited such foundations more severely than was true elsewhere. Specific minimums were prescribed for the endowments of chartered academies and colleges. No religious tests for entrance were permitted. Annual reports had to be rendered to the state superintendent of public instruction. And perhaps because of the symbolism involved, none of the private institutions was to be allowed to assume the name of university.[77]

One man who bitterly opposed the passage of the 1855 act was Henry Philip Tappan, the Easterner who had come to the state three years before to take over the presidency of the University of Michigan. Tappan, in essence, wished to transplant a German-style university to "America's Valley of Democracy." A true university, he wrote, should be something like the University of Berlin. It should be "literally a Cyclopedia where are collected on every subject of human knowledge, cabinets, and apparatus of every description that can aid learned investigation and philosophical experiment, and amply qualified professors and teachers to assist the student in his studies." Clearly he did not associate university work with the mere teaching of general knowledge. The American residential college was equivalent to the German Gymnasium, a school for immature students. The university, in contrast—with its four great faculties of law, medicine, letters and arts, and philosophy and science—should advance knowledge, not merely preserve it. In the American multidenominational setting, such a public institution must be free from ecclesiastical control and therefore could properly have no theological faculty. In addition, it must be free of excessive emphasis on the utilitarian values of learning. The only kind of education for early manhood, when the faculties have been ripened and basic knowledge has been attained, is the university kind, where provision is "made for studying every branch of knowledge in full, for carrying forward all scientific investigation: where study may be extended without limit, where the mind may be cultivated according to its wants, and where, in the lofty enthusiasm of growing knowledge and ripening scholarship, the bauble of an academic diploma is forgotten."[78]

Although unable to realize his wide-ranging dreams in their entirety at the small Michigan establishment of the 1850s, Tappan nevertheless set them down in bold print for all to read. Thus, when we pick up the University of Michigan catalogue for 1853–54, we find a remarkable statement of aims, undoubtedly composed by him: "The System of Public Instruction adopted by the State of Michigan is copied from the Prussian, acknowledged to be the most perfect in the world. . . . In the University, it is designed to organize all the Faculties with the exception of the Theological, which will be left to the different denominations." The catalogue points out that a faculty for science, literature, and the arts had already been organized, but it is careful to describe this as collegiate or undergraduate, corresponding "in general to the course in the Gymnasia of Germany." In this connection, it is asserted that "a system of Public Instruction can never be complete without the highest form of education. . . . The Undergraduate course, after all that can be done to perfect it, is still limited to a certain term of years, and, necessarily, embraces only a limited range of studies. After this must come professional studies, and those more extended studies in Science, Literature and the Arts, which alone can lead to profound and finished scholarship. A system of education established on the Prussian principles of education cannot discard that which forms the culmination of the whole. . . . Nor can it be regarded as consistent with the spirit of a free country to deny its citizens the possibilities of the highest knowledge."

The statement concludes with the hopeful announcement that a course of postgraduate lectures in the highest learning would be established at Michigan "at as early a day as practicable." Admittedly, additional staff, library facilities, and "philosophical apparatus" would be necessary. "A great work, it will require great means; but when once accomplished, it will constitute the glory of our State, and give us an indisputable pre-eminence."[79]

The "All-Purpose" State University: Cornell and Her Sister Institutions

Not until the years following the Civil War did the university-building movement in the United States get going under a full head of steam. In this development, state universities without question played a leading part. Thus, four of the eight American universities which by 1900 boasted enrollments exceeding 2,500 were state institutions.[80] The hopes of Jefferson and Tappan for great publicly supported centers of advanced study were now at last beginning to be realized. What made this possible? The answer lies in the new situation which was taking shape after 1865. On one hand, the federal government was giving public higher education an important stimulus with the substantial financial grants which resulted from the Morrill Acts of 1862 and 1890. On the other, the social and economic fabric of America was being altered sufficiently, with a growing specialization in every aspect of life, so that, for the first time, a really strong public demand was voiced for the kind of broadly inclusive, all-purpose training which many of the state universities were in an admirable position to offer.

The Morrill Acts were unquestionably the most important actions taken by the federal government in the field of higher education in the whole of the nineteenth century. To be sure, the results immediately following the passage of the 1862 act fell below expectations. It was not actually until 1890, when the second of these acts was put into effect, that substantial state support was stimulated. The land-grant colleges prior to 1890 had apparently been expected to live and thrive exclusively on their original Morrill Act endowment. The 1890 act, by providing annual federal appropriations for these institutions, worked to encourage state authorities to furnish similar financial aid. Later measures, such as the Nelson Amendment of 1907 and the Bankhead-Jones Act of 1935, further strengthened the position of the land-grant institutions by increasing the annual federal appropriation to them.[81]

The most significant growth of state universities came where the land-grant funds were added to an existing state university endowment, as in Wisconsin, Minnesota, Georgia, and North Carolina.[82] The Morrill Act grants had the least favorable effect where they were divided up among a number of colleges or used to create a new and separate institution which duplicated in many ways the work of an existing state university. The results in this case, as in Iowa, Kansas, Washington, and Oregon, were low standards of admission and fierce competition for appropriations, with attendant logrolling and wire-pulling at the state legislature. In no less than twenty states a separate college of agriculture and mechanic arts was established in competition with the state university. In Ohio, the state by 1900 came to support three competing state universities! This rampant pluralism in the administration and control of higher education was aggravated in many states by the development of public teachers' colleges and junior colleges, all under separate boards of control.[83]

In certain states, strong leadership prevented such division of public funds. Thus John Sargent Pillsbury in Minnesota pointed out the value of one strong institution in preference to "two or more weak and sickly ones" which might never reach a standard higher than that of a "third-rate college."[84] In New York State, President Andrew Dickson White of Cornell was a forceful opponent of splitting the Morrill Act funds in any way. White saw such dispersion of funds as the main reason for the backwardness of American higher education. He would reduce most of the existing small colleges to the level of intermediate schools like the German Gymnasiums. They could then serve as feeders to the perhaps not more than thirty truly great universities which it would be possible to build up in the nation. In order to further such a plan in his own state, White proposed in 1884 that the Board of Regents of the University of the State of New York become a real examining and degree-granting body.[85]

The crucial question in all of this, as it had been from the very beginning, was the development of a pattern of regular tax support for state institutions of higher learning. This became more common following the passage of the Morrill Acts.[86] Even at such a strong institution as the University of Michigan, no direct annual support was forthcoming from the legislature until 1867. Finally, in 1873, the institution moved on to more solid financial ground: the legislature provided that the proceeds of a tax of one-twentieth of a mill on all the ratable property of the state should regularly go to the university.[87] A number of other populous and wealthy states, such as California, Illinois, and Wisconsin, followed this Michigan precedent. By 1908, these states were each contributing a million dollars or more annually to their respective state universities.[88] In other states, however, efforts to establish such a system provoked long and bitter opposition. This was the case, for example, in Kentucky and Mississippi.[89] In 1878, Charles K. Adams, then a professor at the University of Michigan, wrote to Andrew Dickson White that "the country is full of idiots howling against taxation for higher education, & indeed for any education but A.B.C. education. The tribe is led by such educators as Pres. Eliot, Pres. Anderson, Pres. Magoun, & dear old friend Pres. Andrews."[90] As late as 1898, public support of state universities was being attacked by those who upheld denominational interests or laissez faire. These critics were now even charging the state universities with being "socialistic."[91]

The general importance of our second factor—the scientific and industrial revolution—is quite apparent when one studies the history of American state universities following the Civil War. More and more there was a strong demand that the new sciences be effectively applied to the exploitation of the nation's resources. The state university seemed an ideal mechanism to accelerate this process.[92] Of course, there still remained opposition from advocates of the traditional classical curriculum. It was strong enough in California to make Daniel C. Gilman glad to leave for Johns Hopkins and substantial enough in Minnesota to force William Watts Folwell out of his university presidency.[93] But the current in the state universities was running strongly in favor of a broader "all-purpose" curriculum servicing a multiplicity of vocations.

Another vital factor in the growth of state universities was the rapid expansion of the American public-school system on the precollegiate level. Thus, while there were only 1,026 public high schools with 72,158 enrolled students in 1870, by 1900 the first figure had increased to 6,005 and the second to 519,251.[94] These new public high schools were feeders of ever increasing numbers of students into the state universities. The close relation between democratization of educational opportunity at the secondary-school level and a similar movement in higher education was recognized by many university leaders.[95] The president of the University of Michigan, James Burrill Angell, expressed it this way:

First: I have endeavored to induce every citizen to regard himself as a stockholder in the Institution, who had a real interest in helping make it of the greatest service to his children and those of his neighbors.

Secondly: I have sought to make all the schools and teachers in the State understand that they and the University are parts of one united system and that therefore the young pupil in the most secluded school house in the State should be encouraged to see that the path was open from his home up to and through the University.[96]

It was indeed mainly due to the influence of these state universities (and related institutions such as land-grant colleges) that an ever larger proportion of the total American population was getting a chance at a higher education.[97] Thus we find enrollments at eastern private colleges increasing only 20 per cent between

1885 and 1895, while those at state universities expanded 32 per cent.[98]

As the state universities grew and became established on a firm foundation they came to stand in the American public mind for two dominant ideas. The first was the "all-purpose" curriculum; the second was faithful service to the needs of the community. Most state universities were active in both fields, but the first concept came to be most dramatically associated with Cornell University, and the second was most frequently connected with the University of Wisconsin. It is in this context, then, that we shall discuss them. First let us look at the "Cornell Plan," and then the "Wisconsin Idea."

Cornell, from the day it opened its doors, constituted the very embodiment of the idea of an "all-purpose" curriculum. The statement of its founder, emblazoned on the Cornell University seal, became the watchword of the institution: "I would found an institution in which any person can find instruction in any study."[99] This same theme of complete democracy of the intellect was enthusiastically endorsed by the university's youthful president, Andrew Dickson White. He remembered how in his own undergraduate days at Yale the scientific students at "Sheff" had been separated from the "regular" college boys, with all the inferiority that this implied for the former. He was determined that nothing like this should happen at Cornell. All students and all studies were to be placed on a footing of academic equality.[100]

White's inaugural address of 1868, which came a year before Eliot's well-known inaugural at Harvard, sounded a trumpet blast in the land to herald the coming of an age of university reform. It began by laying down two "foundation" principles for Cornell. First, the new university was to be completely nonsectarian, although not antireligious; secondly, it was to be in much closer relationship with the public-school system than was true elsewhere. In addition, White enumerated a number of "formative ideas" for Cornell, including complete equality between different courses of study, manual work to help students through college and give them valuable educational experience, and the importance of scientific study and scientific method in every field of knowledge. White saw no contradiction between the first of the above ideas and the third one. Separation of "newer" from "older" courses had created an undesirable caste spirit in education. Different minds and different human pursuits required of a college not a single prescribed curriculum but several different courses of study.

White summed up his "formative" ideas by stating most emphatically that America's university structure must be adapted to the American people, to American needs, and to the requirements of modern times, not to English life or German needs, nor to the times of Erasmus or Cotton Mather. This is what he hoped Cornell would represent.

In connection with what he called "governmental" ideas, White pointed out that the Cornell charter provided that trustees were to serve for limited five-year terms rather than the customary life terms and that each year one trustee was to be elected by the university's alumni. In speaking of "eliminated" ideas, he lashed out at the "pedants" and "gerund grinders" ("out upon the whole race of owls") and the "Philistines" who saw no use for any education "beyond that which enables a man to live by his wits and to prey upon his neighbors." He rejected the first because they would substitute "dates for history, gerund-grinding for literature, and formulas for science." And he wished equally to guard higher education from the second group, to whom "Gain is God, and Gunnybags his Prophet."[101]

What was the source of these ideas? Many of them obviously derive from nineteenth-century liberalism. Like Herbert Spencer, White believed in the "new individualism," in freedom from authoritarianism of every kind. This freedom did not, however, extend to Marxists, anarchists, and other radical disturbers of the social order. Individualism needed to be restrained by responsible leadership and social evolution must come about through gradual thoughtful change, not through revolution. Like Jefferson and John Stuart Mill, White put his faith in an intellectual elite which would direct the destinies of the nation and secure rational, intelligent reforms, wherever necessary. Like Guizot, he believed that any nation dominated by only one element disintegrates under the pressure of its own uniformity. Such disintegration might even produce violent insurrection and unenlightened mob leadership. Hence White's opposition to the domination in higher education of sectarianism and the classical curriculum. Hence his objection to everything which might limit the clientele of higher education and thus deny opportunity to superior minds. He particularly feared that a dangerous cleavage between the "haves" and "have-nots" might arise in America as the area of free land disappeared and commercialism increased. To combat this, it was doubly necessary to guarantee enlightened leadership, to establish control by an intellectual elite.[102]

How was this philosophy to be implemented? Early in life White had conceived the idea of building a great American university which would meet the needs of the times; to this he proposed to devote not only his time but a considerable private fortune.[103] Ezra Cornell's educational foundation presented White with the opportunity he had long awaited.[104] For the remainder of an active public career, White worked unceasingly to remove the controls of narrow sectarianism, to develop a broadened collegiate clientele which would be worthy of the instruction offered, to substitute modern methods of instruction by lecture and laboratory for textbook learning, and to instruct the potential leadership in subjects that would bring about desirable social change.[105] He made strenuous efforts to bring Richard T. Ely to Cornell to lecture on "The Labor Question and Its Solution" and he hoped to establish, at Ithaca and elsewhere, "departments for the instruction especially of those who intend entering public life through the newspaper or in the forum."[106] It was his opinion that the young men serving in American municipalities and state legislatures or writing in the great newspapers were "as a rule profoundly ignorant of the simplest history or philosophy."[107] As late as 1906, White was working hard to secure Congressional approval of a scheme, drafted by J. W. Jenks of Cornell, for federal appropriations along the lines of the Morrill Acts to set up departments of commerce and business education in state colleges and universities.[108] In his own chief field of scholarly interest, history, White called for a method of teaching which could "be applied to the immediate needs of our time." The day had not yet arrived, he believed, when America could afford the luxury of "elegant, learned investigations on points of mere scholarly interest."[109] However, he always insisted that the aim of the land grants was to do more than train mere vocationalists; it was to produce future "captains" of industry and agriculture who would also be first-class *men* and *citizens.*[110]

To achieve these objectives, White wanted a democratic, nationwide method of selection of the potential intellectual elite. He visualized this as taking place on a five-level basis. Above the elementary and secondary schools, the most brilliant students would be given scholarships to attend the university. The outstanding university graduates would win fellowships enabling them to study for three more years in American graduate schools. Finally, the top graduate scholars would be given special stipends to study the most difficult problems facing the nation and the world.[111]

In White's view, public control of higher education was absolutely necessary to guarantee the success of such a system. First of all, it would enable the universities to develop leaders who were not committed to any one social element. Also, only under public control could the resources necessary to a real university be concentrated. Moreover, this would free higher education from dependence on sectarian support or precarious private endowments. In line with this, White believed that a university must not discriminate against any member of the student body or faculty because of opinions on religion, or on account of race or sex. Even its board of trustees should be so constituted that no religious or other special interest could ever gain domination.[112]

The Cornell Plan soon attracted nationwide interest.[113] Perhaps, as Carl Becker suggests, Cornell exerted such a widespread influence because it was better situated than other institutions to reflect the dominant temper of the times. Neither wholly eastern nor western, neither altogether a state university nor a private foundation, it was in an excellent strategic position to symbolize the increasing dominance of industrialism in American society after 1865.[114] The earlier humanistic, denominationally controlled higher education preparing for a limited number of learned professions was giving way in the industrial era to a broadly secular higher learning emphasizing preparation for a great variety of specialized and technical occupations. All of this Cornell University actively symbolized. Indeed, Justin Morrill saw Cornell as more nearly approaching "my cherished ideal of what our country most needs than any other hitherto known."[115] And this was to remain an enduring tradition at Ithaca. As recently as 1952, a president of Cornell published a strong defense of the multiservice university. Vocational training in a university, he agreed, should have a substantial "cultural" content. However, on that basis there was no reason to fear that utilitarian preparation would interfere with higher learning's basic devotion to the intellectual life.[116]

University reform was not the exclusive patent of Cornell, however. At the University of Minnesota, for example, William Watts Folwell in 1869 drafted a comprehensive blueprint for a great modern state university. This "Minnesota Plan" bore a striking resemblance to the program which was being followed at Ithaca. Indeed, White and Folwell always kept in close touch.[117] In any case, we find in Minneapolis, as at Ithaca, the same devotion to an "all-purpose" curriculum, "embracing potentially all subjects of human and practical interest"; the same emphasis on equality of subjects; the same belief in the value of scientific research; the same concern with service to the needs of society through the systematic study of commerce, government, and human relations. Folwell foresaw a university which would train experts in legislation and public administration. He foresaw a university which would be open to "all worthy comers," irrespective of race, sex, religion, or economic status. He foresaw a university "not merely from the people but for the people."[118] And he and his fellow state university presidents of the post-Civil War era labored with passionate conviction to bring these far-ranging dreams to pass.

The "Wisconsin Idea"

The University of Wisconsin in the early twentieth century came to realize most completely the other important ideal which has been associated with the American state university. This was the ideal of service to all the needs of the democratic community. In essence, we can trace this concept back to the Jacksonian period, when public education began to be considered as an ameliorative, rather than merely a preservative, function of government. In this context, the state universities represented the very embodiment of Francis Wayland's "hopeful scheme for the preservation of republican social values." It was to be the key to an open society and honest and efficient democratic government. Already with Tappan's regime at Michigan there was the beginning of the articulation of this ideal. Andrew D. White at Cornell and Charles K. Adams, who taught at Ann Arbor, devoted themselves to its realization in later years. White sought federal aid for the program, while Adams worked on a more local basis, collaborating with President Angell to set up a school of political science at Michigan in 1881.[119] William Watts Folwell, as we have seen, worked in Minnesota for the same goal. White and other Easterners concentrated primarily on civil-service reform, while Folwell and Westerners were more concerned with realization of the agrarian dream. All, however, were anxious to make educated intelligence count more effectively in politics. This would help to maintain democracy, would banish partisanship and incompetence, and would equip men for positive human improvement. Thus, the "Wisconsin Idea" was by no means original with Wisconsin.

Why did this idea nevertheless reach its highest state of development in early twentieth-century Wisconsin? Richard T. Ely, then a prominent Wisconsin professor, explains that it was demanded "by the attitude of the people of the

State." The people of Wisconsin "never allowed their university to lose itself in academic unrealities. They knew they wanted something different and new, something responsive to their need, something which they called practical." In Ely's opinion, the university administration and faculty simply reflected this popular demand. Indeed, the concept "that a state-supported university should contribute directly to improved farming, more efficient industry, and better government" was given support by the university's Regents repeatedly during the years following the school's founding in 1848.[120]

How did Wisconsin people come to develop such an attitude? A faith in the values of public education undoubtedly had been implanted by the influential local New England element, while an appreciation of specialized university training had been brought over by German and Scandinavian immigrants. Indeed, it has been argued that the large German immigrant group in Wisconsin helped to create a favorable regard for the university-trained expert and the university professor in public life. This contrasted with the usual American suspicion of the expert.[121]

At the same time, local economic conditions proved favorable to the expansion of the university. By the late nineteenth century, Wisconsin agriculture had begun to shift from a wheat-growing to a dairying basis. The result was a more prosperous and progressive rural economy, one in which more efficient business management and specialized technical knowledge were necessary for success. The university helped to provide these essentials. Its popular agricultural "short course" and the Babcock fat test, developed by its research department, saved Wisconsin dairymen hundreds of millions of dollars.[122] The close relationship between profitable farming and university research created a broad basis of popular support for public higher education. The people of the state came to regard the university as a "good investment" because it returned directly to them, in economic benefits, more than was expended on it.

The height of the university's influence came, appropriately enough, during the Progressive era. "Fighting Bob" La Follette, himself a graduate of the university, was in the governor's chair. Determined to push through a sweeping reform program, he intended that the university should work in close partnership with his administration in reconstructing the state. In 1904, La Follette's personal choice for the presidency of the university, Charles R. Van Hise, was inaugurated in office. A native of Wisconsin, Van Hise had been professor of geology at Madison and had never been formally associated with any other institution of learning. He shared all the preconceptions of the La Follette Progressives and worked in close collaboration with their political aims.[123] Then, too, Van Hise appears to have been influenced to an important degree by William Rainey Harper, president of the University of Chicago. Van Hise had served under Harper as a visiting lecturer at Chicago and was deeply impressed with Harper's Chautauquan ideas of bringing a university to all the people by extending its direct influence far beyond its own campus.[124]

Van Hise's inaugural address of 1904 defined the specific ways in which he intended that the university should serve the objectives of the Wisconsin Idea. It was to be an institution for all the people of the state. It would seek to combine the best features of the English residential college and the German research university. Liberal arts, applied science, and creative research would all go forward together, with students of differing interests profiting from close association with one another. The university would be a "watchtower," taking an active part in improving society, serving as an essential instrument of public service. It would strengthen, in this age of universal knowledge, creative work of all kinds, at whatever cost. Unlike a privately endowed institution, a state university, supported by the state "for all its sons and daughters," could not afford the luxury of selecting some narrow phase of knowledge and confining itself to this. It could place no such bounds upon the lines of its endeavor. Obviously referring to great European institutions, such as the University of Berlin, Van Hise concluded: "For my part, I look forward with absolute confidence to the liberal support by the state of a school whose chief function is to add to the sum of human achievement. I am not willing to admit that a state university under a democracy shall be of lower grade than a state university under a monarchy."[125]

During the fourteen years of the Van Hise administration, the University of Wisconsin made substantial progress in attaining these goals. The "Progressive idea" of a state university reached fulfillment in Madison at the same time that the "Progressive idea" in Wisconsin politics was reaching flood tide. The resultant experiment attracted widespread attention throughout the United States and Europe.

The university during these years cemented the already warm relations it had developed with people throughout the state by maintaining a notably comprehensive system of university extension. Following the example of Cambridge University in England, the Chautauqua movement of the 1880s had pioneered in an effort to bring college courses closer to the great mass of the people. Leaders such as Herbert Baxter Adams, Richard T. Ely, and William Rainey Harper had subsequently worked hard to establish extension work as a definite part of the American university structure. Twelve institutions organized extension teaching between 1891 and 1906; twenty-eight others had joined the procession by 1913. One of the most highly publicized programs of this nature was the one which developed in Wisconsin. This "great, powerful link which connects every part of the university with the individual in the State" reached out into Wisconsin homes near and far. By 1910, over 5,000 people were taking the university's correspondence courses. District Centers of Extension Teaching were planted everywhere. A Bureau of General Welfare answered thousands of factual questions about sanitation, economics, sociology, government, and education. University shops and laboratories tested soils, ores, fuels, clays, and water. A Bureau of Debating and Public Discussion sponsored debates throughout the state on controversial issues and loaned package libraries of selected materials to local discussion groups. The university thus was becoming one with the state; its campus in truth was the whole state of Wisconsin.[126]

While most of Van Hise's faculty applauded his emphasis on the dollars-and-cents value of university-sponsored research in "practical" fields such as agriculture, there were some who were troubled by this facile, promotional approach. Admittedly a minority, they found the president's policies to be "a betrayal of the less tangible but more basic cultural values for which a university should stand."[127]

One of the characteristic features of the Wisconsin Idea was the close partnership which developed between the state government and the university. A veritable "interlocking directorate" arose between the two agencies as La Follette's legislative program was furthered by the continuous research and counsel of university economists, agricultural experts, political scientists, and sociologists. Long before Franklin Roosevelt's New Deal introduced the "Brain Trust" concept into American national politics, La Follette's Wisconsin Idea developed it on a statewide basis. By 1910, thirty-five of the university's professors were giving part of their time to some branch of the state's nonpolitical service. President Van Hise set an example for his faculty by serving on a number of public commissions. In similar fashion, the university's economists served on state railroad and tax commissions, its political scientists helped draft legislative bills, its engineers helped plan road-building programs, and its agricultural scientists furthered the profitable development of the dairying industry. In all of this, physical as well as ideological proximity of state university and state government undoubtedly played a part. The professors on University Hill in Madison were only a mile away from the politicians on Capitol Hill.[128] The Saturday Lunch Club, which met weekly during sessions of the legislature, provided an opportunity for professors such as Ely, Ross, and Commons to exchange views informally with state officials.[129]

There were some who bitterly resented this close identity of the university with the government. Did Wisconsin have a state university or a "university state"? There were mutterings that the university was trying to "rule the state," that it was becoming too expensive.[130] This undercurrent of discontent had burst out years before in an attempt to oust Professor Ely.[131] The trustees had successfully repelled that attack, however, and by the Van Hise period it appeared that the majority of Wisconsinites were well content with their university.

Frederick C. Howe, outstanding "muckraker" and Progressive leader of this period, enthused about these developments as representing a vital experiment in human government. The state of Wisconsin had found a way to fuse efficiency and democracy. The university had become the "Brain of the Commonwealth," making possible the progressive legislation in which Wisconsin pioneered. "It is an experiment station in politics, in social and industrial legislation, in the democratization of science and higher education. It is a state-wide laboratory in which popular government is being tested in its reaction on people, on the distribution of wealth, on social well-being."[132] To all of this the head of the state's Legislative Reference Bureau in 1912 agreed, and added that the Wisconsin Idea amounted in essence to the extensive use of the state university for political reform, economic and social improvement, and human welfare.[133]

The notable success of the Van Hise regime in Wisconsin had the effect of stimulating other state universities to follow similar policies. The idea of service became more than ever one of their fixed principles. Democratic higher education increasingly sought to find new ways in which to serve the needs of American democracy.[134]

A Related Phenomenon: The Municipal University

The rise of state universities was paralleled by a movement for democratic higher education in the fast-growing cities of America. All through the nineteenth century, urban centers played a decisive role in the history of the country. By 1900, they were becoming the controlling factor in American civilization.[135] In this setting it was quite natural that the municipal university should arise and seek to provide, at public expense, a free higher education for the people of the cities. It provided for urban areas the same educational opportunities that the state university and the land-grant colleges afforded to more rural regions. The net result was further to accelerate and broaden the already powerful movement for democratic higher learning.

Although the origins of a few of the municipal universities went back before the Civil War, the movement had to await the full impact of urbanization following 1865 to attain significant proportions. In 1837, Charleston, South Carolina, took over the support and control of a college that had been chartered many years before as a private institution.[136] In that same year, Louisville, Kentucky, took the first steps toward the organization of its municipal university.[137] Next, in 1847, the legislature of New York chartered the Free Academy of New York City. From this small seed was to develop during the next hundred years the New York municipal college system, largest of its kind in the world.[138] This completes the roll call of the ante-bellum foundations.

In 1873, the movement got under way once again when Cincinnati utilized a large private legacy to set up its own municipal university. In 1884, Toledo, Ohio, took similar action, and in 1913 Akron assumed control of Buchtel College, a local denominational institution, as the nucleus for a municipal university. Detroit in 1923; Wichita, Kansas, in 1926; and Omaha, Nebraska, in 1931 took steps to establish their own institutions of this type.[139]

Six of these schools (Charleston, Louisville, Cincinnati, Toledo, Akron, and Wichita) owed their foundation to an act of a city council. Three (City College and Hunter College in New York and Wayne University in Detroit) were creations of a city board of education. Six (Charleston, Cincinnati, Toledo, Akron, Omaha, and Wichita) were established on the basis of already existing private colleges, and six others (Louisville, Wayne, City College of New York, Hunter, Brooklyn, and Queens) were created as completely new public institutions.[140]

It is apparent, then, that the municipal university in America did not conform to a uniform pattern in its administrative development. At the same time, it was by no means successful in completely pre-empting even its own special field of urban higher education. There were many competing public agencies which operated in this area. Such, for example, were state universities, like the University of Minnesota in Minneapolis and the University of California in Berkeley and Los Angeles, which happened to be located in, or near, great centers of population. Such, also, were the state-supported technical institutes, normal schools, and teachers' colleges which were situated in urban communities. Such, especially in the twentieth century, were the many public junior colleges and community colleges which were either state or locally supported.[141]

In addition, a number of privately endowed universities developed in or near American cities which came to be so closely identified with the life of their communities as to approximate the type of the municipal university in everything but support and control. We are referring here to institutions such as New York University, Boston University, Temple University in Philadelphia, the University of Buffalo, the University of Rochester, the University of Pittsburgh, Fairleigh Dickinson University in Rutherford, New Jersey, Washington University in St. Louis, the University of Denver, George Washington University and American University in Washington, D. C., and Western Reserve University in Cleveland.[142] Many of these schools kept pace with the municipally supported universities by pioneering in new fields such as coeducation, university extension, afternoon and evening instruction, and specialized service to the sustaining urban society.

Also, we must remember that there were a few truly great American universities of national and even international reputation which happened to be located in important urban centers. Harvard, Columbia, Johns Hopkins, Stanford, the University of Pennsylvania, and the University of Chicago clearly belong in this category.[143] As a result, they too were obliged to come to grips with local urban problems, and a certain proportion of their student bodies was composed of local residents who lived at home and commuted to class.[144] Indeed, one of the great appeals of all urban institutions, whether public or private, whether predominantly local in clientele or national, was that they enabled many young people in cities who could not afford the costs of going away to a dormitory college, or whose parents preferred that they stay at home, to receive a college education.[145]

In view of the great number and variety of competing colleges and universities which over the course of the years established themselves in American cities, it should not surprise us to learn that the growth of municipal universities has been slow and sporadic. This, however, is not the only reason why they have lagged behind state universities and land-grant colleges. We must also take into account the difficult financial situation which this class of institutions faced.[146] Historically, American state legislatures have plowed most of the funds earmarked for higher education into state universities, state-supported normal schools and teachers' colleges, and state agricultural and engineering colleges. Until the period following the Second World War, little financial aid came from any state treasury to any municipal college or university. In addition, no appreciable financial assistance came from the federal government until the passage of the

G.I. Bill of Rights. Thus the municipal university as a public institution was cut off from the two main sources of support which had built up the state university. Urban communities maintaining their own universities were obliged to rely almost entirely upon their local resources.[147]

Since few private gifts came to these institutions, their main sources of income came to be local tax receipts and tuition fees. This forced many of them to rely more widely on charges for tuition than they would have liked, negating somewhat their basic objectives of furnishing free higher education to the urban masses. Then, too, limited resources kept many municipally supported universities from going as far in providing professional education as the state universities. Few municipal universities, for example, entered the more elaborate and costly fields of professional education, such as dentistry and medicine. Even fewer developed advanced graduate work in the arts and sciences leading to the Ph.D. degree.[148]

Given these obstacles, it is significant that the American municipal university accomplished as much as it did. It survived and expanded as a part of the American system of higher education because it was helping to meet the sweeping public demand for more diversified college courses, greater educational opportunity, and more direct service to a fast-industrializing and urbanizing society. In this respect, it not only paralleled but supplemented the work of the state university. Like the latter, it fostered the concept of "equality of studies"; it sought, and achieved, a close articulation with local systems of public education on the elementary and secondary level; it stressed adult education and popularized the higher learning in every way that it could; and it enthusiastically espoused the "watchtower" idea of service to the life of the sustaining community. The municipal university idea was not, after all, so very different from the Cornell Plan or the Wisconsin Idea.[149]

The Significance of the American State University

The American state university has been a dramatic symbol of something unique in the history of higher education. It has been the very embodiment of the new concept that government should, and indeed must, give a free higher education to the people. As such, it has made manifest the characteristic American faith in the value of formal education and the even deeper commitment on the part of the American people to the principles of democracy and equality of opportunity. President Benjamin Ide Wheeler of the University of California expressed its spirit very well when he said: "A university is a place that rightfully knows no aristocracy as between studies, no aristocracy as between scientific truths, and no aristocracy as between persons."[150]

The American state university has had some real achievements to its credit, especially in the period since 1865. It has helped raise the standards of literate leadership throughout the western country. It has pioneered in introducing accreditation of high-school work in order to raise standards of college preparation.

It has blazed a trail in sponsoring coeducation, university extension, and direct service to the community. It has early experimented with the system of free electives, associated with the work of Eliot at Harvard. It has adapted itself to the influence of the German university, and established programs of advanced graduate training in pure, as well as applied, arts and sciences.[151]

Above all, the state universities have come to stand for the broadest possible courses of study and the broadest possible public services to their constituencies. In so doing, they have reflected the two most important foreign influences upon the development of the American university, namely, the French Enlightenment and German scholarship. The first of these has resulted in the growth of a broad and utilitarian curriculum to serve the needs of the immediate society, and the second has led to an intensification of theoretical study and systematic effort to push back the frontiers of pure knowledge. In the American state university, heroic attempts have been made to keep these two movements under way at one and the same time. Perhaps these attempts have not always been as successful as some might wish, but it remains an open question whether this has been so because the two lines of work are inherently conflicting.

President Coffman of the University of Minnesota summed up the basic state university approach when he said in 1932: "The State universities hold that there is no intellectual service too undignified for them to perform. They maintain that every time they lift the intellectual level of any class or group, they enhance the intellectual opportunities of every other class or group."[152] Directly opposed to this point of view were such critics as Foerster, Flexner, and Hutchins who held that the indiscriminate offerings in such "service-station" institutions of both liberal and vocational studies had produced a chaotic mixture which was of benefit to neither. They further charged that the training of the most highly talented in American society was suffering because of the dominantly equalitarian atmosphere in state university classrooms.[153] It was a matter of record that Wisconsin for years would not publish a student's academic standing with reference to other students. The rationale for this policy seemed to be that democracy in higher education required that all students who earned degrees be considered equally "good." The same type of reasoning may explain why Phi Beta Kappa was banned at Michigan for a time.[154] It is worthy of attention that even so stanch a friend of the state universities as Professor E. A. Ross of the University of Wisconsin felt obliged to note that "the state university is not the ideal resort for the student of an intellectual temper and a disinterested interest in things. The utilitarian spirit of the place leaks in at the keyhole and dulls the edge of speculation."[155]

Many of the weaknesses which critics have found in the American state university may well have arisen as a result of the conditions under which it was obliged to work. Given the tremendous job of mass education which it was expected to do, how could its standards be other than quantitative? Then, too, the adult-education divisions and correspondence courses which men like Flexner attacked most severely were useful and important services which the taxpaying citizens came to demand of "their" university. Since these taxpayers were the institution's principal source of support, it is difficult to see what other course could have been followed. More to the point would be the question whether the rise of "practical" studies has led to an actual neglect of humanistic ones.

Among foreigners who have studied the meaning of the American state university, none has written a more searching analysis than the Briton James Bryce. In his *American Commonwealth,* Bryce recognized the importance of the state university in maintaining democracy and equality of opportunity. "It is the glory of the American universities," he wrote, "as of those of Scotland and Germany, to be freely accessible to all classes of people." He went on to add that in America popularity in clientele was linked with freedom in teaching and control. "While the German universities have been popular but not free, while the English universities have been free but not popular, the American universities have been both free and popular. . . . Accordingly, while a European observer is struck by their inequalities and by the crudeness of many among them, he is also struck by the life, the spirit, the sense of progress, which pervade them."[156]

In an address many years later, Bryce observed that by making higher education accessible to all classes, the American state universities had achieved what had never been done before. They had "led all classes of the people to believe in the value of university education and wish to attain it." This seemed to him to reflect the new concept of the functions of government which was arising in the United States. It was now believed that governmental authority might be usefully extended to all sorts of undertakings for the public benefit which had previously been left to private enterprise. "In committing yourselves to this principle you here in the West seem to have returned to that conception of the functions of the State which prevailed in the Greek republics of antiquity where it was defined as 'a partnership of men in the highest social life,' and you have abandoned that *laissez-faire* doctrine generally held seventy years ago. . . ." Bryce wondered whether the doctrine of ancient Greece and modern Wisconsin or that of the Physiocrats and Benthamites would prove in the long run to be best for mankind.[157]

An American scholar who had no doubts that the Wisconsin Idea would prove triumphant was Frederick Jackson Turner, historian and author of the well-known "frontier thesis." With the passing of the last open frontier on the North American continent, Turner pondered what forces would now operate to preserve the democratic society which the older agrarian order had bred. He concluded that the middle-western state universities would save democracy in the new age of industrial capitalism by producing a trained and responsible leadership. Like White, Folwell, and Angell, he fell back on a faith in the new frontiers of science which the university-trained elite would explore.[158]

The state university thus had the task of adjusting pioneer ideals to the new requirements of American democracy. To do this, Turner emphasized, it "must check the tendency to act in mediocre social masses with undue emphasis upon the ideals of prosperity and politics." It must stay clear of the abyss of conformity to community sentiment, because the state universities were founded "to raise ideals and to point new ways rather than to conform." It must realistically recognize that the overwhelming task of reducing the West "to the uses of civilization" would for a time "overweigh . . . art and literature, and even high political and social ideals." But in these very state universities lay the best chance of ensuring that the ideals of pioneer democracy should survive the inundation of material success. Turner concluded with the hope that "The light of these university watch towers should flash from State to State until American democracy itself is illuminated with higher and broader ideals of what constitutes service to the State and to mankind; of what are prizes; of what is worthy of praise and reward."[159]

9

The Development of The
Graduate School

The impact of German university scholarship upon nineteenth-century American higher education is one of the most significant themes in modern intellectual history. German influence on American educational thought went back at least as far as the European *Wanderjähren* of Everett, Ticknor, Bancroft, and Cogswell in the early nineteenth century. It was at this time that the German universities were beginning to attain leadership in the world of thought. Eighteenth-century Halle and Göttingen had already shown signs of shifting their emphasis from teaching to creative and original research, but this trend was greatly accelerated with the founding of the University of Berlin in 1810. The example of Berlin revitalized older German universities and led to the founding of new ones, such as Breslau (1811), Bonn (1818), and Munich (1826).[1]

The essence of the German university system, which gave it intellectual leadership in the nineteenth century, was the concept that an institution of true higher learning should be, above all, "the workshop of free scientific research." This emphasis on the disinterested pursuit of truth through original investigation led, on one hand, to the development of the concept that a true university must maintain freedom of teaching and freedom of learning within certain carefully defined limits. On the other, it led ultimately to a stress on the various services which higher learning could render to the state. By *Lernfreiheit* ("freedom of learning") the German academician meant that university students should be able to take whatever courses they liked, when and where they liked, with no formal attendance requirements or examinations until the final degree examination. This system he deemed essential for the training of mature scholars and professional men, in contrast with the rigid schoolboy-type discipline of the preparatory Gymnasium. By *Lehrfreiheit* ("freedom of teaching") he meant the freedom of the German university professor to investigate any and all problems in the course of his research and to reveal his findings, whatever they might be, in teaching and in published works.[2]

After the birth of Imperial Germany in 1871, the concept of the university as an instrument dedicated to the service of the state was developed to a high

174

degree. In the age of Bismarck university research and training, especially in the natural and medical sciences, produced important dividends of power and wealth in all aspects of public life.[3] To be sure, this was simply the most dramatic example of a course of development which practically all universities in Continental Europe were then undergoing. Besides being dedicated to the increase of knowledge in the abstract, they were expected to express the national spirit through positive service. In the process, they lost whatever administrative independence they possessed and were subordinated to the state.[4]

This new type of German university soon evolved instructional techniques which reflected its growing preoccupation with pushing back the frontiers of knowledge. The seminar, the specialist's lecture, the laboratory, and the monographic study were introduced as indispensable means of training scholars. The philosophical faculties, hitherto "lower" divisions preparing for the "upper" professional faculties, were the first to be remodeled along these new lines. They soon gained recognition as independent professional faculties on an equal plane with the others and by the middle of the nineteenth century had become "the scientific faculty par excellence." From the philosophical faculties, the influence of these new methods of instruction and investigation, including seminars, laboratory work, and specialized lectures, spread to the faculties of theology, medicine, and jurisprudence. As a result, the German universities became world famous for their success in joining teaching and research and for their ambitious goal of producing, not just the practitioner, but the creative scholar and original investigator in every field of professional endeavor.[5]

As word of German intellectual superiority spread, a remarkable pilgrimage of American students to leading centers of new learning, such as Berlin and Leipzig, took place.[6] Between 1815 and the outbreak of the First World War, more than ten thousand American students passed through the halls of German universities. One-half of this number enrolled at the University of Berlin, and the remainder could be found mainly at Leipzig, Heidelberg, Halle, Bonn, Munich, and Göttingen. In addition, it is notable that more than half of these Americans studied in the philosophical faculties. Fewer of them, proportionately, were interested in studying law, theology, or medicine in Germany.[7]

In seeking to understand this transatlantic scholarly migration, one of the most extraordinary examples of cultural interaction in the history of higher education, it is important to keep in mind certain realities. First of all, there were few places other than Germany to which an American, desirous of advanced study, could go before the Civil War. Oxford and Cambridge retained their Anglican religious tests for degrees until 1871, and even after that date did very little to provide postgraduate instruction.[8] As for the French universities, a residue of suspicion remained from the 1790s with respect to supposed French "infidelity" and "immorality." In any case, French facilities for advanced study in many fields had fallen far behind those of Germany.[9]

A second reality was that at home in America there were few opportunities at this time for the advanced student who wanted to specialize in some phase of the arts or sciences. Daniel C. Gilman and Charles W. Eliot both discovered how difficult it was to attempt graduate study in ante-bellum times.[10] It is true that as far back as 1777 Ezra Stiles had drawn up a plan to make Yale into a university comparable to Leyden or Edinburgh. Nothing had come of this, however, because no funds were available.[11] Certainly Timothy Dwight was accurate when in 1814 he declared that institutions like Yale and Harvard were more like "collegiate schools" of the Eton type than universities.[12] Similarly, Professor Münke of the University of Heidelberg was correct when he commented in a German periodical in 1831 that existing American colleges were most comparable to European *Gymnasien.* He recommended, by the way, that Americans erect true universities entirely separate from such preparatory schools.[13]

As we have seen, heroic attempts were made in a few places in America to build universities before the Civil War.[14] The University of Virginia is perhaps the outstanding example of this movement. The efforts of Ticknor, Nott, Lindsley, Wayland, and Tappan were also exerted in this direction.[15] It was clear to these educational reformers that American advanced scholarship could not hope to rival that of Europe as long as the level of instruction in American colleges remained so lamentably low.[16] Many of these efforts, to be sure, were unavailing. "The prewar reformers left a great deal of unfinished business, but they set the agenda for change." They helped prepare the way for the Eliots and Gilmans of the 1870s and 1880s. "Their experience taught what problems must be solved, their thinking established many of the terms within which others could seek solutions, and their zeal and imagination quickened the will to complete what they had started."[17]

When we keep this situation in mind, we can understand why many American visitors expressed such veneration for the German university. Returning to their native soil, they were anxious to revolutionize the whole system of American higher education by introducing higher standards.[18] They were sure that they had caught a vision of excellence across the seas. More important, they were determined to use what they had seen as a yardstick for the measurement of the efficiency of the American college. The relative youth of the University of Berlin seemed to them to indicate what could be done, with public aid, in a few short years.[19]

Few Americans before 1850 were willing to follow in the footsteps of these educational prophets.[20] In the whole first half of the nineteenth century, not more than two hundred citizens of the United States matriculated at German universities.[21] The real flood tide did not come until much later.[22] It has been suggested that this demonstrates the influence of cultural selection in German-American intellectual contacts.[23] The stream of American students in Germany did not reach its flood until America's own technological and educational needs expanded to a point where this was urgently required. The ante-bellum denominational college had no use for German scholarship and, indeed, rather feared it. Presidents of such institutions evaluated professors mainly on the basis of their moral character and religious orthodoxy. As Noah Porter put it, "The most efficient of all moral influences in a college are those which proceed from *the personal characters of the instructors.* . . . A noble character becomes light and inspiration, when dignified by eminent intellectual power and attainments."[24] To such educational leaders scholarship was not the primary consideration in choosing a faculty. German higher education itself was suspect because of its supposed heretical tendencies.

After the Civil War a new situation began to emerge as American society became more industrialized, urban, specialized, and secular. A demand arose for a new kind of higher education. Specialized skill was now needed in a host of professional and scientific fields. Money was available in important amounts for the endowment of universities which would advance knowledge and train the technical experts needed by modern society. As American higher education became more specialized and secular, a German Ph.D. increased proportionately in the prestige value that it possessed for academic careerists. The scholarly exodus is not to be completely explained by these self-seeking considerations, however. Unquestionably, some of the German-trained American scholars burned with a zeal to reform the crudities of their day and age. Men like Richard T. Ely wished to introduce higher standards of public service and a more effective use of state power to serve the public welfare. Others, such as G. Stanley Hall, Thomas C. Chamberlain, and John M. Coulter sought to bring back from Germany a more thorough and objective scholarship to contribute to the world's knowledge.[25]

As American higher education increased in stature it fed on different aspects of German academic culture. Before 1850, most American visitors to German universities seem to have been impressed primarily by the advanced level of teaching which they encountered there. Those who came in later days, by way of contrast, were most interested in German ideals of scholarly research. Of course, it was only after 1850 that the United States began to develop the kind of society that could profitably utilize scientific research.[26] Selectivity, too, was apparent in the *types* of German influence the returning American scholars brought back with them. Most of them, clearly, brought back the technical rules and outward forms of scholarship, the instructional techniques which relied heavily on the seminar, the lecture, and the research laboratory. But did they also bring back the basic spirit? Did they bring back the philosophic context in which these scholarly mechanisms had arisen? Most of them apparently did not.[27] Nineteenth-century Americans were inclined to see in the German university what they wanted to see. This is why they brought back with them to the New World an outlook which featured exact research and scientific specialization to a much greater degree than was true in the German universities. In other words, German academic *practices* and methods of work impressed American advocates of pure science more than did the German idealistic search for underlying spiritual unities or the German concept of *Wissenschaft* as a form of investigation which would proceed always in a broad, deep, contemplative context.[28] As William T. Harris was to discover, there was simply no market for German philosophic idealism in a busy American culture that was becoming increasingly pragmatist.[29] State university people and advocates of a dominantly utilitarian education were distrustful of the German university with its emphasis on pure research and its undemocratic context. They called for a distinctively "American" university which would reflect their country's "national genius."

In the transplanting of these considerably modified forms of the German university to American soil in the later nineteenth century, the decisive role was played by a highly influential group of persons destined to become presidents of the most important universities in the United States. Included in this notable company were Charles W. Eliot, Daniel C. Gilman, Andrew D. White, James B. Angell, William Watts Folwell, G. Stanley Hall, Nicholas Murray Butler, Charles Kendall Adams, and F. A. P. Barnard. All of these men had their basic conceptions shaped in one way or another by firsthand experience with European universities. All of them were stimulated by this experience to advocate a "New Education" for America. And all of them were agreed upon the vital necessity of building real universities in America which would offer better facilities for professional training and for advanced graduate instruction in the arts and sciences.[30]

The Founding of Johns Hopkins

There were two ways in which American educators sought to transform established patterns of higher education. One, difficult at best, sought to establish wholly independent graduate schools. The other, followed in the great majority of cases, involved superimposing a German-type university structure on the existing English-type college. We turn now to the first of these approaches, as illustrated by the founding of Johns Hopkins University.[31]

Johns Hopkins represents the most important innovation in graduate instruction launched during the whole period between the Civil War and the First World War. With the great Hopkins bequest supporting and Daniel C. Gilman leading, it aimed at national, not local, influence.[32] Gilman's stated purpose was to bring to Baltimore as teachers and as students the ablest minds that he could attract.[33] It is notable that not one member of the original faculty was a Baltimorean or even a Marylander. Similarly, in its course of study the institution determined to break new ground. It would attempt not to duplicate existing colleges but to supply the needs of the United States in certain special learned fields. It would therefore begin "with those things which are fundamental" and move "gradually forward to those which are accessory." To accomplish this it would "institute at first those chairs of language, mathematics, ethics, history and science which are commonly grouped under the name of the Department of Philosophy." Development of vital professional fields, such as medicine, would come later.[34]

Taking his cue from the German university and from his own earlier experience at the Sheffield School of Yale, President Gilman preferred to spend his ample funds for "men, not bricks and mortar." He wanted the best scholars in the world, not the most magnificent buildings. It was important, he wrote, that the "glory of the University should rest upon the character of the teachers and scholars here brought together, and not upon their number, nor upon the buildings constructed for their use."[35] Carrying out this policy literally, he made no provisions for a campus at Hopkins in the early days, nor for football or baseball fields. It was not unusual for a student, coming for the first time, to pass by the university without recognizing it. Even local Baltimoreans were apt to confuse the university buildings with a piano factory! To be sure, there was an ample supply of every facility needed for actual scholarly work. One visitor summed up the situation by remarking: "They have millions for genuine research but not one cent for show."[36] On the other hand, Hugh Hawkins has shown that Daniel Gilman "was not as singled-eyed in his interest in graduate education and research as tradition pictures him, that he bent with the wind of public opinion, that he placed the effect of higher studies on the student over their contribution to the advancement of knowledge." His aims were pluralistic and his methods pragmatic.[37]

With its exclusion of "ecclesiasticism or partisanship," Johns Hopkins heralded in yet another way the coming of a new kind of American university. It was to be a nonsectarian institution dedicated to the unfettered search for truth. Hence it was no mere accident that Thomas Henry Huxley was invited as honored guest to deliver the main address at its formal opening.[38] The whole conceptual framework of knowledge was undergoing reorganization in terms of dynamic change. The reconstruction of American higher education was accelerating precisely because the new concepts of science were falling on fertile academic soil like that at Hopkins.

Gilman's whole approach might be summed up as embodying a high-level eclecticism. As one student of his career has noted, he viewed the American university as "essentially an indigenous phenomenon and its success, in 1876," as involving the "seizing and welding together [of] the *disjecta membra* of the earlier reformers. . . ."[39] A small but eminent faculty was given complete freedom "to carry on the higher work for which they had shown themselves qualified." With men of the stature of Ira Remsen, Henry A. Rowland, Basil L. Gildersleeve, and J. J. Sylvester leading the way, the whole emphasis was on productive research.[40] Students and teachers alike were "afire with the zeal to learn."[41] President Gilman, who took a personal interest in the research projects of his faculty members, put it this way: "Investigation has thus been among us the duty of every leading professor, and he has been the guide and inspirer of fellows and pupils, whose work may not bear his name, but whose results are truly products of the inspiration and guidance which he has freely bestowed."[42] As Abraham Flexner has pointed out, Johns Hopkins made it possible for the first time for the scholar's life in America to be unified. Scholars could now combine teaching and creative research in their own specialized fields.[43]

While thus sponsoring a conception of pure research in many ways bolder and broader than that of Francis Bacon in the *New Atlantis,* Gilman also saw the university in America as having definite social responsibilities. In his view, it should perform certain essential functions for civilization, such as advancing knowledge and applying the fruits of research to problems of daily living. In the central sentence of his Johns Hopkins inaugural of 1876, he expressed the hope that university reform would make "for less misery among the poor, less ignorance in schools, less bigotry in the temple, less suffering in the hospital, less fraud in business, less folly in politics."[44]

In order to develop the kind of high-quality university that was desired, it was soon realized that the Hopkins professors must be given able students who would stimulate them. Gilman was anxious to attract to his first student body "men of mark, who show that they are likely to advance the sciences they profess."[45] But students such as these were not easy to find in the America of 1876. The only way that Gilman was able to get them in the beginning was by "hiring" them by means of a system of well-paying fellowships, a measure with which he had already experimented at the University of California in 1874.[46] And what a remarkable group of young men they were! Among the first students at this "paradise and seminarium of young specialists" were Josiah Royce, Walter Hines Page, Herbert Baxter Adams, Frederick Jackson Turner, John Dewey, J. McKeen Cattell, Albion Small, John R. Commons, Joseph Jastrow, and Woodrow Wilson, to name but a few.[47] One historian of Johns Hopkins maintains that no expenditure in American higher education "has ever had so large and so enduring a return from the investment."[48]

Methods of instruction were similar to those in vogue at German universities —lectures to large groups, a few seminars for intensive research, and laboratories for experimentation. And, like the German university, the academic atmosphere was distinctly laissez faire. Students were free to come and go as they pleased, and take what courses they pleased. An able young student like Abraham Flexner could, under this system of *Lernfreiheit,* enroll in more than one course scheduled for the same hour, and not have this noticed until the examinations came![49] Gilman sponsored the Ph.D. degree as the chief reward for graduate study at the new university. Fledgling scholars, who had only recently taken bachelor's degrees and "came with all our college honors thick upon us," were soon transformed by the exacting Hopkins regimen into disciplined investigators.[50] The president's annual reports make it clear that the Hopkins Ph.D. was not as clearly defined at first as it later became but was developed and crystallized by the experience of the university during the first years of its existence.

Credit for the successful launching of this remarkable experiment in higher learning seems to belong equally to the original trustees of the Hopkins bequest and to President Gilman. The trustees were farseeing enough to follow the advice tendered them by Charles W. Eliot, Andrew D. White, and James B. Angell in a series of crucial conferences during 1874.[51] They refused to yield to the strong temptation to establish a school with a purely local aim, giving "practical" training and nothing more, and with a "favorite son" of Baltimore as president. Instead they decided to build a university. In turn, Gilman, once he had been chosen to head the institution, drafted a blueprint for a more sweeping program of graduate study than any that had been proposed for it up to that time. In so doing, the university would serve the basic needs of American society. He took this advanced position in his first interview with the trustees, and, having gained their approval, made it public in an article in the *Nation* early in 1875.[52] This did not mean that Johns Hopkins began as a purely graduate institution. In 1876, 35 undergraduates were registered at the school as against 54 graduate students. However, enrollments reveal that the emphasis in Baltimore quite clearly was placed on graduate study during the remainder of the nineteenth century. In 1880–81, Johns Hopkins enrolled 102 graduate students and only 37 undergraduates. In 1885–86, the corresponding totals were 184 and 96. In 1895–96, they were 406 and 149.[53]

A review of Gilman's statements on the role of pure research, however, reveals a somewhat ambivalent attitude. It has been pointed out that he really "lacked a scholar's temperament" and that the early achievements of Johns Hopkins may have owed more to the efforts of its first faculty and fellows than to its president. But Gilman's flexible, eclectic policies may have given "the early Johns Hopkins just the protective facade it needed."[54]

When Gilman retired from the presidency in 1901, Johns Hopkins had a faculty of philosophy with thirteen different departments organized for advanced work and a medical school that was rapidly becoming world-famous.[55] During the preceding twenty-five years the institution had played a decisive part in furthering the idea of the university in the United States, although it appears that its most significant contributions were made during its first year of existence. It finally lost its primacy and was financially crippled due to the misfortunes of the Baltimore and Ohio Railroad, in which most of its funds were invested. But its influence persisted in spite of this misfortune. Actually, Johns Hopkins had done its work so well that a number of other schools, Clark, Chicago, Columbia, Harvard, and Wisconsin, paid it the compliment of imitating it. Happily some of these gained access to much vaster funds, which enabled them eventually not only to catch up with Hopkins but even to outstrip it.[56]

In any case, the influence of Johns Hopkins on American higher education was out of all proportion to its size, wealth, or age. In 1926, J. McKeen Cattell found that of 1,000 distinguished American scientists, 243 were Hopkins graduates. Within twenty years of the founding of the Baltimore institution, over sixty American colleges and universities had three or more members of their staffs holding Hopkins degrees. These young Ph.D.'s were going out as dedicated missionaries all over the country to spread the university idea. In 1896, there were already ten of them at Harvard, thirteen at Columbia, and nineteen at Wisconsin.[57] The success of Johns Hopkins encouraged other institutions to seek research scholars for their own faculties.[58] "Whether consciously or not," Gilman and his associates in Baltimore "were building a new profession in America, that of university professor."[59] The opportunities for graduate study in America were being made far greater than they would otherwise have been. And, above all, the name Johns Hopkins had come to have a special significance throughout the world as symbolizing the development of advanced scholarship and teaching in America.

Reorganization of Older Liberal-Arts Colleges into Full-Scale Universities

With all the feverish activity going forward in Baltimore after 1876, it behooved the older liberal-arts colleges to look to their laurels. The most significant growth of university research and teaching in America came, as the fates would have it, not at the pioneering institutions but at the older and larger universities. The latter could draw on wealthy alumni or state legislatures because of the presence of a vigorous undergraduate tradition.[60] This was to be seen clearly at institutions such as Harvard. Charles W. Eliot frankly acknowledged the Johns Hopkins stimulus when he stated in a public address:

> I want to testify that the Graduate School of Harvard University, started feebly in 1870 and 1871, did not thrive, until the example of Johns Hopkins forced our Faculty to put their strength into the development of our instruction for graduates. And what was true of Harvard was true of every other university in the land which aspired to create an advanced school of arts and sciences.[61]

Writing in the 1880s, President Frederick A. P. Barnard distinguished three stages in the history of Columbia University. His classification may well be applied to all the older collegiate foundations of the East which were gradually transforming themselves into universities during this period. The first period, as Barnard saw it, was that of the college. The second was dominated by the adding of various professional schools. The final period was that of the true university, when a comprehensive program of graduate studies was developed.[62]

We have already dealt at some length with the old-time liberal-arts college, which dominated the first division that Barnard had in mind. Stage two, which pertains to the half-century preceding the Civil War, witnessed the expansion of some of the older and stronger eastern colleges through their acquisition of professional schools. Thus Harvard added a medical school in 1814, a law school in 1817, and a scientific school in 1847. Yale established its medical school in 1823, its theological department in 1822, its law school in 1824, and its scientific school in 1854. Yet these institutions were not yet integrated universities by Continental European standards. They might better be described as multiple-faculty institutions. Not only were standards in these early professional schools low, but many of them were only loosely controlled by the colleges with which they were supposed to be affiliated. At the same time, the college faculties gave little or no support to these affiliates.

After the Civil War, a movement got under way to convert these multifaculty institutions into real universities, and in this the influence of Johns Hopkins played an important part. The movement went farther, and encountered less opposition, at Harvard than elsewhere, but eventually Yale, Columbia, and Princeton all joined the procession.

President Eliot's long and continuous rule over Harvard's affairs—forty years —gave him an incomparable advantage in university building. Courses of "university lectures," it is true, had been established under Eliot's predecessor, Thomas Hill.[63] By 1872, however, Eliot had expanded them into a regular graduate department. This was destined to become the nucleus of a Graduate School of Arts and Sciences, formed later by merging the faculties of Harvard College and the Lawrence Scientific School. At the same time, the demands of the times for a more secular system of administration and a more elective curriculum were met. Also, Eliot strove to raise the level of instruction in the various professional schools to true graduate levels. Finally, he sought to unify in his own person the work of Harvard "University," and thus have it merit the name, by actively presiding at the meetings of its various faculties.[64]

At Yale, there was a stiffer battle between those devoted to the old college and those interested in university development. As early as 1847 a new department of philosophy and the arts had been established with a view to giving specialized and advanced instruction.[65] In a very real sense, this was the first "graduate school" of arts and sciences to be set up by an American institution of higher learning.[66] Although handicapped by lack of funds, this program led immediately to the awarding of an earned master's degree and, within a few years, a Ph.D. as well.[67] In 1871, a strenuous effort was made by a "Young Yale" faction among the alumni to initiate a more positive university program. This temporarily came a cropper when the conservative Noah Porter was chosen president.[68] The movement gathered renewed strength, however, when Timothy Dwight the younger succeeded to the presidency in 1886. Dwight was already on record as favoring the university idea.[69] In office, he followed a program closely resembling that of Eliot. The professional schools were now tied more closely to the central college. Graduate instruction was expanded and undergraduate electives were extended. The presidential office was used to help unify the university.[70]

At Columbia, President Frederick A. P. Barnard in 1870 expressed his deep concern with the continuing drop in enrollment and the exodus of young Americans to German universities.[71] He became convinced that the only way to arrest these dangerous tendencies was "by providing here the attractions which are so abundantly offered in foreign lands."[72] As a result, Barnard warmly endorsed the plans developed by young John W. Burgess for the establishment of a graduate department of political science at Columbia.[73] Despite opposition from an "old guard" which feared diminution of the interests of Columbia College, Burgess and his influential ally on the board of trustees, the eloquent septuagenarian, Samuel B. Ruggles, triumphed, and the new graduate faculty was established in 1880.[74] Barnard also worked for the university idea by supporting the expansion of course offerings, the introduction of more electives, and the unification of the work of Columbia's various professional faculties with that of the parent institution.[75] These policies were energetically carried forward under his successors,

Presidents Low and Butler. In 1907, the separate faculties of political science, philosophy, and pure science were combined under Burgess who became the first dean of the university's "Graduate Faculties." In 1912 the trustees voted that what had heretofore been known as Columbia College should now legally be entitled Columbia University in the City of New York.[76]

In 1877 Princeton too began to move in the direction of attaining university status. In that year, a graduate department was established on the recommendation of President James McCosh.[77] Like his colleagues in the other eastern private foundations, McCosh thought of developing universities in America by "superinducing" them upon "a few of our more advanced colleges." In this way, McCosh reassured the college's alumni, Princeton could gain the advantages of a German university without its disadvantages.[78] In 1900, a strong faculty movement led by Andrew F. West brought about the establishment of a full-fledged graduate school. And in 1910 after a battle royal West succeeded in attracting to Princeton a large endowment to finance the elaborate plan for a residential graduate college which was his special dream.[79] When, in 1896, Princeton came to celebrate the 150th anniversary of its founding as the College of New Jersey, it officially changed its name to Princeton University.[80]

The Establishment of New Universities, Hopkins Style

Harvard, Yale, and Columbia had *become* universities; Johns Hopkins had *begun* as one. In the later nineteenth century there were three other institutions which, directly emulating the Baltimore enterprise, were founded as universities. These were Clark University, Catholic University of America, and the University of Chicago.

G. Stanley Hall, who had been a professor at Johns Hopkins, sought to bring the graduate university idea to New England when in 1888 he was appointed to be the first president of the newly founded Clark University in Worcester, Massachusetts. His original faculty was small but of high quality; his first course of study was necessarily limited to a few select fields, but proceeded on an advanced level. In 1899 the university boasted that it was "exclusively what is called in Europe a Philosophical Faculty, or a part of one so far as yet developed, devoted to a group of the *pure sciences* which underlie technology and medicine."[81] However, a misunderstanding soon arose between Hall and the school's founder, Jonas Gilman Clark.[82] The latter came to oppose the president's emphasis on the graduate side of the institution, and withheld financial backing. Clark felt that Hall's emphasis on graduate-level scientific research should be balanced by more concern for effective teaching of undergraduates in such fields as the humanities. Responding to these pressures, the university's trustees in 1900 established an undergraduate college.[83] Even before that date faculty morale had been undermined by the continuous dissension. In January, 1892, several professors resigned in protest. As a result, when William Rainey Harper came along a few months later with the Rockefeller fortune supporting him and offered Clark professors double their present salary to come to the newly founded University of Chicago, a number of them accepted. Thus much of the benefit of Hall's early planning ultimately redounded to the advantage of Chicago.[84]

In 1889, the same year that Clark opened for instruction, the Catholic University of America began its work in Washington, D. C., despite considerable opposition from the more conservative members of the American hierarchy. Having received its apostolic constitution from Pope Leo XIII, it resembled in this respect the great medieval universities which had been canonically instituted under papal patronage as well as under state charter. Bishop John J. Keane, the first rector, had studied Gilman's work at Johns Hopkins very closely, and the whole emphasis in the early days of the institution was on a similar type of purely graduate instruction.[85]

The university began its work with graduate students in the Faculty of Theology as the only ones enrolled. European scholars on the faculty introduced the seminar method. Not until 1904 did the university officially announce its willingness to grant undergraduate degrees and not until 1930 did it establish an undergraduate college. One of the reasons, though not the only one, for initially eschewing any kind of undergraduate work apparently was a desire to remain on good terms with the Catholic liberal arts colleges of the country.[86]

The third of these post-Hopkins foundations was, from every point of view, the most significant. Between 1889 and 1892, John D. Rockefeller, Sr., donated more than $2,000,000, and a number of other individuals gave smaller sums, toward the endowment of a great new University of Chicago.[87] Although it was built upon the foundations of two older institutions, the university was in every sense of the word a new establishment. The master plan which charted its course was entirely the work of its enterprising and dynamic first president, William Rainey Harper. There were to be five main divisions—the University Proper; the University Extension; the University Press; the University Libraries, Laboratories, and Museums; and the Affiliations. This detailed and carefully articulated plan represented, in one sense, an attempt to introduce the efficiency and specialization of modern industrial combinations into the world of American higher education. The plan was not only sweeping; it was novel. Making university extension, publication, libraries, and affiliations an integral part of the academic structure was a new concept in university administration.[88]

A commentator on the history of the modern American university has pointed out that President Harper himself "had trouble in defining just what was distinctive about Chicago (aside from the fact that it had a summer school), although he insisted that it represented a 'new type' of university in America." The dynamic university builder's rhetoric "ran to a generous inclusiveness."[89] On the other hand, one of Harper's most influential faculty members, the sociologist Albion W. Small, saw the president's whole policy as determined by an incisive analysis of the social situation of modern America. Harper's working platform was based, Small suggested, on an examination of the demands that a progressive democracy made upon education. On this basis, there were three essential policies which the Chicago president believed an American university must follow. These were, first, the ceaseless investigation of every realm of knowledge; second, an active ambition to put knowledge to use for human service; and third, a greater accessibility involving the maintenance of more ways of entrance to the university than had been true in the past and many more direct channels of communication with the outside world.[90]

In terms of the influence of Johns Hopkins, the first of the above principles was of course most important. Harper, like Gilman, maintained that he was interested wholeheartedly in fostering advanced instruction and research. He asserted that he wanted to establish a real university, not just another college. Himself an avid scholar in the field of Hebrew literature and culture, he approached original research with an almost religious fervor. For him it was a cosmic principle which transcended mere method, a fundamental not only of the "university spirit" and of free thought, but the key to the greatest truths of the universe itself.[91]

As a result of this viewpoint, Harper early made it clear that promotion for members of the faculty would be directly related to their scholarly research, rather than their teaching.[92] Yet his policy on this matter was equivocal. Many members of the Chicago faculty complained that the university's library facilities were inadequate; Harper preferred to disperse available funds on his many grandiose projects. He also was opposed to programs for the Ph.D. degree that were too narrow or specialized. And he wished to see at Chicago a quadrangle plan that would resemble the way of life of the resident colleges at Oxford and Cambridge.[93]

Johns Hopkins had started with forty graduate students and a small faculty. Clark had begun with but "the torso of a university." But William Rainey Harper, with the vast funds at his disposal, was able to open the doors in 1892 of what was already in actuality, not just potentially, a great university. A faculty of 120 were prepared to give advanced work in no less than 27 subject-matter fields. Already 594 students were enrolled, half of them doing graduate work. Harper's money had enabled him to hire some of the most eminent scholars of his day. Besides those who came from Clark, there were Albion Small, Thorstein Veblen, John Dewey, Hermann von Holst, William Vaughn Moody, J. Lawrence Laughlin, James Rowland Angell, and Jacques Loeb. These men formed a remarkably creative and homogeneous academic circle during the 1890s. And from the intellectual ferment they produced emerged the "Chicago School," a new ideological orientation for America which William James hailed as being more consistently pragmatist than his own pragmatism.[94]

New Instructional Techniques and Expanding Scholarly Activities

The European-educated scholars of the latter half of the nineteenth century brought back to America a number of key research techniques and instructional procedures which radically transformed their native academic landscape. They developed laboratories, established research libraries, organized seminar groups, assigned research papers, subdivided the part of the curriculum which dealt with their subject into many specialized courses, and built up departments composed of like-minded individuals. We have noted, in this connection, how institutions like Eliot's Harvard allowed university methods and subject matter, via the elective system, to penetrate even the undergraduate curriculum.[95] Above all, these scholars helped to establish the ideal of productive research as the guiding star of American higher learning.

Reflecting this emphasis on scientific method and the precise measurement of factual data were three new instructional techniques—the seminar, the experimental laboratory, and the scholarly lecture. These tended increasingly to replace the older method of hearing class recitations. As early as 1869, Charles Kendell Adams had set up something like a *Historische Gesellschaft* at the University of Michigan.[96] This pioneer experiment with seminar work was followed up in the early 1870s at Harvard, where Henry Adams "made use of his last two years of German schooling to inflict their results on his students." The real development of the seminar method in American higher education did not come, however, until after the founding of Johns Hopkins. There Herbert Baxter Adams conducted a widely renowned seminar during the 1880s in history and the social sciences.[97] At Clark, in the 1890s, G. Stanley Hall organized an equally famous seminar in psychology.[98] The results achieved in these pioneering American seminars appear to have varied widely in quality and significance, as indeed was true of many of the prototype groups in Germany at this time.

The widespread popularity of the lecture method and the increasing use of laboratory techniques as a part of scientific instruction also owed much to German influence and, more particularly, to the example of Johns Hopkins. This new rigor in college and university work, this respect for higher standards of accuracy and precision, Daniel C. Gilman traced back to "the introduction of laboratory methods in chemistry by the great teacher Liebig, and subsequently in physics and biology by other men of genius."[99]

Another indication that American learning was coming of age was furnished by the development of great university libraries. Fifty years earlier, such libraries scarcely existed in the country; the ante-bellum college regime had no need for them. The medieval "treasure trove" concept of hoarding books still persisted. In the 1870s, Melvil Dewey and Justin Winsor pioneered a new philosophy for college libraries, claiming that "a book is never so useful as when it is in use." Librarianship began to emerge as a profession. What had formerly been the part-time task of a member of the instructional staff became a technical and specialized occupation. Improved systems of classifying and shelving books were introduced. Library schools were reorganized and integrated with university graduate schools. While research libraries at prominent American universities still had to compete for funds with gymnasiums, athletic fields, dormitories, and landscaping projects, at least the first steps had been taken toward the creation of collections of books adequate to the new scholarly emphasis.[100] Harper of Chicago saw all this as reflecting a new spirit in American university life: "For in every subject . . . the laboratory method and the library method now hold full sway."[101] Indeed, the American talent for practical and efficient organization expressed itself so effectively in the development of university libraries and research laboratories that they came increasingly to be models in their respective fields for other nations.[102]

A related, and equally significant, phenomenon was the appearance of a number of busy university presses. This movement had both English and German antecedents. English university presses, like the famous ones at Oxford and Cambridge, had been operating ever since the sixteenth century and served as obvious prototypes for similar American establishments. German influence was important not so much for actual presses—German commercial publishing was so specialized that there was no need for university presses—as for influencing American higher education to stress graduate studies and research, which in turn necessitated new publishing outlets.[103]

Daniel C. Gilman took an active part in this, as in other, phases of university expansion. "It is one of the noblest duties of a university," he stated in his fifth annual report, "to advance knowledge, and to diffuse it not merely among those who attend the daily lectures . . . but far and wide."[104] By 1878 Gilman had an active publications agency set up in Baltimore. Andrew D. White was also active in this cause and was responsible, at Cornell in 1869, for the earliest use of the term "university press" in the United States.[105] As we have seen, William Rainey Harper at the University of Chicago considered his publications program to be the vital cement that would bind his whole vast academic edifice together.

University presses, despite this distinguished backing, were slow in starting in America. Only three were successfully established before the turn of the century.[106] After 1900, however, the movement picked up momentum. By 1948, there were thirty-five university presses and they accounted for 8 per cent of the total number of titles published in the United States. They also carried on a significant amount of periodical publishing and were rendering a number of services of a nonpublishing nature to their respective universities. Their yardstick for selecting manuscripts was predominantly quality, not potential profit. The presses came to be viewed as an indispensable adjunct in establishing an institution's reputation as well as helpful in attracting able new faculty members. In the 1950s and 1960s university presses experienced boom times as all of American higher education went through an unprecedented period of expansion. By 1968 there were over eighty such presses operating and they published 3,000 titles. Then a decline set in. Inability to secure adequate endowment had always hampered full development of the university presses. But in the early 1970s, as many colleges and universities faced a severe financial crisis due to the reduction of government grants and declining student enrollments, the university presses suddenly found themselves in serious jeopardy. Cost-conscious administrators sharply reduced support for university publishing operations which, because they were accumulating bigger and bigger deficits, came to be regarded as dispensable luxuries. Harvard University in 1972 dismissed the director of its press, which had accumulated a $500,000 deficit. By that year, the total output of academic publishers in the United States had dropped to 1,800 titles. Some presses closed down completely, others trimmed their staffs drastically and greatly reduced the number of manuscripts accepted for publication. It was possible economic pressures might ultimately force the university presses to emphasize commercially viable books at the expense of specialized scholarly works. If this happened it would increasingly be difficult for the presses to fulfill the essential purpose for which they had been founded, namely, to produce books of scholarly excellence that commercial publishers could not afford to bring out.[107]

Another sign of the impact of the European university on American life was the rapid multiplication of learned societies. Again, the effort was to catch up, as much as possible, with the level of scholarly activity in Germany, and in Europe generally, to help realize American intellectual independence. Earlier scholarly organizations in the United States had been either broad in scope or predominantly local in nature. The American Philosophical Society and the Massachusetts Historical Society are good cases in point. By the 1870s, with the growing professionalization, specialization, and institutionalization of American scholarship, they came to be much more specific in interest.[108] One historian has attributed this proliferation of scholarly societies not only to influence from overseas but to a national talent for organization.[109] In any case, the movement went forward so rapidly that by 1908 there were 120 national learned societies in America and 550 local ones.[110] The rise of specialism was bringing about new subdivisions within main subject-matter fields. At the same time, the need for pooling intellectual resources during the First World War brought about the ultimate national expression of the organizational movement in the forming of great federations of related professional associations. In this way, the National Research Council, the Social Science Research Council, and the American Council of Learned Societies made their debut on the academic scene.[111]

Universities played an important part in the development of the scholarly societies and, in turn, reflected in their academic programs the work that these organizations were carrying forward and the point of view that they represented. President Gilman consistently sought to promote the establishment of such associations at Johns Hopkins. Under a Hopkins professor, Basil Gildersleeve, the American Philological Association was established. The Hopkins scholars also organized a Political Science Association, a Scientific Association, a Metaphysical Club, and an Archaeological Society.[112] As other universities followed the example of Johns Hopkins in stressing specialized research and as they turned out ever greater numbers of Ph.D.'s trained for thorough research, the number of learned societies rapidly increased.[113]

A closely related project actively sponsored by such institutions as Johns Hopkins and Chicago was the promotion of scholarly journals. President Gilman specifically stated that he had borrowed from Germany the idea of establishing a sufficient number of scholarly journals to serve America's intellectual and scientific needs.[114] In 1878, he badgered Professor Sylvester into agreeing to edit a mathematical journal, and a year later he persuaded Ira Remsen to inaugurate the *American Chemical Journal.* In 1880, Professor Gildersleeve began the *American Journal of Philology* and in 1881 the *Journal of Physiology* was established, both published under the sponsorship of the university. In later years, to be sure, Gilman had second thoughts about the value of the flood of scholarly publications that he had helped to precipitate. He began to wonder whether scholars would be so inundated by printed matter that they would be unable to find really significant data.[115]

President Harper at Chicago was just as active in promoting an increase in the number of scholarly periodicals in the United States. He was anxious to see each department of the university publish at least one journal to give publicity to its work and to serve as a medium for the printing of the work of other researchers. The first result of this policy was the *Journal of Political Economy.* During the fifteen years of the Harper administration, ten other periodicals were launched at Chicago, including the *Journal of Geology,* the *School Review,* and the *American Journal of Sociology.*[116]

As a result of this influential support from the great universities, scholarly publications mushroomed in America about as rapidly as learned societies. By 1945, according to the American Council of Learned Societies, eighty-six periodicals were being issued in the field of history alone.[117] These "textbooks of scholars" now played the same invaluable role they did in Europe in molding the thought of American specialists and conveying to them the latest findings.[118]

In order further to encourage the productivity of research scholars on their staffs, American universities introduced another new program—the plan of sabbatical leaves. In contrast to the special leaves of absence which a number of colleges had granted on an individual basis since very early times, the new arrangement was specifically designed to give faculty members the opportunity for self-improvement and the time for the completion of research projects. Usually after six or seven years of service, all qualified professors were offered a choice between full salary for a half year or half salary for a full year. The first institution to initiate this system was Harvard in 1880. Cornell and Wellesley followed suit in the middle 1880s, Columbia in 1890, and Brown in 1891. By the turn of the century, Amherst, Dartmouth, Stanford, California, and Illinois also had established sabbaticals. In all, seventy-one institutions of higher learning provided some form of sabbatical leave by 1920.[119]

Honoris Causa

The whole pattern of degree granting arose during the Middle Ages as a form of professional licensure, with both Church and State exercising authority in this field. Teachers and other professional workers came to be licensed, and admitted to ply their craft, just as members of other specialized municipal guilds were. The highest *studia generalia* were recognized as having the power to confer the *jus ubique docendi.*[120] From this is derived the modern *baccalaureate, magister artium,* and *doctor philosophiae,* with all the intangible rights and privileges, and all the economic importance, pertaining thereto.[121] Just as the feudal system gave various vested interests and chartered groups tremendous power in medieval times, so modern colleges and universities, through their power to confer degrees and certificates of professional proficiency, came to "hold the key to a vast body of rights over intangibles, whose potential national importance and possible abuses are roughly comparable."[122]

One of the most serious problems involving this degree-granting power in modern America is the whole thorny question of honorary versus earned degrees. American colonial colleges took over from the English universities the custom of awarding honorary degrees to distinguished men in various fields of scholarship and public service. Thus, under President Dunster, Harvard College asserted the right in 1642 of conferring degrees *pro more academiarum in Anglia.* A statute of 1692 specified that this included the traditional right to confer honorary degrees, and in that year Increase Mather, John Leverett, and William Brattle were so honored. Yale followed Harvard in this regard, as did other colonial colleges. In 1753, for example, Benjamin Franklin received honorary degrees from both Harvard and Yale. With the War of Independence, American colleges no longer had to fear possible vetoes of their awards by the English Privy Council, and they proceeded to confer honorary degrees much more liberally. By 1801, Harvard graduates had already received 179 honorary degrees, and Yale graduates had garnered 144.[123]

During the nineteenth century, degrees such as D.D. and LL.D. were practically "demonetized" by their lavish use as honorary compliments. At this time there was no provision anywhere that such degrees be earned. In a context of Jacksonian democracy and educational laissez faire, obliging state legislatures conferred upon a great number of publicity-hungry small colleges and self-styled "universities" the chartered right to confer any and all academic degrees whatsoever. In the case of the D.D., this practice became so widespread that Peter Cartwright remarked, "Divinity must be very sick because it has so many doctors." In all, nearly two hundred varieties of honorary degrees were granted in the United States between 1870 and 1939, including the degree of D.F.F. (doctor of fortitude and faith). Fifty thousand persons received such degrees. In the twentieth century, a trend became apparent toward awarding honorary degrees to those already holding them. Herbert Hoover achieved the world's record with 52. At the same time, private institutions in particular tended increasingly to award a large number of honorary degrees to leaders in industry and finance. This policy has been characterized by the AAUP as one of "getting ahead by degrees." The obvious hope of such institutions was that they might attract financial aid by means of honorary awards.[124]

Between 1872 and 1900, 4 per cent of all honorary degrees awarded were bachelor's, 31 per cent were master's, and 65 per cent were doctor's. Of the honorary doctorates, 59 per cent were D.D.'s, 29 per cent were LL.D.'s, and 7 per cent were Ph.D.'s. It was in this last category that the most serious conflicts arose. The trend toward awarding an honorary Ph.D. obviously ran counter to the whole concept of university standards of achievement. Bucknell awarded an honorary Ph.D. in 1852, the first American institution to do so, to one Ebenezer Newton Elliott, recognized apparently because of his distinction as "President of the Southern Scientific Institute in the State of Mississippi." Princeton granted an honorary Ph.D. as early as 1866, a dozen years before it awarded an earned one. Indeed, in 1870, more honorary than earned Ph.D.'s were being granted in America. The practice was rife all over the country, with institutions in the Middle Atlantic States leading the way, those in the West following not too far in the van, and even well-known New England colleges participating in the movement. Dartmouth, for example, awarded no less than twenty honorary Ph.D.'s between 1872 and 1885.[125] From 1873 to 1890, nearly four hundred honorary Ph.D.'s were granted. In some cases, "universities" were incorporated for the sole purpose of awarding this degree for a monetary consideration.[126]

Other institutions claimed to grant an earned Ph.D., but advertised conditions for its attainment so lax that it was not very different from a gratuitous degree. In 1899, half the American institutions reporting that they awarded an earned Ph.D. were undergraduate colleges conferring the degree for some sort of work away from the campus.[127] One such school, for example, gave the Ph.D. for a moderate amount of elementary reading *in absentia,* but required that a final examination be taken in the presence of a clergyman! In general, it seemed as if Americans were seeking to justify Thomas Carlyle's observation that their main ambition was "to hobble down to posterity on the crutches of capital letters."[128]

A combination of state action together with increasing pressure exerted by various private accrediting agencies by the time of the First World War brought about a considerable decline in the granting of honorary Ph.D.'s. The great foundations, like the General Education Board and the Carnegie Foundation, helped to drive home the idea that issuing such degrees was bad academic conduct. This they did by demanding that colleges employ only authentic Ph.D.'s to qualify for donations to their pension funds.[129]

Other honorary degrees, particularly the LL.D., continued to be awarded in great numbers by American colleges. One student of the problem has suggested that this was inevitable, since these degrees have played the part in American culture that titles, decorations, and government awards do in other countries.[130] President Benjamin Ide Wheeler of the University of California reflected this point of view when he stated that the people of his state expected the university to "confer the blue ribbon," and that if this practice was given up, some other agency would take it in hand. President Hadley of Yale also approved of the practice of "decorating the festival," if only because this was the sole means of attracting really good speakers to the average American college commencement![131]

Spread and Strengthening of Graduate Degrees

Frederick Jackson Turner, the noted historian, was typical of hundreds of enthusiastic scholarly missionaries in the eighties and nineties who went forth from Johns Hopkins determined to establish the Baltimore idea of the university as the norm for American higher education. Turner found in Wisconsin that it was "not a difficult task to make students here, who contemplate a higher education, come to the conclusion that J.H.U. is much preferable to Harvard."[132] Due to the proselyting efforts of men like Turner, and the growing demand for Ph.D.'s, large graduate schools modeled on Johns Hopkins found their enrollments steadily increasing. We can appreciate the importance of this increase when we realize that in 1850 there were but eight graduate students in the whole United States. By 1900, this total had increased to 5,668, but the greatest expansion was still to come. By 1930, there were 47,255 graduate students in the United States, and by 1950 the figure was 223,786.[133]

The increase in the number of Ph.D.'s granted kept pace with the general expansion of graduate enrollments. Walter C. John estimated that 44 Ph.D. degrees were awarded in 1876 at 25 institutions. By 1918, there were 562 Ph.D.'s being awarded annually. This figure increased to 1,064 in 1924, 3,088 in 1940, and 6,633 in 1950. By the turn of the century, no less than fifteen major graduate schools were in operation in America, and the number increased markedly during the twentieth century. By 1960 more than 175 institutions were granting doctor's degrees and more than 9,000 doctorates were being awarded annually in the United States. At this date the number of earned master's degrees neared the 70,000 mark, while 380,000 bachelor's degrees were granted. By 1965 the number of earned doctorates awarded annually had mounted to 15,000! As American higher education underwent massive expansion in the years following World War II, more doctorates were granted in the United States during the 1950s than in all the years up to that time.[134]

The great increase in graduate study created a demand for standardization of the value of graduate degrees. In a manner characteristic of the American culture this was accomplished primarily by nongovernmental agencies, through the work of national accrediting associations and influential educational foundations.[135]

Although the degrees of *magister artium* and *doctor philosophiae* were not widely different in the medieval university, they later diverged and, in England, the doctorate practically disappeared. The master's degree eventually could be attained merely by keeping one's name on the college rolls. This Oxford and Cambridge pattern was brought over, during the colonial period, to the American college. As late as 1825 the master of arts was awarded "in course" to any holder of a Harvard bachelor's degree after the lapse of three years and the payment of a fee. Ticknor's efforts to make this a meaningful degree by developing graduate instruction proved unavailing. In this period, it was frequently remarked by the townspeople of Cambridge that "all a Harvard man has to do for his Master's degree is to pay five dollars and stay out of jail."[136] This practice was typical of other colleges of the era. In rare instances attempts were made in the colonial period to strengthen the master's degree. Thus, Bishop Berkeley gave an endowment to Yale for the specific purpose of subsidizing young men who were pursuing studies between their first and second degrees. This probably was the first example of an attempt to subsidize graduate study in American educational history.[137]

When university instruction was expanded and reformed during the 1870s, the master's was transformed into an earned degree. Harvard, for example, granted its last M.A. "in course" in 1872.[138] Yale offered its first earned M.A. in 1876. Soon a number of other institutions followed suit, and an enormous increase in the granting of master's degrees occurred. In 1890, only 70 such degrees were awarded in the whole United States, but 14,495 were given by 1930.

As early as 1905, George Burton Adams deplored the great variety of things for which the master's had come to stand: honorary degrees given to people with no academic training; degrees given to an institution's own graduates for courses pursued *in absentia;* degrees for a year of residence study, which was often just a fifth year of undergraduate work; and—sometimes—a degree given for a year of genuine graduate study.[139] Repeated attempts were made by accrediting agencies to establish the last-named standard as the norm for the degrees. In 1932 an investigating committee of the American Association of University Professors still expressed great dissatisfaction with the status of the M.A. degree. In 1957 a Committee on Policies in Graduate Education presented a report to the American Association of Graduate Schools which noted that the M.A. remained in many institutions either a "consolation" degree or a "quick" degree awarded for superficial performance.[140] In April, 1972, the Education Department of the State of New York announced the results of a two-year study of master's programs within its jurisdiction. It found that, regrettably, many of these programs were poor. Far too many of them differed very little in quality from undergraduate programs. "It would seem," said the department's Bureau of College Evaluation, "that an attitude of collusive mediocrity has been adopted among students, faculty, and administration at the master's level."[141]

At Johns Hopkins, the M.A. and the Ph.D. were not at first considered separate degrees. In 1909, Johns Hopkins inaugurated an experiment designed to end the growing chaos in graduate degrees by establishing the M.A. as a degree for college teachers. The Ph.D. would then be reserved for that small group which gave promise of making first-rate contributions to original research. In line with this objective, the new master's was made into a rigorous two-year degree. Although it was not an investigator's degree, neither was it a consolation prize for a Ph.D. candidate who had fallen short of success. Yale followed this lead in 1910 by introducing a strengthened two-year M.A., obviously intended for prospective college teachers. The new experiment was bucking too strong a current to succeed, however. By this time, the master's degree had practically become standardized in America as the badge of the secondary-school teacher. Those planning to become college teachers demanded the Ph.D. J. Franklin Jameson pointed out that graduate students could not be indifferent to the ineluctable logic of "no dissertation, no degree; no degree, no job."[142] Having failed to set up an acceptable M.A. as a standard for college teachers, American universities found themselves saddled, for better or worse, with a doctorate which had the weakness of trying to serve two ends, teaching and research, ends not always distinguished clearly by graduate schools.[143] Professor William A. Nitze of the University of Chicago asserted in an address in 1932 before the Association of American Universities that this had happened "because the few outstanding universities in this country never had the courage to resist public opinion and tell people the facts; namely, that education is necessarily a selection of the best, that it is aristocratic (and not democratic) in effect, and that therefore nothing could have been more futile than to lay hold on a standard of excellence and lower it to the point where it would meet a so-called 'practical demand.' "[144]

The American Ph.D., as we have seen, was directly modeled on its German prototype. The pre-existing master's degree was so well entrenched in America, however, that when the Ph.D. was brought over, it did not supplant it, but was merely superimposed on it. The Ph.D. was awarded for the first time in the United States by Yale in 1861. The Yale doctorate may very well have been the prototype for the one which Daniel C. Gilman established in Baltimore; Gilman was one of the major forces in Yale's scientific school during the early years of experimentation with this degree and one of its leading proponents. After the founding of Johns Hopkins, more and more doctorates were granted.[145] Hopkins, too, helped establish a trend in 1887 by requiring that the doctor's dissertation be printed. "The Hopkins Doctorate became the model for the Protean Ph.D.; it was carefully defined where there had been no definition, and its emphasis was on productive research." At the same time the university established a distinction between admission to graduate instruction and approval for the Ph.D. because Gilman was anxious to welcome the free-lance scholar not in search of any degree.[146]

It soon became obvious that it would be as difficult to establish a uniform standard for the Ph.D. as for the master's degree. Candidates for the degree had varying aims and abilities and graduate schools had varying standards. Beginning in 1893, a number of graduate-student clubs, anxious to protect the meaning of their degrees, carried on a campaign for the establishment of a higher and more uniform standard in the awarding of Ph.D.'s. "The Doctor's degree," they stated, "ought to stand all the world over, as it does in Europe, for research. . . . We ask that the Doctor's degree be given only to persons competent to advance knowledge in some department and trained as resident graduates in some university of high rank."[147] As a result of this agitation, the Association of American Universities was established in 1900, and this organization proceeded to define certain minimum standards of high quality with respect to academic residence, examinations, and dissertation, to which all accredited institutions had to conform in awarding the Ph.D.[148]

Meanwhile it became increasingly obvious that what William James had written about the tyranny of "the Ph.D. Octopus" was literally coming true in America. By the middle of the twentieth century, the great majority of students taking the Ph.D. looked upon it as a "union card" necessary for teaching in a college or university. Most graduate schools continued to orient the degree in the direction of potential research, even though various studies during the 1920s revealed that less than 20 per cent of American Ph.D.'s produced significant research after their dissertations. Indeed, how could they, confronted as they were with many required teaching hours each week, committee assignments, consultative duties, and general lack of interest in research on the part of many college presidents, trustees, and alumni? A careful study in 1927 of the productivity of Ph.D.'s in History stated that an important reason for their lack of production was "the low social value placed on scholarship in the United States as compared with European countries."[149] Critics of the system, while recognizing the difficulty of doing away with it completely, were more and more coming to insist that doctor's degrees really mean something; "that one degree should cease being used as a blanket award to cover all graduate training." The November 1957 report of four prominent graduate school deans to the Association of Graduate Schools recommended that this situation be remedied by "clearly" defining the "protean" Ph.D. degree in terms of certain national standards of high quality. An attempt to achieve just such a clearer definition was already under way. This involved proposals for various new types of doctorates, some designed specifically for college teachers. These remained primarily in the discussion stage. However, as early as 1920 Harvard had introduced the Ed.D. as a higher degree for practicing educators. It did not help to clarify the situation. While the new degree was widely copied, its status soon became as confused as that of the Ph.D.[150]

A study Bernard Berelson published in 1960 for the Carnegie Corporation suggested drastic "streamlining" remedies. Berelson proposed that universities enforce a four-year limitation for doctoral study; accept shorter dissertations; establish closer faculty supervision of graduate work; modify foreign language and oral examination requirements to make them more flexible; require *all* doctoral candidates to have some actual teaching experience, not less than half time for half a year; and experiment, if feasible, with a new two-year "intermediate" doctorate designed for college teachers only.[151]

In the early 1970s attempts were made in a number of institutions to experiment with a new doctorate for teachers. This degree, the Doctorate of Arts, received the endorsement of the influential Carnegie Commission on Higher Education. Some schools went farther than this. A few began to award doctorates for books of poems, novels, even original musical compositions, thus dispensing with the traditional dissertation requirements.[152]

These innovations, however, did not go far enough to satisfy a panel on Alternate Approaches to Graduate Education which had been set up by the U.S. Council of Graduate Schools. In a report published in 1973 the panel demanded far-reaching changes in the structure of American graduate education. It maintained that every discipline, especially at the Ph.D. level, "should include a deliberate and significant component of discipline-related work outside the university walls." It called for preferential treatment "for those hitherto discriminated against in admission to graduate education, namely, women and members of minority groups." To facilitate such a policy, it declared that the graduate schools must end their second-class treatment of part-time students. It recommended that universities develop ways of evaluating systematically the teaching performance of graduate-school professors. It advocated that teaching ability as well as a faculty member's service to the community be given equal weight in the academic world's reward system with the quality of the individual's research. It proposed that a commission be created to develop methods of evaluating the learning that went on off-campus. It asked that universities set up panels of "successful achievers" from outside the academic world which would work with the traditional departments to advise students. It believed that graduate schools should lead the way in exploring the proper uses of new instructional materials and technological aids for teaching. Finally, it expressed the hope that it would become the norm for graduate students and professors to examine carefully the social implications of all projected research, thus linking course work to independent study and, wherever possible, directing student-faculty projects in such a way that meaningful social change might be accomplished.[153]

It remained a serious question whether such sweeping innovations in graduate training would be generally approved or swiftly implemented in the nation's universities. Derek C. Bok, president of Harvard University, doubted whether some of these changes were either necessary or desirable. In his report to the Board of Overseers of Harvard University for 1972–1973 he declared that the proper goal of his institution remained that of "developing scholars." While some members of Harvard's graduate faculty would undoubtedly "create new programs concerned with problems such as arms control or population," he wrote, "any wholesale effort to divert the Ph.D. toward immediate social needs would misdirect the talents of our professors. . . . Any serious effort to grapple with most social problems must draw heavily upon our store of basic knowledge. . . . As a result, the efforts of the faculty in carrying on scholarly work and training new generations of scholars not only serve the important end of enriching our culture; they also help to enlarge the body of basic knowledge on which enlightened social policy must depend."[154]

10

Professional Education

In spite of the long liberal-arts tradition of the American college, there are many who think that the college was basically a professional school in colonial times and a professional school of theology at that. Now it is true, as a matter of fact, that the majority of college graduates in colonial times did go into the professions and that theology attracted more young men than did any other. And it is also true that a predominant purpose in the founding of colonial colleges was the rearing of an educated ministry. Yet, these facts notwithstanding, it is still probably contrary to fact that the colonial college was primarily a professional school, even for theological studies. Professional education in colonial times, in contrast to the common opinion cited, was largely by apprenticeship. Not till the nineteenth century was education for the professions to be had to any considerable extent in formal schools, and not till the latter part of this century were these schools raised to university grade.

Professional Preparation Through Apprenticeship

Preparation for one of the traditional learned professions—law, theology, or medicine—has always had the two dimensions of theory and practice. Under the apprenticeship system the chief accent fell on practice. The professional candidate placed himself under an able and mature minister, lawyer, or doctor and hoped by observation and imitation to be admitted subsequently to professional status. Sometimes, as in the case of the ministry, a candidate associated himself so closely with a practitioner that he went to live in his home. Through assisting a practitioner in the performance of his professional duties, the novice had an opportunity not only to learn professional skills himself but also to repay his benefactor in some degree for both the opportunity to learn and for the direction given to his learning. Indeed some practitioners, notably successful in their teaching of apprentices, charged them a fee in addition to using their services.

In spite of the claim to being learned, the professions under the apprenticeship system made only slight demands on the nature and extent of the apprentice's

198

training prior to signing indenture papers, if any were signed at all. The ministry, perhaps, demanded most by usually expecting the candidate to know the classical tongues and, if he had attended college, to know some theology as well. Terms of study were not exacting either, since there was no determinate length to the apprenticeship as there had been in England, some terms running several months and others several years. Under frontier conditions it is not difficult to believe that terms ran shorter rather than longer.

There were, of course, numerous activities the performance of which at once helped the practitioner and instructed the neophyte. In making copies of papers like wills and deeds the young law clerk learned much of their legal form; in serving writs and filing actions he acquainted himself with judicial procedure; and in being a handyman about the court in term time he picked up the art of the attorney and the ethics of the bar. The would-be physician started making himself useful by washing bottles, later mixing drugs, and perhaps at a still later stage progressing to such routine matters as bloodletting. By being present in the doctor's office and accompanying him on calls he picked up much of the lore of diagnosis and therapy. Again, the prospective clergyman, through "living in" with a minister of the Gospel, became intimately acquainted with pastoral routine and duties, at the same time learning to dedicate himself to the service of God and man.

Important as was the mastery of the details of professional practice, theoretical considerations were not omitted. Theory the apprentice mastered out of books. But here he did not so much pursue a systematic course of readings as he read widely and deeply from whatever library his practitioner happened to possess. In fact one reason the future divine took up residence with an ordained clergyman was to avail himself of the latter's library. Similarly the future lawyer clerked in the office of some attorney in order to "read law" in preparation for the bar. Over and beyond books, of course, law and theology presented innumerable opportunities for master and apprentice to argue fine points of theory. Furthermore, clergymen and lawyers who were conscientious beyond the ordinary in their teaching duties often set theses or questions on which their apprentices presented papers which in turn became the basis for analysis and further discussion.

In evaluating the apprenticeship period of professional training, it must be confessed that the training was very uneven in quality. Nevertheless it developed technical competence as measured by the standards of the day. The future physician at least had the advantage of learning about disease by seeing it at first hand and observing the effect of treatment on it. In the approved pedagogical language of a later day, his was truly a learning by doing. And yet in spite of such advantages there were all too obvious limitations of the apprenticeship system. The man successful in law, medicine, or theology was not necessarily a successful teacher. Not only might he lack talent for instruction, but all too frequently a crowded professional life left all too little leisure to exercise the pedagogical talent he did possess.[1] Perhaps an even more serious limitation of the system was its empirical nature. In spite of the apprentice's reading, emphasis fell heavily on *ad hoc* procedures. The theory undergirding and giving scope and direction to practice was minimized and sometimes overlooked. The legal apprentice tended to learn local procedures and local peculiarities of the substantive law rather than general principles. In the case of medicine the pedagogical emphasis on empirical rule of thumb is probably to be explained by its coinciding with an empirical period of that discipline's development. Happily some economically more favored youth were able to make up such deficits by attending European centers of professional study such as the English Inns of Court for law or the University of Edinburgh for medicine.

Early Professional Schools

Before passing from the period of informal preparation for the professions through apprenticeship to the period of more formal training through professional schools, it will be well to note how some of the colleges had already begun establishing chairs in theology and law as part of their undergraduate offerings. Chairs of theology appeared at Harvard and Yale before the middle of the eighteenth century, and chairs of law began to make their debut at sister colleges after the Revolutionary War. Thomas Jefferson was instrumental in inaugurating the first professorship at William and Mary, a professorship to be copied before the century was out at both the University of Pennsylvania and Columbia. While no doubt students pointing for the ministry or the bar found these courses ultimately useful for professional purposes, probably none would have regarded them as the main avenue to professional life since apprenticeship still dominated the approaches to the professions in the eighteenth century. Even college graduates who planned on the ministry without apprenticing themselves to some local pastor generally stayed on at college after graduation for a period of time to put themselves under the preprofessional guidance of the president, usually a clergyman.[2]

But, professional preparation aside, it is probably true that the courses in theology often had at least as strong a liberal as a professional orientation. Whatever the vocational destination of the young bachelor of arts, there was little doubt in colonial and early national times that religion was the principal integrating factor in any sound liberal education. Much the same may be said for the courses offered in law. The men who taught them—George Wythe at William and Mary, James Wilson at the University of Pennsylvania, and James Kent at Columbia—were likely thinking at least as much in the broad liberal terms of politics and jurisprudence as they were of the immediate practice of the law. This was the spirit in which Blackstone lectured at Oxford from 1768 onward, and certainly his chair was the model for American colleges. Two famous textbooks resulted from these chairs of law: Blackstone's *Commentaries on the Laws of England* and Chancellor Kent's *Commentaries on American Law,* both long and widely read by future law clerks and students.

While chairs in medicine began to appear during this same period, the first seems to have been established in 1765 at the College of Philadelphia, as might have been expected from Benjamin Franklin's interest in the college and in science. King's College followed two years later, Harvard and Dartmouth before the century was out, but Yale and Brown did not follow suit till the first decade of the nineteenth century. It is not so clear in the case of medicine as it is of law and theology that it was studied liberally and this in spite of the fact that Yale made a point of subjecting its medical students to the same college discipline—compulsory chapel and eating at commons—as her undergraduates. Similarly, at a later date Brown insisted that its medical like its academic faculty live on campus. At neither college did such regulations succeed. Yale rescinded its requirement before any serious mischief occurred, but Brown, by persisting in the enforcement of its residence rule in the face of faculty opposition, only succeeded at the expense of driving out its medical faculty.

While the colleges were establishing chairs as initial steps in the long development of professional education, burgeoning forces latent in the apprenticeship system were expanding it into the first real professional schools. Some successful pastors, for instance, were accepting not just one, or even two, but a number of young men to study with them for the ministry. Although not formally organized as schools, these aggregations were widely known as "schools of the prophets." The evolution from apprenticeship to school, however, was even more clear in the case of the law. The first and outstanding school was that of Judge Tapping Reeve at Litchfield, Connecticut. As his law practice was disrupted by the war, the judge apparently compensated by taking on more and more apprentices. In the course of time the teaching of apprentices in his office came to predominate over the carrying on of a law practice, but so gradual was the transition that there is some doubt when in the 1780s to date the beginning of the school. Once transformed, however, from office to school, Judge Reeve's method had many imitators. Medical schools, when they started in the first decade of the next century, had a not dissimilar structure. Instead of teaching their apprentices singly, however, several physicians would band together to teach their apprentices collectively, thus allowing for some degree of specialization in the faculty of their resulting school.

It is noteworthy in both cases, law and medicine, that the schools were run for the financial profit of their proprietors and were therefore for the most part incorporated independently from institutions of higher education like the old established colleges on the eastern seaboard. Since students after completing the course often called their former teachers in as consultants, membership on one of these faculties brought added professional prestige as well as a division of tuitions.[3] This led to a rapid growth in the number of such schools and a commercial exploitation of the American public which discredited the whole system.[4]

These new professional schools tended to be didactic. Lectures replaced empirical training; telling replaced doing. The lecture hall substituted both for contact with client or patient and for presence in court or at sickbed. All this made sense in the era because it enabled the practitioner-teacher to distill his own professional experience in summary form and thus economize the student's time and effort. Moreover, with emphasis on lecturing it was possible to organize a more or less systematic course of instruction to take the place of the somewhat haphazard order in which significant learning experiences arose under the apprenticeship system.[5] Some practitioner-teachers virtually dictated as they lectured, so that at the conclusion of the course, if a student had not had a text at the beginning, he now did. But, like Chancellor Kent, teachers themselves soon began to publish their lectures and thereafter lecturing was often supplemented by recitations based on the text of published lectures. It is said that the Litchfield Law School continued its popularity longer than most proprietary schools because the lectures delivered there were longest delayed in reaching the public press.

Popular as these proprietary schools became, they by no means supplanted the apprenticeship system. Rather they paralleled and competed with it. Unfortunately, as a result, their standards tended to approximate those of apprenticeship training and hardly dared exceed them for fear of losing out in the competition for students. Entrance requirements, for example, were practically nil. Boys would be admitted to these professional schools who could not gain entrance to a college or even to its preparatory department.[6] In his inaugural address at the University of Nashville in 1829, President Lindsley declared that it was easier at the time in Tennessee to qualify for the practice of the law or medicine than to build a dray or shoe a horse.[7] Not only were standards of admission almost nonexistent, but matriculation, too, was irregular. The candidate started professional school as he did an apprenticeship, when the time suited him. The length of time he stayed was also uneven. Under such conditions rigorous examinations, if any at all, were almost out of the question. Harvard, where the standards were as high as anywhere about the time of the Civil War, awarded the medical doctor's degree to any candidate who could pass five out of nine oral examinations all taken on the same day![8] With or without examinations, however, the diplomas awarded were equally impressive. In view of all these circumstances it is small wonder that the prestige of the professional student stood low. So low was it at Bowdoin that the undergraduates there looked down on the medical students on its campus with a disdain that was not above playing pranks on them.[9]

Deplorable as early standards seem to a later day, they were not without their explanation under the influence of Jacksonian democracy. With the accession of Andrew Jackson to the Presidency of the United States, egalitarianism spread, not only to the civil service, but to qualifications for professional training as well.[10] As the common man came to power, his confidence in pioneer versatility caused him to distrust the expert. He claimed the right for all economic classes to enjoy professional privileges as a new principle of no less far-reaching significance in a democracy than the older one that those who exercise professional privileges should be trained to discharge them.[11] Thus, the 1851 Indiana constitution provided that every person of good moral character, being a voter, shall be admitted to practice law in all the courts of the state.[12] While one might reluctantly concede this principle in the case of training for the law, which is so closely akin to training for politics, the fierce egalitarianism of the frontier seemed to know no bounds and extended it to medical education as well, even though there the difference between expert and charlatan might be the difference between life and death.

Obviously neither the professional schools nor the surviving apprenticeship system worked out altogether satisfactorily. Both tended to be too specific in their curriculums. Both needed a broader scholarship. What seemed required was a type of professional education that combined the practical merits of the apprenticeship system with the academic merits of the chairs of law, theology, and medicine in the colleges. President Kirkland of Harvard was early to cry out for something better,[13] but it was Andover Theological Seminary that was early to respond.

The Congregationalists who founded this institution in 1808 had lofty ambitions. At the outset they aimed at a faculty that would give full time to teaching, a student body that would have a college education behind it, and ahead a three-year term of instruction. By starting with a sizable library and by expanding the curriculum to include history and such languages as Hebrew, they hoped to make such demands on scholarship as more nearly to merit being a learned profession. Although these plans were applauded by most thinking persons, nevertheless there was an undercurrent of dissent. There was a fear in some quarters that such a seminary would more likely turn out scholars than sturdy soldiers of the Cross. These quarters still clung conservatively to the notion that education in the privacy and seclusion of the revered "school of the prophets" was more likely to foster humility, patience, and devotion. A pleader for founding a theological seminary at Princeton refuted these anxieties by pointing out an opposite danger in the "school of the prophets," the danger that candidates confined to the provincialisms of the clergymen with whom they lived and studied might turn out to be dogmatic if not bigoted as well.[14]

After something of a false start in the next decade Harvard, under the leadership of Justice Story, finally revamped its law school in 1829 to take in only college graduates or their equivalent and to lift its sights from the study of local to general principles of law.[15] Medical education, too, if low in achievement, was not without its elevated sights. John Morgan, in inaugurating the study of medicine at Franklin's College of Philadelphia, was prophetic in the demands he made. Men coming to the study of medicine, he insisted, should be versed not only in Latin, Greek, and French but also in mathematics and the sciences. Fresh from a sojourn in Europe, he further begged that medicine be studied and taught as a science supplemented by clinical lectures from hospital physicians.[16] Taking much the same stand, Eliphalet Nott at Union College claimed that engineering education would be stronger and more effective if combined with a liberal-arts curriculum on a liberal-arts campus.

Upgrading Professional Education

Notwithstanding the sound ideals enunciated, it was difficult to match ideals with actions in the early nineteenth century. Under existing social conditions the holding power of Andover was not great enough to retain students for the full three-year term and Justice Story too frequently had to admit men to the study of law with less than a bachelor's degree and even less than its equivalent. It must be added that Story only made the fledgling school a part-time concern since at the time he was sitting on the United States Supreme Court. But better times were ahead. Improvement occurred on a number of fronts almost simultaneously.

First, after long preoccupation with opening the doors of opportunity as wide as possible to those bent on professional careers, interest came to center more and more on selective factors. Harvard was among the first to brook the danger of decreased enrollments from raising the entrance hurdles. After the Civil War her youthful and energetic new president, Charles W. Eliot, persuaded her professional schools one by one not only to require a bachelor's degree for entrance but to raise the tuition rate to boot. Enrollments fell at once in accordance with the dire predictions of the old guard, who did not sympathize with the new president. But when the quality of this new product began to make itself felt in professional life, enrollments rose again and Eliot was more than vindicated for the risk taken.[17] Not every college or university felt strong enough to take a similar risk, not even the stronger ones, but a number followed somewhat timidly by requiring at least two years of college. Some excused their timidity in terms of protecting the interests of poor boys who could not afford so long a preparatory period.[18] By the turn of the century the percentage of professional people with no training beyond secondary school was rapidly falling. Indeed better than 10 per cent of lawyers, doctors, clergymen, and college teachers by that time had had both college and professional or graduate instruction in preparation for their careers.[19]

By the first quarter of the twentieth century the mere possession of a bachelor's degree and the tuition fee was no longer enough to command entrance to the better professional schools. When applications for admission outran the number of places available, professional schools were able to pick students with particular kinds of records. Medical schools especially showed favor to applicants who had pursued a premedical curriculum of selected courses in science, such as chemistry and biology. Law and theological schools continued to accept students from a wide variety of curriculums, though specialization of some sort latterly augured greater success than its absence.[20] Of course, all professional schools showed a preference for the college graduate with a good scholastic record. In fact, studies revealed that undergraduate scholastic success was a good prediction of success in professional school.[21]

In raising the tuition as well as the threshold of entrance requirements, it was only proper that the professional schools should offer an enriched program of studies. Here the new vitamins came principally from studying the traditional professions of law, medicine, and theology in the light of neighboring disciplines.[22] Medicine particularly benefited from being studied in conjunction with the sciences of chemistry, physics, biology, physiology, psychology, and the like. Law, too, took on new proportions when studied in the light of history, philosophy, and the social sciences. As this larger scope caught on, students came to study from books whose titles changed from *Cases on the Law of* _____ to *Cases and Materials on the Law of* _____. To promote research into the wider and deeper ramifications of the law, Harvard early in the twentieth century established a graduate department of law that awarded the S.J.D. degree. Not to be outdone, theological schools reinvigorated their traditional courses of study by drawing on the resources of psychology, sociology, and politics in order to give the ministry an informed as well as a sensitive social conscience in such matters as temperance, divorce, human exploitation, racial discrimination, and similar social problems, to say nothing of keeping it abreast of the impact of scientific discoveries on theology.[23] As in the case of the Newton Theological Seminary, there was an outcry against these innovations, a fear that the professional student would lose himself in the labyrinths of theory to the serious neglect of more practical and useful concerns, but the outcry subsided.[24]

As scholarship in professional schools spread out, it became evident that independently incorporated professional schools were at a disadvantage. It was not so easy and convenient for them to draw on closely associated academic disciplines as it was for the affiliated school. Permeated by the academic atmosphere of the university and backed by its broader financial base, professional schools as parts of universities found it easier to move away from one of the great weaknesses of the proprietary school, its part-time faculty, and toward one of full-time teachers.[25] Acutely aware of this and other facts, a number of proprietary schools in the nineteenth century surrendered their independent status and became parts of old-established seats of learning. Thus the Litchfield Law School joined the Yale family of professional schools before the middle of the century, and the College of Physicians and Surgeons in New York City affiliated with Columbia at the century's end. How strong the trend became is witnessed by the fact that out of one hundred law schools at the turn of the century seventy-one were affiliated.[26] While medical schools followed this trend, theological seminaries lagged behind, the more sectarian ones fearing to lose their narrow appeal.

Schools of technology were something else again. The first ones to be founded like Rensselaer Polytechnic Institute and Massachusetts Institute of Technology not only followed the European custom of being separate and independent from the university but have remained so in spite of the centripetal influence of the university on other professional schools. These institutes, however, together with the later land-grant colleges of agriculture and mechanical arts, compensated for their independent position by enlarging their own curricula to include many university studies. Thus M.I.T. has come to offer work in the humanities, including on its faculty a professor of philosophy. In most state universities, of course, law, medicine, and engineering have been integral parts of the university almost from the beginning. Indeed, at the University of Maryland professional schools even antedated the undergraduate college.

Contemporary with strengthening of the curriculum came corresponding innovation in methods of teaching it. Excessive lecturing in medical schools began to give way to the laboratory; the amphitheater lost some of its importance to intensive study in the outpatient department and in the hospital ward. While it had been the custom of medical students to observe diagnosis and treatment, William Osler at Johns Hopkins conceived the idea of having them assist in these activities within the limits of their training.[27] Thus apprenticeship had a rebirth and transformation in the medical internship. Schools of education and social work, like medicine, were also able to include clinical work or practicums, where the candidates came into direct contact with clients as part of their regular curricula. Usually this live contact had been reserved for the end of the professional course but in at least one instance, Case-Western medical school, it was vouchsafed to even first-year students. Similar educational procedures were more difficult to employ in law and business schools, where moot courts and business games were more in vogue.[28]

Law schools also caught the scientific spirit. In introducing the case method of legal study at Harvard, Christopher C. Langdell acted on the assumption that law was capable of scientific study. Only on this assumption was it worthy of university-grade instruction; otherwise, he claimed, it should continue to be treated as a craft and taught through apprenticeship. The case method of teaching proposed to reach legal principles, like scientific ones, by induction.[29] In place of learning principles of law ready made from lectures or texts, the student was disciplined in the art of ferreting out the principles himself from an analysis of concrete adjudicated cases. Thus, taking a page from Aristotle, the student learned the art and not just the product of legal reasoning. In doing so he had the further pedagogical advantage of learning to do precisely what he would be doing later as a counselor at law or, happily even later, as a judge.

Further upgrading of professional education occurred through self-regulation by the professions themselves. Slowly at the end of the nineteenth century, but with rapid acceleration in the twentieth, public standards were raised. A three-cornered set of forces brought it about: state examining authorities, associations of practitioners, and associations of professional schools. At first the standards of state examiners improved no more rapidly than did those of the associations of practitioners themselves.[30] Professional schools, however, impatient with this pace, tended to move well out in front of practitioners. The gap opened up caused some animosity between practitioners and professional faculties, and later on within law faculties themselves, between those who taught competence for local practice and those who taught more general legal theory.[31] The American Bar Association and the American Medical Association both had committees or councils specifically concerned with studying educational requirements for admission to professional ranks. The Association of American Law Schools, for instance, formed by the better ones of their number in 1900, grew out of a committee of the American Bar Association on legal education. By operating directly or indirectly as accrediting agencies the associations of professional schools exerted a leavening and standardizing influence both inside and outside their membership.[32] Thus by 1906 law schools set a three-year term as a minimum, by 1912 required law school libraries to possess at least 5,000 volumes, and by 1915 demanded that their members have at least three full-time professors on their faculties.

The most startling and epoch-making force for the improvement of professional education has yet to be mentioned, the Carnegie Foundation for the Advancement of Teaching. The study of medical education which it sponsored under Abraham Flexner and published in 1910 produced a veritable revolution in medical education.[33] In spite of Harvard's bold leadership, followed by Johns Hopkins medical school when it opened at the end of the nineteenth century, medical education continued to be plagued by a plethora of low-grade medical schools, low in academic standards and low in even rudimentary scientific equipment. In 1890 there were actually 160 schools awarding the M.D. degree. In the next decade this number fell to 126. This drop was largely due to some publicity given to existing conditions by the *Journal of the American Medical Association,* which had started publishing figures showing how well the graduates of the different schools did on various state medical examinations. On the basis of these results the *Journal* made a preliminary rating of schools in three categories, the highest consisting of schools with 10 per cent or fewer failures, next those with 10–20 per cent, and third those with more than 20 per cent.

The American Medical Association followed this up in the first decade of the twentieth century by making an individual visit to each of the then existing medical schools and rating them according to ten basic criteria. Schools rating 70 or better went into class A, those between 50 and 70 into class B, and those below 50 into class C.[34] This paved the way for the far more thorough study of Flexner. During his investigation twenty schools closed on the spot rather than have the devastating evidence about them exposed to public view. The final report named each remaining school and described its circumstances in detail. By 1915 the pitiless light of public scrutiny had brought the number of medical schools down to 95—66 in class A, 17 in class B, and 12 in class C. Five years later the number had shrunk to 85—70 in class A, 7 in B, and 8 in C. Later in that decade only three schools still remained in class B and six in C, all the rest being in A. This upgrading of medical education to such a phenomenally high level in so short a while was nothing short of epoch-making.

The Flexner Report put medical training out in front of other traditional forms of professional education, if by no other means than by making it unequivocally postbaccalaureate. Some schools of law and theology set their standards correspondingly high, but by no means all of them. Study for the ministry still often occupied undergraduate years in the twentieth century. Indeed in a few of the states it was still possible to prepare for the bar through apprenticeship. Notwithstanding a Carnegie Foundation study of legal education, no such startling progress was made as in medical education.

Training for the newer and younger professions—engineering, pedagogy, business, agriculture, journalism, architecture—passed through much the same stages of development that the older ones experienced. Early training for some of these occupations was quite empirical. The teacher, for instance, learned to teach by teaching, *docendo docere*. The son learned to farm from his father. Merchants took on apprentices much as did lawyers and doctors. Johns Hopkins, who left his name and fortune to the great university in Baltimore, started his business career as such. Up to the founding of Rensselaer Polytechnic Institute engineers were largely self-taught. The founding of this institute, however, marked a turning point; it signaled the fact that American life was becoming increasingly complex. No longer would simple empirical techniques be sufficient to meet the intricacies propounded by the growing industrialization of the country. The application of science, not just to medicine, but to all phases of life, began to make demands on occupations which could only be met by more theoretical schooling.

The period of founding schools for these various occupations encountered somewhat the same problems met by the older professions when schools began to supplant apprenticeship there. For one thing there was the old confusion between theory and practice. The public expected these new schools to be practical and yet at the same time to enrich practice with new scientific insights. But where to find a faculty which had this fine balance of theoretical and practical knowledge? For the most part the men who were available for the new colleges of agriculture and mechanics were academicians; they were botanists, chemists, physicists. Although they became the first professors of "applied" science, they were able to supply in the beginning only a very meagerly practical curriculum. Similarly, the only faculty available in the early business schools such as Wharton were professors of economics and political science. If presidents had tried to staff their faculties with practical men possessed of theoretical insight, they would have been even more unsuccessful, for such men simply were not in sight as yet.[35]

Encountered again was also the problem of the academic level for technical instruction. While it was possible to pitch the engineering curriculum at a collegiate level, that of pedagogy, for instance, started as a department in secondary schools, particularly academies. Through the efforts of Horace Mann and Henry Barnard normal schools came to take over this function, but early normal schools were little more than advanced academies. Shortly after the founding of Amherst its faculty made a plea for the incorporation of pedagogy into the college curriculum,[36] but it was not till the twentieth century that teacher training reached college grade and then largely in teachers' colleges separate from academic campuses. Unaffiliated with academic institutions for the most part, they suffered the same inherent weakness as had the proprietary schools of medicine and law.[37] In spite of significant beginnings of a theory of education, the academic mind refused to regard pedagogy seriously. This was even true where at the end of the nineteenth century departments of education emerged on college campuses as offshoots from departments of philosophy and psychology. But for that matter all these junior professions at first occupied a low rung on the ladder of academic prestige, as had the older professions in their early days. No matter how much the practice of these occupations demanded more and more theory to meet the demands of a vastly more complicated America, people, and particularly academic people, ironically regarded them as utilitarian and therefore compared them unfavorably to the liberal arts.[38]

Undaunted, however, the same forces moved in to upgrade the early schools for the junior professions as operated in the more traditional ones. The demands for theory which in the beginning began to lift these professions out of the rut of empirical routine continued to compound themselves and spread over into contiguous disciplines. When Joseph Pulitzer, the great journalist, for example, offered to endow a school of journalism, Charles W. Eliot suggested a curriculum of practical details—newspaper administration, the law of journalism, journalistic ethics, and the like—but Pulitzer directed his benevolence to Columbia and a curriculum much more closely related to liberal arts.[39] Similarly, as pedagogy came to draw strength from a wide range of liberal arts, but especially philosophy, psychology, and the social sciences, it outgrew its tight-fitting skin of methodology and expanded into the broad study of education itself. Also new and better methods presented themselves for teaching these expanded curriculums. Thus, corresponding to the "block" curriculum in medicine, the "project" method in agriculture was developed. Instead of studying botany, chemistry, and economics as isolated courses, the student would undertake a "project" to raise and market a particular crop on an assigned plot of land, the successful completion of which would involve an integrated use of these academic disciplines as resources.

The deeper and broader the scholarship aimed at, the more it became evident that genuine professional competence could not be achieved short of graduate study. Consequently, although much professional study continued at the undergraduate level, leading universities began to establish graduate professional schools in rising fields like education,[40] architecture,[41] and business.[42]

The Harvard Graduate Business School particularly revealed the educational statesmanship of its founders. Even before becoming president, after Eliot's retirement in 1910, A. Lawrence Lowell thought it might "mark an era" if Harvard were to establish a school of business where college graduates, without regard to their specialities in college, might study business, not as political economy, but business as business and yet not to turn out finished administrators but rather to shorten the inevitable period of apprenticeship with the growing body of theory. Business should be flavored with theory, said A. Lawrence Lowell, himself trained in the law, just as the study of law is flavored with jurisprudence in Continental Europe and should be in the United States. How to embody this philosophy in practice was a question—whether to organize the curriculum around particular branches of industrial organization like banking and railroading, around particular jobs such as accountants and statisticians, or according to the art of administration in general.[43] In any case it became quite clear that the best balance between theory and practice was gained by borrowing the case method from the law school.[44]

Repeating the history of the older professions, these newer schools of university grade formed professional associations to accredit sister schools and upgrade their quality. The Carnegie Foundation for the Advancement of Teaching was no little help here as with earlier professional education, conducting studies of engineering[45] and education[46] which, while they did not make such epochal changes as Flexner had for medicine, nevertheless erected important milestones in the improvement of training for these occupations.

Since the Second World War, many innovations have been made in the aims, curricula, and methods of both senior and junior professional schools.[47] Medical, law, and agricultural schools, for instance, have come to state their aims more broadly, in terms of the welfare of man in relation to his environment. To achieve this larger frame of reference they often find the old curriculum too long and too congested. To remedy this situation they are starting to spend less time on required core courses and more on flexible alternatives. To achieve this end there was a strong trend to integrate professional curricula with behavioral and social sciences.[48] This trend in turn led to not only interdisciplinary courses but interprofessional ones as well. Unfortunately this larger scope of professional education had a tendency to overcrowd the curriculum. In part, some thought this overcrowding resulted from adhering to the traditional notion that a candidate should become proficient in each branch of his profession. By abandoning that notion in favor of greater and earlier specialization many thought the congestion could be relieved.[49]

Broader aims and curricula naturally demand more imaginative methods. It is no surprise, therefore, that there is a shift to problem solving techniques. Often professional students are taught to conceptualize their problems in terms of "models" and "game theory." Data processing and the computer as well as programed instruction are among the new methods. The point at which the neophyte student is immersed in the practical aspects of his profession is being advanced to the second and even the first years of professional study. Moreover the clinical or apprenticeship aspects of training are being enriched at some universities by encouraging commercial and industrial concerns to locate their research laboratories on the periphery of the campus. The mutual benefits of this policy are quite obvious.

The Higher Study of Higher Education

So far references to the evolution of the professional study of education have concerned the training of personnel to man the system of elementary and secondary schools. In a history of higher education perhaps a special indulgence may be granted for the separate mention of the preparation of personnel for the higher schools as well. Here, as in the lower schools, the early rule was *docendo docere*. Seventeenth- and eighteenth-century tutors learned to teach by teaching. The ones chosen for this trial by ordeal were those who had recently completed their studies for the bachelor's degree and were waiting call to a pulpit, for the assumption was widely and tacitly held that the only preparation needed to teach was a knowledge of the subject matter to be taught. Inasmuch as the predominant method of instruction was the recitation, wherein the tutor did little more than quiz the student to see that he had read his text,[50] it is not surprising that this assumption remained long unexamined. Unless one regards the four-year college course as an apprenticeship in the liberal arts, there was no practice of any sort under the eye of a master. Perhaps the only change in these conditions of professional training till well into the nineteenth century was one noted by Charles W. Eliot when he himself decided to become a college teacher. He counted it an advance that he unequivocally chose to make a career of teaching and not just to make it a steppingstone or interim employment to some other calling.[51]

Even before the day of Eliot a number of young men were setting a new fashion in preparing themselves for college teaching. Men like George Ticknor, George Bancroft, and Henry Wadsworth Longfellow, after graduating from Dartmouth, Harvard, and Bowdoin respectively, studied in European universities, especially German, in preparation for their later obligations at home. As has already been described, they were but the vanguard of an illustrious line of Americans who returned home to top the Anglo-American college with graduate schools devoted to German ideals of scholarly research.[52] In the course of time the Ph.D. degree, which crowned this graduate instruction, became the indispensable prerequisite to a job in college teaching. Colleges grew to count their blessings in terms of the number of Ph.D. holders on the faculty and the list of the faculty's scholarly publications.[53] By taking this stand colleges and universities assured themselves of faculties which had never before been so well qualified in their mastery of the subject matter they taught. Yet, although modern faculties were far better qualified than their predecessors of the seventeenth and eighteenth centuries, no change had occurred in the underlying theory of their training. Copying German practice confirmed rather than challenged the assumption that a knowledge of subject matter was the principal if not sole preparation needed for college teaching. Not even the gradual advance from the recitation to the lecture during the nineteenth century caused a re-examination of the assumption. Lecturing was just telling, and telling was to be learned empirically by telling.

If there were slight misgivings about this system before the nineteenth century was out, there was a positive clamor of criticism in the twentieth century. The secondary schools, long accused of sending poorly trained students to college, now turned on the colleges and accused them of poor teaching themselves.[54] But the principal criticism during the first two decades of the century came from the liberal-arts colleges themselves. David Starr Jordan, from the vantage point of the presidencies of the University of Indiana and Stanford University, corroborated the complaint of the secondary school by publicly confessing that no worse teaching was to be found than that in freshman year of large colleges.[55] Their lack of success William Rainey Harper of the University of Chicago ascribed to the failure of young Ph.D.'s to realize that a different method was required in teaching freshman and sophomores from the one used in the graduate school.[56] Men like Andrew F. West, who knew the problem at first hand as dean of the Princeton Graduate School, thought that the besetting sin of the embryo Ph.D. was his intensive knowledge of his own specialty and his extensive ignorance about the subjects which bordered on it, an overspecialization purchased at the price of research studies too often of second- and third-rate quality.[57] Going further, Charles William Eliot was saying in his inaugural at Harvard, "The actual problem to be solved is not what to teach but how to teach."[58] Even before the termination of the nineteenth century George Santayana at Harvard was pointing out that young instructors were so intent on becoming scholars that they only became teachers by "accident." A little later Woodrow Wilson was to join him in deploring how modern faculties were losing the close moral and sympathetic personal touch with students which they had formerly possessed.[59]

In spite of these warnings nothing substantial was done to redress the balance between teaching and research. Publish or perish became the code by which faculties lived. In following it faculties were but pragmatically noting which side of their bread was buttered. Advance in academic rank and salary for the most part went to those with long lists of publications rather than those successful in the classroom. Perhaps the college or university administration rewarded research activities because it thought them more worth while, or perhaps because published research was a more tangible and therefore less controversial measure of appraising professional worth.[60] President Edmund Day of Cornell declared that it was up to the faculty rather than the administration to redress this balance, for it was the faculty that resented measures to evaluate the efficiency of teaching in order to put it on a par with research.[61] Although the professional study of higher education would be difficult, he saw no reason for preferring to regard it as a mystery.

The discussion of college teaching ranged far and wide, even to a discussion of the professional prototype itself. As Dean Max McConn of Lehigh observed, training for academic life is self-selective; it attracts to itself preferably thinkers rather than doers.[62] He who can, goes from college into life as a go-getter or reformer; he who can't, goes to graduate school to become a teacher. This penchant of the academic mind for the abstract, some thought, lay at the bottom of the failure of college teaching. Two abstractions in particular were stamped on the student mind—the theoretic separation of fields of specialization from each other and the abstraction of scholarly interests from life itself. Moreover it tended to fashion an ideal of liberal education which strangely resembled the professional stereotype itself, a man who had an esoteric interest in learning on its own account and who eschewed the application of learning to the concrete and specific. It was small wonder, therefore, that the professorial manner often struck the student as impractical, absent-minded, arid, verbose, and even cantankerous.[63]

The penchant for the abstract was, of course, not only the despair but also the crowning hope of the profession. No problem can be studied seriously short of analyzing it into a series of abstractions. Unless the higher learning provides a place for long-term research and unhurried meditation which transcends immediate and utilitarian demands, not even practical concerns will prosper. The happy union of scholarship and practice was notably illustrated during the depression of the 1930's and the Second World War following, when a number of professors were called into public service. If politicians and cartoonists insisted on ridiculing the professor as a "brain-truster" in this period, it but proved the important position he had achieved.[64] In any event, criticizing the teacher with a theoretical proclivity was an old pastime, as witness the fun the dramatist Aristophanes poked at Socrates, one of the greatest teachers of them all.

Whatever the merits or demerits of the professional prototype, complaints about the preparation of college teachers continued on between the two world wars. However ideally research and teaching should supplement each other, the fact nonetheless persisted that the importance of research had grown and continued to grow out of all proportion to that of teaching. At long last a number of professional associations took the problem under study, among them the Association of American Colleges, the Association of American Universities, the American Council on Education, the North Central Association, and the American Association of University Professors, the last subsidized by a grant from the Carnegie Foundation for the Advancement of Teaching.[65]

The American Association of Colleges led off in 1926 with the appointment of a commission on the recruitment and training of college teachers.[66] The work of this commission reached its climax with its third report, in 1929, which recommended that graduate schools ascertain as early as possible which graduate students were planning careers in teaching rather than research. The commission also commended to graduate schools the relaxation of research requirements and the institution of an elective on progressive instructional and curricular movements.[67] There was no new report the next year but the previous one was raked with searing blasts from several influential graduate deans. Nor was the president of the Carnegie Corporation, Henry Suzzalo, able to save the day with his sensible observation that "it is a quite commonplace fallacy among them [college professors] to believe that presentation involving a dozen different techniques may be acquired without conscious effort and thoughtful attention. . . . Deliberate acquisition of skill is necessary.[68]

In spite of Suzzalo the graduate schools refused to relax requirements as they barricaded themselves against the introduction of education courses. Even eminent deans of schools of education like Charles H. Judd of Chicago and Melvin Haggerty of Minnesota opposed required education courses in the graduate school because they did not think there was as yet enough solid research in education to justify it. But Judd's suggestion to make improvement of college instruction a part of the improvement of instruction at lower levels as well ran cold shivers up the academic spine. Not only had professors never identified with teachers on lower rungs of the educational ladder but they feared the possible upward extension of state certification laws to college teaching.

Without trying to side-step responsibility for the avoidable shortcomings of college teaching, it was generally agreed on all sides that extenuating circumstances did account for some of the difficulties. The great expansion of college enrollments after the First World War made good teaching difficult by imposing larger classes, heavier teaching loads, and more administrative responsibilities on even the best instructors. Besides, digging deeper into the barrel of students of college age resulted in a student body of less stimulating academic ability. Teaching dunces in the elementary or secondary school is bad enough, but trying to teach a mature dunce, as Santayana ruefully remarked, is the last word.[69] The situation inspired the disquieting thought that there might be more students in college who could not learn than there were teachers who could not teach.

The rising tide of college enrollments which undercut standards of teaching after the First World War threatened to engulf them after the second. Statistics published in 1957 indicated that only 23 per cent of all new full-time college teachers held earned doctor's degrees. As this was a decline of 8 per cent from 1953 the country was becoming less and less prepared to meet the avalanche of students expected in the next decade. Conversely in the same period the number of new full-time teachers holding less than a master's degree rose from 10 per cent to 23 per cent. Private institutions were maintaining a higher average than municipal ones, and the latter were ahead of state universities, but the prospect for the future was still alarming. Little abatement of the alarm was to be found in the sampling of colleges on which the statistics were based. Of the thousand institutions invited to participate in the study over 80 per cent responded, and from their original number had been excluded junior colleges, theological seminaries, schools of pharmacy, optometry, and the like.[70]

With seeming premonitions of these dangers Howard Mumford Jones again indicted the graduate schools at the war's end for neglecting the problem of training future college teachers for careers in teaching and called on the schools to rethink the problem of graduate instruction.[71] Yet the most serious effort to rethink graduate education, an effort subsidized by the Carnegie Corporation, suggested a number of innovations but no serious ones on the professional study of education.[72] Furthermore, the Council of Graduate Schools, representing over two hundred graduate institutions, dealt an apparent *coup de grâce* in 1961 to any hope for substantial change. As spokesman for graduate study in the United States the council set standards for it along strictly traditional disciplinary lines.[73]

The prolonged student strike at the University of California in 1964–65, however, shook academic complacency on this and other issues. Tremors were felt all the way from Berkeley to New Haven and points in between. One result: Yale proposed a two-year master of philosophy degree and California a two-year doctor of arts for "ABD's" (graduate students who had completed "all but the dissertation").[74] These degrees were reminiscent of Yale's earlier policy of a two-year M.A. for teachers and corresponded to European practice where "candidate" is a recognized title for the "ABD." A year or two later the Ford Foundation gave $40,000,000 to ten universities with leading graduate schools for the improvement of graduate instruction, one phase of which was to better apprenticeship teaching of graduate assistants.[75]

In searching for ways to improve teaching in spite of these handicaps, a number of suggestions were put forward. Some favored a more careful selection of teaching personnel both before training and before placement.[76] While few were willing to relax subject-matter requirements for those accepted, not a few recommended that the subject-matter departments should give some attention to problems of teaching in their fields. It was suggested that some member of each department who himself was an especially good teacher should distill in a few meetings or lectures the secrets of successful teaching.[77] Or, after a young Ph.D. had been added to the staff, some senior professor should take upon himself the duty of visiting and supervising his inexperienced junior colleague.

Some made the more radical proposal of dividing graduate study into two doctorates, the traditional Ph.D. for those specializing in research and a new D.A. (Doctorate of Arts) for those planning careers in teaching.[78] Some hoped that a better crop of teachers might be harvested by having them forego intensive specialization and substitute in its stead a wide course of reading so that in teaching their fields they would be able to relate them meaningfully to a wide context of life.[79] Such a program would certainly afford a corrective to Dean West's complaint.

But the foregoing were but piecemeal palliatives. They underestimated the depth of undergraduate dissatisfaction with the quality of teaching they had been receiving, as witness the students' wanting tenure abolished as academic featherbedding and the haven of the incompetent. Hence students "wanted in" on the selection, promotion, and dismissal of their teachers. If the Council of Graduate Schools did not get the message, three important private foundations did— Carnegie, Danforth, and Lilly. Together they sponsored a report, *Faculty Development in a Time of Retrenchment,* which bore down once again on pedagogy as indispensable.[80] It opposed a two-track program for the doctorate because the prestige of the D.A. would inevitably lag behind that of the Ph.D. Instead the report favored a strong teaching component occurring *within* the normal span of the Ph.D. program. A strong teaching component, it went on to say, should include not only theoretical study of education but a teaching practicum under close supervision and free from other courses.[81]

As a matter of fact, from the conclusion of the First World War onward the higher study of the problems of higher education became a special field in the graduate schools of education of the leading universities of the country. There had been some demand for formal instruction in college teaching in the first decade of the twentieth century,[82] but William H. Cowley claims that G. Stanley Hall had already started giving instruction in the higher learning at Clark University as early as 1893.[83] Yet it was not till the third decade of the new century that such courses became general. After that the policy spread so rapidly that by 1936 there were three dozen institutions offering advanced study of the higher learning.[84] This number doubled and trebled after the Second World War. Most notable, perhaps, was the Carnegie Foundation's establishment of centers for the study of higher education at the University of Michigan, Columbia, and the University of California.

There was some confusion as to what direction this study of higher education should take.[85] As might be expected of a new field of study, much of the early content was little more than descriptive of contemporary practice; it lacked theory. It also lacked research as a base for practice. Oddly enough, academic disciplines seemed to have done research on nearly everything except academe itself. But the social disturbances of the late 1960s, especially those stirred up by the students themselves, brought a reversal here. Higher education came to be seen as unresponsive to the needs of the times. The resulting unrest challenged the legitimacy of higher education's presuppositions so basically that many thought it time to examine the multiplicity of postwar changes with a view to planning the rest of the century.

A number of top universities like California and Columbia conducted self-studies as springboards to new action.[86] Offering broader scope were several nationwide commissions which addressed themselves to the reform of higher education in general. One was the Assembly on University Goals and Governance, which seemed to seek guidance in a nostalgia for older forms of higher education.[87] Another more caustically critical of the contemporary situation was the Newman Report.[88] But by far the most comprehensive and thorough study of higher education ever undertaken in this country was made by the Carnegie Commission on Higher Education appointed in 1967. In the next several years it published its results in over sixty volumes.[89] The general tone of these volumes affirmed a faith in the traditional values of American higher education—its expansion, its increasing diversity, a cautious egalitarianism, and freedom to dissent. Some found fault with it, however, because it stated no embracing or integrating theory of higher education.[90]

In any event these publications made substantial additions to a modest literature of higher education which had blossomed in the 1930s[91] and which came to full bloom in the second half of the century in such books as Bernard Berelson's *Graduate Education in the United States,* Clark Kerr's *The Uses of the University,* Christopher Jencks's and David Riesman's *The Academic Revolution.*[92] Obviously these men were leaving behind the era in which the college professor had been willing to do research on nearly every human activity except his own. It was none too soon, for, with many universities operating under multi-million-dollar budgets, the conduct of higher education was rapidly moving out of the stage where its expertise could be learned on the job or in apprenticeship fashion as in the past.[93]

Reinforcing this new professionalism in higher education was the Association for Higher Education. This association had its genesis as one of the four constitutional departments set up by the National Education Association when it was founded in 1870. The department flourished till 1910, after which it steadily declined till 1924 when it was discontinued. In part the decline can be associated with the rise of such new organizations as the American Association of University Professors and the American Council on Education. Happily the department was revived again in 1942 just in time to afford professional leadership for the post-war boom in higher education. In 1950 the department changed its name to the Association for Higher Education though it still remained federated to the National Education Association. *Issues in Higher Education* has become its annual mouthpiece.

Professional Education and the Higher Learning

It has already been seen how the various professions, the older and the newer ones alike, improved the quality of their training by moving from an empirical to a theoretical stage. As they drew more and more strength from related disciplines, they came more and more to absorb the spirit of the higher learning of the graduate school of arts and sciences. The major characteristic of this spirit was the disinterested pursuit of knowledge on its own account. To qualify as a "learned" profession, therefore, some contended that professional study must be carried on at a strictly theoretical level. While it had undoubtedly been an advance to move from a narrowly practical to a broadly theoretical stage in professional preparation, to advance farther by abandoning the practical altogether required some argument.

Two points were made. On the one hand it was argued that concern with the practical is concern with the specific and the routine. The danger with pitching professional instruction at this level is that it has so limited a range of application and so quickly gets out of date. The decline of theological education President Hutchins of the University of Chicago ascribed to its increasing concern with the pastor's parish problems rather than the problems of theology itself. Law and medicine, therefore, he claimed further, should be closer to the university than to the court and the hospital.[94] Professional study, if it is to remain worthy of the higher learning and not be anti-intellectual, must treat of general principles and fundamental propositions. The commercial milieu of the university is a particular threat to the integrity of professional instruction because through its subsidies it tempts the faculty to subordinate investigation of general laws to finding specific answers for its problems.[95] Indeed, since professional education is more prone to succumb to practical exigencies, a man like Thorstein Veblen was even prepared to separate it altogether from the university, if need be, to preserve the integrity of the graduate school as a place for pure research.[96]

On the other hand Veblen also argued that professional concern with teaching was a second deterrent to the higher learning. The only instruction he would tolerate would be that which, combined with inquiry, helped to train the next generation of scholars. That there were other kinds of teaching, like undergraduate preparation for citizenship, he did not doubt. All he insisted on was that they be kept apart from instruction at the university level. The purpose of the undergraduate college is to drill and convey knowledge. It fits for the higher learning but is distinct from the higher learning itself. Moreover, while a student's health and morals might be a concern of lower schools, it was distinctly not a responsibility of the higher learning.[97] Therefore the difference between the undergraduate and graduate schools is more one of kind than one of degree. Consequently Veblen saw their continued connection in the unitary structure of the university as a "freak of aimless survival."

There was precedent for a university without an undergraduate college, but a university without professional schools would have run counter to traditions dating back to the medieval university. The medieval university, however, Veblen discounted as having emerged out of barbarian times when people were unmitigatedly, if necessarily, pragmatic in outlook. But to insist that the modern university retain this pragmatic quality, he maintained, was but to insist that it remain barbaric. From this position he was not even moved by the advantage, historically proved, that the professional schools and the graduate schools of arts and sciences had mutual need of each other, the professional school drawing on the graduate school for theoretical inspiration and the professional schools providing a context where academic theories might be tested.[98] Hutchins, together with Flexner, though sympathetic with Veblen's polemic against the practical, saw no reason to burn the barn to roast the pig. All that had to be done to retain the professional schools in the university, as they saw it, was to exorcise them of the practical by concentrating fully on the theoretical. To the argument that the medical school at least managed to combine the practical and theoretical in successful proportions, Hutchins took the position that it was an exception because the same conditions could be produced in the university hospital as off-campus in private practice. Similar conditions in law, engineering, or business simply could not be reproduced on the campus.[99]

In spite of this theoretical development of the role of theory in professional education, the great weight of custom favored striking a balance between the theoretical and practical aspects of the higher learning. Indeed there were those who justified in principle the importance of practice. Woodrow Wilson for one, the future president of Princeton, saw an advantage in the close connection between professional and liberal education,[100] and Alfred N. Whitehead, eminent professor of philosophy at Harvard, saw the importance of mating theory with practice in the university.[101]

11

The Federal Government and Higher Education

One of the most interesting aspects of the rise of American universities, both public and private, has been the relation of the federal government to their development. Although the United States Constitution nowhere gives the national government specific power to exercise authority over education in the various states, federal influence has been nevertheless steadily increasing. Examples of federal concern for higher learning can be found in the early years of the Republic, but the most extensive development of national interest in this field has occurred in the twentieth century and, more particularly, since the Second World War. The increasing complexity of modern life and the nation's growing involvement in world affairs have made this inevitable.

This, of course, is but one aspect of the emergence of the modern "positive state." The courts have come to interpret the "general welfare" clause of the Constitution so that Congress may make vast expenditures for purposes such as highways, public health, and education, with the discretion as to drawing the line between national and local welfare left in its own hands. The principal mechanism whereby the appropriations have been made is the federal grant-in-aid to the states. By this means, one authority suggests, the federal government "has become in many matters the architect of the policy administered by the states."[1]

One important qualification, however, must be kept in mind when we consider the relation of this burgeoning federal power to the world of higher education. We must recognize that federal activity before 1965 always operated on the periphery, never at the heart, of higher learning.[2]

Abortive Attempts at a National University

Although the federal government was reluctant to support higher education in general, the first movement to involve the federal government in higher education was of just this sort. This was the project to establish a national university. The proposal, which antedates the founding of the present federal government, has been repeatedly put forward, in one form or another, in the nineteenth and twentieth centuries.

In January, 1787, the Philadelphia physician and man of affairs Benjamin Rush published an article in which he called upon the nation to establish a postgraduate university at its capital city to foster advanced research and instruction of a utilitarian type.[3] Many other proposals of this nature were advanced during the later years of the eighteenth century and the early years of the nineteenth, reflecting the wave of nationalistic thinking which was sweeping the country after the success of the American Revolution. Notable among these plans was that published in 1806 by Joel Barlow, the renowned intellectual and United States minister to France. Following the pattern established by the French Revolution, he recommended placing a great national university at the top of a comprehensive system of American education. This federal institution would sponsor the two indispensable activities of a true university—teaching and research.[4]

At the Constitutional Convention in 1787, some delegates proposed that a definite clause be included in the document, enabling the United States Congress to establish a national university. This was dropped when it was argued that the federal government, having been given control of the capital district, would already possess all the powers necessary to take such action.[5]

The first six presidents of the United States were all agreed that a national university was a desirable project for the young Republic to undertake. In addition, Washington, Jefferson, Madison, and John Quincy Adams sent definite requests to Congress, asking it to establish such an institution.[6] Washington even left a special bequest to Congress in his last will and testament which was to be used exclusively for the purposes of a national university. State-rights sentiments in Congress, sincere doubts about the constitutionality of the proposed institution, and an undercurrent of anti-intellectualism combined to stymie all efforts to secure approval of a national university bill. As for Washington's bequest, it was ignored by the nation's legislators. The gift had consisted of fifty shares of the Potomac River Company; in 1828 the company collapsed and the shares became worthless.[7]

From the close of the administration of the second President Adams down to 1869, the national university movement was dormant. To be sure, in 1819 some friends of Joel Barlow's, seeking to carry out as much of his plan as possible, secured a Congressional charter for the Columbian College and Columbian Institution for the Promotion of the Arts and Sciences, both located in Washington, D. C. While the former eventually developed into the present George Washington University, for a long while it was just another small, privately endowed liberal-arts college, not the national graduate school and research institute which Barlow had contemplated.[8] There was a temporary revival of interest in the 1840s in connection with the debate in Congress as to what was to be done with the Smithson bequest.[9] But no more action resulted from this discussion than had eventuated from previous presidential recommendations, although the National Observatory, established in 1842 in Washington as a result of the persistent efforts of John Quincy Adams, and the Smithsonian Institution, finally organized in 1846, have been properly termed "offshoots of the national university concept."

The American public remained either apathetic or downright hostile to the original national university idea, despite the goodly company of prominent and persuasive spokesmen who supported it. The state-rights philosophy, which prevailed through much of the nineteenth century, helps to explain the movement's failure. A national university was too "federal" to suit the particularistic outlook of the time. It might even necessitate heavier federal taxation. American colleges from earliest colonial times had always been close to the particular states and localities whose interests they served; their constituencies and alumni were predominantly local or regional and no need was apparent for an institution which would be more broadly based. Then, too, the powerful religious denominations which controlled these colleges were hostile to a national university on the ground that it might become a center of secularism and irreligion.[10]

Despite the new surge of nationalism which swept the Republic after the Civil War, realization of the national university project remained as far away as ever. In fact, new obstacles had emerged by this time. The National Academy of Sciences had been established in Washington in 1863, a project of Senator Charles Sumner of Massachusetts, who believed he was following in the footsteps of Joel Barlow. The Johns Hopkins University had been chartered in Baltimore in 1875. Federal agencies such as the Department of Agriculture and the Bureau of Standards were beginning to set up their own research and specialist-training facilities. It was possible now for opponents of the national university to argue that it would merely duplicate the work of existing government bureaus and private universities.

That the movement got under way once again was due mainly to the dedicated purpose and vigorous agitation of one man, Dr. John W. Hoyt. An energetic editor, publicist, and educator, Hoyt spent over thirty years campaigning unceasingly for the cause.[11] He finally succeeded in persuading the National Education Association to endorse the project and secured the support of a number of members of Congress.[12] Beginning with a measure submitted in 1872, more than sixty bills for a national university were introduced in Congress during the next sixty years.[13] Presidents Grant and Hayes forwarded messages to Congress endorsing the measure.[14] Again no action resulted. Hoyt's most redoubtable opponent was President Charles W. Eliot of Harvard. Eliot opposed a national university on the ground that it would inject political interference from the central government into higher education and undermine individual freedom and initiative.[15] In this position, Eliot was supported by most of the presidents of the large private eastern universities and by supporters of the recently chartered American University in Washington, D. C.[16] On the other hand, prominent educators such as President White of Cornell, President Jordan of Stanford, and President Van Hise of Wisconsin endorsed the national university idea.[17]

Though bills for a national university continued to be submitted to Congress as late as the 1930s, it was clear that the movement had failed to generate the necessary momentum to succeed. If anything, the influence of the federal government, as exerted through the Morrill Acts, was to diffuse and scatter the state-sponsored portion of American higher education, rather than concentrate it. This reinforced the tendency already apparent in the private sector of higher education of duplicating "in the structure of higher education the multiple-government structure of American political federalism."[18] Thus the dream of the Fathers of the Republic to utilize federal power directly to sponsor higher learning in the nation's capital has not yet been realized.

The Service Academies

There was one area of higher education in which the federal government was reluctantly permitted by Congress to operate. This involved the establishment and maintenance of special academies for the armed forces. Although these institutions provoked considerable suspicion and opposition during their early years as representing an undemocratic caste system and an unwarranted exercise of federal power, their proponents had more success than the advocates of a national university. This was because it was possible to argue that the service academies represented a legitimate aspect of the obvious federal responsibility under the Constitution to defend the Union. It was, however, an uphill battle all the way. In the period of their inception, the service academies were little more than secondary schools. It was not until the twentieth century that they secured national accreditation as doing work of college grade and only then did political sniping at their activities die down.[19]

General Henry Knox, the nation's first Secretary of War, very early proposed systematic training for American officers. In 1800, Secretary of War James McHenry endorsed a plan for a group of schools to serve the needs of various branches of the armed services. In the state-rights atmosphere then prevalent, the only part of this plan carried out was the establishment in 1802 of the United States Military Academy at West Point.[20]

In the first years, West Point gave a rudimentary training which by no stretch of the imagination could be deemed collegiate. There were few buildings, no textbooks, no regular instruction. The pattern which prevailed was the same apprenticeship system under which most prospective lawyers and physicians were then trained.[21] Cadets served as apprentices to the military profession in the company of a preceptor. In 1817, this situation began to change when Brevet Major Sylvanus Thayer took over the superintendency of the academy. During the next sixteen years, Thayer established a four-year curriculum, divided the cadet corps into small sections for purposes of instruction and grading, posted marks weekly, and established a board of visitors to check up on the work of the institution.

Thayer had been sent by the War Department to France to study foreign methods of military and engineering education. He returned with a fine collection of maps and technical treatises, and also with a determination to transplant to West Point the methodology of the great École Polytechnique of Paris. This he accomplished with great success. Products of the Polytechnique, like Claudius

Crozet, were hired for the West Point faculty. Temporarily, engineering textbooks in the original French were employed. And the United States Military Academy emerged as the leading center in the country for the training of civil engineers up to the time of the Civil War.[22]

During these years, West Point graduates could be found on the engineering staffs not only of military and government projects but also of numerous private railroad, construction, and surveying companies. They played a prominent role in the organization of engineering departments at Harvard, Yale, Rensselaer, and a score of other educational institutions. Still the political sniping continued. It was charged that the academy was an undemocratic sanctuary maintained at federal expense for the sons of the wealthy. Thayer was obliged to resign his superintendency because of the coolness of President Jackson to the academy's policy of steadily raising admission requirements. Much of this criticism was silenced when Congress provided, in the 1840s, that cadets were henceforth to be appointed under a system of selection representing each Congressional district.[23]

In the early twentieth century, the admissions requirements and general academic standards of the academy were upgraded as part of Secretary Root's total reorganization of the United States Army following the Spanish-American War. Well it might be, for the government was now providing at West Point, as at other service academies, what amounted to a full four-year scholarship, covering both tuition and general expenses, for a combined college and professional course. In return, of course, all cadets were required to sign a pledge that they would serve in the armed forces for a certain number of years.[24]

Many of the same difficulties experienced by the Army in developing West Point were encountered by those interested in creating a similar institution for the United States Navy. The principal method of training naval officers during the early years of the Republic was again by apprenticeship. The argument in favor of "learning by doing" seemed to many even more irrefutable in the case of seamen than in that of the military. After all, Commodores MacDonough, Decatur, Perry, and Porter had all come up this way. Nevertheless a movement for systematic shore training got under way by 1821. A number of makeshift schools were set up at Navy yards where midshipmen on leave could "cram" for their examinations for promotion. Meanwhile Presidents and Secretaries of the Navy repeatedly called for establishment of a full-scale academy. Finally, in 1845, Secretary George Bancroft decided to establish the institution by his own fiat. Taking over old Fort Severn at Annapolis, Maryland, as a campus Bancroft detailed naval instructors and midshipmen there without bothering to ask for Congressional authorization or approval. Later this was forthcoming, anyway, as he had anticipated.[25]

Annapolis went through the same stages of gradual, but continuous, elevation of admission standards, lengthening of the course of study, and broadening of the curriculum as West Point. Again the scruples of Congressmen had to be overcome. They would have preferred to keep entrance requirements on a purposely elementary level so that American youths who had been otherwise denied educational opportunities would be able to attend. The development of the public-high-school movement took away much of the force of that argument. In addition, when the system of appointing midshipmen only by Congressional districts was established in 1852, it made the Navy a more national institution and increased the popularity of the academy. The equivalent at Annapolis of the Thayer regime was the superintendency of Vice-Admiral David D. Porter during the later 1860s. He found the institution a high school and left it a college. A tremendous expansion of plant and enrollment occurred in the early twentieth century as part of Theodore Roosevelt's general program for enlarging and strengthening the Navy. By this time the academy had become the basic collegiate unit in a wide-spread network of Navy schools offering a number of different types of specialized training.[26]

In the twentieth century, the principle of the national service academy, as represented by West Point and Annapolis, was so generally accepted in America that it was extended to other branches of the federal service. By 1900, the United States Coast Guard began to develop its own academy at New London, Connecticut, for the training of officer personnel. And by 1956, the federal government was annually expending $3,150,000 for the support of this institution. Similarly, the United States Maritime Administration, working in close collaboration with the Navy, established a Merchant Marine Academy at King's Point, New York. Finally, with the emerging importance of air power, it was inevitable that an Air Force Academy would be created. Congress authorized this step in 1954 and the first class of cadets was admitted in July, 1955. Important as it was, the new institution was but one in a complex network of Air Force educational institutions, collectively known as the Air University.[27]

The Impact of Wars on American Higher Education

The relation of the American federal government to higher education has been influenced markedly by the impact of the major wars in which the nation has participated. Although both the Revolutionary and the Civil Wars had their effects on the colleges, it was not until the twentieth century that the federal government became actively concerned with these results of war's turbulence.

There is no question but that the Revolutionary War had a disruptive influence on all aspects of American intellectual life, including the work of colleges. Scarcely one of the nine institutions founded before 1776 escaped some war damage. Students and faculty were dispersed, buildings either ravaged or converted for use as barracks and military hospitals, and finances exhausted. A majority of American college professors and college presidents ended up as rebels, though there were a number of prominent Tory or neutralist faculty members. As for the students, they appear to have been overwhelmingly pro-rebel.[28]

Conditions were not much better during the Civil War, particularly in the southern states. Colleges were practically emptied of students and professors, and institutions within the territory of the Confederacy, both public and private, were forced to close their doors. In the North, however, there was no such total disorganization of the higher learning. Indeed, many new institutions were founded. Yet the war left its mark. The federal government now directly entered the field of higher education with the passage of the Morrill Act and with this came the war-inspired requirement that there be military training in all colleges benefited by its provisions.[29]

The real impact of war on federal policy toward higher education came in the twentieth century. By this time, wars were becoming more "total," and a similar trend was apparent in the involvement of the federal government in the nation's affairs. Consequently, when college enrollments dropped sharply after America's entry into the First World War, Washington did not follow the same laissez-faire policy as in previous conflicts. The government was actively concerned because this drop threatened a shortage of scientists, technicians, and medical personnel which under modern circumstances might well prove disastrous. To meet this emergency, the federal government deferred from military service students who were receiving training in these vital fields.

Also, a Students Army Training Corps was set up "to prevent unnecessary and wasteful depletion of the colleges." Contracts were made with over 525 institutions for the "subsistence, quarter, and military and academic instruction" of college students who enlisted as cadet officers subject to being called to active service at such time as the War Department deemed it desirable. By October, 1918, more than 140,000 students were enrolled in this program. Meanwhile a closer partnership than ever before had been established between the federal government and the nation's colleges and universities.[30]

Many of the same problems faced the nation once again during the Second World War, only in a somewhat aggravated form. Faced by depleted enrollments and rising costs due to war conditions, the colleges were thrown into an even more desperate dependency on the federal government than during the first war. For its part, Washington followed much the same policy that it had pursued during 1917–18, deferring selected groups of students and setting up Army and Navy specialized training programs by contract with hundreds of educational institutions. As before, the existing faculty and plant of colleges participating in the program were utilized. By 1945, Army and Navy contracts accounted for as much as 50 per cent of the income of some men's colleges. In general, the federal government was tending to expand its investment in various university research projects and training programs as compared with what had been true twenty-five years before. And even more than in the First World War, the ultimate effect was to foster accelerated programs, cooperative research, the growing importance of technical and scientific studies, and the inundation of the colleges by such great numbers of students as had never been seen before.[31]

Peacetime Military Training in Colleges

One permanent heritage of war which remained in America's colleges was the maintenance of federal programs of military training in time of peace. This first made its appearance after the Civil War. Early Union military disasters like Bull Run motivated the inclusion in the Morrill Act of a section which stated that all land-grant colleges aided by the federal government must offer courses of military training. Regular officers of the United States Army were detailed to supervise this program at the "aggie" colleges. The purpose behind this legislation was to equip selected college men with the knowledge and experience necessary to qualify them to serve as officers in a possible emergency army. A small professional army was to be backed up by a large group of trained reservists.[32]

Although all land-grant institutions were required to maintain military training units, the Morrill Act left it to their discretion whether such training was to be made compulsory for all students. Many such colleges did indeed make military training compulsory, usually for two years. Others chose to maintain it on a voluntary basis. There were student protests against military drill in the 1880s at state institutions such as the University of Wisconsin and the University of Illinois. On the other hand, a number of non-land-grant institutions, before the First World War, on their own initiative set up military science units with War Department approval and cooperation. In all, 30,000 American college students were taking military training by 1914. By this date, too, the land-grant institutions had furnished three times more officers to the Army than West Point, including 50 general officers, 2,000 field officers, and 25,000 captains and lieutenants.[33]

As a result of the events of 1917 and 1918, this program was expanded to include all types of colleges throughout the land. The National Defense Act of 1920, which in turn amended and revised previous emergency legislation of 1916, was passed as a consequence of the nation's experiences in the European conflict. It provided for the establishment of a Reserve Officers Training Corps at schools, colleges, and universities. Student members of this corps were to take military training as part of their academic course under War Department supervision. The aim was to prepare future reserve and noncommissioned officers. By way of contrast with the pattern established under the Morrill Act, the program now applied to all colleges, public or private, which wished to participate in it. Once again, the local institution had the right to decide whether this military training was to be made elective or compulsory for all students.[34]

By 1926, 80,000 American students were enrolled in R.O.T.C. units. All was not smooth sailing, however. Almost from the first, peacetime military training in colleges had come under criticism. College presidents as eminent as Charles W. Eliot had objected to aspects of the program. Students at land-grant institutions such as Wisconsin had taken serious exception to compulsory military training under the Morrill Act. During the period between the two world wars of the twentieth century opposition of this kind reached a new peak of bitterness. Some students seem to have been motivated in their attitude by pacifism, others by radicalism. In any case, a number of colleges and universities were obliged at the height of this campaign to make military training optional. The rise of aggressive totalitarianism brought about a change in American student opinion. After Pearl Harbor, many student leaders who had sworn the "Oxford" oath never to bear arms were found fighting for the Four Freedoms in the armed forces of the United States.[35] R.O.T.C. continued to play an important part in the colleges after V-J day. During the academic year 1954–55 a total of 337 colleges had R.O.T.C. units of some kind, enrolling in all no less than 376,000 students.[36] But a decade later student disenchantment with the Vietnam War and the subsequent discontinuance of the military draft led to a severe setback to the whole R.O.T.C. program.

Federal Aid to Higher Education

As we have seen, from earliest times the United States developed a dual system of support and control in higher education. Two spheres of administration emerged, roughly equal in importance—one private and the other public. At the same time, an ever increasing amount of federal aid tended to give a certain advantage to publicly supported institutions. This trend, however, has had its principal effect in the period since 1890. Before this date, most arguments proposing a wider degree of federal participation in education were unsuccessful. Bills in Congress for general federal aid to schools regularly failed of passage. They went against an ingrained American suspicion of centralized governmental power.[37] After 1890, conditions changed. Industrialization and urbanization added new dimensions to American life. Not much government had been needed in the pioneer agricultural society of the early Republic; but now "a high degree of co-ordination, coercion, and restriction" was necessary to meet the complexities created by mass-production industrialism and major world power.[38] The concept developed that government must play a much larger role in providing for the people's welfare. The expanding role of federal power in higher education was but one facet of this total movement.

In the early years of the nation the policy of giving general federal assistance to higher education without federal control gained favor. Since land was the principal form of wealth then available to the government, the first federal donations for colleges were land grants to the new western states. This program actually went back to the university grants made to the Ohio and Scioto Companies in 1787, even before the present federal Constitution went into operation. It was continued when the Ohio Enabling Act was passed in 1802, and was followed, despite the protests of eastern states such as Maryland, upon the subsequent admission of every new western state. The Ohio act granted the state whole townships of federal land for the support of higher education. When Oregon and California were admitted, these grants were increased, and the Oklahoma Enabling Act made even more lavish provisions. In all, thirty-one states received federal grants for education under these acts.[39] Few conditions were imposed on the states. They were required, it is true, to make an accurate accounting of all federal grants received to show that the funds had been used for the general purposes of the appropriation. However, no attempt was made by the federal government to control the type of education that was to be given. This was left entirely to the states and local communities.[40] Another important point to be remembered is that the federal government during these years saw aid to education as a means rather than as an end in itself. Educational benefits remained essentially by-products of a policy that was intended primarily to facilitate the sale of public land, aid the growth of the newer western states, further the objectives of agricultural organizations, and balance the interests of both landed and landless states.[41]

This policy continued on into the later decades of the nineteenth century, but there was superimposed upon it, beginning with the Morrill Act of 1862, a new program of utilizing federal assistance as a means of stimulating special types of education within the states. During the next fifty years, subsequent federal legislation extended this new approach to the stimulation not only of state colleges of agriculture and mechanic arts but also of agricultural research (Hatch Act, 1887), university extension (Smith-Lever Act, 1914), and vocational education (Smith-Hughes Act, 1917). Under these various acts, federal officials in Washington came to control a formidable distribution of moneys for higher education in the states.[42] By 1930, it amounted to $23,000,000 a year. And the federal government was now taking the initiative, previously left to the states, of determining just what educational activities were to be aided by federal money.[43]

Opponents of the original Morrill Act had charged that it would only be an entering wedge for a vast extension of federal power. Subsequent events seemed to bear out this prediction. In 1854, President Franklin Pierce had vetoed a bill granting lands to the states for the benefit of the indigent insane which, from his "strict-constructionist" point of view, seemed unconstitutional. In 1859, President James Buchanan took a similarly narrow view of the "general welfare" clause when he vetoed as unconstitutional Morrill's initial bill for land-grant agricultural colleges. Congress had no authority to appropriate federal money to educate people within the several states, he argued. It could dispose of federal lands, but this did not mean it had the right to give them away. Its educational land grants to states as they entered the Union were, by contrast, constitutional because they had the effect of enhancing the value of the lands in those states still owned by the federal government. But how would an agricultural college in New York or Virginia facilitate the sale of public lands in Minnesota or California?[44]

With the coming of the Civil War an enormous impetus was given to a more nationalistic interpretation of the federal government's power. The Morrill Act was now passed, along with a number of other measures which had previously been blocked by those upholding what they maintained were the exclusively reserved powers of states. The Morrill Act was significant because it initiated the practice of using federal grants-in-aid to achieve certain specific objectives desired by the federal government. This was to prove a powerful weapon during subsequent years in developing various federally controlled programs to improve the "general welfare." The act introduced also the principle of equalization of opportunity, a concept which was to become normative for most federal legislation dealing with education in the twentieth century. This was done by means of taking land from the landed states and giving it to the landless states for educational purposes.[45]

Although the Morrill Act granted large tracts of federal land to states willing to establish colleges of a specified type, there were strings attached. It was provided that none of the grant was to be used for construction of buildings. Thus, the states would have to spend money of their own in order to take advantage of the act. Here was a beginning of the "matching dollars" concept, later developed to a much higher degree.

In subsequent aid to higher education, Congress faced an increasing dilemma. It did not wish to exceed the constitutional limits of its jurisdiction; yet it wished to ensure that the vast grants of federal funds which were now being made would not be misused. Thus, when the Hatch Act was passed in 1887, establishing agricultural experiment stations in connection with the land-grant colleges, an attempt was made to work out a compromise solution. The Commissioner of Agriculture was given certain supervisory powers, greater than anything included in the original Morrill Act. Although he had no power of direct coercion, annual reports and statements of expenditures had to be rendered to him by each experiment station. The states remained in full control of the stations and the land-grant colleges to which they were attached. However, the federal government could, in subsequent years, refuse annual appropriations to the stations if it so chose. This tightening federal control was carried further by the Adams Act of 1906, which limited the types of research to be done and concentrated more supervisory power in the hands of the Secretary of Agriculture. Thus, the conditions of the federal educational grants, during the last century, tended to become increasingly exacting, while their purposes became more and more specific. According to one observer, "It can be said . . . that federal assistance to higher education in the nineteenth century moved from a single, broad scale program of endowment grants to support education to a series of piecemeal efforts to aid education through a broad range of special-interest programs."[46]

When Congress in 1890 passed a second Morrill Act which provided annual federal expenditures for the land-grant colleges, it included more restrictions than had been incorporated in the original act. For one thing, no money was to go to states which denied the education in question to persons because of race. Such education might, however, be provided in "separate but equal" institutions. Secondly, the annual monetary grant could be withheld in the case of any state which failed in any other way to maintain in its institution the standards set by federal law. Thus the "matching dollars" principle was set up as an annual going concern. Finally, a significant portion of the legislation pertained to the curriculum. The original Morrill Act, while specifying that land-grant colleges should teach agriculture and the mechanic arts, had stated that this provision should not be taken to exclude scientific and classical studies. The act of 1890, in contrast with this, enumerated more specifically, and more narrowly, the subject-matter fields for which alone the annual federal appropriations could be used.[47]

However, the federal government established no extensive machinery under the second Morrill Act for supervision or inspection of the institutions which used its funds. Basic administrative control still remained in local hands. The whole trend of the next half-century, however, was in the direction of greater federal insistence on the right to supervise the use by states of the vast sums distributed for education and social welfare purposes. This was illustrated by measures like the Smith-Hughes Act and the Bankhead-Jones Act. Federal control was coming to be more and more of a direct result of federal aid. This did not mean that the federal government had evolved a clearly defined, coherent policy on higher education. Quite the contrary. Actually, what had happened was that a number of federal acts dealing with special aspects of higher education had been passed. These had been pushed through in many cases solely by the lobbying of special pressure groups and were the result of factors other than purely educational ones. In no respect could they be said to be implementations of a comprehensive national blueprint for the encouragement of higher learning.[48]

One further point is that through most of the history of federal aid to education, funds were granted directly to the states or to public institutions through the states. It was not until the 1930s that Washington began to grant assistance in peacetime to private institutions, with which it commenced to deal directly. Even then, it did so by dispensing funds to individuals attending institutions of learning, rather than to the institutions themselves. This practice was nevertheless a departure in federal policy because the educational institutions, both private and public, disbursed these funds to the students and in most cases received the money back as payments for tuition and other expenses.

The first federal program to assist individual students as such to attend institutions of higher education was conducted by the National Youth Administration from 1935 to 1943. During this period, the federal government spent over $93,000,000 on the higher education of 620,000 students. This program would probably never have gone into effect had it not been for the disturbed economic conditions created by the great depression of the 1930s. It was motivated more by temporary economic considerations than by any purposeful plan to give federal aid to college students.[49]

Again due to unusual circumstances, this time brought about by American involvement in the Second World War, the federal government came forward in the 1940s with another program designed to help students attend college. This was set in motion by the provisions of the so-called G.I. Bill of Rights, officially known as the Servicemen's Readjustment Act of 1944. Here again the payment was technically to the individual students, although in actuality it went to the various institutions of higher learning, private and public, in which they were enrolled. The G.I. Bill was obviously motivated by national concern over a specific problem, namely, the welfare of veterans. It constituted one part of a great complex of veterans' benefit legislation which had, by this time, become traditional in American politics. It definitely did not signify a final and purposeful national commitment to the principle of continuing federal aid for all deserving college students, nonveteran as well as veteran. The same observations could be made with respect to Public Law 550 of 1952, passed to aid the veterans of the Korean War. Yet, taken together, these two acts represented the largest scholarship grant to that point in the history of American higher education. Billions of federal dollars were spent on the higher education of millions of veterans.[50]

With the development of vast programs of contract research in the middle of the twentieth century, the federal government began at last to deal directly with all types of institutions of higher learning. As we have seen, federal interest in university research went back at least as far as the Hatch Act of 1887, and began to increase during 1917 and 1918. The impact of the Second World War led Washington to assume 83 per cent of the nation's total research budget in the natural sciences. By 1950, a dozen or more federal agencies were spending over $150,000,000 a year for contract research at various American colleges and universities.[51] Ten years later this figure had mounted to $450,000,000. Here again we have an example, not of a general and permanent federal policy, but of a special program motivated by the government's vital interest in national defense.[52]

Federal policy operated in this respect to reinforce a trend which was already well established in American higher education. For some time it had been apparent that creative American scholars were being produced by only a small group of American colleges. Indeed a study of the situation as it existed immediately following World War II revealed that not more than fifty institutions out of eight hundred granting baccalaureate degrees produced significant numbers of people who became productive research scholars. The authors of this study concluded that the situation "seems . . . to approach a monopoly and to leave undeveloped and unproductive large segments of the American system of higher education."[53]

Reactions to this vast program of federal subsidization were mixed. In 1962 Harold Orlans made a study for the Brookings Institution of the effects of the federal program upon thirty-six universities and colleges. His conclusion was that the government's expenditures benefited the natural sciences greatly and certain social sciences considerably, while having negligible effects on the humanities. Furthermore, it had concentrated the most able faculty and many of the best students at a few leading institutions. The study noted that: "The Government (and vaster historical forces) has divided the liberal arts faculty into a contingent of relatively young scientists and social scientists with lighter teaching loads, higher income, substantial research support, and other perquisites, and another contingent of older humanists, with heavier teaching loads, lower incomes, and little research support."[54]

Another new area of operation for the government where federal funds went directly to higher educational institutions was that of college buildings, student dormitories, supplies, and equipment. After the close of the Second World War the Surplus Property Act of 1944 and subsequent legislation donated or sold at large discounts millions of dollars' worth of surplus military supplies and buildings to colleges hard pressed by the sudden wave of veteran enrollments. Here, then, was a temporary expedient designed to supplement the G.I. Bill of Rights.

The program was put on a more permanent basis in 1950 when Congress passed a bill authorizing the Housing and Home Finance Agency to make up to $300,000,000 in long-term loans to colleges, private as well as public, for the erection of dormitories.[55]

By 1962 over $2,000,000,000 had been loaned under this program to colleges and universities for the construction of dormitories or other revenue-producing facilities. Meanwhile demands were voiced for broader-based federal loans. Estimates were presented that with enrollments expected to double in the 1960s as much as $20,000,000,000 might be needed for capital replacement and for expansion, not just of dormitories, but of classrooms, laboratories, and libraries. The response to this appeal from leaders of the nation's colleges and universities came when Congress passed the Higher Education Facilities Act of 1963 and made available greatly expanded financial support. This bill provided a wide variety of federal loans and grants for the construction of dormitories and many other types of academic facilities (including classrooms and laboratories) for graduate schools, colleges, and technical institutes.[56]

It is notable, too, that the federal government continued a practice, begun during the Second World War, of utilizing a number of colleges and universities for the in-service training of federal personnel. This became another area where contracts were negotiated directly between the federal government and the individual institutions. In 1950, more than 60,000 federal employees, the bulk of whom were in the armed services, were receiving in-service training of this type at various colleges.[57]

Furthermore, the federal government undertook to give thousands of persons advanced training in schools and special courses of its own. This was done with the objective of increasing the competence and efficiency of federal personnel. In addition to the service academies and postgraduate military schools, a number of civilian departments gave training of this kind. In 1947, 85,000 persons were receiving some type of higher education in federally operated schools. The majority of these, again, were in the armed forces.[58]

We conclude this survey of the vast, swiftly expanding federal involvement in higher education by noting two special aspects. First, besides controlling and financing public education of all grades in the District of Columbia, including the local teachers' colleges, the federal government, ever since the nineteenth century, regularly made appropriations to certain private institutions in the federal district, notably Gallaudet College for the deaf and Howard University. By the 1950s the largest part of the budget of the latter institution was provided by the federal government. Second, the federal government through the Fulbright Act (1940), the Smith-Mundt Act (1948), and the "Point Four" Program (1950) sponsored a great number of activities in higher education involving other countries, including the exchange of students, professors, and specialists, the provision of travel and maintenance grants for study overseas, and the development of technical improvement programs staffed by academic personnel.[59]

Thus largely by piecemeal methods, involving immediate responses to the demands of pressure groups or the needs of particular departments, the federal government had carved out for itself, by the middle of the twentieth century, a domain in the higher learning far exceeding the wildest dreams of those who had advocated a national university in the early days of the American Republic. A careful student of the problem found that the total federal financial investment in higher education for the fiscal year 1947 amounted to $2,475,387,000. This was one-half of the total income in that year of all American colleges and universities![60] Some of this total, to be sure, was made up of payments under the G.I. Bill which were later cut back. Nevertheless, this remained an astounding figure.

By 1960 the federal government was spending for research programs alone over $750,000,000 a year in educational institutions and allied research centers. "Research and related activities, then, conducted in or under the auspices of colleges and universities," commented two contemporary students of this phenomenon, "are virtually dominated financially by the Federal Government."[61] Additional hundreds of millions were being dispensed annually in grants to university students by the National Science Foundation and the National Institutes of Health and under the National Defense Education Act of 1958 in student loans to undergraduates, graduate fellowships, and subsidies to university-based teacher-training programs.

The federal government had, by means of many specific programs, become the largest single source of support for America's colleges and universities.

The President's Advisory Commission and Its Report

Despite the rapid development of activities of the federal government in higher education, there was a widespread feeling at the mid-point of the twentieth century that these were not comprehensive enough. Powerful bodies of opinion began to call for a program of much more extensive and direct federal financial aid to colleges and universities. In part, this discontent was due to the leaping costs of higher education, especially in the 1940s. In part, it was motivated by the necessity for tremendous expansion of physical facilities in order to meet the huge increases in enrollment which followed the First and Second World Wars.[62] An underlying factor, unquestionably, was the fundamental American commitment, going back to the age of Jefferson and Jackson, to maintenance of equality of educational opportunity as an underpinning of political and economic democracy. As American society reached new levels of complexity, many felt that the democratic opportunities for an education, which had been made well-nigh universal on the elementary and secondary levels, should now include postsecondary training. This was held to be the chief avenue of social mobility which remained open in an industrial and technological age. The experience with the National Youth Administration program had revealed what many felt to be a very unequal distribution of educational opportunity in the United States.[63] Experience with the G.I. Bill of Rights confirmed the feeling that the federal government must do something to maintain the wider opportunity which it had provided as a sustaining feature of peacetime. Leaders of higher education had approached these questions cautiously during the 1930s, but by the period following the Second World War, opinion was crystallizing in favor of a general program of federal aid to higher education.[64]

In July, 1946, President Truman appointed a commission of twenty-eight distinguished citizens under the chairmanship of George F. Zook, president of the American Council on Education.[65] This commission was asked to "re-examine our system of higher education in terms of its objectives, methods, and facilities; and in the light of the social role it has to play." The commission's report was issued in six volumes, appearing between December, 1947, and February, 1948, under the general title, *Higher Education for American Democracy.*

The main proposal of the commission was that all barriers to educational opportunity be abolished immediately. Every American should be "enabled and encouraged to carry his education, formal and informal, as far as his native capacities permit."[66] In order to attain this objective the commission proposed that the nation plan to double its enrollment in college and universities within a decade. By 1960, it conceived of a potential enrollment of 4,600,000 in institutions of higher education, including 2,500,000 at the freshman-sophomore level, 1,500,000 at the junior-senior level, and 600,000 graduate students. The reason for this projection was the commission's estimate that "at least 49 per cent of our population has the mental ability to complete 14 years of schooling," and "at least 32 per cent of our population has the mental ability to complete an advanced liberal or specialized professional education."[67] The commission assumed that the great majority of individuals with these potentials would ordinarily wish to pursue advanced study, but that many were prevented from doing so by economic handicaps, or by racial, religious, and geographical barriers.

To overcome these handicaps, the commission proposed, first of all, that the American system of free public education be extended upward to include two more years of study beyond the high school. Every state should establish "community colleges" as part of its public-school system to provide easily accessible free education through the sophomore year. These local institutions would emphasize terminal programs in their course of study, but they would also prepare some students to go on to higher levels.

In addition to this basic proposal, the commission recommended that a federal program of college scholarships be established "for at least 20 per cent of all undergraduate non-veteran students."[68] Also, it believed that great numbers of national fellowships should be awarded for graduate study. It called, moreover, for specific legislation to prevent racial and religious discrimination in the selection of college and university students.

Operating on the assumption that the great expansion of facilities for higher education would come in public institutions, the commission proposed that federal financial aid be appropriated to the states to be distributed to publicly controlled colleges and universities to help them meet current expenditures. At the same time, it was recommended that there be a program of federal grants to such institutions for capital outlay.[69]

Minority groups on the commission dissented in the case of two points raised in the report. Four members disagreed with the commission's demand for a ban on racial segregation in public institutions of learning, and two Catholic members protested against the recommendation that federal funds for general expenses and physical plant be appropriated only to publicly controlled institutions.[70]

The publication of this report, as might have been expected, stirred widespread debate among American educators. Many questions were discussed pro and con. Were the statistics used by the commission in reaching its estimates of potential college enrollments reliable? Were there really that many young people of college age competent to pursue a higher education? Do such great numbers really wish to continue their education beyond high school? Was it a question of economic and other barriers or lack of motivation? Would higher education for such large numbers lead to the elevation of national standards or the reduction of all higher learning to a general level of mediocrity? Could the nation afford the cost? Would there be sufficient vocational opportunities for so many highly trained persons? What would be the place in this program of the private institution, the denominational institution, the institution maintaining forms of racial segregation?[71] Would extensive federal aid be followed by tight federal control, extinguishing that freedom which had allowed local institutions to remain flexible and experimental and to make unique contributions to American education?[72] Was the federal government, which was now making vast contributions to public services such as highway construction, social security, agricultural prosperity, hospitals, and military preparedness, contributing comparable support to higher education?[73]

In any case, the argument remained largely academic during the first few years after the commission's report. The two veterans' education bills, Public Laws 346 and 550, kept the colleges well filled, and continuing huge requirements of national defense subordinated other issues. Yet, with the ending of the impact of the Korean "G.I. Bill" and the approach of a greater wave of enrollment than even that of the 1920s or the later 1940s, demands were renewed for implementation of at least some aspects of the commission's ambitious plan.

One response to the growing anxiety came in 1956 when President Eisenhower appointed a Committee on Education Beyond High School. This committee, headed by Devereaux C. Josephs, chairman of the board of the New York Life Insurance Company, was generally more conservative than the Zook Commission in assessing the federal government's role in higher education. Its recommendations concerned the introduction of more order and continuous scrutiny into the administrative and policy-making apparatus of the federal government in this field. These suggestions were spectacularly spotlighted by the propulsion of the first Russian satellite into space in 1957. Federal aid to higher education now had the highest priority. The National Defense Education Act, which incorporated some of the Josephs Committee's recommendations into its framework, was enacted by Congress the following year.

It was not until 1965, however, that Congress responded to the long campaign for federal aid by passing an act which was probably the most comprehensive national measure concerning colleges and universities up to that time. In the past, the federal government had always refused to acknowledge any direct and permanent responsibility for a uniform and coordinated program in the field of higher education. Moreover, many of the special federal grants which had been made to the nation's universities had related, in one way or another, to graduate study and research. The Higher Education Act of 1965 was the first federal measure to provide a broad permanent program of financial aid to both public and private colleges as well as to individual college students. Its major emphasis was on a coordinated program to aid the undergraduate student and to cope with the problems created for undergraduate colleges not only by rising enrollments but by the rising aspirations of young people from every social class.

The omnibus act of 1965 authorized federal financing to enable colleges and universities to assist in the solution of community problems such as housing, public health, and poverty by means of research, university extension, or continuing education programs. It established a program whereby federal funds would be appropriated to help institutions of higher education improve and expand their libraries. It made provision for federal assistance to help raise the quality of developing colleges that "for financial and other reasons are struggling for survival and are isolated from the main currents of academic life." National Teaching Fellowships were established to encourage graduate students and junior faculty members to teach at such institutions. Four types of federal assistance were provided to academically qualified students in financial need, including Educational Opportunity Grants, an expanded program of low-interest insured loans, and increased college programs offering the opportunity for part-time employment. Fellowships were established for the university training of those who wished to enter or re-enter the field of elementary or secondary education. Finally, the legislation made available financial assistance for the acquisition by colleges of laboratory equipment, audio-visual materials, and television equipment and materials for the improvement of undergraduate instruction.[74]

In the early 1970s the federal government's involvement in higher education became even deeper and more far-reaching. As we have seen, Washington began at this time to put into effect a sweeping "Affirmative Action" program which was designed to ensure that colleges and universities gave equal treatment to women and members of minority groups in every phase of their operations. Federal grants would be withheld from institutions found to be unsatisfactory in this regard. This program was significant, but even more important was the Higher Education Act of June 23, 1972. This measure established three major categories of federal aid to colleges. For the first time in the history of the United States, Congress authorized direct federal monetary grants to nearly all institutions of higher education with no strings attached. The schools could use these funds in any way that they chose. In addition, the legislation established that, as a matter of national policy, any college student who could not afford the cost of his education was entitled to get some financial help from the federal government. Such grants were not to exceed $1,400 per student, however. Finally, the already-established student loan program was renovated by the provision that a new agency, the National Student Loan Association, would purchase existing student loans from banks, thus enabling the banks to make additional loans with fresh capital. The total cost of the new program was estimated at more than $20 billion. Thus, the federal government had emerged by 1972 as the principal financier of America's programs of higher education. Certainly no more important federal measure in the field of higher education had been enacted for more than a century.[75]

PART IV

HIGHER EDUCATION IN

THE TWENTIETH CENTURY

12

Articulation of Secondary and Higher Education

So far little attention has been paid to the transition from secondary school to college. Never an easy passage and always the subject of faculty debate, it did not reach the stage of professional discussion till the end of the nineteenth century, when it managed to hold public attention for a score or more years. Ever since colonial times there had been considerable diversity in the way boys prepared for college. Some came up through the Latin grammar school, others through its successor, the academy. Still others tutored, often under some clergyman. Rare individuals like John Muir at a much later time were self-taught.[1] Diversity of preparation presented no particular difficulties in early times, when a candidate's proficiency was tested in relatively few subjects, generally the staples of Latin and Greek.

Confusion only arose when subjects began to multiply, giving scope for each college to emphasize its own idiosyncrasies. Then an academic snarl occurred, and it was some time before order began to appear. Search for a principle of order was far-reaching because it raised questions not only about who was qualified to cross the line separating secondary and higher education but about where that line should be drawn and about what should be taught on each side of it. The discussion of these questions even had a remote reaction on the articulation between college and postgraduate instruction. We turn now to see how this snarl was unraveled.

Obstacles to Smooth Articulation

As long as the college curriculum remained classical there was little occasion for entrance requirements in anything but Latin and Greek. Indeed, to these languages only one new subject for admission was added in the eighteenth century. In 1745 Yale began examining candidates in arithmetic, a precedent followed by both Princeton and Columbia when they were founded. But in the early part of the next century, as the classical curriculum made more and more concessions to modern subjects, proficiency was demanded one by one in three new subjects:

geography, history, and English—grammar and composition at first and literature somewhat later.[2] After the Civil War appeared requirements in modern foreign languages and science as well. Yet, though these new subjects were supposed to test competence to pursue a more modern curriculum, faculties still had more confidence in the older subjects to assure students of college caliber. Thus, paradoxically enough, the Sheffield Scientific School at Yale in its early days made Latin but not science one of its requirements of admission.[3]

Yale's idiosyncrasy here is only one example chosen from among the many colleges that made it difficult for secondary schools to know how to prepare their graduates for college entrance. Colleges were anything but uniform in their demands.[4] For a while Yale required botany and Columbia both physics and chemistry, but Princeton had no science requirements at all. Colleges requiring much the same subjects might differ on the amount of each. They might agree on expecting four years of Latin, but disagree on which authors the candidate should have read or, as in the case of Cicero, which of his orations should have been covered. Colleges sometimes even prescribed the author of the grammar by which the candidate was to prepare himself. In the institutions which admitted by written examination there were often arbitrary differences in grading. Mathematics, for example, might be a "terror" at one institution and a comparative "snap" at another. Obviously high schools and even academies could not make general preparation to meet such a diversity of demands without having almost as many senior classes as colleges for which their graduates were preparing.

If it was difficult for the college preparatory student to make the transition from secondary school to college, it was even more so for the student who, when he entered the lower school, had expected to go no further. In this category there were more than a few since a main purpose in founding academies and high schools had been to provide a terminal secondary education. Indeed the early high school was often known as the "poor man's college." Often, however, expectations changed between entrance into and graduation from secondary school. Perhaps unanticipated intellectual abilities came to the surface or perhaps the economic circumstances of a boy's family improved to awaken college aspirations. Commendable as such aspirations were, colleges usually were so independent, so bent on maintaining a high standard, that they saw no way to satisfy them. In fact eastern colleges in particular suffered from a hardening of entrance requirements resulting in an acute academic sclerosis that obscured their seeing the possibility of the academic college as the logical continuation of the "poor man's college."

A discontinuity seemed to reign between secondary school and college, a discontinuity made the more disrupting by differences of opinion on how to reduce it. Many thought the colleges should use their entrance requirements to compel secondary schools for their own good to come up to a higher scholastic level.[5] A few, like President Bascom at the University of Wisconsin, proposed adapting requirements to the existing state of secondary education. "We should," he claimed, "as soon think of making a tree taller by pulling it half way out of the ground, as to seek to add to the dignity of our State University by conditions of admission beyond the reach of her intermediate schools."[6] Still others tried to reduce discontinuity, not by demanding changes in the secondary schools but by bringing about changes in the college. For students not possessing the traditional college preparatory training some colleges offered an alternative to the traditional liberal curriculum together with an alternative degree such as the bachelor of science or bachelor of philosophy.[7] But this alteration returned to plague its sponsors because, as if obeying an academic Gresham's law, it tended to drive down traditional entrance requirements too.[8]

The difficulty of moving in any direction was aggravated by the relatively low state of secondary schools themselves. Old-established academies, especially in New England, were doing effective college preparation, but there were not enough of them. Besides, in the later nineteenth century they were rapidly being supplanted by the high school as the characteristic American secondary school. Yet the high school of the period, for all its expansive zest, seemed to expend its strength like an adolescent on physical growth and to lack the qualitative stamina which was to come with age. Consequently in the last quarter of the century a gap seemed to yawn between the end of the high school and the beginning of the college course. The latter seemed to begin at some distance beyond where the former left off. Some states, like California, had themselves to blame. In a short-sighted show of democracy they assigned the major share of their school revenues to their elementary schools and thus enjoyed the incongruity of a relatively rigorous system of elementary and higher education without a steady stepping-stone between the two.[9]

In other far western states, such as Washington, Oregon, Idaho, and Wyoming, population was too sparse for strong high schools to arise. But the gap was by no means peculiar to the younger states. In any event, to bridge this gap a number of colleges established "preparatory departments."[10] But the device was not too satisfactory because of the temptation to give college credit for work done at the preparatory level. How prolonged and serious this gap was can be seen from the fact that as late as 1915 there were still 350 institutions reporting preparatory departments to the United States Commissioner of Education.[11]

To compound the difficulty of articulation between secondary school and college still further, it must be said that not a few colleges were themselves little more than secondary schools. Unless this had been so a late-nineteenth-century observer could not have written, "The University requirements are now for entrance what they were fifty years ago for graduation, and the average age of matriculation is now above eighteen years, the time at which our grandfathers were graduated."[12] On the frontier the situation may have been even worse. When Iowa State College opened its doors just before the Civil War, it required entrants to be fourteen years of age, to be able to read and write English with ease, and to pass a satisfactory examination in the fundamentals of arithmetic! Even a decade after the war entrance requirements were still of no more than grammar-school grade—geography, arithmetic, grammar, reading, and spelling. Failing in these, the student was entered in the "preparatory department" (which must have been little better than an elementary school).[13] But these were not just the exigencies of the frontier. Only a generation earlier Francis Wayland was railing against admitting fourteen-year-olds to the Brown campus. They should stay at least two years longer at secondary school, he claimed, because even the brightest of them who succeeded in graduating at eighteen were just then prepared to start all over.[14]

Perhaps the most concrete evidence of maladjustment between secondary school and college was the large number of "conditioned" students who were being accepted into college. As late as 1907 over half of the freshmen matriculating at Harvard, Yale, Princeton, and Columbia had failed to meet their entrance requirements in one particular or another.[15] To some extent, of course, this failure was due to lack of foresight on the part of the student or those guiding his academic destinies in secondary school. But in part the failure was due to excessive variety of requirements. Further, colleges themselves were often at fault because of the discrepancy between the requirements they announced and the ones they actually enforced.[16] Sometimes competition for students, spurred by financial need, caused them to compromise their own requirements. At other times college admission authorities were confronted with a choice between the most promising boys and the boys who had studied certain subjects.[17]

Standardizing College Entrance

The obstacles to the smooth articulation of secondary school and college just described were too intolerable to go long unattended. In one direction the effort at remedy took the form of admission on the diploma or certificate of the secondary school. The University of Michigan seems to have been the first to adopt this practice in 1870. Her model was the practice of German universities in accepting the product of German gymnasia.[18] But of course there was much greater uniformity among German than American secondary schools. To have admitted only on the local diploma in the United States at the time would have risked serious abuse by struggling colleges striving to increase their enrollments. To avoid this pitfall Michigan adapted the German practice to local American conditions by sending representatives of its faculty to visit and inspect individual high schools at regular intervals. This scheme had several advantages. In the first place it drew the secondary school and college closer together by minimizing the barriers between them. High schools were stimulated to better work and colleges learned to comprehend the problems of secondary schools. In the second place the system was more fair both to the student going on to college and to the one remaining behind. The former was judged on his four-year effort rather than the effort of a few hours of examinations.[19] The latter benefited because his teacher did not have to sacrifice him to find time to prepare his college-bound classmate for a crucial final-examination hurdle.[20]

Other states followed Michigan's lead. But salutary as the system was within state boundaries, it did not reach students who wished to cross those boundaries to attend the college of their choice. Neither was it altogether adapted to private secondary schools and colleges. To meet these needs regional associations were formed. In the Middle West the need was met by the formation of the North Central Association in 1894.[21] Precedent for regional standardization of entrance requirements, however, already existed a decade earlier in the formation of the New England Association of Colleges and Preparatory Schools. Later on associations were formed for yet other regions such as the southern and Middle Atlantic states.

In a second direction the remedy for chaotic entrance requirements took the shape of uniform examinations. Probably the "Regents" examinations in New York were the first to perform such a standardizing function. In 1878, in response to a request from the principals of academies, the New York Board of Regents undertook to examine the work of secondary schools in order to establish proper standards of scholarship not only for graduation from secondary school but for admission to the several colleges of the state. Two years later the state took a second step by publishing syllabuses to furnish guidance to schools preparing students for the Regents' examinations.[22] There seems little doubt that these examinations had a beneficial effect in stimulating secondary schools and a unifying effect on the diversity of college demands. Yet Harvard's president, Charles W. Eliot, was not altogether happy about them. Writing after the examinations had been in use a dozen years, he objected to the fact that there were no educators on the Board of Regents and that the maximum salary paid Regents' examiners was insufficient to ensure competence in examination construction.[23]

The most notable effort at a uniform set of examinations was that proposed by Nicholas Murray Butler in the 1890s at a meeting of the Association of Colleges and Secondary Schools of the Middle States and Maryland. On that occasion Butler urged drawing up a uniform set of college admission requirements and the formation of a joint board of examiners. Some defenders of the chaotic laissez-faire policy in the past feared that the formation of such an agency might lead to dictating to the individual colleges whom they should accept and reject. This opposition was silenced when Eliot, who was present, pointed out that the object of the proposed organization was merely to obtain uniformity in requirements and in examinations. The autonomy of any individual institution remained intact, he pointed out amidst laughter, to admit only those who failed if it wished. After that Butler carried the day, and his proposition soon took the concrete form of what was to become the College Entrance Examination Board. In addition to uniformity the examinations of this board offered the further advantages of being held at many geographical centers and not just on the campus of the institution the candidate desired to enter. Moreover, colleges which accepted the results of the board were able to make significant savings of both time and money previously expended on their own individual tests.[24]

The first examinations set by the board were composed with the greatest care in order to win the early confidence of the colleges relying on them. Also, to gain the trust of the lower schools, a secondary-school representative sat on each subject-matter examining committee. Even so confidence came slowly, especially at the more conservative seats of learning. If it came slowly it came nonetheless surely. In its first year of operation the board examined 973 candidates; five years later it examined more than twice that many.[25] Only two institutions, Columbia and New York University, had the courage forthwith to abandon their own examinations. Yale early but hesitantly offered to accept the board's examinations if it could reread and regrade the results, but the board's self-respect would not submit to such terms. Even after the board's first decade of existence Harvard, Yale, and Bryn Mawr were themselves still examining more candidates than they were accepting through the College Entrance Examination Board.[26]

After the brilliant success of psychological testing in the First World War, the College Entrance Examination Board took an increasing if cautious interest in this new form of measurement. The examinations it had set up to this point had been tests of ability to assemble information, power of expression, intelligent appreciation, and courage to express independent judgment. To supplement but not supplant these measures of a candidate the board now sought added tests to estimate his potentiality and his aptitude.[27] By using a combination of test results it became possible to anticipate college success—to save the prospective misfit from the humiliation of failure at college, to search out the gifted early, and to predict the kind of curriculum a student should pursue.[28] In this period, too, much more attention was given to the personal and moral qualities of candidates for admission—qualities such as perseverance, initiative, purposefulness, sense of proportion, and the like.[29]

As colleges gave more attention to aptitude tests and personal qualities, new problems of grave social significance came to the surface. In any selective system of higher education there lurked constant anxiety whether the most deserving were finding their way to college. In a free-enterprise economy many have surmised the contrary, but without being able to prove it exactly. After a careful study of higher education in Pennsylvania by the Carnegie Foundation for the Advancement of Teaching, facts seemed to confirm the surmise.[30] The study showed that in 1928 the liberal-arts colleges in Pennsylvania alone accepted 1,000 students with test scores below the average of all those who were unfortunate enough to go to no college at all and overlooked 3,000 with better scores than the average of the 4,000 they did take. More ominous, however, were the restrictive admissions policies of colleges which sought to adjust enrollments to the physical and instructional capacities of their institutions. No quarrel arose when in addition to intellectual potentiality colleges selected candidates so as to draw them from all parts of the nation. But there was strong evidence at the time of the Second World War and after that colleges were also choosing on the basis of race and religion. Some thought balanced distribution was justifiable here too, but there was a recurrent anxiety about the justice of the proportions.[31]

The attempt to improve the articulation between secondary school and college took yet a third direction. This was the effort to introduce some uniformity into the subject matter demanded for admission. Here the National Education Association took the initiative through a series of its committees which reported between 1893 and 1918.[32] The first committee to report was the famous "Committee of Ten" composed of men prominent in higher education at the time. They wrestled with the basic problem of how to articulate the college with a dual-purpose high school, a high school which had to serve as preparation for college and also as preparation for life. Down to 1893, when the committee reported, the prestige of the college preparatory function had predominated, enabling the colleges to dictate the high-school curriculum. After the report of the committee, however, the high school came to enjoy a more and more independent position.

At the outset the committee frankly recognized that too few boys and girls go on to college to warrant making the high school primarily a college preparatory institution. As the committee put it, the preparation of a few pupils for liberal-arts colleges or scientific schools should be the "incidental and not the principal" object of all secondary schools except, perhaps, the few private ones which made college preparation their chief objective.[33] Yet the committee did not want the doors of colleges and scientific schools to be closed to capable students who creditably completed a high-school course other than the college preparatory. Although entertaining the desirability of such a liberal policy, the committee concluded the time was unripe for recommending it since too many contemporary high schools had terminal curriculums covering many subjects but none thoroughly.

The committee, however, did not stop at this already familiar impasse. On the contrary it went on to make two suggestions. In the first place it unanimously recommended that, whatever the subject taught in the high-school curriculum, "it be taught in the same way and to the same extent to every pupil so long as he pursues it, no matter what the probable destination of the pupil may be, or at what point his education is to cease."[34] In the second place the committee suggested that, if the recommendations of its nine subcommittees on each of the major studies of secondary-school instruction were carried out, these subjects "might fairly be held to make all the main subjects taught in the secondary schools of equal rank for the purpose of admission to college or secondary school."[35] The two suggestions together seemed to provide a neat way to overcome the impasse presented by the dual nature of the high school. They played down the comparative importance of different subject-matter content and played up the common denominator of their formal mental discipline. Differentiation in a pupil's destination could be minimized if subjects were taught on the theory that "They would all be taught consecutively and thoroughly, and would all be used for training the powers of observation, memory, expression, and reasoning."[36]

Solid progress though the committee made, it met criticism at several points. Many were of the impression that the college rather than the secondary-school point of view preponderated in the report. Thus there seemed a strong implication that the dual function of the high school was best served by a college preparatory curriculum; that preparation for college was the best preparation for life even though the pupil never went to college or even finished high school![37] But this bias was easy to explain. The personnel of the committee had been drawn largely from the ranks of higher rather than secondary education.[38]

The item, however, from which repercussions were longest heard was the suggestion that the major subject matters might be considered of equal value for college entrance. Coming at a time when the elective curriculum was in full swing, this suggestion soon took the form that all subjects were of equal educational value if taught equally well. G. Stanley Hall, eminent psychologist and president of Clark University, definitely found himself unable to accept such a principle. Neither could President Hyde of Bowdoin.[39] The latter, a member of the "Committee of Fifteen" on college entrance requirements which reported in 1899, was no doubt instrumental in persuading that committee to enter a caveat against regarding all subjects of equal cultural and disciplinary value.[40]

Reform, even corrected by criticism, made headway slowly. Another committee of the National Education Association, reporting in 1911 on the articulation of high school and college, still complained of the difficulties the secondary school was experiencing in fulfilling its dual function. The dominating position of colleges still laid too heavy a burden on the secondary school in asking it to prepare for life at the same time it was preparing for college. Consequently the committee demanded an "open door" policy so that the secondary school might have as much freedom to explore the adolescent's possibilities for self-realization as the college claimed for itself.[41] But it was in the report of the National Education Association's Commission on the Reorganization of Secondary Education, published in 1918, that the secondary school finally managed to talk back to the college on equal terms. On the commission secondary and public-school personnel predominated as higher-education personnel had on the committee of 1893. Consequently it came as no surprise that they saw higher education no longer limited to the few or secondary education to the relatively few as the first committee had. On the contrary, they saw democracy demanding that liberal education be extended to an increasingly large segment of the population. Just as the secondary school had come to feel a duty to admit all pupils who would derive greater benefit from it than by remaining in elementary school, so too, the committee stated, "higher institutions of learning, taken as a whole, are under a similar obligation with reference to those whose needs are no longer met by the secondary school and are disposed to continue their education beyond that point."[42]

While these were brave words, it yet remained to give convincing demonstration that students with unorthodox secondary-school preparation could actually do successful work in conventional colleges. In 1930 the Progressive Education Association appointed a Commission on the Relation of Secondary School and College which undertook a carefully planned eight-year experimental study of this problem. A selected list of colleges and progressive secondary schools was drawn up for the test. With the exception of Harvard, Yale, Princeton, and Haverford, the colleges selected all agreed to release the selected secondary schools from the usual subject-matter and "unit" requirements for admission for a period of five years. At the end of the experimental period the college product of these schools was matched with the college product of conventional secondary schools on the basis of sex, age, race, scholastic aptitude, home background, and probable future. The resulting differences in college achievement between these two groups, if not great, was rather consistently in favor of the progressive secondary schools. The product of the latter not only had received more academic honors but they had clearer ideas about the meaning of education, demonstrated greater intellectual resourcefulness and curiosity, earned a higher proportion of non-academic honors, showed a better orientation toward choice of vocation, and had a more active concern with what was going on in the contemporary world.

Interestingly enough, the results of the study showed that the more widely the participating secondary schools deviated from conventional requirements, the more noticeable was the college superiority of their product over the conventionally trained students. As a result of the study the commission announced that the time-honored assumption that successful preparation for the liberal-arts college depended on the study of certain prescribed studies was no longer tenable.[43]

A fourth direction taken by the standardization of college entrance requirements needs only brief exposition—the development of the "point," "credit," or "unit" system of college admissions. If some degree of equivalence was to be admitted between subjects presented for entrance, as suggested in the report of the Committee of Ten, the question then arises: What should be the unit of measurement for purposes of academic bookkeeping? Apparently the New York Regents were first in the field with such a unit in 1895, which they called a "count." A "count" they defined as ten weeks of work in one of three studies a day taken five days a week. In 1902 the North Central Association defined the sought-for unit as a course covering a school year of not less than thirty-five weeks, consisting of four or five periods a day of at least forty-five minutes each. The heavy emphasis on the temporal dimension of the standard of measurement led some to call this the "time exposure" method of determining fitness for college. As nothing better seemed available, the Carnegie Foundation for the Advancement of Teaching used a variant of it when it sought to form standardized comparisons of colleges for purposes of its pension fund.[44] Although the foundation did not invent the unit, it so popularized it that it became known as the "Carnegie unit."[45] Successful as the "unit" was in standardizing academic bookkeeping, it nonetheless came to exercise a tyranny of its own, which finally went into eclipse as admission boards gave more and more attention to intelligence and aptitude tests.

In spite of improved college procedures it was reckoned, after Russia's Sputnik frightened the United States into taking inventory of its manpower resources, that less than half of the upper 25 per cent of high school graduates were taking college degrees and only 60 per cent of the top 5 per cent.[46] A principal step to remedy this shocking situation had already been taken in 1953 by the development of advanced placement. Several colleges and secondary schools by then were becoming aware of the need to expedite the transition from high school to college, especially for seniors capable of academic acceleration.[47] Under this new policy unusually capable students were admitted not only to college but to sophomore standing by successfully passing courses of collegiate grade in high school. Obviously this policy had the incidental effect of upgrading the high school curriculum to prepare its seniors for advanced placement examinations.[48] In 1956, 1,229 students from 104 high schools took 2,199 advanced placement examinations for 130 colleges. A decade later the new policy was an overwhelming success with 34,278 students from 2,369 high schools taking 45,110 examinations for 994 colleges![49]

What to Do with the College?

Climbing the educational ladder from the secondary school to the college was a much more complex task than merely ascertaining whether the student was strong enough to take his foot off the secondary rung and raise it to the collegiate one, for, concurrently with the debate on entrance requirements, ran one on how the ladder itself should be constructed. Until the latter part of the nineteenth century few people had stopped to realize how the American educational ladder was the result of more or less accidental historical factors.[50] As emigrants from European shores the colonists brought along an odd assortment of European educational institutions. Elementary education was a mélange of English and German precedents; secondary education, starting with an English grammar school, had shifted to an indigenous American high school; collegiate education was definitely English in origin; and the graduate school, of course, definitely German.

Consequently, by the turn of the century the United States had a rather hodge-podge educational ladder whose upper rungs took their shape and spacing from forces characteristic of three different national traditions. Although each rung made its unique contribution to the American scene, it seemed to many high time that these rungs be viewed not separately but as parts of a single educational ladder. As men turned this relationship over in their minds the critical question seemed to be what to do with the college.[51] If it had been difficult to articulate the college and the high school it was no less so to articulate the college and the graduate school. The English and German traditions of higher education were so diverse that solution of the problem of articulation took a number of directions.

Perhaps most radical was the proposal to dispense with the college altogether. In the original design of Johns Hopkins there was no provision for an undergraduate college. The same was true of the founding of Clark. Both Daniel Coit Gilman and G. Stanley Hall, the respective founders of these first American universities on the German model, deliberately designed their institutions independent of colleges. Even where graduate schools were superimposed on existing colleges there were men like John W. Burgess at Columbia who expected the college to disappear. "I am," he said, "unable to divine what is ultimately to be the position of colleges which cannot become universities and which will not be gymnasia. I cannot see what reason they will have to exist. It will be largely a waste of capital to maintain them, and largely a waste of time to attend them."[52]

This sentiment persisted in high places well into the middle of the twentieth century. Indeed, Jacques Barzun, dean of Columbia's graduate school, went so far as to opine that "the liberal arts tradition is dead or dying . . . sooner or later the college as we know it will find no proper place in the scheme of things."[53] Its place in the scheme of things was jeopardized, Barzun thought, because high schools were doing college work—witness advance placement—and graduate and professional schools, due to the explosion of knowledge, were demanding earlier and earlier specialization. Barzun was not happy about this erosion of the college, as probably Burgess was, and promised to do nothing to advance it. But in spite of promising to do everything to prevent it, these were the facts as he saw them.

Instead of rejecting the college most universities with graduate schools accepted it. One proposal for articulating the two levels of instruction was to organize them quite independently of each other. Both Yale and Princeton pointed their hopes in this direction. There were those at Harvard who agreed, holding that college methods could not be forced to achieve university functions.[54] This, however, proved to be the minority view as Eliot, after defending the importance of college teaching in his inaugural and playing down the role of research, later swung over to adapting the college to the uses of the university. Indeed, in 1890 he sponsored action which organized the undergraduate and graduate faculties as a single faculty of arts and sciences with unitary control over degrees from the bachelor of arts to the doctor of philosophy.

Nearly every American university followed Harvard's lead in this momentous decision, even Yale and Princeton succumbing to it. But whether making the undergraduate college, with its tradition of teaching, the first rung of the ladder to the graduate school, with its tradition of research, allowed the latter to overwhelm the former to the disadvantage of teaching, remained a moot question well into the twentieth century.[55] In reorganizing the University of Chicago just before World War II, Robert M. Hutchins tried to undo Eliot's handiwork not only by separating graduate and undergraduate faculties but by physically separating them too, but it was already very late to turn the clock of history back. When Hutchins left Chicago for the Ford Foundation the college lost its autonomy and was quickly invaded by graduate-school specialists again who generally had been hostile to the idea all along.[56]

Still another proposed disposition of the college was to trim its length and thus reduce the duration of the academic course. At a meeting of the National Education Association in 1888 President Eliot of Harvard touched off a lively controversy on economizing time in education by addressing himself to the question "Can school programs be shortened and enriched?"[57] Whereas President Wayland had had misgivings in the first half of the century over the tender age at which freshmen were entering Brown, President Eliot had misgivings in the latter half of the century at the steadily advancing age at which freshmen were entering

Harvard. If fourteen was too early for Wayland, nineteen was too late for Eliot. With no professional school above, time was an unimportant dimension for Wayland. For him the important consideration was to cover the content of a liberal education thoroughly if it took six or even seven years. With professional education ahead, time was of the essence to Eliot. As he pointed out, if a student entered at nineteen and planned to attend professional school after college, he could not hope to become self-supporting till twenty-six, an obvious hardship for many.

Two principal pressures apparently were insistently demanding more and more time and thus postponing self-support till later and later. Rising college entrance requirements exerted one of these pressures as higher standards demanded more and more time for preparation. The other pressure was that exerted by the greatly improved quality of professional education itself. In the short space of a hundred years professional education had moved from an apprenticeship prescribing no college education whatever to a position where it was asking four years of college as a prerequisite.

But granted there was need of saving time, where was the saving to be made? Some thought the place to economize time was in the lower schools. An eight-year elementary school they viewed as excessively long. In spite of the intensive drill in the last two years, students were really marking time. Why not commence secondary education, and therefore college preparation, two years earlier by replacing some of the elementary-school subjects with secondary ones, for instance, replacing advanced arithmetic with beginning algebra? The Committee of Ten must have thought the idea a good one, for it was included as a recommendation in their report. Others thought that time could be conserved in the secondary school itself. The boldest suggestion here came from William Rainey Harper, president of the University of Chicago. He not only made the radical proposal that the period of secondary education include the last year of the elementary school and the first two years of college, as well as the conventional four years of high school, but also the startling suggestion that this stretch of seven years be accomplished in six by the average student and in five by the brilliant one.

Still others saw the problem of economizing time as one of making some adjustment in the college course itself. This was the more imperative because of the rapid improvement secondary schools were making. Perhaps in the nineteenth century while the high school was coming of age a four-year college was necessary to compensate for the former's deficiencies, but such a situation no longer confronted the twentieth. Much of what was formerly done in the college was now being done in secondary school. As colleges raised their entrance requirements and went on into more advanced collegiate work, they thrust more and more of their former subject matter down into the secondary school. In fact, Nicholas Murray Butler claimed, raising standards had gone so far by the first decade of the twentieth century that, judged by nineteenth-century standards, the student was no longer devoting four but virtually six years to the liberal arts and sciences.[58]

But what adjustment in the college program did such a situation warrant? Some recommended, as Eliot at Harvard, the reduction of the four-year course to three. This idea was not altogether novel, as the Sheffield Scientific School at Yale had long been operating on a three-year curriculum. In support of his recommendation, however, Eliot pointed to British rather than American precedent. Thus he called attention to the fact that the English colleges, prototypes of the American, had long since reduced their four-year curriculum of colonial times to three.[59] Yet, although Harvard, Hopkins, Clark, and Columbia made it optional for a student to get his bachelor's degree in three years, this was one of the few reforms tenaciously backed by Eliot which he was unable to make stick.[60] In some instances the college course was compressed into three years by permitting students to commence their professional specialization in the senior year. The plan must have enjoyed some popularity because 25 per cent of the student body at Columbia between 1892 and 1902 chose to combine liberal and professional education in this fashion.[61]

The Committee on Economy of Time in Education, which reported for the National Council of the National Education Association in 1913, went so far as to recommend the reduction of general education by at least *two* years.[62] Consequently, as the improving secondary schools pushed up from below and the demanding professional schools pressed down from above, the college was so squeezed in between that not a few wondered whether it would be squeezed out of existence.

William Rainey Harper, president of the new University of Chicago, was one of the chief skeptics of the three-year proposal. Like Wayland, he did not orient his thinking to the temporal dimension of the college problem. In fact, contrary to Eliot, he was of the opinion that the entering age of undergraduates had been more constant than Harvard's president realized.[63] Moreover, with secondary schools improving so rapidly, he thought that, if anything, entrance requirements should be lowered rather than continually raised or at least that students should be permitted to enter college with advanced standing.[64] Even if some students could accomplish the four-year course in three, Harper thought that there were probably as many more who should take five. Besides, even if a three-year college course was preferable for some, he saw no reason to legislate a three-year course for all. Those wanting a four-year course should still have it. On this point Columbia's Butler was in agreement with him.[65] But Harper was most apprehensive that a three-year college would lead to the decadence of the small independent college. With the secondary school already stepping on the heels of the college and even overtaking its early years, a three-year college might be so little in advance of the secondary school that it would have little appeal.[66]

The Junior College

The current problem of the college, as Harper saw it, was not so much one of saving time as of realigning the years of secondary and higher education. In his mind the real problem posed by the secondary school, so improved as to be doing work formerly done by the college, was to decide where to draw the line separating the two. Eliot was doubtful such a line could be drawn at all,[67] but Harper was beset with no such misgivings. For himself he drew it between the second and third years of the college course. Below that line he thought studies were "collegiate" in character and were to be assimilated to the work of the secondary school. Above the line studies were of "university" grade and were to be compared to the graduate school.[68] While at first Harper used the terms "collegiate" and "university" to make the distinction he had in mind, before the nineteenth century was out he was using the terms "junior" and "senior" college.[69] But even so the term "junior college" did not gain general currency till perhaps the second decade of the twentieth century.

Harper's distinction was not novel. Michigan had tried to partition the college in the 1850s, Minnesota in the 1870s, and Cornell from 1890 to 1891.[70] The theory of such a partition was based on a comparison of the American college with the German Gymnasium of the time.[71] Men in a position to know, like Tappan at Michigan, Folwell at Minnesota, and White at Cornell, regarded a large part of the work done in the nineteenth-century American college as about on a par with the German secondary school. On the further theory that the university should not be engaged in secondary instruction, Illinois, Michigan, and Stanford debated the proposal that the first two years of the college be dropped altogether.[72] Both the latter two institutions, however, found the suggestion impractical, Michigan because secondary schools, although improving, were still not advanced enough in the 1880s to send up students prepared to enter junior year and Stanford because it feared the financial consequences of losing students' fees for the first two undergraduate years.[73]

Although the idea of the junior college was not original with Harper, it was he who was able to give the idea enduring appeal. His arguments for the partition of the college into an upper and lower division were aimed at various interests. In one direction Harper thought a lower or junior college with an entity of its own might beckon students who otherwise would never attend college. In another direction the partition might incline some students to find it both convenient and respectable to terminate their college course at the end of two years. Providing such terminal facilities, Harper expected, would also appeal to graduate and professional schools because their resulting student body would be more select and therefore permit more advanced work. Again, if terminal facilities at the end of two years could be made respectable, some four-year colleges might be persuaded to become strong junior colleges rather than struggle along as weak four-year institutions. Finally, because he regarded the junior college as providing essentially secondary education, Harper hoped that secondary schools themselves would expand to include the junior-college years in their offerings.[74]

As different institutions started putting these ideas into practice, the traditional American educational ladder began to space its rungs in a variety of ways. Some organized the junior college as a separate two-year institution. Where this was the case the educational ladder resulted in an 8–4–2, 6–3–3–2, or a 6–6–2 pattern. Others organized their educational ladders to include the junior college as an integral part of the secondary schools. This apparently was Folwell's original idea at the University of Minnesota in the 1870s.[75] The resulting ladder then had its rungs arranged in an 8–6, 6–3–5, or a 6–4–4 configuration.

In order to emphasize the fourteenth rather than the twelfth year of schooling as the dividing line between secondary and higher education, it had been Harper's intent to organize the faculties of the upper and lower divisions separately.[76] It remained, however, for one of Harper's successors at Chicago, Robert M. Hutchins, to give thorough expression to this notion. Taking the 6–4–4 plan of organization as his model for the University of Chicago, Hutchins planned to make the latter four-year unit—the last two years of high school plus the first two years of college—into a new four-year college to be capped by the award of the bachelor's degree.[77]

As might be expected, there was an immediate outcry against such a radical realignment of the secondary school and college and college and graduate school. On the Chicago campus those who had always looked on the college as a training ground for the graduate school objected to the plan on the ground that it would break the traditional continuity of specialization. Some in the college faculty which was to devote full time to the new college unit were fearful they might be reduced to the status of high-school teachers. And supporters of the traditional high school feared that this institution would be swallowed up in the college. Off the Chicago campus there was wide objection to disturbing the long-standing currency of the bachelor's diploma as a four-year degree. Surprisingly enough, a large majority of junior colleges, which might have expected to benefit notably from this part of Hutchins' proposal, also opposed it.[78]

Yet, revolutionary as the proposed new bachelor's degree sounded in the decade of the Second World War, Hutchins was far from the first to suggest it. Nicholas Murray Butler had already done that in the first decade of the twentieth century,[79] and Charles Kendall Adams had preceded Butler with the suggestion a decade before that.[80] The forces of tradition, however, were not to be dislodged easily. Opinion generally rose to the support of the traditional four-year college in fear that the proposed four-year college, even if it did not curtail intellectual objectives, would lack the time to develop deep social and moral values formed by the social attrition of undergraduate life and long associated with the college in both England and the United States.[81] Americans easily accepted a graduate school of the German model atop their college, but they resisted partitioning their college to assimilate their high school to a German gymnasium.

The fact that the principle of the four-year college survived should not obscure the further fact that the advent of the junior college did render precarious the status of many weak four-year institutions. A large proportion of these, of course, were already anemic before the junior college put in an appearance. As already intimated, Harper had a solution for this dilemma. Weak institutions should become junior colleges. These, together with high schools and academies which had the energy to stretch up to junior-college stature, were to draw strength from affiliation with or standardization by universities like the University of Chicago or the University of Missouri.[82]

A further word now about the development of secondary schools which Harper foresaw sprouting a thirteenth and fourteenth year of schooling beyond the conventional twelfth year. The high school at Joliet, Illinois, was parent to the first such junior college. There the superintendent and board of education set the stage for a junior college at the turn of the century, when the high school began offering postgraduate studies. With Harper lending encouragement from the wings, Joliet was soon asking and obtaining advanced standing for its post-graduates at such state universities as Michigan and Illinois. As the work grew in extent and importance it became more and more an independent part of the high school's offering. Not only did postgraduate students enjoy a larger measure of freedom than the rest of the student body but the faculty assigned to the work soon became a special committee in charge of it. Occasionally this postgraduate instruction passed under the title of "junior college," but there was nothing official till the First World War. Perhaps it was just as well, for had it been popularized too early Joliet taxpayers might have become alarmed. As it was, they found it easy to accept because they regarded this advanced work as merely an extension of the high school rather than an invasion of the college field. The board of education, however, did not miss the significance of this expansion of public facilities and in due course officially recognized it in name for what it had already become in fact, a public junior college.[83]

As the high school had originally been an "upward extension" of the elementary school, so now the junior college became an "upward extension" of the high school. The democratic energies which had been pushing up from below in the nineteenth century were obviously far from spent in the twentieth. Indeed the upthrust of the high school into the junior-college field was viewed by many as but the logical fulfillment of the high school's claim to being the "poor man's college." With its higher curriculum the junior college by mid-twentieth century had become in reality what the high school pretended to be in name, a people's college.

Not all junior colleges were upward extensions of high schools or decapitated four-year colleges. Some sprang full blown from the plans of their founders. However formed they multiplied rapidly. Down to 1920 private junior colleges multiplied more rapidly than public ones, but thereafter the number of public ones outstripped the private. Their combined total grew spectacularly. It has been estimated that in 1920 there were approximately 52 of the new two-year colleges. A volume of the Carnegie Commission on Higher Education has calculated that ten years later there were 569, which increased to 610 by the advent of World War II. This number diminished during the decade of combat but more than regained its losses ten years later. By 1970 the number of junior colleges had grown to the astounding total of 1,100.[84]

The development of the junior college depended not only on the multiplication of its facilities but also on bringing these facilities geographically within reach of the mass of the people. The further growth of the junior college as a local or "community" college, therefore, was of the utmost importance.[85] Such an institution brought higher education within reach of many students who would otherwise have found prohibitive the expense of board and room and travel away from home. Even if a student had his eye on a four-year college education, he could take his first two years locally and thus save at least that much of his expenses. Many overgrown state universities, incidentally, were relieved to have their work decentralized to this extent. To remain a "community" college for the masses, however, the junior college had to beware concentrating on preparation for senior college. Its most pregnant possibility lay in orienting itself to the needs of the great mass of people who would not be going on.[86]

Transfer and Terminal Curriculums

The growth of the public junior college into a community college for the people was coincident with a tremendous, almost fantastic, expansion of the number of American youth seeking college opportunities in general. In 1830 only one in 3,200 was a college graduate in the United States.[87] Forty years later there were 52,000 students attending higher education, 1.7 per cent of the 18–21 age group.[88] As late as the opening of the last decade of the nineteenth century this figure had risen to 3 per cent and at the turn of the century only 4 per cent, representing a total of 238,000 students. By 1920, however, this percentage had doubled.[89] Mounting to 12 per cent in the next ten years it reached 18 per cent just before the Second World War. The almost fantastic expectation that this percentage would double in the postwar period[90] actually came to pass when 4 million youth or 40 per cent of the 18–21 age group in 1964 were in some institution of higher education. Nor are these figures to be interpreted as a normal function of general population growth. Between 1950 and 1960, for instance, population grew 8 per cent while college and university population was increasing 40 percent.[91]

Save for the growth of the junior college, it would have been impossible to accommodate this phenomenal increase in numbers. At mid-century the President's Advisory Commission on Higher Education was counting on this new rung of the educational ladder to bear the weight of any future increase. It will be well to examine the forces back of these numbers if we are to understand their impact on the aims and curriculums of the junior college. The simplest explanation is that the mounting enrollments were merely an expansion into the twentieth century of forces released by the democratic yeast inherent in the Morrill legislation of the preceding century.[92] Once the American people learned there was a curriculum which more nearly approximated their needs than the traditional humanistic curriculum of the old-line colleges, they kept on asking for more and more.

Two further events in the twentieth century added impetus to this historical trend. The first was the great depression of the 1930s. Because during this period adults, let alone youth, could only hope to find a job by accident, hordes of the latter descended upon the college, preferring to spend their time there rather than in idleness. As Robert Maynard Hutchins said, "The most footless question that university presidents have been debating in recent years is, Who should go to college? Where else is there to go?"[93] The second was the generous G.I. Bill, after the Second World War, which made it possible for returning veterans to go to college to compensate for time spent in the armed services. Not only did large numbers take advantage of this bill but a significant portion of them came from family backgrounds which had never thought of college careers before.

The temporary setback of the depression notwithstanding, the American standard of living remained high during most of the first half of the twentieth century. The basic economy seemed to have the strength to encourage larger and larger numbers of youth in their expectations of attending college as a means of promoting their social mobility.[94] So far, in fact, did the United States go in identifying college attendance with "getting ahead" that modifications began to occur in the common-law duty of parents to provide education for their children. A Vermont court in 1844 refused to support the suit of a minor against his parent for the expenses of a college education on the long-standing rule of common law that parents were only required to provide their offspring with "necessities" and a college education was far from one of them.[95] The old common law had held that even a common-school education was not a necessity unless a child's parents were in unusual circumstances. The Vermont court, however, conceded that times had changed sufficiently by mid-nineteenth-century America to concede the necessity of a common-school education, but not enough to admit the necessity of a college one. By the twentieth century the high court of a western state, Washington, moved ahead to recognize that circumstances had changed still further, so that in 1926 even a college education might be regarded as a necessity. "Nor should the court be restricted to the station of the minor in society," read the decision, "but should in determining this fact, take into consideration the progress of society and the attendant requirements of citizens today. . . . That it is the public policy of the state that a college education should be had, if possible, by all its citizens is made manifest by the fact that the state of Washington maintains so many institutions of higher learning at public expense."[96]

The "progress of society" to which the court referred was not just the standard of living. One draws the inescapable inference from the decision that citizenship in a modern democratic state confronts the individual with such complex problems that little short of a college education will be adequate preparation for its responsibilities. Beyond the complexities of citizenship lay the further enigmas of twentieth-century economic life. The strife of economic systems such as capitalism and communism, to say nothing of the profound readjustments occurring within capitalism itself from such technological improvements as automation, demanded social attitudes and engineering skills of an order higher than those provided by a mere high-school education.[97] The Report of the President's Commission on Higher Education for American Democracy in 1947, echoing the Report of the Commission on the Reorganization of Secondary Education in

1918, summed up these views by declaring, "The time has come to make education through the fourteenth grade available in the same way that high school education is available."[98] Studying the statistics of the armed services in the Second World War, the President's commission was confident that 49 per cent of the youth of college age had the aptitude and capacity for at least the first two years of college.

Stirring sight that it was to see the mass enthusiasm for college education, it was just as striking that not all those headed for college were headed in the right direction. Some students, though capable, did not have the motivation for college work. Many state universities, compelled by law to accept all the graduates of their state high schools, flunked their freshmen classes unmercifully when they failed to meet traditional standards. Of those who survived, relatively few stayed on to graduate—as a matter of fact, less than half the entering classes.[99] This process of attrition proved to supporters of the conventional college that the failures and drop-outs were just not college material. To others, like President Coffman of the University of Minnesota, it indicated an appalling waste of human resources.[100] What impressed the latter group was not the lower quality of students, for that was almost inevitably to be expected with a vast increase in numbers, but the failure of the college to adapt its curriculum to their peculiar needs.

In its early years the junior college conceived its curriculum as the first two years of a regular four-year college. Pre-eminent, therefore, was its "transfer" function, that is to pass its graduates on to some institution with the junior and senior years of college. It early began to appear, however, especially during the depression, that as many as two-thirds to three-fourths did not transfer, went no further. As the junior college, particularly its community-college form, became in fact a terminal institution, authorities devised terminal curriculums to fit the altered circumstances.[101] Indeed it would have been as useless to say that the first two years of a conventional college course should be the same for all, whether or not they were going to transfer, as it had been for the Committee of Ten in the 1890s to claim that the education of all high-school students should be the same no matter how long they stayed in high school and that the college preparatory curriculum of the high school was best not only as a preparation for college but as a preparation for life.

If anyone thought that the great expansion of junior-college facilities would lead to "educational inflation" or to an unemployed "intellectual proletariat" he was mistaken because the product of these colleges was quickly absorbed in "middle jobs." The rise to prominence of "middle jobs" was the result of a profound change in job patterns in postwar technological America. Unskilled jobs suffered a steep decline as technical or semitechnical ones correspondingly increased.[102] While such work did become a substantial part of many junior-college programs, in the course of time a reaction set in against overspecialization.[103] More general education was thought necessary. But if more general education was to be provided, obviously a distinction would have to be drawn between general education for transfer and for terminal students. For the former, general education tended to take its character from the categories into which liberal education in the four-year college were either traditionally cast or were being recently reorganized.[104] For the latter, general education developed a new set of categories based on phases of current living.[105]

In listing these phases general education showed an indebtedness to categories set out in the Report of the Commission on the Reorganization of Secondary Education, known as the "cardinal principles of education." Thus general education was to continue an interest in personal and community health, lay the basis for a satisfying family life, develop an informed citizenship, choose a personally gratifying and socially useful vocation, cultivate skills in oral and written communication, and encourage critical examination of one's social values.[106]

One of the most interesting examples of general education at the junior-college level was that at the University of Minnesota. There, under the leadership of President Coffman, the university organized a special administrative unit, at first called an "Institute for Social Intelligence" and later a "General College." Its aim was to provide general education for those whose abilities did not warrant attempting a conventional liberal-arts program, but who nevertheless still had some distance to go in their cultivation before reaching a point of seriously diminishing returns. As its work gained in dignity and popularity it came to have an independent faculty with a dean of its own.[107] To guide this faculty in its pioneering efforts careful research was done on the nature of the student body attending the General College[108] and on the kind of curriculum best suited to it.[109]

It is of more than passing significance that a number of students, whose abilities might have justified their enrolling in the regular college or some other branch of the University of Minnesota, preferred the General College because the functional curriculum of general education appealed to them more than did the regular one.[110] Indeed so vital did the discussions about "general education" become at Minnesota and elsewhere that not a few used the phrase as a rubric under which to argue the thorough reforms they thought long overdue in liberal education itself.[111] Some seemed to use the terms general and liberal interchangeably.[112] Moreover, a not inconsiderable number of junior colleges, overcome by their own success, abandoned their unique two-year status and sought to become four-year liberal-arts institutions with all their attendant prestige.

Open Admissions

The optimism generated by the junior-college movement boomed in the 1960s into a movement for "open admissions." Two-year colleges were urged by the Carnegie Commission on Higher Education to adopt an "open door" policy admitting all high school graduates and otherwise qualified individuals.[113] The institutions best matched to such lowered entrance barriers were "comprehensive" junior colleges providing both academic and vocational, transfer and terminal, programs. The zooming optimism even overflowed these institutions into colleges "without walls" and "external degree" programs.[114] The idea behind this extension of the educational horizon was to provide an escape from the conventional limitations of entrance, residence, and graduation requirements. On this more flexible basis a student could study off-campus a program uniquely designed for him and present evidence of achievement not ordinarily accepted for internal degree programs.

Unlike those who served on the President's Advisory Commission on Higher Education, there were numbers who did not share the euphoria of an ever-expanding student clientele in higher education. Thinking in the pattern of an older American or even European tradition, they felt that higher education should be selective rather than inclusive. Gallant as it might be for a wealthy nation like the United States to undertake the higher education of so many, they feared the enterprise must inevitably result in watering down the quality of both its student body and its curriculum. To them it was no compliment to be rated by foreign critics as the "best half-educated" people in the world.[115] At home a Vice-President of the United States, Spiro Agnew, deplored the impact of "open admissions," as did a noted sociologist, Daniel Moynihan, after having earlier embraced the idea.[116] But the fear of watering down the quality of students was without substantiation. A study sponsored by the Carnegie Commission on Higher Education covering the years 1925–1961 showed that not only had quality not declined but that it had actually increased.[117]

Whether in or out of favor, "open admissions" challenged a number of higher education's assumptions. In the front rank was the proper role of higher education in American culture.[118] Traditionally it had been an autonomous concern with knowledge itself, its discovery and transmission. Of course only a limited number of students—an elite—had such an interest. Hence the college admissions officer was a talent scout for this elite, a predictor of performance in the world of academe. In the course of time higher education took on the further role, not only of picking the elite, but of generally distributing or allocating places in the occupational and social structure. As the young became aware of this function, there was a mounting desire to get a higher education as a means of increasing their upward social mobility. Indeed, so important did this new role become that the young felt it almost obligatory to go to college. But if college was this important, then all should go; there should be an "open door" to the college. College, which under the traditional view of higher education had been a privilege, should now become a right.[119]

With this added role of higher education came a challenge to assumptions underlying the traditional curriculum. As might be expected, the tide of students admitted through the "open door" policy had little attraction to the traditional interest in knowledge itself. Indeed, they often found it boring and irrelevant. To meet their complaint junior colleges came up with more practical courses, often *ad hoc* in character. To traditionalists the humanitarian motives of the terminal junior college, whether "community" or "general," entailed an unhappy dilution of the curriculum. For them the proliferation of *ad hoc* courses which included something interesting for everyone—the average, subaverage, and even inert—risked endless triviality.[120] A compromise of sorts between these two perspectives on higher education was achieved through a scheme of "tracking." Instead of permitting "open admissions" to overwhelm the four-year college and university a track was set up whereby the most able were routed to the university, the moderately able to the four-year college, and the rest to the junior college.[121]

The minor device of "tracking" directs attention to another perspective on higher education challenged by "open admissions," that of fitting students into an educational meritocracy where merit was measured by inherited genes rather than by inherited social position usually based on wealth. Many saw "open admissions" as a first step in the equalization of higher educational opportunity. While no doubt "open admissions" was a device for upward mobility, it was also true that meritocracy was more interested in equality of opportunity than in equality itself. As long as the distribution of power and privilege among adults remained radically and dramatically unequal there could be little hope for real equality of opportunity even when initiated by an "open door" policy. And even if there were, the question was raised whether there was not something sadistic in making society even more competitive and status conscious than it was.[122] Such an unrelenting competition exacted a toll from both losers, whose self-esteem was damaged, and from winners, who might be more self-righteous about their elite status than was warranted. Therefore some thoughtful critics felt that what was needed was not more mobility but more genuine equality.[123]

Meritocracy based on equality of opportunity rested on the further assumption that psychological tests were a valid way of determining who was to get higher education and how much. Once the darling of liberals and egalitarians, these tests had been seriously questioned because of being culture bound. Whatever contribution they made to meritocracy, they still tended to discriminate against the blacks and the poor.[124] Some frankly recognized the shortcomings of these tests, especially in that they did not measure a student's candor, drive, and diligence, but nevertheless accepted them as the best means at hand to distribute limited opportunities. Consequently they settled for the paradox of an elitism of merit flourishing simultaneously with an educational egalitarianism. They did not feel that it was necessary to choose between quality and equality.[125]

One assumption of higher education, however, seemed to be confirmed rather than challenged by the popular acceptance of the "open admissions" policy, namely that higher education added a plus to the kind of individual a person was. In the immediate post-World War II years a study of the impact of college teaching on the changing of student values led to the discouraging conclusion that the college was having surprisingly small influence in changing the values of most students.[126] It seemed to matter little whether curriculums were conventional, integrated, or problem-oriented; the end effect was to socialize rather than liberalize the undergraduate. Student values remained remarkably homogeneous from freshman to senior year, whether in the Ivy League or the Big Ten, in denominational colleges or state universities, on the East or the West Coast. Students seemed gloriously content to accept current conventions as the context in which to realize their ambitions. Preoccupied with personal status and prestige, few were anxious about the state of national or world affairs. If they concentrated their aspirations on material gratification for themselves and families, they but reflected the outlook of their parents and society at large.

Perhaps this impression resulted because the report was put out in the apathetic fifties. A couple of decades later another study of the Carnegie Commission reversed this impression.[127] In comparing young people who went to college with those who did not the authors of this report were convinced that there was a constantly widening gap between the two groups. The college products not only acquired new knowledge, skills, and interests but were marked by their welcome attitude toward information. They used printed media more, knew more of what was happening in the world, and were more conscious of how society works. College-bred young people, moreover, tended to be more open-minded and less authoritarian, more concerned with cultural and aesthetic values, less preoccupied with material possessions, less apprehensive of job security, more absorbed in the challenging aspects of an occupation, and politically more inclined to support civil liberties. In spite of this praise another Carnegie study, *College Graduates and Jobs*, deplored attending college for its prestige value, noting that one in ten of the college population would prefer to be elsewhere and doing something else.[128]

13

Innovations in Curriculum and Methods

By the middle of the nineteenth century, as already related, instruction in undergraduate classrooms followed three dominant modes—lecture, laboratory, and recitation.[1] Of the three, the lecture and laboratory methods gained a momentum in the balance of the century which carried them with little modification to the threshold of the twentieth century as the most popular forms of instruction. The old-fashioned recitation continued to lose ground throughout this period, successfully surviving only or principally where animated by a Socratic spirit. If little change occurred in methods of instruction in the latter half of the nineteenth century, a profound change came over the curriculum as the elective principle gained ascendancy over prescription.[2] Not only did this reform in the curriculum give play to individual differences of aptitude and preference but it also greatly expanded the number and variety of curricular offerings.[3] Yet, even with a modernized curriculum taught by tested methods, there was a noticeable misgiving at the opening of the twentieth century that all was not well with undergraduate instruction.

Signs of Changing Times

The chief sign foretelling a change in the educational weather came from the college clientele itself. The undergraduate body of the nineteenth century—and of the eighteenth and seventeenth as well—had been a relatively small percentage of the population. Most of them were destined for the professions. As future members of learned callings they expected to read books and deal with ideas, to dedicate themselves to intellectual ideals. Consequently just to go to college set a youth apart.[4] It indicated a resolution on his part to assume moral responsibility for his development.

The educational clientele of the twentieth century, as already seen, was much larger.[5] Following a rising standard of living after the Civil War, a rapidly rising tide of students swept into and out of the secondary schools. It was no time at all before this wave of students was lapping the shores of the colleges. But with the larger segment of the population of college age which sought the higher learning came many who were not headed for the professions and who came from homes which held no particular allegiance to the intellectual life. Rather were they headed for mercantile and industrial pursuits.[6] Far too many were not headed in any direction at all. They came, or perhaps better were sent, for whatever social prestige college might bring. They attended because it was the socially accepted thing to do. With the extravagance possible for the sons of the rich, it is small wonder that college took on some of the aspects of a country club or that the "playboys" among them should rationalize that it was better to have attended college and loafed than not to have attended at all.[7]

The change in number and composition of the undergraduate body was soon reflected in a discrepancy between the traditionally stated aims of the college and the ambitions of the new clientele. Traditionally the aim of the college had been intellectual and moral. In a notable Phi Beta Kappa oration Woodrow Wilson, while still president at Princeton and before his public career as governor of New Jersey and President of the United States, spelled out this intellectual dimension very well. Its aim was not learning (except for the few) but the spirit of learning. "It consists," Wilson stated, "in the power to distinguish good reasoning from bad, in the power to digest and interpret evidence, in a habit of catholic observation and a preference for the nonpartisan point of view."[8] The parallel moral dimension demanded that college form the man of character armed with Christian virtues for which he was willing to stand up and be counted. This moral dimension tended to be subordinated to the intellectual as American higher education began to ape not English but German models which claimed no responsibility for student morals and sought amoral objectivity in its research.[9]

The ambitions of the new undergraduate clientele tended to deviate considerably from this time-honored ideal. Many a twentieth-century father sent his son to college less to sharpen his wits than to polish his manners, especially if the father felt himself to have suffered from lack of a collegiate background. He expected college to round off his son's social angularities and thus enable him to get along well with his fellows in later life, particularly those who might be college-bred. The employment market, he was dimly aware, sought the man who had been well known and popular on the campus by virtue of participation in social clubs, student government, publications, and athletics.[10]

If the traditional ideal had produced the scholar, perhaps it might be said that the newer ideal aimed at the gentleman. Each ideal, of course, had its limitations. Could the college fulfill both and make the undergraduate into both "a scholar and a gentleman?" To many it seemed no more possible for the college to serve both these ideals than to serve God and Mammon. Wilson himself, while ready to concede the social value of a college education, declared that "If young gentlemen get from their years at college only manliness, esprit de corps, a release of their social gifts, a training in give and take, a catholic taste in men, and the standards of true sportsmen, they have gained much but they have not gained what a college should give them."[11] Others, more sanguine, maintained the "all-around man" as their ideal, the man who, if he did not stand out as a scholar or a gentleman, at least combined the harmonious proportions of being intellectually awake, physically sound, socially refined, aesthetically sensitive, and religiously committed.[12]

Confusion or at least uncertainty about the objectives of the higher learning was matched by disappointment in the program of studies. In the first decade of the century one-third of those matriculating dropped out before graduation. Of course unexpected depleting of finances occasioned some of this exodus, but no small part resulted from lack of conviction that the college curriculum was worth the effort to stay.[13] Many businessmen, indeed, encouraged this conviction by spreading the notion that a college education, far from being an asset, was a positive liability for a career in commerce and industry.[14] A number of people, successful enough in life to write autobiographies in mid-twentieth century, recollected the undergraduate curriculum of this period as having little relevance to contemporary life. Corroborating this conclusion, the great popularity of the extracurriculum stood as a mute protest against the aridity of the regular curriculum.[15] In contrast to the latter, which too much resembled "busywork," the former gave challenging scope to intellectual planning and organization. Writing about *Alma Mater,* Henry Seidel Canby described the era from 1890 to 1920 as one in which colleges appealed to students through glittering personalities like William James at Harvard, William Graham Sumner at Yale, and Woodrow Wilson at Princeton rather than through the intrinsic merit of their curriculums.[16]

Some thought that the unattractiveness of the undergraduate program resulted from its being shaped for the average student and designed to prevent him from getting his degree without doing at least some work. As Frank Aydelotte so well said, "The routine designed for this purpose smacks of secondary school practices—frequent tests, short but clear cut daily assignments, profusion of written exercises, sharp rules dealing with cuts and absences. The educational pace is made up of short steps instead of long strides."[17] All of which amounted, as others stated, to a kind of educational paternalism in which there was too much teaching and too little learning. Mr. Dooley, mouthpiece for Peter Finley Dunne, the great American humorist, brought out the same imbalance in the words he put in the mouth of a college president greeting a freshman, "Now my friend," he inquired, "in what subject would you like your thinking done for you by our learned professors?" Still others thought that the undergraduate program of studies was blighted, not so much by being designed for the average, as by being designed as the first steps toward a Ph.D. degree which only relatively few would seek and even fewer attain. Thus the overarching shadow of the graduate school with its emphasis on research not only eclipsed the faculty interest in undergraduate teaching[18] but it also blighted the undergraduate curriculum by making it more relevant to a subsequent interest in research than to a current interest in contemporary affairs.

The elective system, of course, had made an earnest attempt to make the curriculum more meaningful to the undergraduate by allowing him to choose studies for their intrinsic rather than their disciplinary value. But even this gain was offset by a concomitant loss. It won interest but it lost integration. Aided and abetted in the twentieth century by the psychology of individual differences and by the theory of the specificity of learning, which supplanted the theory of formal transfer of training, the elective principle resulted in a fragmentation of the curriculum. With the atomization of the course of study it became possible for students to turn in their credits as if they were clipping so many coupons to get a degree. The whole system was symptomatic of an intellectual agnosticism about any over-all unity or design. Nor did requirements of concentration and distribution, where in force, produce it, since even here individual courses were taught without much conscious attention to their interrelation.

Discontent with the curriculum was accompanied by discontent with the methods by which it was taught. The period from 1890 to 1920 was the time in which the old disciplinary theory of education was disintegrating. The day in which the professor was justified in assuming the role of taskmaster was passing. Both the elective curriculum and the new psychological studies, severely qualifying formal discipline and the transfer of training, destroyed willingness to submit to instruction which was as arid as it was severe. Henry Seidel Canby has left a first-hand account of the types of teaching which characterized this period. One was what he called "hard-boiled." The professor took the attitude of "I have it. Come and get it or stay away." Another type was "indifferent." Here professors gave their first attention to their writing or committee work. If this indifference raised a wall of student resistance, they threw up a wall of academic requirements as counterresistance. They met boredom with boredom. A third type was "factual." It made an ideal of the well-crammed student. Canby likened the outcome of this type of instruction, however, to a soda bottle which fizzed in welcome relief when the examination button was pressed to allow pressure to escape. Some instruction, like the "enthusiastic," he admitted was very good. So too was the "idealistic" kind where questions were slanted to bring out the value of ideas. But Canby reserved his chief scorn for the triviality of the recitation, which he denounced for its incredible "sham, bunk and perfunctoriness."[19]

Obviously a considerable budget of discontent had accumulated for twentieth-century educators to dispel.[20] The times seemed ripe for a better selection of curriculum materials, for greater integration of the materials selected, and improved methods of instruction, especially with reference to the motivation of studies. Colleges made a wide variety of approaches to meet these demands.[21] Among them there was a good deal of overlapping.[22] Perhaps it will be easiest to follow the trend of the times if we start with the plans which disturbed the traditional organization of subject matter least and proceed to those which altered it more and more radically. Thereafter we can note a few new emphases on older methods of instruction necessitated by the reorganization of the curriculum.

Better Use of Traditional Subject Matter

It will be well to get a running start here by reminding ourselves that the budget of discontent with the college program in the twentieth century was in part a balance brought forward from the nineteenth. To meet the changing demands of that hundred-year period, college authorities had gradually permitted the infiltration of the sciences into the program of liberal studies and had also gradually modified the prescribed curriculum till it had become largely if not wholly elective. Yet in spite of these concessions to individual freedom and preference there still remained a considerable and influential opinion that the curriculum was not efficiently enlisting the energies of the undergraduate. Since the introduction of the elective principle into a liberal curriculum augmented by the sciences had not fully mobilized these energies, expert opinion turned for relief in a different direction.

A new diagnosis of the trouble in undergraduate instruction called for placing greater responsibility for his education on the student's own shoulders. Recognizing a pedagogical principle at least as old as St. Thomas Aquinas's *De magistro,* Harvard's A. Lawrence Lowell declared that "all true education in college is self-education; and therefore the student must be induced to desire to make an effort, and a strenuous effort."[23] But how to induce him to do it? Sporadic attempts had already occurred in the nineteenth century. The University of Michigan, for instance, in the 1880s, tried to elicit extra student effort by releasing selected upperclassmen from conventional course requirements in two or three subjects but not waiving the requirement of a final examination therein. The proffered elbowroom for personal initiative stirred a few students but did not generate enough enthusiasm to prevent the plan from lapsing by the turn of the century.[24]

A more enduring attempt to reach the springs of student initiative occurred at the beginning of the new century under the energetic leadership of Woodrow Wilson at Princeton. Hardly had he been installed president before he launched a drive for the installation of a preceptorial plan of instruction. By adding to the faculty fifty preceptors—chosen for gentility as well as scholarship—he hoped to capture some of the benefits of individualized instruction at least for part of the program of each upperclassman. Although the expense of this type of instruction prevented him from having as low a student-preceptor ratio as he originally hoped, Wilson was successful in infusing a new spirit into undergraduate instruction. This spirit aimed at an intimate, informal association between student and teacher where, without forcing, intellectual interests would become contagious. The preceptor was to stimulate and guide, not drill and quiz. Students were to read books not to make a creditable showing at the preceptorial conference, but to master the ideas contained therein as a normal part of building their own personal points of view.[25]

Harvard's approach to implementing Lowell's desire to stir the student to self-exertion made a different emphasis. As Lowell saw it, the problem was not so much to push the average student to raise his minimum achievement as it was to excite the superior one to his maximum attainment. The average, perhaps, cannot expect to achieve more than mediocrity, but it is a major misfortune to thrust mediocrity on the talented. To create a favoring environment that would reward the exertion of outstanding ability, Lowell tried to capture for Harvard some of the English distinction between "honors" and "pass" courses. Instead of applying the distinction to courses, he applied it to results on a final examination designed to test, not a student's achievement in individual courses, but his ability to integrate the results of his labor in a whole field of study. The fundamental organization of the curriculum into individual subject-matter components was left untouched, but the student was encouraged to transcend their limits by organizing his thinking for the final examination in terms of broad general ideas underlying or interrelating his chosen field. Lowell feared, and with some reason, that gifted American students would not elect in sufficient numbers a special honors course if offered, but they might rise to the bait of achieving honors in an examination which would test their resourcefulness in exploring and organiz-ing a whole area.[26] At first only the department of history and government experimented with the device, but success soon won adherents in other depart-ments. In time the general examination proved so demanding that students found need of special help to prepare for it. To provide individual assistance Harvard instituted a tutorial system. Harvard tutors, however, unlike preceptors at Prince-ton, were drawn from all ranks of the faculty and did not form a subordinate rank of the teaching staff.[27]

Still a third application of the English system to American colleges occurred at Swarthmore after the First World War. There Frank Aydelotte, himself a former Rhodes Scholar, organized the undergraduate program, as Lowell had been reluctant to do, by recognizing honors instruction as something beyond and distinct from regular course work. While everyone at Princeton had some precep-torial work and every student at Harvard took the general examination, only those took honors at Swarthmore who elected them and who were certified by their lower-division instructors as capable of carrying them. Under tutorial guid-ance this selected group of students enjoyed considerable autonomy to organize their time and studies as they saw fit in their last two years. To insure that they would study the field of their interest and not the idiosyncrasies of the faculty teaching it, final examinations were set not by the Swarthmore faculty but by external examiners. By this sort of examination it was possible to evaluate the effectiveness of the faculty as well as the achievement of the student body.[28]

The heart of the honors program was the colloquium, the dialogue between faculty and student. Happily this form of instruction appealed to increasing numbers of students at Swarthmore. Whereas only 11 out of 227 chose honors at the outset of the program at Swarthmore, there were 146 out of 331 on the eve of the Second World War.[29] Not only did the idea spread among students but it also spread to other colleges. Expanding rapidly at first to count 93 by 1927 the rate of growth was much slower during the depression and subsequent world war period so that by the war's end there were only 116. The large-scale promo-tion of honors programs occurred from this point on. Much of the new momen-tum came from the formation of the Inter-University Council on the Superior Student and the newsletter it published as a clearinghouse on honors programs in hundreds of colleges over the country.

A close cousin of honors work was the program of "independent study."[30]

While obviously an important ingredient of honors work was encouragement of the student to assume considerable individual responsibility for planning and executing his studies, there were some who thought that "independent study" should characterize the instruction of many more than just honors students. In the elective curriculum, Americans had copied some of the self-determination characteristic of the German university, but a number wanted to go further and copy the self-reliance of independent study, too, as far as possible. The model they had in mind was described by an American returning from foreign study after the Civil War. The German student, he said, is "accountable only to himself for his opinions and mode of living, he shakes off spiritual bondage and becomes an independent thinker. He *must* think for himself, for there is no one set over him as a spiritual adviser and guide, prescribing the work for each day and each hour, telling him what he is to believe and what to disbelieve and marking him up or down accordingly."[31]

The advantage of capturing this attitude for the American student was obvious. If there was any drawback it was that this kind of instruction might cost as much as 25 per cent more than conventional instruction.[32] But a noted college trustee had a solution for this exigency. With more independent study there could be fewer formal classes; with fewer class sessions, the number of faculty could be curtailed; the salaries thus saved could be set against increased instructional costs.[33] Some institutions gave the solution a try, but others thought the economy more apparent than real.

In addition to Swarthmore two other smaller colleges made notable efforts to reinvigorate academic studies. Reed College in Oregon was launched just before the First World War on the announced platform of being an institution where intellectual enthusiasm was to be dominant. To insure this aim, extracurricular activities—the "side shows" as Woodrow Wilson called them—were uncompromisingly eliminated from competing with the main tent.[34] Thus a student had to pass a qualifying examination to enter the senior year and had to write a thesis on which he was orally examined before he graduated. In this way William T. Foster, Reed's first president, hoped to make his college a Johns Hopkins for undergraduates, the Balliol of America.[35] Antioch College took off in a different direction to bring a serious vein to its campus by splitting the academic year between academic studies and full-time gainful employment.[36] Taking a leaf from the experience of the University of Cincinnati, but also sobered by the impact of the depression, Antioch organized its program into alternating periods of work and study. Weeks in the classroom were followed by weeks on a real job earning a living, in turn followed by another stretch of studies succeeded again by work. A number of advantages sprang from the program. Sandwiching work between layers of the academic program led both to a better understanding and motivation of academic studies and to more responsible attitudes toward work. All of which was to say nothing of the more efficient use of the physical plant of the college made possible by platooning the students.

Correlation and Integration of the Curriculum

The foregoing devices for improving the quality of the undergraduate program achieved their success without seriously disturbing the traditional organization of the curriculum into discrete units of subject matter ruled by more or less autonomous departmental faculties. The general or comprehensive examination did, however, call attention to the desirability of biting off larger chunks of subject matter than represented by conventional courses. How well the student succeeded in digesting these larger bites was an open question. Instead of changing the metabolism or integration of the curriculum as a by-product of studying for an examination, some colleges proceeded more directly to a reorganization of the curriculum itself.

Before indicating their procedure, however, it may be well to pick up the story in the nineteenth century. There was a time then when the curriculum consisted of such large constellations of subject matter as natural philosophy, moral philosophy, and belles-lettres. To maintain their sway over these vast fields faculties found it necessary to invoke the principle of *divide et impera,* dividing in order to rule. Toward the end of the century, therefore, specialization forced a fragmentation of the traditional curriculum. Natural philosophy proliferated into such sciences as physics, chemistry, biology, and geology. Moral philosophy subdivided into political science, economics, sociology, and anthropology.[37] And the study of belles-lettres became the study of poetry, drama, and the novel. Worried by the diversification of courses, President Stiles of Yale at the end of the eighteenth century tried to introduce some integration into a largely prescribed if variegated curriculum by delivering a series of lectures variously styled as the "cyclopedia of literature" or the "circle of the sciences." There, discoursing on language, geography, mathematics, natural philosophy, and astronomy, he endeavored to give students a coherent perspective of human learning.[38]

In the nineteenth century Eliot's elective principle emphasized specialization rather than prescription and integration. To restore some comprehensiveness, Lowell, in the early twentieth century, required the student to distribute his electives over a wide sampling of subjects at the same time that he was permitted to retain a generous share of time for concentration on one of them.

The history of the curriculum, thus, had taken the form of a vast Hegelian triad wherein the thesis in the early nineteenth century had been prescription, the antithesis in the later nineteenth century had been election, and the synthesis in the twentieth century had been concentration and distribution. But at best this synthesis was artificial. It was only a cross section of courses from specialized and usually unrelated departments. The mere addition or juxtaposition of such courses without any effort at bending them to each other and toward some broad central aim was mechanical at best. Hence the kind of synoptic integration characteristic of liberal education went by default. The search for unity centered in what came to be called "general education."[39] This phrase has had many meanings. One—general education for the terminal junior-college student—has already been noted.[40] A second—general education in the four-year college—now needs explication. At the outset one may note the close similarity between general and liberal education. General education, however, was not so much a synonym for liberal education as it was a way of organizing it. As a facet of liberal education it developed two dimensions. On the one side it faced the great proliferation of subjects and tried to determine what everyone ought to know regardless of departmental organization. On the other it tried to interrelate subjects into some meaningful whole.

Blame for the lack of unity was initially laid at the door of the colleges and their multiplication of courses in the curriculum. As early as 1902, however, John Dewey was pointing out that congestion in the curriculum stemmed not from faulty pedagogical organization but from rapidly expanding knowledge of the arts and sciences. What was needed, he said, was "a survey, at least, of the universe in its manifold phases from which a student can get an 'orientation' to the larger world."[41] One of the earliest to try to implement Dewey's suggestion was Alexander Meiklejohn. While dean at Brown before World War I he introduced a course in "social and economic institutions" into the undergraduate course of study. A decade later he was advocating two kinds of general or survey courses, one for beginners and another for seniors. The latter became a forerunner of senior symposia like that at Reed College in 1924 whose stated purpose was to help the student achieve a synthesis of the various factors—historical, literary, scientific, political, and the like—making up contemporary society and inciting him to face the question of his own philosophy of life.[42]

Columbia and Dartmouth, however, were most prominent in developing what came to be known as "survey" courses. During the First World War Columbia had offered a course on "War Issues" to members of its Student Army Training Corps. Since these issues were complex it was necessary to approach them almost simultaneously on a variety of fronts—history, philosophy, economics, politics, and the like. The definite success of this interdisciplinary attack led to the query, if it was a good educational procedure in wartime, why might it not be equally good in peacetime as well? Assuming the affirmative, Columbia came forward with its later widely known "Introduction to Contemporary Civilization." At first "C.C." was a one-year course but in 1929 a second year was added. In 1937 a similar survey course was offered in humanities which also a decade later became a two-year offering. A similar science sequence was short-lived, lasting only from 1934 to 1941.

Since the interdisciplinary approach had been so successful in organizing a single course, some concluded that it might be equally successful in organizing a whole year or even two years of undergraduate study. Indeed this was precisely the tack taken by Alexander Meiklejohn in setting up his "experimental college" at the University of Wisconsin. In the first year of its two-year program he proposed that students devote the whole year to a study of an ancient civilization such as the Greek or Roman. To penetrate the spirit of such a culture as that of the Greeks it would be necessary to come at it from all sides—its poetry, its drama, its philosophy, its politics, and its economy—but none except in relation to all the rest. In the second year Meiklejohn proposed taking up a modern, most likely American, civilization in the same manner. The main aim would be not so much to gain information, although that was important, as to develop a philosophical habit of mind in grasping the over-all significance of the way the various parts of a culture interact.[43] This promising innovation lasted a few years and then folded its tent, not for want of merit, but for want of students, who were actively discouraged from electing it by a midwestern philistinism emanating not only from politicians but even faculty.[44]

If there had been no unity in the curriculum it was because, as Meiklejohn pointed out, curriculum-makers had not assumed the unity of knowledge. But now that they were starting from this assumption, on what was unity to be predicated? Some thought there was a correlation among disciplines, that synoptically all disciplines had a logical relation to each other. From a nineteenth-century angle this unity paralleled the emphasis Herbartians had been placing on "correlation" of subjects in the elementary and secondary schools. But the interesting innovation in "survey" courses was that they took their point of departure, not from the logic of subject matter, but from the logic of events. "The sense of the plan," as Jacques Barzun pointedly put it, "can be seen at once by starting, not from the college, but from the world."[45] The advantage of such a starting point is that unity cuts straight across subject-matter lines. By doing so it assures the student not only a wide acquaintance with different disciplines but also an inescapable integration of them. Furthermore, crisscrossing the various disciplines, whether to understand "war issues," "problems of democracy," or "area" studies (popular during and after World War II to get an integral view of a country by interrelating its history, politics, religion, economics, and the like) had the merit of broadening rather than specializing college education.[46] It put stress in introductory courses on what is important for everyone to know, whether academically minded or not, and regardless of vocational destination. Furthermore, it avoided the persistent complaint that conventional introductory subject-matter courses were mainly designed to be prerequisites to a major or even a subsequent Ph.D. in that field.

On looking at the reverse side of the coin, it will not be surprising that conservative faculty members had reservations about, if they did not actually oppose, the survey course as thin and diffuse.[47] The endeavor of survey courses to understand the contemporary world rather than systematic subject matter took on added importance during the depression when colleges were wrestling with the "youth problem." Such courses seemed ideally suited to many young men and women who ordinarily might not have attended college but who entered and tarried there because the employment market was unready to absorb them.

Although many colleges successfully copied the survey course in various forms, the faculty of the University of Chicago examined it and found it wanting. But it also found wanting the contemporary system of liberal education with its conglomeration of electives and credits, all subserving specialization in the graduate school. Eschewing mere amendment of the traditional pattern, this faculty tried to rethink the problem of liberal education from the ground up. First of all, as already seen, it set up a new college unit of four years, consisting of the last two years of high school and the first two years of college, whose principal function was to concern itself with general or liberal education free from bias toward the graduate school.[48] The curriculum for this school was to include the subject matter indispensable to every educated person whatever calling he might be headed for, whether medicine, law, engineering, business, education, or what. In taking responsibility for deciding what is indispensable, they agreed that they must avoid the atomization of the elective system and yet achieve a general education more thorough than that secured by the survey. To implement this conclusion they telescoped the multidepartmental organization of subjects, which had become entrenched behind the elective system, into four divisions—biologic science, physical science, social science, and the humanities. Each student had to give evidence of mastery of the basic materials tightly packed into each of these four divisions, together with evidence of a command of a clear prose style. While the faculty was unequivocal about the content of these divisional courses, student attendance at them was voluntary. Moreover, a student could sit for examinations not only at the end of the term but any time before then that he might think he was ready. As at Swarthmore, the examining function was separated from the instructional. With the energetic support of President Hutchins this Chicago plan became one of the most talked-about reorganizations to be found in college education during the second quarter of the twentieth century.[49]

Yet, advanced as he regarded the "divisional" organization to be, Hutchins did not think it went far enough. Neither did he think such further evidences of the popularity of interdisciplinary integration as Harvard's "roving professorships" or Yale's Institute of Human Relations more than a palliative to the basic problem. To recapture the unity which liberal education enjoyed when theology reigned as queen of the disciplines, it was necessary that general education be grounded in the "fundamental and permanent studies."[50] These studies, he claimed, were to be found in the "Great Books" curriculum spawned at Columbia, encouraged at Chicago, and actually put in operation at St. John's College in Maryland.

This course had its inception in the mind of John Erskine—professor, author, and musician—while serving on the faculty of Columbia University during the First World War.[51] He challenged the indictment against contemporary youth that they had no interest in the great classics of Western civilization. To test his conviction he proposed a course running throughout the last two years of college in which students would read a classic a week and then meet for an extended period to discuss it informally. Fellow faculty members scouted the notion that a week per classic could more than scratch the surface of serious criticism. Erskine reminded them, however, that the charge against youth was not inadequate scholarship but unwillingness to read great books. When after the war he received consent to try out his scheme, it proved a surprising success. So many students elected it, as a matter of fact, that it had to meet in sections. No small part of its later success was owing to such remarkable section leaders as Mortimer J. Adler and Mark Van Doren, who both subsequently became its public champions. But it was Stringfellow Barr and Scott Buchanan from the faculty of the University of Virginia who finally went to St. John's via the University of Chicago to incorporate the "Great Books" as the very heart of that college's curriculum.[52]

How many "great books" are there?[53] The round number of 100 became associated with the St. John's program. Erskine's course included only about half that number. Obviously the total number is relatively unimportant. More significant is the question, What is the criterion of a great book? Hutchins put it neatly when he explained, "A classic is a book that is contemporary in every age."[54] Of course the variety of books which meet this test is great, but the tie which binds them together and thus restores unity to the curriculum is metaphysics, for in these classics, in these "permanent studies," are to be found the perennial rational principles that undergird the universe. Needless to say, studies possessing such perennial qualities were to be the same for one and all at St. John's. For proponents this was a strong point in the program; for critics, a point of attack.[55]

General education continued to win adherents in the post-World War II era. The most notable recruit, probably, was Harvard. Even while the war was in its later stages, a committee of the Harvard faculty was trying to peer ahead and divine the curriculum changes postwar conditions would demand. Their conclusions were published under the title of *General Education in a Free Society.*[56] Though widely discussed throughout the country, they were never fully implemented at Cambridge. Indeed at Chicago and Columbia general education had some difficulty maintaining its prewar momentum, particularly where general education reached into a second year. The increasing demand for early specialization, especially in the natural sciences, exercised considerable braking force.

As colleges began to review and re-examine their general education programs it was Columbia where a new defense was put forward.[57] A one-man faculty report there took issue with the idea that general education was being ground down between the nether millstone of advanced placement in the secondary school and the upper millstone of demand from the graduate school for early specialization. It recognized that secondary schools might encroach on higher education in the college in logical fields like mathematics, but it claimed that the high school was much less a threat in fields like the humanities. As for the graduate school it maintained that specialized and general education had more interests in common than in opposition. Supporting argument here started with the observation that facts learned in general education age faster than the student. To avoid obsolescence, therefore, general education must concentrate on theory rather than fact. But even theories, the basic conceptualizations of disciplines, are changing 20 to 100 times faster today than a century ago. Obviously, if general education will concern itself with how disciplines form and reform their basic conceptualizations and how the basic conceptualizations of different disciplines can be linked together, it will have been justified *both* as an invaluable end in itself and as an indispensable preparation for specialization.[58]

Individualized and Life-Adjustment Curriculums

As the second half of the twentieth century rolled on, attempts to reconstruct the undergraduate curriculum became bolder. Up to this point even the boldest plans largely confined themselves to giving an existing and long-standing intellectual heritage a new scheme of organization. It was not long, however, before innovating minds turned their attention from the organization of the heritage to the content of the heritage itself. Instead of accepting inherited content at its own assessment, they took virtually none of it for granted. Careful not to pour the new wine of democratic endeavor, fermented notably by the Morrill Acts, into the old bottles of liberal education, they decided to build a curriculum each constituent of which was recommended, not by age-old intrinsic values, but by its contemporary significance. Like Barzun, they started with the world—and the contemporary world at that. Believing with Darwin that structure follows function, they set about constructing a curriculum based on the functions which contemporary men and women perform.

Perhaps the clearest illustration of building a functional curriculum was to be found at Stephens, a two-year college for women in Missouri. There the administration was committed to a program of collegiate education for women as women. To direct such a program it engaged a curriculum expert, Werrett W. Charters. Using techniques which had become popular in the so-called scientific construction of elementary- and secondary-school curriculums, Charters set out first to ascertain the "needs" of young women which a college education was to satisfy. This he did by asking some 300 women to keep diaries for the period of a week, noting therein a record of their activities, intellectual and emotional. All 300 were college graduates, some recent and some of longer standing. Half were married and among those gainfully employed nearly a dozen and a half vocations were represented. Moreover the 300 were distributed over 37 of the 48 states. Material from these diaries was finally collected under some two dozen categories, which later were reduced to seven—communications, physical health, mental health, humanities, social and civic relations, consumer training, philosophy and religion. Natural science and family relations were added later. To meet the "needs" of these categories new courses were constructed.[59] Of course they included more than might be expected of traditional materials; but if they did, it was not because of their historical prestige but because of their functioning in the contemporary scene.

While Stephens, Minnesota, and other like-minded colleges were working out new custom-made functional curriculums, experimental colleges such as Bennington and Sarah Lawrence were tailoring similar functional curriculums to each individual student. When the entering student came on their campuses an individual inventory was made of her capacities, interests, and previous experiences. Taking off from this point into the contemporary world, the student with the help of an adviser selected problems or areas of interest which she wished to explore.[60] Intellectual materials in library, laboratory, or studios were next suggested as resources that might prove fruitful in the exploration. What the student learned in following up these suggestions became her curriculum. Indeed, as President Harold Taylor of Sarah Lawrence said, "The curriculum . . . will have to be conceived as a name for the total active life of each person in college."[61] Thus no fixed historical content of liberal studies formed a Procrustean bed on which she had to lie. Yet it was recognized, to be sure, that the bed of her own making did not always fit either. Consequently early curriculum choices tended to be tentative and subject to change. If some time was lost in fitting the curriculum to the student, it was more than compensated by the student's more effective learning when she and her adviser finally found the curriculum which both recognized as genuinely meaningful to her.[62]

At their best the problems selected for study came out of the context of the contemporary world. Atomic fission with its complex ramifications might be a good example. Here the student would not only probe scientific profundities concerned with physical fission but also a whole tangle of social consequences in the field of international relations, morals, public power, and the like which cut quite across conventional subject-matter lines. To unravel the tangle she would have to go to each of these disciplines, as in the case of the survey course. The difference would be, however, that in the individualized approach she would have to be a much more active agent in planning her own strategy and ultimately organizing the results of her study. In this respect her study plan would resemble "honors" work, but again it would differ in that she would be organizing, not conventional fields of study into some logical mosaic, but intellectual resources for the solution of some vital problem of the day.[63] Incidentally, faculties like those of Bennington and Sarah Lawrence held the conviction that integration is something to be sought in the individual student, not in the curriculum.

The educational impieties involved in such radical curriculum departures did not escape criticism. Some questioned the desirability of the life-adjustment principle, for, in learning to adjust to present problems, the student might paradoxically find himself out of adjustment by the time he graduated because in a rapidly changing world problems might be quite different then.[64] Similarly others feared that such a curriculum failed to provide systematic instruction in subjects of perennial significance.[65] Still others doubted that many adults have even occupational interests which would sustain spontaneity in a problem organization of the college curriculum.[66] Lastly were those who deplored having something for everyone in the curriculum at the expense of exacting high standards for the elite.[67]

One need not probe far beneath the surface of these individualized, life-adjustment curriculums to detect their connection with the "progressive education" movement in the elementary and secondary schools of the time. As it was only possible to break the academic lockstep in the elementary and secondary schools by experimental schools, so too it was felt that experimental colleges were the only means to bring about the fundamental reforms of which liberal education stood in need. The "progressive" device of casting the college curriculum in problematic form, together with selecting materials from the intellectual heritage in terms of their pragmatic relevance, brought once again to the surface the extensive impact of John Dewey on American education.

Innovative forces in the college curriculum abated during the war years and the succeeding apathetic '50's. But in the activistic '60's they reasserted themselves.[68] In one direction there was an effort to politicize higher education. Where this occurred, the curriculum was not only oriented to problems—much as in the earlier experimental colleges—but it sought to be an actual force in social outcomes. Here Antioch again catches the eye. Although never wholly radicalized the faculty there were more politically polarized than anywhere else. In another direction there was an effort to concentrate on the affective aspects of life. Innovators here saw not only St. John's but even the problem-oriented curriculums as too verbal, too intellectual. One kind of curriculum to embody the neglected aspect of feeling centered on the aesthetic. The best early example was perhaps Black Mountain College. Another kind was the "communal-expressive" curriculum as evidenced in Johnston College, an experimental offshoot of the University of Redlands and Kresge College of the University of California at Santa Cruz. Humanistic psychologists provided these colleges not only with an ideology but also techniques like the encounter group.

The Demand for Relevance

The educational innovations launched during the first half of the century continued to work themselves out in the decade following the war. The placid fifties, however, were followed by the turbulent sixties. However satisfied academicians might have been with the earlier decades of progress, there was a latent student discontent with their academic diet. This discontent surfaced almost explosively with the student disruptions of the Vietnam War period. The rallying cry heard almost everywhere was that the curriculum lacked "relevance." Nor was this complaint limited to the activist minority. The Carnegie Commission on Higher Education found from a questionnaire that 91 per cent of a 70,000 student sample polled wished for a greater relevance! Striking support for this statistic was found in the fact that 71 per cent of faculty similarly polled agreed with them. Nor was the impact of these figures lessened by the fact that approximately 70 per cent of both groups were satisfied with higher education in general.[69]

Just what criteria were the students using for relevance? For one thing, they thought that the conventional curriculum held inexcusably aloof from contemporary moral and political forces in their environment such as war, race riots, psychedelic drugs, sex—indeed, a whole new counterculture. Perhaps pertinent materials were packed away somewhere in the cultural storehouse but little or none of them were brought to bear directly on the specific problems "bugging" them. For another thing, students thought the conventional curriculum irrelevant because they saw its academic demands merely as stepping stones to a career or simply as hurdles that the "establishment" put in their way to test their obedience, endurance, and conformity, a configuration they rejected *in toto*.[70] For a last thing, the financial stringency of the seventies settled the issue of relevancy for an increasing number of students by making practical or vocational studies more attractive than liberal ones.[71] The student demand for relevance was effective in two directions. In a few established colleges like Brown and Brandeis students were outstanding figures in curriculum reform.[72] But it was in the "free university" movement—and there were a hundred such universities scattered in more than three dozen states—that relevance had its heyday.[73] These universities took their model from Paul Goodman's *The Community of Scholars,* which laid a heavy emphasis on freedom.[74] The "free university" thus was a voluntary association of those who wanted to learn with those who wanted to teach. Nothing was either prescribed or proscribed. The curriculum reflected student interests; otherwise the instructor had no students. Such *ad hoc* courses were offered as the drug culture, sex, the Vietnam War, race, civil liberties. True to voluntarism, moreover, no pressure was exerted on the curriculum through a system of grades, degrees, or accreditation. Typically the "free university" charged no fees, and if it had to, they were paid as voluntary contributions.

A special and very important instance of relevance was the generation of black studies programs. At the height of racial protest in the second half of the sixties many blacks awoke to a new feeling in pride of race. To develop self-confidence in that new pride they found the white culture of the conventional college and university somewhat dysfunctional. Consequently they demanded a "black" curriculum relevant to the "black" experience. With 30 million blacks in the country the demand could hardly be denied. In fact, since the student protests arose, over 1,200 institutions of higher learning came to offer a "major" in the field. At City College of New York enrollment in black studies rose from 750 to 1,500 students in a single year. Whether these new courses should be organized as offshoots from conventional departments or have a separate status of their own presented problems initially. Some blacks contended the black experience was so unique that only blacks could teach a black curriculum. Others contended that true scholarship was independent of skin color. In any event, black studies have come a long way toward academic respectability since their early days.[75]

Many individual faculty members also sharpened up their courses to make them more relevant. But the spirit of relevance also sparked and reinforced numerous other academic innovations.[76] Between 1962 and 1965, for instance, the Carnegie Commission on Higher Education found that there had been a better than 20 per cent change in departmental offerings among colleges sampled.[77] One prominent suggestion for invigorating the curriculum which had the support of the Carnegie Commission was to reduce the time taken by the undergraduate course to three years, a suggestion which had enjoyed a brief popularity early in the century.[78] Columbia thought undergraduate and professional studies could be made more relevant to each other. Instead of postponing specialized career education until the completion of general education, Columbia proposed some specialized education begin at once and some general be reserved for graduate years.[79] A number of people thought relevancy could be heightened by including a period of public service somewhere in the undergraduate experience.[80] Still others experimented with the academic calendar.[81] Thus some advocated a year-round calendar to speed up entry on an active career. Dartmouth and Goucher adopted 3–3 plans wherein the academic year was divided into trimesters in which each student took three intensive courses each trimester.[82] Similarly Colorado College resurrected the earlier Hiram College plan of studying just one course at a time for blocks of three to four weeks.[83] One very popular rearrangement of the academic monthly calendar was the 4–1–4 plan because the midterm period permitted such a variety of activities satisfying the demand for relevancy. Here there could be a de-emphasis on credits and great flexibility for adjusting student and faculty roles to each other.

The Motivation of Learning

Whatever the form of curriculum revision, a large measure of its success was going to depend on molding methods of instruction by the same spirit governing the curriculum revision itself. Yet, as a matter of fact, there was only mild attention paid to innovation in that direction. Lecturing was still popular but there was a lessening demand for it as students took over growing responsibility for working up a field through their own reading. Instead of competing with the printed page as a purveyor of information, the lecture took on the function of interrelating and interpreting that information.[84] The increasing popularity of the discussion method indicated a marked swing from the didactic to the dialectic in instruction. Its nineteenth-century antecedent, the recitation, in which the teacher cited and the student recited, went into the pedagogical discard. But the recitation as a Socratic dialogue flourished and took on greatly enlarged significance.[85] The technique used so effectively by Mark Hopkins, Eliphalet Nott, and Francis Wayland in the early nineteenth century was perpetuated at its end by men like Charles E. Garman at Amherst[86] and in the twentieth by William H. Kilpatrick at Columbia, together with a host of others, especially unsung tutors and preceptors.

If there was only little interest in method, what little there was possessed an insightful quality. On the whole the curriculum revisions of the first half of the twentieth century represented a shift in the center of gravity from subject matter to the student. While older methods took the intrinsic values of subject matter for granted and therefore concentrated on transferring them to the student, newer methods were more inclined to take hold of the interests of students as the handle to teaching the values inherent in the curriculum. Older methods, for the most part, not only disregarded the interest of the student but even counted it a point in their favor that they disciplined the student to apply himself to subject matter without or even against the inclination of interest. William Lyons Phelps, one of

Yale's most beloved teachers, remembered being warned, when he was breaking into teaching before the turn of the century, that being too interesting a teacher might be an obstacle to his academic advancement.[87] Fortunately the contrary situation obtained after the turn of the century. But the colleges were much slower than the lower schools to become preoccupied with the problem of how to elicit the spontaneous energies of the student in favor of his studies.[88]

The problem of generating interest was not an easy one and never had been. Alexander Meiklejohn put one of its principal difficulties in perspective when he pointed out that American students came to college shaped by a society which by and large did not have a high regard for books.[89] The student often reflected this social matrix by contenting himself with a "gentleman's C" in academic achievement. How could the college counteract this subtle but powerful climate of opinion? Interestingly enough, this climate did not pervade the professional school. There it was fashionable to study because only the obtuse failed to appreciate the connection between application to books and subsequent professional success.[90] The liberal-arts curriculum labored under the disadvantage of conventionally being connected to nothing; it had to be studied on its own account and for its own intrinsic worth.[91]

The quick and easy remedy to overcome student apathy to study had usually been the employment of secondary motivations.[92] Negatively, faculties tried to prod the student to his books by appeal to his anxieties—threatening him with low grades, exclusion from participation in extracurricular activities, or even suspension from college. Positively, it tried to arouse intellectual activity through appealing to his vanity—placing high-standing students on the "dean's list," excusing the superior from regular class attendance,[93] flattering them with academic honors such as Phi Beta Kappa, or graduating them *cum laude*.[94] But the trouble with all such secondary motivations had been that the minute they were relaxed or removed motivation slumped. There had been nothing self-sustaining about them. In fact such devices had easily degenerated into immoral attitudes because in making no sustained contribution to the student's own voluntary powers of intellectual improvement they had unfortunately taught him irresponsibility.[95]

In the face of the failure of secondary motivations the only recourse was an appeal to primary ones. In primary motivation, as Meiklejohn, Ordway Tead, and others so clearly saw, there had to be a direct connection between student purposes and the learning tasks assigned.[96] In the traditional motivations already mentioned, the connection was roundabout. In doing his lessons the student responded directly or primarily to relieve his anxieties or boost his vanity. Any spur to or benefit from his lessons was indirect or secondary. The goal of reformers was to promote studies to the position of primary stimulant, where the student would see them as the direct means to satisfying his personal longings and ambitions. Should such an outcome occur, the objectives of college education would play a much more important part than ordinarily realized. They would not only give direction to the student's educational effort but they would also supply it with its motive power. But to be sure that that power reached its destination, the objectives had to be the student's own. They could not be assigned. This fact did not deny that the student would need help from the faculty in formulating his objectives, but it did affirm that ultimately the objectives would have to be of his own acceptance or choosing. Attaching so much importance to student purpose, it should be made explicit, did not necessarily mean an abdication of discipline. Indeed, quite the contrary, those emphasizing the voluntarism of the student held that an even higher and more ethical form of discipline resulted when the student himself deliberately chose a course of study and then autonomously persisted to its conclusion in the face of distraction and perplexity.[97]

The problem method proved most popular in enlisting the student's interest. Early in the twentieth century some saw the possibilities of using in the college the problematic approach common to graduate instruction in research.[98] A little later President Lowell of Harvard wished that the vitality of the case method of teaching law could be captured for the undergraduate college as well.[99] His thinking, however, seems to have stalled before the difficulty of framing problems appropriate to that level of instruction. After World War II Dartmouth instituted a course organized around the "great issues" of the day. Although widely copied for the realism it seemed to infuse in the curriculum, a score of years later it had lost its power to galvanize student energies. By then students seemed to feel that their own activism—their direct involvement in public issues like civil liberties, the war in Vietnam, and the like—must take the place of vicarious concern with "great issues."[100]

It was John Dewey perhaps more than any of these who, influenced by the impact of science on modern culture, showed how the problem method might be used.[101] The point of departure, as he saw it, was to choose some perplexity in which the student had a sense of involvement. Such perplexities might run all the way from large-scale problems taken from public life to the less pretentious ones of private life. Thus, intrigued by the tensions between East and West, a student might want to study some aspect of Russia as it impinged on the Western world. Or he might want to probe deeply into the philosophical or psychological ramifications of some moral strain agitating him personally. Once past the point of departure, there followed the familiar steps in the problem method of gathering data, forming hypotheses, and testing them so far as academic limits permitted.

But in any event the young college instructor was well advised to commence his instruction at the point where the student was in his personal development. In an annual report in 1914 President Butler urged his faculty at Columbia to observe the difference between the logical and psychological organizations of the well-taught lesson.[102] Taking esoteric delight in contemplating the symmetry of their own subject-matter fields, college instructors were prone to forget that the order in which the mature scholar organizes a field of learning is not necessarily the easiest one by which to introduce a neophyte to it. The learner may run a tortuous course to his goal, unable to see or even use the short cuts that seem so logical to a savant.

Running through the new approach to teaching was an emphasis on student activity as an important ingredient of motivation. Some stated it psychologically. Interest involves an emotional drive which the professor, suffering overoften from the occupational disease of hyperintellectualism, is likely to overlook.[103] Interest, however, does not so much beget activity as activity begets interest. In either case it was a psychological error to think that the student first learned passively and then, having learned, engaged in activity to apply what he had mastered. Alfred North Whitehead, England's gift to the Harvard philosophy faculty, justified the activity principle in learning on epistemological grounds with which Dewey would certainly have concurred. "In the process of learning," he said, "there should be present, in some sense or other, a subordinate activity of application. In fact, the applications are part of the knowledge, for the very meaning of the things known is wrapped up in their relationships beyond themselves. Thus unapplied knowledge is knowledge shorn of its meaning."[104]

To take the view that the meaning of the curriculum depended on the consequences of acting on it provided a lively stimulant to study. Certainly it appealed to the twentieth-century-college clientele more pertinently than did the objective of contemplating ideas for their own sake. Nevertheless academic faculties feared the motivation of practical consequences because it so easily led to an emphasis on vocation, the context in which human drives are often most powerful and yet a context which tends to distort the role of the liberal arts. Danger that technology was to liberal education, Robert M. Hutchins nevertheless was willing to admit it into the liberal college, but strictly as a matter of method of instruction and by no means as a component of the curriculum.[105] Most faculties of liberal arts, however, were extremely wary of letting the camel of pragmatism get even this much of his nose into the academic tent.

Encouraging the student to rely on books rather than lectures inevitably enhanced the importance of the college library as compared with its status in earlier centuries. As one librarian put it, the great switch in instruction was from the "few books" to the "many books" method. Whereas formerly students had taken few books out of the library and usually textbooks at that, the new emphasis in instruction encouraged them to go to the library with syllabus or bibliography in hand to examine numerous sources, many of them original. Colleges unwilling to adopt the "Great Books" program of St. John's nevertheless welcomed a wider reading of classic authors within the frame of reference of their own campuses. As a result of the new importance of books, college libraries found it necessary to establish open bookshelves, increase the space allotted to reserved books, and multiply the number of duplicates.[106] But the most exciting development in the use of the library, the computerization of its resources, was just coming into sight after mid-century. Its potentialities seemed fantastic.

New Approaches to Methods of Instruction

In spite of the foregoing improvements in methods of handling curriculum materials teaching remained the Achilles heel of the American undergraduate college in the seventh decade of the century.[107] If there was anything clear from the student protests of that period it was a disenchantment with the quality of teaching students were getting. The demand for relevance in the curriculum was not only a complaint that subject matter was poorly selected but that often when it was well chosen it was taught poorly. For the protesters the cardinal element in method again was interest. The primary component in interest was feeling. By contrast the faculty was too academic, too intellectual. According to the existentialists among the students, man feels before he thinks. Therefore there must be a redressing of the balance between the two in the method of instruction. There must be more self-initiated and self-appropriated learning. If anything, there had been too much teaching and not enough learning for one truly learns only that which he voluntarily accepts to learn and he learns that only insofar as he genuinely accepts it.[108]

The thrust of student discontent did not so much initiate new methods as it spurred and reinforced movements already afoot. Learning was made a more cooperative endeavor; student and instructor made joint inquiry into problematic situations. The student helped choose the ends governing instruction and the materials appropriate to achieving these ends. Colloquiums replaced classrooms and even the informality of the dormitory was enlisted to make learning more attractive. Highly stimulating to the imagination, moreover, was the new educational technology with its employment of electronic media.[109] Audiovisual centers including closed-circuit television, language laboratories, and video cassettes were explored. Computerized instruction, to say nothing of the computerized library, opened up almost unimagined vistas for the future. Some institutions collected these exciting new devices into new specially constructed buildings called "learning centers."[110]

Some thought that the revolution in pedagogy caused by the new technology still lay ahead. Faculty had availed themselves of the new media only grudgingly, in part probably because they were suspicious of materials provided by others.[111] But even at best there was some discouragement about advance in methodology. A survey made for the Carnegie Commission on Higher Education revealed innovative teaching as only a very small part of contemporary practice. On occasion the surveyor found it difficult to obtain admission to classes because a professor still regarded his classroom as his castle. On the whole he found faculty not hostile to teaching. Yet, while they respected it, they were not enthusiastic about it. Few were devoted to teaching and few treated it as a fine art.[112]

The innovative-minded professor had a plethora of directions in which to move.[113] There was some complaint, however, that too few of the directions were charted by substantial research.[114] Indeed, some of the research available seemed to discourage innovation. Thus at least two studies seemed to indicate that such variables as class size, team teaching, discussion versus lecture method, programmed instruction, and the like made no significant statistical difference in learning accomplishment.[115] Although these studies could be attacked for viewing learning as mere subject-matter mastery and for underplaying concomitant learnings difficult to measure, they were a warning that the professoriate had to become more sophisticated about what went on in the classroom.[116] With the financial stringencies of the seventies the public was beginning to apply the test of accountability to instruction, that is, judging it by faculty performance rather than catalogue promises.[117]

In this era of complaint about college teaching one problem of long standing —examinations and academic standards—came up for a new review. For long it had been assumed that the role of higher institutions of learning was to educate and examinations were to measure whether that objective was being achieved. But activist students of the sixties and seventies pointed out that the real as against purported role of examinations was to certify, that degrees and diplomas certified one to the next level of education, to particular rungs on the economic ladder, and to social status in general.[118] Being disenchanted with this establishmentarian order they found themselves seriously at odds with the whole examination system. Some wanted to do away with credentialing while others tried to draw its fangs by a system of pass-fail grades.

As for the former alternative, it made little headway even though there was already some precedent for separating teaching from examining. Dartmouth had tried the idea in 1831,[119] and Eliot recommended it in his inaugural in 1869.[120] But it remained for the next century to give it full play at Swarthmore and the University of Chicago.[121] In addition to encouraging the student to concentrate on the complexities of his subject matter rather than the idiosyncrasies of his instructor, there was the advantage of ultimately developing regional universities whose major function would be to examine. In this way candidates might receive credit for skills and knowledge acquired in a variety of ways other than the conventional academic.[122] The separation of education from examining, however, did not have a popular spread to other institutions. In the majority the two functions remained joined and the main emphasis was on whether the system worked fairly.[123] Fairness was sought in one direction by developing objective tests of the "true-false" and "multiple-choice" variety since a careful study of subjective marks on the old essay examination afforded statistical proof of their unreliability.[124]

As for the latter alternative, the attack on academic standards, there was a slight retreat. In the fifties excellence was the ruling standard. The launching of Russia's Sputnik in this decade, however, created considerable intellectual anxiety because the United States had been beaten at its own specialties, science and technology. The colleges and universities demanded excellence in order to catch up. But in the next decade the student opposition to the establishment not only tried to disassociate higher education from the military-industrial complex but was very sympathetic to minority groups, especially blacks, whose cultural handicap made it difficult for them to compete with whites for the favors distributed by the examination-certification system. Hence it demoted excellence as an academic standard. In addition there was an existential or voluntaristic strain stemming from Paul Goodman which disparaged external pressures like examination grades. All this seems to have been reflected, for one thing, in a decline, commencing in 1963, in the average S.A.T. (scholastic aptitude test) scores. At first the decline was gradual but shortly there was a marked decline each year over the preceding one which was not halted till the compiling of scores for the academic period 1973–1974.[125]

Unable to dislodge the examination system itself, many students opted for a pass-fail system of grades to relieve pressures of the establishment. But very few institutions adopted pass-fail grading for the whole curriculum. Usually a student was allowed only one or two courses in which he would be rated on a pass-fail basis to explore courses outside his major or minor. But graduate schools cast a jaundiced eye at the system. So, too, did the public. They knew that problems of war and peace, labor and management, health and poverty, politics and economics, religion and morals required a system of higher education governed by excellence.[126] Nature was neither so bountiful, nor technology so adequate nor humanity so benign that mankind could stay on top of such problems with less than its optimum effort.[127]

14

The Philosophy of Higher Education

Higher education in the United States was nearly two hundred years old before any considerable number of educators took occasion to give explicit statement to its underlying philosophy. Up to this time its philosophy had been largely implicit. And even afterward it tended to be piecemeal rather than comprehensive. Certainly no one projected higher-education programs based on systematic academic philosophies of the day. At first men theorized about that phase of higher education known as liberal education. The concern in liberal studies was largely with what kind of individual to form. The basic idea seemed to be to make a man first and if that was done successfully then one could turn with confidence to his education as a professional man, a captain of industry or commerce, a statesman, and the like. Later this order seemed to be reversed; liberal education came to be subordinated to research and research to public service. When this occurred the theory of higher education focused more on the nature of knowledge and whether public service tended to distort it.

Mental Discipline

In the colonial period thus, nearly everyone took for granted, as his forbears in Europe had since Hellenic times, that *liberali liberaliter instituendi*—"gentlemen should be educated like gentlemen." But what was a gentleman? The education of gentlemen had long proceeded on two little examined dualisms, one about human nature and the other about the nature of society. The one about man considered him to have both a rational and an appetitive nature. The one about society held to its dichotomous class structure. The educational consequence of combining the two dualisms required that man's rational nature be trained to reign sovereign not only over his physical body but over the body politic, the latter composed of freemen like himself on the one hand and lower-class people on the other. Liberal education reflected this situation, being notably intellectual and theoretical compared to the practical and vocational education of the masses.

In the seventeenth and eighteenth centuries young gentlemen or freemen attending college were usually bound for the learned professions. The gateway to these professions, so far as it lay through the college, consisted of a study of the learned languages, Latin and Greek. In this regimen there was scarcely any perceptible difference between cultivation of the mind and preparation for the professions. The classical or humanistic curriculum accomplished both at one and the same time. In the nineteenth century, however, what had been a barely perceptible fissure in the unity of liberal education at the end of the eighteenth, spread so wide that its implicit theory could no longer be taken for granted. It now demanded explicit statement and critical examination.

Discontent with the traditional form of liberal education expressed itself at first, not by the statement of a new set of principles refuting the old, but by the emergence of a different set of practices. These practices were embodied in such new institutions of higher education as the University of Virginia, founded in 1819, and Rensselaer Polytechnic Institute, founded in 1824, both giving lodgment in their curriculums to the agricultural and industrial arts.[1] In part these institutions were legacies of the rationalistic Enlightenment of the preceding century. In part they were a protest against the almost exclusive concern which the colleges up to that time had shown in the traditional subjects of Latin, Greek, and mathematics. This protest was not altogether new since a similar one against the Latin grammar school in the middle of the eighteenth century had resulted in the founding of academies with a curriculum including surveying, navigation, and bookkeeping engrafted on the traditional one of linguistic and mathematical subjects.

The demand for these more technical subjects in both secondary and higher schools represented a changing attitude on the part of patrons of these two levels of learning. In a developing America, especially under the lash of the Industrial Revolution, new careers were opening up and old ones were becoming much more technical by reason of scientific advances. Eager to participate in the growth of their country but with limited funds to spend for this end beyond the secondary school, young men—and their parents—clamored for a more practical sort of higher education.

Obviously the new programs of instruction together with the motivation back of them were enough at variance with the traditional pattern of liberal education to throw down a direct challenge to it. Aware of the danger, the sponsors of the traditional pattern felt compelled to give explicit and systematic statement to the principles hitherto taken for granted in their program. Taking the lead in the formulation of such a statement was a committee of the Yale faculty whose famous report of 1828 long determined the theory of liberal education in the nineteenth century.

Addressing itself to the divisive forces and trying to reintegrate them, the committee declared: "The two great points to be gained in intellectual culture, are the discipline and the furniture of the mind; expanding its powers, and storing it with knowledge."[2] Of these two points the committee leaned toward the former as the more important. The mental philosophy (psychology) which undergirded this conception of discipline held, as Aristotle had stated centuries earlier, that the psyche or soul was a self-active principle manifesting itself in various powers or faculties such as memory, reason, and imagination. By exercising these powers or faculties, students developed mental power which could be transferred at will from one study to another and from studies in general to the occupations of life.[3] Thus the committee saw no incongruity in asking the future lawyer to study chemistry or the future clergyman conic sections since both led to a "balance of the mental powers." Indeed a young man would not know what powers he had, James McCosh, the philosopher-president of Princeton, was later to declare, unless he was required to explore the full range of prescribed studies.[4] The claim that such a curriculum had no practical value disturbed Mark Hopkins not a bit in his inaugural at Williams, for what, he cried, could be more practical than a mind disciplined to turn its power in any direction?[5]

The disciplinary theory of liberal education had a moral as well as a mental dimension. The fact that the syntax of ancient languages was difficult or their content irrelevant to contemporary concerns was reckoned an advantage, not a disadvantage. The persistence it called forth, the self-denial and self-reliance it demanded, were thought to strengthen character and add cubits to one's moral stature. Indeed there were some colleges like Amherst where morality and piety took precedence over intellectual virtues. Mathematics no less than Latin and Greek had a moral impact because it demonstrated that some principles were *a priori* and therefore warranted the courage to be steadfast in the face of curriculum values that seemed to be crumbling due to cultural lag.[6]

Where the formal training of the mind was so important, its furnishing with content could only be of somewhat less consequence. Yet there was so much furniture with which one might store the mind that the Yale committee felt it necessary to state some theory of values. Holding the view that one could not learn everything in a four-year course, the committee took the firm ground that the college should not furnish the student mind with knowledge which might easily or more effectively be gained outside college walls. Consequently, the committee shut the door on admitting professional studies into the curriculum. Having barred professional studies, so it also excluded mercantile, mechanical, and agricultural pursuits as well. These occupations, it held, could best be learned through practice in the counting room, the workshop, and on the farm. By keeping such studies out of the college curriculum the committee hoped to preserve room for such literary and scientific studies as the students might never have time or opportunity again to pursue in the course of a busy practical life. In this manner, although the college might not offer training peculiar to specific occupations, it would provide the broad theoretical foundation logically prior for them all.

Later in the century President Porter of Yale, like McCosh also a philosopher, lent his great influence to guarding the college curriculum of Latin, Greek, and mathematics against the invasion of such polytechnical studies as were taught at Rensselaer or even the sciences as taught at Yale's own Sheffield Scientific School.

His argument here was different from the Yale Report forty years earlier and more like that of Cardinal Newman's *Idea of a University,* which he probably had read.[7] He claimed that liberal studies were undertaken for their own sake and without any ulterior end. Being self-sufficient in themselves they were superior to practical studies, which derived their value from the ends to which they were instrumental.

It was all well and good to say that a liberal education stood on its own pretensions, that its proper motivation was intrinsic, but the fact was that relatively few responded to this ideal, especially in the new clientele attracted to college in the latter part of the nineteenth century. Undergraduates reacted much more readily where they could see the instrumental value of their studies. The fact that utilitarian studies could release student energies more spontaneously, however, did not shake Noah Porter's confidence in holding that liberal studies were intrinsically superior to scientific and technological ones.[8]

Others of this period emphasized liberal education as education of the "whole" man, the "all-around" man. Such an education was to be "symmetrical" and, so far as possible, "complete." Contrariwise it was feared that specialization would produce only a fraction of a man. To avoid narrowness liberal education was to attend to rounding men out physically and morally as well as intellectually. It was to cultivate imagination, lengthen perspective, sober judgment, and refine taste at the same time it gave life direction and purpose. No single curriculum, like the classical, it soon became apparent, monopolized the approach to liberal education so broadly described. A curriculum of modern languages and science had to be recognized as an alternate route.[9]

In stating that their aim was both to form and inform the student mind the Yale faculty were following in the classical tradition of liberal education. They were adhering to its primarily intellectual character. It does not appear, however, that their preference for intellectual studies to the exclusion of practical ones was due, as in Hellenic times, to their regarding the latter as undignified or unworthy of freemen. Perhaps the South cherished the ideal of an Hellenic democracy based on slavery, but the North and much of the West, as might be expected in a frontier society, had a genuine regard for the sturdy sons of toil. Indeed, no small portion of undergraduate bodies were drawn from homes where work was hard and toil unremitting.

Tight grip that mental discipline held in college circles in the nineteenth century, it was not without challenge. A mid-nineteenth-century committee of the Massachusetts legislature lodged a two-fold complaint against the traditional liberal-arts college when it said: "A college should be open to boys who seek specific learning for a specific purpose. It should give the people the practical instruction that they want, and not a classical-literary course suitable only for an aristocracy."[10] On the point of utility the legislature had popular support. Horace Greeley, for instance, advised the farm boy poring over Greek verbs or Hebrew roots that he was wasting his time if he expected mental discipline from it. The mind, he said, is best disciplined by its own proper work, presumably, solving problems of the workaday world.[11] And Daniel Coit Gilman, in a statement prepared for the governing board of the Sheffield Scientific School at Yale some years before he became president at Johns Hopkins, picked up the same note when he contended that there is discipline in the acquisition of all knowledge and not just that which exhausts itself on pure mental gymnastics while rejecting or neglecting the acquisition of content. Thus Gilman implied that not only had there always been a measure of discipline in trades handed down by the guilds but that now this discipline had been vastly increased as science became infused in many trades.[12]

The other side of the coin in the argument on utility and also the second complaint against the disciplinary theory of liberal education concerned its social and political repercussions. The tradition of liberal education inherited from abroad was aristocratic. It opposed the liberal to the servile or utilitarian. To perpetuate this tradition without amendment would endanger republican institutions.[13] Hence Francis Wayland urged that the college be the center of intelligence for all classes. Besides being a preparatory school for those bound for the professions, he exhorted, let it also be a "Lowell Institute," diffusing every kind of knowledge to all classes in the community.[14] A little later, after the Civil War, President Chadbourne of Williams recognized that the tendency to make college semitechnical could not easily be checked, nor should it be, seeing that the American theory of government demands a broad culture for its people.[15] If this was the view in New England it was even stronger in the frontier states where Jonathan Baldwin Turner claimed that the industrial classes were just as entitled to understand the science and philosophy underlying their pursuits as the professional classes were theirs. And James Burrill Angell was unable to conceive anything more unrepublican, more undemocratic, even more unchristian, than a system which would confine the priceless boon of higher education to the rich.[16]

Although weakened by these attacks, mental discipline continued into the twentieth century as the favored theory of liberal education. But it did not hold this favored position long. Some had already suspected at the beginning of the last quarter of the nineteenth century that a better psychology was at hand to replace the grindstone theory.[17] However it was not till the twentieth century that this proved to be the case. In the first decade of this new century began a long series of scientific experiments designed to test the precise amount of transfer of learning which could be expected from one subject to another.[18] When mounting evidence made it clear that the extent of transfer was nowhere near so large nor so automatic as had been assumed for centuries, the popularity of formal mental discipline slipped into eclipse. No longer could college presidents or professors justify a curriculum of liberal education composed of studies admittedly useless except for their formal qualities.[19]

Many, however, were still unwilling to relinquish altogether the theory of discipline.[20] They were convinced that there was an important kernel of truth in the theory which remained unshaken by the new experimental evidence. On close examination it appeared to them that these findings did not completely deny transfer of training, but that they did require much more careful statement of the conditions under which it occurred. Two conditions stood out. First, to get transfer, the instructor had deliberately and consciously to strive for it because it was only likely to occur as a subconscious by-product in very talented students.[21] But second, transfer was most likely where there were identical elements in the items learned and the items to be improved by transfer.

Such identical elements were principally of two sorts. On the one hand they were habits of mind, as for example, learning to extract the implications of a premise with remorseless rigor or learning the exactness of measurement and verification in empirical investigation.[22] On the other hand they were the basic concepts of a discipline with which it organized and interpreted related subject matters. The thought here was that transfer was not so much a matter of the psychology of learning—formerly poorly stated in terms of faculty psychology—as it was a matter of the structure of knowledge.[23] Once men hoped to discover (literally uncover) truth in its naked reality, but latterly the facts of scientific knowledge have been restated, not so much as substantive truths as principles of inquiry. Liberal education should be concerned, therefore, according to a post-World War II theory, not so much with substantive liberal arts, as with their basic concepts seen as fluid inquiry.[24]

Humanism

Knocking out or at least transforming the doctrine of transfer of training as the chief prop for the inclusion of "useless" subjects in the college curriculum gave much freer play to the rising tide of forces which favored a more utilitarian and democratic inclusion of courses. It will be well to examine these forces before looking at the humanistic reaction they incited. Obviously they were nothing new. For a while in the nineteenth century the mental disciplinarians had succeeded in stemming them, but even before the century was out these forces were gathering momentum again.

Rensselaer Polytechnic Institute was followed by other similar institutions, such as the Massachusetts Institute of Technology. The Morrill Act passed by Congress in 1862 led to spanning the nation with a whole system of agricultural and mechanical colleges. Bright new patches showed even on staid old seats of learning like Harvard and Yale where the Lawrence and Sheffield Scientific Schools respectively had been stitched on. Cornell proclaimed itself an institution where anyone could learn anything, and state universities were soon adopting the "Wisconsin idea" of being public-service institutions.

Reinforcing these utilitarian tendencies were other educational developments. Pre-eminent among them was that educational offshoot of nineteenth-century liberalism, the elective curriculum championed so ardently and effectively by Charles W. Eliot of Harvard. The emphasis it placed on individual student interest encouraged students to pick courses in line with life-career motives. Progressive education, inspired by the pragmatic philosophy of John Dewey, also stressed the significance of motivating studies by showing their instrumental value in solving current problems. Although this pragmatic influence was at first felt in the elementary and secondary schools, it was not long before experimental progressive colleges such as Bennington and Sarah Lawrence began to appear in which curriculums were designed to be at least functional if not utilitarian and pragmatic.[25] Perhaps going even further in this direction were such "general" colleges as the one at the University of Minnesota.[26] Here the democratization of higher education initiated by the land-grant colleges came to full tide.

The trend of events was all too evident. Critics took off in all directions.[27] For traditional humanists the dominance of a middle-class business culture was undermining the priceless heritage of liberal education. By constantly finding practical answers to the question what liberal education was good for, those responsible for its destinies were overlooking why liberal education was good on its own account. Consequently they regarded it as a fallacy to make it a prime duty of the college to prepare the student to solve the problems of his day. In their view the college could only have a high degree of relevancy to the current scene in a very stable world where the future was easily predictable—obviously not the situation in the twentieth century.[28]

Or again, the critics found fault with the obvious trends in higher education because of their implied pragmatic yardstick. Pragmatism they saw as an outgrowth of the theory of evolution. By prizing novelty and contingency and discouraging the quest for certainty, educational policies based on this theory ran into serious conflict with the "wisdom of the ages." Instead of trying to transcend this phenomenon of flux, contemporary higher education was surrendering to it. In doing so it cultivated the variant in human nature rather than the constant. Anxious not to thwart student individuality, it encouraged a kind of educational impressionism in which the individual inbred his own temperament. All this resulted in a naturalism which was uncongenial to the religious inclinations of most humanists.[29]

This variant of liberal education the humanists saw as a holdover from the scientism of the eighteenth-century Enlightenment. The empiricists then and the pragmatists contemporarily seemed to be saying that the world is out of joint. It can only be set right by science. What science did for solving the enigmas of nature it can also do for the study of man and society. Perhaps it could, but Norman Foerster, a leading humanist, questioned it.[30] He ridiculed study of the facts of social science as a substitute for study of the values brimming over in the humanities. No doubt the earlier rationalism and the later pragmatism offered a possible theory of postsecondary education, but, Foerster pleaded, do not call it liberal education. Liberal education has permanent qualities, or at least had them from Plato and Aristotle in the fourth century B.C. till Newman and Arnold in the nineteenth. Consequently, let those who would derive prestige from use of the honorable phrase "liberal education" abide by its ancient and enduring meaning. And let those who favor a drastic redefinition of the term find some other name for their efforts.[31]

Another leading humanist, Irving Babbitt, blamed humanitarianism for the decline in the quality of liberal education.[32] This humanitarianism had two main ingredients, a scientific one derived from Bacon and a sentimental one stemming from Rousseau. The educational statesman most notably prompted by such motives, Babbitt thought, was President Eliot of Harvard. He regarded Eliot's elective curriculum addressed to student interest as definitely resting on a sentimental as well as a utilitarian appeal. The danger the humanist saw in such an appeal was that the humanitarian would view college as a means of uplift for the many rather than as a means of thorough training for the few. Consequently, by trying to bring the bachelor's degree within reach of ever widening numbers, he would run the imminent risk of cheapening the degree itself. Although there is an attractive democratic quality about the humanitarian attempt to elevate mankind as a whole, Babbitt inclined to the more aristocratic or "selective democratic" temper of humanism.

Paul Shorey, another notable humanist, pushed the place of science and vocationalism to one side in order to focus attention squarely on the comparatively small number of students capable of disciplined taste and critical enjoyment of the rich heritage of the past.[33] Unless liberal education fastened attention steadfastly on this group, many feared that educated man would become obsolescent. They conceived the ideal of the educated man quite apart from his social status or vocational destiny. Of course they were not disappointed if their educational program resulted in an effective citizen and an able worker, but the proper view of liberal education hardly regarded man's usefulness as his greatest asset. If he turned out useful, it was rather the by-product of his own inner worth. The humanist cultivated this intrinsic worth most effectively through language. Apt use of the written and spoken word he regarded the chief currency of the educated man, a currency spent most wisely on the insatiable curiosity of the mind. Of course he shared with others what his curiosity unearthed, but he never lost sight of the fact that his main preoccupation was with the cultivation of his own worth. In this fashion education became a personal possession of great price. Like a jewel, the student never ceased to polish and cherish it.

When the humanist spoke of education of the whole man he had in mind the harmony of man's rational and emotional natures. He made little provision for finding that harmony through commitment in social action. Rather he proceeded on the assumption that knowledge is a good and commitment will follow from understanding it. Consequently curriculum reform for the humanist was chiefly concerned with subject matter with little or no need for recourse to the behavioral sciences. If the humanist curriculum seemed more formal and structured it was because clear thinking arose from the unity of subject matter based on an objective order in nature.[34]

Rationalism

Foerster, Babbitt, and Shorey were merely the van of the critics of early twentieth-century tendencies in higher education. They pointed to dangers but were ineffective in stopping or diverting them. The gathering forces of resistance, however, finally found a more redoubtable champion in Robert M. Hutchins, president of the University of Chicago. By his vigorously written lectures on *The Higher Learning in America,*[35] published in 1936, he was able to rally lay and professional opinion for a fundamental reconsideration of the philosophy of higher education. Apparently the time was ripe for such a reassessment. The confidence of the country in its political and economic institutions had been deeply shaken by the economic depression of the 1930s and by the apparent success of communism and fascism in meeting similar problems. As the country re-examined its fundamental social philosophy, it also took a searching look at the educational philosophy of its colleges and universities.

The remedy for such elastic and confusing times Hutchins sought in a rationalistic philosophy which would be more perennial and perduring than the educational philosophy of change with its attempt to keep continually abreast or even ahead of the times. He and his able colleague on the Chicago faculty, Mortimer J. Adler,[36] looked back with nostalgia to colonial times or even medieval Europe when theology lent some unity and stability to the higher learning.[37] Agreeing that there was no possibility of restoring theology to its former importance, they proposed to substitute in its stead a metaphysics which drew upon absolutes from Aristotle and St. Thomas Aquinas about the nature of man, the nature of truth, and the nature of value.[38] The program was boldly launched by Hutchins in his oft-quoted syllogism "Education implies teaching. Teaching implies knowledge. Knowledge is truth. The Truth is everywhere the same. Hence education should be everywhere the same."[39] Of course he was too clever to overlook differences of local custom and habit, but these he dismissed as accidental details. His sweeping absolute applied to essentials. What truth might happen to be at any time on some issue might well be highly controversial. Indeed, a university in which there was not continuous controversy about important issues was hardly a university.

The essential feature of human nature, distinguishing man from the brute, was rationality. Rightly understood, therefore, the essence of education was the cultivation of the intellect. And since human nature was the same everywhere and always, intellectual excellence was the proper aim of education in all societies. The kind of intellectual excellence Hutchins and Adler had in mind was very different from the nineteenth-century conception of mental discipline. Indeed Hutchins specifically rejected that notion.[40] His was a more classic rationalism, more like that of Aristotle or St. Thomas, which glorified the life of the mind as the good life. Instead of seeking merely the formal discipline of human faculties, as in the formal study of Latin and Greek grammar, he sought to steep them in the content of the liberal arts—the "wisdom of the ages," the "great books." Here lay the great storehouse of rational principles undergirding the universe which but waited to be grasped by the rational insight of the student. Any idea that all the subjects in the array from aesthetics to zoology were all of equal intellectual worth was repugnant to Hutchins and Adler. On the contrary they saw the contents of the vast storehouse of human learning arranged in a hierarchy based on their ability to bring out the human in man. Besides, the value of the liberal arts did not depend on their being elected by the subjective mood of the student. Rather did they possess an inherently objective character of their own.

If in the nineteenth century Amherst and similar colleges had put piety ahead of intellect among the outcomes of college training, Hutchins and rationalists of his ilk now reversed this order, stating that the principal role of higher education was intellectual and not moral.[41] The issue here was of long standing. The Greeks first posed it when they asked, "Can virtue be taught?" Obviously the question is ambiguous. Did it mean forming the student's mind about virtue or forming actual habits of virtuous conduct? Undoubtedly Amherst meant the latter. Forming moral character, however, Hutchins held to be an art. This art required practice over a period of time and in the context of the neighborhood and community. The unique capability of higher education, however, was to form the mind. Its classrooms could provide instruction in conceptualizations about morals—for instance, the history, sociology, psychology, or philosophy of morals—but it was poorly equipped as a place to practice morals.

Sciences were to take their place by the side of the humanities in a liberal education, but there must be no mistake about their yielding to the logical if not psychological priority of philosophy.[42] To the leaders of this school of thought, science was too empirical, often anti-intellectual, in its complete absorption in the accumulation of facts alone. Yet, claiming not to encroach on the empirical nature of science, they insisted on the priority of rational first principles as a framework in which to set science. Concurring, Foerster in addition claimed that the cultivation of intelligence as a main object in the higher learning had two different meanings when applied to things and their forces and to men and their mores.[43] Following humanist Babbitt he further comforted naturalists by asserting that humane thinking, as against naturalistic thinking, sought to gather the scattered elements of knowledge and coordinate them not only with intellect but also with taste and character.[44]

Reference has just been made to steeping the student in the liberal arts as the best way to realize his human potentialities. According to Adler, however, any admixture of vocational studies or even the vocational point of view so current in the first decades of twentieth-century America would not only adulterate the liberal arts but would deprive the college student of his humane birthright. The value of liberal studies, he held along with Noah Porter, did not depend on the use to which they could be put in the world of affairs but were rather self-contained, valuable in and of themselves. Following the lead of Aristotle, Adler attributed superiority to self-contained or intrinsic values as compared with dependent or extrinsic ones because the former were reflected in the improvement of the man and the latter merely in the improvement of the transaction of affairs. Hence the inescapable superiority of liberal over vocational subjects in college courses.

To support this thesis further Adler went back to the ancient Greek distinction between the education of a class maintained in leisure and of one having no leisure.[45] The education appropriate to the leisure class, as is well known, was superior to that appropriate to the class of slaves or artisans. Instead of ascribing this superiority to the power structure of Greek society, Adler preferred to give it a philosophical rationalization. The slave or artisan was extrinsically motivated to work. Provision for his subsistence was the reward for his labor. The leisure class, on the other hand, was intrinsically motivated. Freed from the compulsion of obtaining the necessities of life, it could choose activities which were self-rewarding. Therefore the studies which fitted for the wise use of leisure enjoyed an honor and dignity which were barred to preparation for making a livelihood. Moreover, since the word "school" etymologically derives from the Greek word σχολή meaning "leisure," it was positively a misuse of higher schools to include any vocational training at all. They were definitely a place to learn for the sake of learning and not for the sake of earning. Conversely, to include vocational training without compensation in higher institutions was not even education at all. And similarly, to regard the pursuit of the liberal arts as work was to disclose oneself as still a child, for a child may still need extrinsic motivation to study, but it is a sign of approaching maturity to be able to respond voluntarily to the intrinsic merits of the liberal arts.

A final reason for keeping the liberal arts pure and undefiled by vocationalism resembled the early nineteenth-century Yale Report by asserting again that there was no reason to teach in college what could be learned outside. To Hutchins and his followers, however, this policy did not recommend itself only on grounds of economy of time and resources.[46] Like the attitudes of Veblen and Flexner toward professional education,[47] the college and university had a unique function to perform in American society, namely to train for thinking in long-range theoretical perspective. Such training was not the unique function of any other institution and consequently would constitute an irreparable social loss if not carried out in its higher schools. To concentrate exclusively on thinking did not mean that politics, vocation, and religion were unimportant. Indeed, an important part of thinking is thinking about just such activities. What the college and university had to guard themselves against was permitting their courses to multiply and become *ad hoc,* fragmented, and consequently trivial, as they were where largely empirical in content and designed to meet the myriad specific needs of contemporary social and vocational adjustment. Specific applications should be left to technical institutes so that colleges and universities could be free to concentrate on the general aspects of thinking.[48]

The proponents of the foregoing philosophy of higher education were not unaware that they might be criticized for being undemocratic or even aristocratic. Anticipating and countering this complaint, they maintained that the liberal education they had in mind was for everyone.[49] This they could well do since the Industrial Revolution had now given everyone some measure of leisure and since the political revolutions of the late eighteenth century had made everyone free. If everyone was politically and economically free, then the objective of education should be, as Rousseau said on the threshold of these revolutions and John Stuart

Mill a century later, not the vocational one of training a magistrate, soldier, or priest but the liberal one of making a man. Such an education, far from being illiberal or aristocratic, they claimed with pride and conviction, was the only one which would guarantee a common universe of discourse so necessary for the solidity of democratic institutions.[50]

Pragmatism[51]

How successful the Hutchins-Adler school of educational philosophy had been by mid-twentieth century in stemming the naturalistic-utilitarian tendencies of higher education was a moot point. Catholic colleges generally drew satisfaction from this point of view and felt confirmed by it. One non-Catholic college, St. John's, in Maryland, made an about-face in its conventional program when it reorganized under a new Chicago-inspired leadership.[52] Many changes occurred at the University of Chicago itself, but the faculty there was far from being of one mind with its president.[53] Yet, if the new medievalism, as some called it, failed to capture a majority opinion on many campuses, it nevertheless provided a rallying point for strong minorities who were genuinely alarmed at the course of events. An even more important service, which the writings of Hutchins and Adler performed, was to focus such lay and professional attention on the underlying philosophy of higher education in America as had never before occurred in the over three hundred years of its existence.

For one thing it provoked the exponents of naturalistic and pragmatic tendencies since the time of Eliot's elective system to come forward at last and state explicitly and systematically the principles upon which they were acting. As might have been expected, these principles turned out to be an extension of John Dewey's pragmatism. But even their restatement in the context of higher education was a gain, since there were many who thought that while his *Democracy and Education*[54] had been an appropriate platform from which to reform elementary and secondary education, it would hardly serve in higher education where the problems were so different.

It may be well to introduce this position first by way of noting exceptions it took to the rationalist position just stated. Among the first to take issue with Hutchins' *Higher Learning in America* was Dewey himself.[55] He expressed concern at the authoritarianism implied in a higher education resting on a metaphysic of ultimate first principles. Someone must decide which principles ultimately come first. To undertake such a decision in an area so uncompromisingly divided against itself posed for Dewey a dangerous threat to the intellectual freedom of higher institutions of learning. Moreover, the threat was not lessened by undertaking this task in the name of Truth. Dewey was careful not to identify Hutchins as a fascist, but he could not refrain from pointing out the dangerous affinity of fascism for authoritarian notions.

One of Dewey's most able pupils, Sidney Hook, took further exception to the rationalist-humanist position.[56] Agreeing with Hutchins and Adler that the aims of education should take their origin in a conception of man, Hook quarreled with them on the approach to human nature and its implications for educational theory. In the first place he dissented from the metaphysical conclusion that, from what a man is, the educator can determine what he should become. This doctrine was predicated on the old Aristotelian notion that a man's excellence consists in the realization of his potentialities, especially his unique potentiality of reason. What a man is, of course, limits the range of what he may become but, Hook counterclaimed, it hardly determines any specific fulfillment for an organism with so plastic a nervous system as man. Even granting, in the second place, that man's nature is uniquely distinguished from the brute by his rationality, Hook still refused to give it such exaggerated educational priority as did Hutchins and Adler. He thought emotions too were highly important and cited Alfred North Whitehead for the latter's remark that it is fatally erroneous to conceive of the education of intellect divorced from emotion. Going even farther, Harold Taylor alleged that modern man was not a Greek combination of reason and appetite but a much more subtle and complex combination of characteristics revealed through medical, psychological, and sociological research.[57]

Perhaps the most serious exception taken to the Chicago school of thought by Dewey and his sympathizers concerned the relation of theory and practice. For one thing, they objected to isolating conceptualization to colleges and universities and practice to life and technical institutes. They gravely doubted whether concepts could be taught or learned apart from the context in which they were embodied. In considering how concepts were known, the educator had to keep clearly in mind that concepts were not themselves primary objects of knowledge. Rather were they ways of knowing reality. In the development of knowledge logic could not fruitfully either precede or succeed learning. It had to pervade both stages.[58] For another thing, the rift left between theory and practice by Hutchins and Adler seemed to lead to a further rift between the learning of facts and values. If the scientists seemed to pile up facts with faint sense of their bearing on social policy, it was because of this tragic split, a split in which there was a dualism between science and art. On the one side science disclosed a world of nature operating according to laws quite independent of man's wishes, and on the other art etched a world in which man realized his wishes as a producer of artifacts and a transformer of his environment. Standing astride the dualism, man seemed to be in the world but not of it. He seemed to have the choice between being intelligent, realistic, and scientific or retreating to an ivory tower to enjoy the spiritual edification of the liberal arts. But such a philosophy of liberal education was a mockery to anyone denying the basic dualism and holding that liberal education was a moral as well as an intellectual ideal.[59]

It is time now to state more positively the position taken by John Dewey and those making common cause with him. While the rationalists thought of liberal education as having a constant quality no matter what the century or the country, Dewey and his followers thought of it as necessarily undergoing alterations to meet the changing demands of time and place. Instead of taking their departure from a fixed point of reference, a metaphysical view of the nature of man, they took off from more flexible premises rooted in democracy, liberalism, and pragmatism. Let us consider each in turn.

Some approved and encouraged naturalistic trends in higher education as an obvious concomitant of the democratic process. "Nothing in our educational history is more striking," wrote Frederick Jackson Turner, the great historian of the American frontier, "than the steady pressure of democracy upon its universities to adapt them to the requirements of all the people."[60] The tremendous growth in American affection for and support of higher education has undoubtedly been due in large part to its willingness to meet the needs and demands of the populace. Nor was meeting these popular requirements an abandonment or denial of qualitative standards. It was merely substituting a democratic for an aristocratic yardstick. The social egalitarianism of democracy had filed down the sharp distinction between those who worked and those who did not. Indeed in twentieth-century democracy nearly everyone worked. Where work was well-nigh universal it would be difficult to maintain the traditional division between liberal and illiberal subjects.[61] The liberal studies of any age, therefore, were those concerned with the problems of that age. While each age had its own peculiar problems, this did not mean that the experience of earlier ages was irrelevant. Pragmatists were not anti-historical. On the contrary, they were willing to read the "great books" too, but as a means of shedding light on current problems and not just as an aesthetic end in themselves.

The democratization of the aim and content of liberal education was the natural outgrowth of encouraging ever larger numbers of American youth to attend higher institutions of learning. This expansion of numbers, however, had two dimensions, one Jacksonian and the other Jeffersonian. Down to the middle of the nineteenth century Jeffersonian selective principles kept the numbers in college small and the quality high. After that time Jacksonian principles emphasizing the egalitarianism of the common man increased the numbers but adulterated their average quality. Jacksonianism in higher education reached its high tide in mid-twentieth century, whence numbers were expected to go on to even monumental proportions but coincident with a renewed interest in affording superior students superior opportunities.

A further dimension to the naturalistic trend in higher education drew its inspiration from the liberalism of Charles W. Eliot of Harvard. His stress on liberty and initiative for the student led him to formulate the "elective" system.[62] Through electives many values of the common man gained admittance into the curriculum which had not been there formerly. Permitting election among the liberal arts, however, severely strained the traditional notion that these arts possessed intrinsic values which could be scaled in a fixed hierarchy of worth.[63] For many the absence of a fixed hierarchy implied an egalitarianism in educational values.

Thus it will be remembered that the report of the Committee of Ten in 1893 seemed to establish the principle that one subject was as good as another for college entrance if taught an equal length of time and under equally competent instruction.[64] As a matter of fact this was only a half-truth; if subjects were equal it was only in the unusual sense that each was *sui generis* and therefore really incommensurable. To the liberal pragmatist subjects in the curriculum, while unique, had neither a fixed intrinsic nor a dead-level equality of value. Rather were subjects relatively more or less valuable depending on the uses for which they were studied. These uses, of course, were as diverse as the individual differences among students. The end effect of nineteenth-century liberalism, therefore, was to emancipate the individual from the traditional uniformity of liberal education.

The liberalism of the nineteenth century brought out and gave new emphasis to another dimension inherent in the theory of liberal education. While it was common to say that liberal education was the education worthy of freemen, many in the nineteenth century turned the statement about and said that only men with a liberal education were worthy to be free. The reference here, of course, was to cultivating a state of mind in which the student learned to emancipate himself from provincialism and from the distortion of subjective bias. If he was to liberate himself, he had first to govern himself. Self-government depended on learning to judge and plan autonomously. He had to learn the art of self-criticism enjoined by Socrates when he declared that the unexamined life is not worth living. A liberal education fitting for these duties, naturally, demanded an academic freedom or laissez faire of the mind so that creative individuality might be liberated. One twentieth-century liberal went so far as to give the liberal-arts college a normative role in freeing energies for social reconstruction.[65]

The naturalistic trend of twentieth-century higher education drew support from the philosophy of pragmatism as well as that of liberalism and democracy. Greatly influenced by modern science, Dewey and his cohorts[66] saw a different relation between theory and practice from what Hutchins and Adler did. For Deweyites theory was an instrument of inquiry. Confronted with a problem—scientific, economic, political, or the like—they used theories as proposed lines of solution. Whether the theory was sound or not had to be tested in action. Theory and practice thus went hand in hand, theory anticipating consequences and practice telling whether consequences corroborated theoretical expectations. The method was the same, moreover, whether study was an inquiry into facts or values.

The role of intelligence in such a philosophy was clear; it was the means by which man overcame the precarious or contingent forces in his environment. Since intelligence held this key position, it bothered many that Dewey was indicted as having an anti-intellectual influence on higher education.[67] Obviously he was not demeaning the importance of thinking; rather he was trying to improve it by noting its critical role in experimentation.[68] To call him anti-intellectual, therefore, merely pointed out that his brand of intellectualism was different from the classical variety of the rationalists and humanists. The latter two treated intelligence as an end while the pragmatists treated it as a means.

With such premises it would be hard to miss the importance of keeping higher education closely attuned to current affairs, for it was there that problems arose and in that context that solutions had to be tested.[69] As many of these problems came to a sharp focus in occupational life, it is easy to see how vocational concerns became a vital part of the pragmatist's curriculum. It would be a grave mistake, however, to think that because of these close affinities, a philosopher like Dewey favored a metamorphosis of liberal into vocational education. As he himself said, *"The problem of securing to the liberal arts college its due function in democratic society is that of seeing to it that the technical subjects which are now socially necessary acquire a humane direction."*[70] Hostility to technical studies grew up in pretechnical times, when vocations were not only largely carried on by slaves but were also largely empirical in character. By the twentieth century industrialization had worked a revolution in most vocations. As a result of discoveries in mathematics, physics, chemistry, biology, and other sciences, earlier empirical rule-of-thumb procedures had become technological. The introduction of scientific theories had tremendously increased the intellectual content of technical studies and infinitely enlarged their cultural potentialities. Not only that, but the social consequences of technology made it necessary to establish extended and lively connections with history, economics, politics, sociology, ethics, aesthetics —indeed, most of the liberal arts. Moreover, Dewey saw that the instrumental value of these subjects could not be fully realized unless they were first enjoyed on their own account, that is, aesthetically. Hence, however egregiously many of Dewey's followers may have erred in promoting a narrow vocationalism at the expense of the liberal arts, the error did not find its source in Dewey's writings.

The Obsolescence of Liberal Education

In mid-twentieth century no one seemed to doubt the relevance of liberal education. There were two basically different philosophies supporting it, to be sure, but the main problem was not to justify their relevance but to see whether they could be accommodated to each other. On the one hand were those who saw liberal education as a creature of historical forces. When imported into this country it reflected the aristocratic class interests which had dominated Europe from the Renaissance back to Hellenic times. After the political and economic revolutions at the end of the eighteenth century it responded with ever greater sympathy to ascendant democratic forces. On the other hand were those who thought the idea of liberal education, far from throbbing to the heartbeat of history, was the same for all men everywhere and always. Rooted in a metaphysical view of man and knowledge, it was independent of history.

Could the two views be reconciled? Huston Smith thought a synthesis possible of the absolutism of metaphysics and the relativism of history. There are objective values in higher education, said he, but one must be cautious about overgeneralizing them for all students and one must remember that these values are only gradually discovered over long periods of time.[71] Father Courtney Murray, too, thought the two theories of higher education could be brought into a common universe of discourse. There is a "decay of argument" in the modern university, he pointed out, such a contrariety of voices that, with no basic agreements, there is no way to compare the arguments on both sides. The only hope, therefore, is to form a postmodern university where, it is hoped, there may be a common universe of discourse.[72] But just what could be agreed upon even there was not altogether clear.

Less synthetic and more eclectic in its endeavor to face the schism of theory in higher education was the Harvard Report on *General Education in a Free Society.*[73] "The true task of education," the committee stated very succinctly, "is therefore so to reconcile the sense of pattern and direction deriving from heritage with the sense of experiment and innovation deriving from science that they may exist fruitfully together. . . ."[74] But what was the formula for reconciliation? Educators read the report in vain to find it. Perhaps most enlightening was a subsequent statement by a philosopher member of the committee. Although not planned to be so, the Harvard Report was Aristotelian in spirit. It took the two regnant theories of Hutchins and Adler on the one hand and Dewey on the other and tried to strike a mean between them.[75] As a matter of fact, few were satisfied with the balance the committee struck.[76] The defenders of "heritage" regarded the report as too brash and the defenders of "experiment" regarded it as too mild. Some regarded the language of the report as leaving the chasm between the two philosophies as unbridgeable as ever. Those who thought they were achieving a synthesis by placing science, with its appeal to ordinary experience, in the same spectrum or on the same continuum of learning with art and literature, with their "absolute vision" and "total insight," were simply deceiving themselves. Trying to weave such incompatible strands of doctrine together balked any idea of real synthesis. The best that could result was an eclecticism and a rather contradictory one at that.

Already much earlier Irving Babbitt had been less optimistic. Since the impasse between the genteel tradition of European art and letters and the new proletarian and technological culture went to the root of first principles, he saw no possibility of mediation. In fact he deemed moderates disposed to compromise as being only muddleheaded.[77] Mortimer J. Adler also saw the conflict as irreconcilable. Indeed he saw it as no longer a philosophical but a political problem. Consequently the only way to solve it was to refer it to a choice by the public.[78] Their voice, however, from the Morrill Acts onward had been a rising crescendo in favor of a higher education amenable to their changing needs.

Almost exactly a hundred years after the first Morrill Act student disruptions brought on by the Vietnam War and racial injustices drew attention away from trying to reconcile divergent theories of liberal education to justifying whether liberal education had any relevance at all to existing conditions. The question was, had liberal education become obsolescent? Some even asked whether the liberal arts were dead or if not dead then terminally ill. The long-time faith in liberal education was predicated on its relevance to the development of an individual able to transcend the parochialisms of his day, envision new and better worlds, and exemplify a style of life characterized by grace, responsibility, and courage. By the 1960s several factors had eroded this ideal. The university had overwhelmed the college, the graduate school had overshadowed baccalaureate programs, and the professional scholar had replaced the college teacher. The traditional goal of providing a liberating experience gave way to that of advancing and only incidentally transmitting knowledge. Hence the exposure to great models of human conduct became more exclusively cognitive, technical, and professional. The adoption of the Ph.D. as a prerequisite for professorial rank transformed the professor from practitioner of the liberal arts into an investigator of them. Meantime the liberal arts themselves just about died in the process of becoming professionalized disciplines.[79]

Furthermore the relevance of liberal education was challenged not only by scholarly developments in academia but also by changes in industrial society. As the knowledge taught in colleges became more and more useful for political, economic, and social life, students were motivated to choose and study courses for utilitarian reasons.[80] Indeed, the liberal arts themselves were seen as instrumental. They were a prelude to postgraduate careers dominated by the work ethic. In the postindustrial era, however, it was predicted, affluence could be increasingly taken for granted. What mattered then would not be more security and success but more experience of joy, more free expression of self.[81] In such a new period of self-realization the liberal arts in their original role of liberating the individual could be reborn.[82] Hence obsolescence, though a current threat, might not be a long-term one.

"Value-Free" Higher Education

The force of student unrest in the 1960s was not spent with working out the implications of relevance but continued on to challenge other assumptions of higher education hitherto taken for granted. To give perspective to this reexamination it is necessary to go back to the end of the nineteenth century when the American graduate school was being modeled after the German university. Two important characteristics of that university were incorporated into the philosophy of the American university—autonomy and *Wertfreiheit*. One American student returning in the nineteenth century from study in Germany described the university there as a "detached organism . . . growing in accordance with its own laws."[83] The laws that validated this detached or autonomous character were the canons by which truth itself was authenticated. On the one hand, truth must be "value-free" *(Wertfreiheit)*, that is, disinterested, unaffected by the personal values of the investigator. The elimination of personal bias, which has always been notoriously variable, gave truth an objectivity that commanded general if not universal acceptance. On the other hand, since only experts in assaying truth are sufficient judges of truth, the faculty must enjoy autonomy in determining it. Neither political nor ecclesiastical authorities should interfere.

While much research in the American graduate school was exactly like its German counterpart, there was a notable tendency at the turn of the century in the United States to put research results at the service of the public. Woodrow Wilson of Princeton caught the spirit of the time when he spoke of the "university in the nation's service." In serving society, however, he did not mean that the university should be subservient to society. The service Wilson had in mind was essentially indirect rather than direct. Even as late as the 1930s Robert Nisbet found it difficult to recall more than the barest number of instances where the university contributed directly to the working machinery of society.[84] Thereafter, however, and especially from the Second World War onward, the university became more and more directly involved in government and industry. Financial subsidies from both amounted to a kind of "academic capitalism." Indeed, so dependent did higher education become that for many the simile that best described the university was the "service station." A prime difficulty with this characterization was that in serving social values the university abandoned neutrality on controversial issues and thus endangered not only its claim to objectivity of truth but its claim to autonomy.[85] Truth was no longer clearly "value-free." Some, like the pundit Walter Lippmann, actually justified the trend, holding that the time had come for the university to become expert in questions of value as well as those of fact.[86] If so, it marked a fundamental change in the conventional wisdom as to the American philosophy of higher education.

Whatever changes were afoot, they were brought to a near crisis stage by the student disturbances of the 1960s. In lashing out at the injustices of the social order the students were very critical of the role played by the university, especially its claim to being neutral or "value-free" on the great issues of the day. On the one hand they saw the claim as a sham and a hypocrisy since the university was so thoroughly establishmentarian[87] and nowhere more so than in its working hand in glove with the military-industrial complex in the Vietnam War. On the other hand, departing from the German-American academic tradition, they did not think the university should be "value-free" in the first place but should rather adopt an adversary role in social affairs. Indeed, their philosophy went so far as to politicize the university.

But in politicizing it the students rejected what they called the "liberal establishment" where politics were conducted by compromise, conciliation, and negotiation. Theirs was a politics of feeling rather than intellectual analysis, of moral outrage rather than ideological conviction.[88] Hence they were quick to resort to direct action and confrontation. Surprisingly, a number of students made a virtue of intolerance because toleration dulled the edge of outrage and protest.[89] Indeed, the leaders of student protest were skeptical of academic objectivity as giving higher education too intellectual a cast.

They mistrusted rational and conceptual modes of activity, preferring a greater emphasis on emotion and sensory experience. Thus a point of view was justified if sincerely believed in. Obviously such a philosophy had strong overtones of existentialism.[90] In fact, a former president of the City College of New

York described an "existentialist university" as operating on the counterculture.[91] As such it had a life-style all its own, favoring immediacy[92] to postponement, involvement to neutrality, commitment to suspended judgment, and confrontation to deliberation.[93]

A number of faculty, especially younger ones, also thought the university should surrender some of its value-free stance and adopt a more activist or adversary position on controversial issues of its day. They gave force to their conviction by forming "caucuses" within their disciplinary societies known as the New University Conference (NUC), which tried to incline these learned societies toward the new left.[94] But older faculty were appalled at its anti-intellectual implications.[95] Most of them vigorously reasserted the university's value-free philosophy and nonpolitical stance.[96] Enthusiasm for the New University Conference peaked between 1967 and 1969, after which it declined rapidly with inflation and worsening job opportunities.

But even as the stress and strain of the period subsided, there were concerned friends of the university who were apprehensive that it might be on the brink of subtle changes in its character and philosophy. As an eminent historian, C. Vann Woodward, saw it, many of the university community were already reconciling themselves to the new demands, indeed "eager for the institutional for personal advantages they expect to derive from it. Others find in the transformation or 'modernization' of the university the means of realizing humanitarian or political, though non-academic goals—that is, the traditional goals of scholarship and teaching. Some advocates of modernization see the emergence of the university as a secular church promising self-discovery and 'identity' or group therapy for distraught or alienated post-adolescents; others see the university becoming a new melting-pot for assimilating alienated minorities into a middle-class meritocracy; still others would foster super-research instituted available for crash programs to solve 'crises' of welfare, environment, energy, health, birth-control, or nuclear-arms-control."[97]

In spite of the identity crisis through which higher education was going, no comprehensive and coherent philosophy of its role emerged. Traditionally few faculties taught in the light of any consciously stated philosophic frame of reference, as a survey of a number of liberal-arts colleges revealed after the First World War.[98] It was a disappointment to many that well after the Second World War the Carnegie Commission on Higher Education did not devote one volume of its multivolume report to this urgent task. To be sure, one volume did give extensive consideration to dozens of aims in higher education but the approach was encyclopedic rather than philosophical.[99] Beyond that the commission seemed fearful of the diversity of philosophical viewpoints and tried to play them down by lumping them together in a brief historical summary. "Academic life has been refined through long-term academic experience in many countries, has come to place supreme emphasis on cultivation of the intellect, on rationality, on attempted objectivity based on facts and logical argument. . . . Its methods have evolved to be non-coercive, relying on persuasion, not power. Wide latitude has come to be given to individual freedom. The principal test of achievement has become the quality of intellectual performance—not politics, not creed, not power."[100] This "unwritten academic constitution," as the commission called it, was oversimplified for the highly strained academic world that had called the commission into being. What higher education still needed was philosophy / philosophies of higher education intentionally thought out in detail and integrated in some overall design.[101]

15

Academic Freedom

The right of the professor to follow an argument whithersoever it may lead either in his research or in his teaching is a claim at least as ancient as Plato. The establishment of this claim, however, in the hearts and minds of the American public has undergone numerous vicissitudes. In the colonial college practically no claim was laid to academic freedom. Religious orthodoxy was rather the rule. As the intellectual frontier shifted from religion to politics during the eighteenth century, the spirit of liberty accompanying the French and American revolutions began knocking on academic portals. But it was not until the introduction of German graduate methods of research onto American campuses in the late nineteenth century that academic freedom became a *cause célèbre*. Yet even as late as the twentieth century the professional right to academic freedom had not received an altogether secure lodgment in the pattern of American thinking. Recurrent social crises of war, economic depression, and international tension periodically threatened its very existence. To appreciate the later extent and temper of academic freedom, it will be necessary now to relive its various viscissitudes at some length.

The Era of Orthodoxy and Conformity

However anciently Plato may have claimed the right to follow an argument whithersoever it may lead, by the day of the founding of the colonial colleges in America little doubt remained that the course of theological argument led directly and incontrovertibly to Christian conclusions. Consequently those responsible for collegiate policies were diligent to see that the youth in their charge were exposed only to "sound doctrine" and taught by none, as the General Court of Massachusetts in the seventeenth century directed, who "have manifested themselves unsound in the fayth, or scandelous in their lives, and not giueing due satisfaction according to the rules of Christ."[1]

In such an atmosphere as this it will not be surprising that when Harvard's first president, Henry Dunster, followed theological argument on the question of infant baptism to a different conclusion from that held by his constituency, he had to resign his office. So too did President Cutler at Congregational Yale a century later when he decided to become an Episcopalian. The only question which arose on both these occasions was whether Dunster and Cutler were right or wrong on the substantive issues of theology. No one thought of raising the methodological question whether, right or wrong, learned men were entitled to reason independently to their own conclusions. In the colonial mind truth was not plural but unitary. Moreover religious truth was certified by revelation. To raise doubts under such circumstances was folly indeed. No wonder evidences of infidelity provoked Jonathan Edwards to reproach some colleges for endangering rather than protecting the piety of their students.[2]

Harvard was far from alone among colonial colleges in making orthodoxy the rule of its campus. If anything Yale was even more interested in the security afforded by orthodoxy than was Harvard. There in the middle of the eighteenth century President Thomas Clap zealously strove to preserve Yale as a place where Congregationalists of his stripe could train future clergy in their own way. To this end he succeeded in requiring assent to the Westminster Confession and submission to the Saybrook Platform of 1708 as religious tests for holding office at Yale.[3] A similar Calvinistic yoke was proposed for the neck of the Harvard faculty about the same time, but nothing came of it. Such tests were not limited to New England, for the professors of William and Mary were required to subscribe to the Thirty-nine Articles of the Church of England right down to the American Revolution.[4] Though not threatening the imposition of any such test at Princeton, the trustees of the College of New Jersey were nonetheless vigilant in scanning the writings and lectures of its faculty to ensure their orthodoxy.[5] The idea that such orthodoxies should yield to the rule of tolerance on the academic campus carried no popular backing in these early times. Indeed, when a body of Yale seniors took up a subscription for reprinting Locke's *Essay on Toleration,* President Clap reprimanded them and insisted that, under penalty of forfeiting their degrees, they make a public confession of their sin in undertaking the project.[6]

The tradition of orthodoxy or conformity to dominant modes of thought in the American community long held the college campus securely in its grasp. The only thing that changed was the public issue on which conformity was demanded.[7] After the eighteenth century, religious rivalries gave way to political ones. Perhaps chief among these in the next half-century was the issue of slavery. As late as 1830, apparently, it was still possible to speak freely on this issue within southern academic walls. But toward the end of the ante-bellum period college presidents and professors put their tenure in jeopardy by taking such liberties. Going even farther, Southerners pressed the slavery issue to a point where they campaigned to persuade southern youths to withdraw from northern colleges and to exclude northern textbooks, like Francis Wayland's *Moral Science,* from southern colleges.[8] The demand for conformity, always greater in the South, was not altogether absent from northern institutions. President Lord of Dartmouth, for instance, had to resign because, like many Southerners, he believed slavery was divinely ordained of God.[9]

After the Civil War science, particularly the new Darwinian theory of evolution, roused the parties favoring orthodoxy on college campuses. This doctrine propounded a theory of the origin and nature of man so at variance with the accepted Biblical account that its teaching more than once became the occasion for heresy trials.[10] Indeed, a survey of college campuses in 1880 showed that evolution was inadmissible as a topic of instruction at such seats of learning as Princeton, Williams, Lafayette, and Amherst. Earlier, at Harvard President Felton was moved to write the mother of John Fiske, brilliant student convert to Darwinism, that he considered it "a great and lamentable misfortune to a young man, when, in the conceit of superior wisdom, he openly avows himself an infidel." And, the president added, "any attempt to spread the mischievous opinions which he fancies he has established in his own mind" will require his removal.[11] At Yale William Graham Sumner, a Social Darwinist, ran afoul of President Porter, who regarded Sumner's classroom use of Herbert Spencer's *Principles of Sociology* an attack on theism.[12]

The substantive theories of science, like evolution, seem to have engendered more anxiety in the camp of orthodoxy than did its method. This is not surprising when one stops to remember the methods of instruction regnant at the time.[13] The prevalance of the recitation with its catechetical spirit obviously placed more emphasis on a knowledge of scientific classification than it did on the method of discovery or invention. Even where laboratory demonstrations were employed, the intent was didactic and too often entertaining. The net effect of such instruction created anything but intellectual friction and challenge. But then it must be remembered, too, that a major interest of the public in the teaching of science at this time, as witness the founding of the land-grant colleges, centered not in its riddles but in its application to the practical problems of life.

At the turn of the century the intellectual frontier shifted to political and economic issues again. This time bimetallism, public regulation of private enterprise, labor unions, and similar issues absorbed public attention. These in time gave way to questions of national allegiance during the First World War, to the threat of socialism after the war and during the depression, and finally to communism after the Second World War. But before taking up the constricting impact of these problems on the status of the college professor, we must go back and pick up the origin and nurture of the forces of intellectual freedom which opposed those of conformity.

The Growing Demand for Freedom

Overwhelming as was the support for orthodoxy, especially in colonial colleges, some allowance for deviation appeared from early times. Thus when dispute arose at the end of the seventeenth century over Harvard's orthodoxy, dissatisfied elements in Cambridge lent encouragement to the founding of Yale and the perpetuation of a different orthodoxy there. The founding of Princeton in turn was in part a protest against the state of orthodoxy at Yale. In the course of time each denomination came to have a college of its own—Congregationalists, Presbyterians, Anglicans, Baptists, Dutch Reformed, and the like. Thus the student or his parent had at least a choice between orthodoxies. And, in the case of the Congregationalists, he had a choice between the "old light" and the "new light" orthodoxies. But even this narrow choice gave the grandparent of one Dartmouth freshman a sense of freedom, for he wrote President Wheelock:

> The Education at Yale is not liberal: they are too Contracted in their Principles and do not encourage a free Enquiry. Error never flourishes in any soil so Luxuriantly as where a free Enquiring after Truth is not permitted, I might say encouraged. I thought myself before I again renewed our Old Acquaintance that you had fallen into that Error yourself but was agreeably disappointed.[14]

However limited this freedom, the rich diversity of colleges—denominational and undenominational, public and private—which soon covered the United States came to constitute one of the chief bulwarks of its intellectual freedom.

From the middle of the eighteenth century onward the diversity of belief which had been a by-product of the founding of new colleges became a conscious objective within the academic walls of single institutions. Thus from their founding both King's College and Brown threw their doors wide open to students from all denominations. Pennsylvania at its reorganization in 1779 provided for representation on its governing board of each of the leading religious denominations, including the Catholic.[15] Some colleges, similarly, rejoiced in the fact that their faculties were drawn from a variety of faiths. Brown probably went farthest among colonial colleges in nurturing contrariety of thought by including in its first charter the statement, "sectarian differences of opinions shall not make any part of the public and classical instruction: although all religious controversies may be studied freely, examined and explained."[16]

Just how far there was genuine intellectual freedom at Dartmouth or Brown as measured by later standards may well be a moot point. At any rate the first man to formulate intellectual freedom as a formidable academic policy was Thomas Jefferson. Such a policy proceeded for him almost inexorably from principles of the eighteenth-century Enlightenment which had so largely entered his thinking. The University of Virginia, cherished child of his lifelong thought, was to be a "revolutionary"[17] university incorporating the new liberalism of that century. As he wrote to his long-standing collaborator, Joseph C. Cabell, his "university was dedicated to promoting progress . . . not infinitely as some have said but indefinitely, and to a term which no one can fix and foresee."[18] To replace a static ideal of the perfect state of man with a dynamic ideal of continuing social and intellectual progress as the chief aim of higher education required a new cast of the academic mind. Striking off the shackles of old orthodoxies and combining insights drawn from Plato and Milton, Jefferson made this cast clear to an English correspondent when he stated that the University of Virginia would be based on the ". . . illimitable freedom of the human mind. For here we are not afraid to follow truth wherever it may lead, nor to tolerate error so long as reason is left free to combat it."[19]

Yet, bold and liberal as Jefferson was in calling for an "illimitable freedom of the human mind" in theory, he nevertheless did set boundaries to it in practice. In another letter to Cabell he let slip his lack of complete faith in his own ideals. Apropos of the textbooks to be used at the University of Virginia he wrote that he favored leaving the selection to the faculty but, as a matter of fact, with the backing of another great exponent of freedom, James Madison, he prevailed on the Board of Visitors of the University of Virginia to adopt a resolution listing the specific books to be read in the course on government.[20] Apparently his mistrust of the writings of Federalists like Hamilton, Marshall, and the Adamses, got the better of his preference in this instance for following the argument whithersoever it might lead.

Not only did Jefferson set a limit to "illimitable" freedom of the mind but he was unable to implement that freedom fully. One liberal, Thomas Cooper, whom he had picked for the first faculty, he was unable to seat at the University owing to opposition from forces of religious orthodoxy. Prevented from occupying the chair to which Jefferson had designated him, Cooper subsequently became president of South Carolina College. There in the 1830s he was attacked in the legislature and charged with harming the college because his unorthodox materialistic opinions deterred parents from sending their sons thither. Invoking the clauses on freedom in the state constitution, he defended himself ably. No advantage is to be gained, he declared, in retreating from intellectual difficulties which are unpopular or concealing fundamental doubts that will return to haunt the student later. On the contrary, Cooper continued, the lasting reputation of the college should be based on satisfying the student's just expectation of being taught "fully, impartially, and honestly."[21]

The Rise of Academic Freedom

Forerunner of academic freedom that Jefferson was, his was a voice which, if not crying alone, was nonetheless one crying in an academic wilderness still largely brooded over by a pervading orthodoxy. Some years later President Quincy of Harvard, probably prompted by glowing praise of the state of academic freedom in German universities brought back by returning students like George Ticknor, professed to foresee the end of the period when the academic mind would be vassal to sects in the church and parties in the state.[22] Obviously he did not anticipate the attempt of late-nineteenth-century plutocracy to become its overlord. From its entrenched position on college governing boards this plutocracy attempted a series of such startling professorial dismissals at the turn of the century that the lay and professional public became aroused in unprecedented fashion.[23]

A leading early case was that of President Andrews of Brown, who took the side of free silver in the bimetallism controversy at the turn of the century. His board of trustees were gold-standard men. Fearing that Brown was losing important benefactions because of the stand of the president, the trustees begged him, if he would not renounce his views, that he would at least forbear expressing them in public. Rather than submit to such a humiliating restriction President Andrews resigned.[24] Happily a loud outcry from the lay and academic public led to his reinstatement. Far across the nation another advocate of bimetallism, Professor Edward A. Ross, found himself in difficulty at Stanford. At first President David Starr Jordan stood loyally by him. But later he reluctantly let him go when Ross further made remarks favoring municipal ownership of street railways and publicly criticized Oriental immigration as a threat to the American standard of living, remarks which incurred the implacable displeasure of Mrs. Leland Stanford, who still held the financial fate of the infant institution in her grasp.[25] It was a criticism of railroad operators which also brought about the dismissal of Professor Edward Bemis from the new University of Chicago and by William Rainey Harper at that, outstanding advocate of academic freedom for university research.[26] Not least famous of all the cases was that of Professor Richard T. Ely at the University of Wisconsin. German-trained in modern research methods, Ely was bent on building up a reputable graduate department of economics at Madison. As a scholar he had written on labor problems, corporate abuses, and even Marxist socialism. Forces antagonistic to his views charged him with fomenting public unrest. As there was in fact considerable unrest at the time, which happened to coincide with the depression of 1893, a committee of the University Regents was appointed to investigate the charges. Fortunately this committee exonerated Ely completely.[27]

A last case may be mentioned as also helping to build up pressure for a fresh appraisal of the role of intellectual freedom. This was the Scott Nearing case at the University of Pennsylvania, which was especially disturbing because of the circumstances of dismissal. Nearing was on one-year appointment in the Wharton School of Finance and Commerce there. Although his faculty recommended his reappointment, the board of trustees not only abruptly terminated his connection with the university, but also steadfastly refused to assign a reason for their action.[28] Although well-founded suspicion seemed to light on Nearing's liberal social views, the galling part of this and similar dismissals was the implication that professors were mere employees on contract who could be hired and fired at will. Time had been when professors were not on contract but enjoyed the status of a guild of scholars. It was painful for them to be reminded that as guild control had given way to control by a lay governing board, professors had settled into this subordinate position.[29] The reminder was all the more painful since the original advent of lay control in the eighteenth century was in part a liberal protest against an excessive orthodoxy on the part of the college faculty. Now at the end of the nineteenth and beginning of the twentieth centuries these roles were reversed and it was the lay board that was ultraconservative and the faculty that represented the forces of liberalism.

Latter-day American faculties were much more sensitive to the threat which this situation bore to intellectual freedom than earlier ones because increasing numbers of them had been trained in German universities where the rule of academic freedom protected the professor in teaching and publishing ideas which laymen might not be ready to accept.[30] The roots of intellectual freedom already seen developing prior to the advent of German influences in American higher education had largely stemmed from English and French sources. They were part of the constitutional evolution of civil liberties calling for a free market of ideas.[31] While civil liberty, however, was designed to guarantee the citizen against political interference with freedom of expression, it carried no protection for him against economic boycott or reprisal. It was just this added kind of protection which academic freedom afforded the German professor. Not only was he free to teach and publish the truth as he saw it but he could do so without fear of losing his position.

Jefferson had appreciated the need for this sort of immunity inasmuch as he tried to attract the great Nathaniel Bowditch to the University of Virginia with the bait that the post carried tenure for life. But Jefferson was ahead of his time. As the century wore on, however, professors began to emerge from the quiet precincts of moral philosophy into the rousing arena of social science. Their application of trained intelligence to practical problems was a new assertion of an old belief, especially of the eighteenth century, that man by taking thought could improve his lot in this world. The American Economic Association for one, sensing the world was out of joint, urged its members to play an active role in setting it aright. In doing so, however, they ran at cross-purposes with businessmen who at the turn of the century constituted two-thirds of college and university boards of trustees. So sharp was the disagreement that many came to think that there was a conspiracy on the part of "big business" to throttle academic freedom or, if not that, that there was an essential incompatibility between business and academic cultures.[32] As might be expected, the agitation stirred debate at a number of points.

Alton B. Parker, former judge of the New York Court of Appeals and later presidential candidate on the Democratic ticket in 1904, put the case well for conservative, propertied interests. Granted that the professor should have freedom to express his views, he inquired, why should not donors of the moneys which support higher education also have freedom to determine the doctrines their bounties support? Undoubtedly he spoke for many when he placed the freedom of the donor paramount to that of the professor.

Therefore, when in opposition to the wishes or without the consent of the supporters of the institution, any of the faculty persists in a course that must tend to impress upon the tender minds of the young under his charge theories deemed to be false by the foundation whose servant he is, or which, if not strictly false to it, are deemed so by a vast majority of the most intelligent minds of the age, it seems to me that he has abused his privilege of expression of opinion to such an extent as to justify the governing board in terminating his engagement.[33]

Leading university presidents, however, took a contrary view. "No donor," William Rainey Harper of the University of Chicago emphatically declared, "has any right before God or man to interfere with the teaching officers appointed to give instruction in a university."[34] There must be no interference because, as Charles William Eliot of Harvard stated, no one will believe instruction suspected of being warped. Nevertheless Eliot was willing to concede that benefactors were entitled to some consideration, at least to have their opinions treated respectfully and not contumaciously. But ultimately he looked for release from this sort of embarrassment, not in the fact that living benefactors would die, but in the fact that the burning questions would continually change in the future.[35] At Columbia Nicholas Murray Butler boasted that no one was rich enough to buy control of Columbia's educational policy and backed it up by pointing to the fact that during over thirty years of his administration $9,000,000 had been declined in gifts because strings attached to them hindered the freedom of their administration.[36]

A second point of controversy arose over the right of the professor to pursue the consequences of his research right into the hurly-burly of contemporary affairs. The German professor stopped short of this temptation. He made it a rule to refrain from participation in politics for fear it would make an opportunist of him, which in the end would be bound to distort his disinterested pursuit of truth. If he kept his academic skirts clear of political bias, the state was more likely to respect the objectivity of his research. Many American laymen took a similar view, holding that when the professor enters the arena of practical affairs, he does so as a partisan and forfeits his position as an unbiased scholar.[37] By contrast many American professors were unwilling to impose such a restriction upon themselves. Influenced by the pragmatism of William James and John Dewey they inevitably tested truth by its practical consequences.[38] In this account they felt tenure was necessary to complement freedom and thus redress the balance of power between faculty and lay boards of control and offset the disadvantages of a merely contractual situation into which professors had slowly slipped in the course of two centuries. Indeed, as time wore on it became quite obvious that tenure was the only guarantee that the professor's freedom was real and not a mere shadow.[39]

Nowhere was this better exemplified than at the University of Wisconsin. There the tie between university and state, theory and practice, was so close that it was quipped Wisconsin had a "university state" rather than a state university.[40] As this was in the "progressive" era of party politics there were many who thought that professors were surrendering scholarship to partisanship. As a president of the University of Iowa was to say later, "it may be difficult to draw the line between research and the application of its results in the promotion of state activities, but it is a line which, if not drawn will eventually lead to the impairment if not loss, of the university's freedom."[41] Yet in a celebrated case involving academic freedom in the South, where a professor at Trinity, later Duke, published an article favorable to the cause of blacks, President Kilgo put up a stout defense for the right of the college to enter the arena of practical affairs and take a stand on controversial issues such as trade, politics, and religion.[42]

As scholars were drawn more and more into the arena of public affairs, a third difficulty arose. Were scholars entering this arena as citizens or professors? Was the extraordinary protection of freedom from loss of their jobs, which they sought under the rubric of academic freedom, to be accorded to them whenever they spoke on *any* controversial issue? Evidently some professors thought it did, but in doing so they misled the public by confusing the difference between academic freedom and civil liberty. No one distinguished the two conceptions more successfully than President Lowell of Harvard during the First World War.[43] The critical point to bear in mind, he pointed out, is whether the professor is speaking inside or outside his chair, within or without his field of specialization. If he spoke or wrote inside it, he was entitled to the protective cloak of academic freedom. If not, he was just talking with the competence of any other citizen and was entitled to no greater consideration than anyone else exercising his civil liberties. The average citizen, with only a layman's understanding, is protected from fine or imprisonment for unpopular utterances but not against loss of public esteem or economic status. The professor, with an expert's understanding, must enjoy protection against loss of economic status as well because only so can society guarantee its crucial stake in his technical competence.

Unfortunately this useful distinction did not clear up difficulties in this area. When professors spoke, the public did not always stop to inquire whether or not they were speaking within their competencies. Consequently, the public tended to attach as much significance to their remarks as citizens as to their remarks as professors. Since professors were no more exempt than other citizens from making intemperate statements or mistakes of judgment, there was the constant risk that they would bring discredit not only on themselves but on the institution with which they were connected. Some found a ready remedy for this situation. Putting the good name of the institution ahead of the interests of any individual in it, they asked the professor to trim his exercise of civil liberty. The trustees of the University of Wisconsin, for instance, conceded that President Bascom was entitled to his convictions as a prohibitionist but opposed his openly joining the Prohibitionist party as compromising the university.[44] Others like Kilgo rallied against the notion that professors should not be just as free as other citizens; indeed, informed opinion came to insist that they should enjoy tenure whether speaking inside or outside their chairs.[45]

To make doubly sure of the interests of the university, some invoked the German distinction in *akademische Freiheit* between freedom inside and outside the university. Inside the university there was wide freedom. Yet even here some favored only a freedom born of *consensus gentium.* Thus President Harper at Chicago insisted that his faculty confine themselves to their specialties and only pronounce on them when confirmed by colleagues in their departments.[46] But most university men thought no consensus should be required since knowledge advances by clash of opinion as well as by consensus. Outside the university freedom was to be more restricted and coordinated with official policy. This division of inner and outer freedom was reminiscent of Luther's spiritual freedom combined with temporal obedience.[47]

Another remedy for protecting the university or college against the individual professor's unwise exercise of civil liberty required him to submit any proposed public utterance for approval by the administration prior to its being made public. But to do this, as President Lowell so well pointed out, put the institution in the unhappy position of being responsible for everything its professors succeeded in saying in public. This too would be intolerable. Better, therefore, in the ultimate interest of freedom and vigorous teaching to let the professor exercise his civil liberty whatever the temporary embarrassment to the university.[48]

Latent in the whole development of academic freedom for the individual professor was the question of the corporate role of the university in social affairs. Did the increasing involvement of the professor in public affairs mean that the university had a normative function to perform in social progress? Hitherto it had been readily accepted that the university should transmit the social heritage and push out its bounds by research, even make that research available to the citizenry as a public service.[49] But should it now go a step further and practice the alchemy of transmuting knowledge into wisdom, interpreting facts from the perspective of values, of social philosophy? Walter Lippmann, noted commentator on public affairs, said it should.[50] His view was reminiscent of George S. Counts at the onset of the depression in the 1930s when he addressed American public school teachers with his ringing appeal *Dare the Schools Build a New Social Order?*[51] Yet, as American professors traveled back and forth between the campus and Washington, many were apprehensive that the practice of cultural alchemy was endangering the autonomy of the American university.

Finally, granted freedom to teach the truth, there was debate how it should be taught. As John Dewey pointed out, there seemed to be two kinds of institutions of higher education at the opening of the twentieth century, those devoted to perpetuating and transmitting a certain view of truth and those devoted to investigating and discovering truth.[52] The conditions of academic freedom were different at each. In the former there was freedom within a framework, and in the latter freedom was itself the frame of reference. Except that the former tended more to retain dogmatic methods of indoctrinating its basic philosophy, both suggested methods of teaching which definitely departed from the old recitation and even lecture procedures.[53] Subjects had to be taught so as to provoke thought and encourage inquiry. As early as his inaugural Eliot was hinting that the way to teach science was the way science was itself nourished. It had to be recognized, of course, that different disciplines were in different stages of development, and therefore some warranted more cautious teaching than others. Alluding to these less-settled disciplines, he said:

Philosophical subjects should never be taught with authority. They are not established sciences: they are full of disputed matters, open questions, and bottomless speculations. It is not the function of the teacher to settle philosophical controversies for the pupils, or even to recommend to him any one set of opinions as better than another. Exposition, not imposition, of opinions is the professor's part. The student should be made acquainted with all sides of these controversies. . . . The very word "education" is a standing protest against dogmatic teaching. The notion that education consists in the authoritative inculcation of what the teacher deems true may be logical and appropriate in a convent, or a seminary of priests, but it is intolerable in universities and public schools, from primary to professional. The worthy fruit of academic culture is an open mind, trained to careful thinking, instructed in the methods of philosophic investigation, acquainted in a general way with the accumulated thought of past generations, and penetrated with humility.[54]

To ensure that both sides of controversial issues would be presented adequately at Cornell, Andrew D. White invited lecturers from each side to present its case.[55] Noah Porter at Yale, on the other hand, while agreeing heartily with Eliot and willing to make a last-ditch stand for free discussion, did not feel that this stand required him to call representatives of every shade of opinion, as, for instance, antireligionists, to the academic platform.[56]

The transition from dogmatic instruction to cultivation of the open mind under the aegis of academic freedom indicated fundamental changes in the scholar's theory of knowledge. The drift was clear in a statement of the committee which exonerated Richard T. Ely at the University of Wisconsin. "We cannot for a moment believe," said they, "that knowledge has reached its final goal, or that the present condition of society is perfect. . . . We feel that we would be unworthy of the position we hold if we did not believe in progress in all departments of knowledge."[57] Perhaps the author of that passage was still thinking of progress as steady advance toward a "final" or "perfect" goal which would indefinitely escape man's grasp. But perhaps, too, the committee was dimly becoming aware of the full implication of Darwinian evolution, from which it might follow that there is no fixed limit or perfect form of knowledge and that, on the contrary, truth is always tentative and indefinitely undergoing verification.

The American Association of University Professors

However cogent the argument for academic freedom, there was no way to enforce its strictures at the turn of the century. Certainly professors had no recourse to the law for redress of grievance at the violation of their academic freedom. One principal reason why the courts took no cognizance of academic freedom was their disinclination to interfere in the internal administration of colleges and universities. They were willing to examine the legal authority for acts of the administration but not their propriety. Academic freedom they regarded as a matter of propriety rather than legal right.[58] The tardiness of the courts in this matter is more easily understood when one considers that the phrase, academic freedom, had little currency at the time. Thus the phrase did not appear in the 1909 edition of the most widely used unabridged American dictionary nor even in its 1918 supplement. In fact it had not appeared in the legal dictionary of *Words and Phrases* as late as 1937. Since under the circumstances it was vain to expect presidents and governing boards to guide themselves by mere discussion of principles, it was necessary for the professors to have recourse to other methods of self-protection. This came in 1915 in the formation of the American Association of University Professors.

Before describing its organization note should be taken of several significant precedents leading up to it. The first occurred in connection with the dismissal of Professor Ross from Stanford. His case attracted such national attention that the American Economic Association appointed a committee to investigate. The committee brought in a report in 1901 favorable to Ross. Although it did not succeed in restoring him to his former post, it did make history by constituting the first instance where a professorial dismissal had been reviewed by others than the parties involved. A decade later occurred the forced separation of Professor John M. Mecklin from Lafayette. A liberal in philosophy, he had long had a running battle with his president, who was also chairman of the board of the conservative Princeton Theological Seminary. Following the precedent established in the Ross case, the American Philosophical and the American Psychological Associations, in both of which Mecklin was a member, appointed a joint committee headed by Professor A. O. Lovejoy of Johns Hopkins to investigate. The president and board of Lafayette resented this interference and gave the committee little cooperation beyond equivocal statements. In the end the committee found for Mecklin, but it went beyond the immediate concern of the case to censure the college severely for even an appearance of unwillingness to make a full and frank statement of the facts involved. Warning the college that such action jeopardized the confidence of both the lay and professional public, the committee laid it down as a matter of principle that "No college does well to live unto itself to such a degree that it fails to recognize that in all such issues the university teaching profession at large has a legitimate concern."[59]

Already a movement was afoot to push that concern. Three learned societies —the American Economic Association, the American Sociological Society, and the American Political Science Association—had appointed a joint committee to explore next steps. Finally, after considerable deliberation involving other groups, Professors John Dewey and A. O. Lovejoy issued a call for a meeting to form a "more comprehensive" professional organization than that afforded by the individual subject-matter organizations of long standing. To this initial meeting, which resulted in the formation of the American Association of University Professors, came 867 professors representing sixty different institutions.[60]

In spite of the imposing sponsorship there were some notable names missing from the initial roster. Charles A. Beard of Columbia as well as Barrett Wendell and Albert Bushnell Hart of Harvard held aloof. Their absence was in part indicative of earlier misgivings about the nature of the new organization. In the past the chief interest that bound professors together had been their separate fields of subject-matter specialization. This had resulted in a plurality of individual professional organizations. There was no common overall loyalty as a total group and much less so any "vertical" loyalty which would have included elementary- and secondary-school teachers in the group as well. Protection of job tenure to ensure intellectual freedom now seemed to provide a common rallying point for the profession as a whole. Yet there were those who feared this placed material advantage ahead of service and thus contradicted long-standing genteel ideals of professional ethics. If the AAUP—as the organization soon became known—was to assimilate its tactics to those of trade unionism, there were those who would have none of it. So strong was this antipathy that John Dewey, who presided at the organizational meeting, was prompted to remark that he did not expect the defense of academic freedom to be more than an incidental activity in the new association.[61]

In addition to this more or less passive resistance, the new AAUP met some active opposition. The *New York Times,* for instance, let go with a most unrestrained blast against the "organized dons" and defined academic freedom as "the unalienable right of every college instructor to make a fool of himself and his college by vealy, intemperate, sensational prattle about every subject under the sun, to his classes and the public, and still keep on the payroll or be reft therefrom only by elaborate process."[62] Opposition also came from professional quarters such as the Committee on Academic Freedom of the Association of American Colleges. This committee, composed of college presidents, considered that it could speak more effectively for the professors than could the professors themselves through the AAUP.[63]

In taking this position the presidents apparently did not appreciate how wide the breach of distrust between faculty and administration had grown in this period.[64] Indeed so great was the misgiving that from the outset presidents were excluded from membership in the AAUP like foremen from labor unions, although probably only a relatively small if powerful proportion of the body of presidents were really objectionable and a number of others had sided with the professors in the battle for academic freedom. Even the membership of deans was hedged by provisos which showed clearly that they did not enjoy the full confidence of the professorial body.[65]

The main achievement of the American Association of University Professors when initially organized was the declaration of a body of principles.[66] On the whole this declaration managed to crystallize in systematic form much of the debate which had been going on in the quarter-century prior to 1915. The kernel of the declaration asserted that the prime nature of the academic calling is to deal first hand, after prolonged technical training, with the sources of knowledge. To discharge this function properly professors must be free to come to conclusions about knowledge unaffected by factors which are irrelevant to the validity of that knowledge. While the lay public is under no obligation to accept the conclusions of the academic mind, it is nevertheless of the utmost importance to society that the conclusions of the men trained and dedicated to the pursuit of truth be their own and "not echoes of the opinions of the lay public or of the individuals who endow or manage universities."[67]

The professor's major responsibility, therefore, the declaration went on to say, is to society and not to the governing board of the university. The professor should no more be responsible to the board than the federal judiciary is to the

President. The board, like the President, may "appoint" but it does not "employ." Termination of an appointment, when the time comes, should result from the judgment of one's professional peers and not of a board of lay officers. Responsibility to the lay public is no simple affair because public opinion, while a democratic safeguard against the tyranny of an autocrat, can itself also be tyrannical. The role of the university in public opinion should be to help inform that opinion and make it more circumspect and self-critical. Obviously this function is impaired by any restriction imposed on academic freedom. Public opinion, therefore, should regard the university as "an intellectual experiment station, where new ideas may germinate and where their fruit, though still distasteful to the community as a whole, may be allowed to ripen until finally, perchance, it may become a part of the accepted intellectual food of the nation or of the world."[68]

Lastly, the declaration asserted that the professor should be free to broadcast the fruit of experimental ideas both inside and outside the classroom and both inside and outside his academic chair. But, if he is permitted to enjoy this privilege, he also has the burden of presenting his views responsibly[69] and only after carefully winnowing them. And then he should express them with dignity and courtesy in temperate language. Furthermore, in the case of immature students he should strike a helpful balance between giving them the benefit of his own mature judgment and encouraging them to examine other opinions in coming independently to ones of their own.[70]

Although this declaration was the main success of the association's first year and although Dewey had expected the defense of academic freedom in individual cases to be a mere incident in its activities, it was surprising to all what an overwhelming amount of time was devoted by officers of the association to the investigation of cases thrust upon them. As Dewey himself said in his presidential address of 1915, to have failed to undertake these initial demands would have been cowardly and would have destroyed all confidence in the new organization as anything more than a talking body. Yet contrary to his expectation, the number of cases did not abate but continued to grow. In fact in but a short time Committee A of the AAUP became the leading and most effective defender of academic freedom in the country. At the height of the McCarthy era there were 165 cases pending.[71] And that figure does not include the many cases that were settled quietly and amicably without formal proceedings.[72]

In acting as a pressure group the AAUP had neither the finances nor the personnel to follow up each case. Besides, its main effectiveness did not lie so much in redressing individual grievances as in the warning its resulting publicity gave not only to offending institutions but ones on the brink of offense. In the case of offending institutions there was much disagreement in the association over whether they should be blacklisted. The argument against such a policy was that the penalty was visited on the innocent as well as the guilty. A compromise resulted wherein the offending institutions were placed on a "nonrecommended" list to warn people away from contaminated areas.[73] So brilliantly did the AAUP succeed in the long run that many colleges and universities voluntarily brought their policies into conformity with the association's declaration of principles without even the threat of being placed on the dreaded "nonrecommended" list.[74]

The success of the American Association of University Professors can be measured in two directions. In the one it greatly influenced subsequent declarations of principle on academic freedom by such other organizations as the Association of American Colleges, the Association of American Universities, the National Education Association, the American Civil Liberties Union, and the American Federation of Teachers.[75] In the other direction its success was measured by its sturdy growth. From a membership of less than 900 it had grown fifty years later to well over 60,000, and at that its membership was less than 40 per cent of its potential. The number of local chapters expanded from some 50 in 1920 to over 800 at the association's fiftieth anniversary.[76]

New Crises

Hardly had the American Association of University Professors organized itself and declared its principles than academic freedom had to meet a new series of crises. In the period ahead social stability was to be sorely tried by two world wars and an intervening depression, to say nothing of a "cold" war as well. The great advantage of freedom in legislative as well as academic halls was that it provided a means of turning up a rich variety of resources for meeting human problems. The fact that this variety could also be socially divisive frightened some people, especially on occasions when a wholehearted and united effort seemed necessary not only to maintain stability but perhaps to save the state. This situation posed a great paradox: May it sometimes be necessary to curtail freedom in order to preserve it?

The first test of this question arose during World War I. Professors took positions on the war all the way from the pro-Germanism of Professors Munsterberg at Harvard and Schaper at the University of Minnesota to the outright pacifism of Professors Cattell[77] at Columbia and Whipple of the University of Virginia. To permit the expression of opinions such as these under the guise of academic freedom, many thought, invited a hazardous rocking of the ship of state as it was embarked on stormy seas. Nicholas Murray Butler of Columbia took the problem posed as the subject of his commencement address in the spring of 1917. He sought to solve it by underscoring the distinction between the practice of academic freedom before and after the United States' declaration of war. While the country was making up its collective mind it was the duty of the university to guarantee complete freedom of discussion, no matter how deplorable the views just mentioned might seem. So soon as the country had spoken through Congress, however, this guarantee could no longer be given. Eccentric views formerly tolerable then became intolerable, possibly even seditious.[78] Consequently, Schaper, Whipple, and Cattell had to leave their institutions.[79] Harvard's A. Lawrence Lowell, however, made no distinction between war and peace and shielded Munsterberg to the end.[80] He did, as already seen, make a distinction between academic freedom and civil liberty, between teaching inside and outside one's chair,[81] but he did not press it in this case.

Whether patriotic necessities set limits to academic freedom prompted the AAUP to appoint a committee on "academic freedom in wartime" whose report seemed to many a retreat from the 1915 declaration and certainly added nothing to the prestige of the fledgling AAUP.[82] A decade later the American Council on Education called a meeting to digest and refine ten years of experience with academic freedom. From this effort emerged the 1925 "conference Statement on Academic Freedom and Tenure" adopted by the AAUP and both the Association of American Universities and the Association of American Colleges. Both this and the 1940 statement of the AAUP dealt extensively with procedure to implement the 1915 declaration of principles.[83]

The next test of the paradox of curtailing freedom to preserve it came during the great depression of the 1930s. So severe was that economic shock that political and economic institutions were jarred at all angles from the upright, especially abroad. Again many thought that academic freedom managed to tilt institutions into still more precarious postures. To discourage opinions which might topple institutions altogether and to ensure that others squared with the constitutional perpendicular, a number of the forty-eight states enacted "teacher-oath" statutes. Ordinarily the essence of these statutes was the requirement of an affirmation of loyalty to the state and federal constitutions. Interestingly enough, they were not the first instance of a teacher loyalty oath in this country. On the founding of Dickinson College in 1783 the trustees of that infant institution swore allegiance to the Commonwealth of Pennsylvania and, renouncing obedience to the King of England, swore to uphold the sovereignty and independence of the United States.[84] The chief difference between this oath and those 150 years later was that the earlier was voluntarily undertaken and joyfully executed while the latter were externally imposed and reluctantly subscribed to.

Whether the latter kind of oath was a threat to academic freedom was not altogether clear on the surface. After digging beneath it a committee of the AAUP concluded that the length any ominous shadow cast depended on the intent of the statutes. If they merely asked professors to obey the law of the land they were unobjectionable, although unnecessary, since every citizen is expected to do that without a formal oath. Incidentally, if it was intended to exact the oath of professors as public officers rather than citizens, the committee pointed out that the courts had repeatedly ruled that teachers were not "officers," especially those in private institutions. If again, and this seemed the critical point, the statutes' intent was to cause professors to refrain from criticizing or suggesting changes in the fundamental law of the country, then the committee definitely opposed them as an unwarranted limitation of academic freedom. If this was the intent, moreover, it seemed more than likely that such statutes would also be contrary to public policy since state and federal constitutions contemplate their own amendment. However, at the time the committee reported, 1937, no court had as yet been called on to interpret their wording. In trying to preserve an area for critical-mindedness the committee gave assurance of fair treatment for it by reiterating the AAUP's longstanding policy that the professor should not seek to win students to his point of view of controversial issues, much less to do so by presenting warped or incomplete facts. Finally, if the loyalty statutes were not denying opportunity for difference of opinion but merely reminding professors that there were some American principles so well grounded in history as to admit of little or no controversy in instruction, the committee could not help but agree so long as tolerance of diversity of opinion was one of them.[85]

On the whole in the 1930s the bark of loyalty-oath legislation was more menacing than its bite. It was not till after the Second World War that a bite of this sort of legislation drew academic blood. The howl of protest against it was loudest at the University of California but persistent enough in the states of Oklahoma and Washington to be heard all the way to the United States Supreme Court. There two landmark decisions were laid down. In the first state, professors were required to swear that they were not members of certain subversive organizations. The court struck this oath down because it recognized that membership could be innocent of subversive intention and therefore to punish the swearer amounted to guilt by association.[86] In the second state the court found the definition of such words as "subversive" so vague as to render the statute constitutionally unenforceable.[87] In the Oklahoma case Justice Black, great protagonist of civil liberties, excoriated oath legislation, saying, "Test oaths are notorious tools of tyranny. When used to shackle the mind they are, or at least should be, unspeakably odious to a free people."

The battle between the faculty and the Board of Regents of the University of California was long and acrimonious. Even the Regents were so evenly divided among themselves that during most of the debate only a thin majority favored the oath. After minor concessions on both sides many of the recalcitrant faculty signed a modified version of the oath. But a hard core of thirty-nine remained obdurate to the end and were ultimately dismissed. They took their case to the highest court of the state, where the oath was thrown out on the reasoning that the conventional constitutional oath of office already pre-empted the ground so effectively that the university Regents were not justified in singling out professors for additional obligations.[88]

The struggle at the University of California was more decisive on the matter of loyalty oaths than it was on the question of communism. The Regents of the university aimed a blow at the Communist professor but did not quite bring him down. The loyalty oath proved a clumsy weapon for their purpose because it unnecessarily alarmed professors over their academic freedom and because opportunistically minded Communists on the faculty would not hesitate to conceal their identities. As a matter of fact, the number of Communists actually turned up was insignificant compared with the animosities and timidities released among both faculty and students. It was a question, indeed, who was doing the greater harm, the outright opponents of American institutions or the overzealous protectors of them.[89] The surprisingly and relatively few Communists turned up in

California and elsewhere did not discourage legislators, both state and federal, from relentlessly hunting down these few.[90] Investigating bodies like the Congressional Un-American Activities Committee subpoenaed suspected professors and asked them point-blank under oath whether they were or had been Communists. Proved or admitted membership in the party often led almost automatically to their dismissal from their academic posts. Consequently, to protect their academic tenure many professors fell back on their civil liberties guaranteed in the Fifth Amendment and refused to answer questions about their relations to communism on grounds that their replies might incriminate them. In many instances pleading the Fifth Amendment was taken as self-admission of membership, and the professor was fired just the same.

One of the purposes of this oath legislation had been to screen out card-bearing Communist or Communist-leaning professors. After the First World War there had been anxiety about "socialists" on college faculties. No less a person than President Calvin Coolidge saw them stalking the colleges for women.[91] There was some resulting strain on academic freedom, but Nicholas Murray Butler's fear, that stretching academic tolerance to the extreme demanded by postwar radicalism would be the suicide of academic freedom, turned out to be unfounded.[92] The situation after the second world conflict proved much more ominous. The Cold War with Russia increased national tensions to a point where apprehension about our national security belied our national strength. In this atmosphere a considerable public opinion, increasingly impatient with tolerating the diversity of opinion demanded by academic freedom, was insisting on national conformity in the public opposition to communism. But even so the opposition was directed more against Communist professors than communism itself. More enlightened leaders of public opinion recognized the necessity for studying the ideology and strategy of communism as a means of combating it, but they nevertheless objected to professors who were card-bearing members of the party. Sooner or later, the issue had to be squarely faced whether preventing Communist professors from occupying their chairs was an unwarranted diminution of academic freedom.

The middle of the century witnessed a lively debate of this issue. The opponents of Communist professors made a strong case against them, their major point being that Communist commitments to party discipline actually unfitted professors for the privilege of academic freedom. Since members of the party were expected to follow the party line in their own thought and action no matter how it meandered or contradicted their personal views, Communist professors surrendered the most distinctive and precious asset of academic freedom, the right to arrive at their opinions independently of any influences save the rational process of determining truth itself.[93] There was no question about the right of the professor as a citizen to be a Communist, only question about the advisability of such a citizen being a professor.

The defenders of Communist professors did not so much take issue with the importance of professors' maintaining independence of mind as they did with uncritically accepting, as the governing boards of higher education had so frequently done, membership in the party as sufficient proof by itself of the loss of that independence. By contrast they insisted on substantial evidence in each case that the professor had in fact in the classroom or in his published research hewed to the party line in an unscholarly fashion. To dismiss him from his chair on less proof than this was to convict him unjustly of guilt by association. For similar reasons they objected to dismissing professors merely because the latter pleaded the Fifth Amendment.[94]

Addressing itself to this last point, a special committee of the AAUP declared that "satisfactory performance in teaching or research, and good character in relation to these functions, are the matters to be judged" when academic tenure is at stake in pleading the Fifth Amendment.[95] To judge these professional matters the committee favored frankness on the part of the professor pleading the amendment, "but it does not follow that it is wise or right to place his professional survival in jeopardy by demanding that he not only talk freely but also refute unspecified inferences drawn by his accusers from the refusal to testify. The adoption of such a policy tends to substitute economic punishment for the criminal punishment against which the amendment is designed to guard; and it impairs in direct proportion the constitutional guaranty."[96] In any event, as Ralph Barton Perry wrote to the *New York Times,* the university and not a governmental investigating body must be the judge of these matters.[97]

During the first decade of the Cold War the professor and academic freedom seem to have been definitely on the defensive. The public, overanxious to win security from the tensions released by this war, repressed tendencies not only toward Communist patterns of thought but even toward liberal ones as well. Reactionary forces were so strong that professors, students, and research workers developed a cautious timidity rather than the bold adventurous spirit becoming a university. With truth crushed to earth by Communists abroad and almost crushed in the protective embrace of conservatives at home, there were some who came to distrust the grounding of academic freedom, as had the AAUP declaration of 1915, in the sufferance of an enlightened public opinion. What if that opinion were unenlightened? Pitted against the odds of the day perhaps the battle of truth against error might not always be open, and truth, as witness the recent histories of Nazi Germany and Communist Russia, might not always prevail as Milton in his *Areopagitica* was confident it would. To avoid this calamity perhaps academic freedom should be grounded in the natural law and ultimately in religion. The professor then would become the bearer of the "word" (λόγος) and should, like Socrates, owe his allegiance to God rather than to the populace.[98]

Fortunately the dark cloud that hung over academic freedom during this decade had a silver lining too. The courts, which formerly had taken no notice of academic freedom,[99] began to fashion it into a Constitutional right.[100] In one or another of four cases reaching the United States Supreme Court between 1952 and 1959, all nine justices went on record as recognizing academic freedom as both a substantive and a procedural right.[101] Procedurally the professor was entitled to "due process," that is, basically, presentation with a statement of charges against him and an opportunity to be heard thereon. The minimal legal procedure, however, was supplemented by what has come to be called "academic due process." This happy phrase was foreshadowed in the 1915 declaration of principles by the phrase "good academic custom and usage." To illustrate, every effort was made to conciliate a difficulty before it became an adversary affair. If it reached that point, it was then laid before a committee, not of laymen as in the courts, but of one's professional peers who were expert in academic affairs. Moreover the professor was entitled to choose from the faculty an academic adviser who was a person of established position, wisdom, and judicial temper. By such fairness an effort was made to protect not only the heavy investment made in the expertise of the individual but also the reputation of the institution.[102]

The substantive right to academic freedom was best elaborated in *Sweezey* v. *New Hampshire.*[103] There the attorney general had been authorized to investigate and prosecute subversive activities within the state. Pursuant to this directive the attorney general charged Sweezey, among other things, with teaching communism at the state university. At his trial the defendant swore that he was not a Communist but refused to answer such questions as "Did you tell the class socialism was inevitable?" "Did you advocate Marxism?" and "Did you espouse dialectical materialism?" on the ground that they violated his constitutional freedoms. The New Hampshire court convicted, but the highest court in the land reversed the conviction. Apparently the lower court thought the state's interest in self-protection took precedence over the individual's freedom. The Court in Washington struck the opposite balance. It saw a dire peril to the nation unless there were to be free inquiry in its universities. Not only that, but scholarly inquiry could not flourish in an atmosphere of suspicion and distrust. Fearlessness is a quality of academic work which is as fragile as it is indispensable for the scholar, not only in making amendments to an accepted social frame, but in fundamentally re-examining the frame of reference itself.

While the Sweezey case settled academic freedom as a constitutional issue, it left open some questions about tenure that had come to be closely associated with this freedom. The idea of tenure antedated that of academic freedom. At Yale in the eighteenth century both rector and masters held tenure *quamdiu bene se gesserint,* that is, during good behavior. Columbia did the same for both professors and tutors. Meantime Harvard was noting the "inconvenience" of appointing very young tutors without limitation of time because, if they had good talents, they would soon be induced to go elsewhere and, if they did not have them, they would remain to embarrass the college indefinitely. It is to Columbia's credit that removals could ensue only after a full hearing. Unfortunately this rule seems to have fallen into disuse in the nineteenth century for the essence of tenure has always been, not guaranteed life employment, but an assured hearing before dismissal. With the founding of the AAUP in the twentieth century judicial procedures for terminating a professor's tenure were spelled out in considerable detail.[104] At first in 1925 these judicial benefits were limited to tenured professors, but after 1940 tenure was divorced from academic rank and tied to years of service, a recommended seven of which might be probationary.[105] Even then tenure was not absolute because it could be abrogated by an institution's financial stringency. These conditions of tenure received general acceptance by both the AAC and the AAU in the prosperous postwar period.

Another dimension of the perennial battle for the freedom of the academic mind received some exploration during the turbulence of the late sixties and early seventies. This period raised the question, not for the first time, to be sure, whether there were any limits to academic freedom.[106] The Vietnam War raised one of them. A number of universities were engaged in war research which required that results, being classified information of potential use to the enemy, could not be published. This ran quite counter to the academic tradition of making new knowledge available for the benefit of mankind.[107] Then many activist students went further and protested that since wars are inimical to mankind, higher education should not be engaged at all in their promotion. Other students, many of them black, but many whites too, objected to research that led to the conclusion that some races are genetically inferior.[108] Whatever the academic gain, they thought, there could only be a political loss here. This raised the further question whether the academic fraternity should not have a greater sense of social responsibility for the uses to which its findings, from atomic energy to molecular biology, might be put. One member of that fraternity, however, distinguished between finding out the truth and applying it. If there were to be curbs, he said, they should be on application, not investigation.[109]

The most shortsighted limits to academic freedom in this period were posed by university students themselves.[110] Some tried not only to "shut it down" by strikes, arson, and "trashing" but to shout it down as well. By stirring up noisy commotions they disrupted unpopular speakers on university platforms and unpopular professors in their classrooms. Worse yet they forced physical confrontations with the police when summoned to restore order to the campus, thus supplanting reason with force in the very citadel of reason. Some times motivated by theories of anarchism and nihilism they showed an anti-intellectualism that was any thing but conducive to the open mind.[111] With the conclusion of the war and the return of a normal pattern of academic life it is notable that Yale, ashamed of its own students' treatment of controversial speakers, published a ringing affirmation of principles for free speech on the campus in future times of stress. Although it proposed clear-cut rules for recent kinds of misconduct, it nonetheless realized that "Rules and their enforcement must rest upon a consensus of the whole community . . . and a genuine concern over violations."[112]

It is noteworthy that the great growth of academic freedom in the nineteenth and especially the twentieth centuries was accompanied by the increasing secularization of higher education. In the eighteenth and even early nineteenth centuries Americans had difficulty in thinking of higher education unrelated to denominational religion. Indeed, one objective of founding colleges had been the propagation of denominational religion. Most Christian sects, however, had a double standard of truth, one for natural phenomena and another for supernatural. Freedom was permissible in applying the former but not the latter. Professors were free to follow the argument wherever it might lead in the natural realm, but in the supernatural they were constrained by revelation. There was no compromising the inevitable struggle. Either religion had to submit to free inquiry, or the college and university had to become secular. The 1915 statement of the AAUP made that issue crystal clear. Church-related colleges that preferred to remain sectarian were declared proprietary institutions. Many leading Protestant colleges and universities, originally church-related, had long been cutting their denominational connections rather than be regarded as proprietary. Catholic colleges and universities resisted this secular trend longest. But with the *aggiornamento* launched by Pope John XXIII in 1962 Catholic institutions of higher education began to re-examine their academic stance. Though clinging staunchly to the notion of a distinctly Catholic college or university they began to demand that they enjoy the same academic freedom associated with the great secular institutions of the country.[113] Whether Catholic colleges and universities would also succumb to secularization as a result remained a moot point for the future.

16

Reintegration of Curriculum and Extracurriculum

The history of American college life resembles the swinging of a pendulum in a wide arc. First there was the era of the church-dominated college with its unity of curriculum and extracurriculum, with its cohesive, self-contained life. Next came the changes characteristic of the years from 1865 to 1918, when there arose what one observer has called the "bifurcated college."[1] In their own "students' university," undergraduates improvised a strenuous "college life" which was independent of, and frequently worked at cross-purposes to, the central intellectual concerns of American higher learning. The sideshows were now in a fair way of swallowing up the main tent.[2]

By the time of the First World War, the pendulum was ready to swing back again. Many leaders of higher education were now coming to feel that the perfervid flourishing of the extracurriculum represented a challenge, rather than a menace. What indeed was the danger confronting American higher education? They would answer that it did not lie in the proliferation of various student activities per se, hectic as they might be, but rather in the failure of the colleges to do anything constructive about them. The solution involved taking positive action to reintegrate the curriculum and the extracurriculum. By linking student activities to the basic purposes of the college, classroom and campus could be brought together again.

How specifically was this new unity to be achieved? The answer most frequently given was that the life of the student must be placed more and more in the center of academic concern. The curriculum, and every other aspect of college life, must be closely related to the student's total personal development. To this end, extensive personnel services should be developed which would give attention to the student's problems of self-support and job placement, counsel him on health and personal problems, give him educational guidance, and help him "adjust" to college and life. To this end, too, a new concern should be developed with student housing, with a view to establishing that residential system which would best facilitate academic and personal development. In addition, a broader and more spontaneous student participation in athletics must be fostered. Finally, every effort should be made to steer fraternities and other student organizations into constructive channels and to seek to stimulate a sense of responsibility by widening the scope of student government.

Student Personnel Services

The characteristic expression of this new concern for the "whole student" and for the establishing of a new unity in the American college in the twentieth century came to be the student personnel movement. This is the development which has interested educational visitors from abroad more than any other aspect of American higher learning. In most other countries, students in institutions of higher education have been regarded as responsible adults, and the province of the university has been thought to be strictly that of training the mind. In the United States by way of contrast, college students have been thought of as immature adolescents, requiring guidance at every turn. Student misconduct outside of class, or even academic failure in class, was regarded as reflecting on the university, not on the individual. A more different outlook from that of the Continental European university, with its intellectualistic, impersonal attitude, cannot be conceived.[3]

In part, this American attitude went back to the very origins of the colonial colleges. The seventeenth-century English "collegiate" foundations were not just institutions of higher learning; they were "organized residential associations" for the purpose of inculcating specific patterns of religious belief and social conduct.[4] Their attitude toward the student was one of acting *in loco parentis*. Although the English universities, from which this philosophy was derived, came to evolve a somewhat different application of it in the nineteenth century, the American church-related college remained much closer to the original prototype. With its deep concern for saving the student's soul and overseeing his moral life, it was involved in much more than merely the education of the intellect. American parents expected this, and the conditions of the time seemed to demand it. Under this regime of paternalism, the clerical presidents and professors constituted what might be called the first body of "personnel" officers. The record indicates that they were constantly dealing with a host of problems which involved counseling or the supervision of extracurricular affairs.[5] Seen in this light, the more recent concern with the cultivation of the physical, social, and moral aspects of a student's life as well as the intellectual side may be traced back to the early church-dominated American collegiate "societies."

After the Civil War, American Ph.D.'s, who had been trained in Germany, tried to introduce a more impersonal, intellectualistic approach modeled on the Continental European university. However, the paternalistic tradition had by this time attained such a strong influence upon the American college that it could not be completely eliminated.[6] To be sure, the unity of the old-time college was shattered as the curriculum grew broader and more diversified, as the elective system spread, as the undergraduate population became larger and less homogeneous, and as secular influences became stronger. Many of the newer faculty members were more interested in scholarly research than in personal dealings with students, and it was becoming increasingly apparent that promotion depended upon published research, not on student counseling. In the main, however, American college students were not converted to this intellectualist view of the higher learning. They were not interested in taking advantage of the opportunity to become mature scholars, European style. In the activist atmosphere of the American campus, they considered this to be an approach suitable only for professors and "grinds." Instead they developed enthusiastic support for strenuous extracurricular activities and contented themselves with a "gentleman's C." There is no indication that in the expansive, utilitarian American culture of this period their parents urged them to any other view.

The American college, at this point, showed signs of developing a split personality. The old "college life" continued to flourish. But now it was developing distinctly apart from, and frequently in opposition to, the intellectual side of higher learning. "Campus opinion" came to exercise a sway more imperious, more tyrannical, than anything the old paternalistic college rules had been able to impose.

When the personnel movement arose in the twentieth century, it thus represented not only a major effort to restore a unified life to the American college but also a revival of the old-time college's concern for the nonintellectual side of the student's career. This reaction to the temporary vogue of German impersonalism expressed itself, however, in different ways from the clerically dominated pattern of earlier times. As a result of the greater size and complexity of American institutions of higher learning, it was no longer possible for the president and teaching faculty to function as active personnel officers. This task now had to be assumed by special staff members who devoted all of their time to it. In addition, the new sciences of human relationships, which in our own time have increasingly come to be known as the "behavioral sciences," played an important part in shaping college personnel programs.[7] Mental testing, in particular, as developed by Cattell, Thorndike, and other research psychologists and as stimulated by Army programs during World War I and industrial relations work after it, was significant in this connection.[8] Finally, the changing nature of college populations gave a special direction to the modern personnel movement.[9] Not only had they increased greatly in size but they had become more diverse in make-up than ever before. The small college, with its tiny faculty in close personal touch with a student body of two hundred or so, all of whom were of similar social origin and had similar life objectives, was a thing of the past. Now the watchword was increasingly becoming "education for all," and after 1918 this was interpreted by many as meaning "college for all."[10] New groups were coming into the colleges with a variety of curricular, social, and vocational needs. They were finding existing programs based on the primary goal of subject-matter mastery unrelated to their situation.[11] At the same time, high schools were no longer preparing students for the traditional kind of college to the extent that had once been the case.

More and more beginning collegians saw social and vocational objectives as having greater significance for their lives than intellectual ones. A survey made by Dr. Henry Chauncey of the Educational Testing Service in 1964 revealed this to be the case. His study of 13,000 freshmen entering a broad cross-section of American colleges indicated that social life, extracurricular activities, and the formation of new friendships were for 50 per cent their major interests in college. Some 26 per cent gave top priority to vocational goals, and only 18 per cent listed the cultivation of intellect as their primary goal.[12]

What were the colleges to do under these circumstances? They could admit all who wished to enter, but fail many of these after the first year. Advocates of a more active counseling program called this "callous and uneconomical." They could refuse admission to all except those of the highest intellectual capacity. State laws made this impossible in most publicly controlled institutions. Finally, they could frankly acknowledge the increasing heterogeneity of the student body and seek to "adapt the institution's procedures to the students."[13] This is where the personnel movement came into the picture. Along with the "general education" movement, which we have already described,[14] and the introduction of new instructional methods, personnel work was American higher education's answer to the problem of huge and heterogeneous enrollments.[15]

The net result of all these developments was a profound shift in emphasis in American higher education. The "sink-or-swim" outlook of Eliot's elective system was discarded. With it went the nineteenth-century faculty psychology, with its concept of a dualism of mind and matter and its belief that the independent faculties of the mind—such as judgment, will, and imagination—could be cultivated through mental discipline. In their place organismic psychology, with its emphasis on viewing the individual as a whole person, began to serve as a basis for what came to be called a "holistic" approach to the college student.[16] According to this new view, the college must assume responsibility for the student's total personality development—physical, social, and emotional as well as intellectual.[17] It should recognize that what happens outside the classroom—living conditions, study habits, emotional problems—might vitally influence classroom performance. It should seek a new understanding of the motives back of undesirable conduct. It should realize that merely to set up severe entrance requirements or rigorously to eliminate the academically unfit was an inadequate solution of the problem of "adjusting" the student to his environment. It should view with skepticism the traditional measure of success in college, namely grades in subject matter, because of their lack of objectivity and failure to measure many important characteristics. It should in addition recognize no inherent opposition between the curriculum and the extracurriculum: The college existed for the sake of the student, not for that of special subjects of instruction.[18] Above all, it must not knowingly allow students to fall by the wayside. As one of the leading exponents of this point of view put it: "Once a college has admitted a student it has a moral obligation to do everything within reason to help him succeed."[19]

The similarity between this new emphasis in higher education and the viewpoint being introduced in many elementary and secondary schools by John

Dewey and his followers becomes obvious when we read in one contemporary study of college personnel work: "Students are developing organisms demanding a personalized learning experience if they are to profit from college."[20] In any event, as a result of this "personalistic" approach to education, strenuous attempts were made to apply the findings of scientific psychology so that all the details of the student's personality might be ascertained. It would then be the task of professional counselors and personnel workers to utilize this data to give whatever help was indicated.

In actuality, two distinct movements aiming to "individualize" the college took shape after World War I—the attempt to individualize instruction, as in Harvard's tutorials and Swarthmore's honors plan,[21] and the development of student personnel services. Although it has been pointed out that these two approaches were not mutually exclusive, that, indeed, they did exist at many institutions parallel to each other, it was really the second which most completely reflected the "personalistic" philosophy of higher education.[22] As a matter of fact, one leader of the personnel movement insisted that individualized techniques of instruction could be, and had been, used to attain the "intellectualistic" objectives of men like Flexner and Hutchins. The "personalistic" school of thought, on the other hand, was represented as being intrinsically interested in the role which nonintellectual factors—such as attitudes and emotions—as well as intellectual factors play in college education.[23] The latter emphasis reflected what was perhaps the dominant current in twentieth-century American higher education. An observer of student life in 1966 pointed out that even the academically superior in top-flight schools very often viewed good grades as simply "an instrumental rung" on the ladder of professional success. Few sought knowledge for its own sake. The activist culture of the land did not encourage the committed intellectual.[24]

Although the major influence of the personnel movement came to be exerted after 1918, there were pioneering efforts launched in certain American colleges in the later nineteenth century. Thus President Daniel Coit Gilman instituted a system of student counseling at Johns Hopkins soon after its foundation. The English influence here is easy to identify since it was largely at the suggestion of Professor Charles D'Urban Morris, former Fellow of Oriel College, that the Hopkins adviserships were set up. And yet one usually thinks, and with much justification, of Johns Hopkins as the supreme example of German university influence in the United States![25]

Equally important in this early period was the interest of William Rainey Harper, president of the University of Chicago, in the total personal development of undergraduates. In an address at Brown in 1899 he predicted that what he called "the scientific study of the student" would eventually be made an integral part of the work of the American university.[26]

At this time, too, the rapid development of student extracurricular activities compelled some colleges to appoint special officials to see that this phenomenon did not get completely out of hand. Thus Harvard in 1870 appointed Professor

Ephraim Gurney as what might be termed the first college "dean." Professor Gurney was primarily an "academic dean." He did little counseling. His main task, apart from teaching, was to take the burden of discipline off President Eliot's shoulders. In 1890, a Board of Freshman Advisers was set up at Harvard and the deanship was divided into two offices. This involved essentially a division of labor between an academic dean and a dean of student affairs. LeBaron Russell Briggs, who became a Harvard dean in 1890, came increasingly to perform the latter role and, anticipating the later personnel movement, took on many functions besides purely disciplinary ones.[27]

This pattern tended to become general in middle western and western universities in the early twentieth century; soon it was established in eastern institutions as well. Everywhere two types of deans appeared: "academic deans" of colleges or special faculties (people who were primarily educational administrators) and "deans of students"—deans of men or women as the case might be—whose concern was with the extracurricular life of undergraduates.[28] Then, as enrollments continued to mount, various forms of specialized counseling began to branch off from the latter office. The sheer physical burden of handling student problems was becoming too great for one man, especially in the larger universities. By the time of the First World War the administrative staffs dealing with these problems began to proliferate and diversify. Directors of admission now came to be appointed, and placement and health officers too. The modern phase of the personnel movement was born.

Many writers began to call attention to the new trend,[29] but perhaps the most significant note was sounded in 1909 by Abbott Lawrence Lowell in his inaugural address as president of Harvard. In this he warned that the recent emphasis upon graduate education and research scholarship was sabotaging the unique function of the American college. Undergraduates must be helped to develop as well-rounded individuals as well as scholars. "Among his other wise sayings," Lowell pointed out, "Aristotle remarked that man is by nature a social animal; and it is in order to develop his powers as a social being that American colleges exist. The object of the undergraduate department is not to produce hermits, each imprisoned in the cell of his own intellectual pursuits, but men fitted to take their places in the community and live in contact with their fellow men."[30] Forecasting as it did a notable change in emphasis from that of Lowell's predecessor, Charles W. Eliot, this address was indeed a turning of the road in the history of American higher education.

After the First World War the personnel movement received a tremendous impetus all over America. Mental testing and counseling had been developed on a large scale by the Army, and as soon as peace came "army psychologists transposed to the colleges the many techniques of counseling and diagnosis perfected in army personnel."[31] The field assumed more and more of the aspects of a distinct profession, growing out of the stage of "sentimentalized intuition" and entering that of systematic differentiation and specialization of personnel functions.[32] A solid body of scientific knowledge was being built up that could be applied in counseling situations. Personnel workers of every variety—psychiatric, religious, social, vocational, educational—began to appear in large numbers.[33] At institutions such as the University of Minnesota under President Lotus D. Coffman an independent and comprehensive personnel program was put into effect (at the same time as the "General College" experiment) and professional counselors were given extensive powers of waiver and assignment over students.[34] Great national foundations were becoming interested in coordinating and stimulating the personnel work that was going forward at dozens of campuses across the nation. With the backing of the Rockefeller Foundation and the General Education Board, the American Council on Education initiated an extensive study of personnel practices, achievement tests, rating scales, and vocational monographs. As a result, not only were personnel procedures standardized all over the country, but in 1948 the council joined with the Carnegie Foundation and the College Entrance Examination Board in creating the Educational Testing Service, a nationwide cooperative experiment in the use of achievement tests.[35] To sum up, then, in the years following 1918 the student personnel movement in colleges had gained national recognition and professional stature; it was becoming self-conscious, confident, and widely influential.[36]

New Trends in Student Housing

One of the areas where exponents of the new "personnel point of view" felt much could be done to reintegrate curriculum and extracurriculum was that of student housing. The relative unconcern of the late nineteenth century about the way in which the student lived outside of the classroom was being replaced now by a greater interest in the development and improvement of undergraduate residential facilities. Research studies were bolstering this "personalistic" emphasis by revealing that a student's academic performance was affected in an important way by his surroundings and, particularly, by his housing.[37] More and more college presidents were coming to the conclusion that "Good housing contributes to academic success, and the securing of proper housing is as important as providing proper classroom instruction."[38]

Even at the height of late-nineteenth-century impersonalism, eastern institutions such as Yale continued to be strongly influenced by the old English belief in the values of residential college life. This philosophy began to play an important role once again on the national stage when a former Yale professor, William Rainey Harper, became president of the University of Chicago in 1892. While devoted to scholarly research, Harper was convinced of the educational value of student housing and promoted one project after another to foster a "common element" on the campus reminiscent of the ante-bellum college. Although denounced by some of his contemporaries as "aristocratic," "pro-British," and "medieval," Harper assigned over half the cubage of the original University of Chicago buildings to dormitories.[39] This was a radical departure for the Middle West of that day. In addition, as early as 1893 he had established a House System, founded on residence halls which were to have their own heads, counselors, and house committees. It was hoped that a healthy rivalry would develop between these units. Early, too, he sponsored the building of a well-equipped student clubhouse. Finally, in 1905, toward the end of his administration, he announced a plan to reorganize the junior colleges of the university into four small residential institutions for men and four for women, modeled on the colleges at Oxford and Cambridge.[40]

One can only speculate as to what influence, if any, Harper's announced plans of 1905, which he did not live to carry out, may have had upon Woodrow Wilson's decision, two years later, to sponsor a Quadrangle Plan at Princeton. Like Harper, Wilson proposed to establish residential units which would house both students and unmarried faculty members. Like Oxford and Cambridge, these quadrangles would be tied in with a preceptorial system of individualized instruction; this, it should be remembered, had already been established at Princeton. They would thus become agencies for education as well as body shelters. Wilson wanted more than a mere change in dormitory arrangements. He sought an English-style university which would stimulate a rebirth of liberal culture in the highly fragmented American college curriculum, bringing meaningful unity to what was increasingly becoming academic chaos. Wilson needed $2,000,000 to carry out his ambitious concept; he could not get it because many of the alumni of Old Nassau were antagonized by his proposal to abolish the existing fraternal eating clubs and substitute instead the new residential quadrangles. Although Wilson had lost "the Battle of Princeton," national attention had now been focused on the Quadrangle Plan;[41] all of this was to bear fruit twenty years later through the Harkness donations to Harvard and Yale.

Meanwhile, interest in student housing began to increase elsewhere in the country. Columbia University built its first dormitory in 1896 and Cornell in 1914. Western state universities such as Minnesota, Michigan, and Illinois took similar action before America's entry into the First World War.[42] Graduates of the residential women's colleges of the East, coming to the coeducational universities of the West to serve as deans of women, spread the gospel of student residential housing.[43] More and more, as fraternity chapter houses and private rooming houses sprang up to meet the students' need for housing, university officials were insisting upon careful inspection and supervision of these off-campus facilities. Then, too, many state universities began to construct student union buildings to meet the recreational and social needs of their undergraduates. Designed to bring together "in a wholesome, democratic way all persons on the campus by providing common means of recreation," this movement swept the country after the University of Michigan erected its union building by popular subscription.[44]

By 1939 three-fourths of the institutions examined for accreditation by the North Central Association reported that they were making an effort to vitalize their student housing facilities. This was clearly a nationwide trend, but the problem remained, to which Harper and Wilson had called attention, of finding a way to integrate more closely American provisions for the living arrangements of college students with the educational objectives of higher learning. Alexander Meiklejohn tried to do this as part of the work of his experimental college at the University of Wisconsin, but he succeeded only in antagonizing the fraternity group and alienating the bulk of the undergraduates.[45]

Somewhat more successful in attaining this goal were the new housing units donated to Harvard and Yale in the late 1920s by the millionaire philanthropist Edward S. Harkness, Yale, '97. These units, called "houses" at Harvard and "colleges" at Yale, provided for between 250 and 300 upperclassmen under the direction of resident masters and other faculty members. Each house or college had its own dining room, common room, library, and athletic facilities. In assigning students to these residences, an attempt was purposely made to cut across all lines of differentiation, whether of economic status, geographic origin, race, creed, preparatory-school background, or field of specialization.[46]

For Harvard under Lowell this represented the fruition of a plan which had been maturing for a long time. Ever since 1914 Lowell had been working on the social side to revive dormitory life and on the intellectual side to individualize instruction through honors work and tutorials.[47] The Harkness donation gave him a chance to unite the two lines of development along modified English lines by subdividing Harvard into a residential college system. In New Haven, too, President James Rowland Angell had been showing an increasing interest in carrying through a similar reorganization of Yale.[48] In 1930, after many vicissitudes, Harkness agreed to give the money that enabled his alma mater to construct eight units (or colleges) to serve as the basis for a Yale Quadrangle Plan.[49]

The English influence in all of this was direct and unmistakable. Harkness apparently became interested in the whole program of student housing by repeated visits to Oxford and Cambridge. When the donations to Harvard and Yale were finally proposed, Angell, Lowell, and a number of other college officials from Cambridge and New Haven made special trips to England to study every aspect of the British universities at first hand. For "two or three years these ancient universities must have been crawling with American inquisitors."[50]

Did the Harvard houses and Yale colleges, then, actually realize the dreams of Harper and Wilson? Did they make college residences into positive educational agencies in the way that Oxford and Cambridge had linked a complete tutorial system of instruction with a residential and quadrangle way of college life? Not entirely. At Yale, it was found that the English tutorial system transplanted bodily to America would be much too expensive to maintain and almost impossible to staff. The well-entrenched student institutions of fraternities, secret societies, and intercollegiate athletics would not fit in easily with the English system of completely autonomous residential colleges. At Harvard, the tutorials established by Lowell could be staffed in the face of continuously mounting enrollments only by using large numbers of graduate students, many of whom had little knowledge of how to make the system work.[51] At both institutions, complete adoption of the English system was impeded by the fact that Harkness had given his donation for buildings only, not for tutorial instruction. Without adequate endowment for tutors, the quadrangle residence halls in America were destined to remain primarily social, rather than educational, units.[52] Indeed, Harkness and others who were working closely with him in planning these residences seem to have been perfectly satisfied with this result. These gentlemen apparently believed that educational values would arise, as it were, spontaneously out of the common life that the new quadrangles made possible. Some, like the president of Lafayette College, seemed almost romantically and sentimentally attached to the aesthetic values of beautiful college buildings.[53] Others, with Stephen Leacock, would first provide a smoking room and a dormitory, and, if any money was left over, then employ a professor.[54]

Elsewhere in the United States attempts to introduce the partial version of the English residential system, such as had been established at Harvard and Yale, were limited by a number of factors. Most important of all, few institutions could afford the expensive plant which was necessary to subdivide their undergraduate body into residential quadrangles. Then, too, urban American institutions, where the bulk of students were commuters, could no more readily put the plan into effect than the urban British universities were able to do.[55] Indeed, the world might well have outgrown its need for a secluded collegiate way of life. The modern American university had certainly become huge, complex, and diverse in its interests. It was for this reason that George Santayana felt the "house plan" at Harvard came at least twenty years too late.[56]

One critic has pointed out that the mere expenditure of vast sums on American student housing after 1918 did not of itself ensure that the full educational benefit of this program would be realized. Thus many "collegiate Gothic" residence halls built in this era might impress visitors with their expensive exteriors, while inside were small, cramped, poorly lighted rooms—gloomy, vaulted, darkly paneled. Here, in truth, was an educational embodiment of Veblen's theory of "conspicuous consumption." Or was it "conspicuous waste"?[57] Other observers have wondered whether the tutorial pattern in residence halls could ever be developed to its fullest extent in an American culture which has not traditionally given the same approval to the intellectual life that Europe has done.[58] To William McDougall, former Fellow at Oxford and Cambridge, and, in 1930, professor of psychology at Duke, this anti-intellectualism was reflected in the fact that most student residences in America showed no appreciation of the necessary conditions of intellectual work. Students were herded together two, three, or four in one set of rooms. That these rooms were still primarily sleeping quarters was attested by the appellation "dormitory" commonly applied to them. On many campuses not as well endowed as Harvard or Yale, students were still forced to do all their studying in the common reading room of the university library, "too often under the constant distraction of the near presence of attractive young women," and all their eating in various public places. The herd spirit was always predominant in this setting, and a profoundly noisy, anti-intellectual herd spirit at that. The average American undergraduate still had "no place where he can sit down in comfort with a book and pipe and possess his soul in quietude, no place where he can entertain his chosen friends, where in a score of ways he can express and develop his taste and personality, his individuality."[59]

Employment and Health Services

Along with proper housing, the personnel movement came increasingly to concern itself with the welfare of college students as reflected in their employment opportunities and their health needs. In the late nineteenth century American colleges began to follow the system already established at Oxford and Cambridge of providing a special office to help students find positions. The English placement officials, however, were interested mainly in placing graduates in a few select professions, while their American counterparts from the first were concerned with finding remunerative employment for students while still in college and also in placing them in a much wider range of occupations after college.[60] Indeed so widespread did the self-help movement become on American campuses that in 1940 between one-third and one-half of all students in the nation were pursuing some form of part-time employment. These working students averaged twenty hours of outside employment a week, and between 10 and 20 per cent of them managed in this way to earn all of their college expenses.[61]

There was considerable difference of opinion among educators as to the effect of such outside employment upon studies. Some claimed the results were seriously detrimental, producing strain and frustration. Others rejoined that self-help was a vital part of higher education, teaching undergraduates at first hand about modern diversified economic and social life and giving them an insight into human relations.[62] Reflecting this latter view, Antioch College put into effect a "work and study" plan which resembled in part the manual labor philosophy of a century before. This program was intended not only to aid a student to earn his way through college but also to be an integral part of the institution's educational program.[63] Although the majority of American educators came to feel that a moderate amount of part-time employment might not be harmful to students, and might even have some educational value, I. L. Kandel raised a more basic question: Can there be real equality of opportunity between those college students who receive scholarships and those who have to work their way through?[64]

In any case, the movement for the providing of placement services spread very rapidly in American higher education. By 1925, organized placement bureaus supervised by specialists had been set up in 44 per cent of all large universities, 12 per cent of the medium-sized institutions, and 11 per cent of the small ones.[65] There was a close connection between this placement movement and the more general field of personnel work. From an early concern with bridging the gap between college and career, placement officers often turned to a discussion of personnel problems in general. Professional organizations such as the Association of Eastern College Personnel Officers arose out of meetings of college placement workers in the early 1920s.[66]

Student health, like placement, had long been a concern of American colleges. As far back as 1825 Harvard had introduced methods of physical education involving mass calisthenics modeled on those developed in Germany and Scandinavia. Within the next few years, Yale, Williams, Dartmouth, and Amherst had instituted gymnastic programs of their own. The idea swept the country that physical exercise was something of a panacea for all problems involving the health of college students.[67]

The first college to take an active interest in broader aspects of student health was Amherst. Under Presidents Stearns and Hitchcock, it organized a distinct department of hygiene and sought to prevent any physical illnesses which would be likely to interfere with a student's academic work. By 1870, a number of other eastern colleges were developing programs of this nature. Infirmaries were established, and eventually physical examinations were given to all students at least once a year. This program made progress despite the opposition of some members of the medical profession who denounced colleagues entering the student health field as undertaking a "pernicious form of contract practice."[68]

By the turn of the century, many college health programs began to reflect the influence of the advance of bacteriology and the resultant public health movement. Committees were appointed to supervise sanitation and the control of communicable diseases. Increasingly, a shift in emphasis became apparent, however. From a concern with environmental influences such as public health, the college health departments came to pay more and more attention to the individual student's special problems.

In 1907, the University of California set up a broadly inclusive health service, under full-time college physicians, including preventive, curative, and health education programs. A number of other colleges and universities followed suit. By 1920, these institutions had banded together to form the American Student Health Association.[69] As time went on, it became customary to charge students a yearly fee for these services. In this latest stage, many and diverse problems, such as malnutrition and faulty health habits, came under study and were found to have a definite correlation with absence from class and poor academic performance.[70] The new phase was described by one expert in the field as not just diagnosis and treatment, nor even preventive medicine, but positive "building health."[71] Many held high hopes for important advances in knowledge regarding health conservation as a result of research carried on in connection with these various student health programs.[72] The place of systematic research in such programs remained highly controversial, however. In any event, small colleges naturally found it difficult to finance comprehensive, thoroughly developed student health programs. A detailed survey made in 1953 revealed that only 20 per cent of all institutions of higher education in the United States had such complete health services.[73]

The most significant trend in college health work after 1918 was a growing concern with the crucial field of mental health.[74] This, more than anything else, demonstrated how the health services were coming increasingly to reflect the "student personnel point of view." It served as a natural bridge between health counselors and those specialists who were working in other forms of student counseling. These people frequently shared the same approach and followed the same philosophy. Often their work tended to overlap.

The position of the mental hygiene movement was that health was far more than the mere absence of illness. It was a condition of well-being which embraced mental and emotional, as well as physical, aspects. This condition should be a leading concern of educators because it controlled to a large extent personal and social behavior. Students should not be allowed to drift through college without gaining any insight into their vital personal problems. Idiosyncrasies overlooked by an instructor could develop later in psychotic trends. Intellectual achievement could bestow power, but this could be turned to unsocial or abnormal ends unless emotional maturity accompanied it.[75]

Increasingly, in the 1930s, psychoanalysis entered the mental hygiene picture. Refugee psychologists fleeing from fascist countries associated themselves in the United States with mental hygiene or "child development" groups. As a result, orthodox Freudian influence was strengthened in the student counseling movement.[76] In some places, faculty and administrative officials distrusted the new field as too closely identified with Freudian psychoanalysis and undue emphasis on sex aberrations. At other colleges, mental hygiene was regarded as much too expensive a luxury. In many communities, psychiatry itself remained a new and unfamiliar medical specialty. Then, too, initial student distrust of anything that smacked of mental disease had to be overcome.[77]

Despite these obstacles, a number of colleges began after the First World War to introduce systematic work in mental hygiene for their students. By 1930, there were fourteen such institutions, and the number was growing with every year that passed.[78] After 1926, a particularly interesting program got under way at Yale that was financed on an experimental basis by the Commonwealth Fund. Four resident psychiatrists were involved in this program, which serviced both the college and the city of New Haven. The service was identified with both the School of Medicine and the university's department of health. No effort was made to sugar-coat the new service for the students or to disguise the nature of its work.[79]

The concepts of college mental health work tended to broaden as time went on. At first, psychiatrists were only brought in when an acute emergency arose involving the mental illness of a student or faculty member. Gradually it came to be recognized that mental health really depended on the way people got along with each other on the college campus. Increasingly, it was seen that it was closely tied up with morale at the college, with the presence or absence of conflicts in the environment or within the personality. This, in turn, involved a host of factors —the system of discipline, the athletic establishment, the role of the students in government of their affairs, the attitudes of faculty members toward each other and toward their students, even the architecture of the dormitories and other college buildings.[80]

Counseling

The increased concern with student mental health after 1918 helped increase the demand for student counseling of every kind—physical, emotional, academic, and spiritual. This counseling movement came to express itself in two main ways —general and individual. For general guidance, the device most often resorted to was some form of orientation course or program. In a number of cases, this assumed the definite form of a "Freshman Week," an introductory period of from one to seven days preceding the regular work of the term and devoted to the task of adjusting the entering student to his new environment.[81] In contrast to this, the general orientation course, while attacking much the same problems, extended the time over a longer period varying from two weeks to a full college year. While only six American colleges offered such courses in 1915–16, ten years later eighty-two did. Courses of this type usually tried to teach freshmen how to use the library, how to study, what the purposes and aims of the college were, and how to participate in campus activities.[82]

In the new age of impersonality and mass enrollments, general orientation devices, however valuable, did not completely solve the problem of guiding college students. It was soon recognized that such measures, bolstered by psychological tests of aptitude and achievement for purposes of diagnosis, had to be supplemented by individual counseling in a host of fields, not just in freshman year but throughout a student's college career.[83] This reflected the new emphasis on the "twilight zone" between the classroom and the extracurriculum. It was obvious that all through the student's college career he was confronted with the necessity of making increasingly complex and significant choices. Older and more experienced minds could help him to do this.[84] Research studies revealed that expert counseling of this kind could be an important part of the learning process. It could produce significant improvement in academic performance and reduce the number of eliminations from college.[85]

Programs of individual counseling assumed three or four main forms after 1918. The work developed at the University of Chicago in this period may well serve as an example of the national trend. There we find well-defined and specialized programs in the fields of educational counseling, vocational counseling, personal counseling, and religious counseling. They were all posited on the assumption that higher education should concern itself with the successful development of the whole personality of the student, including nonintellectual as well as intellectual factors.[86]

Educational counselors not only helped to plan individual study programs, but dealt with such problems as poor scholarship and preparation for comprehensive examinations. Vocational counselors provided job information and aided in planning academic programs to realize vocational ends. They sought to induce the student to make self-analysis the basis for vocational choice, and to ensure that the ultimate responsibility for choice would be the student's. Counselors dealing with student personal problems had to grapple with a wide range of questions. They came into contact with problems of physical health; they had to deal with emotional problems involving mental hygiene; they were consulted about financial issues; and, finally, they often found themselves dealing with questions of a moral or religious nature. To help solve these problems they frequently had to call in the expert aid of health officials, psychiatrists, placement agencies, scholarship committees, and religious counselors.[87]

In general, the place of religion on the American campus of this period may be said to be a varied one. In public institutions, the separation of Church and State which was part of the American constitutional system prevented the teaching of special doctrinal beliefs and practices. Nevertheless, in the period after World War I a new emphasis on religious values developed in tax-supported institutions; and many of them now frequently offered elective courses in religion, organized departments of religion, and cooperated with private religious foundations on or near the campus.[88]

In American private colleges, the situation was even more diversified. There it ranged from continuing extreme denominationalism, founded on rigid doctrinal instruction, to an attempt at objective analysis on a broad, nonsectarian basis.[89] In general, it appeared that American higher education was developing a renewed interest in religion in the years following the First World War.[90] Increasingly it was being recognized that higher learning had a responsibility for the moral instruction of young people as well as for their intellectual development. For knowledge to be meaningful, students must be morally perceptive, must learn the art "of living with self, with fellow men, and with nature."[91] To a large extent, this new emphasis on religion was related to the growing interest in guidance and counseling. The assertion that on psychological grounds higher education must concern itself with the "whole" person led inevitably to the argument that, on this ground alone, the religious life of the student should not be slighted.[92]

Athletics, Intercollegiate and Intramural

Even in the field of college athletics there were growing indications, after 1918, of an effort to integrate this highly publicized side of student life with the actual teaching services of higher education. One of the most obvious illustrations of the new trend was the development of intramural athletics. Another sign of the times was the tendency to make athletic coaches members of the faculty and to require them to do teaching as well as coaching. Finally, there was an increasing predisposition in some institutions to transfer the administration of intercollegiate athletics from the control of a semi-independent committee, dominated by alumni, to a new central executive authority under more direct regulation of the university itself.

This did not necessarily mean that "big-time" college football had ceased to have the aspects of a commercial enterprise. If anything, it developed a larger public following than ever before. The 1920s constituted in many ways a "Golden

Age of Sport." Both spectator and participatory sports had become enormously popular, coincident with the impact upon American culture of the automobile, the movies, and radio. And of all the spectator sports, intercollegiate football attracted the greatest public attention. In 1927, thirty million spectators paid $50,000,000 for tickets to college football games. The total capacity of the concrete stadiums which many colleges had mortgaged themselves to build was estimated by 1930 at two million.[93] The Carnegie Foundation Report of 1929, with its disclosures of obvious professionalism and overemphasis, did little to change the situation. The depression of the 1930s did not permanently dampen mass enthusiasm, while the Second World War and the rise of television had the effect of popularizing football still further. Attempts of the National Collegiate Athletic Association to police intercollegiate competition in the 1950s did not eradicate professionalism. College football had too firm a hold on a sports-hungry public. At the same time, many institutions which had gone deeply into debt to construct expensive stadiums saw the recruitment of a winning, professionally coached football team as the only way to attract the gate receipts that were needed to pay off that debt.[94] Within a quarter century after the Second World War there were many calling for a second Carnegie investigation of the economic and ethical crisis gripping intercollegiate sports.[95]

Demands continued to be voiced in many quarters for reform of the situation and "de-emphasis." And at the top of almost every list of proposed reforms was a recommendation that a program of "athletics for all" be substituted for big-time football. This amounted to the introduction of a comprehensive system of intramural sports in which teams would compete, but representing subdivisions of the college, not the college as a whole.[96]

In a sense all student athletic activities in ante-bellum days had been intramural in nature. With the development of varsity teams after 1865 the athletic needs of the ordinary student tended to be increasingly neglected. Then, in the late nineteenth and early twentieth centuries, a new emphasis began to be placed on the intramural approach. The sports clubs of the English universities and the "house system" of competition in the English public schools attracted increasing attention among American collegians. Then, too, college teachers of physical education saw that interest in their work might be increased if a competitive element was introduced. In any event, interclub, interclass, and interfraternity athletic competition began to develop on many campuses. The whole movement was hit-or-miss at first, but eventually college athletic associations stepped in and established uniformity. By 1913, the University of Michigan had established a department of intramural athletics and Ohio State University did the same thing soon thereafter.[97]

The great expansion of the intramural movement came after the First World War. More and more separate sports were included in organized intramural programs. Emphasis was placed to a greater degree on sports that had a "carry-over" value for later life, such as golf, tennis, badminton, and swimming.[98] Some critics nevertheless charged that intramurals were not attracting widespread and enthusiastic student interest, mainly because participants in them did not achieve the same amount of prestige on campus as the varsity athlete.[99] One wonders, however, if intramural development in America was limited by lack of student interest or by lack of adequate financing. At Harvard and Yale an extensive program of intramural competition and "sports for all" was developed after the First World War, closely coordinated with the residential "house" and "college" plans, but this was only possible because an extensive investment of money was made.[100] It is notable that these universities looked upon such expenditures as a justifiable cost of their over-all educational program, comparable to the cost of maintaining a library or a laboratory. Thus, in 1952, President Conant characterized Harvard's $433,000 annual excess of athletic expenditure over athletic income as not so much a "deficit" as a "cost of operation."[101] But how many of the country's colleges and universities were in a position to finance an intramural program on such a grand scale?

Some Evaluations of the Personnel Movement

It would not be historically accurate to conclude our discussion without pointing out that many educators, both American and foreign, have remained profoundly suspicious of the personnel movement. To some, it was as useless as a "fifth wheel." The funds devoted to counseling and related services might better, in their opinion, be used for teaching or research.[102] Others echoed Abraham Flexner in the view that personnel services were overprotecting students, "coddling" them, and sapping them of all self-reliance and sense of individual responsibility.[103] They held, with Robert Hutchins, that a student should not come to a university unless he is intelligent and interested. Since the university was not a custodial establishment, it should not be expected to give the student either character or interest.[104]

Critics of the personnel movement have been quick to point out that it has not been free of a "cultism" of its own. They have noted with care the extravagant claims made by some people in personnel work.[105] They have closely observed the subdivision of the field into smaller and smaller specialties, the same trend which earlier had robbed the college curriculum of some of its basic unities.[106] They have been somewhat amused by the antagonisms which have come almost inevitably to develop between various branches of the personnel movement, such as between the deans of students as a group and the deans of women as a group.[107] Their greatest wrath, however, has been reserved for those institutions which sponsored the organization of an independent personnel division, with important powers of student assignment, but not part of the regular instructional faculty and responsible only to the president's office.[108]

Foreign visitors to American universities and colleges tended, on the whole, to be somewhat skeptical of the student personnel movement. It appears that personnel services and counseling were not carried to as high a pitch of development abroad as in the United States. The Fulbright scholars from many countries who conferred at Haverford College in 1953 raised many important questions about American personnel programs. They pointed out that their universities, in the main, were more highly selective in their admissions policies than many American institutions; that their students bore much greater responsibility for their individual and collective lives than did American students; that part-time employment of students was generally discouraged, lest it interfere with academic work; that the students, rather than the universities, were generally expected to make whatever arrangements might be necessary for housing, food services, and social relationships; and that in many areas, such as the Middle East and the Orient, attempts at personal counseling would be regarded as interference with a person's private life and infringement on parental authority. In general, these foreign observers received the impression "that we are overly solicitous of our students, that we tend to develop in them a sense of continuing dependence."[109]

Defenders of the personnel movement replied to these criticisms by stressing that its aim was to offer individualization and guidance, not spoiling or tyranny. It was no more objectionable for a counselor to give a student data about himself so that he could competently manage his own affairs than it was for a physician to give physical examinations to patients. Even mature and intelligent adults relied on professional counselors when confronted with legal, medical, psychological, or religious difficulties. It was the conviction of personnel workers that students in college should have the same services.[110]

Moreover, it was argued that the personnel movement grew out of the very nature of American academic culture. The United States was committed to a policy of extending the advantages of higher education as widely as possible, of giving each person a chance to make the most of his particular abilities. Both national tradition and current educational philosophy considered this to be the necessary foundation of a democratic society. As a result, there could be found in most American institutions of higher education students of a wider range of ability, and much younger in years, than the majority of foreign university students. To serve their needs, student personnel services of a highly developed type were obviously essential. But some educators justified their existence on other grounds than mere expediency. American higher education, they argued, did not exist for the rich, well born, or specially gifted, but for the masses. It was not limited to fostering pure intellectualism or scholarship; it was also concerned with helping each citizen to fulfill his political, economic, and social aspirations. The personnel movement, therefore, embodied, according to this point of view, one important aspect of the American search, through education, for freedom, equality, and greater material well-being.[111]

Ordway Tead has pointed out the very important influence that the personnel movement has had on the growth of character of the American college student. United with a new sense of moral purpose in all the works of the college, it could aid in re-establishing a truly holistic college life in America comparable to that which existed in the church-controlled colleges of ante-bellum times.[112] By the mid-1960s, however, there were indications that the effort to weld a new integrated context in which the "whole" student could find meaning for his life had not entirely succeeded. Not only were such "nonintegrated" types as the political activists, the Bohemian "disaffiliates," and the willful "underachievers" popping up on leading campuses, but even the professionally oriented superior students seemed to find a wall existing between their academic preparation for success in a complex, technological civilization and the separate interests and goals of their private, purely personal life.[113]

There was no question but that the American college student had become by this time the most thoroughly guided and counseled student in the world. Increasingly, in the 1960s, many American undergraduates gave strong indications that they believed they were far *too closely counseled* and supervised. They seemed to be impatient of all official or adult restraint on their lives, suspicious of anything that smacked of the traditional *in loco parentis* regime. Student attitudes on this question were influenced by a number of factors. Involvement in the civil rights and anti-Vietnam war movements fostered antagonism to obeying laws for their own sake. More tolerant judicial rulings on alleged pornography in movies and books may have helped generate a questioning attitude toward all regulations designed to implement moral codes. Increasingly, too, some parents and university officials seemed to be ready to adopt a more tolerant and permissive response to deviations from accustomed norms.

The most dramatic example of readjustment in policy on the part of university authorities involved the modification of campus parietal rules in the direction of a greater freedom. Some commentators declared that such a trend was inevitable in an age which was variously labeled the era of "the permissive society" or "the sexual revolution." George S. May, dean of Yale College, was quoted in the *New York Times* as saying: "We are not interested in the private lives of students as long as they remain private." Ruth Darling, assistant dean for residence halls at Cornell, declared: "We don't ask what they do and don't want to know. We don't ask because the girls are presumed to be responsible." She added, however, that "we know that all are not responsible." Dean Harris A. Schwartz, in charge of residence halls at Columbia University, observed: "Students today are too bright to be treated as children. They should be allowed greater permissiveness but without letting them destroy themselves or hurt themselves for the future."

The main change in parietal rules involved relaxation of the regulations pertaining to the visiting hours for women in men's dormitories, especially after a number of all-male colleges transformed themselves into coeducational institutions and even established coed dormitories. Where college administrations, such as that of Hobart College in Geneva, New York, refused a student demand that undergraduates be permitted to keep liquor or entertain girls in their bedrooms, half the student body picketed the school's administration building in angry protest. One Cornell student was quoted as commenting: "If the university moves to tighten parietal rules, even the prudish Quakers among us will take a libertarian line."

A closely related factor at many colleges was the availability of off-campus housing. At schools such as New York University, Fordham, and Barnard many students resided off-campus where university officials were unable to enforce visiting hours. At Yale and Princeton, however, virtually all undergraduates lived in dormitories. As a result, liberalized visiting privileges were considered particularly important on those campuses, and the local student newspapers came out in favor of coeducation. At Cornell nearly 45 per cent of the institution's 7,140 male undergraduates lived off-campus in a nearby residential section of Ithaca known as "college town."[114]

Student Activism

The foregoing change in parietal rules resulting from the "sexual revolution" of the times was but a small part of the student revolution of the 1960s, which was, without doubt, the most portentous upheaval in the whole history of American student life. Students of the decade after World War II were known as the "silent generation." Perhaps because of the anti-Communist agitation of the postwar era, students—and not only students but faculty, too—were cowed by the threats of Senator McCarthy. At any rate, as noted by an Amherst faculty committee in 1955, undergraduates were unwilling to assume real responsibility, preferring, as they said, to "stay loose."[115] In the opening years of the next decade, however, activism rather than passivity came to characterize the student mind. Concomitantly the "New Left" was born.

Perhaps one can date this birth from February, 1960, when a sit-in movement was initiated and carried on by black students in the South. This touched off sympathy picketing by northern students at local branches of national variety-store chains, especially Woolworth's, whose southern branches refused to serve blacks at their lunch counters. Hundreds of these same northern students even went into the Deep South at considerable personal risk to work for the Student Non-Violent Coordinating Committee (SNCC) and other civil rights groups. The righteous imperative of the moral and political issues posed by the civil rights movement seemed to them clear and undeniable. Blacks were merely demanding rights that whites had long taken for granted.[116]

The pace of student activism began to accelerate with the rise of the Berkeley "free speech movement" (FSM) in the fall of 1964. The chief significance of this event was that it brought home to the university campus itself the principles and tactics of the civil rights movement.[117] Next year's escalation of the tempo of the war in Vietnam further aggravated student activism. Indeed, from the middle of 1965 onward this war was the overriding political issue that powered student discontent for the rest of the decade. At first students protested along conventional lines with marches and mass meetings. The teach-in at the University of Michigan, which spread to many other campuses, was the only major innovation in this nonviolent phase of protest. After the spring of 1967, however, the students began to take more coercive measures.[118] There was serious resistance to the military draft and obstructive tactics were used against symbols of the military such as the ROTC and recruiters for war suppliers like the Dow Chemical Company. Another development was the increasing sabotage of university facilities. This violence escalated from "trashing" at Columbia and arson at Stanford to mob violence at Berkeley, armed confrontation at Cornell, and homicide at Wisconsin. It reached its apex in the Kent State University slaying of four students by the Ohio National Guard in 1970.[119]

The principal student organization that sparked the student resistance of the New Left was the one known as Students for a Democratic Society (SDS). This body grew out of a much older one, the Student League for Industrial Democracy (SLID), which was an offshoot from the League for Industrial Democracy. That in turn originated in the Intercollegiate Socialist Party before World War I with such notable early members as Walter Lippmann, Clarence Darrow, Upton Sinclair, and Morris Hillquit. SDS had hundreds of campus chapters and at its peak some 75,000 members. But in spite of its Port Huron declaration of principles its diverse membership prevented any tight cohesion. Indeed, at its 1969 spring meeting it split asunder, one faction identifying with the Progressive Labor Party, a left-wing group that had split from the Communist Party in 1961, and the other, more violent and known as the Weathermen, going underground.[120]

SDS, however, was by no means the only student organization of this or earlier periods.[121] A minority of students who were oriented in the direction of the "Social Gospel" but who were not Marxists could be found in the ranks of the Student Christian Movement. The majority of collegians who were active at all in social causes and political agitation (and these were never representative of the bulk of America's campus population) tended to affiliate themselves with such middle-of-the-road organizations as the National Student Federation, an association which was founded at Princeton in 1925. Campus militants maintained that the situation contrasted sharply with that in some nations of Europe, Asia, and Latin America, where university students traditionally played a prominent role in political agitation.[122]

Certainly before the 1960s only a very small fraction of the American student body had been interested in social issues of the day. In the first half of the century most students were apolitical, even apathetic. To the extent they were interested it was largely in a moral rather than political, an educational rather than an activistic, way. If they did organize, they tended to work closely with adult organizations which themselves were frequently in disarray. What thrust they had was not in the direction of the university itself, and there was no evidence, as later on, of a generation gap.[123]

In the second half of the decade the escalation of violence became an increasing concern of public and university officials. A voluntary group of some twenty congressmen visited over fifty university campuses to analyze the causes of disruption and propose remedies.[124] In addition a National Commission on the Causes and Prevention of Violence gave a whole chapter of its report to the politics of student protest.[125] But easily the most important was the President's Commission on Campus Unrest in 1970. This well-chosen commission, representing many facets of the problem and chaired by former Governor William Scranton of Pennsylvania, made very fair findings of fact and conciliatory recommendations aiming to preserve the student right to dissent but to stop short of disruption.[126] President Nixon received the report but unfortunately declined to be guided by it although the report called on him to exercise moral leadership in healing the generational rift in the body politic. Instead, at a later time he bitterly referred to the protesting students as "bums," and Vice-President Spiro Agnew called them "an effete corps of impudent snobs." These remarks only gave greater provocation to efforts of defiance.

Needless to say, university authorities were no less concerned with mounting student violence, the very antithesis of the rational mode of the university. Many saw it as the destruction of academic freedom, a kind of academic genocide.[127] At first the administration met disruption with conventional disciplinary measures —probation, suspension, and expulsion, in that ascending order. Since the university stood *in loco parentis* no one doubted the warrant for such measures.[128] Yet, as early as 1957 and well before disruption on the campus became common, the question arose in some minds whether students were being pushed around without due regard to their civil liberties.[129] In the next decade widespread confrontations of academic authorities provided repeated opportunities for the courts to test and delimit this area.[130]

The First and Fourteenth Amendments to the Constitution proved to be critical here. Students, it was held, were entitled to the same protection as other citizens. The student editors of campus papers were entitled to First Amendment freedoms of speech,[131] and college authorities were enjoined from adopting rules that operated as a prior restraint on the right of students to peaceably assemble to protest their grievances.[132] Fully as important were cases involving the due-process clause of the Fifth and Fourteenth Amendments. On the procedural side of due process it was decided that students were entitled to notice and hearing before the imposition of severe disciplinary penalties,[133] and on the substantive side they were protected from arbitrary and unreasonable regulations of the university.[134] An eminent university president, James Perkins of Cornell, feared that this extension of due process to higher education might well deal a fatal blow to its autonomy, but on the whole the academic community counted the extension of civil rights to the campus as one of the few unalloyed gains of student activism.[135]

It needs noting that activist students in risking disciplinary measures from confronting administrative authorities came to protest not only the Vietnam War and racial injustice but also the shortcomings of higher education as well. More radical student activists were so alienated from the university that they wished to pull it down. Less radical ones would have been content just to close it down. Fortunately both these were a very small minority of the minority of all student activists, estimated at 3 to 10 per cent of the total student body.[136] But nearly all activists sought a restructuring of the university in which "student power" and "participatory democracy" would play a large role. They wanted to get their hands on the levers of control. And by that they did not mean a rejuvenated conventional or traditional student government which they regarded now as "mickey mouse."[137] They "wanted in" on such matters as choice of curriculum content, promotion and dismissal of faculty, and determination of parietal rules.[138]

Many, both students and faculty, did not realize the extent to which the traditional power structure of the university was already crumbling.[139] Fundamentally, the basis for the doctrine of *in loco parentis* had been disintegrating for some time. Increasingly parents were abandoning status and command in the control of their children for reason and suggestion. In similar vein students formerly "sent" to college now went because they realized it was a necessary condition of living in the current world. Equally significant in the breakdown of collegiate paternalism was the changed character of the student body itself.[140] This body was the product not only of better elementary and secondary education, but also of the communications revolution. Because of its exposure to television and the film industry it was more maturely sensitive to life in all its dimensions than any previous generation.

The scope of student protest through the New Left had a broader target than just social injustice and faulty higher education. Beyond such immediate objectives the students were disenchanted with the whole adult "establishment." They felt alienated from the values of their parents and purported to trust no one over thirty, thus forming the much discussed "generation gap."[141] Outwardly they registered their alienation by hippie hairstyles, vagabond dress, uncouth manners, and often obscene speech. The culture and higher education of the establishment, they thought, had lost legitimacy. A new basis had to be found in the so-called counterculture.[142]

The counterculture was hardly of one piece. Rather was it a composite of various themes. A small group of student activists in the counterculture seemed to be nihilists. They wanted to destroy the university, and some actually tried through arson and "trashing." But asked, as the nihilist in Turgenev's novel *Fathers and Sons,* what they would install in its place, they postponed saying till the ground had first been cleared.[143] A larger group of student activists seemed to be anarchists. They favored an unorganized spontaneity (a "happening") wherein there would be no structured curriculum, certainly no requirements, and no grades or degrees leading to certification. A decontrolled voluntarism would take their place.[144]

Akin to anarchism and easily the most prominent theme of the activist counterculture was existentialism. Of the various modes of this philosophy the counterculture put emphasis on the student's search for sentience. Experience was defined as awareness. The purpose of existence was not to alter the world to create new experiences, but rather to change the self to increase its awareness, its sensitivity in search for heightened feeling, direct passion, and pure impulse.[145] To the extent that the drug culture lent itself to this end it had a worrisome place in the student counterculture. Not unexpectedly, immediacy of enjoyment rather than postponement and self-denial, as in the culture of the establishment, laid its own demands on student existentialists. Moreover, in a tradition extending back to Rousseau, students conceived of individuality in restorationist terms, that is, that social reform demands the restoration of the individual as the bearer of an inviolable dignity and will.[146] The obverse of this romantic existentialism was its often defiant rejection of rationality and objectivity. More than anything else it was this rejection of conception and logic that was most difficult for the academic mind to comprehend and accept.[147]

As the twentieth century approached its three-quarter stage a marked change in mood came over the campus.[148] By that time students had lowered their voices and hairstyles had improved in neatness. Civility returned to manners and the alienation causing the generation gap greatly abated. There was indeed a resurgence of middle-class values. On the campus students were again interested in grades, getting into graduate school, and striving for good jobs in the establishment. Yale and Princeton reported crowded libraries. Yet, though quiet had returned to the campus, Kingman Brewster of Yale remarked that it was an "eerie" quiet and warned against mistaking tranquility for a new apathy.

What caused this about-face? Most notable, of course, was the end of the Vietnam War and the end of the military draft to feed it. The campus was thus relieved of a troublesome body of involuntary students whose main interest in college had been avoidance of the draft.[149] With the decline of these irritants there seemed to follow an emotional fatigue from the high excitement of protest. Economic recession had its part to play too. The affluence that had lubricated protest evaporated. The job market revealed an oversupply of Ph.D.s and a dearth of other jobs. With the costs of higher education mounting and subsidies from the federal government phasing out, students assumed a new seriousness toward their studies. All this seemed to have dissipated some of the gleam from higher education as a must for young people.[150]

In retrospect the decade 1960–70 seemed to many like a bad "trip." A number of former activists felt that little or nothing had been accomplished. A close student of the counterculture concluded that its agony consisted in its becoming infected with the very violence that it had opposed.[151] Moreover it never reconciled its program of radical political change with its contradictory tendency to seek self-gratification. Writing more positively, a noted opinion researcher concluded that what had seemed a generation gap was in fact the leading edge of a new morality in quest of self-fulfilling life-styles.[152] On the educational side student activism did set up the "free university" as a counter-image by which to evaluate conventional higher education. How lasting a deposit these countermeasures would leave, either directly or indirectly in current practice, awaited the future for an answer. Nevertheless, there can be little doubt, as witness the appointment of the Carnegie Commission on Higher Education, that student activism of the New Left and the counterculture did provoke more earnest thinking by academicians and the lay public about the manifold problems of higher education than at any previous time in the twentieth century.

17

Enlarging Scope of the Administration of Higher Education

It is a credit to the builders of American higher education that the foundations which they laid down in colonial times for the organization and administration of higher education were still standing in the twentieth century. Although in the meantime the colonial college had become a modern university, although student bodies had grown from hundreds to thousands, and although budgets had skyrocketed from thousands to millions of dollars, the frame of academic government remained basically unchanged as late as the 1950s. The source of power and even its distribution remained much the same. However, beginning in the 1960s, startling increases in the size of the educational establishment and shifting pressure groups in the public brought important modifications and a number of proposals for even more fundamental changes.

Incorporation and Standardization

In spite of the squirming of Harvard and Yale to come into existence without the sponsorship of a royal charter,[1] the need for some kind of charter was never doubted. After the Revolution most new colleges derived their charters from state governments. At first there was a tendency to depend for incorporation on a special act of the legislature. At least two difficulties arose from this method. Shifting majorities in the legislature were one, as witness the University of Michigan. There in 1817 the territorial legislature set up a university under the grandiloquent title of "Catholepistemiad." In spite of several legislative reorganizations, the institution did not prosper. Searching for a reason, the people of the state concluded that the frequent reorganizations were preventing the university from taking root and growing normally. Consequently, in their new constitution of 1850 they caused the governing board of the state university to be popularly elected as a coordinate branch of the state government instead of subordinate to the legislature as hitherto.[2] Not fully awake to the constitutional significance of this move, the legislature continued to lend an interfering hand in directing university policy. But the Regents successfully rebuffed this encroachment with

354

the aid of several important decisions of the state supreme court which emphatically affirmed the constitutional autonomy of the Regents.[3] The Regents were, so the Michigan Supreme Court said, the highest juristic person known to the law, a constitutional corporation, virtually a fourth branch of government. Thereafter the university enjoyed a stability that helped make Michigan a pre-eminent state university. Minnesota and several other states copied Michigan's organization,[4] but others, such as Kansas, Nebraska, and Missouri, preferred the older precedent of legislative control.[5]

A second difficulty grew out of the commendable interest of a young democracy in multiplying educational opportunities. Ever eager to encourage learning, legislatures issued charters with great generosity. As a result the country was soon oversupplied with struggling colleges of such meager income and limited curriculums that standards fell far short of the founders' ambitions and ideals. As a result of financial undernourishment, to say nothing of educational mismanagement, the mortality rate among these colleges was exceedingly high.[6] While it may have served the thinly settled frontier of the early nineteenth century to sprinkle it with even weak colleges, toward the end of the century it became evident that it was no longer in the public interest to risk precious capital on institutions whose life expectancy was short or which, if they survived, offered a distressingly low grade of work.

Obviously, the time was at hand when state legislatures would need some standards by which to guide their generous intentions. For one thing, from 1850 onward states increasingly relieved themselves from *ad hoc* pressures by passing general statutes under which new corporations could be formed. Educational provisions in these general acts continued to multiply and expand, but even by the third decade of the twentieth century they were far from exacting, let alone uniform, in the various states. Barely a quarter of the states laid down any regulations for the educational programs and the degrees to be granted by higher institutions of learning. Indeed, about half of them exercised no supervision over their colleges once they were incorporated, neither by visitation nor by requiring annual reports. Moreover, in spite of the fact that the Dartmouth College Case had put American democracy on guard to protect the aims of higher education preferred by a changing public opinion, more than half of the states continued granting perpetual charters. Some states did not even put the granting of a charter at the discretion of an educational official but left it to the secretary of state or some other ex officio agent.[7]

New York State was something of an exception to the general pattern. There at the end of the eighteenth century the State Regents set some early precedents. Till a general statute on corporations was passed in mid-nineteenth century it shared with the legislature authority to incorporate new colleges. Not only that but as early as 1811 it had laid down such standards as requiring that new foundations have financial backing to the extent of at least $50,000. From an early date, too, the Regents held the right of visitation and for a while exercised it personally. Later they substituted the requirement of an annual report but this proved ineffective when the Regents demanded a report on Eliphalet Nott's financial management of Union College and the latter's trustees successfully refused because it was thought that they were protected by the Dartmouth College Case.[8]

By the end of the century the Regents, through their energetic secretary, Melvil Dewey, author of the decimal system for library cataloguing, were actively exercising visitorial powers again. Through his staff Dewey received annual reports on each institution of higher education in the state and from them compiled a list of institutions in good standing. Not only that but in 1892 he recommended legislation setting minimum standards which by the depression in the 1930s had grown to require new institutions to have at least an 8,000-volume library and eight full-time professors holding the Ph.D. degree or its equivalent, teaching no more than sixteen hours per week. Furthermore, its bachelor's degree must be predicated on an academic term of thirty-four months of not less than fifteen periods a week. To undergird even less of a program, the state had long demanded that an institution start with financial resources of no less than $500,000.[9] While New York was striving upward, happily the North Central Association was keeping pace, having required a productive endowment of $200,000 in 1922, $300,000 a year later, $400,000 in 1924–25 and $500,000 in 1926–27.[10] Paltry as half a million dollars was to back a minimum program, it was generous compared with the $25,000 required by Ohio and munificent compared with the $500 by Nevada.[11] Yet contemporary opinion believed that no more than 120 of some 300 existing institutions could have met New York's standards in the academic year 1889–90.[12] Perhaps this was why as late as 1934 only twenty of the forty-eight states had enacted this kind of legislation.[13]

The continuing laissez-faire attitude of most states toward the regulation of higher education led to increasing embarrassment as the twentieth century got under way. For one thing, it led not only to the founding and encouragement of institutions of low grade but, worse yet, to fraudulent ones as well. In 1972 the director of the accreditation staff of the United States Office of Education estimated that 110 "diploma mills" were operating in the country. Within the preceding ten years the number of such unaccredited institutions had tripled and the greatest number were to be found in Florida, Illinois, and California.[14] To prevent this imposition on the public, New York State was out in front again by prohibiting the use of the term "college" or "university" without permission of its State Board of Regents. Furthermore, it posted legal penalties for selling or otherwise issuing fraudulent degrees.[15] Even though other states might still shout *caveat emptor* to citizens seeking higher education, here was one acting on the principle of *caveat vendor* and itself closely scrutinizing applicants for the prerogative of incorporating higher institutions of learning.

For another thing, as transportation facilities improved across the nation, there was a growing number of students traveling from one part of the country to another who wanted to have credits earned at one institution transferred to another. In the absence of federal control of higher education, let alone local state control, it was well-nigh impossible to determine equivalence of work done. The situation was confused both at the point of transition from secondary school to college[16] and increasingly so at the point of transition from college to graduate school. At this latter point the situation was rendered critical when in 1905 the faculty of philosophy at the University of Berlin informed the Association of American Universities that it would recognize the bachelor's degree of American universities as the equivalent of the German Gymnasium's *Maturitätszeugniss,* but only if taken at a member institution of the association. The association had never conceived of itself as performing such a standardizing function for American higher education. If anything, its members tended to resent and look askance at official scrutiny of their affairs by outside agencies.[17] Nevertheless, addressing itself to this unwanted responsibility, a committee of the association, whose chairman was Charles W. Eliot, urged that "It is the duty of this Association either to standardize American universities, and thus justify the confidence which foreign governments repose in them, or to notify those governments that there are American universities outside this Association whose work and standing are not inferior to universities now members of the Association."[18] Yet, in spite of this strong statement, it was not till the eve of the First World War that the Association of American Universities finally and reluctantly decided to assume the burden.

At first the association hoped that it would be relieved of this responsibility by some other body. Indeed, it even urged the United States Bureau of Education to be that body and to use its long-standing list of colleges as the basis for standardizing them.[19] In drawing up its first list in 1870, the bureau had to take the initial step in classification of deciding what institutions qualified as colleges. Taking the feeble step of recognizing as colleges all institutions granting degrees, the bureau posted a list of 369 colleges on its first compilation. By the twentieth century this simple criterion was no longer satisfactory in spite of minor improvements during the years. Changes were imminent when in 1910 Congress established the office of "specialist in higher education" within the bureau. The first incumbent of this office made it one of his early duties, with the cooperation of the American Association of Universities, to draw up a list of colleges whose recipients of bachelor's degrees were fitted for doing further graduate study. The actual records of graduate students were examined and their undergraduate colleges classified according to the success of their product. Colleges whose graduates completed their master's degree in one year were put in class I, and so on to class IV, which included colleges whose product was totally unprepared for graduate study. The classification was submitted in galley proof form for criticism to a number of graduate-school deans, but premature newspaper publicity of the impending publication resulted in enough pressure being exerted on President Taft so that he requested the Commissioner of Education to withhold the list indefinitely. When Taft's successor, Woodrow Wilson, himself a former university president, took no steps to reverse this decision, the national government dropped efforts at standardization.[20]

In the meantime another likely regulatory prospect appeared, this time a private, nongovernmental agency. In 1905 the Carnegie Foundation for the Advancement of Teaching commenced the administration of its munificent endowment of $10,000,000 to provide retirement allowances for professors in American colleges and universities. Determining the institutions whose professors were eligible for pensions was greatly complicated, once more, by the diversity of institutions calling themselves colleges and universities. In drawing up a roster the foundation modeled its yardstick after New York's legislation of the previous decade. "An institution to be ranked as a college," it announced, "must have at least six professors giving their entire time to college and university work, a course of four full years in liberal arts and sciences, and should require for admission not less than the usual four years of academic or high school preparation or its equivalent, in addition to the preacademic or grammar school studies."[21] Furthermore the college had to underwrite this program with a productive endowment of at least $200,000. Because institutions of higher education were so anxious to qualify their professors for retirement benefits, this yardstick exerted a powerful influence in standardizing the quality of American higher education.[22] Consequently, when the federal Bureau of Education was thwarted in exercising standardizing functions, there were some in the American Association of Universities who turned to the Carnegie Foundation as the logical candidate to perform this service. With the foundation, however, standardization had been purely a by-product of its main purpose, and it did not care to undertake any larger responsibility for it.

Happily, yet another agency was concurrently pointing the way toward the standardization of higher education. The North Central Association of Colleges and Secondary Schools, which had started out at the end of the nineteenth century as an agency to accredit secondary schools, found it to its advantage in the first decade of the next to accredit colleges as well. It laid down ten requirements drawn in part from data used earlier both by the Carnegie Foundation and the United States Bureau of Education. Over and above previously mentioned requirements of high-school preparation and a four-year college curriculum, the association demanded that the faculty have scholastic attainments at least equivalent to a master's degree from a member institution, that laboratories and libraries be adequate, and that graduates be able to enter study for advanced degrees at reputable institutions without conditions.[23] Other regional associations took similar steps.[24]

But effective as these regional associations became, there still was no accrediting agency national in scope. The National Association of State Universities had shown enough interest in this direction to lay down criteria for standardization, but its influence had been slight because it had provided no machinery of enforcement.[25] As the need for nationwide standards of accreditation continued unabated, the executive committee of the Association of American Universities finally put aside its distaste for the task and in 1914 published a list of American institutions whose bachelor's degrees should be accepted by foreign universities such as the University of Berlin. The list contained, naturally, members of the association, but also nonmembers which were on the accepted list of the Carnegie Foundation or would have been except for sectarian connections.[26] By this time almost ten years had elapsed since the University of Berlin had prodded the association, and almost twenty since New York had enacted the first forward-looking statutory regulation. In this period a vast change in point of view had occurred. Instead of relying on or waiting for governmental agencies to police it, higher education had achieved the professional maturity to form voluntary associations for its own self-regulation.[27]

As can be seen, accreditation was in the air during this period. Standardizing agencies not only multiplied but abounded. The various religious denominations started policing the ranks of church-related colleges.[28] A study of colleges for blacks by the United States Bureau of Education revealed only two colleges, Fisk and Howard, as coming up to collegiate grade.[29] State universities and state departments of education soon were leading in accrediting institutions within their boundaries.[30] If anything, this commendable effort at self-improvement began to show evidences of being overdone. Indeed, as early as 1906, at the instance of the National Association of State Universities a number of organizations interested in the matter of standards convened to form a joint committee, the National Conference on Standards, to interrelate their various efforts. The original agencies represented on this committee included the National Association of State Universities, of course; the regional accrediting associations of New England, the South, the Middle Atlantic states, and the Middle West; and the College Entrance Examination Board and later the Carnegie Foundation and the United States Commissioner of Education. More interested at first in standards of admission from secondary school to college, by the end of the First World War the committee was discussing college standards as well.[31]

During this war another coordinating agency arose, the American Council on Education. Originally organized to coordinate the war effort of American colleges and universities, it proved so useful that its existence was continued into peacetime. In the 1920s it took over the National Conference on Standards as its own committee on standards. Although it never became an accrediting agency itself, the council through this very important committee made recommendations which later were adopted and applied by nearly all individual accrediting associations.

Other efforts at coordination and simplification of existing accrediting associations followed, but, these efforts to the contrary notwithstanding, there was a growing criticism of the whole movement by the opening of the 1930s. In one direction there was a feeling that standards had become too inflexible. The rigid quantitative enforcement of each category in a set of standards could easily miss an over-all qualitative appraisal. Thus there was a temptation to assume that if an institution had adequate buildings, laboratories, libraries, high-school graduates for students, and a faculty with Ph.D. degrees, it was a good institution whereas, in reality, these factors were only indicators, not guarantors of quality.[32]

Some institutions could satisfy all the external requirements and yet be inferior, while others could fall short here and there and still be superior as measured by the performance of their students. Moreover, accreditation seemed to encourage uniformity at the expense of experimentation. The North Central Association was sufficiently impressed with this situation to revise its evaluations so as to judge institutions on their total pattern as well as their individual ingredients.[33]

Yet, even with this important modification, criticism continued in other directions. The American habit of looking for a mark of approval—whether derived from *Good Housekeeping,* consumer research organizations, Duncan Hines, or elsewhere—was leading to a conformity which stifled individuality and experimentation. Not only that, but individually standardized departments tended to obtain the lion's share of college and university budgets, to say nothing, as already mentioned, of foreclosing a view of the institution's educational program as a whole. Then there was not a little complaint that there were too many accrediting agencies, resulting in duplication of information demanded, too frequent inspections, and excessive costs of accreditation.

By the time of the Second World War there were many who were ready to abandon accreditation altogether. In fact the Association of American Universities did abandon it in 1948. Men like Samuel P. Capen, former specialist in higher education in the United States Bureau of Education and later chancellor of the University of Buffalo, acknowledged the undoubted contribution of these bodies of educational vigilantes but considered their historic mission fulfilled.[34] Others, unwilling to take such a radical step, nevertheless did not blind themselves to the fact that mischiefs still remained to be exorcised. These forces found expression at mid-century in the formation of the National Commission on Accrediting,[35] composed of the major associations of universities and colleges, both public and private, but excluding all accrediting agencies. The primary objective of the new organization was to accredit the accrediting agencies. By 1966, six regional and thirty professional accrediting agencies met the National Commission's criteria for acceptance. By 1972, they had accredited 2,700 of the 3,000 colleges and universities in the United States. The National Commission sought to maintain a certain amount of uniformity and coordination between the efforts of the various regional organizations and the professional associations. It hoped to eliminate the chaos and confusion that had prevailed hitherto in the field of accreditation.[36]

The Control of Higher Education

Development in the organization and standardization of higher education was paralleled by changes in the personnel whose hands were on its controls. No one should overlook the fact that as the administrative pattern grew in size and power, the hands of business replaced those of the clergy. It was the clergy, as already seen, who by and large occupied the presidential chairs and sat on the governing boards of colleges during the seventeenth and eighteenth centuries.[37] Many in the nineteenth century, too, thought of higher education as a special preserve of religion. Although the First Amendment to the federal Constitution pointed to the divorce of Church and State, nevertheless, various denominations still fought against the separation of religion from the state's university as well. But there were others during this century who, more in the spirit of the Bill of Rights, were making their voices heard for the first time in favor of secular interests in college and university. As a result sectarian and secular interests waged a running battle all during the nineteenth century to control higher education. Naturally somewhat different results occurred in public, denominational, and private but non-denominational colleges.

No doubt Thomas Jefferson was the first great protagonist of the public secular university. Having succeeded in disestablishing the Episcopal Church in Virginia, he followed up this victory by holding the Church at arm's length from the University of Virginia. He held it inimical to both educational and religious freedom to grant any one denomination a preferred status in higher education.[38] Henry P. Tappan at Michigan in mid-nineteenth century was no less insistent on the same principle. Plagued by sectarian bickering which was more interested in the denominational affiliation of appointments to the university faculty than in their educational qualifications, Tappan was provoked to remark: "The University of Michigan is neither religious nor political in its character, but purely scientific and literary. . . . The constitution recognizes in its organization no religious denominations and no political parties. . . . It [the university] belongs not to political parties and religious sects as a field in which they may carry on their conflicts for predominance. It belongs simply to the people, and to all the people whether they belong to political parties or to none; whether they belong to religious sects or have no religious connections."[39]

Thwarted by Jefferson, Tappan, and others, sectarian interests turned to founding institutions of their own where they could tightly bind administration and instruction to the propagation of their credal convictions.[40] Catholic colleges, of course, had long been familiar with this type of organization. In the beginning Catholic college foundations developed under diocesan control.[41] While at first the bishop and his priests might have constituted the faculty, latterly the bishop had come merely to preside over the governing board. Still other colleges were sponsored by teaching orders, which consequently were the parent organizations to petition for a charter from the state. Ordinarily members of the order constituted the governing board,[42] but after mid-twentieth century lay membership was encouraged.

Protestant practices varied. In the case of the Methodists, for instance, control took several forms, such as a board of visitors composed of bishops, a board of trustees elected by the church, or a board confirmed by a general conference of the church. While Catholic colleges remained steadfast against secular trends, there was some defection among Methodist colleges as well as the colleges of other Protestant denominations. The announcement of the Carnegie plan to pension retired professors put great strain on denominational bonds because professors of denominational colleges were excluded from its largess. Yet the terms on which this much-needed security was offered professors were so generous that it is no wonder that a number of church-related colleges went through elaborate contortions to convince the officers of the fund that they were not really related after all.

Henry S. Pritchett, who was called from the presidency of Massachusetts Institute of Technology to administer Mr. Carnegie's vast bounty, was strict in screening colleges that were to participate in the plan. If the college was an agency to advance denominational empire, he thought it ought to expect no support from resources such as he administered. If a college regarded itself as mainly educational, then he called upon it to test its singleness of purpose by showing an interest in higher education whatever the auspices. Pritchett doubted that the average denominational college could pass this test. Moreover, as he saw it, their preferred interest in denominational empires was one of the factors which had spawned more colleges than could be supported, a fact which resulted in lower standards among church-affiliated institutions than obtained in public ones. Governed by this opinion, he strongly insisted that Carnegie funds should not be a compensating crutch on which this infirmity could lean.[43] Many institutions underwent severe soul-searching about whether to maintain or weaken their sectarian ties. In the end not a few institutions—Vanderbilt, for example—were pulled loose from their denominational moorings by the magnet of the Carnegie pension system.

It was not the last time that church-affiliated institutions of higher education would feel a similar magnet. In the middle of the twentieth century the state of Maryland appropriated public funds for the support of four colleges with sectarian ties. This legislation was immediately tested in the Maryland supreme court to see whether it violated the state's constitutional provision against allocating public funds for sectarian instruction. The case turned on a question of fact. Were these four institutions sectarian within the meaning of the constitution? In deciding to let the appropriation stand for one college but to deny it to the three others the court asked itself such questions as, What is the purpose and public image of the institution? Who are the personnel in charge? Who owns the property and provides the financial support? and What is the nature of the program of studies? If the answers to these questions showed a preponderantly ecclesiastical influence, public funds would have to be withheld.[44] Whether in the future similar institutions would become more secular in order to win public funds as many had to win Carnegie ones remained an open question.

It was Noah Porter of Yale in the second half of the nineteenth century who perhaps most vigorously supported clerical control of the private but nondenominational colleges. Living in the twilight of the period when the clergy were the outstanding intellectual leaders in the American community, Porter still preferred their leadership for the time being to that of laymen. Confident in the breadth of their scholarship, he took exception to the criticism that the clergy were not well enough versed in science to be in control of the modern college.

More willing to admit that they might not be sufficiently versed in finance to manage the increasing size of the corporate affairs of higher education, Porter claimed that they at least knew enough to ask those who did. To the objection that clerical control caused higher education to suffer from sectarianism he countered that public or nonsectarian institutions were godless. Better that colleges be the property of some denomination than a vacuum beckoning any aggressive religious group.[45]

Yet Porter's own college was already drifting away from his convictions. As early as 1745 a new charter for the "collegiate school in New Haven" had dropped the requirement that its corporation be drawn exclusively from the Congregational clergy. Oddly enough, notwithstanding being released by the charter, the college continued to choose Congregational clergy for its corporation right up to the last quarter of the nineteenth century. The clergy then finally relinquished this privilege in fact as well as by charter but did so voluntarily because they saw that a clerical majority on the corporation was an anomaly in the face of the gigantic financial and administrative problems confronting it in the twentieth century.[46] Most other colleges of colonial origin took the same course.[47]

As clerical and denominational interests receded from control of public and many private institutions of higher education, secular interests replaced them. These secular interests represented principally two groups, businessmen and alumni. While there was some overlapping of these two categories, alumni nevertheless deserve special mention because they represented a growing kind of self-rule by alma mater with the aid of her offspring. The mounting number and popularity of businessmen on governing boards reflected both a change in the power structure of American society and a growth in college endowments which demanded trained and experienced management. The increasing need of sage financial advice has already been noticed as making itself felt at Harvard as early as the eighteenth century.[48] The rise of business in the power structure, slow in the eighteenth and early nineteenth centuries, accelerated rapidly with the industrial expansion of the country after the Civil War.[49] Thus it has been reckoned that while businessmen constituted about one-fifth of the governing boards in 1860, they had become one-third of those boards by 1930.[50] As a result the economic segment of the population, made up of bankers, lawyers, merchants, manufacturers, and capitalists, was better represented than any other.[51] Farm and labor groups tended to be slighted, and three-quarters of the country's occupational groups had no representation at all. What was more, the age of nearly half of the governing boards was over sixty and their political beliefs generally conservative.

Some people had doubts about this general situation. To some it seemed that proprietary interests predominated to a point where there was danger that the government of higher education would become plutocratic.[52] It was even a question in some minds whether the business interests had the unique competence to manage higher education which was ascribed to them.[53] Thus, by employing investment counsel did not most boards betray a lack of self-confidence in the kind of judgment for which they were chosen? Or, again, in spite of educational attainments much above the average of the population, did not board members lack special training in educational problems?[54] In 1974 a former trustee stated that in his opinion the office of college trusteeship was moribund, that trustees "have for decades now betrayed their trust by neglecting to live up to their powers and responsibilities." A survey in 1967 of 10,000 trustees of American colleges found no evidence that these officials were speaking out on the important issues confronting higher education or were assuming leadership roles as spokesmen for their institutions.[55] To be sure, the representation of educators on governing boards doubled from 5 per cent in 1860 to 10 per cent in 1930. But was it enough? The fact remained, as Thorstein Veblen wrote, that for decades America had been reluctant to trust the management of its higher education to other than men of pecuniary substance in the belief that, by acquiring or otherwise being possessed of considerable wealth, they had demonstrated their fitness for the direction of academic affairs.[56]

The rise of the college alumnus to a position of power on the governing board of his alma mater started with the formation of alumni associations. As early as 1792 it had become the custom at Yale, where class spirit was unusually strong, for each class to appoint an alumni secretary. But in spite of this head start it was Williams in 1821 which organized the first alumni association.[57] The idea became popular immediately with other colleges. The purpose of these early organizations ranged from keeping undergraduate memories fresh to keeping intellectual interests alive, from enticing student patronage to alma mater to soliciting supporting funds for her. Usually the initiative in forming these associations came from the alumni themselves, but college administrations were not slow to appreciate the importance of keeping them both alive and strong. Neither were they long in finding out that the twin of support was control, a desire for a voice in the determination of alma mater's policies. Not later than the middle of the nineteenth century a Yale professor was predicting that if the alumni met together year after year with nothing to do but talk and time enough for that, they soon would be trying to govern the faculty.[58] He was right. Not long after, Harvard alumni gained the privilege of electing members of the Harvard Overseers. Before the century was out the policy had become general.[59] A survey in 1966 of eighty-two public and private colleges revealed that thirty-one of the schools had elected alumni trustees serving on their governing boards; an additional twenty-four had trustees nominated by alumni. In addition, nearly all had a number of alumni serving as trustees who were not holding places specifically reserved for graduates.[60]

The participation of the alumni in university affairs was not an unmixed blessing. True, alumni associations did give generously of their time and money for alma mater. Indeed their heartfelt loyalty was almost a species of patriotism. But like patriotism it had its jingoistic aspects. This became evident as intercollegiate athletics developed into a principal lever for stirring alumni loyalties. Unfortunately, the loyalty bred of this type of rivalry all too frequently exaggerated the physical at the expense of the intellectual prowess of the university.[61] Forgetting the main purpose of the higher education, many alumni were more interested in the staff of coaches than they were in the staff of professors, in gymnasia and stadia than in libraries and laboratories.[62] Alumni influence was by no means limited to athletics, however. At times, alumni showed an active interest in the educational programs of their alma mater. At Princeton, alumni pressure during the 1890s helped achieve a broader implementation of the elective principle.[63]

In many cases introducing a new group like the alumni into the governing board was only possible by enlarging the number on the board. But then the historical tendency of governing boards had been to grow in size, even after their founding.[64] In order to recruit wide interest, private colleges and universities tended to have larger boards than public institutions. Not till the twentieth century, however, was serious thought given on principle to the optimum number the board ought to have. The same might be said for the method of election as well. Many early boards were self-perpetuating. Others were chosen by church bodies to which they belonged. The coming of state universities witnessed various practices, such as appointment by the governor, election by the legislature, and election by the people themselves. Alumni usually selected their own representatives.[65] Where the governor was given the power of appointment, he sometimes had the power of removal as well, which on occasion proved a dangerous threat to the integrity of the board.[66]

Changes and Increases in Administrative Personnel

Increased enrollments and greatly increased endowments not only hastened the transition from boards of control dominated by clergymen to ones dominated by businessmen but they also accelerated the choice of laymen rather than clergy as incumbents of the presidential office. A sampling reveals that while 90 per cent of the college presidents in 1860 were trained for the ministry, only 12 per cent had such training in 1933.[67] By the latter date the great majority of presidents had come up through the faculty and the avenue of scholarship.[68] Clerical training remained longer in demand for the liberal-arts college than for the new land-grant colleges of agriculture and mechanical arts. But even there the administrative abilities of the clergy matched the average, and certainly the most conspicuous failures were not clergymen.[69]

While the college president of only a few generations back often wrote all his official correspondence longhand and a president like James B. Angell at Michigan registered entering students as well as taught them in addition to his other presidential duties,[70] a marked change came over the office toward the end of the nineteenth century. President Hadley of Yale drew the dividing line between the old and the new when his predecessor, Timothy Dwight, grandson of Yale's first President Dwight, accepted the Yale presidency only on the stipulation that he have no teaching duties.[71] Hadley further delineated the change by relating how when he visited old President Porter he like as not found him reading Kant, but when he called on President Dwight he was more likely to find him examining a balance sheet.[72] On Porter's desk, too, he found manuscripts, on Dwight's the catalogues of competing institutions. It was in keeping with these differences, Hadley noted incidentally, that he called on Porter in his study but on Dwight in his office.

The new type of president tilled a broad field. Its breadth was nonetheless taxing of human energy where, as at Harvard in the third decade of the nineteenth century, steps had already been taken to allow the president to concentrate on oversight of the college.[73] Consequently, when Eliot came to the office after the Civil War, it is no surprise that he emphasized this aspect of his office. Thus he regarded the president as the chief executive officer of the deliberative bodies of the university, both of the governing boards and of the faculties. As chief executive officer his first duty was supervision. Consequently Eliot insisted on being ex officio a member of every board with supervisory duties and the presiding officer on each of the several faculties of the university. Appointments to these faculties he saw as one of his most exacting duties, for he suffered no more bitter disappointment than being daily confronted with the evil fruit of a bad selection. In leading his faculties he was careful not to force his measures through, although he was aware that by controlling the purse strings he held great power over educational policy. Viewing the wide domain of his responsibilities, Eliot was not insensitive to the importance of delegating duties. The administrative officer who tried to do everything himself, he wrote, would in the end do little and that little ill.[74]

Obviously, the presidency as Eliot described it had become a powerful office. While it had been customary to describe the old college president as *primus inter pares,* the newer one was simply *primus.* Even so, the wise president, as Hadley observed, held his power in reserve rather than allowed it to obtrude. But there was no denying that he had it. He not only had it but he needed it for the vast tasks in hand, tasks so vast that some favored strong centralization of authority in the presidency, as in business corporations. Even the University of Virginia, where Jefferson had tried to minimize the office by substituting a rotating chairman of the faculty, finally succumbed to instituting a president at the turn of the century in order to maintain her competitive position vis-à-vis her sister institutions.[75] As the problems of higher education demanded presidential powers commensurate with their size and gravity, so it is notable that the problems bred a generation of college and university presidents whose abilities brilliantly matched their opportunities. Eliot was most outstanding, but deserving to be mentioned in the same breath with him were others like Gilman at Hopkins, Harper at Chicago, Angell at Michigan, and Butler at Columbia.[76] Further attesting their eminence is the fact that they not only left an imprint on academic affairs but led public thought outside academic walls.[77]

In its march to power it would be difficult to say whether the legal powers of the presidency were greater thirty years after the turn of the century than they were thirty years before. What did take place for certain in this sixty-year period was a tremendous expansion and differentiation of the administrative function. After the Civil War the administration of higher education was still pretty much a one-man affair. The smaller the institution at the beginning of this period, the more likely the president might act as chief disciplinarian, watch over the books in the library, keep the vital records of the college, take charge of business details, invest the funds of the institution, and act as secretary of both faculty and governing board. In larger institutions some differentiation of these functions had already been occurring, but from this period onward expansion of the administrative function was little short of phenomenal.

The order in which subordinate offices developed varied considerably from institution to institution.[78] On the whole the first specialization of the presidential function to occur was the appointment of a librarian. Next, recognition was extended to the office of registrar. The 1880s can be taken as the median period of its greatest growth. That the office emerged when the elective curriculum was on the rise is probably no accident, as academic bookkeeping then became much more involved and complicated than under traditional prescription. The median decade for the appearance of deans was the 1890s, with the subdivision into deans of men and deans of women coming some time later. The way in which he was selected, whether by presidential appointment or faculty election, determined whose man the dean was. Business officers, directors of public relations,[79] directors of admissions, and many other posts were the product of the next century.

Some of the larger institutions had vice-presidents in the later nineteenth century, but this office had its best growth in the twentieth century. In some instances, instead of creating an office just below the presidency, an office just above such as that of the chancellor was set up. In either case the objective was to free the top executive officer of the university still further from the duties of administration, which continued overwhelming, and to afford him more time to devote to educational policy, to be the educational seer which Eliot envisioned.

In their slow evolution nearly all these offices originally included some teaching duties. Thus the librarianship was only a part-time job of some member of the faculty. So too was the registrarship. Sometimes the librarian was also registrar or perhaps secretary of the faculty. In small colleges the offices of dean and registrar were often combined. All sorts of variations occurred to suit local exigencies. Of course, as the duties of each of these offices increased, less and less time was devoted to teaching till none at all was left except as here and there a dean or even a president like David Starr Jordan[80] insisted on keeping a hand in teaching in order to be more sensitive to the pulse of the student body.

The multiplication of academic personnel in administration was as nothing compared to the nonacademic. In fact so rapidly did administrative personnel multiply that by 1950 the University of Minnesota employed 4,000 nonacademic workers of one sort or another such as clerks, statisticians, dietitians, truck drivers, and the like![81] Even at small liberal-arts colleges in New England, in the fifty-year period prior to the depression, the ratio of students to nonacademic personnel fell from 1.57 to 1.21, while the ratio of students to faculty remained practically constant at 1.11. Stated from a slightly different angle, the 17 per cent of titles which were noninstructional in the college catalogue of 1883 had doubled by 1933.[82]

While nonacademic personnel were increasing in number and administrative importance, academic personnel—the faculty—seemed to be declining as a significant group in the administration of higher education. Originally, it will be remembered, instructional and administrative duties were united in one person, the president. It was not long, however, before the increase of students necessitated that the president have tutors and later professors to help him. That these men assisted not only in instruction but also in the administration of the college is visible as early as the seventeenth century, when Harvard set up the president and faculty as the "immediate government" of the college. President and faculty exercised legislative, executive, and judicial functions; they decided academic policies, executed them, and sat in judgment on their infringement. Some faculties exercised all three of these functions as late as the late nineteenth century.[83] The smaller the college remained, the longer it was possible for president and faculty to preserve this democratic organization. The larger the college grew, especially the larger its faculty grew, the more it became necessary to specialize and delegate duties.

This specialization or differentiation operated in two directions. In one direction, that of organization for academic instruction, faculties began to subdivide themselves into departments of instruction. The beginnings of departmental organization are easily discernible at both Harvard and the University of Virginia in the second quarter of the nineteenth century.[84] These beginnings were subsequently strengthened by the specialization which the introduction of German research methods necessitated and also by the individualization which the elective curriculum permitted. In some places departments not only almost superseded faculty functions but loyalty to the subject matter specialization they represented exceeded that to the college or university itself. Thus, the increasing autonomy of departments fostered a tendency toward fragmentation of the academic structure. Indeed, the forces of compartmentalization did not spend themselves till the twentieth century, and even then they only slackened long enough to organize departments into divisions in order to recognize the growing importance of interdisciplinary studies. In any event, the importance of the departments in the university's administrative structure should not be minimized. They had become the indispensable vehicle for disciplinary and professional specialization. On many campuses departments played an important role in determining actions on personnel, curriculum, and research facilities.[85] It "soon became apparent that the reputation of a university depended upon the reputation of its departments and the scholars within them. Autonomy in the development of a department became a necessity if the university was to achieve a national reputation."[86] Yet a critic of this trend was to write in 1971: "As a university becomes overcompartmentalized and categories harden, departments and the professors in them become isolated and ever more narrow. Exploration and development of promising new fields . . . are thereby retarded or denied."[87]

Following World War II, a number of American universities developed a more complex administrative structure which moved beyond the departmental pattern of organization. Institutes, bureaus, and centers of specialized research and teaching emerged, funded either by the federal government or the foundations. Very often these new academic units cut across traditional departmental boundaries in pursuing their specialized goals. A study in 1970 found some nine hundred institutes and research centers in operation at fifty-one land-grant colleges and universities. The University of Oklahoma had forty-four institutes on one campus alone. The rise of these new academic units raised some serious questions: Would the institutes bridge the gap between the various competing departments and schools on campus or would they bring about even greater administrative chaos and confusion?[88]

In a second direction, that of administration, faculties organized themselves increasingly into committees—committees on discipline, on admissions, on athletics, and the like. In the course of time even these committees tended to bog down with details, so that faculties were glad to shift these duties to such emerging new administrative officers as deans of discipline, directors of admissions, and directors of athletics. Glad as faculties were to rid themselves of executive and judicial duties and thus free themselves for instruction and investigation, they still jealously prized their deliberative or legislative control of the aims, content, and methods of instruction. Yet even here increasing size of faculties, particularly in large institutions, made the faculty meeting, the last stronghold of their power, a rather cumbersome part of college or university administration. While Eliot still found the clash of academic minds in faculty meeting useful in forming his own educational views, after his time academic business grew so complex that it only came before the faculty after it had been carefully digested by administrative officials. This procedure expedited business but it minimized debate and so undermined the legislative importance of the faculty.[89] At Columbia a university council composed of administrative officers and faculty representatives came to transact important business. But the result was the same; as President Butler commented, the faculty was ground down between the university council above and the powerful departments below.[90] Even where faculties were small or did retain some measure of their former deliberative or legislative importance, they often discredited themselves as strongholds where academic traditionalism could entrench itself almost indefinitely to postpone academic progress.

Distribution of Power in the Academic Hierarchy

Just as the faculty seemed in the course of relinquishing its legislative as well as its executive and judicial duties to become a purely teaching body, a substantial threat to its academic integrity roused the academic community to such indignation that it fought desperately to cling to what little power it still retained. From

1890 to 1920 a number of attempts were made to dismiss prominent and coura-
geous professors because their opinions were viewed as socially radical. Regarded
as responsible for these attempted ousters were the new proprietary interests
lodged on boards of control.[91] But presidents were as much the object of faculty
ire as trustees because, selected by the board, they were often identified as siding
with the trustees rather than the faculty. In trying to resist board and presidential
encroachment on their academic freedom,[92] faculties found themselves almost
powerless. Not only had they been shorn in the early eighteenth and nineteenth
centuries of much of their ancient power but the recent aggrandizement of the
presidency and the domination of governing boards by business interests had
upset the balance of power in the academic hierarchy more than anyone had
stopped to realize. When faculties woke to the crisis at hand, they broke out into
a storm of protest and demanded a redress of the power structure.

They lodged a double complaint against the administration of higher education. One complaint was directed against the president, that his enhanced power
had made him autocratic.[93] Whereas formerly he had been *non dominus sed dux*
("a leader not a master"), he seemed now to have reversed his role. He gave
direction from above rather than sought cooperation from below. Some excused
the accretion of presidential power on grounds that it came from force of circumstance.[94] The forces of rapid growth thrust power on the president just as rapid
urbanization had caused the power of the city superintendent of schools to swell
all out of proportion to its former size and had caused him too to be regarded
as autocratic. Others conceded that the presidential system had redounded to the
financial success of the colleges and universities but, like the English critic Harold
Laski, held it too great a price to pay for the timidity induced in the faculty when
standing in the presidential shadow.[95] Nicholas Murray Butler tried to make his
shadow less ominous by claiming that he held his office like a British prime
minister, but his critics claimed he was more like a German chancellor under the
Hohenzollerns.[96]

The other complaint was aimed at the board of trustees and was double-
barreled. Criticism in the one barrel was leveled at boards which were constantly
interfering in the administration of their institutions and failing to observe their
proper functions as legislative rather than executive bodies. This malpractice was
of long standing. It was part of Tappan's difficulties at the University of Michigan
in the middle of the nineteenth century. There the Regents insisted on modifying
courses of instruction, shifting professorships, and making purchases for the
library without consulting the faculty. Tappan took the ground that these were
details of administration which should be left to the expert judgment of the
professional staff.[97] Not long after, President Bascom had much the same problem
at the University of Wisconsin, as did F. A. P. Barnard at Columbia.[98] Happily,
Andrew S. Draper could point out that statutes of the University of Illinois, where
he was president till shortly after the turn of the century, specifically stated that
the function of its trustees was legislative and not executive.[99]

Critics used the other barrel to draw a bead on the inclination of businessmen on governing boards to treat institutions of higher learning like business corporations.[100] Most obnoxious here was the way in which boards dismissed professors whose opinions they disliked. They treated the professor as if he could be hired and fired like any employee in one of their firms. Indeed, when the trustees of Cornell fired Professor William C. Russell from the vice-presidency of the university in the late nineteenth century, they did not so much as assign a cause. Questioned about such a highhanded procedure, one of the trustees told a reporter of the *New York Times* that the trustees did not think it necessary to defend themselves publicly in such a case. Nicholas Murray Butler even justified this practice on the ground that to be dismissed "at the pleasure" of the board left no stain on a professor's reputation, whereas a dismissal on preferred charges would. The Columbia charter, he noted, provided specifically that officers of instruction should serve at the pleasure of the trustees.[101]

Whether or not a professor is more than an employee is an issue which has had a long history. As early as the eighteenth century a professor at William and Mary sought to save himself from ouster by claiming that he held a freehold in his position. A freehold was originally an interest in land in return for services to its owner. The professor claimed he had such an interest in the estate of the college and could not be divested of it without a hearing and show of cause. Attorney for the college, none other than the young John Marshall, argued that since William and Mary was a private corporation no such property right existed and the Virginia court so held.[102] With no freehold in his position the professor's status became one of contract.[103] Though forced to recognize this change, the American Association of University Professors has contended that the professor is more than a mere employee, that he is rather an appointee. In 1940 the Association of American Colleges and the AAUP issued an influential "Statement of Principles on Academic Freedom and Tenure." The statement declared that tenure helped maintain academic freedom and made the profession of college teaching attractive to able persons, thus realizing the full value of higher education for society. To this end, it recommended that after "the expiration of a probationary period," faculty members should have "permanent or continuous tenure" to be terminated "only for adequate cause, except in the case of retirement for age or under extraordinary circumstances because of financial exigencies." Furthermore, it asked that terms of academic appointment should be stated in writing and that the probationary period of full-time service should not exceed seven years. Principles such as these came to be observed in the great majority of American colleges. By 1972 tenure plans were in effect in all public and private universities, all public four-year colleges, and 94 per cent of the private colleges. Approximately 50 per cent of American faculty members had tenure appointments at this time.[104]

Ironically, just as tenure seemed to have become the norm in American higher education, it came under attack. The economic difficulties of the late 1960s led to demands for its modification or abolition. Graduate schools continued to provide an oversupply of Ph.D.s in spite of a declining economy. Tenure was seen under the circumstances as imposing an inflexible financial burden on public and private financial resources. Furthermore, viewed as a kind of civil service job security, the system seemed to diminish a faculty's sense of accountability as witness its diminished interest in teaching.

Vehement attacks on tenure now came from disaffected junior faculty, from politicians critical of university financial policies, from administrators seeking ways to get rid of academic "deadwood," and from leaders of women's groups and minority groups who wanted more faculty openings for the previously disadvantaged. Indeed, an educational periodical at this time raised the question: "Can a college have tenure and Affirmative Action, too?"[105] Activist students attacked tenure because it prevented the university from ridding itself of ineffective teachers. As the onslaught mounted, the AAUP remained firm in its advocacy of the tenure principle. It worked to define detailed procedural standards for use in dismissal hearings and stated its firm opposition to the setting up of tenure quotas for faculties. At the same time, a Commission on Academic Tenure in Higher Education sponsored by the Ford Foundation recommended tightening requirements for admission to tenure and affirmed that the tenure principle was of overriding importance to freedom of teaching and investigation.[106]

In July, 1974, tenure for college professors happily received strong support in the courts of New Jersey. At that time, Superior Court Judge Melvin P. Antell ruled that Bloomfield College had not been justified in abolishing tenure and dismissing thirteen faculty members the previous year. The judge found that the motive for these actions was not primarily financial stringency, but a desire to abolish the tenure system itself. And he declared that tenure in colleges should be protected vigorously, because it was not merely an act "of solicitude for the staff of academic institutions, but of concern for the general welfare by providing for the benefits of uninhibited scholarship and its free dissemination."[107]

Whatever the professor's legal status none in the professoriate castigated the governing board, which engaged him, in more scathing terms than did Thorstein Veblen. In his view governing boards were an "aimless survival" from the days of clerical rule and their retention "an unreflecting deferential concession" to the corporate organization and control found advantageous in the pursuit of private gain in business.[108] Not everyone, however, accepted Veblen's analogy between governing boards of business and of higher education.[109] The analogy, they claimed, broke down principally because a university is not run for profit. While the directors of a business corporation could scan a balance sheet and decide how their business was getting along, no similar profit-and-loss statement could be drawn for the trustees of an institution of higher learning.[110] Universities, moreover, existed to spend rather than make profits. Finally, in a business the governing boards are stockholders or representatives of stockholders whereas in a university they are trustees and so called because they hold the university property in trust.

Still, how to rectify the balance of power? J. McKeen Cattell, himself a victim of presidential wrath at Columbia and therefore impatient with the abuse of power by presidents and governing boards, favored a reorganization of the whole administrative structure at once.[111] After polling nearly 300 of his professorial colleagues he found that 85 per cent favored greater faculty sharing of responsibility for the management of university affairs.[112] This proposal was not altogether surprising, coming, as it did, in the midst of the Progressive era in American politics when reform was in the air and reformers sought to make all government more responsible to the people.[113]

Somewhat earlier an eminent Harvard professor of European background, Louis Agassiz, contended that the United States would never understand the nature of a university as long as its intellectual interests were determined, not by professors inside the university, but by a board of outside lay governors.[114] Of course Agassiz's view was not a new one. It had been a main issue at Harvard in both the early eighteenth and nineteenth centuries. Was the faculty to be regarded as a republic of scholars? This old guild idea stirred real nostalgia in men like Cattell. The guild was based on the notion of expertness. Only experts, that is, guild members, were competent to judge of their own expertness. Some thought it high time for the guild to close its gates in order to be master within its own walls. Indeed, instead of fighting rear-guard actions in defense of their autonomy the faculty should actually go over on offense. As a matter of fact, however, the day was past for such isolationist tactics. Isolationism had led to making many faculties strongholds of reaction. With the rising "service" role of the university it was becoming time to redefine the boundaries between lay and expert control of higher education.

President A. Lawrence Lowell of Harvard made perhaps the single best statement of this new relation for the twentieth century. Since a college or university is supposed to be a self-governing guild of scholars, he asked, does it need a separate board of trustees at all? And, if it does, should final authority lie with the lay board? Lowell answered both these questions in the affirmative. On the first point, the management of higher education must have both lay and expert components. Without the expert influence higher education would become ineffectual and without the lay, it might in time become narrow and out of harmony with the public interest. Yet Lowell cautioned against experts sitting on lay boards and lay boards trying to direct experts in their expertness. In case of conflict ultimate authority must lodge with the lay board because over the years higher education has become so vested with a lay interest.[115] Obviously higher education had come a long way since the Dartmouth Case when John Marshall found the college vested with no public interest.

Addressing himself to the same issue, Nicholas Murray Butler distinguished between the government and the administration of higher education in a way very similar to the distinction drawn between "internal" and "external" aspects of college administration a century or more earlier. Government, he asserted, dealt with the formulation of principles and policies, while administration concerned their execution. Government was a proper function of deliberative bodies like a board of trustees or faculties, but administration properly belonged to presidents and deans,[116] a view strongly seconded by his own exceptionally able dean, Herbert E. Hawkes.[117] To those accepting this distinction the plea for "democracy in administration" made little or no sense.

Similarly David Starr Jordan contrasted administration and instruction.[118] The role of administration, he held, was to expedite instruction. In this vein some, like Charles William Eliot, sincerely doubted that faculties were really desirous to participate in administration.[119] To share power might be gratifying, but to share it also involved accountability and accountability incurred onerous and time-consuming committee work which not a few faculty members considered an encroachment on teaching and scholarship.

While many joined in weighing the historical and theoretical pros and cons of greater faculty participation in administration, others were pointing out how democracy existed in fact in the administration of at least one of the major institutions, Yale.[120] To find it existing there of all places was a surprise, since it was Yale that took the lead in colonial days in departing from the European precedent of faculty control and vesting control in the president and Corporation. Whatever Yale's responsibility for this origin, in his long incumbency, 1817–46, President Jeremiah Day pursued the custom of discussing and deciding important policies in meetings with the faculty. Indeed, by the end of his regime so strong a precedent had been set that the Yale Corporation would take no action without recommendation or assent of the faculty. Consequently, by the turn of the century it was a common saying that at Yale the faculty legislated, the president concurred, and the corporation ratified.[121]

While the Yale pattern was admired, it was difficult to adopt *in toto* where academic shins were already badly bruised. Various institutions, however, did make an honest effort to improve communications between faculty and administration. At Cornell, for instance, two members of the faculty were admitted to the governing board, where they had a right to be heard but not to vote. At Princeton provision was made for a committee of the faculty to sit quarterly with another from the trustees to discuss curriculum problems. California and Michigan also had bodies that worked closely with their boards.[122]

Fully as significant, if not more so, was the fact that the newly formed American Association of University Professors made faculty-administration relations a matter for early consideration by one of its top committees. After the First World War the association published a statement of principles which it thought should govern the two bodies. It asked for closer understanding between faculties and boards of control than that provided by the intermediation of the president. Furthermore it asked for participation with trustees in the selection of both presidents and deans, and in general for consultation on appointments, promotions, and dismissals. Within their own precinct of instruction, it recommended supremacy of faculties in policy making.[123] Following this lead, it is worth noting, several colleges—Vassar, Mount Holyoke, and Colgate among them—drew up statutes or manuals defining the respective powers and obligations of faculty and administration.[124] But in spite of such improvements, a 1939 check of 177 institutions by the American Association of University Professors disclosed that 132 had no plan for faculty-board exchanges of views.[125]

After the Second World War the situation changed considerably. Faculties came to have greater power. They began to control appointments and promotions, academic calendars, work schedules, even certification for entrance to many professions. Faculty assumed these powers either by explicit delegation from governing boards or with tacit trustee approval.[126] In 1974 an observer commented: "The real decision-making power in a university has shifted to the faculty. . . . faculty leaders sit on the board; they dominate internal councils. . . ."[127]

The principal vehicle for implementing this more active faculty voice in university affairs was the academic senate. Senates with strong faculty representation had long been on the scene, but by the early 1970s they had evolved into influential policy-making bodies on many campuses.[128] The American Association of University Professors reported about this time that governing boards were consulting much more frequently than before with faculty representatives about budgetary policies, salary schedules, and tenure.[129]

The increase in faculty power was paralleled by a notable increase in student power. Earlier in the twentieth century, Antioch, Bennington, Bard, Denison, and Sarah Lawrence had experimented with student participation in college government. However, it was not until the campus disorders of 1968–1969 that any considerable movement in this direction took place. In April, 1970, the American Council on Education's special committee on campus tensions reported that student power had become an issue in about three-quarters of the institutions where disruptions occurred, while the Vietnam War was an issue in only 38 per cent of these schools.[130]

Many of the student protests in 1968 and 1969 included demands for student participation in the hiring and firing of faculty and the determination of a "relevant" curriculum. By and large, these demands found a sympathetic reception from university administrators. Many administrators believed that a reform of the university's authoritarian structure was long overdue. Others may have viewed reform "as a means of defusing much current student unrest while at the same time demonstrating that colleges and universities in a time of rapid social change are able to reform themselves. . . ."[131]

In addition to student activism, a number of other factors combined to strengthen the movement for student power. The lowering of the voting age to eighteen, the huge increase in college enrollments, the considerable increase in the percentage of the American population that was under twenty-five, and the greater prominence of child-centered concepts in the rearing of children and in elementary and secondary schooling all played a part.[132] These developments helped to shape a new attitude on the part of youth in the United States and elsewhere in the world. Youth now had a feeling of new strength, "of being part of a powerful new kind of generation, a fairly cohesive group . . . which can represent them and promote their aims in the outside world."[133]

The student power movement produced changes in patterns of university government which were potentially of great significance. A survey of 875 institutions of higher education in 1969 found that 88.3 per cent of them admitted students to membership on at least one of their policy-making bodies. Of these, 2.7 per cent gave students voting privileges on boards of trustees; 41 per cent permitted student observers to sit on committees dealing with matters such as selection of faculty, promotion, and tenure.[134] And these trends continued in the years that followed. In 1971, the American Council on Education made a survey that found that 14 per cent of all American institutions of higher education were now including student representatives on their boards of trustees. A few others were planning to do so.[135]

Students were also increasingly active on committees of the faculty. Moreover, a number of schools began to use student evaluations to judge the teaching performance of their faculty and to make decisions on the effectiveness of particular courses in the curriculum. Some institutions even permitted students to serve on committees interviewing applicants for positions on the faculty and the administrative staff. Others had student advisers assigned to work with their admissions staff to recruit prospective students and to interview them.[136]

What was the significance of the new era of "participatory democracy" in university government? Some found student judgments to be quite helpful in certain situations. Others wondered whether the new system did not waste an inordinate amount of faculty and administrative time. In any event, it soon became apparent that the student would not wish his participation in academic government to encroach on scholastic effort or prevent taking an outside job that might be needed to help meet college expenses. An even more fundamental question related to the nature of the university itself. It was argued by some that a university might well be considered an institution with very special functions. Because of these functions, it might not easily be able to follow the democratic model of government. Depending as it did on "an expertise that is inherent in its very purpose," its specific mission might require different and unequal roles for professors and students. These differing roles might well be "built into the essence of the institution."[137]

Revenues and Expenditures

The financial problems of higher education take their cue, as have most of the problems of organization and administration, from the constantly increasing size of the educational establishment. At the base of this increase lay the growing number of students seeking a college education.[138] More particularly, it was a rapidly rising standard of living predicated on the unprecedented exploitation of the country's rich natural resources after the Civil War that made possible the tidal wave of students which inundated colleges in the twentieth century. The first educational warning of this rise occurred in the phenomenal expansion of secondary education. Between 1870 and 1890 the number of high schools quintupled.

Twenty years later the 2,500 high schools existing in 1890 had become 10,000 and in another two decades 24,000. While the population as a whole rose 60 per cent between 1900 and 1940, the secondary-school population rose 1,200 per cent![139] Such stupendous growth was soon reflected in a corresponding enlargement of higher education in all dimensions. The over-all picture can be gathered by a glance at figures compiled from reports of the federal government. (See page 378.)

Such unrelenting pressure in all directions gave higher education a voracious financial appetite. In the national period of our history there have been three principal ways of feeding this appetite—endowments, taxes, and tuitions. Endowments, which have been the mainstay of private institutions, accumulated slowly down to the period of the Civil War. Charles Thwing, college president and historian of higher education, estimated that at the beginning of the nineteenth century the total productive funds of *all* institutions of higher learning then in existence amounted to less than half a million dollars.[140] Between the Revolutionary and Civil Wars the record discloses only about a dozen large gifts for the use of the higher learning, and these ranged between $20,000 and $175,000.[141] When Princeton made a drive in 1830 for $100,000, an ambitious undertaking in those days, the largest single gift was $5,000.[142] Probably this was a good showing for a country with a mixed economy of agriculture and commerce.

Generous as the givers of this period were, they were quite eclipsed by those of the post-Civil War period. Rapid industrialization in the balance of the century resulted in a number of large personal fortunes, some of which were dedicated to the higher learning. Ezra Cornell started the college that bears his name with $500,000, thus in a single gift matching the total endowment of all colleges at the opening of the century. Cornelius Vanderbilt gave $1,000,000 for the institution named after him. Johns Hopkins bequeathed $3,500,000 to start Johns Hopkins in Baltimore. Here in a single gift was an endowment which matched the endowment it had taken Harvard almost 250 years to accumulate.[143] But greater munificence was yet to come. Stanford University commenced with a memorial gift from Leland Stanford of $20,000,000, and Chicago ultimately became the beneficiary of $30,000,000 of the Rockefeller fortune.

In the twentieth century large-scale giving took a different turn. Not millions but now hundreds of millions of dollars were poured into philanthropic foundations by men like Carnegie, Rockefeller, and Ford, to mention but three of the most notable givers. These foundations spent their income and sometimes their principal, not to found new institutions, but to strengthen older ones and sometimes modify their direction. In disbursing their funds they tried to develop policies which would be constructive and not just palliative.[144] One such early policy made gifts conditional on institutions' matching them with funds raised by themselves. This policy tended to enlarge not only the total fund available but also the circle of contributors.

Another policy called for concentrating disbursements in wealthy and heavily populated areas in order to add force to the effectiveness of the gift. But there was also criticism of this policy because by the 1930s twenty universities were

	1889–1890	1899–1900	1909–1910	1919–1920	1929–1930	1939–1940	1949–1950	1959–1960	1969–1970
Resident college enrollment	156,756	237,592	355,213	597,880	1,100,737	1,494,203	2,659,021	3,216,000	8,498,000
Percentage of 18–21-year-olds in college		4.01	4.84	8.14	12.19	15.32	19.27	33.2	48.0
Staff, instruction and administration	15,809	23,868	36,480	48,615	82,386	131,152	210,349	298,910	551,000
Income*	21,464	35,084	76,053	172,929	483,065	571,288	1,833,845	5,786,000	21,515,000
Expenditures*					377,903	521,990	1,706,444	5,601,000	21,043,000
Value of physical property*	95,426	253,599	460,532	741,333	1,925,095	2,753,780	5,272,590	14,612,000	46,054,000
Endowment*	78,788	197,998	323,661	569,071	1,512,023	1,764,604	2,644,323	5,445,000	10,884,000

* Data in thousands of dollars (i.e., ooo omitted).

Statistics compiled from *Biennial Survey of Education in the United States, 1948–1950*, Chap. 4, sections 1 and 2, pp. 6 and 35 and U.S. Bureau of the Census, *Statistical Abstract of the United States, 1974*, 95th ed. (Washington, D.C., 1974), pp. 133–137.

For the further over-all financial picture, see Robert A Crummel, "The Development of Higher Education in the United States, 1900–1953," *Educational Record*, Vol. 38. October, 1957, pp. 320–328; and Seymour E. Harris, *A Statistical Portrait of Higher Education* (New York, McGraw-Hill, 1972) Chaps. 2.2, 2.5, 4.1–4.9.

receiving 75 per cent of all foundation grants, the remaining 25 per cent going to 310 institutions, leaving 700 others without any subsidy at all.[145] The General Education Board long made it a policy to disburse its funds by making additions to college and university endowments, but as costs mounted faster than additions it came to lose faith in this policy. In giving to public institutions the Carnegie Foundation for the Advancement of Teaching made it a policy to seek the consent not only of the institution's president and board of trustees but also that of the governor and even the state legislature. Perhaps this policy was reminiscent of Senator La Follette's refusal to let his state university, Wisconsin, receive foundation money because it was "tainted" by being derived from fortunes made through exploiting the American people.[146] As time passed foundations altered their policies so as to subsidize not so much institutions as ideas, such as Swarthmore's "honors" program or Minnesota's "General College." Here they were interested in demonstrating the feasibility of an idea and then pulling out, leaving it to local funds to sustain it.[147]

Large giving had continually to be supplemented with smaller gifts. Nearly every institution at one time or another put on endowment drives of its own. Usually these were directed at the alumni. Yale was the first, in the 1890s, to organize annual alumni giving. In the first solicitation 385 alumni gave $11,000. Thirty years later this giving was so well organized that upward of 8,000 alumni were giving close to a half million a year to the university.[148] By mid-century they were contributing millions annually. Other colleges and universities did not fail to take note.[149] But in spite of the best-organized efforts, the cost of higher education soared far more rapidly than did the rate of giving.[150]

If capital accumulated slowly among older institutions on the Atlantic seaboard, where population was concentrated and the chief commercial interests were situated, it accumulated even more slowly on the frontier. It is natural, therefore, that the Morrill Act of 1862 should have looked to the public domain for endowment of the new colleges of agriculture and mechanical arts to spring up there. Unfortunately land was cheap and could not be held for appreciation, as there was a generation in being needing higher education. Consequently the early sale of lands did not always bring the handsome endowment that was expected. Cornell was an exception. At the instance of its patron-founder Cornell postponed selling its scrip till it realized the exceptional sum of $5,000,000. Michigan and Oklahoma appear to have realized the next largest sums, nearly a million dollars apiece. Eleven states realized less than $150,000 and another six, unhappily, realized less than $100,000. More melancholy was the fact that in some states these funds were used for other purposes than higher education. Fortunately the states no longer in possession of their original funds have nonetheless paid their universities 5 per cent interest on them as if they had never lost them. Five per cent was the return required by the Morrill Act, but it was not always easy to make investments at that rate. Hence states had to find various ways to make up the difference between the actual rate of yield and the rate required by law.[151]

But even with the full 5 per cent yield there was little expectation that endowments were to be the main means of financing the expanding higher education of the middle western states. Indeed, with or without the supplementary income from land-grant funds, state universities were already tapping the much larger financial resources of public taxes. At first state universities depended on annual legislative appropriations to meet expenses. The main drawback with this method of support was that lay opinion in the legislature was often at odds with professional opinion in scrutinizing items in the university budget. This necessitated development of a university lobby at the state capital. Some presidents, like Charles Kendall Adams at Wisconsin, were eminently successful with their state legislatures. But it was a better arrangement from the university point of view when in 1873 James B. Angell persuaded the Michigan legislature to make an annual grant to the state university of 1/20 of a mill. This provision not only gave the university a more stable income on which it could count but it also enabled the university to transfer funds within its budget without always asking the specific approval of the legislature.[152] The resulting financial stability of the University of Michigan soon became the envy of other states such as Wisconsin and Minnesota, which ultimately adopted the same practice. Before the end of the century Michigan was granting 1/10 and Wisconsin at one time as high as 17/40 of a mill.[153]

While endowments and taxes bore the brunt of financing higher education, it would be a mistake to underestimate the importance of student tuitions. The average fee in 1860 was $31; in 1933 it was $238, a 650 per cent increase and more![154] As a matter of fact, there had been an almost continual rise in tuition during this approximate seventy-five-year period. The rise was relatively slow during the nineteenth century, but it mounted rapidly after 1900 and rose almost vertically after the First World War.[155] Between 1940 and 1960 tuition in public higher education doubled and in private higher education trebled.[156] Even with this steep rise in tuition fees, the president of Oberlin estimated that they paid only half the cost of a student's college education.[157] In other words, every student was enjoying a half-scholarship whether he needed it or not. During the depression and after the Second World War there was a tendency to question this practice. Some of the experimental colleges, such as Bennington, decided to make tuition pay the full cost of instruction.[158] Although there was provision for scholarship aid, the social implications of this move ran counter to long-standing American prejudices. A number of state universities, such as Missouri, had hoped to be tuition-free.[159] Even Stanford, a private institution, started on this basis.[160] If such founding fathers as Washington, Jefferson, Adams, and Madison did not go this far, they all did favor the public's bearing a large portion of the expense of higher education.

In the interval between 1930 and 1960 expenditures for higher education rose from 0.56 per cent to 1.12 per cent of the gross national product which itself increased from $91 billion to $502 billion in this same period.[161] And still colleges and universities did not have enough to pay the twentieth-century costs of higher education. As in the past, growth in numbers and educational offerings continued to outstrip income. But even worse, three forces unmentioned as yet were adding almost insuperable obstacles to balancing university income and outgo. First was the great depression of the 1930s. During this period enrollments jumped 20 per cent because industry and commerce were unprepared to employ the annual crop of high-school graduates. At the same time college and university income fell; stocks and bonds yielded appreciably less, and legislatures reduced taxes.[162] Second, the twentieth century witnessed two world wars. The credit inflation necessary to pay for these wars greatly reduced the purchasing power of university income, especially where it was dependent on conservatively invested endowment. In the decade 1940–50 it is estimated that government monetary policies cut this income in half.[163] These stringencies were especially hard on the smaller, weaker institutions, a situation silhouetted by the fact that less than a quarter of all institutions of higher education held 89 per cent of the total endowment of higher education.[164] But third, it seemed that perhaps the day of large adding to private endowment had run its course. Steep increases in both inheritance and income taxes to pay for modern wars and for dozens of new social services seemed to signal the end of the kind of philanthropy which inaugurated universities like Hopkins, Chicago, and Stanford and also added richly to the existing endowments of the private universities on the Atlantic seaboard.[165] In noting this trend of the times as early as the First World War, Nicholas Murray Butler sounded the alarm for higher education but to no avail.[166]

By mid-twentieth century the financial crisis in higher education was acute.[167] Noted as a cloud on the horizon thirty years earlier,[168] it now darkened the whole academic sky. With new sources of private endowment drying up, inflationary policies halving income, and tuition as high as it could go without turning away deserving young men and women, what was to be done? Some looked to increased subsidies from the federal government and, as already seen, were not disappointed in its unprecedented largesse.[169] Others preferred tax exemption as an indirect governmental subsidy to higher education.[170] Still others turned to private industry.

As industry benefited from the trained leadership of the college graduates it employed, so now industry was asked to defray some of the costs of that education as a legitimate charge against profits. During the Progressive era but especially during the great depression the public had become disenchanted with the American private corporation as a benign social influence. In an effort to rehabilitate their public image these corporations engaged in a kind of "welfare capitalism." Under this rubric they made charitable gifts to such organizations as the Red Cross and the Community Chest. In the 1930s Sears, Roebuck and Allied Chemical made similar gifts to higher education. Yet, generous as was this gesture of good will, the question lurked in the minds of many whether it was legal for a private corporation to share its profits with others than its stockholders. To settle this issue New Jersey in 1950 passed a law permitting private corporations to divert earnings from stockholders to eleemosynary institutions such as those of higher education.[171] Indeed, recognizing their indebtedness to higher education for the trained leadership it provided industrial and commercial corporations, leading industrialists formed the Council for Financial Aid to Education as a means of encouraging private corporations to give liberally to higher education. Through efforts of this council 207 companies contributed over $34,000,000 in 1956, $42,000,000 in 1958 and $50,000,000 in 1960. Some companies like General Electric and General Motors matched contributions of their employees to their individual alumni funds.[172]

Many institutions tried to augment their resources by improving their investment policies. Thought was given to the best form of investment management. Whereas formerly this had variously been the function of the board, a committee of the board, the president, treasurer, business manager, or some combination of these officers, it was now recommended that the full board be responsible but rely for advice on special investment counsel.[173] Thought was also given to the custom of investing institutional funds in well-secured equities such as bonds and mortgages. While security and assured income were at a maximum in such investments, they were subject to the infirmity of depreciation in times of inflation. To avoid falling behind in such times, modern investment policy called for larger percentages of funds in common stocks. Amherst was an interesting case in point. In 1875, 60 per cent of its productive funds were in bonds, 20 per cent in stocks, and the balance in a miscellany of real estate, notes, and the like. In 1924, bonds had mounted to 91 per cent with only 6 per cent in stocks. During the depression 72 per cent was still in bonds, while stocks had risen again but only to 17.5 per cent. By the middle of the war decade, bonds were down to 30.5 per cent and stocks were up to 63 per cent.[174] In 1967, however, McGeorge Bundy, president of the Ford Foundation, sharply criticized college endowment managers for their timidity and lack of imagination. He felt that universities had set their investment sights too low. In 1972, a new Ford Foundation study of the problem argued for more aggressive investment policy by university endowment funds, with the aim of securing higher rates of return. This might necessitate going more heavily than heretofore into volatile common stocks and even growth stocks.[175]

The situation was complicated by demands that began to be voiced in the early 1970s that universities recognize a responsibility for the social policies of the corporations in which they held stock. Thus, if certain corporations were engaged in racist policies, in pollution of the environment, or in the manufacture of products that were injurious to human health, it was held that universities should dispose of the stock they held in such organizations, or at the very least vote their proxies against the management. In 1973, Yale University responded to these demands by announcing that it would henceforth follow "ethical investor" guidelines in the management of its endowment. On the other hand, despite protests by black militants in 1972, Harvard University refused to sell its Gulf Corporation stock (Gulf was then operating in Portuguese-occupied Angola) and the result was mass picketing and a week-long occupation of the Harvard president's office.[176]

Problems relating to university endowments were only one aspect of a situation in the 1960s and 1970s which confronted American higher education with the gravest financial crisis in its history. This crisis was compounded of many elements. College enrollments, which had boomed following World War II, tended to level off. Colleges found themselves with openings for students that were not being filled. Contributing to this state of affairs were the increasingly depressed economic conditions in the country, the growing doubts among young people about the value of a college degree, the swiftly rising tuition charges which were pricing potential students out of the college market, and the larger role assumed by relatively inexpensive two-year community colleges. News that college graduates were encountering great difficulties in finding gainful employment in a recession-constricted economy also may have discouraged prospective applicants. In their desperation, some colleges sought to attract enrollments by flamboyant promotional techniques, radio commercials, direct-mail campaigns, and tuition rebates for students who were able to recruit others. Some institutions hired commercial recruiting firms which, for a fee, undertook to find students for them.[177]

Higher education's financial crisis was aggravated by the fact that operating costs, in an era of runaway inflation, tended to soar out of sight. Meanwhile contributions to the university exchequer from both public and private sources steadily declined. The full impact of this unhappy situation where costs were increasing at a much faster rate than available income began to be felt by many schools in 1967 and 1968. Earl F. Cheit observed that all of this happened, ironically, after American colleges had gone through a decade of unprecedented growth. He added: "Contrary to what might be expected, that growth had not protected the schools but may well have made them more vulnerable to a downturn. Many were undercapitalized, overextended, moving into enlarged areas of responsibility without permanent financing, or still raising quality standards. Because the increasing demands on the schools (both from without and from within) for research, for services, for access, and for socially current programs are an important part of the reason for cost increases, the cost-income problem is far more than the consequence of inflation, overextension, and an external economic downturn."[178]

Whatever the cause of the "new depression in higher education," its results were indisputable. A detailed on-site survey of the financial condition of forty-one colleges and universities prepared for the Carnegie Commission on Higher Education in 1970 found that 71 per cent of these institutions were either "headed for financial trouble" or were already "in trouble." Only those colleges representing less than one quarter of the nation's total enrollments were stated to be "not in trouble."[179] A similar study by the Carnegie Commission two years later did not discover notable improvement in the finances of these schools.[180] The hardest hit institutions were the private ones. Public higher education was more generously subsidized by this time than the private sector, even though the trend in many states was toward reduction of the annual appropriations earmarked for higher education.[181]

The cost situation, already bad, was made worse in 1973 and 1974 as the Arab oil embargo sent the price of fuel soaring and the worsening American inflation made food costs increasingly prohibitive. These developments inevitably threatened already shaky university budgets.[182] All across the country colleges strove to contain their expenditures by cutting down on services, reducing the size of faculties, making no new appointments, abolishing some departments outright, and discontinuing special programs. Some schools were obliged to sell off assets, dip into principal, postpone all salary increases, and boost tuition charges drastically.[183]

Young Ph.D.s, looking for their first college teaching jobs, were particularly hard hit. Many were unable to locate any kind of academic position.[184] The American Association of University Professors reported that it had received more than 1,100 complaints during 1973 from faculty members who had been dismissed from their positions. The University of Wisconsin sent out layoff notices at this time to eighty-eight tenured faculty members on nine of its campuses. Southern Illinois University dismissed 104 faculty and staff members, 28 of them tenured.[185]

Surveying this dismal scene, Clark Kerr, chairman of the Carnegie Commission on Higher Education, ventured the prediction that American higher education would run a $26 *billion* deficit by 1980, and that even if the federal government increased its aid to colleges substantially, these institutions would need to save at least $10 billion through retrenchment and increased efficiency to barely break even.[186]

Efficiency of Management

Colleges and universities had long sought to stretch their resources by trying to use what they had with greater efficiency. First steps were taken in this direction well before inflation, depression, and new tax policies took their toll of university income. As early as the first decade of the twentieth century there was some misgiving about the effectiveness of our institutions of higher learning.[187] New York State might have succeeded in laying down criteria of what a college must be to incorporate, but this still left unanswered whether any given institution satisfactorily met these criteria. First to raise this question seriously was Henry C. King of Oberlin in his annual report as president in 1908–09. Determined to do something about the matter, he had appointed a faculty committee to consider the problem. As a result of its deliberations the committee drew up a list of strategic questions to direct inquiry into a college's efficiency, and King made them part of his report.[188]

Although nowhere in this report did the word "survey" appear, nonetheless this action of Oberlin is generally taken to be the beginning of the survey movement in higher education. Shortly thereafter Virginia made a statewide survey of higher education, which it published in 1912. Flexner's famous report on medical education was the first instance of a survey of higher education national in scope. In 1910 the United States Bureau of Education appointed a specialist in higher education whose services were to be available for college and university surveys. Almost immediately there were a dozen requests on the bureau's docket, many of which were undertaken by the distinguished specialist Samuel P. Capen.

The popularity of the movement at the time is not difficult to understand. These years happened to coincide with the period when industry was making scientific studies of its own efficiency under the leadership of Frederick W. Taylor. They also coincided with the timely and contemporary development of scientific techniques in educational measurement.[189] As a matter of fact colleges and universities had engaged in self-studies before the twentieth century[190] but from its second decade onward it was possible to predicate administrative decision on much more exact data than formerly. Mobilizing and organizing such data became the function of bureaus of research which appeared as important adjuncts of the organization and administration of higher education after the First World War. By the Second World War and after, their activity assumed the name of "institutional research" and those engaged in it formed a professional Association for Institutional Research. Prior to 1955 only 10 institutions of higher education could boast this kind of administrative agency. Yet, less than ten years later 115 had them and through them were exploiting modern management techniques in the administration of higher education.[191]

The large educational foundations also had a hand in the drive for greater efficiency. Apparently President King drew his inspiration for a study of academic efficiency from attending a meeting of the Carnegie Foundation for the Advancement of Teaching, which was then considering criteria for determining which colleges were worthy to benefit from its pension plan. Because of the size of this and other benefactions it contemplated, the corporation wanted to ensure that it was aiding well-managed institutions and not shoring up tottering ones. Consequently it paid particular attention to financial management. On close inspection it found careless and slipshod practices far too widespread. Few institutions had cost-accounting systems.[192] Many failed to distinguish between educational and business budgets. Most regrettable was the failure of a number of institutions to draw a sharp line between endowment funds and funds for current expenses.[193] By refusing to aid institutions till these loose practices were tightened, the foundations added immeasurably to more efficient administration.

Another direction in which colleges and universities sought greater efficiency in the use of their resources was in the educational program itself. The vulnerable point here could be seen almost at a glance; it lay in the duplication of offerings, not so much within institutions as between them. States that supported more than one institution of higher education were particularly vulnerable, especially the states which had set up separate land-grant colleges instead of making their state university the beneficiary of the Morrill Act. For instance, the state university of course taught basic science. But the land-grant colleges frequently offered basic science also to undergird study in agriculture and engineering, to say nothing of some work in liberal arts, the province of the state university. Much the same problem arose where several institutions in an area each offered an expensive type of instruction—e.g., a school of veterinary medicine—when the area really needed only one such program.

State institutions of higher education had some difficulty in overcoming duplication. If savings were to be made, at the expense of which campus would it be? The competitive position of each institution did not make it easy to find an answer to this question. Furthermore, each institution usually had its own independent board of control and made its own independent approach to the legislature for funds. Toward the end of the nineteenth century, however, some states felt more and more frustrated in seeking their ends through autonomous or semi-autonomous institutions of higher education because of their competitive factionalism.[194] As this competitive factionalism increased in the twentieth century an energetic effort was made to overcome it by including higher education in the general tendency toward centralization of administration in state government, a movement which gained momentum after 1917 with Governor Lowden's introduction of the executive budget in Illinois.[195]

As applied to higher education centralization took two principal forms, an early one through existing governmental agencies and a later one through specially created coordinating boards of higher education. In the first category the earliest coordinating agency, if it may be called that, was the state legislature. Every time it created a new institution of higher education or enlarged the scope of an old one, wittingly or unwittingly it was planning the scope of institutions and their geographic distribution over the state. In the twentieth century, however, state functions had so broadened in scope and complexity that the governor supplanted the legislature as the chief coordinator of state services. The efficiency of his coordination depended in turn on a staff differentiated into such offices as budgeting, accounting, purchasing, and the like.[196]

In addition to the legislature and the governor many states have added a third echelon of coordination, a state coordinating board of higher education. These state boards have been roughly of two sorts. One is represented by North Dakota which as early as 1889 replaced the individual boards of its various state institutions of higher education by a single statewide board of control. Ten other states followed this precedent in the twentieth century, including Florida, Iowa, and Kansas. While they have stuck to this pattern of administration they have found that internal administration of individual institutions tends to claim the major portion of their time rather than statewide coordination. The other kind of state coordinating board, very popular after 1940, was a master board placed above the individual local boards which were left in operation. Oklahoma pioneered this model, followed by such other states as California, Texas, Illinois, and Wisconsin. Some master boards have chosen chancellors to be their executive officer.[197]

Coordination by these boards has had two dimensions, one vertical and the other horizontal. In the former the concern has been with the pyramid of educational programs leading from the bachelor's through the master's to the doctor's degree. In the latter the concern has been geographical distribution of academic programs over the state. Obviously, the problems of horizontal coordination easily extended beyond state boundaries to whole regions; hence the formation of such regional boards of higher education as the Southern Regional Education Board and the Western Interstate Commission for Higher Education.

At first state coordination and governing boards often directed higher education in rather *ad hoc,* even haphazard, fashion. They indulged in expediency, easing pressures in higher education where the shoe pinched. It was not long, however, before they saw the shortsightedness of such a policy. Consequently, instead of reacting to problems as they arose, boards tried to anticipate them before they emerged. Thus some states like California formulated "master plans" for higher education in their states. In these plans they tried to define the role and scope of existing institutions, lay down criteria for establishing new ones, decide on priorities for physical plant renovation and construction, and approve new programs, not in terms of local pressures but in terms of potential students and public need. It was not always easy to implement such blueprints. A proposal in 1971 for a similar master plan in New Jersey produced considerable public debate and angry responses from colleges which saw their programs threatened by it.[198]

A few states like Colorado and Ohio thought they could obtain the benefits of coordination by voluntary cooperation rather than statutory compact. Neither was notably successful.[199] More promising was the voluntary cooperation of the "Big Ten's" Committee on Interinstitutional Cooperation and regional associations of small private colleges such as the Great Lakes College Association.[200] Yet another kind of voluntary cooperation occurred between colleges located close together like the Claremont Colleges. Here were several independent liberal-arts colleges—Scripps, Pomona, and Claremont—which were close neighbors geographically. Because no one of them alone could offer a strong program of graduate studies, they united to pool their library and faculty resources for a single strong offering. The Quaker colleges of Haverford, Swarthmore, and Bryn Mawr cooperated to form a similar constellation.[201] These two federations of colleges bore some resemblance to the universities of Oxford and Cambridge, but neither was as tightly bound together as their English prototypes.[202]

Some thought they saw in these events the passing of the autonomy of the university. Protective bulwark that this ancient conception had been for the expertness of the faculty in the past it was now becoming an obstacle to statewide patterns of higher education. Whereas at one time many admired the constitutional autonomy of the University of Michigan, now fewer and fewer states revised their constitutions in this direction. Not only that but an increasing number of functions of higher education were coming to be administered from off campus. Indeed, universities were inviting outside agencies to help them with test services, setting standards, future planning, and the like. Just as the walls of the republic or guild of scholars earlier seemed to be collapsing, so the spirit of autonomy now seemed to be giving way to that of cooperation and coordination.

Universities employed other approaches to improve efficiency. With the rise of computer science following World War II, universities began to use computers to prepare their payrolls, process financial data, manage student records and schedules, prepare statistical reports, and turn out class lists. By the early 1970s some ten thousand computers were being used in various American educational institutions. A student of this development commented: "The computer may not produce improved institutional research, but it makes it feasible within existing economic, temporal, and personal constraints, thus fostering improved planning and resource allocation."[203]

One last attempt at greater efficiency needs mention, the more efficient use of physical plant. For long the system of two academic semesters, one commencing in the autumn and the other in the winter, reflected the exigencies of an agrarian economy where young men were needed summers on the farm. When the University of Chicago opened its doors just before the turn of the century it divided the calendar year into four academic quarters. Other colleges and universities followed suit coincident with the First World War in order to accelerate the academic careers of boys bound for the armed services. But when the war was over many institutions slipped back into the practice of semesters again. But year-round operation in either quarters or trimesters became popular again after the Second World War to meet the avalanche of students. Thus state legislatures preferred the added expense of year-round operation of existing facilities to that of erecting new ones operating on the semester plan. Besides that, the explosion of knowledge, requiring a broader curriculum and a longer term of study, also made time a precious resource to be conserved.[204]

Despite all the efforts by universities to improve their performance, dissatisfaction with that performance grew more acute in the 1960s and 1970s. The student disruptions on a number of campuses were widely publicized and led to public distrust of universities. It was a time when taxes were rising steeply while the income of business organizations and private individuals was shrinking. This led to demands that universities be made to justify what they were doing by proving the efficiency and effectiveness of their work. Coincidentally a movement had been gathering steam for years in business and government which stressed the importance of systems of quantitative analysis to aid management in fiscal matters. This approach correlated with a trend that had long been evolving in the field of educational measurement, namely, a heightened concern with precision, reliability, and validity in the handling of data. Management experts and educational measurement specialists were primarily concerned with the study of clearly observable phenomena, because only those could be reliably measured. With this goal in mind, branches of the federal government that made grants to higher education, state legislatures, and education departments came to demand a precise accounting of the results being attained by colleges and universities. Taxpayers shared this outlook. More than ever before, they demanded that universities be held "accountable," be made to justify the expenditures that society made on their behalf.[205]

Studies of university "productivity" and efficiency did little to reassure the public. One of these used growth in number of credit hours as an indicator of growth in instructional output and compared this figure with totals for instructional input. The conclusion reached was that there had been "no productivity change . . . in higher education over the time period" 1930 to 1967.[206]

Universities, thrown on the defensive by the accountability movement, found themselves more vulnerable than ever before because more of them were publicly controlled than ever before. In the early twentieth century approximately half the students enrolled in colleges and universities were in public institutions and half in private. By the 1970s, however, 76 per cent were enrolled in public institutions and only 24 per cent in private ones. Publicly controlled universities, by their very nature, had less autonomy and flexibility and tended to be more strictly accountable to voters, taxpayers, state officials, and federal bureaucrats.[207]

And what items were being placed high on the accountability agenda? David D. Henry, formerly president of the University of Illinois, saw them as "equal access to higher education for women and minority groups both as students and employees; cost regulation; managerial efficiency; codification of internal decision-making processes; behavioral accountability (the outcomes of learning); relevance of managerial technologies; and centralizing management while decentralizing educational functions."[208]

The most ambitious accountability effort during the early 1970s was that sponsored by the Western Interstate Compact for Higher Education. This organization set up a national center for higher-education management systems. By 1973 it was able to announce that some eight hundred institutions of higher education from all fifty states were participating members of the center. The center was subsidized by the U.S. Department of Health, Education, and Welfare and had a program that aimed to improve institutional management, perfect statewide coordination of higher education, and bring about improvement in decision-making processes relating to higher education on the national level.[209]

There was suspicion of the accountability movement on many campuses, even downright hostility. Quantification of academic work was "almost an alien concept" to many college educators and the introduction of workload surveys and other modes of statistical analysis to improve efficiency was strenuously opposed by them.[210] National scholarly associations also disapproved of this trend. The American Historical Association adopted a resolution that condemned attempts to control academic courses "through performance-based or behavioral objectives set unilaterally by outside agencies." Many of these critics of accountability in higher education wondered how the intangible component in college work was to be measured. As Chancellor William H. Danforth of Washington University put it: "None of us quarrels with pleas for increased accountability; however, none of us believes that the tools of cost accounting can quantify the life of the mind."[211]

The demand for accountability obviously raised the question of how much autonomy was feasible for the university in the 1970s. As John J. Corson phrased the issue, "Will society any longer entrust to an individual institution what are now socio-educational decisions, as well as the fiscal decisions of higher education?" A study committee at the University of Rhode Island believed most emphatically that society should continue to do so. In a report to the State Board of Regents in March, 1974, the committee declared: "The process of gradually establishing a workload reporting system which is based upon careful formulation of rules appropriate to each individual unit is necessarily slow, but it is . . . vastly preferable to any 'efficient' or 'simple' system that disregards the diverse objectives of a university which is engaged in liberal arts as well as professional and fine arts education, undergraduate as well as graduate teaching, and research as well as extensive public service."[212]

By way of rebuttal, Paul L. Dressel and William H. Faricy argued in a book published in 1972 that "the luxury of autonomy for individual institutions can no longer be tolerated." In earlier times, they asserted, such autonomy might have been appropriate because higher education then "was still in its adolescence" and also "numbers were not large, and usually limited to the elite." But in the present day, they declared, "higher education must be regarded as a state and a national resource and must be coordinated and controlled so as to fulfill the needs of society."[213]

Salaries and Pensions

After every effort to gain more income and to squeeze each cent from the purchasing power of the dollar, it was still necessary to confess to the financial undernourishment of higher education. Which item in the academic budget suffered most from decade after decade of undernourishment? Probably the largest item, faculty salaries. At a superficial and cursory glance faculty salaries seem to have been on the rise in the nineteenth century. In the second quarter of the century professorial salaries ranged up to $1,200, in the third up to $2,500, and in the final quarter up to $4,000 and beyond in a few exceptional cases such as the University of Chicago. But we have no careful study for this period which tells us whether this gradual rise represented an improvement vis-à-vis the purchasing power of the dollar.

Such a study, fortunately, is available for the next century.[214] It shows that average professorial salaries in state universities and land-grant colleges were $2,000 in 1904 and $7,000 in 1954. But when this apparently gratifying rise in salary was corrected by the purchasing power of the dollar, it turned out that in terms of 1904 dollars a 1954 salary of $7,000 was worth only $1,956, a melancholy decline of 2 per cent. Corrected salaries of assistant and associate professors showed actual gains of 3 per cent and 6 per cent respectively, with instructors gaining most, 38 per cent. But these gains were paltry compared with the 101 per cent for elementary-school teachers, 137 per cent for railroad firemen, 140 per cent for workers in automobile factories, 163 per cent for coal miners, and even 48 per cent for the sister profession of medicine. In comparing top executive salaries in railroading with top executive salaries in large universities for only the second half of this fifty-year period, it appeared that railroad presidents registered an 11 per cent gain while university presidents suffered a 26 per cent loss!

It is not easy to account for this comparative decline in the economic status of academic life. No doubt inflation and depression had their effect,[215] but these forces raised havoc with salaries and wages in other occupations too. Perhaps in part it was due to expanding college enrollments. A careful study at Yale showed that the university budget for salaries in 1918 was $468,232 and in 1927, $1,174,650, an impressive increase of 151 per cent. But while this increment was occurring the faculty grew from 159 to 294 members, an increase of 74 per cent. Nearly half of the enlarged salary budget, therefore, went into increasing the size of the faculty.[216] Looking beyond his own academic walls and suspecting deeper forces at work, President Hadley of Yale, himself an economist, claimed that faculty salaries were being pulled down because the supply of talent in the academic market outran the demand.[217] In part, he pointed out, the oversupply came about because universities were offering graduate instruction at a nominal price to any young man with a good college record who could show that he needed a subsidy. Thus universities appeared to be more interested in making it easy to enter the profession of college teaching than in making it worth while to stay there.

The law of supply and demand also had a qualitative dimension often overlooked, but not by William Graham Sumner, Yale's great political scientist. As early as the post-Civil War period he was complaining about the inferior talent that was going into college teaching. But what better was to be expected, he queried, when other occupations were paying more for the best talent? If the college offered remuneration below the market, it had to be content with second-rate men. Moreover, it was no excuse for the public to think of professors as a class of talented men who were willing to sacrifice fame and fortune for the opportunity to lead the intellectual life. "If such a class ever existed," wrote Sumner, "it is now extinct. The laws of supply and demand, of the relation between price and quality, rule here as everywhere else."[218] If professors were tempted to neglect their teaching to turn a penny on the side—a temptation of long standing, as nineteenth-century presidents Francis Wayland and F. A. P. Barnard could testify[219]—and if they were scorned as "yokels" or "pitiful proletarians"[220] in the twentieth century, the public had in part to bear the responsibility.

The more affluent colleges and universities sought to enhance the attractiveness of academic employment by offering a variety of "fringe benefits." Among these were group insurance and various plans for health insurance. Some, like the University of Michigan, gave its faculty periodic medical check-ups. Perhaps oldest among these appurtenances was sabbatical leave. Harvard initiated this paid leave of absence for travel, study, and research as early as 1880. The custom caught on slowly: only ten other institutions had followed suit by the end of the nineteenth century. However, as the twentieth century wore on more and more institutions decided to offer paid sabbaticals to their professors.[221]

Many other suggestions were made on how the professor should exert leverage on society to bring his economic status more in harmony with his social expectations. Many were favorably impressed by an idea of the economist Fritz Machlup. Through Committee Z he prevailed on the AAUP to set up salary scales by which to grade and compare colleges and universities as to mean, average, and median salaries at the various academic ranks. This committee saw it was useless to mount an aggressive attack on low salaries when an institution simply did not have the resources to pay better. On the other hand to show an institution whether it was in an A, B, C, D, E, or F category of salaries based on a national comparison could easily prick its pride into exerting itself to the utmost to move into a higher category with the added advantage of being able to attract a more talented faculty.[222]

In the mid-1960s, most American college teachers were not prepared to go beyond the Committee Z approach. By and large, they regarded trade-union tactics and collective bargaining as "unprofessional" and unsuitable for the campus. Then a change in attitude began to occur. Unquestionably, the worsening economic conditions in the country and in higher education brought this about. As college funds shrank, faculty positions in many fields became scarce and faculty salaries were frozen. Professors found that their salaries were insufficient to enable them to cope with the rampant inflation that beset the economy. The federal government was at the same time cutting back on the research contracts that had provided income for some professors. And as if this were not enough, attacks on the principle of tenure by legislative and public spokesmen were multiplying. Thus American college professors felt that they were being assailed on all sides with respect to their professional standing and job security. It was at this point that they began to consider the possibility of union organization with greater interest and sympathy.[223]

For many years, the National Labor Relations Board had discouraged collective bargaining in higher education; it did this by refusing to assume jurisdiction over cases involving nonprofit organizations. During the mid-1960s, however, a majority of the states passed laws authorizing collective bargaining by their public employees. At first it was thought that these measures did not apply to the faculties of public institutions of higher education, but a few years later it was established that they did in fact include college teachers. Then, in 1970, the NLRB ruled in a landmark case involving Cornell University that all private educational institutions with incomes of at least $1,000,000 were covered by the collective-bargaining provisions of federal law.[224]

With the new professorial interest in unionism and federal legal approval of this activity, three national organizations came forward to compete for the allegiance of college teachers. These were the American Federation of Teachers (an affiliate of the AFL-CIO), the National Education Association, and the American Association of University Professors. The AAUP had long held aloof from collective-bargaining activities, but in May, 1972, it reversed this stand and voted to "pursue collective bargaining as a major additional way of realizing . . . goals in higher education."[225] The whole situation on American college campuses began to change. Strikes by college professors, hitherto unheard of, began to occur with increasing frequency. In 1966 there was a large-scale walkout at St. John's University; in 1969 there was a particularly bitter one at San Francisco State College.[226]

By June, 1974, faculty members had selected collective-bargaining agents on 338 campuses; they had rejected collective bargaining on 29. The National Education Association (NEA) had won the largest number of these collective bargaining elections, 133, mainly because of the overwhelming edge it possessed in unionizing the staffs of public two-year junior and community colleges. The American Federation of Teachers was second in number of campuses organized with eighty, but again two-year colleges made up the bulk of its total. The American Association of University Professors had successfully unionized twenty-nine campuses by 1974; of these, twenty-six were four-year institutions. In the meantime, twenty states had passed laws specifically authorizing collective bargaining by faculty members at all levels of postsecondary education. This, naturally, served as a further encouragement to faculty unionism.[227]

Despite the flurry of union activity, many faculty members still sat on the fence, undecided whether to join any one of the competing collective-bargaining organizations. Indeed, it appeared that the majority of American college campuses would remain unorganized. Perhaps hesitant professors shared David Riesman's fear that trade unionism would dissolve the academic community and create in its place a "high-level civil service mentality." Others feared that the trade-union philosophy would make the faculty "employees" rather than leaders of the academic community. They would no longer be able to make good their claim that they should share with administrators the task of governing and developing the university, because an adversary relationship would emerge with the faculty always on one side of the bargaining table and the administration on the other. Then, too, some predicted that collective bargaining in higher education would inevitably move to statewide levels, thus further diminishing the autonomy of individual departments, schools, and campuses. Some of the ramifications of the question were well stated in a work that appeared in 1972: "Can professors truly share in a system of authority and responsibility for planning and carrying out the work of colleges and universities? . . . Or do they wish to stress the adversary relationship between themselves as employees and the organization's managers, not only using whatever bargaining power they can muster to compel the managers to increase their salaries but also conceding to management the entrepreneurial functions of assuming risks and deciding basic policies?"[228]

Another factor that influenced the economic well-being of American professors was the development during the first half of the twentieth century of various programs of retirement allowances. Columbia, Yale, and Harvard successively established retirement benefits in the 1890s, but it was not till 1905 that a more widespread system of pensions for college professors was inaugurated by Andrew Carnegie, the great steel magnate and philanthropist. Disturbed by the deplorably low economic status of the profession, Carnegie sought to elevate it by assuring its members the prospect of economic security in old age.[229] To this end he set up the Carnegie Foundation for the Advancement of Teaching with the princely endowment of $10,000,000, the income from which was to provide professors who had taught a minimum of fifteen years with a pension equal to 60 per cent of their salary at age sixty, and their widows with a pension equal to half of that.[230] Unfortunately, not every institution wishing to qualify its professors for such a retirement allowance could be recognized. Indeed, the diversity of institutions calling themselves colleges and universities, earlier encountered by the federal Bureau of Education, now plagued the foundation so that it was driven into the business of screening and classifying those whose professors were deserving of pensions.

By 1910 there were 215 professors from 73 qualified institutions receiving Carnegie pensions. In addition there were 53 widows. By 1915 the number of professors rose to 289 and widows to 95.[231] Actuarial studies undertaken during this period revealed that both benefits and beneficiaries were increasing more rapidly than the endowment could maintain at its original scale of disbursement. As it later became apparent, too, life expectancy was rising while interest rates were declining, thus deepening the crisis which was in the offing for the Carnegie pension system.[232] But in addition to being inadequate, the system was also operating unfairly. Many were disturbed that it operated heavily in favor of the larger and stronger institutions, of which an undue percentage were in the North, particularly in New England.

Moreover, it actually depressed salaries in some cases. Because of their inclusion in the plan some institutions were able to outbid nonmembers for the services of leading professors, but then took advantage of their bargaining position by offering lower salaries.[233]

This budget of difficulties added up to the necessity for a change in the principles of administering the pension fund. Obviously, the main difficulty lay in the fact that the fund was noncontributory and needed to build up a reserve. Consequently, in 1918 the Carnegie Foundation decided to reorganize its pension activities on strictly actuarial principles. With an added gift from the Carnegie Corporation for this purpose, the foundation incorporated the Teachers Insurance and Annuity Association under the laws of the state of New York. Under this new plan the professor made an annual contribution of up to 5 per cent of his salary to a future pension, and this contribution was matched by his college or university. This arrangement had the further advantage of being an annuity contract between the T.I.A.A. and the professor in which the employing institution had no equity and which could therefore be transferred whenever the professor changed positions.[234]

There was considerable outcry against this fundamental change of policy, even though the foundation agreed to carry out all obligations incurred under its former plan.[235] A committee of the newly formed American Association of University Professors was particularly loud in protest.[236] Nevertheless the T.I.A.A. went forward and proved so successful that institutions such as Yale and Harvard, which at first kept up their earlier individual pension plans, finally discontinued them in favor of the new system. The principles defined by the T.I.A.A. were essentially the same as those which were later followed in 1935, when the federal social security system was established. But even with this success it was startling to learn that as late as 1939 barely a third of the institutions qualifying as colleges and universities had funded plans for retirement income for their faculties.[237] This was in part compensated by the social security legislation of the federal government, yet even then the inclusion of higher educational institutions in the final legislation was almost omitted.

After mid-century it became evident that, popular as T.I.A.A. had become, it was unable to keep pace with rising prices in the postwar era. To remedy this situation C.R.E.F. (College Retirement Equities Fund) was brought forth in 1952 to complement T.I.A.A. This was a kind of investment trust into which professors were permitted to place up to 50 per cent of the contribution they and their institutions were making to T.I.A.A. By investing these funds in common stocks C.R.E.F. sought to hedge against inflation and thus increase the size of the professor's retirement annuity.

By 1970 T.I.A.A. and C.R.E.F. enrolled some 300,000 college teachers and administrators in their programs. These people belonged to the staffs of nearly 2,000 educational and scientific institutions in the United States. The reserves invested in these two pension programs totaled $2.5 billion by 1970. Alan Pifer, president of the Carnegie Corporation, declared that because of "the security that colleges and universities could offer to their faculty members and administrators" due to the contributions of T.I.A.A., "higher education has been able to a considerable degree . . . to measure up to the immense challenges it has faced."[238]

PART V

IN PERSPECTIVE

18

Distinguishing Features of American Higher Education

Higher education in the United States is today over three hundred years old. In the span of three centuries it has yielded a variety of forms—among them the New England hilltop college, the state university, the school of technology, the complex municipal college or university, the community or junior college. Each of these represents a significant stage in the growth of American civilization. Yet in the midst of this diversity we may well ask whether there are any features which distinguish the evolution of American higher education. We think there are such distinguishing features, possessing a common imprint—democracy.

European institutions had been evolving for many centuries in the soil of a well-defined culture with well-recognized and distinct traditions, traditions which governed the interrelated sphere of politics, religion, and society. Going back to the time of the ancient Greeks and from there forward to the Renaissance, Reformation, and Enlightenment, this European higher learning had the specific objective not only of transmitting to the next generation an intellectual heritage which was held to be valuable, but of training a select segment of the population to be an elite.

The American was impelled by every facet of his culture to transform this traditional system which he brought with him from the Old World, although he used it as the foundation stone of his own higher learning. His cultural pattern and intellectual climate had a greater simplicity, a greater democracy, precisely because they had arisen along the frontier of Western civilization in a dynamic era of industrial, scientific, and political change. The most acute foreign observers, from the time of Crèvecoeur to that of Tocqueville and Bryce, immediately saw that the American was in many ways a "new man." Of course, Europe was by no means immune to the shock of change implicit in the development of modern world civilization. Its powerful and constraining traditions, however, absorbed more of the impact than the freer and less inhibited American environment did.

In taking over the established forms of higher education from Western Europe, the American people have broadened and democratized them so that more and more persons have the opportunity to secure some form of post-secondary training. They have at the same time increasingly sought to make higher learning more functional and more closely related to the daily concerns of the average American, thus producing many new and unique developments, including a more flexible curriculum and a broader, more inclusive scheme of university organization. Moreover, they have not only broadened the clientele and curriculum of higher education but they have also broadened the concept of the college or university student himself.

The higher learning now addresses itself to the totality of his life, not just to its intellectual aspect. In short, American higher education as we know it today represents the end product of a long period of interaction between the Western European university heritage and the native American physical and social environment. From this process of transplantation and continuous adaptation have emerged those aspects of academic culture which we have come to recognize as "characteristically American."[1]

The process was slow at first, but gained momentum in recent times. Indeed, in the course of the past seventy-five years, as President Conant of Harvard acutely observed, "the forces of democracy had taken the European idea of a university and transformed it."[2] The resultant American system of higher education became essentially *sui generis*. It fused native and borrowed elements in a unique way to produce something new in educational history. The eclectic flavor of the ensuing product, as has recently been noted, is testified to by the fact that while democratic and utilitarian values inevitably gave tone to the entire structure, other outlooks, such as those of pure research and liberal culture, continued to exist (in somewhat modified form) within the framework and were not totally assimilated to the dominant ethos.[3] To explain this novel educational pattern further, we cannot do better than to examine a number of its most salient and distinguishing characteristics.

Popularization of Opportunities for Higher Education

As a consequence of the American commitment to democracy in education, more Americans by the middle of the twentieth century were taking some form of postsecondary training than any other people on the face of the globe. By 1956 over three million students were registered in programs leading toward degrees offered by American colleges and universities. Another million or so adults were registered in nondegree programs. According to the American Council on Education, 6,928,000 students were enrolled in various postsecondary programs in 1968. This total far exceeded that of any other nation and appears even more remarkable if expressed in terms of the percentage of the college-age population enrolled, which amounted to 43 per cent of the eighteen to twenty-one age group. This phenomenal growth in student population was a continuous process. From 1875 to 1950 American college enrollments doubled every fifteen years. During the 1950s and 1960s these enrollments approached an amazing 100 per cent growth rate for each decade. Then, as we have seen, they began to level off. Older institutions expanded their programs and founded new campuses to cope with the incoming student tide. New institutions arose seemingly overnight, still further popularizing opportunities for higher education. Fairleigh Dickinson University in New Jersey, founded as a tiny junior college in 1941, about the time Pearl Harbor was bombed, became in just a quarter of a century a large multi-campus institution with 20,000 students and a variety of programs.

The college population in the United States increased almost 1,000 per cent between 1900 and 1948, while the census of the total population showed an increase of only 100 per cent. In Great Britain the total population in 1948 was 47,000,000. If the same percentage of youth had gone to college there as in America, enrollment in British colleges and universities should have been approximately 800,000. Actually it was less than 80,000. The same situation was true in other countries; a much smaller percentage of eligible youth got higher education than in America. By the 1970s, only Japan, Canada, Australia, New Zealand, India, and the U.S.S.R. came anywhere near the United States percentage of mass involvement in higher education. We must, of course, make allowance for the fact that at least half of the American students—those in the first two years of college—would probably not be classified in Western Europe as being on the "university level." Nevertheless, the differential is remarkable.[4]

On the brink of adolescence Europe made a conscious separation of the small minority of youth who were to take a course preparatory for the university (and thus become the future elite of the country) and the great majority who were to go on for a time with a purely vocational, nonuniversity training. America rejected such rigid and open selectivity, whether based on superior intellectual ability or social position or both, but it was not until the twentieth century that the full consequence of this rejection began to become evident. By that time a "big change" was under way which amounted to the establishment of democracy in education in fact as well as in theory. The palpable proof was a tremendous expansion in numbers and in the proportion of eligible population in attendance on both secondary and college levels. The secondary education of the country was expanded and reorganized in terms of a single educational ladder and a "comprehensive" high school with more than 90 per cent of all eligible youth in attendance. The resultant pressure led to the development of a concept of "higher education for all" (or nearly all) with a steadily increasing percentage of the eligible population enrolled in some form of postsecondary training.

During the Second World War, Ralph E. Turner summed up the fundamental principle of American democracy as "the free access of all individuals to the full content of the advancing body of knowledge."[5] So devoted has the American become to this doctrine that attempts began to be made to protect this freedom by giving it legal status. New York in 1948 and Massachusetts in 1949 sought to maintain equality of opportunity for higher education by passing fair educational practices acts. Under the terms of these pioneering measures it became illegal for an educational institution to discriminate against applicants for admission "because of race, religion, creed, color, or national origin," or to make inquiries respecting these matters of applicants for admission.[6] In a nation as polyglot in its population make-up as the United States, legislation such as this indicated a serious intention to keep the doors of educational opportunity open as wide as possible for all qualified youth.

Despite such measures problems involving equality of opportunity for members of minority groups to secure a college education persisted in America in the middle of the twentieth century. There was, however, increasing evidence that real progress was being made in solving them. Thus in 1948 the American Council on Education found that despite the continuance of some discriminatory practices, 87 per cent of all Jewish students who applied for admission to liberal-arts colleges were admitted.[7] Also, educational opportunity for blacks expanded significantly for a number of reasons. For one thing, institutions for blacks such as Howard, Fisk, and Hampton began to place their graduate and professional programs on a more advanced basis. In addition, a number of Supreme Court decisions from 1936 to 1952 outlawed segregation or exclusion of black students at public institutions of higher learning. By 1953 it had became the law of the land that all states, North and South, must provide equal educational opportunities for blacks in their state universities. By that year all states, with the exception of five in the South, were admitting black students to their graduate and professional schools. Two years later, due to pressures of various sorts, 125 other institutions of higher education in the South, formerly all-white, including land-grant colleges, municipal colleges, and private institutions of all types, were admitting blacks. In addition, formerly all-black colleges were now admitting white students. At the same time more and more black scholars were attaining eminent positions on the faculties of leading American universities such as Columbia, Chicago, Minnesota, and Wisconsin, and black studies programs were added to the curriculums of colleges from coast to coast.[8]

The United States also went farther than most other nations in modern times in eliminating ancient barriers due to sex. Coeducation became much more the general rule in America than it was in Europe and elsewhere in the world. The numerous and excellent opportunities for women to secure higher education in the United States never ceased to amaze visitors from abroad. In the early 1970s Affirmative Action programs sponsored by the federal government sought to do away with all remaining instances of discrimination in American universities against women as students or as staff members. At the same time, the main effect of federal financial aid to higher education was to strengthen already powerful tendencies toward egalitarianism and mass education.

Broadening the Scope of Higher Education

The rationale under which this uniquely American venture in higher education went forward involved not only equalization of educational opportunity but another closely related and enormously significant principle, respect for all occupational groups. Needless to say, belief in egalitarianism was a helpful factor in inducing this respect. Thus the idea of an intellectual elite never took root in the United States because it defied deep-seated American traditions of the dignity of all work as well as the worth of each person. American democracy was willing to recognize that some individuals might be better at certain types of work than others. It was even ready "to respect the methods and honor the achievements of specially trained people."[9] It was not, however, willing to accept ancient notions of the scholar as belonging to a class apart from and above the mass of the people. It was not ready to accept the implications of the dualism of mind and body or materialism and idealism which some have seen in Plato's concept of the philosopher-king, in medieval scholasticism, or even in modern forms of "elitist" rationalism as represented by Babbitt, Foerster, and Hutchins.

James B. Conant has summed up the significance of this basic outlook which thus "almost unconsciously" shaped the growth of the modern American university as "none other than a philosophy hostile to the supremacy of a few vocations . . . a philosophy moving toward the social equality of all useful labor." Bringing this about was not only the tremendous expansion of secondary education but also the resultant greater heterogeneity in objectives and backgrounds of the growing army of applicants to American colleges and universities. Then, too, due to the increasing complexity of modern industrial life, the public came to demand more and more formal postsecondary education for more and more of its children. This obliged American colleges and universities to offer specific training for a host of vocations with which they had not been concerned and to place these fields on at least an approximate par with the more traditional specialties. Under these circumstances the word "profession" came to have a much more elastic meaning than ever before.[10]

The traditional European university had four great faculties—law, medicine, theology, and arts. It is true that this structure was somewhat broadened and diversified in the twentieth century, but in the United States there has been much greater divergence from the established pattern. American universities have demonstrated a much greater readiness to admit new and different fields of study as integral members of the academic family.[11] Schools of journalism, education, engineering, pharmacy, nursing, business, public health, agriculture, library service, and public administration came in the United States to be accepted as proper and accredited parts of the academic structure.

Without question, these new university faculties, many of them dealing with so-called "second echelons of intellectuality,"[12] serve areas of human life which are of the greatest importance. What, for example, has been more important in modern Western civilization than the development of business enterprise?[13] And what has been more vital, particularly in the United States, than the improvement of the nation's vast system of public elementary and secondary schools?[14] A similar argument could be made for the usefulness of university work in other new fields. Here "professions" and "semiprofessions" were arising out of what had formerly been trades and vocations. Like the more traditional fields, these new areas were proceeding to develop their own scholarly and theoretical basis by compiling a body of scientific data which could serve as a basis for constructive generalization and research rather than the merely empirical trial-and-error applications of trades.

From one point of view, this catholicity and adaptability of the American university has been interpreted as illustrating the pragmatic genius of the American people, their readiness to try anything new at least once if it only promised to yield valuable results. From another, it has been denounced as a deplorable excursion into vocationalism which would disintegrate the university as an organic whole, a "service-station" concept of education which was both unseemly and unscholarly.[15] But an important question arises. Were not the older professional curriculums which first arose during the Middle Ages also markedly "vocational"? Is not every important advanced study—whether law, medicine, or business administration—at bottom vocational? Such studies, including the liberal arts, would have questionable values if aimed at a disembodied culture and divorced from the realities and problems of this world. It nevertheless remained essential to make sure that all such specialized university curriculums were organized in a systematic way, with a definite theoretical structure and body of scholarly content. And American higher education had ever since the era of Eliot and Gilman been increasingly aware of the need to aim at the development of true "professions," not merely apprentice-type, trial-and-error vocations.

The Idea of Service

What distinguished the American idea of the higher learning from other modern conceptions of the university was not only its essential democracy, but even more its positive dedication to the service of an evolving dynamic, democratic community. To the English concept of the general culture of the educated gentleman and the German concept of scholarly research for its own sake, the American university added another dimension; namely, that higher education to justify its own existence should seek to serve actively the basic needs of American life.[16] It is precisely this aspect of American higher education which has made the deepest impression on European visitors. Some have seen this intimate relation of the modern American university to the sustaining community as closest to the ancient Greek concept of wisdom.[17] Lord Bryce, as we have seen, found it to be unique in the modern history of education.[18] Josiah Royce, the noted idealist philosopher, viewed this idea of service as representing not gross materialism and utilitarianism, but rather the highest form of idealism which was broadening and deepening the entire national life.[19] Charles McCarthy's *Wisconsin Idea* documents this kind of approach at great length. McCarthy, head of the Wisconsin Legislative Reference Library, played a leading role in revitalizing the University Extension Division in 1906. He was responsible for the legislation which in 1911 made this program the nucleus for an extensive system of vocational and adult education to serve the needs of the people of Wisconsin.[20]

There seems little doubt that American colleges have realized their ideals of service. They have never been isolated "ivory towers" but, rather, high "watch-towers." They have played a decisive role in the advancement of American democracy. They have furnished the professional training needed by a growing nation. They have contributed to the efficiency of its economy by making possible the specialization required by a technological age. They have helped advance man's knowledge of himself and of his universe. And, all the while, they have thus been increasing the health, wealth, and power of the United States.

Specific examples of this American emphasis on the social utility of higher education, on what has been called "intelligence-in-action,"[21] can be found in the research programs of the land-grant colleges, which seek to improve local politi-cal and economic conditions (as seen in the work of the agricultural experiment stations) and the carrying of the results of this work to the people (by means of the many flourishing university extension systems).[22] Discoveries produced by these means in the field of agricultural chemistry alone have added hundreds of millions of dollars to the annual income of American farmers and plant-food manufacturers. Another case in point, significant in the industrial age, has been the increasing activity of American colleges and universities in the crucial field of labor relations, trade-union problems, and workers' education.[23] In addition, American higher education has worked in close conjunction with the public-school systems of the land to produce coherence and national unity out of a great variety of immigrant groups. Due to their joint efforts, *e pluribus unum* became less of a vague ideal and more of a concrete reality as differences of origin were transcended in the opportunities of a new social mobility. Many of these service activities in colleges and universities were sponsored initially by the federal gov-ernment or by various state governments. The aim was to secure expert help in coping with a number of social, economic, health, and environmental problems. About the same time the great philanthropic foundations turned to the universi-ties for aid in solving similar problems. In order to advance knowledge in these areas, both the government agencies and the foundation managements sponsored the establishment of a network of specialized research centers, institutes, and laboratories on the campuses of the nation.[24]

In "applied" research, American ideals of service in higher education pro-duced everything from Salk vaccine to hybrid corn. But this does not mean that what has been called the area of "pure" research was overlooked. Here university scholars were busily at work on everything from atomic physics to Elizabethan literature. Indeed, there were few places in American society other than the colleges and universities where original researchers in the "pure" sciences or the humanities could find a living and a long-term subsidy. Increasingly, too, workers in the creative arts—music, poetry, dramatics, painting—found similar patronage in university grants or appointments.

Unsystematized Diversity

Closely related to our basic theme of democracy in higher education is the great variety of educational opportunities afforded by the different kinds of American colleges and universities. American higher education has never conformed to one uniform pattern, whether of organization, administration, or support. The Dartmouth College Case of 1819, the absence of a state church, the presence of a highly competitive denominationalism, and the deeply ingrained American suspicion of centralized power have all combined to produce educational diversity. There was never any one ministry of the central government in America, as in Europe, to establish norms of university procedure and control. Projects such as those calling for a national university always ran afoul of this aversion to concentration of power in any field, including higher education.

The result has been a relatively unregimented and unsystematized academic situation. The most diverse types of institutions of higher education have been founded in the United States, all claiming to be "colleges" or "universities." Among the nation's 1,855 institutions which were listed by the United States Office of Education in 1955 as deserving a place within that broad classification known as "higher education in America" were 732 liberal-arts colleges, 288 separately organized professional schools, 192 teachers' colleges, 505 junior colleges, and 281 municipal institutions. In addition to these, there were great complex universities, land-grant colleges, military institutes, and schools of technology.

This absence of monolithic structure in American higher education has provoked the ire of some critics, who have held that it has led to chaos, low standards, and scattering of effort.[25] It has been upheld by others as one of the strong points of American higher learning. Many years ago, President Gilman pointed out that diversity was a result of American dedication to the fundamental principle of local self-government and American freedom from political and ecclesiastical control. The United States preferred the lesser to the greater evil: If our universities were suffering from excessive spontaneity, as Gilman said, they were at least free from extreme forms of intellectual despotism.[26] William Rainey Harper, whose early form of "multiversity" in Chicago was labeled "Harper's Bazaar" by some of the irreverent, added that just as the universities of Cambridge and Oxford were an expression of English aristocracy, and those of Berlin and Leipzig were representative of German imperialism, so "the small colleges in Ohio and Missouri, in Iowa and South Carolina . . . are the expression of the democratic spirit, which is the true American spirit."[27]

Indeed, who can say that Harper was wrong? American educational diversity and localism certainly helped to broaden and democratize higher learning by opening college doors to large numbers of people who otherwise would not have been able to enter. For many Americans in varied economic circumstances it was not really a question of going to Harvard or Yale or to a small college, but rather of going to that small college or getting no higher education at all.

Obviously, higher education could not well have been organized in any other way in a country as vast and heterogeneous as the United States. And one can agree with the committee of the Association of American Universities which held that this situation had basic value since it reflected "the characteristics of a free society and of the role of higher education therein."[28] Diversity, said the committee, had furthered equality of educational opportunity, with all that this meant for American social mobility. It had made it easier to maintain freedom in general, and academic freedom in particular. It had afforded the opportunity for original and fruitful experiment, for the serving of the public need with a multiplicity of institutional types and academic programs, for a healthful competition which might never have existed under a more authoritarian and centralized system. As the committee noted, American educational history has been one of avoiding, wherever possible, dangerous concentrations of power.

The Role of Voluntary Cooperation in Setting Standards

In the absence of centralized control the responsibility for establishing standards in every branch of American higher learning and for coordinating effort has devolved upon various nongovernmental authorities. They have proceeded to take important action in these fields, on a local, state, regional, or national basis, entirely by means of voluntary cooperation, with little or no governmental dictation. Indeed, it has been remarked that voluntary associations of this type were essentially "an American equivalent of the official ministries which regulate education in some other countries."[29]

Many important things have been accomplished by this voluntary pooling of effort. Standards of work in both secondary and higher education have been raised by the establishment of accrediting associations. Ultimately six regional associations of this type have been founded, jointly covering the whole of the United States, together with twenty national organizations concerned with standards of training within specific professions. A National Commission on Accrediting was established in 1949. In addition, great philanthropic foundations working in the educational field, such as the Carnegie, Rockefeller, and Ford foundations, have by means of their donations been enabled to impel important and beneficial changes in both the administration and the course of study of American colleges and universities, while at the same time inducing a trend toward standardization at a higher level of efficiency in these fields.[30] National organizations which were concerned with advancing the interests of higher education, such as the American Council on Education, the Association of American Universities, the American Association of Land Grant Colleges, the Association of American Colleges, and the American Association of Junior Colleges, have played a similar role.[31]

The various scholarly societies of the nation have worked both separately in their own national organizations and jointly in associations such as the American Council of Learned Societies to improve standards of teaching and research in their respective fields. Special organizations such as the American Association of University Professors have had an important influence in leading to the introduction of more secure tenure provisions in colleges and other benefits for faculty members. The whole vital area of admissions to college has been vastly improved by the work of the College Entrance Examination Board and the Educational Testing Service.

The voluntary method, too, has led to outstanding progress in coordinating

American higher education. Examples of this can be seen in the Midwest Inter-Library Center; the joint university library in Nashville, Tennessee; the Lowell Institute in Boston; the University Center in Richmond, Virginia; the Institute for Nuclear Studies at Oak Ridge, Tennessee; the St. Louis Education TV Commission; and the graduate school program and University Without Walls undergraduate curriculum of the thirty-four-member Union for Experimenting Colleges and Universities, a group which included leading institutions from all across the country.[32] Even more important in setting a pattern was the Southern Regional Education Board, which was established in 1948. Here ultimately sixteen states compacted together to coordinate their systems of higher education so that uneconomical duplications of services would be avoided and more effective use of joint facilities would be made possible. Educational compacts of a more limited scope, but nonetheless following this precedent, were established by a number of far western states in 1953 and by the New England states in 1954. The net result of these agreements, as in the case of the other instances of voluntary cooperation which we have cited, was a general improvement of American higher education. At the same time, they led to a vast extension, on the national level, of bureaucratic patterns in university management. Thus, interestingly enough, essentially "voluntary" measures in America came to counteract, in the administrative if not the philosophic sphere, the diversity and lack of homogeneity in higher education and ultimately introduced a large measure of sameness and identity of structure.[33] In this connection, a foreign observer noted in 1972: "This standardization makes possible the integration of the system. There are practically no blind alleys in it. One can always transfer from one level to another, and it is easy to transfer from one institution to another, especially between degrees."[34]

The Corporate Structure of College Government

The democratic diversity of higher education in America has been especially evident in the varying systems of support and control that have developed in college administration. Fundamentally, of course, the situation followed the lines of dualism, with two great categories of colleges and universities growing up in America—the private and the state-supported—but there were important differences within each classification. In particular, the private sources of support for American colleges have been very diverse—individual, denominational, corporate, and philanthropic.[35] Of the 1,203 private institutions in existence in 1955, 723 were under the control of religious denominations (470 Protestant, 248 Catholic, 5 Jewish) and 480 were nonsectarian. The public institutions, in turn, were controlled either by local communities, the states, or the federal government.

A kind of balance of forces helping significantly to maintain the freedom which we have noted as a fundamental characteristic of American higher education resulted from the roughly equal importance that these private and state-supported spheres came to have. Of the total of 1,855 American colleges and universities in 1955, 1,203 were private and 652 public. However, the one-third which were publicly controlled enrolled three-fifths of the students. During the 1950s and 1960s subsidies from the federal government and increased expenditures on higher education by the states enlarged still further the public sector. In addition, the phenomenon of the quasi-public institution became an increasingly important one, particularly in large urban communities, as state and federal funds came to underwrite large portions of the budgets of universities which had formerly been entirely private.[36]

In any event, private benefaction has played a significant role in the history of American higher education. At times it has made possible valuable experiments, such as those launched by the donations of Johns Hopkins and Jonas Gilman Clark, experiments which might otherwise never have been initiated. Finally, the dividing line in America between public and private institutions of higher education has never been absolute. Private institutions have always been publicly chartered and regulated; some of them have even received public subsidies. Public institutions have likewise received endowments from private sources and have been obligated to take into account the opinions and attitudes of many nongovernmental groups. As we have seen, this blending of public and private characteristics became pronounced by the time the Higher Education Act of 1965 and the major amendments of that act in 1972 were written into the statute books, and the effect of this legislation was to make such distinctions less sharp than ever before.

Whatever the type of private or public support and control which came to prevail in American colleges and universities, they nearly all ultimately followed the same characteristic form of college government. This involved government by corporate boards of nonresident trustees and by resident administrative officials known as presidents. It contrasted sharply with systems of academic government in England and Continental Europe, where either the immediate faculty or some more remote governmental or ecclesiastical authority exercised decisive control. Since American college boards of trustees were nonresident, they were obliged to delegate a large part of their power over the more immediate problems of academic administration to college presidents, who thus came to possess important continuing authority. Thus was born a new kind of official in the history of higher education, much more powerful than the English "vice-chancellor" or German "prorector." Indeed, to some foreign observers the American college president's powers have seemed too autocratic.[37] However one interprets his role, in the American type of academic government it has been decisive: An Eliot or a Gilman could make his university world-famous; a poor president could set his school back for many years.

As early as 1905, Henry S. Pritchett, president of the Carnegie Foundation, noted that American colleges and universities were conducted under an administrative system which was closer in form to that of a modern business corporation than to anything else in the history of higher learning.[38] There were the same boards of trustees, the same professional executives, as in large corporate enterprises. Although Pritchett was correct in pointing out that modern American academic government came to utilize many of the managerial techniques developed by the business world, it is also important to note that the colleges in other respects reflected in their system of organization the atmosphere of democratic control and freedom which gave higher education in the United States a distinctive cast. Thus the pattern of government by nonresident trustees or regents rather than resident faculty members was in large part based on the philosophy that in this way a broad representation would be given to the interests and views of the sustaining community. Members of these corporate college boards customarily served voluntarily without pay, regarding their work as a form of public service. It was this system which furthered the close relationships between the college and the democratic community so characteristic of American higher learning.

In the second place, no one agency of American college government, not even the board of trustees, was able under ordinary circumstances to wield absolute power. Just as in the federal government, a rough system of checks and balances emerged.[39] Boards of trustees and professional administrators tended to check each other. As if this were not enough, both had to reckon with the growing power of organized faculties (which were coming to exercise varying degrees of control over a wide range of administrative matters), organized alumni (who were increasingly represented on advisory councils and important academic boards), the general public (with its many pressure groups, whose favorable opinion was vital to the progress of any American institution of higher learning), and, finally, the student body, which in the 1960s and 1970s began to play an influential role in academic governance with the rise of "participatory democracy."[40]

All of these checks and balances *within* college government were reinforced *without* by a diversity of institutional types in American higher education which struck a balance of forces, preventing the predominance of any one of them. Also important in this regard was the fact that, as we have seen, educational standards were being set and policies formulated by dozens of agencies of voluntary cooperation. We are thus presented with the picture of a system of college and university government whose main emphasis is on initiative rather than uniformity, freedom rather than constraint, responsiveness to the public will rather than imposition by remote authority.

The Place of the Extracurriculum

The higher learning in the United States has always been organized for informal "education" as well as formal "instruction." It has come to be interested in "the whole student"—in forming character as well as intelligence, in preparing men and women to be desirable citizens and persons as well as specialists and savants. Here, again, we may well see in this unique "college life" the powerful influence of the democratic American community upon patterns of higher education. Certainly these characteristics mark off American student life from that of Continental Europe and even from that of the parent universities in England.[41]

At Oxford and Cambridge "college life" was traditionally considered to be an integral part of baccalaureate training, but it was never developed on the organized basis which became true in America. One modern British observer, noting this difference, has interpreted the activistic life of the American campus—the "big-time" intercollegiate athletics, the publications, the fraternities—as resulting from the serious need for socialization and acculturation in a democratic, mobile, heterogeneous nation.[42] This informal side of the higher learning has, however, helped to make the American college more popular with the community than has been true in many other cultures. More than elsewhere, college graduates in America have come as a result of this "college life" to identify themselves closely with their alma mater, to take a personal pride in its progress, and, most important, to work actively as organized alumni for its financial benefit. Visitors from foreign universities have noted this phenomenon with more than a touch of envy.

In the early twentieth century, many observers of the American college scene felt that a deplorable gap was opening up between the curriculum and the extracurriculum. It was even suggested that these two main aspects of the modern American college—the intellectual and the socio-athletic—which had worked in harmony in earlier, simpler times, were now working at cross-purposes and producing a war of campus versus classroom.[43] After the First World War, however, attempts were made to produce a new synthesis of the principal elements in American college life. The role of the rapidly expanding student personnel movement was vital in this connection. Largely as a result of its "personalistic" point of view, a number of important specialized services were developed to help the individual student in every phase of his college career. This new concern for the totality of the student's life was illustrated by the rise of health and employment services, better housing arrangements, personal and educational counseling, and intramural sports for all. It was evidenced also by the revival of interest in ethics and religion, by the reconstruction and reformation of fraternities and sororities, by the rise of student "unions," and by the introduction of plans of student government. Efforts were made by college administrations to link the work of the classroom with the life of the campus, whether in dormitory and residence hall, student newspaper office, playing field, or college theater.

The widespread, and sometimes violent, student unrest of the 1960s and early 1970s, with accompanying development of a youth "counterculture," illustrated graphically how difficult it would be to synthesize a unified and coherent college life that would serve the needs of the young people of the later twentieth century. Indeed, two sociologists speculated at this time that the very increase in the autonomy of the modern student, with the resultant reinforcement of "permissive and supportive aspects of the socialization environment," actually contributed to the disturbances and the stresses and strains which appeared on many campuses.[44] In any event, university leaders redoubled their efforts to make all dimensions of the campus experience more meaningful to the often questioning and skeptical student.

Concluding Estimate

In September, 1774, Barnabas Binney, A.B., valedictorian at the public commencement of the College of Rhode Island, predicted that his alma mater (and the other colonial colleges) would bring forth "her sons of genius and virtue; till she had covered the earth with a glorious race of American Homers, Ciceros and Newtons, who shall bless mankind, and raise her fame above old Athens."[45] Looking back from the vantage point of the twentieth century, we may well ask: Has the history of American higher education justified the high hopes of Barnabas Binney and his generation?

If we look at the positive contributions made by the colleges to the training of the nation's leadership, the maintenance of democratic opportunity for equal access to and popular utilization of knowledge for the public weal, and the untrammeled freedom for innovation and experimentation which have flourished, our answer cannot be any other than an unequivocal "yes!" From the early nineteenth century down to the period following the Second World War, studies of the social and economic structure of the American culture have revealed that the persons of achievement, the persons who held the key positions, were in the majority of cases college graduates.[46] The significance of this fact is that it does not reflect, as has traditionally been the case, the power structure of a caste-ridden society. On the contrary, this leadership by the college-educated has gone forward in a nation where opportunities for some kind of postsecondary training have been made more readily available to the great masses of the people than anywhere else in the world. American higher education, far from reinforcing caste, has helped to foster social mobility; instead of ratifying the recruitment of an elite by ascription, it has thrown its influence in the direction of the selection of a leadership by achievement.

The very freedom of American higher education, its diversity and absence of enforced unity, has been attacked as making for a lack of coherence. This situation was seen as one making possible the invasion of quackery of all kinds, "wild, uncontrolled, and uncritical expansion."[47] Critics were worried by what they saw as an "indiscriminate faith in magnitude and development," an excessive materialism, an absence of qualitative standards which ignored the able and intelligent, a turning away from the past to concentrate upon the pressing claims of the present and the dreams of a golden future.[48] While there are elements of truth in this critique—not all of American higher education has actually been "high" in every respect—a balanced review of higher learning in the United States suggests that the indictment is considerably overdrawn.

There have been qualitative triumphs in America as well as quantitative ones. Moreover, how can we be sure of a valid measure of such a perplexing intangible as "intellectual quality"? In any case, it might be argued that the immense vitality and force generated by American institutions of higher learning itself constitutes a pattern. They have given the world an example of tremendous drive and venturesomeness, great energy, verve. The ceaseless renovation and expansion of the curriculum, the fruitful experimentation with new methods of teaching, have been made possible by the absence of mandatory conformity, by the healthy rivalry which has existed between states, municipalities, religious denominations, and private groups of every type, all working in the field of higher education. More might be lost than gained by attempting to impose an artificial coherence on these diverse institutions. Assuredly this would be the case if the attempted new synthesis robbed the American system of its flexibility.

Foreign visitors have noted many of the dominant characteristics of the American university which we have catalogued. They have been impressed by the local autonomy which prevailed in higher education and the freedom of initiative. They have admired the superior physical equipment and plant of New-World institutions. They have found American professional training superior in certain fields to that in their own countries. They have taken note of the extensive public support given to higher education in the United States and the continuing interest which organized alumni groups manifested in the welfare of their alma maters. They have praised the technical superiority of American university libraries and laboratories. They have been interested in the many services provided for American students by the personnel movement. They have observed with approval the thoroughgoing democracy and equality of opportunity which animated American higher learning and the semireligious dedication of the people to the values of formal education. They have seen American colleges and universities as contributing to the life of the Republic the things it most needed—higher political standards, liberal culture, and a desire to ameliorate social injustice.[49]

These observers did not approve everything that they saw, however. One criticism which keeps cropping up in their published commentaries alleges a lack of genuine individualism in the life of American undergraduates. There was too much complacency and self-satisfaction among American youth, too little independence of opinion. There was too much "babying" of college students, too much standardized teaching and learning which emphasized externals rather than the inner spirit of learning.[50] There was not "the eager desire to understand the universe which keeps the Oxford undergraduate awake o'nights, the teacher's anxiety to embark upon a great subject and make it his own."[51]

Some of these visitors thought that they detected an American tendency to emphasize physical equipment and monumental buildings at the expense of individual scholars and teachers of pre-eminent ability. The salaries of American professors were too low and their social standing was not high. In too many cases, university professors were regarded as mere schoolmasters, rather than as advocates of knowledge.[52] The Continental European observer was impressed by the problem of status because the situation of American college teachers contrasted somewhat with that of his own university professors, who, being government "officials," had approved social standing comparable to that of diplomats and civil servants. Fundamentally, this more honorific position had in the past derived from the hierarchical structure of European society, with its feudal and monarchical tradition, but by the 1970s powerful forces of popular unrest and social change were circumscribing, or at least redefining, the professor's role in many countries.[53] The American democracy, with its egalitarian national heritage, had never recognized a superior caste, and certainly not a professor's caste.

More to the point than the issue of social prestige was the question whether the American attitude led the New World to undervalue pure scholarship, whether inside or outside the university. Some commentators have insisted that this was so. They have argued that the American university environment was not as favorable a place as Europe for the development of original scholars; that the young American Ph.D. entered into a world which did not care for his creative work unless it had some immediate practical applications.[54] Unquestionably there is some truth in this analysis. America has been so predominantly a pioneering, pragmatic culture that its higher learning has inevitably in past times tended to center its attention on creating an active and useful intelligence. This did not always create the best setting in which to develop scholarship for its own sake, to originate great theoretical insights into the foundations of knowledge. Yet even the most pragmatic culture depends fundamentally upon such insights for its effective progress.

In a sense, America had lived for many years on the "borrowed capital" represented by the important theoretical insights which she imported from Western Europe. With the founding of Johns Hopkins, America took steps to develop her own original thinkers. There remained, of course, even among people like Gilman, a suspicion of "genius" if it was linked to excessive eccentricity or unconventionality. "It is neither for the genius nor for the dunce," asserted the president of Johns Hopkins, "but for the great middle class possessing ordinary talents that we build colleges."[55] Be that as it may, it is a fact that the research methods of Europe were enthusiastically adopted by American universities. Men of mark in the world of original thought began to come forward from American academic halls—Willard Gibbs, Benjamin Peirce, Asa Gray, William James, Thorstein Veblen, John Dewey. The American university "became the principal home" of American science. In the early twentieth century, great educational foundations poured forth vast sums to subsidize extensive projects of cooperative research. Some, indeed, have felt that this institutionalized, organized, technically efficient approach was in itself an expression of the American spirit in the realm of scholarship. The founding of the Institute for Advanced Study at Princeton, New Jersey, in 1933 gave evidence, not only of an intention to shelter refugee scholars fleeing Hitlerite oppression, but also of a desire to provide a center for study for the native generation of original scholars which had arisen in America.[56] In the middle of the twentieth century, with the dramatic impact of the launching of the Russian Sputniks, American higher education began to enter a period of profound soul-searching. Had it perhaps been too immediately utilitarian in its emphasis? Could a truer balance on the whole question of original scholarship be established? Many began to ask whether American academic culture could not, while retaining its valuable emphasis on "intelligence-in-action," make a larger place for original thought and investigation. Some even felt that national survival itself depended upon such a development.

A dramatic example of the progress of advanced scholarship in America was afforded by the flourishing of postdoctoral work, often aided by government subsidy, in the years following the Second World War. This area expanded to such a degree that it might almost be called a "fourth level" of American higher learning, superimposed on the pre-existing layers of baccalaureate, masters, and doctoral training. By 1959, no less than 151 postdoctoral programs were being offered at 40 universities in the field of psychology alone. A considerable number of postdoctoral fellowships were being awarded at this time, most of them in the sciences.[57] At Columbia University, the University Seminars furnished a vehicle for a "Community of Scholars" to explore a wide range of problems.[58] Such organizations as the National Science Foundation, the Atomic Energy Commission, and the National Institutes of Health were particularly active in the 1960s and 1970s in subsidizing advanced study and research on the postdoctoral level. As the National Institutes of Health began large-scale subsidization of medical research, university medical schools became the chief recipients. As the Department of Health, Education and Welfare began to make large sums available to finance studies in public health, welfare, and related social areas, the bulk of these funds went to the universities.[59]

One trend of the last fifty years seems indisputable. As the United States gradually attained importance as a global power, her higher education similarly acquired more and more of a global significance. This has been signalized in various ways. American missionary efforts resulted in the establishment of outposts of higher learning in Turkey, Lebanon, Syria, Africa, China, Japan, and Egypt. The American School of Classical Studies in Athens, Greece, did important research work in the field of antiquities. Thousands of young people began to come to study at American universities from Europe, Asia, Africa, and Latin America.

As early as the period 1865–85, more than 230 Japanese came to study in American universities. After their return to Japan, 51 per cent of these students came to occupy positions of leadership and made an important contribution to the Westernization of Japanese governmental, business, and academic life. American educational influence during these years induced Japan to set up an American-style single-track school system. During World War I the same type of influence contributed to the passage of the University Act of 1918, which gave official recognition to private institutions. American impact on Japanese education reached its maximum after 1945, during the post-World War II occupation period.[60] In 1948, just before the Communist triumph in China, there were no less than thirty institutions of higher learning of American origin in that country. Four of these were medical schools.[61] In the Near East, American institutions such as Robert College in Turkey, Aleppo College and Damascus College in Syria, the University of Baghdad in Iraq, the American University of Beirut, Lebanon, and the American University of Cairo, Egypt, played a significant role in the educational development of the region.[62]

Already, by 1908, there were 1,500 foreign university students in the United States; by 1932, there were more than 10,000 of them. International Houses were erected in New York, Chicago, and Berkeley to shelter them. In 1948 there were 25,464 foreign students in the United States. This figure climbed to 47,245 by 1958. In the 1960s, Fulbright scholarships and the Agency for International Development Grants produced a sharp increase in these numbers. The foreign student population began to grow at the rate of ten thousand a year and by 1970 the Institute of International Education reported that it had reached an all-time high of 144,708.

In turn, American students and professors in ever larger numbers went forth to study and do research in foreign lands. In 1972, 32,148 Americans were reported to be studying abroad. No longer did they concentrate predominantly in one country, as they had in nineteenth-century Germany; now they could be found all over the world. After World War II, American universities began to set up their own centers[63] for overseas study in distant areas. In 1964, Fairleigh Dickinson University acquired Wroxton Abbey in England, once Lord North's country seat, as a center for English studies. In 1966, Stanford University opened a center for the study of British culture at Harlaxton Manor, Grantham, in Lincolnshire, its fifth European campus. By this date, there were nearly a dozen American university centers in Italy. Exchanges of students and university scholars between the United States and other countries were stimulated most notably after the Second World War by the enactment of measures such as the Fulbright Act and the Smith-Mundt Act.[64]

The global significance of American higher learning can be seen, too, in the growing influence upon world thought of scholars such as William James and John Dewey.[65] In addition, American influence appears to have played a positive role in the 1898 reorganization of French universities, which established a new doctorate in an effort to combat the international influence of the German university.[66] Furthermore, Great Britain and France, following the First World War, established new graduate degrees for the openly professed purpose of attracting more American students. Oxford, for example, established the degree of D.Phil. in 1917 as a result of a "broad hint" from the British Foreign Office that such action was necessary to rival German educational influence and attract foreign students (particularly Americans). The other British universities soon followed suit. For her part, France, in 1921, threw open to foreigners all of the state doctorates in her universities.[67] The British authorities, indeed, were so eager to attract representative students from the United States that Oxford about this time even abolished one of its requirements for the Rhodes scholarships, namely, the examination in Greek. Only 1 per cent of American college students in 1920 were studying Greek. Cambridge, in turn, followed this measure by abolishing its requirement of Greek for some of its degrees. This, too, was expected to induce more American students to come.[68]

In closing, we may confidently express the feeling that American higher education has by no means even yet arrived at an equilibrium. It remains in a state of dynamic evolution, much like the culture which surrounds it and sustains it. To be sure, the main themes of democracy and responsiveness to change stand out in bold relief for all to see. But as mankind explores the new horizons of the space age we can more validly than ever echo the statement of David Starr Jordan over seventy years ago: The true American university lies in the future.[69]

Notes

1. Beginnings

1. Before 1646, nearly one hundred Cambridge University men had come to New England, together with about thirty Oxford graduates.
2. Samuel Eliot Morison, *Founding of Harvard College* (Cambridge, Mass., Harvard University Press, 1935), pp. 5, 25–26, 40, 47, 127, 337.
3. Clifford K. Shipton, *Biographical Sketches of Those Who Attended Harvard College in the Classes 1722–1725* (Boston, Massachusetts Historical Society, 1945), p. 36.
4. Courtlandt Canby, "A Note on the Influence of Oxford University on William and Mary," *William and Mary Quarterly*, Series 2, Vol. 21, July, 1941, pp. 243–244.
5. Burns B. Young, "What Is a College?" *Educational Record*, Vol. 30, October, 1949, p. 404. The thesis forms used at the first Harvard commencement followed those of Edinburgh so closely and were so radically different from those of contemporary Oxford and Cambridge as to suggest that they may have been directly borrowed from the Scottish institution.
6. A. Bailey Cutts, "Educational Influence of Aberdeen in 17th Century Virginia," *William and Mary Quarterly*, New Series, Vol. 15, July, 1935, pp. 236–241, 242–243, 248–249; Charles F. Thwing, *History of Higher Education in America* (Englewood Cliffs, N.J., Prentice-Hall, 1906), pp. 56–57.
7. Hastings Rashdall, *The Universities of Europe in the Middle Ages* (Oxford, Clarendon Press, 1895), Vol. II, pp. 370–388, 464–518.
8. John Tate Lanning, *Academic Culture in the Spanish Colonies* (New York, Oxford University Press, 1940), pp. 3–17, 22–33; Jerome V. Jacobsen, S.J., "Educational Foundations of the Jesuits in Colonial Hispanic America," in Herbert E. Bolton, *Greater America* (Berkeley, University of California Press, 1945), p. 122.
9. John George Bourinot, *The Intellectual Development of the Canadian People* (Toronto, Hunter, Rose, 1881), pp. 24–25; Richard M. Saunders, "The Cultural Development of New France before 1760," in Ralph Flenley (ed.), *Essays in Canadian History* (Toronto, Macmillan, 1939), pp. 325–327; Francis Parkman, *The Old Regime in Canada* (Boston, Little, Brown, 1901), pp. 221–223.
10. George H. Williams (ed.), *The Harvard Divinity School* (Cambridge, Mass., Harvard University Press, 1954), pp. 298–299.
11. Samuel Blair, *An Account of the College of New Jersey* (Woodbridge, N.J., James Parker, 1764), pp. 5–7.
12. A good illustration of this intellectual position is to be found in an address delivered by President Charles Chauncy of Harvard College in 1655: "Gods Mercy, Shewed to his People, in Giving them a Faithful Ministry and Schools of Learning for the Continual Supplyes Thereof."
13. Perry Miller, *The New England Mind: The Seventeenth Century* (New York, Macmillan, 1939), pp. 75–79, 85.
14. Williams, *op. cit.*, pp. 241–245, 300–304, 344–345, 348–350.
15. Frederick B. Tolles, *Meeting House and Counting House, The Quaker Merchants of Colonial*

Philadelphia 1682–1763 (New York, Norton, 1948), pp. 150–153.

16. Colonial Society of Massachusetts, *Collections,* Vol. 15, Harvard College Records, I, p. 24.

17. Herbert B. Adams, *College of William and Mary,* U.S. Bureau of Education, Circular of Information No. 1, 1887.

18. Shipton, *op. cit.,* pp. 44–45. This same president, Thomas Clap, made life as uncomfortable as he could for Episcopalian students at Yale. He maintained that he could not give privileges to students who regarded his own clerical gown as a forgery. He began to be more liberal in 1765, when he permitted non-Congregational students to attend Sabbath services of their own denomination. He was careful to add, though: "Yet, if . . . any should take Pains to infect the Minds of their Fellow-Students with such pernicious Errors, as are contrary to the Fundamentals of Christianity, and the special Design of founding this College so that Parents should justly be afraid of venturing their Children here it is probable that some Notice should be taken of it."

19. Alison B. Olson, "The Founding of Princeton University: Religion and Politics in Eighteenth-Century New Jersey," *New Jersey History,* Vol. 87, Autumn, 1969, pp. 133–150.

20. For the declared purposes of the various colleges, see Thomas J. Wertenbaker, *Princeton, 1746–1896* (Princeton, N.J., Princeton University Press, 1946), pp. 11–21; Dorothy R. Dillon, *The New York Triumvirate* (New York, Columbia University Press, 1949), pp. 31–34, 38–40; David McClure, *Memoirs of The Reverend Eleazar Wheelock* (Newburyport, Mass., E. Little & Co., 1811), p. 62; Walter C. Bronson, *History of Brown* (Providence, R.I., Brown University Press, 1914), pp. 4–5, 14–33; William H. S. Demarest, *A History of Rutgers College* (New Brunswick, N.J., Rutgers University Press, 1924), pp. 75–76.

21. Henry Van Hoesen, *Brown University Library* (Providence, R.I., 1938), pp. 32–34.

22. For these colonial charters, see Bronson, *op. cit.,* pp. 1–4; Wertenbaker, *op. cit.,* pp. 11–12; Blair, *op. cit.,* pp. 7–10.

23. Beverly McAnear, "College Founding in the American Colonies, 1774–1775," *Mississippi Valley Historical Review,* Vol. XIII, June, 1955, pp. 24–26; Robert L. McCaul, "Whitefield's Bethesda College Project and Other Attempts to Found Colonial Colleges," *Georgia Historical Quarterly,* Vol. 44, September, 1960, pp. 270–277; *ibid.,* December, 1960, pp. 381–398.

24. James B. Conant *et al., History and Traditions of Harvard College* (Cambridge, Mass., Harvard Crimson, 1936), p. 14.

25. Richard Hofstadter and C. DeWitt Hardy, *Development and Scope of Higher Education in the United States* (New York, Columbia University Press, 1952), pp. 7–8; A. Meiklejohn, *The Liberal College* (Boston, Marshall Jones, 1920), pp. 16–23.

26. Shipton, *op. cit.,* p. 34.

27. Willard Smith, "Relations of College and State in Colonial America" (unpublished doctoral dissertation, Columbia University, 1949), p. 67.

28. As quoted in Miller, *op. cit.,* p. 84.

29. *Ibid.*

30. Clifford K. Shifton, "Secondary Education in the Puritan Colonies," *New England Quarterly,* Vol. VII, December, 1934, pp. 646–658; "Puritanism and Modern Democracy," *New England Historical and Genealogical Register,* Vol. CI, July, 1947, pp. 181–198.

31. On this, see Samuel Eliot Morison, *The Puritan Pronaos* (New York, New York University Press, 1936), pp. 82–104.

32. Alexander Cowie, *Educational Problems at Yale College in the Eighteenth Century* (New Haven, Conn., Yale University Press, 1936), p. 5; Harold Rhodes, "Educational Factors Affecting Requirements of Yale College" (unpublished doctoral dissertation, Yale University, 1940), pp. 3–6.

33. Cowie, *op. cit.,* pp. 4–5; Samuel Eliot Morison, *Three Centuries of Harvard* (Cambridge, Mass., Harvard University Press, 1936), pp. 103–104.

34. Colonial Society of Massachusetts, *op. cit.,* pp. 25–26.

35. Robert Middlekauf, *Ancients and Axioms: Secondary Education in Eighteenth Century New England* (New Haven, Conn., Yale University Press, 1963), pp. 76–77.

36. Edwin C. Broome, *Historical and Critical Discussion of College Admission Requirements* (New York, Macmillan, 1903); Wertenbaker, *op. cit.,* p. 91; Blair, *op. cit.,* p. 33; Herbert and Carol Schneider, *Samuel Johnson, Career and Writings* (New York, Columbia University Press, 1929), Vol. 4, p. 225; Demarest, *op. cit.,* pp. 227–228.

37. Broome, *op. cit.* The order in which the new required subjects first made their appearance was

as follows: geography (1807, Harvard); English grammar (1819, Princeton); algebra (1820, Harvard); geometry (1844, Harvard); ancient history (1847, Harvard and Michigan); modern history (1869, Michigan); English composition (1870, Princeton).

38. George B. Adams, "The College in the University," *Educational Review,* Vol. 33, February, 1907, pp. 132–133.

39. C. C. Crawford and Leonard V. Koos, "College Aims Past and Present," *School and Society,* Vol. 14, December, 1921, pp. 505–506; George P. Schmidt, "Cross-currents in American Colleges," *American Historical Review,* Vol. 42, October, 1926, p. 47.

40. The first year will teach rhetoric; the second and third, dialectic; the fourth will add philosophy (*ibid.,* p. 47).

41. Samuel Eliot Morison, *Harvard College in the Seventeenth Century* (Cambridge, Mass., Harvard University Press, 1936), Vol. I, pp. 141–147.

42. For Yale, see Cowie, *op. cit.,* pp. 11–17; for Dartmouth, see Leon B. Richardson, *History of Dartmouth* (Hanover, N.H., Dartmouth College Publications, 1932), Vol. I, p. 248; for Princeton, see Blair, *op. cit.,* p. 24.

43. Benjamin Silliman, looking back to his own student days at late eighteenth-century Yale, recalled: "Classical learning was . . . the principal object of attention, and so it continued to be until my time. To train young men to write and to speak was the great effort of the instructors. Theological, ethical, and metaphysical subjects were much cultivated, and logic was also a prominent topic." George P. Fisher, *Life of Benjamin Silliman* (New York, Scribner, 1866), Vol. I, p. 88.

44. Edward J. Young, "Subjects for the Master's Degree in Harvard College from 1655 to 1791," *Proceedings of the Massachusetts Historical Society,* Vol. 18, June, 1880, pp. 121–122; Franklin B. Dexter (ed.), *The Literary Diary of Ezra Stiles* (New York, Scribner, 1901), Vol. III, pp. 306, 397.

45. Richard M. Gummere, *The American Colonial Mind and the Classical Tradition* (Cambridge, Mass., Harvard University Press, 1963), pp. 55–75.

46. William T. Costello, "The Scholastic Curriculum at Early Seventeenth Century Cambridge" (unpublished doctoral dissertation, Harvard University, 1952), pp. i–ix, 271–278.

47. Miller, *op. cit.,* pp. 121, 143–144, 152, 160, 165, 175–176. There were held to be "more worthy" and "less worthy" arts. The "less worthy" ones were those, such as calligraphy, typography, horseshoeing, and agriculture, which were considered to be utilitarian and to have bearing only upon a limited subject.

48. Egbert C. Smyth, "The New Philosophy against which Yale Students were warned in 1714," *Proceedings of the American Antiquarian Society,* New Series, Vol. 11, October, 1896, p. 252. In Johnson's manuscripts there is entered for 1719–1720 "Locke's Essay Concerning Human Understanding," and for 1721–1722 "Isaac Newton's Principia."

49. Edmund Morgan, "Ezra Stiles, The Education of a Yale Man, 1742–1746," *Huntington Library Quarterly,* Vol. XVII, May, 1954, pp. 260–268. By 1750, it seems likely that Locke's *Essay Concerning Human Understanding* was used as a principal text at Yale for the junior and senior years.

50. Francis L. Broderick, "Pulpit, Physics and Politics," *William and Mary Quarterly,* Vol. VI, Third Series, January, 1949, pp. 58–63; Wilson Smith, *Professors and Public Ethics: Studies of Northern Moral Philosophers before the Civil War* (Ithaca, N.Y., Cornell University Press, 1956), pp. 37–41.

51. Perry Miller (ed.), *American Thought from the Civil War to the First World War* (New York, Holt, Rinehart & Winston, 1954), p. x.

52. Phyllis Allen, "Scientific Studies in the English Universities of the Seventeenth Century," *Journal of the History of Ideas,* Vol. X, April, 1949, pp. 250–251.

53. Broderick, *op. cit.,* pp. 44–46.

54. David C. Humphrey, "Colonial Colleges and English Dissenting Academies: A Study in Transatlantic Culture," *History of Education Quarterly,* Vol. 12, Summer, 1972, p. 192. Also see Broderick, *op. cit.,* pp. 50, 54–55; Wertenbaker, *op. cit.,* pp. 88–92, 97; Morison, *Three Centuries of Harvard,* pp. 89–91; Van Hoesen, *op. cit.,* p. 63.

55. Theodore Hornberger, *Scientific Thought in the American Colleges, 1639–1800* (Austin, University of Texas Press, 1945).

56. Frederick C. Waite, "Position of Astronomy in American Colleges of the Colonial Period," *Bulletin of the Association of American Colleges,* Vol. 26, November, 1940, pp. 416–420. At

the College of Rhode Island the first five professorial appointments lay in the field of science! See Donald Fleming, *Science and Technology in Providence, 1760–1914* (Providence, R.I., Brown University Press, 1952), pp. 20–21.

57. Shipton, *op. cit.,* pp. 34–36.
58. Fisher, *op. cit.,* Vol. I, pp. 88, 92–93. Stiles was said to have cherished the hope that in the future life he would be permitted to visit the planets and examine the rings of Saturn and the satellites of Jupiter.
59. I. Bernard Cohen, *Some Early Tools of American Science* (Cambridge, Mass., Harvard University Press, 1950). However, in America, as in Europe, the greatest creative activity in eighteenth-century science took place outside college halls, carried on by nonacademic investigators such as Franklin, Colden, Bartram, Logan, and Garden.
60. Howard C. Rice, Jr., *The Rittenhouse Orrery* (Princeton, N.J., Princeton University Press, 1954), pp. 16–17.
61. Schneider and Schneider, *op. cit.,* pp. 217–281.
62. Harris E. Starr, "William Smith," *Dictionary of American Biography,* Vol. 17, p. 354; Guy E. Snavely, "The College of Mirania," *Bulletin of the Association of American Colleges,* Vol. 27, May, 1941, pp. 281–282.
63. William Smith, *Works* (Philadelphia, Maxwell and Fry, 1803), Vol. I, pp. 180–182, 200–228.
64. William Smith, *Account of the College, Academy, and Charitable School of Philadelphia* (Philadelphia, University of Pennsylvania Library, 1951), pp. 15, 22–27, 35–36.
65. Gilbert W. Mead, "William Smith—Father of Colleges," *Bulletin of the American Association of Colleges,* Vol. 27, May, 1941, pp. 276–277.
66. See the estimate in Charles A. and Mary R. Beard, *Rise of American Civilization* (New York, Macmillan, 1930), Vol. I, pp. 172–173.
67. Julian P. Boyd (ed.), *The Papers of Thomas Jefferson* (Princeton, N.J., Princeton University Press, 1950), Vol. II, pp. 305–333, 526–545.
68. Robert Polk Thomson, "The Reform of the College of William and Mary, 1763–1780," *Proceedings of the American Philosophical Society,* Vol. 115, No. 3, June, 1971, p. 213. Also see Paul L. Ford (ed.), *The Works of Thomas Jefferson* (New York, Putnam, 1904), Vol. III, pp. 251–256.
69. This could not be said to be true, for example, of degrees like the modern German *Diplom Volkswort* and *Diplom Ingeniert.*
70. Alfred Z. Reed, "Contribution of the Medieval University to American Higher Education," *Carnegie Foundation for the Advancement of Teaching,* 31st Annual Report, 1936, pp. 60–61. Thus, medieval universities paralleled the older craft guilds, with their regulation of apprentice training and certification of independent practitioners.
71. Colonial Society of Massachusetts, *op. cit.,* Vol. 15, pp. 26–27.
72. Schneider and Schneider, *op. cit.,* Vol. IV, p. 226.
73. Morison, *Harvard College in the Seventeenth Century,* Vol. I, pp. 139–148.
74. Colonial Society of Massachusetts, *op. cit.,* pp. 26–27. King's College, in 1755, specified, however, that the candidate during his three years of study after his bachelor's shall "have been guilty of no gross immorality."
75. For example, we find the following "parts" being presented at colonial Harvard: "Can Jesuits be good subjects?" discussed from the negative point of view, 1697; "Does a college education incapacitate a man for commercial life?" neg., 1724; "Is civil government originally founded on the consent of the people?" aff., 1725; "Can the price of articles for sale be regulated by law?" aff., 1725; "Is the voice of the people the voice of God?" aff., 1733. Young, *loc. cit.,* Vol. 18, June, 1880, pp. 123–124.
76. Thwing, *op. cit.* No earned doctorates existed in colonial or early nineteenth-century America.
77. Jared Sparks (ed.), *Library of American Biography,* Second Series (Boston, Little, Brown, 1845), Vol. VI, pp. 60–61. In 1783, when Stiles awarded a doctorate to Professor Samuel Stanhope Smith of Princeton, the Yale president arranged for Smith to appear on the stage and participate in an imposing ceremony. This experiment was tolerably successful, "except that the candidate seemed not to have well studied his part; and the consequent embarrassment created some diversion in the audience."
78. It was not until after the American Revolution, in the new Massachusetts constitution of 1780, that the power to grant degrees was specifically given to Harvard.
79. Morison, *Harvard College in the Seventeenth Century,* Vol. I, p. 69.

80. Young, *op. cit.,* pp. 402–405.
81. *New England's First Fruits* (London, 1643), pp. 31–32.
82. Lucy M. Salmon, "The College Commencement," *Educational Review,* Vol. 9, May, 1895, pp. 427–447.
83. James W. Alexander, *Princeton, Old and New* (New York, Scribner, 1898), p. 48.
84. Becker, *op. cit.,* pp. 7–8.
85. Thwing, *op. cit.,* pp. 104–105.
86. Conant *et al., op. cit.*
87. Richard Hofstadter and Walter P. Metzger, *The Development of Academic Freedom in the United States* (New York, Columbia University Press, 1955), pp. 316–317.

2. Early Patterns of Organization and Administration

1. Jurgen Herbst, "The First Three American Colleges: Schools of the Reformation," *Perspectives in American History,* Vol. 8, 1974, pp. 7–52. See also Edward H. Reisner, "The Origin of Lay Boards," *Columbia University Quarterly,* Vol. 23, March, 1931, pp 63–64, and James B. Conant, "Academical Patronage and Superintendence," *Harvard Educational Review,* Vol. 8, May, 1938, pp. 314–316.
2. William H. Cowley, "Professors, Presidents, and Trustees" (unpublished manuscript; cited with permission of the author), Chap. 2. The author cites even earlier precedent for control by a lay board. In the medieval Italian university at Florence the faculty appealed to the town council for help in breaking the almost despot control which students exercised over the university. In hearkening to this appeal the council set up a lay body to administer financial grants to the faculty and later to supervise the recipients thereof.
3. Cowley, *op. cit.,* Chap. 1.
4. Charles W. Eliot, *University Administration* (Boston, Houghton Mifflin, 1908), pp. 48–49. Both Amherst and the University of Georgia started with bicameral governing bodies.
5. When the University of Michigan was first established in 1817 as the "Catholepistemiad," the charter provided that the "president and didactors" should be a self-governing agency, but this was discontinued three years later. John E. Kirkpatrick, *Academic Organization and Control* (Yellow Springs, Ohio, Antioch Press, 1931), Chap. 9.
6. Timothy Dwight, *Dwight's Travels in New England and New York* (New Haven, Conn., published by the author, 1821), Vol. 1, pp. 212–213.
7. Edward P. Cheyney, *History of the University of Pennsylvania* (Philadelphia, University of Pennsylvania Press, 1940), pp. 188–194, 286–287.
8. Samuel Eliot Morison, *Harvard College in the Seventeenth Century* (Cambridge, Mass., Harvard University Press, 1936), pp. 3–21. See also Robert J. Wert, "The Impact of Three Nineteenth Century Reorganizations upon Harvard University" (unpublished doctoral dissertation at Stanford University, 1952).
9. For details see Perry Miller, *The New England Mind: The Seventeenth Century* (New York, Macmillan, 1939), pp. 456–486.
10. See pp. 104, 105, 288–290.
11. *Statutes and Laws of the University in Cambridge, Massachusetts* (Cambridge University Press, Hilliard and Metcalf, 1826).
12. John Lowell, *Remarks on a Pamphlet Printed by the Professors and Tutors of Harvard University Touching Their Right to the Exclusive Government of that Seminary* (Boston, Wells and Lilly, 1824), p. 32. Modern authors often make the distinction between external and internal control as that between the government and the administration of the university. For the general context in which these "remarks" were made see David B. Tyack, *George Ticknor and the Boston Brahmins* (Cambridge, Mass., Harvard University Press, 1967), pp. 115–119.
13. *Bracken* v. *William and Mary,* 3 Call (Va.) 507 (1790).
14. Kirkpatrick, *op. cit.,* Chaps. 10–12.
15. Francis Wayland, *Thoughts on the Present Collegiate System in the United States,* quoted in Richard Hofstadter and Wilson Smith (eds.), *American Higher Education: A Documentary History* (Chicago, University of Chicago Press, 1961), pp. 335–346; Jasper Adams, "On the Relation between the Board of Trustees and Faculty of a University" quoted in *ibid.,* pp. 325–327.
16. Herbst, *op. cit.,* pp. 38–40, 43–45.

17. Morison, *op. cit.*, p. 23; Walter C. Bronson, *History of Brown University, 1764–1914* (Providence, R.I., Brown University Press, 1914), p. 29.
18. Yale was founded by act of the Connecticut legislature in 1701. Clap's successful legal ruse has led some authorities to think that Yale was founded a year earlier, in 1700. This led to some subsequent confusion. Thus Yale's 150th anniversary was celebrated in 1850 but its 200th and 250th were honored in 1901 and 1951 respectively, thus indicating that 1701 is now the accepted date of founding. See Richard Warch, *School of the Prophets* (New Haven, Conn., Yale University Press, 1973), pp. 25–26, and Louis L. Tucker, *Puritanical Protagonist* (Chapel Hill, University of North Carolina Press, 1962), Chaps. 9 and 10.
19. Sheldon S. Cohen, "The Parnassus Articles," *History of Education Quarterly,* Vol. 5, September, 1965, p. 177.
20. Franklin B. Dexter (ed.), *The Literary Diary of Ezra Stiles* (New York, Scribner, 1901), Vol. 3, pp. 460–464. For a more detailed chronology of this Yale episode, see M. Clapp (ed.), *The Modern University* (Ithaca, N.Y., Cornell University Press, 1950), p. 78, and Edmund S. Morgan, *The Gentle Puritan* (New Haven, Conn., Yale University Press, 1962), Chap. 25.
21. Leon B. Richardson, *History of Dartmouth College* (Hanover, N.H., Dartmouth College Publications, 1932), Vol. I, Chap. 6.
22. *Dartmouth College* v. *Woodward,* 1, N. H. 111.
23. Cited in Charles Warren, *The Supreme Court in United States History* (Boston, Little, Brown, 1922), Vol. I, p. 484.
24. *Dartmouth College* v. *Woodward,* 4 Wheaton (U.S.) 518. For subsequent college cases citing this precedent, see Gordon R. Clapp, "The College Charter," *Journal of Higher Education,* Vol. 5, February, 1934, pp. 79–87.
25. James Kent, *Commentaries on American Law,* Vol. I, pp. 415–416, 826–830.
26. For a fuller account of this report, see pp. 104, 105, 288–290.
27. E.g., Charles K. Adams, "State University," *North American Review,* Vol. 121, October, 1875, pp. 365–408.
28. Frank W. Blackmar, *The History of Federal and State Aid to Higher Education* (Washington, D.C., Government Printing Office, 1890), pp. 131–148. See also, Morgan, *op. cit.,* p. 408.
29. Beverly McAnear, "The Raising of Funds by the Colonial Colleges," *Mississippi Valley Historical Review,* Vol. 38, March, 1952, pp. 591–612.
30. *Ibid.*
31. Warch, *op. cit.* p. 152.
32. Richardson, *op. cit.,* Vol. I, pp. 242–246. See also Donald O. Dewey, "The Cost of an Education in 1799," *AAUP Bulletin,* Vol. 48, September, 1962, pp. 266–267.
33. Frederick Rudolph, "Who Paid the Bills? An Inquiry into the Nature of Nineteenth Century College Finance," *Harvard Educational Review,* Vol. 31, Spring, 1961, pp. 144–157.
34. Wayland, *op. cit.,* pp. 361–368.
35. William Brickman, "Tax Exemption Privileges for Professors of Brown University," *History of Education Quarterly,* Vol. 6, Winter, 1966, pp. 65–78. It is interesting to note that Brown's colonial charter also in medieval fashion exempted professors from military service.
36. Thomas J. Wertenbaker, *Princeton 1746–1896* (Princeton, N.J., Princeton University Press, 1946), pp. 52–55.
37. Josiah Quincy, *History of Harvard University* (Boston, Crosby, Nichols, Lee, 1860), Vol. II, pp. 247–257. See also Seymour E. Harris, *The Economics of Harvard* (New York, McGraw-Hill, 1970) Chaps. 29–33; and Margery S. Foster, *"Out of Small Beginnings . . .": An Economic History of Harvard College in the Puritan Period, 1636–1712* (Cambridge, Mass., Belknap Press of Harvard University, 1962).

3. Early Student Life

1. In addition, the status of 65 parents in this group could not be determined. There were also seven listed as "physicians and schoolmasters." See Samuel Eliot Morison, *Harvard College in the Seventeenth Century* (Cambridge, Mass., Harvard University Press, 1936), Vol. II, p. 451.
2. Clifford K. Shipton, "Ye Mystery of Ye Ages Solved, or, How Placing Worked at Colonial Harvard & Yale," *Harvard Alumni Bulletin,* Vol. 57, December 11, 1954, pp. 258–263.
3. Samuel Eliot Morison, *Three Centuries of Harvard* (Cambridge, Mass., Harvard University Press, 1936), pp. 200–201; Thomas J. Wertenbaker, *Princeton, 1746–1896* (Princeton, N.J.,

Princeton University Press, 1946), pp. 192–193; Amos A. Stagg, *Touchdown!* (New York, McKay, 1927), p. 20. There were some among the older colleges, however, that tried to keep costs down. For example, Dartmouth in its 1822 catalogue announced the probable annual expenses of a student as totaling $98.65. Of this, $26 was for tuition, $2.40 for incidentals, $52.25 for board, and $10 for wood and light. Leon B. Richardson, *History of Dartmouth College* (Hanover, N.H., Dartmouth College Publications, 1932), Vol. I, p. 377.

4. Morison, *Three Centuries of Harvard,* pp. 200–201; Wertenbaker, *op. cit.,* pp. 192–193. The Princeton experiment proved unsatisfactory.

5. William Lathrop Kingsley (ed.), *Yale College: A Sketch of Its History* (New York, Holt, Rinehart & Winston, 1879), Vol. I, p. 142. He is quoted as fearing that Yale might turn into a center for sons of the rich, proud of their accidental advantage and lacking any incentive for intellectual achievement.

6. Charles W. Eliot, "The History of American Teaching," *Educational Review,* Vol. 42, November, 1911, p. 359.

7. Thomas LeDuc, *Piety and Intellect at Amherst College* (New York, Columbia University Press, 1946), pp. 6–7. President Hitchcock of Amherst maintained that his institution "was founded specially for indigent students" and that many of its students were extremely poor. Edward Hitchcock, *Reminiscences of Amherst College* (Northampton, Mass., Bridgman & Childs, 1863), p. 47.

8. Frederick Rudolph, *Mark Hopkins and the Log* (New Haven, Conn., Yale University Press, 1956), p. 65. During the presidency of Hopkins even Williams became more and more expensive to attend, as fees and living expenses increased.

9. Union College, *Catalogue,* 1852, p. 20. They were awarded only to those willing to sign a pledge never to use "intoxicating liquor as a beverage, or tobacco in any of its forms."

10. Rufus Choate of the class of 1819 at Dartmouth paid only $13.59 in cash of the $93.73 he owed the college for that year. He gave his note for the balance, and repaid it later. Richardson, *op. cit.,* Vol. I, p. 384.

11. John Todd, *Plain Letters Addressed to a Parishioner in Behalf of the Society of Collegiate and Theological Education at the West* (New York, Leavitt, Trow, 1847), p. 22. In a similar vein, the Princeton theologian, Reverend Samuel Miller, maintained that: "It is well known that the greater part of the students in our colleges belong to families in very moderate, and not a few of them in straitened circumstances. . . ." Samuel Miller, *Letters from a Father to his Sons in College* (Philadelphia, Presbyterian Board of Publication, 1852), pp. 203–204.

12. Dixon Ryan Fox, *Union College, an Unfinished History* (Schenectady, N.Y., Union College, 1945), pp. 18–19; Francis Wayland, *Thoughts on the Present Collegiate System* (Boston, Gould, Kendall & Lincoln, 1842), p. 30.

13. Morison, *Harvard College in the Seventeenth Century,* Vol. II, pp. 499–500; William P. and Julia P. Cutler, *Life, Journals and Correspondence of Rev. M. Cutler* (Cincinnati, Robert Clarke, 1888), Vol. II, p. 31; Wayland, *op. cit.,* p. 129; Theodore R. Crane, "Francis Wayland and the Residential College," *Rhode Island History,* Vol. 19, July, 1960, pp. 67–69.

14. William H. Cowley, "History of Student Residential Housing," *School and Society,* Vol. 40, December 1, 1934, pp. 705–710.

15. Charles F. Thwing, *History of Higher Education in America* (Englewood Cliffs, N.J., Prentice-Hall, 1906), p. 381. A play entitled *The French Revolution,* which was staged by Dartmouth's United Fraternity in this period, shows marked anti-church tendencies. United Fraternity at Dartmouth College, *The French Revolution* (New Bedford, John Spooner, 1793), p. 67.

16. Winfield Scott, *Memoirs Written by Himself* (New York, Sheldon, 1864), Vol. I, pp. 9–10.

17. Clarence P. Shedd, *Two Centuries of Student Christian Movements* (New York, Association Press, 1934), pp. 36–37, 48–49; George P. Schmidt, *The Liberal Arts College, A Chapter in American Cultural History* (New Brunswick, N.J., Rutgers University Press, 1957), p. 27.

18. Merle E. Curti, *Growth of American Thought* (New York, Harper & Row, 1943), p. 83.

19. As quoted in Laurence R. Veysey, *The Emergence of the University* (Chicago, University of Chicago Press, 1965), p. 34n.

20. Shedd, *op. cit.,* pp. 48–49; Cornelius Van Santvoord and Taylor Lewis, *Memoirs of Nott* (New York, Sheldon, 1876), pp. 221, 223–224; James B. Angell, *Reminiscences* (New York, McKay, 1912), pp. 33–34.

21. LeDuc, *op. cit.,* pp. 29, 31–32. At Union College about the same time a clergyman utilized the death of one of the students to begin a revival. The corpse was laid out in the Reverend's study.

"He assembled the students around the lifeless remains of their departed friend, and conversed and prayed with them in the most solemn manner." Francis and Heman L. Wayland, *A Memoir of the Life and Labors of Francis Wayland, D.D.* (New York, Sheldon, 1867), Vol. I, pp. 106–107.

22. William Otis Carr, *Amherst Diary, 1853–1857* (Guilford, Conn., Shore Line Times Publishing, 1940), pp. 15–18.

23. Claude M. Fuess, *Amherst: The Story of a New England College* (Boston, Little, Brown, 1935), p. 89.

24. Charles R. Williams (ed.), *Rutherford B. Hayes, Diary and Letters* (Columbus, Ohio State Archaeological Society, 1922), Vol. I, pp. 36–37.

25. Shedd, *op. cit.,* pp. 18–19, 26–31; Thwing, *op. cit.,* pp. 381–382.

26. George R. Cutting, *Student Life at Amherst* (Amherst, Hatch & Williams, 1871), pp. 60–63; Shedd, *op. cit.,* pp. 54–60, 69, 74–75.

27. Francis Wayland, *Dependence of Science upon Religion* (Providence, R.I., Marshall, Brown, 1835), p. 40.

28. Fox, *op. cit.,* pp. 44–45. See also Union College, *Catalogue,* June, 1824, p. 4; Yale College, *Catalogue,* 1841–42, p. 30; William Watts Folwell, *Autobiography and Letters* (Minneapolis, University of Minnesota Press, 1933).

29. Allen Tankersley, *College Life at Old Oglethorpe* (Athens, University of Georgia Press, 1951), pp. 67–68.

30. Arthur H. Cole (ed.), *Charleston Goes to Harvard* (Cambridge, Mass., Harvard University Press, 1940), p. 65; Mark Hopkins, *Early Letters* (New York, John Day, 1929), p. 116.

31. William G. Hammond, *Remembrance of Amherst* (New York, Columbia University Press, 1946), p. 187.

32. F. D. Huntington, "Public Prayers in Colleges," *Barnard's American Journal of Education,* Vol. IV, 1857, pp. 23–24, 30–31.

33. Seniority at colonial Harvard ran as follows: freshman, sophomore, junior, senior, junior bachelor (first-year student for the master's degree), middle bachelor, senior bachelor, junior fellow (bachelor of arts), junior fellow (master of arts), senior fellow of the house, president. Morison, *Harvard College in the Seventeenth Century,* Vol. I, pp. 58–59, 65–66; and *Three Centuries of Harvard,* p. 107.

34. Samuel Wolcott, *Memorial of Henry Wolcott* (New York, Anson Randolph, 1881), p. 225.

35. Charles Beecher (ed.), *Autobiography, Correspondence, etc. of Lyman Beecher, D.D.* (New York, Harper & Row, 1864), Vol. I, pp. 40–41.

36. G. Stanley Hall, "Student Customs," *Proceedings of the American Antiquarian Society,* 1900–1901, p. 97.

37. Kingsley, *op. cit.,* Vol. I, p. 142; Beecher, *op. cit.,* Vol. I, p. 40; Morison, *Harvard College in the Seventeenth Century,* p. 37; Timothy Dwight, *Theology Explained and Defended* (New York, Harper & Row, 1864), Vol. I, p. 23.

38. Henry D. Sheldon, *History and Pedagogy of American Student Societies* (Englewood Cliffs, N.J., Prentice-Hall, 1901), pp. 97–109.

39. David Potter, *Debating in Colonial Chartered Colleges* (New York, Teachers College, Columbia University, 1944); LeDuc, *op. cit.,* p. 119; Hall, *op. cit.,* pp. 100–101; Sheldon, *op. cit.,* pp. 89–94; Charles W. Lomas, "The Lighter Side of the Literary Society," *Quarterly Journal of Speech,* Vol. 39, February, 1953, pp. 45–48.

40. The society libraries were particularly important, because they represented the one place on the campus at this time where students got a chance to explore modern literature and to secure information on the topics of the day. LeDuc, *op. cit.,* pp. 119–120; Cutting, *op. cit.,* p. 20.

41. Hitchcock, *op. cit.,* pp. 326–327; LeDuc, *op. cit.,* p. 119; Sheldon, *op. cit.* Nineteenth-century American students may not have been as deeply involved in violent political action as their Latin American or Continental European contemporaries, but they did from time to time debate fateful issues. This suggests that they may have been just as much interested in the disputed issues themselves as in the technical means by which they were presented. For example, we find a literary society at Oglethorpe University, Georgia, debating in 1859 "Does the Harper's Ferry insurrection justify secession of the South?" and in 1860 "Has the advancement of the southern States in power and wealth been retarded by the institution of Slavery?" Tankersley, *op. cit.,* pp. 51–57.

42. Saul Sack, "Student Life in the Nineteenth Century," *Pennsylvania Magazine of History and Biography,* July 1961, pp. 270–273.

43. Wertenbaker, *op. cit.,* pp. 201–208; James W. Alexander, *Princeton—Old and New* (New York, Scribner, 1898), pp. 4–6, 9–10; Ashbel Green, *Life of Ashbel Green* (New York, Robert Carter, 1849), pp. 139–141; Henry Clay Cameron, "History of the American Whig Society," *Addresses and Proceedings at the Celebration of the One Hundredth Anniversary of the Founding of the American Whig Society of the College of New Jersey* (Princeton, N.J., Stelle and Smith, 1871), pp. 12–13.

44. Thomas S. Harding, *College Literary Societies: Their Contribution to Higher Education in the United States, 1815–1876* (New York, Pageant Press, 1971), pp. 317–319.

45. Morison, *Three Centuries of Harvard,* pp. 62–63, 180–183; James B. Conant *et al., History and Traditions of Harvard College* (Cambridge, Mass., Harvard Crimson, 1936), pp. 20–23.

46. Cutting, *op. cit.,* pp. 54–56, 124–126.

47. United Fraternity at Dartmouth College, *op. cit.,* pp. iii–vi; Wertenbaker, *op. cit.,* pp. 29, 195; Morison, *Three Centuries of Harvard,* pp. 91–92.

48. Samuel Willey, *Dartmouth Reminiscence, 1840–1845* (Hanover, N.H., Dartmouth College Library, 1955), pp. 10–11; Wertenbaker, *op. cit.,* pp. 195–198; Morison, *Three Centuries of Harvard,* p. 202.

49. Bruce, *op. cit.,* Vol. II, pp. 318–319; Wertenbaker, *op. cit.,* pp. 197–198.

50. Wertenbaker, *op. cit.,* pp. 193–200, 245, 252; David A. Weaver, *Builders of American Universities* (Alton, Ill., Shurtleff College Press, 1950), Vol. I, pp. 150–151; Bruce, *op. cit.,* Vol. II, pp. 336–337.

51. Morison, *Three Centuries of Harvard,* p. 207; Folwell, *op. cit.,* p. 61.

52. Hall, *op. cit.,* p. 85.

53. Willey, *op. cit.,* p. 7; Andrew P. Peabody, *Harvard Reminiscences* (Boston, Ticknor, 1888), pp. 200–201.

54. Philip Lindsley, *Educational Discourses* (Philadelphia, Lippincott, 1859), Vol. I, pp. 39–40; Weaver, *op. cit.,* Vol. I, pp. 156–157; Rev. Jesse Appleton, *Addresses* (Brunswick, Me., Joseph Griffin, 1820), p. 10.

55. President Hitchcock of Amherst complained that public sympathy in the American community was rarely with a college faculty, almost always with an offending student. "A college Faculty are looked upon by many as an aristocratic, arbitrary and tyrannical set, whom every humane man is bound to oppose. . . ." This attitude, he felt, is what encouraged student rebellions. Hitchcock, *op. cit.,* pp. 316–317.

56. At Yale President Stiles even regulated the wearing of hats within the College Yard. On the early college rules and punishments, see Colonial Society of Massachusetts, *Collections,* Vol. 15, Harvard College Records, I, pp. 26–27; Samuel Blair, *An Account of the College of New Jersey* (Woodbridge, N.J., James Parker, 1764), pp. 19–22; Leon B. Richardson, *History of Dartmouth* (Hanover, N.H., Dartmouth College Publications, 1932), Vol. I, p. 164; William H. S. Demarest, *A History of Rutgers College* (New Brunswick, N.J., Rutgers University Press, 1924), pp. 228–230; Walter C. Bronson, *History of Brown* (Providence, R.I., Brown University Press, 1914), pp. 182–192, 212; Alexander Cowie, *Educational Problems at Yale College* (New Haven, Conn., Yale University Press, 1936), pp. 6–10; Morison, *Three Centuries of Harvard,* pp. 110–116, 177, and *Harvard in the Seventeenth Century,* Vol. I, pp. 86, 112–118, 121–122, 329; Franklin B. Dexter (ed.), *Literary Diary of Ezra Stiles* (New York, Scribner, 1901), Vol. III, p. 299; Edward J. Power, *A History of Catholic Higher Education in the United States* (Milwaukee, Wisc., Bruce Publishing, 1958), pp. 123–126.

57. Crane, *op. cit.,* pp. 69–71.

58. Schmidt, *op. cit.,* pp. 83–85; Veysey, *op. cit.,* pp. 33–35.

59. Morison, *Three Centuries of Harvard,* pp. 117–118; Wertenbaker, *op. cit.,* pp. 185–187; Cowie, *op. cit.,* pp. 18–19. A whole account of Harvard's early history has been written from the standpoint of student insistence on good food. See Alma D. M. Bevis, *Diets and Riots* (Boston, Marshall, Jones, 1936).

60. Nathaniel Hawthorne was fined for playing cards for money at Bowdoin. Harry S. Warner, *Alcohol Trends in College Life* (Methodist Board of Temperance, 1938), pp. 5–6; Philip Lindsley, *Improvement of Time* (Trenton, N.J., George Sherman, 1823), pp. 7–8; Morison, *Three Centuries of Harvard,* pp. 120–122; Shipton, *op. cit.,* Vol. VII, pp. 45–46; Hammond, *op. cit.,* p. 211; Miller, *op. cit.,* p. 102; Fuess, *op. cit.,* p. 265; Beecher, *op. cit.,* Vol. I, p. 43.

61. On a more innocent level, we do have evidence that there was much student partygoing and dancing with girls. Morison, *Three Centuries of Harvard,* p. 116; Earnest, *op. cit.,* pp.

106–112; Powhatan Robertson, "Diary," *William and Mary Quarterly*, New Series, Vol. II, January, 1931, pp. 61–67.

62. Williams, *op. cit.*, Vol. I, pp. 53–54; Fuess, *op. cit.*, p. 15; Wayland and Wayland, *op. cit.*, Vol. I, pp. 264–265; Van Santvoord and Lewis, *op. cit.*, pp. 149–150; Timothy Dwight, *Theology Explained and Defended* (New York, Harper & Row, 1846), Vol. I, pp. 23–24.

63. Roy J. Honeywell, *Educational Work of Thomas Jefferson* (Cambridge, Mass., Harvard University Press, 1931), pp. 143–145; Bruce, *op. cit.*, Vol. II, pp. 258–266, 311–317.

64. President Willard of Harvard comforted Ashbel Green of Princeton on this account: "I am persuaded it must be a difficult task for the immediate Governors to preserve that regularity among the students, which could be wished, while they so generally come from those parts of the Union where youth are little accustomed to subordination and where disorganizing and loose principles greatly prevail." Chamberlain MSS., Boston Public Library, Joseph Willard to Rev. Dr. Ashbel Green, November 26, 1802. See also, on this problem, James Benson Sellers, *History of the University of Alabama* (University, University of Alabama Press, 1953), Vol. I, p. 200; John N. Waddel, *Academic Memorials* (Richmond, Va., Presbyterian Committee of Publication, 1891), p. 267; Ellis M. Coulter, *College Life in the Old South* (New York, Macmillan, 1928), pp. 84–85.

65. Bruce, *op. cit.*, Vol. III, pp. 111–133; Henry Tutwiler, *Address Before the Alumni Society of the University of Virginia* (Charlottesville, Chronicle Book and Job Office, June 29, 1882), pp. 10–11; W. Gordon McCabe, *Virginia Schools Before and After the Revolution* (Charlottesville, Chronicle, 1890), p. 43; John S. Patton, *Jefferson, Cabell and the University of Virginia* (New York, Neale Publishing, 1906), pp. 155–161; Lucian Minor, *Discourse on John A. G. Davis* (Richmond, Shepherd and Colin, 1847), p. 23.

66. Green, *op. cit.*, pp. 291–292, 360–362, 373–375. In a report to the trustees in 1814 Green told of a tremendous explosion "of what has been denominated the *big cracker*. . . . About two pounds of gunpowder were confined and exploded in the cavity of that log. . . . It was also now apparent that the original design was to have fired it in the prayer hall, before the pulpit, at the time when the building was burning; and this has accordingly been since confessed by the actors in this diabolical affair." On the Princeton rebellions, see Wertenbaker, *op. cit.*, pp. 134–150; and John E. Pomfret, "S. S. Smith," *Dictionary of American Biography*, Vol. 17, p. 344.

67. The 1830 rebellion occurred because the Yale sophomores declined to recite their mathematics lessons according to the rules required by their professor.

68. William H. Cowley, "The College Guarantees Satisfaction," *Educational Record*, Vol. 16, January, 1935, pp. 20–21; Fitzgerald Flournoy, "Hugh Blair Grigsby at Yale," *Virginia Magazine of History*, Vol. 62, April, 1954, p. 179; Kingsley, *op. cit.*, Vol. I, pp. 137–138; Hammond, *op. cit.*, pp. 127, 195, 295; Hopkins, *op. cit.*, pp. 104–105, 117.

69. Charles W. Eliot, *Harvard Memories* (Cambridge, Mass., Harvard University Press, 1923), p. 125; Andrew D. White, *Autobiography* (London, Macmillan, 1905), Vol. I, p. 353. In one of the early Harvard student rebellions, that of 1818, Ralph Waldo Emerson was one of those ordered "rusticated" for a few weeks to recover his equilibrium. Morison, *Three Centuries of Harvard*, pp. 208–210.

70. White, *op. cit.*, Vol. I, pp. 348–349.

71. Van Santvoord and Lewis, *op. cit.*, pp. 152–154.

72. Morison, *Three Centuries of Harvard*, pp. 252–253; White, *op. cit.*, Vol. I, p. 348. At least one of the rebellions achieved tangible results. After student riots in 1823, the Harvard Board of Overseers instituted an investigation of the whole college program. From these findings came the modified curriculum with some provision for elective work which was put into effect in 1825; Frederick F. Harcleroad, "Influence of Organized Student Opinion on American College Curricula: An Historical Survey" (unpublished doctoral dissertation, Stanford University, 1948), pp. 75–76, 199–200.

73. Fisher, *op. cit.*, Vol. II, pp. 336–337.

74. White, *op. cit.*, Vol. I, pp. 348–349; Charles W. Eliot, "The History of American Teaching," *Educational Review*, Vol. 32, November, 1911, pp. 362–363.

75. Crane, *op. cit.*, p. 75.

76. Wertenbaker, *op. cit.*; Earnest, *op. cit.*, pp. 105–106.

77. See Chapter 7 for greater detail on this change in student attitudes.

4. Multiplication and Variation of Colleges

1. "The American Idea was thus in its premise and its intent the idea of a One whose being consists in the co-operation of the unequal Many on equal terms . . . it is always *e pluribus unum.*" Horace M. Kallen, *The Education of Free Men* (New York, Farrar, Straus & Giroux, 1949), p. 113.
2. Merle E. Curti, *Growth of American Thought* (New York, Harper & Row, 1943), pp. 344–345.
3. Donald Tewksbury, *Founding of Colleges and Universities Before the Civil War* (New York, Teachers College, Columbia University, 1932).
4. Ralph H. Gabriel, *Course of American Democratic Thought* (New York, Ronald Press, 1940), pp. 4–5.
5. Although an intensive age of college founding was from 1790 to 1859, 134 more colleges were added in the years 1860 to 1890 and another 135 between 1890 and 1929. John D. Millet, *Financing Higher Education in the United States* (New York, Columbia University Press, 1952), p. 92.
6. John M. Thomas, "Report of the Commission on the Distribution of Colleges," *Bulletin of the Association of American Colleges,* Vol. VII, May, 1921, pp. 19–21.
7. Arthur J. Klein and Franklin V. Thomas, "Cooperation and Coordination in Higher Education," *American Council of Education Studies,* Series I, Vol. II, No. 5, April, 1938; Daniel J. Boorstin, *The Americans: The National Experience* (New York, Random House, 1965), pp. 153–160.
8. George W. Pierson, "American Universities in the Nineteenth Century," in Margaret Clapp (ed.), *The Modern University* (Ithaca, N.Y., Cornell University Press, 1950), p. 68.
9. Charles Forster Smith, "Southern Colleges and Schools," *Atlantic Monthly,* Vol. 54, October, 1884, pp. 545–547. At the same time, the combined income of all 36 colleges and universities of Ohio was less than that of Harvard! Also, the 43 New England preparatory schools reported nearly twice as much endowment and property as the 69 weakest southern colleges.
10. William R. Harper, *The Trend in Higher Education* (Chicago, University of Chicago Press, 1905), p. 377; on this problem, see also Heman Humphrey, *Discourse before the Connecticut Alpha* (New Haven, Conn., L. H. Young, 1839), pp. 15–16, and Truman H. Safford, "Why Does the Number of Students in American Colleges Fail to Keep Pace with the Population?" *Academy,* Vol. 3, November, 1888, p. 491.
11. Noah Porter, *American College and the American Public* (New Haven, Conn., C. C. Chatfield, 1870), pp. 254–258. Presidents McCosh of Princeton and Harper of Chicago endorsed the "affiliation" idea, but nothing came of it at this time.
12. Rossiter Johnson, "College Endowments," *North American Review,* Vol. 136, May, 1883, pp. 490–491.
13. The École Polytechnique, founded in Paris in 1794, had a great influence on American developments, as did the École Centrale des Arts et Manufactures, established in 1829. Other important European precedents for American technical education were the Königliches Gewerbe Institut of Berlin (1821), the Polytechnisches Institut of Vienna (1815), the Technische Bohmische Standische Lehranstalt of Prague (1806), and the Polytechnische Schule zu München (1827). Franklin Greene, *Rensselaer Polytechnic Institute* (Troy, N.Y., Palmer C. Ricketts, 1933), pp. 3–4.
14. The first use of the word "technology" in America is to be found in Jacob Bigelow's textbook, *Elements of Technology* (Boston, Hilliard, Gray, Little & Wilkins, 1831).
15. Rensselaer Polytechnic Institute, *Annual Register,* 1858, p. 2; Ethel McAllister, *Amos Eaton* (Philadelphia, University of Pennsylvania Press, 1941), p. 2; Palmer C. Ricketts, *History of Rensselaer Polytechnic Institute* (Troy, N.Y., Rensselaer Polytechnic Institute, 1930).
16. McAllister, *op. cit.,* pp. 515–517.
17. Greene, *op. cit.,* pp. 13–14; Rensselaer Polytechnic Institute, *op. cit.,* pp. 17–19; McAllister, *op. cit.,* p. 517.
18. Union College, *Catalogue, Third Term,* 1856, pp. 23–24; Dixon Ryan Fox, *Eliphalet Nott* (Princeton, N.J., Newcomen Society, 1944), p. 12.
19. Samuel Eliot Morison, *Three Centuries of Harvard* (Cambridge, Mass., Harvard University Press, 1936), pp. 279–280.

20. Russell H. Chittenden, *History of the Sheffield Scientific School* (New Haven, Conn., Yale University Press, 1928), Vol. I.
21. Institutions such as Case, Worcester, Drexel, Pratt, Stevens, and Carnegie were strongly influenced by the Massachusetts Institute of Technology.
22. Richard G. Axt, *The Federal Government and the Financing of Higher Education* (New York, Columbia University Press, 1952), pp. 59–60. During the 1880s, more than 4,000 engineering graduates were turned out in the United States.
23. U.S. Commissioner of Education, *Report, 1900–1901* (Washington, D.C., Government Printing Office, 1902), pp. 1722–1723; Aaron John Brumbaugh, *American Universities and Colleges* (Washington, D.C., American Council on Education, 1948), pp. 81–88. The mid-twentieth-century total is divided between independent polytechnic institutes and engineering schools affiliated with land-grant colleges, state universities, municipal universities, or privately endowed institutions.
24. Francis Wayland, *Report to the Corporation of Brown University* (Providence, R.I., G. H. Whitney, 1850), p. 57.
25. Earl D. Ross, *Democracy's College* (Ames, Iowa State College Press, 1942).
26. *Ibid.;* Margaret T. Riley, "Evan Pugh of Pennsylvania State University," *Pennsylvania History,* October, 1960, pp. 340–359; Mary T. Carriel, *Jonathan Baldwin Turner* (Urbana, University of Illinois Press, 1961).
27. It was largely due to pressure from the Grange and the Farmers' Alliance that the second Morrill Act of 1890 was amended to provide that federal funds could be used only for instruction in agriculture, mechanics, English, mathematics, science, and economics, "with special reference to their applications in the industries of life." The first Morrill Act had contained no such restriction. Axt, *op. cit.,* pp. 56–57.
28. *Ibid.,* pp. 48–49; Arthur J. Klein (ed.), *Survey of Land Grant Colleges* (Washington, D.C., Government Printing Office, 1930), Vol. I, pp. 19–22.
29. Ross, *op. cit.,* pp. 113–115.
30. W. O. Thompson, "Spirit of the Land-Grant Institutions," *Proceedings of the Association of Land Grant Colleges,* Vol. 45, 1931, p. 106.
31. White, *op. cit.,* Vol. I, p. 369.
32. Axt, *op. cit.,* pp. 56–57, 60–63; Ross, pp. 170–171. The second Morrill Act was passed despite the opposition of leaders of private colleges, like McCosh of Princeton and Eliot of Harvard, who charged that further federal subsidy to land-grant institutions constituted discrimination against their schools. Then, too, there was a bloc in Congress which preferred a bill for federal aid to common schools.
33. Iowa State Agricultural College, *Fourth Biennial Report of the Board of Trustees, 1871* (Des Moines, G.W. Edwards, 1872), pp. 9–10.
34. Thomas Woody, *History of Women's Education in the United States* (Lancaster, Pa., Science Press, 1929), Vol. II, pp. 137–140. In 1848, militant American feminists issued a Declaration of Women's Independence at Seneca Falls, N.Y.
35. *Ibid.,* pp. 141–142. The New England intellectual, Catherine Beecher, was an early advocate of collegiate education for women. In her essay, "The True Remedy for the Wrongs of Woman," published in 1851, she criticized existing "female colleges" as only high schools, and not worthy of the name of college.
36. Emma Willard, at one time, commented pointedly on "the absurdity of sending ladies to college."
37. One author comments: "The standard of work done at Georgia Female College fell far short of that done in the men's colleges of the period." Oliver C. Carmichael, "Change in Higher Education," *Bulletin of the Association of American Colleges,* Vol. 32, October, 1946, pp. 355–356. It was a former president of Judson, Milo P. Jewett, who persuaded Matthew Vassar to devote a large part of his fortune to founding a women's college.
38. Mount Holyoke, founded in 1836, did not grant collegiate degrees at first. Brumbaugh, *op. cit.,* pp. 16–17.
39. Woody, *op. cit.,* Vol. II, pp. 151–157, 173.
40. *Ibid.,* pp. 203–210; Anna Brackett (ed.), *Education of American Girls* (New York, Putnam, 1874), pp. 202–203, 208–209, 315–317. By the end of the nineteenth century, convincing evidence had accumulated showing that girls could do as well as boys in college work.
41. Mabel Newcomer, *A Century of Higher Education for American Women* (New York, Harper & Row, 1959), pp. 21–31.

42. Thorstein Veblen, *Theory of the Leisure Class* (New York, Macmillan, 1912), pp. 375–377.

43. Even at Oberlin there was a great deal of opposition at first to admitting women to "full" college privileges. Stress was placed on the preparation of girls for their domestic role in society. As part of their manual-labor assignment, Oberlin girls proved very useful to the college community, waiting on table, washing dishes, scrubbing floors, and mending clothes for their male fellow students. In the early years, there seems to have been no concept that the higher training of these young women might prepare them in any way for the professional privileges which were then monopolized by men. Robert S. Fletcher, *History of Oberlin College* (Oberlin, Ohio, Oberlin College, 1943), Vol. I, Chaps. 16, 24; Vol. II, p. 718.

44. Robert S. Fletcher, "The First Coeds," *American Scholar,* Vol. 7, Winter, 1938, pp. 76–86. In 1838, Miss Zeremiah Porter had received a "diploma" (not an A.B.) after completing a course in the "Ladies Department" of Oberlin. It is interesting that as late as 1869 the president of the University of Wisconsin was opposed to women graduates receiving the "bachelor's" degree. He changed his opinion in that year, however, when he learned that the dictionary meaning of the word could be "unmarried woman"! Merle E. Curti and Vernon Carstensen, *History of the University of Wisconsin* (Madison, University of Wisconsin Press, 1949), Vol. I, pp. 369–381.

45. This cleavage followed markedly sectional lines. The stronghold of the separate women's college was in the East. West of the Appalachians only five non-Catholic liberal-arts colleges for men were founded. On the Pacific Coast there are today few non-Catholic women's colleges. Lynn White, Jr., *Educating Our Daughters* (New York, Harper & Row, 1950), p. 50; Power, *op. cit.,* pp. 139–143.

46. Woody, *op. cit.,* Vol. II, pp. 140–150. We should not overlook, in this connection, the establishment of Wells College (1868) and Goucher College (1888), both in the East, and Mills College (1885) in California.

47. This same tradition of separatism was strong in the southeastern states. Thus, between 1885 and 1910, eight states in this region established separate tax-supported colleges for women. Carmichael, *op. cit.,* p. 355.

48. M. H. Maguire, "The Uniqueness of Radcliffe," *Radcliffe Quarterly,* May, 1948, pp. 3–9. Harvard flatly declined, however, to "annex the 'Annex' " and later a joint understanding with Radcliffe was worked out which was officially ratified in 1943.

49. John W. Burgess, *Reminiscences of an American Scholar* (New York, Columbia University Press, 1934), pp. 173–174, 241–242. President Barnard had wished to introduce complete coeducation in Columbia, but his plans were frustrated by student and alumni pressure, aided and abetted by some members of the faculty.

50. Tulane University, *Register, 1919–1920* (New Orleans, La., Tulane University, 1920), pp. 13–14.

51. Walter C. Bronson, *History of Brown* (Providence, R.I., Brown University Press, 1914), pp. 450–458. Another example of a women's college of this type is the Flora Stone Mather College of Western Reserve University.

52. U.S. Commissioner of Education, *Report, 1900–1901,* Vol. II, p. 1719; Brumbaugh, *op. cit.,* pp. 1022–1023; Newcomer, *op. cit.,* pp. 14–15.

53. Mary Mariella Bowler, *Catholic Colleges for Women* (Washington, D.C., Catholic University of America, 1933), pp. 123–124. Although it started late, the Catholic college movement for women spread so rapidly that by 1921 there were 38 such institutions and by 1930 there were 74. All these schools were exclusively for women.

54. White, *op. cit.,* Vol. I, pp. 399–401; Charles F. Thwing, *History of Higher Education in America* (Englewood Cliffs, N.J., Prentice-Hall, 1906), Chap. 16; Woody, *op. cit.,* Vol. II, pp. 241, 248–249; President of the University of Michigan, *Annual Reports,* 1872, pp. 11–12; President of the University of Chicago, *Report,* 1897–98, p. 11.

55. White, *op. cit.,* p. 51; Louis B. Wright, *Culture on the Moving Frontier* (Bloomington, Indiana University Press, 1955), pp. 225–226; Ross, *op. cit.,* pp. 128–129, 157–158; Brackett, *op. cit.,* pp. 200–202. William Rainey Harper attributed the progress of coeducation to the more advanced outlook of the West, a spirit "splendidly modern and higher than the older spirit of the monastery and the convent." Harper, *op. cit.,* p. 301.

56. Woody, *op. cit.,* Vol. II, pp. 255–280; James B. Angell, *Reminiscences* (New York, McKay, 1912), pp. 239–241; James B. Sellers, *History of the University of Alabama* (University, University of Alabama Press, 1953), Vol. I, pp. 473–483; Curti and Carstensen, *op. cit.,* Vol. I, pp. 369–381; Orrin L. Elliott, *Stanford University* (Stanford, Calif., Stanford University

Press, 1937), pp. 132–136. In certain western universities, such as Wisconsin, Northwestern, and Stanford, a reaction against full coeducation set in about the turn of the century. Demands were voiced for coordinate colleges, as at Harvard and Brown, but nothing came of this.

57. Parts of the Southeast remained adamant against coeducation, even at state universities. See Bruce, *op. cit.*, Vol. IV, pp. 63–69; Vol. V, pp. 92–103.

58. G. Stanley Hall, "Co-education," *NEA Proceedings*, 1904, pp. 538–542.

59. William F. Russell (ed.), *Rise of a University* (New York, Columbia University Press, 1937), Vol. I, p. 254.

60. Quoted in Schmidt, *op. cit.*, p. 132. As early as 1837, a dismissed student wrote a scurrilous pamphlet against Oberlin College, charging that joint education of the sexes there amounted to free love! Needless to say, this pamphlet had a wide circulation. Fletcher, *op. cit.*, pp. 80–81.

61. White, *op. cit.*, Vol. I, pp. 399–401.

62. U.S. Commissioner of Education, *Report for 1900–1901* (Washington, D.C., Government Printing Office, 1901), Vol. II.

63. *Ibid.*, pp. 1308–1309, 2406; U.S. Commissioner of Education, *Report for 1882–1883* (Washington, D.C., Government Printing Office, 1884), pp. cxxxiv–cxxxv.

64. Gabriel Compayré, "La Coéducation des Sexes aux États-Unis," *Revue Pédagogique*, Vol. 49, October 15, 1906, pp. 325–326. In Britain, however, there was a choice between the separate, coordinate colleges, as at Oxford or Cambridge, and coeducation, as at the Scottish universities, the University of London, and the new "civic universities" of Wales and the North of England. In his inaugural address at Harvard, President Eliot declared that American liberal treatment of women grew out of a democratic spirit which disliked disabilities of all sorts. Samuel Eliot Morison, *Development of Harvard University Since the Inauguration of President Eliot, 1869–1929* (Cambridge, Mass., Harvard University Press, 1930), pp. 69–70.

65. Carmichael, *op. cit.*, pp. 355–356.

66. White, *op. cit.*, pp. 52–55.

67. *The Chronicle of Higher Education*, Vol. 8, June 24, 1974, pp. 1, 4; July 8, 1974, pp. 8–9.

68. Statistics compiled from late nineteenth-century Bryn Mawr show the great majority of women graduates going into teaching. The same trend is apparent in Catholic women's colleges. Kate Holladay Claghorn, "The Problem of Occupation for College Women," *Educational Review*, Vol. 15, March, 1898, pp. 217–230; Bowler, *op. cit.*, p. 94.

69. For example, the 1898 catalogue of Agnes Scott College in Georgia declared: "Its great object from the very first has been, the glory of God in the higher Christian Education of young women." This was stated to be necessary in order to "fit woman for the greatest efficiency in her God-given sphere and work." Agnes Scott Institute, *Tenth Annual Catalogue and Announcement*, 1898–99.

70. Roberta Wein, "Women's Colleges and Domesticity, 1875–1918," *History of Education Quarterly*, Vol. 14, Spring, 1974, pp. 31–47; White, *op. cit.*, pp. 32–35, 59–61. The same problem insofar as it related to the development of Catholic colleges for women in America is discussed in Power, *op. cit.*, pp. 182–197.

71. *Godey's Lady's Book* criticized the early course of study at Vassar on this ground. Harriet Beecher Stowe and Horace Greeley also called for a more original and independent approach by the women's colleges. *Educational Yearbook*, 1943, p. 277; Julius Sachs, "The Intellectual Reactions of Coeducation," *Educational Review*, Vol. 35, May, 1908, pp. 466–475; Woody, *op. cit.*, Vol. II, pp. 192–198.

72. Constance Warren, *New Design for Women's Education* (New York, Stokes, 1940), pp. 6–7; Woody, *op. cit.*, Vol. II, pp. 210–217; M. Carey Thomas, "Present Tendencies in Women's Education," *Educational Review*, Vol. 32, January, 1908, pp. 64–65.

73. *The Chronicle of Higher Education*, Vol. 7, May 7, 1973, p. 3.

74. Of the nearly 600 accredited liberal-arts colleges existing in the United States in the middle of the twentieth century, more than 300 were church-affiliated. Willard Sperry, *Religion in America* (Cambridge, Eng., Cambridge University Press, 1946).

75. Frederick J. Kelly and Ella B. Ratcliffe, *Privately-Controlled Higher Education*, U.S. Office of Education Bulletin, 1934, No. 12, p. 22. Skeptics and anticlericals did not endow private colleges in America at this or later times.

76. Tewksbury, *op. cit.* By 1860, 180 permanent colleges had been founded by various religious

denominations. Of these, 14 were Roman Catholic and the remainder Protestant. The Protestant colleges included 49 Presbyterian institutions, 34 Methodist, 25 Baptist, and 21 Congregationalist.

77. By 1900, of 664 American colleges and universities, 403 were professedly Protestant and 63 Roman Catholic. Kenneth S. Latourette, *The Great Century, 1800–1914* (London, Eyre and Spottiswoode, 1941), pp. 418–419.

78. William Warren Sweet, *The American Churches* (New York, Abingdon, 1947), pp. 59–60; William Warren Sweet, *Religion in the Development of American Culture* (New York, Scribner, 1952), pp. 164–165; Schmidt, *op. cit.,* p. 36.

79. Albea Godbold, *Church Colleges of the Old South* (Durham, N.C., Duke University Press, 1944), pp. 107, 147–148; Latourette, *op. cit.,* p. 220. The main emphasis of the early Congregationalist and Presbyterian colleges was on high-quality ministerial training. This objective was faithfully pursued, despite the fact that the atmosphere prevailing along the western frontier was, at times, dominantly anti-intellectual. By way of contrast, the Methodists, Baptists, and Disciples of Christ were more interested in general Christian college education for all the people, not just the preparation of ministers. These denominations held that no amount of advanced training could make up for lack of divine "call," and that, in fact, no elaborate training was needed to preach the Gospel.

80. Thus the pattern which was characteristic of European settlement of the American coastline during the colonial period was now duplicated in the new setting of the nineteenth-century frontier movement beyond the mountains. Frederick Jackson Turner, *The United States, 1830–1850* (New York, Holt, Rinehart & Winston, 1935), pp. 339–340.

81. Evarts B. Greene, "The Puritan Counter-Reformation," *Proceedings of the American Antiquarian Society,* Vol. 42, New Series, 1932, pp. 39–41.

82. Howard Mumford Jones, *Theory of American Literature* (Ithaca, N.Y., Cornell University Press, 1948), pp. 85–87.

83. Stewart Holbrook, *Yankee Exodus* (New York, Macmillan, 1950), pp. 301–302, 304–308. Yale, Dartmouth, Amherst, and Williams served as models for the New England-type denominational colleges founded in the West. Examples of such institutions were Western Reserve and Oberlin in Ohio, Wabash College in Indiana, Illinois College, Iowa College at Grinnell, Beloit in Wisconsin, and Carleton College in Minnesota. This Yankee influence, by the way, was not limited to Congregationalist institutions, but affected others as well.

84. Green, *op. cit.,* pp. 39–41.

85. Dixon Ryan Fox (ed.), *Sources of Culture in the Middle West* (Englewood Cliffs, N.J., Prentice-Hall, 1934), pp. 56–58; LeDuc, *op. cit.,* pp. 40–41. In these colleges, of course, it was essential that the president be not only an effective administrator but also a clergyman considered by his own denomination to be sufficiently orthodox. If a president-elect in such an institution were not a clergyman, he would have to become one to assume his office. For example, in 1846, when Theodore Dwight Woolsey, professor of Greek, was elected president of Yale, he was required by the Yale Corporation to be ordained to the Christian (Congregationalist) ministry before he was inaugurated as head of the college. *Discourses and Addresses at Ordination . . . and Inauguration of Theodore Dwight Woolsey as President of Yale* (New Haven, Conn., B. L. Hamlen, 1846), pp. 3–4.

86. The whole movement was a reflection in the field of higher education of the trend toward forming a common interdenominational front for American orthodox Protestantism. Dixon Ryan Fox, "The Protestant Counter-Reformation in America," *New York History,* Vol. 16, January, 1935, p. 25; Wright, *op. cit.,* pp. 179–181; Tewksbury, *op. cit.*

87. Kelly and Ratcliffe, *op. cit.,* pp. 27–28, 31–36; Sweet, *Religion in the Development of American Culture,* pp. 168–170; C. Harve Geiger, *The Program of Higher Education of the Presbyterian Church in the U.S.* (Cedar Rapids, Iowa, Laurance Press, 1940), pp. 224–225; David A. Weaver, *Builders of American Universities* (Alton, Ill., Shurtleff College Press, 1950), Vol. I, p. 128; Floyd W. Reeves and John Dale Russell, *College Organization and Administration* (Indianapolis, Ind., Disciples of Christ, 1929), pp. 30–31, 52–53; Donald J. Cowling, "The Congregational Foundation for Education," *Bulletin of the Association of American Colleges,* Vol. 8, May, 1922, pp. 138–139; Floyd W. Reeves *et al., The Liberal Arts College* (Chicago, University of Chicago Press, 1932), pp. 4–6.

88. Bertram W. Korn, *Eventful Years and Experiences* (Cincinnati, Ohio, American Jewish Archives, 1954), pp. 152–158; Eric E. Hirshler (ed.), *Jews from Germany in the U.S.* (New York,

Farrar, Straus & Giroux, 1955), pp. 142–143; Rufus Learsi, *The Jews in America* (New York, World Publishing, 1954), pp. 121–122, 209–210.

89. Andrew M. Greeley, *From Backwater to Mainstream: A Profile of Catholic Higher Education,* Carnegie Commission of Higher Education (New York, McGraw-Hill, 1969), p. 4.

90. Holy Cross College in Worcester, Massachusetts, which would accept only Catholic students, was refused a state charter in 1849. David R. Dunigan, *History of Boston College* (Milwaukee, Wisc., Bruce Publishing, 1947), p. 98; Edward J. Power, "Formative Years of Catholic Colleges," *Records of the American Catholic Historical Society,* Vol. LXV, December, 1954, p. 32; Curti, *op. cit.,* pp. 492–493; Gabriel, *op. cit.,* pp. 53–54; Francis Cassidy, *Catholic College Foundations* (Washington, D.C., Catholic University of America, 1924), pp. 86–96; Wright, *op. cit.,* pp. 143–145.

91. A new departure was the addition at many American Jesuit schools of a new department, unknown in the Ratio, which was called the Commercial Course. This was a shorter utilitarian course preparing for business, and was recognized by an honorary certificate rather than a bachelor's degree. Raphael N. Hamilton, *The Story of Marquette University* (Milwaukee, Wisc., Marquette University Press, 1953), pp. 18–19, 21–27; Edward J. Power, "Historic Foundations of Catholic Colleges," *Catholic Educator,* Vol. 26, January, 1956, p. 278; February, 1956, pp. 361–362; Power, *op. cit.,* pp. 30–49.

92. Fox, *op. cit.,* pp. 33–34; see also LeDuc, *op. cit.,* pp. 9–10.

93. Turner, *op. cit.,* pp. 339–340.

94. Buchtel College, *History and Dedication, with the Inauguration of President McCollester* (Akron, Ohio, *Daily Argus,* 1867), pp. 29–30; Wright, *op. cit.,* pp. 179–181.

95. George P. Schmidt, "Crosscurrents in American Colleges," *American Historical Review,* Vol. 42, October, 1936, pp. 61–62; LeDuc, *op. cit.,* p. 60; Leslie K. Patton, *Purposes of Church-Related Colleges* (New York, Teachers College, Columbia University, 1939), pp. 58–59, 71–72; Jesse Appleton, *Lectures Delivered at Bowdoin College* (Brunswick, Me., J. Griffin, 1820), pp. xiv–xv; Union College, *Dr. Potter's Discourse at the Fiftieth Anniversary* (Schenectady, N.Y., Riggs, 1845), pp. 21–22; Francis Wayland, *Dependence of Science upon Religion* (Providence, R.I., Marshall, Brown, 1835), pp. 21–22; Stow Persons, *American Minds: A History of Ideas* (New York, Holt, Rinehart & Winston, 1958), pp. 189–194.

96. Rev. Truman Marcellus Post, *Religion and Education: An Oration at Iowa College, July 30, 1856* (Davenport, A. P. Luse, 1856), pp. 10, 14–15, 21–24.

97. Gabriel, *op. cit.,* p. 13.

98. Our italics. This passage is quoted in Walter M. Kotschnig (ed.), *The University in a Changing World* (London, Oxford University Press, 1932), pp. 132–133.

99. Natalie A. Naylor, "The Ante-Bellum College Movement: A Reappraisal of Tewksbury's The Founding of American Colleges and Universities," *History of Education Quarterly,* Vol. 13, Fall, 1973, p. 271.

100. The number of American institutions for the higher education of blacks increased from one in 1854 to 105 in 1950. These institutions remained comparatively small, however. U.S. Office of Education, *Biennial Survey of Education in the United States, 1948–1950* (Washington, D.C., Government Printing Office, 1952), Section I, p. 9.

101. This was at Bowdoin. Before the Civil War, a few blacks were attending Oberlin, Franklin, and Rutland Colleges and the Harvard Medical School. John Hope Franklin, *From Slavery to Freedom* (New York, Knopf, 1947), p. 228.

102. Charles S. Johnson, *The Negro College Graduate* (Chapel Hill, University of North Carolina Press, 1938), p. 7.

103. Ashmun Institute, founded in 1854, received aid from the Presbyterian Church for the purpose of training missionaries for Africa. It eventually received a college charter as Lincoln University in 1866. Franklin, *op. cit.,* pp. 228–229; Ruth D. Wilson, "Negro Colleges of Liberal Arts," *American Scholar,* Vol. 19, Autumn, 1950, pp. 462–463.

104. Dwight O. W. Holmes, *Evolution of the Negro College* (New York, Teachers College, Columbia University, 1934); and "Seventy Years of the Negro College," *Phylon,* Vol. 10, 1949, pp. 307–313.

105. Ruth D. Wilson, *op. cit.,* p. 462; Willard Range, *Rise and Progress of Negro Colleges in Georgia* (Atlanta, University of Georgia Press, 1951), p. 21; Johnson, *op. cit.,* p. 286.

106. Gabriel, *op. cit.,* pp. 139–140.

107. Ruth D. Wilson, *op. cit.,* p. 461. A few educated black leaders, such as Frederick Douglass,

feeling that only instruction in the liberal arts would give the black man equal status and remove the badge of servility, supported this overambitious approach.

108. Because of the almost complete lack of high schools for blacks, it was mandatory for these missionary institutions to maintain their own subcollegiate preparatory divisions. As late as 1914, there were only forty-seven four-year public high schools for blacks in the entire South.

109. Howard, destined to become the largest of all American institutions for blacks, received regular federal appropriations from the Department of the Interior. Holmes, *Evolution of the Negro College*, pp. 49–54; Ruth D. Wilson, *op. cit.*, p. 466.

110. Frank Bowles and Frank A. De Costa, *Between Two Worlds: A Profile of Negro Higher Education* (New York, McGraw-Hill, 1971), pp. 28–34; Alan Pifer, *The Higher Education of Blacks in the United States* (New York, Carnegie Corporation of New York, 1973), pp. 11–12.

111. Ruth D. Wilson, *op. cit.*, pp. 462–463.

112. *Ibid.*, pp. 462–464. By this time, both North and South accepted the principle of "white supremacy." This policy, in essence, amounted to a denial in this specific case of the American democratic faith. Gabriel, *op. cit.*, p. 140.

113. Kenneth H. Ashworth, *Scholars and Statesmen* (San Francisco, Jossey-Bass, 1972), pp. 80–81. Under the first Morrill Act, only three states—Mississippi, Virginia, and South Carolina—chose to use some of the federal funds to support the higher education of blacks. These states gave them as subsidies to existing schools for blacks, which later attained the status of colleges. There were no specifications in the act ensuring that southern blacks would share in its benefits.

114. Holmes, *Evolution of the Negro College*, Chap. 11. There were no white members on the staffs of state colleges for blacks, as there then were on the staffs of private colleges for blacks. Southern whites would not take such positions, and northern whites were not welcomed to these faculties either. Some southern states even made it illegal for whites to teach in publicly supported institutions for blacks.

115. This was at the Florida A. and M. College.

116. In 1923, North Carolina took over support of the National Religious Training School of Durham, North Carolina. In 1947, this became the North Carolina College at Durham, a state-supported liberal-arts college for blacks. Franklin, *op. cit.*, p. 538; Ruth D. Wilson, *op. cit.*, pp. 465–466.

117. Taken all together, the various educational funds from 1914 through 1933 contributed over $31,000,000 for the higher education of blacks. Ruth D. Wilson, *op. cit.*, pp. 464–465; Fred J. Kelly, *National Survey of the Higher Education of Negroes*, U.S. Office of Education (Washington, D.C., Government Printing Office, 1942–43), pp. 13–14, 28–29.

118. In 1943, a United Negro College Fund was established whereby a number of privately supported liberal-arts colleges, instead of competing with each other for funds, shared the money raised for operating costs. In 1948, this amounted to $1,157,000. Ruth D. Wilson, *op. cit.*, pp. 465–466.

119. Kelly, *op. cit.*, pp. 10–13. From 1826 to 1936, 25,697 blacks received academic degrees from colleges for blacks and only 5,393 from northern colleges which would admit blacks. Johnson, *op. cit.*, Chap. 5; Frank Bowles and Frank A. De Costa, *op. cit.*, p. 57.

120. By 1940, there were 13,147 students in public institutions of this type, either state or municipally supported, and only 8,561 attending private colleges for blacks. Kelly, *op. cit.*, pp. 4–5; Franklin, *op. cit.*, p. 383.

121. Franklin, *op. cit.*, pp. 539–540; Ruth D. Wilson, *op. cit.*, p. 467.

122. John S. Brubacher, *The Law and Higher Education: A Casebook* (Rutherford, N.J., Fairleigh Dickinson University Press, 1971), Vol. I., pp. 34–40; *The Courts and Higher Education* (San Francisco, Jossey-Bass, 1971), pp. 5–8; Holmes, *Evolution of the Negro College*, pp. 79–84; Edward C. Elliott and Merritt M. Chambers, *The Colleges and the Courts* (New York, Carnegie Foundation, 1936), pp. 12–13; Felix C. Robb and James W. Tyler, "The Law and Segregation in Southern Higher Education: A Chronology," *Educational Forum*, Vol. 16, May, 1952, pp. 475–480.

123. "Desegregation," *The Chronicle of Higher Education*, Vol. 8, July 8, 1974, p. 4; Alan Pifer, *op. cit.*, pp. 22–25.

124. *New York Times*, February 12, 1972, pp. 1, 27; June 7, 1974, p. 1; June 28, 1974, p. 1; Louis G. Heller, *The Death of the American University* (New Rochelle, N.Y., Arlington House, 1973), pp. 114–128.

125. *New York Times,* June 7, 1974, pp. 1, 20.
126. *The Chronicle of Higher Education,* Vol. 7, March 26, 1973, p. 1; Vol. 8, April 29, 1974, pp. 1, 6–8; May 6, 1974, p. 3; *New York Times,* April 30, 1974, p. 20.
127. Frank Bowles and Frank A. DeCosta, *op. cit.,* pp. 78–82.
128. Alan Pifer, *op. cit.,* pp. 29–30.
129. Wilson Record, "Some Implications of the Black Studies Movement for Higher Education in the 1970's," *The Journal of Higher Education,* Vol. 44, March, 1973, pp. 197–202.
130. Thomas Sowell, "Colleges Are Skipping over Competent Blacks to Admit 'Authentic' Ghetto Types," *New York Times Magazine,* December 13, 1970, p. 50.
131. Alan Pifer, *op. cit.,* pp. 31–32.
132. Carnegie Commission on Higher Education, *From Isolation to Mainstream* (New York, McGraw-Hill, 1971).
133. *New York Times,* October 11, 1971, p. 26.
134. Lloyd E. Blauch, *Educational Service for Indians,* Staff Study No. 18, Advisory Committee on Education (Washington, D.C., Government Printing Office, 1939), pp. 69–70. These policies can better be understood when it is remembered that, up to the time of the Grant Presidency, the official United States policy had been that the Indian must be driven westward. Then there was a shift in attitude to the concept that the Indian should be considered a primitive "ward" of the federal government. It was at this time, 1873, that the government began to assume primary responsibility for the education of Indians on reservations, seeking to introduce them, on a fairly rudimentary basis, to the white man's civilization. Curti, *op. cit.,* pp. 496–498.
135. Gustavus E. E. Lindquist, *The Indian in American Life* (New York, Friendship Press, 1944), p. 95.
136. Gustavus E. E. Lindquist, *The Red Man in the United States* (Garden City, N.Y., Doubleday, 1923), p. 45.

Chapter 5. Early Methods of Instruction

1. George P. Fisher, *Life of Benjamin Silliman* (New York, Scribner, 1866), Vol. I, p. 50.
2. American Historical Association, Annual Report, Vol. 2, *Calhoun Correspondence,* 1899, p. 80.
3. *Reports of the Course of Instruction in Yale College by a Committee of the Corporation and the Academical Faculty* (New Haven, Conn., Hezekiah Howe, 1828), p. 11.
4. James B. Angell, *Reminiscences* (New York, McKay, 1912), pp. 28–29.
5. Andrew P. Peabody, *Harvard Reminiscences* (Boston, Ticknor, 1888), p. 201.
6. Henry Adams, "Harvard College 1786–1787," in *Historical Essays* (New York, Scribner, 1891), p. 86.
7. Andrew D. White, *Autobiography of Andrew Dickson White* (London, Macmillan, 1905), Vol. I, pp. 26–29. At Princeton in 1846 a professor who punctuated Greek grammar and syntax with sallies into the delights of Greek literature had to resign. Thomas J. Wertenbaker, *Princeton 1746–1896* (Princeton, N.J., Princeton University Press, 1946), pp. 234–235.
8. Julian M. Sturtevant, *Julian M. Sturtevant, An Autobiography,* quoted in Richard Hofstadter and Wilson Smith (eds.), *American Higher Education: A Documentary History* (Chicago, University of Chicago Press, 1961), p. 275.
9. Francis and H. L. Wayland, *A Memoir of the Life and Labors of Francis Wayland, D.D.* (New York, Sheldon, 1867), Vol. I, pp. 230–234.
10. *Ibid.,* pp. 35–36.
11. Frederick Rudolph, *Mark Hopkins and the Log* (New Haven, Conn., Yale University Press, 1956), pp. 48–52. See also, John Bascomb, *Things Learned by Living* (New York, Putnam, 1913), pp. 99–107.
12. Samuel H. Frisbie, "The *Ratio* at Yale," *Woodstock Letters,* Vol. 28, 1899, pp. 21–23.
13. Allan P. Farrell, *The Jesuit Code of Liberal Education* (Milwaukee, Wisc., Bruce Publishing, 1938), pp. 416–418.
14. John T. Desaguliers, *A Course of Experimental Philosophy* (London, J. Senex, 1734).
15. London, T. Longman, 1745.
16. William Duncan, *The Elements of Logic* (London, W. Otridge, 1800), pp. 272–276. For a full discussion of the theory of early methods of instruction, see Carl A. Hangartner, "Movements to Change American College Teaching, 1700–1830" (unpublished doctoral dissertation, Yale University, 1955), pp. 137–146. Picking up the discussion again later in the century is Paul

Buck (ed.), *The Social Sciences at Harvard, 1860–1920* (Cambridge, Mass., Harvard University Press, 1965).

17. *Ibid.,* p. 10.
18. Noah Porter, *The American Colleges and the American Public* (New Haven, Conn., Charles C. Chatfield, 1870), Chap. 4. See also, Charles W. Eliot, *Inaugural Address,* quoted in Hofstadter and Smith (eds.), *op. cit.,* pp. 603–604, 610. In his inaugural Eliot gives a somewhat more balanced summary of the complementary advantages and disadvantages of both methods.
19. Frederick H. Pratt, "The Dangers and Uses of the Lecture," *Educational Review,* Vol. 24, December, 1902, pp. 484–496.
20. Palmer C. Ricketts, *History of Rensselaer Polytechnic Institute* (New York, Wiley, 1934), pp. 11–12.
21. *Ibid.,* pp. 33, 43–44.
22. There are good illustrations of early "apparatus" in Hangartner, *op. cit.,* pp. 150–151, 154, 157, 159, 163, 166.
23. Earle D. Ross, "The Manual Labor Experiment in the Land Grant College," *Mississippi Valley Historical Review,* Vol. 21, March, 1935, pp. 513–528.
24. Edmund S. Morgan, *The Gentle Puritan* (New Haven, Conn., Yale University Press, 1962), pp. 394–398.
25. Diary, Vol. 3, July 21, 1784.
26. Columbia College, *President's Annual Report,* 1869, p. 37.
27. Charles W. Eliot, *Inaugural Address* (Cambridge, Mass., Sever and Francis, 1869), p. 37.
28. Leon B. Richardson, *History of Dartmouth College* (Hanover, N.H., Dartmouth College Publications, 1932), Vol. I, pp. 263–265.
29. Stiles, *op. cit.,* April 5, 1785. See also Morgan, *op. cit.,* p. 401.
30. Mary L. Smallwood, *An Historical Study of Examinations and Grading Systems in Early American Universities* (Cambridge, Mass., Harvard University Press, 1935), p. 44.
31. Columbia College, *Annual Report of the President,* 1887, p. 27.
32. William H. Cowley, "A Century of College Teaching," *Educational Record,* Vol. 39, October, 1957, p. 315.
33. Smallwood, *op. cit.,* pp. 70–74.
34. F. A. P. Barnard, "On Improvements Practicable in American Colleges," *Barnard's American Journal of Education,* Vol. 1, 1855, pp. 275–277.
35. Francis Wayland, *Thoughts on the Present College System* (Boston, Gould, Kendall, and Lincoln, 1842), pp. 36–40.
36. Timothy Dwight, *Decisions of Questions* (New York, Jonathan Leavitt, 1833), pp. 154–156.
37. Richardson, *op. cit.,* Vol. II, pp. 441–445; George Ticknor, *Remarks on Changes in Harvard College* (Cambridge, Mass., Cummings, Hilliard, 1825), p. 5.
38. Richardson, *op cit.,* p. 612.
39. Louis Shores, *Origins of the American College Library, 1638–1800* (Nashville, Tenn., George Peabody College, 1934), p. 56.
40. *Ibid.,* pp. 121–140.
41. Richardson, *op. cit.,* Vol. I, pp. 250–251.
42. Wertenbaker, *op. cit.,* p. 310.
43. H. L. Webb, "Student Reading at Union College a Hundred Years Ago," *Journal of Higher Education,* Vol. 11, December, 1940, pp. 476–478.
44. George Ticknor, letter to Stephen Higginson, May 20, 1816, quoted in Hofstadter and Smith (eds.), *op. cit.,* pp. 256–257.
45. George Bancroft, *Journal of the Proceedings of a Convention of Literary and Scientific Gentlemen . . . in . . . the City of New York,* quoted in Hofstadter and Smith, *op. cit.,* p. 303.
46. Samuel Eliot Morison, *The Development of Harvard University Since the Inauguration of President Eliot, 1869–1929* (Cambridge, Mass., Harvard University Press, 1930), p. 62.

Chapter 6. The Elective Struggle

1. Samuel P. Capen, *The Management of Universities* (Buffalo, N.Y., Foster and Stewart, 1953), p. 110.
2. William T. Foster, *Administration of the College Curriculum* (Boston, Houghton Mifflin, 1911), pp. 26–28; A Citizen of Philadelphia (Benjamin Rush), "An Inquiry into the Utility of a

Knowledge of the Latin and Greek Languages," *American Museum,* Vol. I, June, 1789, pp. 525–535.

3. This is from the *Progress of Dulness* (1772), as quoted in Howard Mumford Jones, *Theory of American Literature* (Ithaca, N.Y., Cornell University Press, 1948), pp. 30–33.

4. The students there were given "ye liberty of attending whom they please, and in what order they please, of all ye different lectures in a term if they think proper." Herbert B. Adams, *The College of William and Mary* (Washington, D.C., U.S. Bureau of Education, 1887), pp. 39–40, 50, 56; Earl G. Swem, *Kentuckians at William and Mary* (reprinted from the *Filson Club History Quarterly,* July, 1949), pp. 12–13.

5. Philip A. Bruce, *History of the University of Virginia* (New York, Macmillan, 1920), Vol. I, pp. 223–512.

6. "Every student is free to attend the schools of his choice, and no other than he chooses; provided, that if under the age of twenty-one, he shall attend at least three professors . . ." University of Virginia, *Catalogue, 1832–33* (Charlottesville, D. Deans, 1833), p. 16. Jefferson himself was a dedicated student of the classics, however, and the original Enactments of the university provided that no one should receive a diploma from the institution who had not passed an examination in the Latin language. *Enactments by Rector and Visitors of the University of Virginia* (Charlottesville, 1825).

7. *Ibid.,* pp. 3–10. The number of these "schools" increased later on. Bruce, *op. cit.,* Vol. I, pp. 330–332; James M. Garnett, *The Elective System at the University of Virginia* (reprinted from *Andover Review,* April, 1886), pp. 2–3.

8. University of Virginia, *Catalogue, 1832–33,* pp. 24–25.

9. During the early years, the only degree awarded was the master's. However, in this period less than a tenth of the students stayed for a full three-year course, and less than one-hundredth for four. In 1848 the university reluctantly confessed defeat and established a B.A. degree. Bruce, *op. cit.,* Vol. II, pp. 61–65, 68–73, 135–140. Garnett, *op. cit.,* pp. 5–6, 8–9; Richard Storr, *The Beginnings of Graduate Education in America* (Chicago, University of Chicago Press, 1953), pp. 13–14.

10. Francis Wayland, Horace Holley, and Philip Lindsley seem to have been inspired, at least in part, by what was being done in Charlottesville. Bruce, *op. cit.,* Vol. III, pp. 244–255; George P. Schmidt, "Crosscurrents in American Colleges," *American Historical Review,* Vol. 42, October, 1936, pp. 57–58; Rev. Horace Holley to George Ticknor, May 23, 1825, Chamberlain Manuscripts, Boston Public Library.

11. Orie W. Long, *Thomas Jefferson and George Ticknor* (Williamstown, Mass., McClelland Press, 1933), pp. 30, 38–39; see also Henry Grattan Doyle, *George Ticknor* (Washington, 1937), reprinted from *Modern Language Journal,* Vol. 22, October, 1937.

12. Ticknor felt that "We must therefore change, or public confidence, which is already hesitating, will entirely desert us." George Ticknor, *Life, Letters, and Journals* (Boston, Houghton Mifflin, 1909), Vol. I, p. 359.

13. George Ticknor, *Remarks on Changes Lately Proposed or Adopted in Harvard University* (Cambridge, Mass., Cummings, Hilliard, 1825), pp. 7–8.

14. President J. T. Kirkland had been interested for some time in introducing into Harvard some of the features of the specialized training characteristic of European universities. John T. Kirkland, "Literary Institutions—University," *North American Review,* Vol. 7, July, 1818, pp. 270–274; *Report of a Committee of the Overseers of Harvard College* (Cambridge, Mass., Hilliard and Metcalf, 1825).

15. Samuel Eliot Morison comments on these laws as follows: "There can be no doubt that if the Faculty and the New England public had been prepared for so radical a change . . . Ticknor's reforms would have put Harvard College a generation ahead of her American rivals, and made her equal to the smaller European universities, and offered a much sounder basis for introducing new subjects into the curriculum than the atomic subdivision subsequently adopted under Eliot." *Three Centuries of Harvard* (Cambridge, Mass., Harvard University Press, 1936), p. 233.

16. Storr, *op. cit.,* p. 21.

17. President Eliot later wrote of Ticknor as a "reformer fifty years in advance of his time." Long, *op. cit.*

18. This section further provided "that each division thus made shall be carried forward as rapidly as may be found consistent with a thorough knowledge of its subjects and studies." Ticknor

regarded this principle "as the broad corner stone for beneficial changes in all our colleges." Ticknor, *Remarks on Changes Lately Proposed or Adopted in Harvard University* (Cambridge, Mass., Cummings, Hilliard, 1825), pp. 7–8, 35–41.

19. Morison, *op. cit.*, p. 233.
20. Under the circumstances, the new system was continued only in Ticknor's own department.
21. The Massachusetts Education Commissioners, for example, handed in a report to the state legislature in 1826 denouncing the "monkish" colleges for not furnishing training appropriate to the business and laboring classes of the country. "A Proposed Institution in Massachusetts," *American Journal of Education*, Vol. I, 1826, pp. 87–88, 152–153.
22. The head and the moving force in this experiment was Jacob Abbott, later famous as the author of the "Rollo" books and an advocate of better teacher training. The petition warned that if curricular modifications were not immediately forthcoming, new educational institutions might spring up detrimental to the existing colleges. Amherst College, *Substance of Two Reports of the Faculty* (Amherst, Mass., Carter and Adams, 1827), pp. 5–6; Gail Kennedy (ed.), *Education at Amherst* (New York, Harper & Row, 1955), pp. 10–11.
23. Amherst College, *op. cit.*, pp. 10–12, 20–22.
24. When the Amherst trustees abandoned the new program, Abbott resigned from the faculty. Claude M. Fuess, *Amherst: Story of a New England College* (Boston, Little, Brown, 1935), pp. 99–101.
25. *Ibid.*, pp. 173, 222–223; Thomas LeDuc, *Piety and Intellect at Amherst College, 1865–1912* (New York, Columbia University Press, 1946).
26. R. Freeman Butts, *The College Charts Its Course* (New York, McGraw-Hill, 1939), pp. 131–132.
27. Marsh had been deeply influenced by German thought and scholarship, as well as by the English philosopher Coleridge. The four major fields provided for in his plan were mathematics and physics, English literature, languages, and philosophy. Ronald Wells, *Three Christian Transcendentalists* (New York, Columbia University Press, 1943), pp. 16–17; Schmidt, *op. cit.*, pp. 52–53.
28. Dixon Ryan Fox, *Eliphalet Nott* (Princeton, N.J., Newcomen Society, 1944), pp. 13–17, 21–23; Robert F. Seybolt, "Eliphalet Nott," *Dictionary of American Biography*, Vol. 13, pp. 580–581. Nott once told the Greek professor at Union: "I care less for Greek than you do, and less for books, generally, as a means of educational discipline. But a college must have a wide curriculum, to be varied or enlarged as circumstances may demand. All kinds of men and minds are needed." Cornelius Van Santvoord and Lewis Taylor, *Memoirs of Eliphalet Nott* (New York, Sheldon, 1876), p. 176.
29. Union College, *Catalogue, 1833–34*, pp. 16–17; *Catalogue, September, 1845*, p. 19; *Catalogue, Third Term, 1849*, p. 22. A "partial" course was authorized at Union by the catalogue provision that "Students not regular members of College, are allowed, as University Students, to prosecute any branches for which they are qualified."
30. Schmidt, *op. cit.*, pp. 50–53. This kind of resistance to giving equal dignity to the new courses is illustrated by an article in the *North American Review* in 1829. Here the author insists that the traditional meaning of the B.A. degree be preserved, as properly belonging to those who have completed a true liberal education, including a thorough classical knowledge. Alpheus Spring Packard, "College Education," *North American Review*, Vol. 28, April, 1829, pp. 302–309.
31. Harry E. Edwards, "Trends in the Development of the College Curriculum within the Area of the North Central Association" (unpublished doctoral dissertation, University of Indiana, 1933).
32. Elbert V. Wills, *The Growth of American Higher Education* (Philadelphia, Dorrance, 1936), pp. 173–180; Butts, *op. cit.*, pp. 132–134; Milton Haight Turk, "Without Classical Studies," *Journal of Higher Education*, Vol. 4, October, 1933, pp. 339–346. Most of these new courses of study were soon abandoned by the colleges which had experimented with them. Internal opposition and lack of popular demand for these programs seem to have been responsible.
33. University of Rochester, *Catalogue, 1851–52*, pp. 15–16.
34. The presence of Rensselaer in nearby Troy, New York, seems to have been one of the factors that accelerated the development of scientific courses at Union College.
35. See pp. 222–223.
36. William Arba Ellis (ed.), *Norwich University, Her History, Her Graduates, Her Roll of Honor*

(Montpelier, Vt., The Capital City Press, 1911), pp. 2–5.

37. See pp. 86, 90.

38. One part of the report was written by President Jeremiah Day and the other by Professor James L. Kingsley. The widespread influence of the report may be accounted for by the active part Yale then played, along with Princeton, in training the presidents and faculty members of the new frontier colleges. George P. Schmidt, "Colleges in Ferment," *American Historical Review,* Vol. LIX, October, 1953, p. 23; Cornelius C. Felton, "Characteristics of the American College," *Barnard's American Journal of Education,* Vol. 9, 1860, pp. 115, 124–126; Frederick A. P. Barnard, "On Improvements Practicable in American Colleges," *Barnard's American Journal of Education,* Vol. I, 1885, pp. 183–184; Yale College, *Catalogue, 1841–42,* pp. 28–29.

39. To use the words of the Yale Report: "The cornerstone must be laid, before the superstructure is erected."

40. Yale College, *Reports on the Course of Instruction in Yale College* (New Haven, Conn., Hezekiah Howe, 1828), pp. 3–10, 14–15, 18–19, 23, 25, 29–30, 34–37, 52; Laurence A. Veysey, *The Emergence of the American University* (Chicago, University of Chicago Press, 1965), pp. 23–31.

41. Ralph Waldo Emerson, "The American Scholar," in Frederick I. Carpenter, *Emerson: Representative Selections* (New York, American Book, 1934), pp. 64–70.

42. Josiah Quincy, *Remarks on the Nature and Probable Effects of Introducing the Voluntary System in the Studies of Greek and Latin* (Cambridge, Mass., John Owen, 1841), pp. 7–8, 9–10, 15–16.

43. Morison, *op. cit.,* pp. 262–263. Harvard students taking electives were allowed for them only half the marks they would get for other courses.

44. Francis Wayland, *Thoughts on the Present Collegiate System in the United States* (Boston, Gould, Kendall, 1842), pp. 80–87, 102–103, 154–156. Like his mentor Eliphalet Nott, Wayland, an ordained minister of the Gospel, saw no conflict between science and religion. Francis and Heman L. Wayland, *Memoir of the Life and Labors of Francis Wayland* (New York, Sheldon, 1867), Vol. I, pp. 40–41, 57.

45. *Report to the Corporation of Brown University on Changes in the System of Collegiate Education* (Providence, R.I., George H. Whitney, 1850), pp. 51–52. Brown University, *Catalogue, 1834–35,* pp. 16–17; *1846–47,* p. 26; *1847–48,* p. 22; *1850–51,* pp. 17–18; *1852–53,* p. 26.

46. Walter C. Bronson, *History of Brown University* (Providence, R.I., Brown University Press, 1914), pp. 263–265, 321–325, 403; Donald Fleming, *Science and Technology in Providence, 1760–1914* (Providence, R.I., Brown University Press, 1952), pp. 37–38.

47. Francis Wayland, *The Education Demanded by the People of the United States* (Boston, Phillips, Sampson, 1855), pp. 28–29. Although a modern critic has denounced Wayland's book as "a tract probably productive of more mischief than any other in the history of American education" (Morison, *op. cit.,* p. 286), his younger contemporaries attributed to him the most beneficial of influences. Charles W. Eliot, many years later, publicly acknowledged his debt to Wayland. William G. Roelker, *Francis Wayland: A Neglected Pioneer of Higher Education* (Worcester, Mass., American Antiquarian Society, 1944). James B. Angell of the University of Michigan similarly testified to the important effect of Wayland's ideas on him when he was an undergraduate at Brown. James B. Angell, *Reminiscences* (New York, McKay, 1912), pp. 107–108.

48. In a book published in 1851 Tappan maintained that Germany had produced "the most perfect educational system in the world." Henry P. Tappan, *University Education* (New York, Putnam, 1851), pp. 291–292.

49. *Ibid.,* pp. 12–15. For many years, Tappan worked on a project for a great university system in the city of New York which was to cost half a million dollars. At times, he believed the plan was near realization, but final success eluded him. Storr, *op. cit.,* pp. 82–86.

50. Tappan, *op. cit.,* p. 64.

51. *Ibid.,* pp. 50–51.

52. University of Michigan, *Catalogue, 1853–1854,* pp. 33–34; Wills, *op. cit.,* pp. 178–180; Henry P. Tappan, *A Discourse Delivered on the Occasion of His Inauguration as Chancellor of the University of Michigan* (Detroit, 1852), pp. 21, 39–42.

53. Kent Sagendorph, *Michigan: The Story of the University* (New York, 1948), p. 80; Tappan, *op. cit.,* p. 22; Henry P. Tappan, *Public Education* (Detroit, 1857), p. 14.

54. Edwin McClellan, "The Educational Ideas of Henry Philip Tappan," *Michigan History,* Vol. 38, March, 1954, pp. 67–78.

55. Andrew D. White, *Autobiography* (Englewood Cliffs, N.J., Prentice-Hall, 1905), Vol. I, pp. 291–292.

56. Storr, *op. cit.,* pp. 50–53.

57. Harvard University, *Catalogue, 1847–48,* pp. 60–62.

58. *Ibid.,* p. 61. However, there was provision in the new school for considerable freedom in choice of courses on the part of the students. Attendance at lectures and recitations was declared to be voluntary. A full course of "laboratory exercises," in which the students were to participate, was projected.

59. Yale College, *Catalogue, 1849–50,* p. 44; Russell Chittenden, *History of the Sheffield Scientific School* (New Haven, Conn., Yale University Press, 1928), Vol. I, pp. 82–83, 140–143; Vol. II, pp. 303–311, 483–489. In New Haven, as in Cambridge, subject matter which was excluded from the "regular" college curriculum was taken up in the scientific school, but at the same time there were also the same lower entrance standards and, for a time, no degree requirements.

60. White, *op. cit.,* Vol. I.

61. Fuess, *op. cit.,* p. 137.

62. Dartmouth was legally bound by deed of gift to set these low requirements.

63. Leon B. Richardson, *History of Dartmouth College* (Hanover, N.H., Dartmouth College Publications, 1932), Vol. I, pp. 422–427. A notable exception to the decline of the pre-Civil War "experimental" colleges was Union College under Nott. This institution's flexible curriculum apparently attracted a large student enrollment, although some critics charged that the real reason for this was lower admission standards. In any case, in 1829 Union ranked third in the nation in student enrollment and in 1839 was second only to Harvard. Dixon Ryan Fox, *Union College* (Schenectady, N.Y., Union College, 1945), pp. 16, 21–22.

64. As cited in Veysey, *op. cit.,* p. 21.

65. On this problem, see William Graham Sumner, "Ways and Means for Our Colleges," *Nation,* Vol. II, September 8, 1870, p. 153.

66. Wilson Smith, *Professors & Public Ethics* (Ithaca, N.Y., Cornell University Press, 1956), pp. 168–170.

67. James Harvey Robinson, "The Elective System: Historically Considered," *International Quarterly,* Vol. 6, September–December, 1902, p. 194.

68. Frederick H. Hedge, "University Reform," *Atlantic Monthly,* Vol. 18, September, 1866, p. 301; Orie W. Long, *Frederick Henry Hedge* (Portland, Me., Southworth-Anthoensen, 1940), pp. 40–41.

69. Samuel Eliot Morison, *Development of Harvard University Since the Inauguration of President Eliot, 1869–1929* (Cambridge, Mass., Harvard University Press, 1930), pp. lxiv–lxv. Eliot felt sure that election would foster scholarship by giving free play to inborn preference and stimulating enthusiasm for chosen work. This, he believed, would improve the tone of class work. See also Charles W. Eliot, "The New Education," *Atlantic Monthly,* Vol. 23, February and March, 1869, pp. 203–220, 358–367.

70. Charles W. Eliot, *Educational Reform* (Englewood Cliffs, N.J., Prentice-Hall, 1898), p. 1; Morison, *Three Centuries of Harvard,* p. 342.

71. Morison, *Three Centuries of Harvard,* p. 346. "He had the patience of an Indian and the persistence of a beaver." LeBaron Russell Briggs, "President Eliot, as seen by a Disciple," *Atlantic Monthly,* Vol. 144, November, 1929, p. 597.

72. Morison, *Development of Harvard University,* pp. xlii–xliii; Richard Hofstadter and C. DeWitt Hardy, *Development and Scope of Higher Education in the United States* (New York, Columbia University Press, 1952), p. 51.

73. Hugh Hawkins, "Charles W. Eliot, University Reform, and Religious Faith in America, 1869–1909," *Journal of American History,* Vol. 51, September, 1964, pp. 191–201.

74. Noah Porter, *The American College and the American Public* (New Haven, Conn., C. C. Chatfield, 1870), pp. 15–16; Noah Porter, "The Class System," National Education Association *Proceedings,* 1877, pp. 95–105.

75. James McCosh, "The Course of Study in Princeton College," *Education,* Vol. 5, March, 1885, p. 354; *The New Departure in College Education* (New York, Scribner, 1885), p. 4.

76. Andrew F. West, "Must the Classics Go?" *North American Review,* Vol. 138, February, 1884,

pp. 152–159; "What Is Academic Freedom?" *North American Review,* Vol. 140, May, 1885, pp. 432–433, 439–442; *A Review of President Eliot's Report on Elective Studies* (New York, J. K. Lees, 1886); *The Value of the Classics* (Princeton, N.J., Princeton University Press, 1917), pp. v–vi, 359–360, 381–383.

77. For typical arguments of this type see West and McCosh, already referred to, and also Richard Rogers Bowker, "The College of Today," *Princeton Review,* Vol. 13, January, 1884, p. 93. For twentieth-century restatements of the traditionalist position, see Robert M. Hutchins, *The Higher Learning in America* (New Haven, Conn., Yale University Press, 1936), pp. 70–71; and Edward K. Rand, "Bring Back the Liberal Arts," *Atlantic Monthly,* Vol. 171, June, 1943, pp. 80–81.

78. Edward L. Godkin, "Yale and Harvard," *Nation,* Vol. 34, January 19, 1882, pp. 50–51; George H. Palmer, *The New Education* (Boston, Little, Brown, 1887), pp. 27–28, 40–41.

79. Charles Francis Adams, Jr., *A College Fetich* (Boston, Lee and Shepard, 1883), pp. 18–19.

80. William S. Gray, *Provision for the Individual in College Education* (Chicago, University of Chicago Press, 1932), pp. 14–20.

81. Palmer, *op. cit.,* pp. 15–17; Charles Eliot Norton, "Harvard University in 1890," *Harper's Magazine,* Vol. 81, September, 1890, p. 587.

82. William Graham Sumner, "Our Colleges before the Country," in *War and Other Essays* (New Haven, Conn., Yale University Press, 1911), pp. 361–362.

83. Clarence King, "Artium Magister," *North American Review,* Vol. 147, October, 1888, pp. 376–381. This writer, engineer, and soldier of fortune maintained that the classical curriculum had failed because it had not produced great American poets or dramatists, or even original literary scholars. It made young men hate literature. Far better that the young man with literary inclinations "be a cowboy, with the Bible and Shakespeare in his saddle-bags . . . than to have life, originality, and the bounding spirit of youthful imagination stamped out of him."
    A modern literary critic has insisted, however, that with the death of the classical college American literary production and literary style suffered a marked decline. Van Wyck Brooks, *New England: Indian Summer* (New York, Dutton, 1946), pp. 106–107.

84. Thorstein Veblen, *Theory of the Leisure Class* (New York, Macmillan, 1912), pp. 396–398.

85. Eliot, *University Administration,* pp. 131–134, 150, 226–228; Harvard College, *Annual Reports of the President and Treasurer,* 1884–85, pp. 45–46; Henry James, *Charles W. Eliot* (Boston, Houghton Mifflin, 1930), Vol. II, pp. 44–49; Brooks, *op. cit.,* p. 104.

86. Hazen C. Carpenter, "Emerson, Eliot, and the Elective System," *New England Quarterly,* Vol. 24, March, 1951, pp. 13–34.

87. As early as 1859, Spencer had called for a larger place for science in the curriculum on the purely utilitarian ground that it had the greatest value for the chief functions of modern living. Herbert Spencer, *Education* (London, G. Manwaring, 1861), pp. 93–96. Eliot frequently praised Spencer's writings and appointed the Darwinist and positivist John Fiske to lecture at Harvard in 1869 on these controversial subjects. Richard Hofstadter and Walter P. Metzger, *The Development of Academic Freedom in the United States* (New York, Columbia University Press, 1955), p. 338.

88. It was not until 1890 that a system of student counseling was set up at Harvard to aid young men in the selection of those programs which were best suited to their needs and interests.

89. George W. Pierson, "The Elective System and the Difficulties of College Planning, 1870–1940," *Journal of General Education,* Vol. IV, April, 1950, p. 165; Butts, *op. cit.,* p. 246; Orvin T. Richardson, "Requirements for the Bachelor's Degree, 1890–1940" (unpublished doctoral dissertation, University of Chicago, 1946), pp. 120–121.

90. Sherman B. Barnes, "Learning and Piety in Ohio Colleges, 1865–1900," *Ohio Historical Quarterly,* Vol. 69, October, 1960, pp. 336–352.

91. D. E. Phillips, "The Elective System in American Education," *Pedagogical Seminary,* Vol. 8, June, 1901, pp. 210–212.

92. Phillips, *op. cit.,* p. 212; Walter P. Rogers, *Andrew D. White and the Modern University* (Ithaca, N.Y., Cornell University Press, 1942), pp. 2–4, 92–98.

93. At Columbia, election was applied to the major portion of the junior and senior years in 1880. Princeton began to allow more election to upperclassmen after McCosh became president in 1868. Between 1884 and 1893, Yale worked out a plan whereby the first half of the college course was required and the second half was elective. Thomas J. Wertenbaker, *Princeton, 1746–1896* (Princeton, N.J., Princeton University Press, 1946), pp. 235–236, 293, 303–307, 386–387; William F. Russell (ed.), *The Rise of a University* (New York, Columbia University

Press, 1937), pp. 95–96; George W. Pierson, *Yale College, An Educational History, 1871–1921* (New Haven, Conn., Yale University Press, 1952), pp. 191–192.

94. The "minor" usually required about two-thirds as much work as that of the "major." Merle E. Curti and Vernon Carstensen, *The University of Wisconsin, A History* (Madison, University of Wisconsin Press, 1949), Vol. I, pp. 395–402, 622–630; University of Michigan, *President's Annual Report, 1873*, p. 10; *1874*, pp. 7–8; *1884*, p. 6; Phillips, *op. cit.*, p. 210.

95. Johns Hopkins University, *Official Circular*, June, 1877, pp. 5–6; John C. French, *History of the University Founded by Johns Hopkins* (Baltimore, Md., Johns Hopkins Press, 1946), p. 109; P. Stewart Macaulay, "The Group System at Johns Hopkins," *Bulletin of the Association of American Colleges*, Vol. 31, December, 1945, pp. 614–615. Another prominent institution which followed the "group system" was the University of Pennsylvania. Phillips, *op. cit.*, p. 211.

96. Harvard College, *Annual Reports of the President and Treasurer*, 1884–85, pp. 33–35, 40, 47–49; Charles S. Moore, "The Elective System at Harvard," *Harvard Graduates Magazine*, Vol. 11, June, 1903, pp. 530–534; Paul Hanus, "Graduate Testimony on the Elective System," *ibid.*, Vol. 10, March, 1902, pp. 354–359.

97. Morison, *Development of Harvard University, 1869–1929*, pp. xlvi–xlix.

98. There was a similar report by a Yale Faculty Committee in 1903, which led to a parallel tightening up of controls at New Haven. Pierson, *op. cit.*, p. 174.

99. A. Lawrence Lowell, *At War with Academic Traditions in America* (Cambridge, Mass., Harvard University Press, 1934).

100. Morison, *Development of Harvard University*.

101. See pp. 271–272.

102. Veysey, *op. cit.*, p. 257.

103. Rand, *op. cit.*, p. 81. Rand recalls that in his own college days under Eliot students at Harvard were sure that they were enjoying a liberal education. "We felt that despite the diversity in the feast of learning that tempted us to different dishes, we were sitting at the same table."

104. Charles W. Eliot, "The Case against Compulsory Latin," *Atlantic Monthly*, Vol. 119, March, 1917, pp. 360–361.

105. David Starr Jordan, *The Days of a Man* (Yonkers, N.Y., World Book, 1922), Vol. I, p. 80.

106. F. W. Clarke, "American Colleges *vs* American Science," *Popular Science Monthly*, Vol. 9, July, 1876, pp. 467–475.

107. LeDuc, *op. cit.*, pp. 78–79.

108. Rogers, *op. cit.*, pp. 114–115.

109. Edward H. Cotton, *Life of Charles W. Eliot* (Boston, Small, Maynard, 1926), pp. 164–165; Wertenbaker, *op. cit.*, pp. 271–274, 308.

110. Richard F. Axen, "Four Perspectives of Union College" (unpublished doctoral dissertation, University of California at Los Angeles, 1952), pp. 23–25, 84–85.

111. Schmidt, *op. cit.*, p. 37.

112. See Eliot's views in Charles W. Eliot, "The New Education," *Atlantic Monthly*, Vol. 23, March, 1869, pp. 365–367.

113. For a discussion of this trend, see Edmund E. Day, "Notes on the Reorientation of Liberal Education," *Bulletin of the Association of American Colleges*, Vol. 32, October, 1946, pp. 340–341.

114. William A. Neilson, *Charles W. Eliot, the Man and His Beliefs* (New York, Harper & Row, 1926), p. 77.

115. Spencer, *op. cit.*, pp. 93–96.

116. Edward L. Youmans, *The Culture Demanded by Modern Life* (Englewood Cliffs, N.J., Prentice-Hall, 1867), pp. 53–56; E. A. Bryan, "The Spirit of the Land-Grant Institutions," *Proceedings of the Association of Land-Grant Colleges*, Vol. 45, 1931, pp. 92–94; Veblen, *op. cit.*, pp. 390–391.

117. Isaac Todhunter, *The Conflict of Studies* (London, Macmillan, 1873), pp. 30–31.

118. Elizabeth C. Agassiz, *Louis Agassiz, His Life and Correspondence* (Boston, Houghton Mifflin, 1886), Vol. II, pp. 619–622.

119. *New Yorker*, Vol. 27, December 1, 1951, p. 50.

120. David A. Weaver, *Builders of American Universities* (Alton, Ill., Shurtleff College Press, 1950), Vol. I, pp. 277–382; for a similar analysis, see Edwin E. Slosson, *Great American Universities* (New York, Macmillan, 1910), pp. 510–511.

121. John Bascomb, *Things Learned by Living* (New York, Putnam, 1913), pp. 73–74; Willis Rudy,

The Evolving Liberal Arts Curriculum: A Historical Review of Basic Themes (New York, Teachers College, Columbia University, 1960), pp. 8–11, 35–47.

122. Stowe, *op. cit.,* p. 18. On this phenomenon, see C. Wright Mills, *White Collar: The American Middle Classes* (New York, Oxford University Press, 1951), p. 131.

123. W. H. Widener, "The College in a Pecuniary Culture," *Educational Record,* April, 1936, pp. 191–192; Abraham Flexner, *Universities, American, English, German* (New York, Oxford University Press, 1930), p. 70.

124. Fox, *op. cit.,* p. 40.

125. Morison, *Three Centuries of Harvard,* p. 384; David Starr Jordan, "University Tendencies in America," *Popular Science Monthly,* Vol. 63, June, 1903, p. 145. Flexner, in particular, was highly critical of "bargain-counter" *ad hoc* courses, such as principles of advertising, business English, and elementary costume design, which he felt properly had no place in a college or university curriculum. Flexner, *op. cit.,* pp. 55–56, 72, 140–144, 151–152.

126. Elizabeth B. Young, *Study of the Curricula of Seven Selected Women's Colleges of the Southern States* (New York, Teachers College, Columbia University, 1932), pp. 198–199.

127. Bachelor's degrees were offered now in fields as diverse as music, nursing, "homemaking," and "oratory."

128. William Tucker, *My Generation* (Boston, Houghton Mifflin, 1919), pp. 337–338.

129. LeDuc, *op. cit.,* p. 58. A similar type of argument can be found in Allan P. Farrell, *The Jesuit Code of Liberal Education* (Milwaukee, Wisc., Bruce Publishing, 1938), pp. 409–412.

130. W. DeWitt Hyde, "Policy of the Small College," *Educational Review,* Vol. 2, November, 1891, pp. 314–315.

131. Sherman B. Barnes, "Learning and Piety in Ohio Colleges, 1900–1930," *Ohio Historical Quarterly,* July, 1961, pp. 214–242.

Chapter 7. The Period of Fraternities and Athletics

1. Edward A. Birge, "A Change of Educational Emphasis," *Atlantic Monthly,* Vol. 103, February, 1909, pp. 190–191.

2. Laurence R. Veysey, *The Emergence of the American University* (Chicago, University of Chicago Press, 1965), pp. 272–275.

3. Woodrow Wilson, "What is a College for?" *Scribner's Magazine,* Vol. XLVI, November, 1909, pp. 572–575.

4. See pp. 41–42.

5. Noah Porter, *The American College and the American Public* (New Haven, Conn., C.C. Chatfield, 1870). On this see also "College Dormitories," *Barnard's American Journal of Education,* Vol. 30, 1880, pp. 741–742.

6. William H. Cowley, "History of Student Residential Housing," *School and Society,* Vol. 40, December 1, 1934, pp. 710–711.

7. *Ibid.;* Charles M. Perry, *Henry Philip Tappan* (Ann Arbor, University of Michigan Press, 1933), p. 232.

8. Edward Hitchcock, *Reminiscences of Amherst College* (Northampton, Mass., Bridgman & Childs, 1863), pp. 142–144; P. H. Mell, "College Government—The Dormitory System," *Barnard's American Journal of Education,* Vol. 30, 1880, pp. 65–67.

9. Frederick Pike, *A Student at Wisconsin* (Madison, Wisc., Democrat Printing, 1935), pp. 28–30; Cowley, *op. cit.,* pp. 711–712.

10. Samuel Eliot Morison, *Three Centuries of Harvard* (Cambridge, Mass., Harvard University Press, 1936), p. 422; Philip A. Bruce, *History of the University of Virginia* (New York, Macmillan, 1922), Vol. IV, pp. 69–71; George W. Pierson, *Yale College, An Educational History, 1871–1921* (New Haven, Conn., Yale University Press, 1952), pp. 411–412; W. S. Currell, "Why Students Leave College Before Graduation," *School Review,* Vol. 12, March, 1904, pp. 246–252; Edward F. Pothoff, "Who Goes to College?" *Journal of Higher Education,* Vol. 2, June, 1931, pp. 294–295.

11. At Yale, for example, students in 1902 earned over $38,000 as a result of work obtained through the college's bureau of self-help. Many others held scholarships. Pierson, *op. cit.,* p. 412.

12. Ernest Earnest, *Academic Procession* (Indianapolis, Bobbs-Merrill, 1953), pp. 210–213.

13. Charles W. Eliot, *University Administration* (Boston, Houghton Mifflin, 1908), pp. 216–220.

14. Robert Strozier *et al., Housing of Students,* Studies on Student Personnel Work, Series VI, No.

14 (Washington, D.C., American Council of Education, 1950), pp. 2–3.

15. James McCosh, "Discipline in American College," *North American Review,* Vol. 126, May-June, 1878, pp. 432–433; Francis and Heman L. Wayland, *Memoir of the Life and Labors of Francis Wayland* (New York, Sheldon, 1867), Vol. I, pp. 224–225. Any sampling of the histories of the ante-bellum colleges will illustrate this situation. For more details, see Chapter 3.

16. Bliss Perry, *And Gladly Teach* (Boston, Houghton Mifflin, 1935), pp. 65–66; G. Stanley Hall, *Life and Confessions of a Psychologist* (Englewood Cliffs, N.J., Prentice-Hall, 1923), p. 158.

17. As quoted in Veysey, *op. cit.,* pp. 295–296.

18. Samuel Eliot Morison, *The Development of Harvard University Since the Inauguration of President Eliot, 1869–1929* (Cambridge, Mass., Harvard University Press, 1930), pp. lxviii–lxix; Andrew D. White, *Autobiography* (London, Macmillan, 1905), Vol. I, pp. 430–431; Columbia College, *President's Report, 1869,* pp. 19–20; Orrin L. Elliott, *Stanford University, The First Twenty-Five Years* (Stanford, Calif., Stanford University Press, 1937), pp. 408–410; William F. Russell (ed.), *Rise of a University* (New York, Columbia University Press, 1937), Vol. I, Chaps. 9 and 11.

19. William Rainey Harper, *The Trend in Higher Education* (Chicago, University of Chicago Press, 1905), pp. 328–329.

20. Nathaniel S. Shaler, "Discipline in American Colleges," *North American Review,* Vol. 149, July, 1889, pp. 13–14.

21. E. A. Miller, "Moral Conditions in Ohio Colleges," *Educational Review,* Vol. 39, May, 1910, pp. 500–510; Stephen Vincent Benét, *The Beginning of Wisdom* (New York, Holt, Rinehart & Winston, 1921), pp. 125–126; Harry S. Warner, *Alcohol Trends in College Life* (Methodist Episcopal Church, 1938), pp. 8–9; Thomas J. Wertenbaker, *Princeton, 1746–1896* (Princeton, N.J., Princeton University Press, 1946), pp. 315–317, 361–362; Edward M. Burns, *David Starr Jordan: Prophet of Freedom* (Stanford, Calif., Stanford University Press, 1953), pp. 18–20, 168; Elliott, *op. cit.,* pp. 379–429; Perry, *op. cit.,* pp. 65–67.

22. Arthur T. Hadley, "Wealth and Democracy in American Colleges," *Harper's Magazine,* Vol. 113, August, 1906, p. 450.

23. James B. Angell, "Discipline in American Colleges," *North American Review,* Vol. 149, July, 1889, p. 6.

24. Richard Rogers Bowker, "The College of Today," *Princeton Review,* January, 1884, pp. 106–107.

25. William Le Conte Stevens, "Correspondence re: Self-Government in Colleges," *Popular Science Monthly,* Vol. 19, September, 1881, p. 697. For a detailed description of one of these early schemes, see George Rugg Cutting, *Student Life at Amherst* (Amherst, Hatch & Williams, 1871), pp. 93–94.

26. Henry D. Sheldon, *History and Pedagogy of American Student Societies* (Englewood Cliffs, N.J., Prentice-Hall, 1901), pp. 255–260; Bruce, *op. cit.,* Vol. IV, pp. 109–112; William M. Sloane, *The Life of James McCosh* (New York, Scribner, 1897), pp. 224–225; Louis C. Hatch, *History of Bowdoin College* (Portland, Me., Loring, Short & Harmon, 1927), pp. 206–209; James B. Conant *et al., History and Traditions of Harvard College* (Cambridge, Mass., Harvard Crimson, 1936), pp. 64–65.

27. As quoted in Veysey, *op. cit.,* p. 297. Also see John M. Gregory, "An Experiment in College Government," *International Review,* Vol. VI, June, 1881, pp. 512–513; Sheldon, *op. cit.,* pp. 258–261.

28. M. C. Fernald, "Cooperative Government," National Education Association *Proceedings, 1890,* pp. 685–690.

29. Earle D. Ross, *History of Iowa State College* (Ames, Iowa State College Press, 1942); Merle E. Curti and Vernon Carstensen, *The University of Wisconsin, A History* (Madison, University of Wisconsin Press, 1949), Vol. II, pp. 503–511.

30. Claude M. Fuess, *Amherst: The Story of a New England College* (Boston, Little, Brown, 1935), pp. 220–222; William S. Tyler, *History of Amherst College* (New York, F. H. Hitchcock, 1895), pp. 238–243; Thomas LeDuc, *Piety and Intellect at Amherst College, 1865–1912* (New York, Columbia University Press, 1946); Hatch, *op. cit.,* pp. 203–206.

31. Louise S. B. Saunders, "Government of Women Students in Colleges and Universities," *Educational Review,* Vol. 20, December, 1900, pp. 475–498; Thomas Woody, *History of Women's Education in the United States* (Lancaster, Pa., Science Press, 1929), Vol. II, pp. 202–203.

32. In some institutions, enforcement of the system was placed under the jurisdiction of student committees, while in many others the faculty had charge.

33. Bird T. Baldwin, *Present Status of the Honor System in Colleges and Universities* (Washington, D.C., Government Printing Office, 1915); C. Alphonso Smith, "Honor in Student Life in Colleges and Universities," *Educational Review,* Vol. 30, November, 1905, pp. 384–395; John Patton, *Jefferson, Cabell, and the University of Virginia* (New York, Neale Publishing, 1906), pp. 166–167, 174–175; Bruce, *op. cit.,* Vol. IV, pp. 170–175; Vol. V, pp. 254–260; James W. Alexander, *Princeton, Old and New* (New York, Scribner, 1898), pp. 31–32; McMillan Lewis, *Woodrow Wilson of Princeton* (Narbeth, Pa., Livingston Publishing, 1952), pp. 29–31; Sheldon, *op. cit.,* p. 265; Charles F. Thwing, *History of Higher Education in America* (Englewood Cliffs, N.J., Prentice-Hall, 1906), p. 238; Charles Fordyce, "College Ethics," *Educational Review,* Vol. 37, May, 1909, pp. 492–500.

34. Henry T. Claus, "The Problem of College Chapel," *Educational Review,* Vol. 46, September, 1913, pp. 177–187; C. H. Patton and W. T. Field, *Eight O'Clock Chapel* (Boston, Little, Brown, 1927).

35. McMillan, *op. cit.,* pp. 54–56; Henry C. Tuck, *Four Years at the University of Georgia* (Athens, Ga., published by the author, 1938), p. 25. In some of the state universities religious services were prohibited by law.

36. Benét, *op. cit.,* pp. 54–55.

37. Alfred Stearns, *An Amherst Boyhood* (Amherst, Mass., Amherst College, 1946), pp. 95–96, 102–103.

38. Claus, *op. cit.;* Abraham Flexner, *Daniel Coit Gilman* (New York, Harcourt Brace Jovanovich, 1946), p. 87; Morison, *Three Centuries of Harvard,* pp. 366–368, and *Development of Harvard University, 1869–1929,* pp. xli–xlviii; White, *op. cit.,* Vol. I, pp. 402–403; Jessica T. Austen, *Moses Coit Tyler* (Garden City, N.Y., Doubleday, 1911), p. 123.

39. Hugh Hawkins, "Charles W. Eliot, University Reform, and Religious Faith in America, 1869–1909," *Journal of American History,* Vol. 51, September, 1964, pp. 191–213.

40. Pike, *op. cit.,* pp. 78–80; Curti and Carstensen, *op. cit.,* Vol. I, p. 176; James E. Pollard, *History of Ohio State University* (Columbus, Ohio State University Press, 1952), Chap. 5.

41. Clarence Shedd, *Two Centuries of Student Christian Movements* (New York, Association Press, 1934).

42. Walter M. Kotschnig (ed.), *The University in a Changing World* (London, Oxford University Press, 1932), pp. 98–99.

43. Founded at William and Mary College, Phi Beta Kappa became a national organization in 1780 and 1781, when it issued charters to chapters at Yale and Harvard. In later years it changed into what it remains today, a national honorary and scholarly fraternity. Lily Jay Silver, "Phi Beta Kappa and the Nation," *Education,* Vol. 74, March, 1954, pp. 401–413; William T. Hastings, "Phi Beta Kappa as a Secret Society," *Key Reporter,* Vol. 31, Autumn, 1965.

44. The attitude of President Nott at Union College was friendly toward fraternities. He did require them, however, to forgo secrecy and cooperate with his administration. Cornelius Van Santvoord and Tayler Lewis, *Memoirs of Eliphalet Nott* (New York, Sheldon, 1876), p. 32; Union College, *Catalogue,* 1847, p. 29.

45. Hatch, *op. cit.,* pp. 312–315; also Wayne Musgrave, *College Fraternities* (New York, Interfraternity Conference, 1923), pp. 88–93; Hitchcock, *op. cit.,* pp. 325–326; William G. Hammond, *Remembrance of Amherst* (New York, Columbia University Press, 1946), pp. 169–170; Reginald H. Phelps, "One Hundred and Fifty Years of Phi Beta Kappa at Harvard," *American Scholar,* Vol. I, 1932, p. 62; Silver, *op. cit.,* pp. 402–411; Theodore R. Crane, "Francis Wayland and the Residential College," *Rhode Island History,* Vol. 19, July, 1960, pp. 77–78.

46. William Baird, *Manual of College Fraternities* (New York, College Fraternity Publishing, 1915), pp. 6–9, 16–19, 33–35; Musgrave, *op. cit.,* pp. 6–19, 28–29.

47. Veysey, *op. cit.,* p. 293; Stearns, *op. cit.,* p. 104; Pike, *op. cit.,* p. 175; LeDuc, *op. cit.,* pp. 123–127; Dixon Ryan Fox, *Union College, An Unfinished History* (Schenectady, N.Y., Union College, 1946), pp. 14–15. The sponsorship of social events such as dances by fraternity chapters at denominational colleges, it should be realized, represented something of a revolution in American college mores.

48. Edwin E. Aiken, *The Secret Society System* (New Haven, Conn., O. H. Briggs, 1882); H. L. Kellogg (ed.), *College Secret Societies* (Chicago, Ezra A. Cook, 1874); John Bascom, *Secret Societies in College* (Pittsfield, Mass., 1868); J. T. McFarland, "College Fraternities, Their

Influence and Control," National Education Association *Proceedings, 1890,* pp. 707–711; Sloane, *op. cit.,* pp. 221–222; Wertenbaker, *op. cit.,* pp. 322–324.

49. Pike, *op. cit.,* Walter B. Palmer (ed.), *Minutes of the Eleventh Session of the Interfraternity Conference,* November 29, 1919, pp. 61–64; Thwing, *op. cit.,* p. 379; Ernest E. Lindsay and Ernest O. Holland, *College and University Administration* (New York, Macmillan, 1930), pp. 511–521; Edward C. Elliott and Merritt M. Chambers, *The Colleges and the Courts* (New York, Carnegie Foundation, 1936), pp. 13–15. The reasoning of the Mississippi court was that since the state university student was a beneficiary of the state's largess, he would have to accept it on the conditions laid down by the state. The United States Supreme Court found this in no way coming within the prohibitions of the Fourteenth Amendment.

50. William H. P. Faunce, "The Relation of the College Faculty to Fraternities," National Educational Association *Proceedings, 1910,* pp. 348–357; Lindsay and Holland, *op. cit.,* pp. 513–520; Baird, *op. cit.,* Mary Irwin (ed.), *American Universities and Colleges* (Washington, D.C., American Council on Education, 1956), p. 38; Christian E. Burckel, *The College Blue Book* (Baltimore, Md., 1956), p. 284.

51. Andrew D. White, "College Fraternities," *Forum,* Vol. III, May, 1887, pp. 246–253. See the statements by Benjamin I. Wheeler, David Starr Jordan, Jacob Gould Schurman, James R. Day, and Frederick P. Keppel in W. A. Crawford, *The American College Fraternity* (Arkadelphia, Ark., 1903). See also the balanced estimate in Eliot, *op. cit.,* pp. 224–225.

52. Albert S. Baird (Chairman), *Report of the Committee on Relations between Colleges and Fraternities to the 1912 Interfraternity Conference* (New York, Interfraternity Conference, 1912), p. 28; Musgrave, *op. cit.,* pp. 23–25; Curti and Carstensen, *op. cit.,* Vol. I, pp. 664–668.

53. Sheldon, *op. cit.,* pp. 172–192, 221–229; Musgrave, *op. cit.,* pp. 94–98.

54. Alfred McClung Lee, "Can Social Fraternities Be Democratic?" *Journal of Higher Education,* Vol. 26, April, 1955, pp. 174–176; S. Willis Rudy, *The College of the City of New York, A History, 1847–1947* (New York, City College Press, 1949), pp. 68–70, 178, 295, 399; Lindsay and Holland, *op. cit.,* pp. 511–520.

55. Kellogg, *op. cit.,* pp. 7–9; John A. Porter, "The Society System of Yale College," *New Englander,* Vol. VII, New Series, pp. 390–391.

56. Benét, *op. cit.,* pp. 62–64; George Frazier, "Yale's Secret Societies," *Esquire,* September, 1955, pp. 106–116.

57. Charles M. Flandrau, *Diary of a Freshman* (London, William Heinemann, 1901), pp. 213–215; Morison, *Three Centuries of Harvard,* pp. 418–428.

58. Owen Wister, *Philosophy Four* (New York, Macmillan, 1903). On the other side of the picture, we find Professor Charles Eliot Norton insisting in 1890 that the "rich students' " clubs exerted little influence; that "student life at Harvard is essentially and healthily democratic." Charles E. Norton, "Harvard University in 1890," *Harper's Magazine,* Vol. 81, September, 1890, pp. 585–586. In an effort to keep it so, the *Harvard Crimson,* in the autumn of 1904, decided to stop printing the membership lists of any student clubs or organizations, with the exception of Phi Beta Kappa. Harvard Crimson, *Seventy-Fifth Anniversary* (Cambridge, Mass., Harvard University Press, 1948), p. 21.

59. Alexander, *op. cit.,* pp. 14–18; F. Scott Fitzgerald, *This Side of Paradise* (New York, Scribner, 1920), p. 47.

60. Ray Stannard Baker, *Woodrow Wilson, Life and Letters* (Garden City, N.Y., Doubleday, 1927), Vol. II, p. 262; Arthur S. Link, *Wilson: The Road to the White House* (Princeton, N.J., Princeton University Press, 1947); Lewis, *op. cit.,* p. 47.

61. The first intercollegiate debate was held in 1881, and this form of competition began to attract increasing interest among undergraduates. David Potter, *Debating in Colonial Chartered Colleges* (New York, Teachers College, Columbia University, 1944); see also Pike, *op. cit.,* pp. 77–78, and John C. French, *History of the University Founded by Johns Hopkins* (Baltimore, Md., Johns Hopkins Press, 1946), pp. 265–267.

62. Sherman B. Barnes, "Learning and Piety in Ohio Colleges, 1865–1900," *Ohio Historical Quarterly,* Vol. 69, October, 1960, pp. 334–335; Cutting, *op. cit.,* pp. 111–113; Edward A. Ross, *Seventy Years of It* (Englewood Cliffs, N.J., Prentice-Hall, 1936), p. 14; Francis A. Walker, *Discussions in Education* (New York, Holt Rinehart & Winston, 1899), pp. 260–262; Laura H. Moseley (ed.), *Diary of James Hadley* (New Haven, Conn., Yale University Press, 1951), p. 309; William Otis Carr, *Amherst Diary, 1853–1857* (Guilford, Conn., Shore Line Times Publishing, 1940), pp. 3–4; William W. Folwell, *Autobiography and Letters of a Pioneer of*

Culture (Minneapolis, University of Minnesota Press, 1933), p. 61; Richard T. Ely, *The Ground Under Our Feet* (New York, Macmillan, 1938), pp. 30–31; John W. Burgess, *Reminiscences of an American Scholar* (New York, Columbia University Press, 1934), pp. 58–59.

63. The first Harvard-Yale crew race took place in 1852.

64. Mark Hopkins, *Miscellaneous Essays and Discourses* (Boston, T.R. Marvin, 1847), pp. 244–245; Hitchcock, *op. cit.*, p. 68; Hammond, *op. cit.*, pp. 179–180; Morison, *Three Centuries of Harvard*, pp. 314–316; Howard Savage, *American College Athletics* (New York, Carnegie Foundation, 1929), pp. 13–20.

65. Amos Alonzo Stagg, *Touchdown!* (New York, McKay, 1927), pp. 50–51; Savage, *op. cit.*, p. 20.

66. Guy Lewis, "The Beginning of Organized Collegiate Sport," *American Quarterly*, Vol. 22, Summer, 1970, pp. 222–227.

67. Veysey, *op. cit.*, p. 276. See also Savage, *op. cit.*

68. One source has estimated that the athletic receipts at Yale alone in 1906 were more than five times the total income of the college seventy-five years before! Clarence F. Birdseye, *Individual Training in Our Colleges* (New York, Macmillan, 1907), pp. 158–164. On this question, see Savage, *op. cit.*, pp. 22–29; Stagg, *op. cit.*, pp. 71–82, 180–181.

69. Savage, *op. cit.*, pp. 28–29.

70. Ely, *op. cit.*, p. 202; Curti and Carstensen, *op. cit.*, Vol. I, p. 578. Adams retained on the rolls able football players of little intellectual ability, despite strenuous objections from his faculty.

71. Amos Alonzo Stagg to his family, January 20, 1891; University of Chicago Archives, as quoted in Joseph E. Gould, "William Rainey Harper and the University of Chicago" (unpublished doctoral dissertation, Syracuse University, 1951), pp. 122–123.

72. John F. Crowell, *Personal Recollections* (Durham, N.C., Duke University Press, 1939), pp. 45–46, 230–231. On one occasion, Crowell wrote that a Trinity defeat of the University of North Carolina's football team "gave notice that the little college up in Randolph had come out from under."

73. Savage, *op. cit.*, p. 24; William A. Neilson, *Charles W. Eliot, The Man and His Beliefs* (New York, Harper & Row, 1926), pp. 119–120; Edward C. Elliott, *The Rise of a University* (New York, Columbia University Press, 1937), Vol. II, pp. 442–447; Burns, *op. cit.*, pp. 169–170; James F. Kemp, "The Proper Function of Athletics in Colleges and Universities," *Educational Review*, Vol. 35, February, 1908, pp. 170–177.

74. The religious press objected to the moral relapses and excessive drinking which were reputed to accompany many of the "big games." Crowell, *op. cit.*, p. 226. The denominational attitude is illustrated by President John C. Kilgo of Trinity College, North Carolina, who reversed Crowell's big-time sports program there. Kilgo maintained that the fortunes of a denominational college should hang on faith in Christ, not the record of a football team. Paul N. Garber, *J. C. Kilgo, President of Trinity College* (Durham, N.C., Duke University Press, 1937), pp. 156–162.

75. White, *op. cit.*, Vol. I, pp. 352–353; E. Benjamin Andrews, "The General Tendencies of College Athletics," National Educational Association, *Proceedings, 1904*, pp. 549–557.

76. Walter Camp, *Book of College Sports* (Englewood Cliffs, N.J., Prentice-Hall, 1910), pp. 2–8.

77. Harvard even abolished football for a couple of years, while she studied the situation. Morison, *Three Centuries of Harvard*, pp. 409–410; Conant *et al.*, *op. cit.*, pp. 50–51; Savage, *op. cit.*, p. 22.

78. These figures included both high-school and college competition. Stagg, *op. cit.*, p. 253.

79. Savage, *op. cit.*

80. Fox, *op. cit.*, pp. 35–36; Burns, *op. cit.*, pp. 169–170, Stagg, *op. cit.*, pp. 253–255; Curti and Carstensen, *op. cit.*, Vol. II, pp. 533–547. Henry O. Severance, *Richard Henry Jesse* (Columbia, Mo., published by the author, 1937), pp. 151–152; French, *op. cit.*, pp. 293–294; Bruce, *op. cit.*, Vol. V, pp. 292–298; LeDuc, *op. cit.*, pp. 132–133; Sheldon, *op. cit.*, pp. 245–253.

81. In 1894, the Southern Intercollegiate Athletic Conference was established. The Big Ten was formed the following year, and the Northwest Conference made its debut in 1904. Stagg, *op. cit.*, pp. 114–116; Savage, *op. cit.*, pp. 26–27; Curti and Carstensen, *op. cit.*, Vol. I, pp. 693–709.

82. Savage, *op. cit.*, pp. xx–xxi, 31–32, 310–311.

83. William H. P. Faunce, "Character in Athletics," National Education Association, *Proceedings, 1904*, pp. 558–565.

84. *The Chronicle of Higher Education,* Vol. 8, July 8, 1974, p. 13.

85. Edwin E. Slosson, *Great American Universities* (New York, Macmillan, 1910), pp. 506–507; Stagg, *op. cit.,* pp. 174–175. To Thorstein Veblen, this whole business was simply an expression of the "barbarian temperament." Just as fraternities displayed the primordial heritage of clannishness, so athletics manifested the predatory instinct, pure and simple. This is why, he declared, they were so closely connected. Thorstein Veblen, *Theory of the Leisure Class* (New York, Macmillan, 1912), pp. 278–379.

86. LeDuc, *op. cit.,* pp. 132–133.

87. Walker, *op. cit.,* pp. 259–260.

88. Ernest Barker, "Universities in Great Britain," in Kotschnig (ed.), *op. cit.,* pp. 98–99.

89. Arnaud C. Marts, "College Football and College Endowment," *School and Society,* Vol. 40, July 7, 1934, pp. 14–15.

90. A. Lawrence Lowell, "College Rank and Distinction in Life," *Atlantic Monthly,* Vol. 92, October, 1903, p. 519.

91. George Fitch, *At Good Old Siwash* (Boston, Little, Brown, 1911), p. 291.

92. W. Carson Ryan, *Literature of American School and College Athletics* (New York, Carnegie Foundation, 1929), pp. xi–xii.

93. Edwin G. Dexter, "Accidents from College Football," *Educational Review,* Vol. 25, April, 1903, p. 417.

94. Crowell, *op. cit.,* pp. 226–227; Thwing, *op. cit.,* pp. 388–389; Richard Hofstadter and C. DeWitt Hardy, *The Development and Scope of Higher Education in the United States* (New York, Columbia University Press, 1952), pp. 112–113.

95. Fox, *op. cit.,* p. 35; Norton, *op. cit.,* pp. 586–587.

96. Denis W. Brogan, *The American Character* (New York, Knopf, 1944), pp. 142–143.

97. Arthur T. Hadley, "Wealth and Democracy in American Colleges," *Harper's Magazine,* Vol. 113, August, 1906, p. 452.

98. Brogan, *op. cit.,* p. 142.

99. Flandrau, *op. cit.,* pp. 100–101.

100. Frank L. Mott, *History of American Magazines* (Cambridge, Mass., Harvard University Press, 1938), Vol. II, pp. 99–100; James Bruce and J. Vincent Forrestal, *College Journalism* (Princeton, N.J., Princeton University Press, 1914), pp. 3–4.

101. "Our Magazine," *Yale Literary Magazine,* Vol. I, February, 1836, p. 39; Benét, *op. cit.,* p. 60; *Yale Literary Magazine,* Centennial Number, Vol. CI, February, 1936, pp. xiv–xvii. William Lyon Phelps writes in this issue: "I wanted to be on the *Lit.* board more than I wanted anything else. I wanted it more than I wanted Phi Beta Kappa, and about three hundred times more than I wanted an election to a Senior Society."

102. Donald Hall (ed.), *The Harvard Advocate Anthology* (New York, Twayne, 1950), pp. 11–13, 21–25.

103. Mott, *op. cit.,* Vol. I, pp. 172, 488–489; Vol. II, pp. 99–100; Vol. III, pp. 165–166.

104. Bruce and Forrestal, *op. cit.,* p. 4; Harvard Crimson, *The Crimson, 1873–1906* (Cambridge, Mass., 1906), pp. 1–22; Harvard Crimson, *Seventy-Fifth Anniversary, 1873–1948* (Cambridge, Mass., 1948), pp. 1–10; Irwin, *op. cit.,* pp. 39–40.

105. Harvard Lampoon, *Fiftieth Anniversary, 1876–1926* (Cambridge, Mass., 1926), pp. 1–2, 15, 18–27; Mott, *op. cit.,* Vol. I, p. 427; Vol. III, pp. 268–269.

106. Wilbur Cortez Abbott, "The Guild of Students," *Atlantic Monthly,* Vol. 128, November, 1921, pp. 623–624; E. Lloyd-Jones and M. R. Smith, "Campus Customs: Sense and Nonsense" (unpublished manuscript). For novelistic treatment of this phenomenon, see Charles K. Field and Will Irwin, *Stanford Stories* (San Francisco, A. M. Robertson, 1913), pp. 268–269; and George Fitch, *At Good Old Siwash* (Boston, Little, Brown, 1911), pp. 289–290.

107. William Lyon Phelps, attending Yale in the 1880s, recalled later how he "would at any moment gladly have died for my class flag." William L. Phelps, *Autobiography with Letters* (New York, Oxford University Press, 1939), pp. 134–135. On this subject, see also Sheldon, *op. cit.,* pp. 83–87, 123–124, 172–177; and Hall, *op. cit.,* p. 113.

108. Alexander, *op. cit.,* pp. 27–29; Edward H. Cotton, *Life of Charles W. Eliot* (Boston, Small, Maynard, 1926), pp. 27–29; Field and Irwin, *op. cit.,* pp. 58–59.

109. Edward Augustus Freeman, *Some Impressions of the United States* (London, Longmans, Green and Co., 1883), pp. 192–193.

110. Leon B. Richardson, *History of Dartmouth College* (Hanover, N.H., Dartmouth College Publications, 1932), Vol. II, p. 721. Some welcomed this change as making possible the realization

of a fuller individuality. For example, Dean Briggs of Harvard argued that students should be free to choose their intimate associates irrespective of class. Where Greek and chapel are elective, he said, baseball should not be compulsory. Conant *et al., op. cit.,* pp. 43–49.

111. Fuess, *op. cit.,* pp. 276–277. The older pattern is described for us as follows in one memoir: "The resources of distraction were limited in a small college town: the automobile did not exist and the 'safety' bicycle in vogue after the dangerous high-and-low wheel machines, was not a socializing agent. So the distraction of books had its excuse!" James M. Baldwin, *Between Two Wars* (Boston, Stratford, 1926), Vol. I, p. 29.

112. Elliott, *op. cit.,* pp. 206–207; Abbott, *op. cit.,* pp. 620–621.

113. Henry Seidel Canby, *Alma Mater: The Gothic Age of the American College* (New York, Farrar Straus & Giroux, 1936), pp. 125–131.

114. As quoted in Veysey, *op. cit.,* p. 285.

115. *Yale Literary Magazine,* Centennial Number, Vol. CI, February, 1936, p. 30.

116. William Lyon Phelps, *The Excitement of Teaching* (New York, Liveright, 1931), pp. 44–45.

117. Owen Johnson, *Stover at Yale* (New York, Stokes, 1912), p. 246.

118. Canby, *op. cit.*

119. Burges Johnson, "Campus against Classroom," *Harper's Magazine,* Vol. 167, July, 1933, pp. 218–219.

120. Abbott, *op. cit.,* pp. 624–625.

Chapter 8. The American State University

1. Richard Hofstadter and C. DeWitt Hardy, *Development and Scope of Higher Education in the United States* (New York, Columbia University Press, 1952), p. 30.

2. Pierson has cited three markedly different English dictionary definitions of the meaning of the word from the late eighteenth century down to 1891. George W. Pierson, "American Universities in the Nineteenth Century," in Margaret Clapp (ed.), *The Modern University* (Ithaca, N.Y., Cornell University Press, 1950), p. 60. On this question, see also "The University," *Barnard's American Journal of Education,* Vol. 9, 1860, pp. 49–50.

3. Norman Foerster, *The American State University* (Chapel Hill, University of North Carolina Press, 1937).

4. Note, for example, Thomas Jefferson's justly renowned Virginia Statute for Religious Freedom (1786). Such acts cleared the way for state secular higher education.

5. Willard W. Smith, "Relations of College and State in Colonial America" (unpublished doctoral dissertation, Columbia University, 1949), pp. 144–155.

6. Allen Oscar Hansen, *Liberalism and American Education in the Eighteenth Century* (New York, Macmillan, 1926).

7. This controversy, principally involving proponents of the claims of the University of North Carolina and the University of Georgia, revolved around the question whether the "beginning" of a university should be dated from the first provision for it in a constitution, the granting of a charter, or the year when it first opened for instruction. Frank P. Graham, "The First University of the People," *School and Society,* Vol. 59, January 1, 1944, p. 18.

8. Henry S. Pritchett, "The Use of the Term University in the United States," *Carnegie Foundation for the Advancement of Teaching, Second Annual Report,* 1907, pp. 84–85.

9. See John S. Whitehead, *The Separation of College and State* (New Haven, Conn., Yale University Press, 1973). Also see James B. Conant, "America Remakes the University," *Atlantic Monthly,* Vol. 177, May, 1946, p. 41.

10. *Trustees of the University of North Carolina* v. *Foy* (5 North Carolina 58); Alexander Brody, *The American State and Higher Education* (Washington, D.C., American Council on Education, 1935), pp. 45–47; see also Edward C. Elliott and Merritt M. Chambers, *The Colleges and the Courts* (New York, Carnegie Foundation, 1936), pp. 116–118. The Dartmouth College decision of 1819, which drew a sharper line between "public" and "private" institutions, was also applied to prevent changes in existing chartered state foundations. Thus the University of Maryland, incorporated in 1812, had its board of regents abolished by the legislature in 1825 and a new board of trustees set up. Thirteen years later the courts held this act void on the basis of the precedent established by the Dartmouth College Case. *Regents of the University of Maryland* v. *Williams* (9 Gill and J. 365).

11. This is well illustrated by the early history of the University of Georgia. See Rev. Isaac V.

Brown, *Memoirs of the Rev. Robert Finley, D.D., Late Pastor of the Presbyterian Congregation at Basking-Ridge, New Jersey, and President of Franklin College, Georgia* (New Brunswick, N.J., Terhune and Letson, 1819), pp. 133–136.

12. Ernest V. Hollis, "Columbia Almost a State University," *Educational Forum*, Vol. 4, May, 1940, pp. 409–414; Dorothy R. Dillon, *The New York Triumvirate* (New York, Columbia University Press, 1949); Herbert and Carol Schneider, *Samuel Johnson* (New York, Columbia University Press, 1929), Vol. IV.

13. John B. Pine, "The Origin of the University of the State of New York," *Educational Review*, Vol. 37, March, 1909, pp. 284–291.

14. Carl Becker, *Cornell University: Founders and the Founding* (Ithaca, N.Y., Cornell University Press, 1943), pp. 14–16; William Warren Street, *Religion in the Development of American Culture, 1765–1840* (New York, Scribner, 1952).

15. G. Stanley Hall, "Student Customs," *Proceedings of the American Antiquarian Society*, October, 1900, pp. 122–123.

16. In place of rationalism, a great vogue now arose for the Scottish "common sense" philosophy, which could be used as a philosophical grounding for orthodox faith. Herbert Schneider, *History of American Philosophy* (New York, Columbia University Press, 1946), pp. 246–249.

17. For examples, see Eliphalet Nott, *Address to Candidates for the Baccalaureate, May 18, 1805* (Albany, N.Y., Charles R. Webster, 1805), pp. 9–11; Theodore Dwight, Jr., *President Dwight's Decisions of Questions Discussed by the Senior Class in Yale College* (New York, Jonathan Leavitt, 1833), p. 227; Samuel Stanhope Smith, *Lectures, Corrected and Improved, which have been delivered for a series of years at the College of New Jersey* (Trenton, Daniel Fenton, 1812), Vol. II, p. 303.

18. Earl G. Swem, *Kentuckians at William and Mary College* (reprinted from *Filson Club History Quarterly*).

19. In the same way, any plan for centralized public control of education was quickly denounced as "Bonapartism" and dictatorship.

20. Dixon Ryan Fox, "Civilization in Transit," *American Historical Review*, Vol. 32, July, 1927, pp. 761–762. The reason most of the clergymen who were hired during this early period had to be brought down from the North was that the southern "gentleman" saw little dignity in teaching. For a college-trained person, law and theology were then considered the only honorific "professions," aside from managing a plantation; Alma P. Foerster, "The State University in the Old South" (unpublished doctoral dissertation, Duke University, 1939), pp. 106–117.

21. Frederick Jackson Turner, *The United States, 1830–1850* (New York, Holt, Rinehart & Winston, 1935), pp. 201–202.

22. Julian P. Boyd (ed.), *Thomas Jefferson Papers* (Princeton, N.J., Princeton University Press, 1950), Vol. II, pp. 305–324, 534–544.

23. Henry Tutwiler, *The Early Years of the University of Virginia* (Charlottesville, Chronicle and Job Office, 1882), pp. 7–8.

24. James M. Garnett, *The Elective System of the University of Virginia* (reprinted from *Andover Review*, April, 1886), pp. 4–5.

25. Joseph C. Cabell to Thomas Jefferson, January 14, 1822, in Thomas Jefferson and Joseph C. Cabell, *Early History of the University of Virginia as Contained in the Letters of Thomas Jefferson and Joseph C. Cabell* (Richmond, Va., J. W. Randolph, 1856), pp. 232–237.

26. Thomas Jefferson to Joseph C. Cabell, February 26, 1818, *ibid.*, pp. 128–129.

27. Joseph C. Cabell to Thomas Jefferson, January 14, 1822, *ibid.*, pp. 232–237.

28. Philip A. Bruce, *History of the University of Virginia* (New York, Macmillan, 1922), Vol. III, pp. 8–14. In 1856, the Virginia legislature repealed the law providing free board at the University for "state scholars." It was alleged at the time that this provision was encouraging "idle habits" among some of these young men.

29. Jefferson and Cabell, *op. cit.*, pp. 201–202, 239–240, 260–261.

30. Thomas Jefferson to Joseph C. Cabell, December 28, 1822, *ibid.*, pp. 260–261.

31. *Enactments By the Rector and Visitors of the University of Virginia* (Charlottesville, 1825), pp. 3–10.

32. Bruce, *op. cit.*, Vol. I, pp. 332–333; See pp. 97–98.

33. Roy J. Honeywell, *The Educational Work of Thomas Jefferson* (Cambridge, Mass., Harvard University Press, 1931), pp. 56–62. In terms of foreign influence, Jefferson seems to have been

principally impressed by the models furnished by the University of Geneva, the "revolutionary" University of France, and even the University of Edinburgh. It surprises some that he was not interested in the newly founded University of Berlin. Yet one observer argues that he may have rejected the idea of having one American-style college president with real power serve continuously because of the example of the annual election of a *rector magnificus* in German universities. Garnett, *op. cit.,* pp. 3–4.

34. "Had we built a barn for a college, and log huts for accommodations, should we ever have had the assurance to propose to an European professor of that character to come to it? Why give up this important idea, when so near its accomplishment that a single life more effects it?" Thomas Jefferson to Joseph C. Cabell, December 28, 1822, in Jefferson and Cabell, *op. cit.,* p. 260.

35. William P. Trent, *English Culture in Virginia* (Baltimore, Md., Johns Hopkins Press, 1889), pp. 16–17, 24–27. At one time, Jefferson hoped to attract to the university "three of the ablest characters in the world to fill the higher professorships." These were Dr. Thomas Cooper; the Abbé Correa, a famous naturalist; and Say, the noted French economist. Jefferson, however, was disappointed in these expectations.

36. Thomas Jefferson to Joseph C. Cabell, January 25, 1822, in Jefferson and Cabell, *op. cit.,* pp. 239–240.

37. Thomas Jefferson to Joseph C. Cabell, January 31, 1821, *ibid.,* pp. 201–202. The Missouri Compromise of 1820, it should be remembered, had restricted slavery in the Louisiana Purchase to a line south of latitude 36° 30′.

38. Thomas Jefferson to Joseph C. Cabell, January 28, 1823, *ibid.,* pp. 270–271.

39. Thomas Jefferson to Joseph C. Cabell, January 13, 1823, *ibid.,* pp. 266–268.

40. *Ibid.*

41. Daniel J. Boorstin, *The Lost World of Thomas Jefferson* (Boston, Beacon Press, 1960), pp. 217–225.

42. Pritchett, *op. cit.,* p. 85.

43. Bruce, *op. cit.,* Vol. I, pp. 332–333.

44. Orie W. Long, *Thomas Jefferson and George Ticknor, A Chapter in American Scholarship* (Williamstown, Mass., McClelland Press, 1933).

45. Turner, *op. cit.,* pp. 201–202.

46. Foerster, *op. cit.,* pp. 116–117, 181–186, 208–209, 461–466.

47. For the strong vein of utilitarianism in Jefferson's educational thinking, see Boorstin, *op. cit.,* pp. 216–225.

48. Philip Lindsley, *Educational Discourses* (Philadelphia, Lippincott, 1859); Henry C. Witherington, *Higher Education in Tennessee* (Chicago, University of Chicago Libraries, 1931); John F. Woolverton, "Philip Lindsley and the Cause of Education in the Old Southwest," *Tennessee Historical Quarterly,* March, 1960.

49. Louis B. Wright, *Culture on the Moving Frontier* (Bloomington, Indiana University Press, 1955), pp. 61–63; Robert E. Riegel, *America Moves West* (New York, Holt, Rinehart & Winston, 1947), pp. 288–289; Niels H. Sonne, *Liberal Kentucky, 1780–1828* (New York, Columbia University Press, 1939), pp. 240–261; Henry G. Baker, "Transylvania: A History of the Pioneer University of the West" (unpublished doctoral dissertation, University of Cincinnati, 1949).

50. See pp. 102–103.

51. See pp. 106–107.

52. See p. 62.

53. Egbert R. Isbell, "The Universities of Virginia and Michigania," *Michigan Historical Magazine,* Vol. 26, 1942, pp. 39–53; Willis Dunbar, "Public Versus Private Control of Higher Education in Michigan," *Mississippi Valley Historical Review,* Vol. 22, December, 1935, pp. 388–389.

54. We have already noted the exception represented by the University of Vermont, founded in 1791.

55. Examples are the Universities of Indiana (1821), Michigan (1837), Iowa (1847), Wisconsin (1848), and Minnesota (1851). It should be noted that state universities continued to be founded at this time in the South. Thus we find Delaware establishing such an institution in 1833, Missouri in 1839, Mississippi in 1844, and Louisiana in 1853.

56. Cyrus Northrup, *Addresses, Educational and Patriotic* (Minneapolis, H. W. Wilson, 1910), pp. 507–509; Theodore C. Blegen, *The Land Lies Open* (Minneapolis, University of Minnesota

Press, 1949), pp. 143–144; Frederick Jackson Turner, *The Frontier in American History* (New York, Holt, Rinehart & Winston, 1921), p. 354; George F. Magoun, "Source of American Education—Popular and Religious," *The New Englander,* Vol. 36, July, 1877, pp. 476–477.

57. Charles M. Perry, *Henry Philip Tappan* (Ann Arbor, University of Michigan Press, 1933), pp. 223–227.

58. William P. and Julia P. Cutler, *Life, Journals, and Correspondence of Reverend Manasseh Cutler* (Cincinnati, Robert Clarke, 1888), Vol. II, pp. 321–323; Richard G. Axt, *The Federal Government and the Financing of Higher Education* (New York, Columbia University Press, 1952), pp. 26–27.

59. David S. Hill, *Control of Tax-Supported Higher Education* (New York, Carnegie Foundation, 1934), pp. 29–30; Hofstadter and Hardy, *op. cit.,* pp. 38–39; Axt, *op. cit.*

60. The territorial legislature of Indiana in 1804 celebrated the action of Congress in giving a township for the support of a seminary of higher learning by authorizing the establishment of Vincennes University, "for as much as literature, and philosophy, furnish the most useful and pleasing occupations, improving and varying the enjoyments of prosperity, affording relief under the pressure of misfortune, and hope and consolation in the hours of death." Quoted in Wright, *op. cit.,* pp. 106–107.

61. James A. Woodburn, *The History of Indiana University* (Bloomington, Indiana University Press, 1940), pp. 121–123.

62. Donald G. Tewksbury, *The Founding of Colleges and Universities before the Civil War* (New York, Teachers College, Columbia University, 1932), p. 184.

63. University of Michigan, *President's Annual Report,* 1887, p. 17.

64. John N. Waddel, *Academic Memorials* (Richmond, Va., Presbyterian Committee of Publication, 1891), p. 297; Alonzo Church, *Report of Alonzo Church, D.D., President of Franklin College, University of Georgia, Read before the Senatus Academicus, Nov. 10, 1853* (Athens, Ga., Franklin College, 1853), p. 8.

65. These disputes often arose in connection with the allocation of the congressional land grant. The church-related colleges would sometimes struggle among themselves for shares of this grant, thus unintentionally helping to strengthen the case for a state university. Merle Curti and Vernon Carstensen, *The University of Wisconsin: A History, 1848–1925* (Madison, University of Wisconsin Press, 1949), Vol. I, pp. 14–19.

66. Sherman B. Barnes, "Learning and Piety in Ohio Colleges, 1865–1900," *Ohio Historical Quarterly,* Vol. 69, October, 1960, pp. 328–331.

67. Wright, *op. cit.,* pp. 106–107. Woodburn, *op. cit.,* pp. 121–123; Harry E. Edwards, "The College Curriculum in the Area of the North Central Association, 1830–1930" (unpublished doctoral dissertation, University of Indiana, 1933), pp. 75–76.

68. Willis Dunbar, *The University and Its Branches* (reprinted from *Michigan Alumnus Quarterly Review,* July 20, 1940, Vol. XLVI, No. 24).

69. Quoted in Dixon Ryan Fox, "Civilization in Transit," *American Historical Review,* Vol. 32, July, 1927, pp. 765–766.

70. See such representative statements of this era as Heman Humphrey, *Discourse Before the Connecticut Alpha, August 14, 1839* (New Haven, Conn., L. H. Young, 1839), pp. 5–14; Worthington Smith, *Popular Instruction* (St. Albans, Vt., E. B. Whiting, 1846), pp. 10–16.

71. Woodburn, *op. cit.,* pp. 122–123; Richard W. Leopold, *Robert Dale Owen* (Cambridge, Mass., Harvard University Press, 1940), p. 286.

72. In 1856, the largest reported enrollment was at the University of Virginia, with 514 students, 184 of whom were listed as "professionals." The next largest was at the University of Michigan, which had 288 students. Of these, 133 were in the medical branch. Clarence Shedd, "Higher Education in the United States," in Walter M. Kotschnig (ed.), *The University in a Changing World* (London, Oxford University Press, 1932), pp. 136–137.

73. Curti and Carstensen, *op. cit.,* Vol. I, p. 187.

74. Turner, *The Frontier in American History,* p. 354; Wright, *op. cit.,* pp. 106–107.

75. Blegen, *op. cit.,* pp. 152–159.

76. Willis Dunbar, "Public Versus Private Control of Higher Education in Michigan, 1817–1855," *Mississippi Valley Historical Review,* Vol. 22, December, 1935, pp. 390–392.

77. *Ibid.,* pp. 395–404; Dunbar, *The University and Its Branches, op. cit.*

78. Henry Philip Tappan, *University Education* (New York, Putnam, 1851), pp. 61–68, 82–95; Perry, *op. cit.,* pp. 223–229.

79. University of Michigan, *Catalogue, 1853–1854* (Ann Arbor, S. B. McCracken, 1854), pp. 20–23.
80. Pierson, *op. cit.*, p. 62.
81. W. O. Thompson, "The Influence of the Morrill Act upon American Higher Education," *Proceedings of the Association of American Agricultural Colleges and Experiment Stations,* Vol. 26, 1912, p. 93; Axt, *op. cit.*, pp. 57–59; Dean W. Kuykendall, "The Land-Grant College: A Study in Transition" (unpublished doctoral dissertation, Harvard University, 1946).
82. James B. Angell, *Reminiscences* (New York, McKay, 1912), pp. 121–122; Shirley W. Smith, *James Burrill Angell* (Ann Arbor, University of Michigan Press, 1954), p. 79; Wright, *op. cit.*, pp. 146–148; Henry S. Pritchett, "Shall the University Become a Corporation?" *Atlantic Monthly,* Vol. 96, September, 1905, p. 292; Witherington, *op. cit.*, pp. 135–136. Ultimately, twenty-six states donated their Morrill Act grants to their state university. *Education Yearbook,* 1943.
83. Henry S. Pritchett, "Spirit of the State Universities," *Atlantic Monthly,* Vol. 105, June, 1910, pp. 745–747; "The State as a Unit in Educational Administration," *Carnegie Foundation for the Advancement of Teaching, Third Annual Report,* 1908, pp. 80–81; Charles Riborg Mann, "Federal Relations to Education," *Educational Record,* Vol. 11, April, 1930, p. 94; Hill, *op. cit.*, pp. 367–370; Earl D. Ross, *History of Iowa State College* (Ames, Iowa State College Press, 1942), pp. 197–214; Association of American Universities, *Proceedings,* Sixth Annual Conference, January, 1905, p. 27. By 1943, there were nineteen separate land-grant colleges for white students and seventeen for Negro students. *Education Yearbook,* 1943.
84. Blegen, *op. cit.*, pp. 172–173, 178–179; for the Minnesota development, see also Northrup, *op. cit.*, pp. 407–409, 507–508.
85. In the older states of the East, White proposed that public and private aid be concentrated upon a small number of "the broadest and strongest foundations already laid," while in the West he believed that it should go exclusively to build up state universities "for the highest literary, scientific, and industrial instruction." White could very well have gotten these ideas from President Tappan of Michigan, under whom he served as a professor of history during the 1850s. See Walter P. Rogers, *Andrew D. White and the Modern University* (Ithaca, N.Y., Cornell University Press, 1942), pp. 203–205; Andrew D. White, *Advanced Education: A Paper Read Before the National Education Association, August 5, 1874; Some Important Questions in Higher Education* (Boston, Office of Old and New, 1874).
86. Pritchett, *op. cit.*, p. 146.
87. University of Michigan, *President's Annual Report,* 1875, pp. 17–18; 1885, pp. 8–9; Angell, *op. cit.*, pp. 243–244; Richard Price, *Financial Support of State Universities* (Cambridge, Mass., Harvard University Press, 1924), p. 156, and *Financial Support of the University of Michigan* (Cambridge, Mass., Harvard University Press, 1923), pp. 37–38, 40–41, 54–55. See Chap. 17.
88. Pritchett, *op. cit.*
89. W.J. Kerr, "Spirit of the Land-Grant Institutions," *Proceedings of the Association of Land-Grant Colleges,* Vol. 45, 1931, pp. 74–75; Waddel, *op. cit.*, pp. 294–295.
90. Charles K. Adams to Andrew D. White, January 8, 1875, White Papers, Cornell University (courtesy of Professor Thomas LeDuc, Oberlin College); according to White, the proposal for a second Morrill Bill was defeated in Congress in 1873 due to the influence of this same group. Andrew D. White to Daniel C. Gilman, March 1, 1873, Gilman Papers, Johns Hopkins University (courtesy of Professor Thomas LeDuc).
91. Charles K. Adams, *State Aid to Higher Education* (Baltimore, Md., Johns Hopkins Press, 1898).
92. See Pierson, *op. cit.*, pp. 63–64. A concrete example of how these demands affected one state university is afforded by Michigan, where pressure from the mining interests of the Upper Peninsula led to the establishment by the legislature of a School of Mines at Ann Arbor. University of Michigan, *President's Annual Report,* 1875, pp. 14–15.
93. William Watts Folwell to Andrew D. White, April 30, 1879, in William Watts Folwell, *Autobiography and Letters* (Minneapolis, University of Minnesota Press, 1933), pp. 190–196, 219–220; Ross, *op. cit.*, Curti and Carstensen, *op. cit.*, Vol. I, pp. 100–101; Wright, *op. cit.*, pp. 146–151; William Ferrier, *Origin and Development of the University of California* (Berkeley, Calif., Sather Gate Book Shop, 1930), pp. 359–361. For a critique of the narrowing impact of science teaching at the University of Wisconsin in the 1870s, see John Bascom, *Things Learned by Living* (New York, Putnam, 1913), pp. 67–68.
94. *Ninth Census of the United States, 1870* (Washington, D.C., Government Printing Office, 1870), p. 46; U.S. Commissioner of Education, *Report for 1899–1900* (Washington, D.C., Government Printing Office, 1901), Vol. II, p. 2119.

95. Charles W. Eliot, *Educational Reform* (Englewood Cliffs, N.J., Prentice-Hall, 1898), p. 334.
96. Angell, *op. cit.*, p. 255. Angell upheld the essentially Jeffersonian position that higher education should be accessible to the talented individual, regardless of financial status, in the interests of fully utilizing the intellectual potential of the nation. See James B. Angell, *Higher Education: A Plea for Making it Accessible to All* (Ann Arbor, 1879).
97. University of Michigan, *President's Annual Report,* 1885, pp. 20–24; Edward F. Pothoff, "Who Goes to College?" *Journal of Higher Education,* Vol. 2, June, 1931, pp. 294–295; Curti and Carstensen, *op. cit.,* Vol. I, pp. 661–662; Edward A. Ross, *Changing America* (Englewood Cliffs, N.J., Prentice-Hall, 1912), pp. 191–192. Of course, we must be careful not to overlook, in this connection, the parallel influence in the late nineteenth and early twentieth centuries of Chautauqua lecturers, the development of university extension, the multiplication of "reading circles" and summer schools, and many other related movements in the popularization of learning in America.
98. Adams, *op. cit.,* pp. 13–14.
99. This concept was also emphasized in the Cornell charter, which explicitly stated: "The leading object of the corporation hereby created shall be to teach such branches of learning as are related to agriculture and the mechanic arts, including military tactics. . . . But such other branches of science and knowledge may be embraced in the plan of instruction and investigation pertaining to the university as the trustees may deem useful and proper." Becker, *op. cit.,* pp. 88–90.
100. Andrew D. White, *Autobiography* (London, Macmillan, 1905), Vol. I, p. 341.
101. *Ibid.,* pp. 341–342. White never swerved from his basic objectives during his long administration of Cornell's affairs, although he did modify his stand on certain minor points, such as student self-government. In his annual report for 1884, a year before he left the Cornell presidency, White reiterated the same principles he had stated in his inaugural address. Cornell University, *President's Annual Report,* 1884, p. 61.
102. Rogers, *op. cit.,* pp. 210–215.
103. White, *Autobiography,* Vol. I, pp. 287–295.
104. *Ibid.,* pp. 294–339.
105. A clause in the bill which founded Cornell is illustrative of this theme. It provided that the university should be open to all applicants "without distinction as to rank, class, previous occupation, or locality." Rogers, *op. cit.,* pp. 61–62.
106. White wanted to get Ely to come to Ithaca because the latter knew "all about the cooperative system on the Baltimore and Ohio RR which I have been trying to get Depew to try on the N.Y. Central." Andrew D. White to Charles K. Adams, April 7, 1886, White Papers, Cornell University (courtesy of Professor Thomas LeDuc).
107. The University departments he wished to establish for the training of American journalists and legislators were to be modeled on a similar program at the University of Tübingen in Germany. White was an enthusiastic, and sometimes uncritical, admirer of Bismarck and the German university. Andrew D. White to Charles K. Adams, May 17, 1878, *ibid.*
108. *Ibid.*
109. Andrew D. White to Charles K. Adams, May 17, 1878, *ibid.*
110. Rogers, *op. cit.*
111. White, *Autobiography,* Vol. I, pp. 390–396.
112. Again, the Cornell University charter was very explicit on this question. It stated that "persons of every religious denomination, or of no religious denomination, shall be equally eligible to all offices and appointments." Becker, *op. cit.,* pp. 88–90.
113. Edward McN. Burns, *David Starr Jordan: Prophet of Freedom* (Stanford, Calif., Stanford University Press, 1953), pp. 4–5, 68, 368; Earl D. Ross, *Democracy's College* (Ames, Iowa State College Press, 1942), pp. 152–153.
114. Becker, *op. cit.,* pp. 21–22, 135–136.
115. Morrill added: "That is to say, an institution fully equipped to furnish all that is required not only by the literary or clerical professions, already perhaps overcrowded, but also all that can be useful to most and the . . . ambitions of the forty-five millions out of fifty hardly provided for twenty years ago." Justin S. Morrill to Andrew D. White, May 24, 1883, White Papers, Cornell University (courtesy of Professor Thomas LeDuc). This statement has to be accepted with considerable caution, however, because there is a strong possibility that Senator Morrill wrote letters in a similar vein to other land-grant-college presidents.

116. Edmund E. Day, *Education for Freedom and Responsibility* (Ithaca, N.Y., Cornell University Press, 1952), pp. 57–58, 68–69.
117. Folwell, *op. cit.*
118. Blegen, *op. cit.*, pp. 186–190.
119. The Michigan school was directly modeled on a similar institution which had been successfully established at the University of Tübingen in Germany. Michigan declared that the purpose of the new school was to furnish "proper training for the duties of the public bureaus and of civil service in general." University of Michigan, *President's Annual Report,* 1881, pp. 2–4.
120. Richard T. Ely, *The Ground Under Our Feet* (New York, Macmillan, 1938), pp. 195–196; Vernon Carstensen, "The Origin and Early Development of the Wisconsin Idea," *Wisconsin Magazine of History,* Spring, 1956, pp. 181–187.
121. This reflected the dominant concept in the German empire "that it pays the state to concern itself in the betterment of human beings and the protection of human welfare, in order that it may receive in return a rich reward for this investment." Charles McCarthy, *The Wisconsin Idea* (New York, Macmillan, 1912), p. 24.
122. Frederic C. Howe, *Wisconsin, An Experiment in Democracy* (New York, Scribner, 1912), p. x.
123. Ely, *op. cit.*, pp. 206–207.
124. Maurice M. Vance, *Charles Richard Van Hise, Scientist Progressive* (Madison, State Historical Society of Wisconsin, 1960), pp. 85–87.
125. Charles R. Van Hise, *Inaugural Address, June 7, 1904* (Lancaster, Pa., 1904). In subsequent addresses, Van Hise continued to elaborate the concept of a university dedicated to the promotion of human progress. To do this effectively, however, it must have complete *Lehrfreiheit* and *Lernfreiheit,* freedom to teach and freedom to learn. Reactionaries must not be allowed to crush the university's intellectual freedom, because it was the real source of constructive evolution and orderly advance in the human community. This would, of course, require the supporting society to display a notable largeness of view, but Van Hise was hopeful that this would prove to be possible. See Charles R. Van Hise, *The Spirit of a University, A Commencement Address, June 19, 1912;* "The Place of a University in a Democracy," National Education Association, *Proceedings, 1916,* Vol. 54, pp. 68–73.
126. McCarthy, *op. cit.,* p. 127; Edward A. Ross, *Seventy Years of It* (Englewood Cliffs, N.J., Prentice-Hall, 1936); A. Stephen Stephan, "University Extension in America," *Harvard Educational Review,* Vol. 18, Spring, 1948, pp. 100–107.
127. Vance, *Charles Richard Van Hise,* pp. 93–94.
128. Ely, *op. cit.,* p. 207; Ross, *op. cit.,* pp. 206–208.
129. Roberts Maxwell, *La Follette and the Rise of the Progressives* (Madison, State Historical Society of Wisconsin, 1956), pp. 58–59.
130. Ely, *op. cit.,* pp. 206–207.
131. See pp. 313, 318.
132. Howe, *op. cit.,* p. vii.
133. McCarthy, *op. cit.*
134. For examples of other public institutions of higher education where comprehensive service programs were being implemented just before World War I, see Bruce, *op. cit.,* Vol. V, pp. 60–61; Edmund J. James, "Function of the State University," *Science,* Vol. 22, November 17, 1905, pp. 625–628. See also the material on the administration of President Lotus D. Coffman at the University of Minnesota in the 1920s and 1930s in Lotus D. Coffman, *The State University: Its Work and Problems* (Minneapolis, University of Minnesota Press, 1934).
135. Arthur M. Schlesinger, "The City in American History," *Mississippi Valley Historical Review,* Vol. 27, 1940, pp. 42–66; Willard Thorp, Merle E. Curti, and Carlos Baker, *American Issues: The Social Record* (Philadelphia, Lippincott, 1944), p. 739.
136. College of Charleston, *Catalogue, 1941–1942* (Charleston, 1942), pp. 20–21; Roscoe H. Eckelberry, *A History of the Municipal University of the United States* (Washington, D.C., U.S. Office of Education, 1932), pp. 10–16, 20.
137. Edward S. Jouett, "The University of Louisville," in *A Century of Municipal Higher Education* (Chicago, Lincoln Printing Co., 1937); University of Louisville, *Catalogue, 1919–1920* (Louisville, Ky., University of Louisville, 1919).
138. S. Willis Rudy, *The College of the City of New York: A History, 1847–1947* (New York, City College Press, 1949), pp. 69–70, 382–394, 460–463. See also *Addresses at the Opening of the Free Academy of New York, January 27, 1849* (New York, 1849); *The C.C.N.Y. Collegian,* Vol. I, No. 7, February 20, 1867, p. 3.

139. University of Cincinnati, *Catalogue, 1919–1920* (Cincinnati, Ohio, University of Cincinnati, 1919); University of Toledo, *Bulletin, Catalogue Issue,* Vol. XV, June, 1938, pp. 2–3; Parke R. Kolbe, *History of the Establishment of the University of Akron* (Akron, Ohio, 1914), pp. 1–8; University of Akron, *Annual Catalogue, 1939–1940* (Akron, Ohio, 1939); Municipal University of Wichita, *Biennial Catalogue Bulletin,* Vol. XLVI, No. 4, April, 1942; Wayne University, *Bulletin,* Vol. 29, February 15, 1951, No. 4 (Detroit, Mich., 1951), pp. 20–21; Raymond Walters, *Historical Sketch of the University of Cincinnati* (n.p., 1941).
140. Parke R. Kolbe, *Urban Influences on Higher Education in England and the United States* (New York, Macmillan, 1928), pp. 149–150; Eckelberry, *op. cit.,* pp. 165–169; "The University and the Municipality," *U.S. Bureau of Education Bulletin,* 1915, No. 38, pp. 16–18.
141. John S. Diekhoff, *Democracy's College* (New York, Harper & Row, 1950), pp. 30–31; Kolbe, *Urban Influences on Higher Education,* pp. 139–140.
142. Boston University, *General Catalogue, 1872–73* (Boston, Riverside Press, 1873); Boston University, *Bulletin, Vol. XXII,* April 18, 1933, No. 16, pp. 7–9; New York University, *Bulletin, Catalogue Number,* 1940–41, Vol. XLI, No. 2, pp. 121–127; Temple University, *Bulletin, College of Liberal Arts and Sciences,* 1948–49 (Philadelphia, 1948), p. 19; Charles E. Bevry, *Responsiveness: The Place of the Urban University* (Philadelphia, Temple University, 1936); University of Pittsburgh, *Training to Win* (Pittsburgh, University of Pittsburgh, 1943); *Proceedings and Addresses at the Celebration of the Twentieth Anniversary of the Inauguration of Samuel P. Capen as Chancellor of the University of Buffalo* (Buffalo, 1943).
143. Horace H. Furness, *Address at the Commencement of the University of Pennsylvania, June 7, 1894* (Philadelphia, 1894); Robert Herrick, *Chimes* (New York, Macmillan, 1926), pp. 15–16, 41–43. In this connection, it has been argued that the modern university needs the limitless possibilities of metropolitan life—the great museums, hospitals, libraries, art galleries, and concert halls—to realize its highest potential as a center of creative scholarship and learning. On this point, see John Erskine, *My Life as a Teacher* (Philadelphia, Lippincott, 1948), pp. 32–35; and Samuel P. Capen, "A Program for Progress in Education," *Educational Record,* Vol. 4, January, 1923, pp. 5–7.
144. This urban movement in modern higher education has by no means been confined to the United States. It is illustrated also by the leadership assumed during the last one hundred years by the great universities of London, Paris, Berlin, and Vienna, by the rise of the "red-brick" civic universities in Great Britain, and by the founding of municipally supported institutions of higher learning at Frankfort on the Main, Hamburg, and Cologne in Germany. Kolbe, *Urban Influences on Higher Education,* pp. 9–11, 92–94, 105–113; Ernest Barker, "Universities in Great Britain," in Kotschnig, *op. cit.,* pp. 96–97.
145. Diekhoff, *op. cit.,* pp. 29–30; Eckelberry, *op. cit.,* pp. 169–174.
146. Frederick C. Hicks, "Selected Problems of Municipal Universities," in *Inauguration of George F. Zook as President of the Municipal University of Akron, January 22, 1926* (Akron, Ohio, 1926), p. 58.
147. University of Toledo, "President's Report, 1954," *Bulletin of the University of Toledo,* Vol. 32, No. 3, November, 1954, pp. 4–15; Diekhoff, *op. cit.,* p. 44; Thomas E. Coulton, *A City College in Action, Struggle and Achievement at Brooklyn College, 1930–1955* (New York, Harper & Row, 1955), pp. 46–47. An exception has been the program of state aid in New York, given for the specific purpose of teacher training in the municipal colleges of New York City.
148. Kolbe, *Urban Influences on Higher Education,* pp. 151–160; Eckelberry, *op. cit.,* pp. 179–185; Hicks, *op. cit.,* pp. 59–61. It is notable, however, that America's largest and wealthiest metropolis, New York City, over the century-long period from 1847 to 1947 appropriated approximately $200,000,000 from its own tax funds to provide a free higher education for residents of the city in four municipal colleges. This compares favorably with the total public appropriation for any one of the state universities during this same period. Rudy, *op. cit.,* pp. 38–41, 90–91, 116–125, 357–360.
149. On this question, see George F. Zook, "The Contribution of the Municipal University," in *Inauguration of George F. Zook as President of the Municipal University of Akron,* pp. 19–27; A. Monroe Stowe, *Modernizing the College* (New York, Knopf, 1926), pp. 2–3; "How the University Serves the City," *Municipal Exhibit of the City of Cincinnati* (Cincinnati, Ohio, October 1–15, 1913); Carl Holliday, "The Municipal University," *School and Society,* Vol. 6, October 13, 1917, pp. 427–431; November 10, 1917, pp. 546–549; November 24, 1917, pp. 601–604.

150. As quoted in Laurence R. Veysey, *The Emergence of the American University* (Chicago, University of Chicago Press, 1965), p. 66.

151. John D. Hicks, "Development of Civilization in the Middle West, 1860–1900," in Dixon Ryan Fox (ed.), *Sources of Culture in the Middle West* (Englewood Cliffs, N.J., Prentice-Hall, 1934), pp. 90–92; Pritchett, *op. cit.,* p. 292.

152. Coffman, *op. cit.,* pp. 205–206.

153. Foerster, *op. cit.;* Abraham Flexner, *Universities, American, English, German* (New York, Oxford University Press, 1930).

154. Veysey, *op. cit.,* p. 63.

155. Ross, *op. cit.,* pp. 196–197.

156. James Bryce, *The American Commonwealth* (London, Macmillan, 1889), Vol. II, pp. 550–551, 567–568.

157. James Bryce, *University and Historical Addresses* (New York, Macmillan, 1913), pp. 160–163.

158. Henry Nash Smith, *Virgin Land* (Cambridge, Mass., Harvard University Press, 1950), p. 258. Smith sees this Turner concept of the state university as rather unconvincing and unrealistic.

159. Frederick Jackson Turner, *The Frontier in American History,* pp. 156–157, 287–289, 354–355.

Chapter 9. The Development of the Graduate School

1. Friedrich Paulsen, *German Education, Past and Present* (London, T. Fisher Unwin, 1908), pp. 184–186; Reginald H. Phelps, "The Idea of the Modern University, Göttingen and America," *The Germanic Review,* Vol. 29. October, 1954.

2. Merle E. Curti, *Growth of American Thought* (New York, Harper & Row, 1943), p. 582; Richard Hofstadter and Walter P. Metzger, *Development of Academic Freedom in the United States* (New York, Columbia University Press, 1955), pp. 386–395; J. Leo Wolf, in *Journal of the Proceedings of a Convention of Literary and Scientific Gentlemen* (1830), as quoted in Richard Hofstadter and Wilson Smith (eds.), *American Higher Education, A Documentary History* (Chicago, University of Chicago Press, 1961), Vol. I, pp. 308–311.

3. Paulsen, *op. cit.,* pp. 192–193; Ralph Henry Gabriel, *Course of American Democratic Thought* (New York, Ronald Press, 1941), pp. 296–297.

4. Paul Farmer, "Nineteenth Century Ideas of the University in Continental Europe," in Margaret Clapp (ed.), *The Modern University* (Ithaca, N.Y., Cornell University Press, 1950), pp. 4–8.

5. Paulsen, *op. cit.,* pp. 188–189.

6. David B. Shumway, "Göttingen's American Students," *American-German Review,* Vol. III, June, 1937, pp. 21–24. Actually, Benjamin Smith Barton was the first American to receive a German university degree, that of doctor of medicine from Göttingen in 1787. He went on to a useful career as the first professor of natural history at the University of Pennsylvania.

7. Charles F. Thwing, *The American and the German University* (New York, Macmillan, 1928), pp. 40–44.

8. James Bryce, *The American Commonwealth* (London, Macmillan, 1888), Vol. II, p. 542. For the same reason, few Americans went to the south-German Catholic universities, which still retained their religious oaths. Hofstadter and Metzger, *op. cit.,* p. 392. On the English universities, see Charles C. Gillespie, "English Ideas of the University in the Nineteenth Century," in Clapp, *op. cit.,* pp. 30–49.

9. Thwing, *op. cit.,* pp. 68–71.

10. Daniel C. Gilman, *Launching of a University* (New York, Dodd, Mead, 1906), pp. 8–9; Charles W. Eliot, "The History of American Teaching," *Educational Review,* November, 1911, pp. 356–357. Eliot, in his early career at Harvard, experienced the difficulties confronting all would-be scholars in this period when he sought to combine teaching with advanced study. Charles W. Eliot to Charles Eliot Norton, September 18, 1860, Norton Papers, Harvard University.

11. Ezra Stiles, *Plan of a University* (New Haven, Conn., Fellows of Pierson College, 1953).

12. Theodore Dwight, Jr., *President Dwight's Decisions of Questions Discussed by the Senior Class in Yale College, in 1813, and 1814* (New York, Jonathan Leavitt, 1833).

13. Richard Shryock, "The Academic Profession in the United States," *AAUP Bulletin,* Spring, 1952, p. 38.

14. See Chapter 6.

15. Philip Lindsley, *Works* (Philadelphia, Lippincott, 1859), Vol. I, pp. 354–355; Union College,

Catalogue, 1852, Third Term; 1853, Third Term; W. Carson Ryan, *Studies in Early Graduate Education* (New York, Carnegie Foundation, 1939), pp. 9–10.

16. C. F. Jackson, "American Scholarship," *The Knickerbocker,* Vol. 28, July, 1846, pp. 9–13.
17. Richard J. Storr, *The Beginnings of Graduate Education in America* (Chicago, University of Chicago Press, 1953), pp. 129–134.
18. Richard T. Ely, "American Colleges and German Universities," *Harper's Magazine,* Vol. LXI, July, 1880, pp. 253–260.
19. Alonso Potter, "Consolidation and Other Modifications of American Colleges," *Barnard's American Journal of Education,* Vol. I, 1855, pp. 472–474.
20. James M. Hart, *German Universities: A Narrative of Personal Experience* (New York, Putnam, 1874).
21. James W. Bell, "German Universities," *Education,* September, 1881, pp. 49–50, 60–63.
22. More than two thousand Americans were studying in German universities during the 1880s. Thwing, *op. cit.,* pp. 42–43.
23. Hofstadter and Metzger, *op. cit.,* pp. 367–369.
24. Quoted in Laurence R. Veysey, *The Emergence of the American University* (Chicago, University of Chicago Press, 1965), p. 45.
25. Curti, *op. cit.,* pp. 580–581; George W. Pierson, "American Universities in the Nineteenth Century," in Clapp, *op. cit.,* pp. 63–68; Arthur M. Schlesinger, *The Rise of the City, 1878–1898* (New York, Macmillan, 1933), pp. 211–212; Gabriel, *op. cit.,* pp. 296–297.
26. Hofstadter and Metzger, *op. cit.,* p. 375.
27. Thomas LeDuc, *Piety and Intellect at Amherst College, 1865–1912* (New York, Columbia University Press, 1946).
28. Hofstadter and Metzger, *op. cit.,* p. 402.
29. Willis Rudy, "Josiah Royce and the Art of Teaching," *Educational Theory,* Vol. II, July, 1952, pp. 164–166.
30. Student life in Germany "intensified" White's desire "to do something for university education in the United States." It "almost remade" G. Stanley Hall, and it left Nicholas Murray Butler with "an ineffaceable impression of what scholarship meant." Andrew Dickson White, *Autobiography* (Englewood Cliffs, N.J., Prentice-Hall, 1905), Vol. I, p. 291; G. Stanley Hall, *Life and Confessions of a Psychologist* (Englewood Cliffs, N.J., Prentice-Hall, 1923), p. 219; Nicholas Murray Butler, *Across the Busy Years* (New York, Scribner, 1935), Vol. I, p. 126. On this theme, see also James B. Angell, *Reminiscences* (New York, McKay, 1912), p. 102; Gilman, *op. cit.,* p. 275; George S. Merriam (ed.), *Noah Porter, A Memorial by Friends* (New York, Scribner, 1893), p. 95; Timothy Dwight (the Younger), *Memories of Yale Life and Men* (New York, Dodd, Mead, 1903), p. 223; Henry James, *Charles W. Eliot* (Boston, Houghton Mifflin, 1930), Vol. I; Solon J. Buck (ed.), *William Watts Folwell; The Autobiography and Letters of a Pioneer of Culture* (Minneapolis, University of Minnesota Press, 1933), p. 88; Charles Forster Smith, *Charles Kendall Adams, A Life Sketch* (Madison, University of Wisconsin, 1924), pp. 12–13; John Fulton, *Memoirs of Frederick A. P. Barnard* (New York, Macmillan, 1896), p. 362; John W. Burgess, *Reminiscences of an American Scholar* (New York, Columbia University Press, 1934), p. 121; Charles W. Eliot to Charles Eliot Norton, January 28, 1864, Norton Papers, Harvard University.
31. The two aspects of university building were not rigidly separated, however. See Willis Rudy, "Eliot and Gilman: The History of an Academic Friendship," *Teachers College Record,* Vol. 54, March, 1953, pp. 307–318; also, Charles W. Eliot to Daniel C. Gilman, July 1, 1874, Eliot Papers, Harvard College Archive.
32. A. Lawrence Lowell, "Universities, Graduate Schools, and Colleges," *Atlantic Monthly,* Vol. 150, August, 1932, p. 216.
33. Gilman, *op. cit.,* p. 12.
34. Johns Hopkins University, *Official Circular, June, 1876,* p. 2; *February, 1877,* pp. 15–16; Daniel C. Gilman, *First Annual Report of the Johns Hopkins University,* 1876, pp. 15–16, 20–22.
35. Gilman, *First Annual Report,* p. 15; *Launching of a University,* pp. 41–42.
36. Rockwell D. Hunt, "Johns Hopkins Forty Years Ago," *Johns Hopkins University Alumni Magazine,* November, 1934, p. 25; Richard T. Ely, *The Ground Under Our Feet* (New York, Macmillan, 1938), pp. 100–103.
37. Hugh Hawkins, *Pioneer: A History of the Johns Hopkins University, 1874–1889* (Ithaca, N.Y., Cornell University Press, 1960), p. 66.

38. *Addresses at the Inauguration of Daniel C. Gilman as President of Johns Hopkins University* (Baltimore, 1876). On this, see Fabian Franklin, *The Life of Daniel Coit Gilman* (New York, Dodd, Mead, 1910), pp. 220–221.

39. Francesco Cordasco, *Daniel Coit Gilman and the Protean Ph.D.* (Leiden, Netherlands, E. J. Brill, 1960), pp. 80–81.

40. Gilman, *Launching of a University*, pp. 140–141.

41. Abraham Flexner, *Universities: American, English, German* (New York, Oxford University Press, 1930), pp. 73–74.

42. Gilman, *Launching of a University*, p. 134; for Gilman's active interest in research, see Hall, *op. cit.*, pp. 246–247.

43. Abraham Flexner, "The Graduate School in the United States," *Proceedings of the Association of American Universities*, 1931, pp. 114–115.

44. *Addresses at the Inauguration of Daniel C. Gilman*, p. 30.

45. Gilman, *Launching of a University*.

46. See the estimate of this procedure in Pierson, *op. cit.*, pp. 74–75.

47. The phrase was G. Stanley Hall's. See Hall, *op. cit.*, p. 246; see also the reminiscences of student life in the early days in Baltimore by Josiah Royce in *Scribner's Magazine*, Vol. 10, September, 1891, p. 383.

48. John C. French, *History of the University Founded by Johns Hopkins* (Baltimore, Johns Hopkins Press, 1946), p. 41. The great initial interest in the Hopkins Fellowships is shown by the fact that there were more than 150 applications for the first twenty fellowships granted.

49. Flexner, "The Graduate School in the United States," *op. cit.*, pp. 114–115.

50. Gordon Laing, "The Interlocking of Graduate and Undergraduate Courses," *Proceedings of the Association of American Universities*, 1925, pp. 73–75.

51. J. B. Angell to Reverdy Johnson, chairman of the Johns Hopkins trustees, April 21, 1874, Johns Hopkins University Archive (courtesy of Professor Thomas LeDuc, Oberlin College); French, *op. cit.*, pp. 2–35; Franklin, *op. cit.*, pp. 182–183.

52. Abraham Flexner, *Daniel Coit Gilman: Creator of the American Type University* (New York, Harcourt Brace Jovanovich, 1946), pp. 195–196.

53. See the description of the progress of Johns Hopkins in President Gilman's *Annual Reports* for 1886, 1891, and 1892. Johns Hopkins University, *Annual Reports, 1886–1892*.

54. French, *op. cit.*, pp. 130–142; Lowell, *op. cit.*, p. 216; Hawkins, *op. cit.*, pp. 124–125, 316–323.

55. Richard H. Shryock, *The Unique Influence of Johns Hopkins University on American Medicine* (Copenhagen, Denmark, Ejnar Munksgaard, Ltd., 1953), p. 10.

56. Gilman, *Launching of a University*, p. 135; Hall, *op. cit.*, p. 242; Flexner, *Universities, American, English, German*, pp. 73–74; Hawkins, *op. cit.*, pp. 126–134.

57. W. Stull Holt (ed.), *Historical Scholarship in the United States, 1876–1901* (Baltimore, Md., Johns Hopkins Press, 1938), pp. 183–184, 252–253; Gilman, *Launching of a University*, p. 139.

58. "Your scale of salaries is a liberal one, and will secure you good men." Charles W. Eliot to Daniel C. Gilman, November 29, 1876, Eliot Papers, Harvard College Archive.

59. Veysey, *op. cit.*, pp. 170–173.

60. James, *op. cit.*, Vol. I, pp. 221–224; Vol. II, pp. 3–5; George Newsome, "American University Patterns, 1776–1900" (unpublished doctoral dissertation, Yale University, 1956).

61. Johns Hopkins University, *Celebration of the Twenty-Fifth Anniversary of the Founding of the University, and Inauguration of Ira Remsen as President* (Baltimore, Md., Johns Hopkins Press, 1902), p. 105.

62. William F. Russell (ed.), *Rise of a University; The Later Days of Old Columbia College* (New York, Columbia University Press, 1937), Vol. I, pp. 373–375.

63. At these lectures, the audiences tended at first to be made up predominantly of "young women who have no call to business or matrimony." Francis J. Child to Charles Eliot Norton, March 26, 1871, Norton Papers, Harvard University. See *Announcement of Harvard University Lectures, 1870–71*.

64. Harvard College, *Annual Report*, 1876–77, pp. 18–21; James, *op. cit.*, Vol. II; Samuel Eliot Morison, *Three Centuries of Harvard* (Cambridge, Harvard University Press, 1936), pp. 306–307, 372–373. Under Eliot, there was even an attempt to introduce something like the German *Privatdocent* system. In 1897, the faculty was permitted to authorize any doctor of philosophy in Cambridge, whether connected with the university or not, to offer a course of his own, and fix and collect fees. Nothing much came of this experiment, however.

65. Yale College, *Catalogue, 1847–48*, pp. 42–43; 1856–57, p. 43.
66. Edgar S. Furniss, "The Beginning of Graduate Work at Yale," *Ventures*, Vol. 4, Fall, 1964, pp. 6–10.
67. Pierson, *op. cit.*, pp. 79–80; Edward L. Godkin, "President Woolsey," *Nation*, Vol. 13, July 6, 1871, pp. 6–7; Ryan, *op. cit.*, pp. 8–9.
68. The "Young Yale" faction wanted to make Daniel C. Gilman, then a leading figure on the faculty of the Sheffield Scientific School, Woolsey's successor as president.
69. Timothy Dwight (the Younger), *Yale College: Some Thoughts Respecting Its Future* (New Haven, Conn., Tuttle, Morehouse and Taylor, 1871). The university controversy at Yale was going on as late as 1885, however. See William Bliss, "Yale College or Yale University," *New Englander*, Vol. 44, September, 1885, pp. 736–743; Simeon E. Baldwin, "Yale University," *ibid.*, November, 1885, pp. 882–887.
70. Pierson, *Yale*.
71. Columbia College, *President's Report*, 1866, pp. 27–29; 1868, pp. 31–32.
72. Russell, *op. cit.*, p. 379.
73. Burgess, *op. cit.*, pp. 198–204, 230–231.
74. R. Gordon Hoxie, *A History of the Faculty of Political Science, Columbia University* (New York, Columbia University Press, 1955), pp. 3–31.
75. Columbia College, *President's Report*, 1883, pp. 37–38; 1884, pp. 22–23; 1885–86, 49–53.
76. A graduate Faculty of Philosophy was created in 1890 and a general University Council was set up in that year to coordinate the work of all the faculties. In 1891, the College of Physicians and Surgeons became an integral part of Columbia, while the Union Theological Seminary formed an alliance with it. The Faculty of Pure Science was established in 1892. In 1893, Teachers College became another of its affiliates. Russell, *op. cit.*, Vol. I, pp. 373–375; Hoxie, *op. cit.*, pp. 103–104.
77. Thomas J. Wertenbaker, *Princeton, 1746–1896* (Princeton, N.J., Princeton University Press, 1946), pp. 302–303, 339–340.
78. James McCosh, "What an American University Should Be," *Education*, Vol. 6, September, 1885, pp. 44–45.
79. Arthur Link, *Wilson: The Road to the White House* (Princeton, N.J., Princeton University Press, 1947), pp. 59–66, 76, 88–91; Andrew F. West, *The Graduate College of Princeton* (Princeton, N.J., Princeton University Press, 1913), pp. 27–28.
80. Wertenbaker, *op. cit.*, pp. 368–369.
81. Edmund C. Sanford, "A Sketch of the History of Clark University," in *Publications of the Clark University Library*, January, 1923, pp. 2–4, 6–8; *In Memoriam, Jonas Gilman Clark, 1815–1900;* William Edward Story and Louis N. Wilson (eds.), *Clark University 1889–1899* (Worcester, 1899), p. 9.
82. How a misunderstanding could have arisen on either side is puzzling in view of the letter Hall sent to Clark, before formally accepting the presidency, in which the former specifically states his understanding to be that ". . . the development of the college is to proceed in time, but in plans and endowment the University is to be the more important ulterior end in view." G. Stanley Hall to Jonas G. Clark, April 5, 1888, in N. Orwin Rush (ed.), *Letters of G. Stanley Hall to Jonas Gilman Clark* (Worcester, Mass., Clark University Library, 1948), pp. 2–3.
83. Harry Elmer Barnes, who taught at Clark in the later Hall era, claims that "Clark never fulfilled any decent fractional part of his promises to President Hall in the way of financial support for this university." Harry E. Barnes, "Clark University," *American Review*, Vol. III, May, June, 1925, pp. 272–277.
84. Sanford, *op. cit.;* see also the analysis by George H. Blakeslee in Wallace W. Atwood (ed.), *The First Fifty Years* (Worcester, Mass., Clark University, 1937), pp. 3–7; G. Stanley Hall, "President Harper," *Biblical World*, Vol. 27, March, 1906, pp. 233–234.
85. On this, see John L. Spaulding, *An Address Delivered at the Laying of the Cornerstone of the Catholic University, May 24, 1888* (Peoria, Ill., B. Cremer & Bros., 1888), pp. 17–18; also, John Tracy Ellis, *The Formative Years of the Catholic University of America* (Washington, D. C., American Catholic Historical Association, 1946), pp. 20–38, 99–113, 193–194, 398–399; Patrick H. Ahern, *The Catholic University of America, 1887–1896* (Washington, D.C., Catholic University of America Press, 1949), pp. 87–96; Peter E. Hogan, *The Catholic University of America, 1896–1903* (Washington, D.C., Catholic University of America Press, 1949), pp. 76–78, 81–82, 95–100.
86. Jurgen Herbst, "Liberal Education and the Graduate Schools: An Historical View of College

Reform," *History of Education Quarterly,* Vol. 2, December, 1962, pp. 246–248; Power, *op. cit.,* pp. 228–237.

87. Allan Nevins, *John D. Rockefeller* (New York, Scribner, 1940), Vol. II, p. 232; John D. Rockefeller, Sr., *Random Reminiscences of Men and Events* (Garden City, N.Y., Doubleday, 1933), pp. 176–177.

88. Joseph E. Gould, "William Rainey Harper and the University of Chicago" (unpublished doctoral dissertation, Syracuse University, 1951), pp. 173–175, 209–210.

89. Veysey, *op. cit.,* p. 377; For a highly favorable estimate of the University of Chicago in its early days by a foreign visitor, see Henri Moissan, "L'Université de Chicago," *Revue Scientifique,* Vol. 8, October 30, 1897, pp. 557–560. See also Thomas W. Goodspeed, *Story of the University of Chicago* (Chicago, University of Chicago Press, 1925), pp. 53–55, 72; University of Chicago, *The President's Report,* 1897–1898, pp. 33–34; John Merlin Powis Smith, "President Harper," *University Record,* July, 1932, p. 169; Lyman Abbot, "William Rainey Harper," *ibid.,* March, 1906, pp. 58–59.

90. Albion W. Small, "Harper as University President," *Biblical World,* Vol. 27, March, 1906, pp. 217–218.

91. William R. Harper, "The Old and the New Testament Student," *Biblical World,* Vol. 18, March, 1897, p. 161.

92. "This, more than anything else, set the academic style and nourished what William James was later to call 'the Ph.D. octopus.' " Mortimer Adler, "The Chicago School," *Harper's Magazine,* Vol. 183, June, 1941, pp. 378–379. Harper first announced this policy in an unpublished first report to the board of trustees in 1892, but it soon became generally known to the faculty. Gould, *op. cit.,* p. 209.

93. Veysey, *op. cit.,* p. 376.

94. President's Report, *Decennial Publications of the University of Chicago* (Chicago, University of Chicago Press, 1903), Vol. I; Adler, *op. cit.,* pp. 378–382; Joseph Dorfman, *Thorstein Veblen and His America* (New York, Viking Press, 1934), pp. 91–94; Gould, *op. cit.,* pp. 152–155, 160–166, 231–232.

95. See Chapter 6.

96. Charles K. Adams, *Questions for History Students* (Ann Arbor, University of Michigan, 1871); Smith, *op. cit.,* pp. 14–18; *Memorial of Charles Kendall Adams* (Madison, University of Wisconsin, 1903), p. 7.

97. Henry Adams, *Education of Henry Adams* (Boston, Houghton Mifflin, 1930), p. 303, and *Syllabus for History II, 1873–1874,* Harvard College Archive; *Harvard University Curriculum: Notices, 1870–1871,* Harvard College Archive; Harold D. Cater (ed.), *Henry Adams and His Friends* (Boston, Houghton Mifflin, 1947), pp. xxxviii–xxxix; Herbert Baxter Adams, "Special Methods of Historical Study," in Andrew D. White, Charles K. Adams *et al., Methods of Teaching History* (Boston, D. C. Heath, 1896), pp. 113–114; Ely, *op. cit.,* pp. 10–11; Johns Hopkins University, *President's Annual Report,* 1886, pp. 12–13.

98. Ryan, *op. cit.,* pp. 77–79.

99. Gilman, *Launching of a University,* pp. 152–153.

100. Johns Hopkins University, *President's Annual Report,* 1877, pp. 31–32; 1890, pp. 16–17; Frederick Jackson Turner, *Address at Dedication of John Carter Brown Library Building, May 17, 1904* (Providence, R.I., 1905), pp. 55–56; A Lawrence Lowell, "Some Functions of Higher Education," *Yale Review,* Vol. 31, Autumn, 1941, pp. 78–85; Henry E. Bliss, "Departmental Libraries in Universities and Colleges," *Educational Review,* Vol. 43, April, 1912, pp. 387–409; Guy Redvers Lyle, *The Administration of the College Library* (New York, H. W. Wilson, 1944); Harvie Branscomb, *Teaching With Books* (Chicago, Association of American Colleges, 1940), pp. 5–6, 103–108; Veysey, *op. cit.,* p. 178.

101. William Rainey Harper, *The Trend in Higher Education* (Chicago, University of Chicago Press, 1905), pp. 126, 134.

102. Edouard Rod, "American Universities," *North American Review,* Vol. 169; September, 1899, p. 416; Flexner, *Universities: American, English, German,* p. 77; Hugo Münsterberg, *American Traits* (Boston, Houghton Mifflin, 1901), p. 86.

103. Chester Kerr, *A Report on American University Presses* (Washington, D.C., Association of American University Presses, 1949), p. 16.

104. See also Johns Hopkins University, *President's Annual Report,* 1887, p. 9.

105. Kerr, *op. cit.,* p. 264.

106. These were Johns Hopkins, Chicago, and Columbia.

107. Kerr, *op. cit.*, pp. 40–41, and *The American University as Publisher: A Digest of a Report on American University Presses* (Norman, University of Oklahoma Press, 1949); Floyd Henry Reeves, *et al.*, *The University Faculty* (Chicago, University of Chicago, 1933), pp. 281–282; Flexner, *Universities: American, English, German*, p. 79; Merle E. Curti (ed.), *American Scholarship in the Twentieth Century* (Cambridge, Mass., Harvard University Press, 1953), p. 13; Robert Reinhold, "Crisis of the University Press," *New York Times Book Review,* May 7, 1972, pp. 30–32; *New York Times,* June 24, 1972, p. 29; June 26, 1972, p. 18.

108. Curti, *Growth of American Thought*, pp. 586–588; Ralph S. Bates, *Scientific Societies in the United States* (New York, Wiley, 1945); Harrison R. Steeves, *Learned Societies and English Literary Scholarship in Great Britain and the United States* (New York, Columbia University Press, 1913).

109. W. Stull Holt, "Historical Scholarship," in Curti, *American Scholarship in the Twentieth Century,* p. 88.

110. Curti, *Growth of American Thought,* p. 588.

111. Guy Stanton Ford, *On and Off the Campus* (Minneapolis, University of Minnesota Press, 1938), p. 141–142; Homer P. Rainey, "Educational Councils and Similar Associations," *Proceedings of the Association of American Universities*, 1940, pp. 79–81; Charles H. Haskins, *ibid.*, 1920, pp. 39–40; American Council of Learned Societies, *Bulletin No. 1,* October, 1929, pp. 2–6; Curti, *American Scholarship in the Twentieth Century,* p. 6.

112. Gilman, *Launching of a University;* French, *op. cit.*

113. It was during this era that the following scholarly societies were founded: Archaeological Institute of America (1879), Modern Language Association (1883), American Historical Association (1884), American Economic Association (1885), American Psychological Association (1892).

114. Gilman, *Launching of a University,* pp. 135–136.

115. French, *op. cit.*, pp. 45–56; Hawkins, *op. cit.*, pp. 112–113.

116. Ryan, *op. cit.*, pp. 130–131.

117. Curti, *American Scholarship in the Twentieth Century,* p. 13.

118. Bates, *op. cit.*, p. 174.

119. Walter Crosby Eells, "The Origin and Early History of Sabbatical Leave," *Bulletin of the American Association of University Professors,* Vol. 48, September, 1962, pp. 253–256.

120. This meant that the recipient was qualified to teach his special subject anywhere.

121. In the Western world, degrees of this type have come to be symbolized by a distinctive form of academic dress. This evolved from medieval forms. Caps and gowns, for example, derived from the cassock and hood worn by monks and scholars during the Middle Ages. Academic hoods were originally designed to be put over the head, and were lined with fur in winter and silk in summer. The mortarboard developed from the square cap of the Middle Ages, with the corners stiffened and a tassel added.

   European universities in modern times retained considerable individuality and diversity in academic dress, but America, with characteristic efficiency, introduced the factor of standardization. After a magazine article on academic costume was published by Gardner C. Leonard in 1895, a conference was held at Columbia University to set up a standard code. Leonard's suggestions were approved by this gathering, and promulgated as the Intercollegiate Code for Academic Costume. In 1902, a bureau was chartered by New York State to administer this code. Thorstein Veblen attributed this increasing insistence on scholastic ritual to the growth of wealth in a pioneer culture which produced "a leisure-class sentiment of sufficient volume in the community to support a strong movement of reversion towards an archaic view as to the legitimate end of education." Thorstein Veblen, *Theory of the Leisure Class* (New York, Macmillan, 1912), pp. 371–372. See also Winslow S. Anderson, "Academic Costume in American Colleges," *Bulletin of the Association of American Colleges,* Vol. 32, October, 1946, pp. 416–417; Frederick R. S. Rogers, *The Story of University Degrees and Academical Dress* (Sutton, Surrey, 1952), pp. 14–15.

122. H. W. Widener, "The College in a Pecuniary Culture," *Educational Record,* Vol. 17, April, 1936, pp. 184–186; Alfred Z. Reed, "Contribution of the Medieval University to American Higher Education," Carnegie Foundation for the Advancement of Teaching, *31st Annual Report, 1936,* pp. 63–69; "Professional Recognition, Accrediting, and Licensure," *32nd Annual Report, 1937,* pp. 43–61; "Origins of Licensing in the Learned Professions," *33rd Annual Report, 1938,* pp. 71–78.

123. Theodore Dwight Woolsey, "Academical Degrees," *Century,* Vol. 28, July, 1884, pp. 365–376;

Edward D. Perry, "The Ph.D. in the United States," *Columbia University Quarterly*, Vol. 6, June, 1904, p. 260; George E. Vincent, "Honorary Degrees," *Proceedings of the Association of American Universities*, 1914, pp. 28–30.

124. Stephen E. Epler, *Honorary Degrees, A Survey of Their Use and Abuse* (Washington, D.C., American Council on Public Affairs, 1946); Perry, *op. cit.*, pp. 260–262; Adolph E. Meyer, "The Farce of Honorary Degrees," *American Mercury*, Vol. 67, July, 1949, pp. 104–110.

125. In 1901, Santa Clara College in California granted seven honorary Ph.D.s and "American University" of Harriman, Texas, granted nine. Perry, *op. cit.*, p. 262; Epler, *op. cit.*; R. Andrew Lady, "An Examination of the Doctor of Philosophy Degree *Honoris Causa*" (unpublished manuscript, Wyoming College, Williamsport, Pa.).

126. Epler, *op. cit.*

127. Carter V. Good, "History of Graduate Instruction in the United States," National Society for the Study of Education, *Fiftieth Yearbook* (Chicago, published by the Society, 1951), Part I, pp. 5–6.

128. Vincent, *op. cit.*, pp. 29–30; Perry, *op. cit.*

129. Vincent, *op. cit.;* Good, *op. cit.* In 1892, the *Educational Review* threatened to publish a list of institutions offending academic sensibilities by granting honorary Ph.D.'s. Five years later it carried out this threat with great effectiveness.

130. Epler, *op. cit.*

131. *Proceedings of the Association of American Universities*, 1914, pp. 35–40.

132. Holt, *op. cit.*, pp. 66–67, 151–152.

133. Walton C. John, *Graduate Studies in Universities and Colleges in the United States*, U.S. Office of Education, Bulletin No. 20, 1934; Council of State Governors, *Higher Education in the Forty-Eight States* (Chicago, n.p., 1952), p. 43.

134. Nelson B. Henry (ed.), National Society for the Study of Education, *Fiftieth Yearbook*, 1951, Part I, p. 8; Johns Hopkins University, *Celebration of Twenty-Fifth Anniversary*, pp. 78–79; Mary Pierson, *Graduate Work in the South* (Chapel Hill, University of North Carolina Press, 1947), pp. 106–107. Fellowship grants helped to swell these totals of graduate students, although the value of "hiring students" came increasingly to be doubted in terms of attracting the superior type of student wanted for Ph.D. training. Charles W. Eliot to James B. Angell, February 29, 1896, Eliot Papers, Harvard College Archive; Gilman, *Launching of a University*, p. 135; Columbia College, *President's Report*, 1866, p. 18; Bernard Berelson, *Graduate Education in the United States* (New York, McGraw-Hill, 1960), pp. 32–34; Everett Walters, "The Immutable Ph.D.," *Saturday Review*, January 15, 1966, pp. 62–63.

135. See Chapter 17.

136. Morison, *Three Centuries of Harvard*, p. 107; John, *op. cit.*, pp. 1–5, 41–44; "GSAS: Professional Method for Professional Scholars," *Harvard Crimson*, November 12, 1954, p. 3.

137. In this period, if one already held either a bachelor's or a master's degree, he could apply for the same degree—*ad eundem gradum*—at a sister institution and expect to receive it without further academic study. Yale awarded the bachelor's degree *ad eundem gradum* as late as 1900 and Wesleyan the master's as late as 1915. Stephen E. Epler, *Honorary Degrees, A Survey of their Use and Abuse* (Washington, D.C., American Council of Public Affairs, 1946). See also Graham P. Conroy, "Berkeley and Education in America," *Journal of the History of Ideas*, Vol. 21, April-June, 1960, pp. 211–221.

138. Samuel Eliot Morison (ed.), *Development of Harvard University, 1869–1929* (Cambridge, Mass., Harvard University Press, 1930), p. 452.

139. George Burton Adams, "The Degree of Doctor of Philosophy," *Educational Review*, Vol. 30, June, 1905, pp. 35–36.

140. John, *op. cit.*, pp. 41–44; *Proceedings of the Association of American Universities*, 1934, pp. 37–38; A. A. Grusendorf, "The Master's Thesis," *Journal of Higher Education*, Vol. 12, February, 1941, pp. 85–88; *New York Times*, November 13, 1957, p. 28.

141. *New York Times*, April 3, 1972, p. 1.

142. Johns Hopkins University, *Official Circular*, June, 1887, p. 10; French, *op. cit.*, pp. 344–389; Glenn Reed, "Fifty Years of Conflict in the Graduate School," *Educational Record*, Vol. 33, January, 1952, pp. 12–13; William A. Nitze, "Course Requirements *vs.* Research Requirements for the Degree of Doctor of Philosophy," *Proceedings of the Association of American Universities*, 1932, pp. 60–61.

143. Charles H. Judd, "Production of Good College Teaching," *Association of American Colleges Bulletin*, Vol. 15, March, 1929, pp. 93–94.

144. Nitze, *op. cit.,* pp. 60–61.
145. Yale College, *Catalogue,* 1860–61, p. 54. In 1863, Yale conferred one of these early earned doctorates on J. Willard Gibbs, "perhaps the greatest theoretical physicist since the time of Newton." Charles A. Kraus, "The Evolution of the American Graduate School," *AAUP Bulletin,* Vol. 37, Autumn, 1951, p. 499.
146. Johns Hopkins University, *Official Circular,* June, 1877, p. 10; *President's Annual Report,* 1887, pp. 45–46.
147. Committee of the Graduate Club of Harvard in Cooperation with a Committee of Similar Clubs at Cornell, Johns Hopkins, and Yale, *Graduate Courses: A Handbook for Graduate Students, 1893–1894* (Lexington, Mass., Ginn, 1894); John, *op. cit.,* pp. 23–26.
148. Frederick J. E. Woodbridge, "The Present Status of the Degree of Doctor of Philosophy in American Universities," *Proceedings of the Association of American Universities,* November, 1912, pp. 19–20.
149. Marcus W. Jernegan, "Productivity of Doctors of Philosophy in History," *American Historical Review,* Vol. 33, October, 1927, pp. 1–22. This percentage, however, at least in the field of history, tended to increase in the 1930s and 1940s. See William B. Hesseltine and Louis Kaplan, "Doctors of Philosophy in History," *American Historical Review,* Vol. 47, July, 1942.
150. Flexner, *Universities, American, English, German,* pp. 124–125; Lowell, *op. cit.,* p. 216; Reed, *op. cit.,* pp. 12–13; Everett Walters, *op. cit.,* pp. 62–63; Bernard Berelson, *op. cit.,* pp. 234–258.
151. *New York Times,* January 12, 1966, p. 65.
152. *New York Times,* February 11, 1974, p. 30.
153. *The Chronicle of Higher Education,* Vol. 7, December 3, 1973, pp. 7–15.
154. *The President's Report to the Members of the Board of Overseers of Harvard University, 1972–1973* (Cambridge, Mass., Harvard University, 1973), p. 10.

Chapter 10. Professional Education

1. Mary L. Gambrell, *Ministerial Training in Eighteenth Century New England* (New York, Columbia University Press, 1937), p. 140.
2. *Ibid.,* Chap. 5.
3. William R. Williams, "The Teaching of Medicine," *Educational Review,* Vol. 34, December, 1907, pp. 466–67.
4. William F. Norwood, *Medical Education in the United States before the Civil War* (Philadelphia, University of Pennsylvania Press, 1944), p. 143.
5. Harvard College, *Annual Report of the President to the Overseers* (Cambridge, Mass., F. W. Metcalf and Co., 1830), pp. xxxv–xxxvi.
6. Merle E. Curti and Vernon R. Carstensen, *The University of Wisconsin, A History, 1848–1925* (Madison, University of Wisconsin Press, 1949), Vol. I, pp. 452–459.
7. Philip Lindsley, *The Works of Philip Lindsley,* Leroy J. Halsey, ed. (Philadelphia, Lippincott, 1866), Vol. I, pp. 221–222.
8. Edward H. Cotton, *The Life of Charles W. Eliot* (Boston, Small, Maynard, 1926), pp. 128–129.
9. Louis P. Hatch, *History of Bowdoin College* (Portland, Me., Loring Short, and Harman, 1927), Chap. 12.
10. Merle Curti, "Intellectuals and Other People," *American Historical Review,* Vol. 60, January, 1955, p. 267; Dixon R. Fox, "Civilization in Transit," *ibid.,* Vol. 32, July, 1927, pp. 763–764.
11. Alfred Z. Reed, *Present Day Law Schools in the United States and Canada* (New York, Carnegie Foundation for the Advancement of Teaching, Bulletin No. 21, 1928), pp. 5–6.
12. William K. Selden, *Accreditation* (New York, Harper & Row, 1960), p. 59.
13. John T. Kirkland, "Literary Institutions—University," *North American Review,* Vol. 7, July, 1818, p. 275.
14. Philip Lindsley, *Plea for Theological Seminary at Princeton* (Trenton, 1821), pp. 14–15.
15. Charles W. Eliot, *Harvard Memories* (Cambridge, Mass., Harvard University Press, 1923), p. 49. See also Arthur E. Sutherland, *The Law at Harvard* (Cambridge, Mass., Belknap Press, 1967), Chap. 4.
16. Donald H. Fleming, *William H. Welch and the Rise of Modern Medicine* (Boston, Little, Brown, 1954), pp. 4–5.
17. Eliot, *op. cit.,* p. 135.
18. Morris Hadley, *Arthur Twining Hadley* (New Haven, Conn., Yale University Press, 1948), pp. 158–159.

19. E. G. Dexter, "Training for the Learned Professions," *Educational Review,* Vol. 25, January, 1903, pp. 31–37.
20. Ernest Havemann and Patricia S. West, *They Went to College* (New York, Harcourt Brace Jovanovich, 1952), p. 148.
21. F. C. Ferry, "Report of the Commission on Faculty and Student Scholarship," *Bulletin of the Association of American Colleges,* Vol. 8, March, 1922, pp. 131–133.
22. Herman Oliphant, "Parallels in the Development of Legal and Medical Education," *Annals of the American Academy of Political and Social Science,* Vol. 167, May, 1933, pp. 160–163.
23. Charles W. Eliot, *Educational Reform* (Englewood Cliffs, N.J., Prentice-Hall, 1898), pp. 61–86.
24. Henry James, *Charles W. Eliot* (Boston, Houghton Mifflin, 1930), Vol. I, pp. 278–279; Edward C. Elliott, *Rise of a University* (New York, Columbia University Press, 1937), Vol. II, p. 292.
25. One of Harvard's most brilliant professors of law, James Barr Ames, had never practiced law when appointed in 1873. Cotton, *op. cit.,* p. 154.
26. James B. Scott, "The Study and Teaching of Law," *Educational Review,* Vol. 28, September, 1904, pp. 130–151.
27. John C. French, *A History of the University Founded by Johns Hopkins* (Baltimore, Md., Johns Hopkins Press, 1946), p. 426.
28. Edgar H. Schein, *Professional Education* (New York, McGraw-Hill, 1972), pp. 118.
29. Joseph Redlich, *The Common Law and the Case Method* (Carnegie Foundation, Bulletin No. 8, 1914), pp. 15, 24–25, 39.
30. James G. Rogers, "The Standardization Movement in American Law Schools," *Educational Record,* Vol. 13, July, 1932, pp. 220–223.
31. Reed, *op. cit.,* pp. 397–398.
32. For details of accrediting in the various professions, see Fred J. Kelly *et al., College Accreditation* (U.S. Office of Education Bulletin, 1940), pp. 23–24, 73–74, 85–93, 156–157; John D. Russell, *The Outlook for Higher Education* (Chicago, University of Chicago Press, 1939), Chap. 15.
33. Abraham Flexner, *Medical Education in the United States* (Carnegie Foundation, Bulletin No. 4, 1910).
34. Irving S. Cutter, in Kent, *op. cit.,* Chap. 10.
35. Alfred C. True, *A History of Agricultural Education in the United States, 1785–1925* (Washington, D.C., Government Printing Office, 1929), p. 192; Walter P. Rogers, *Andrew D. White and the Modern University* (Ithaca, N.Y., Cornell University Press, 1942), pp. 115–123; Thurman W. Van Metre, *A History of the Graduate School of Business, Columbia University* (New York, Columbia University Press, 1957), Chap. 1; Curti and Carstensen, *op. cit.,* pp. 459–475.
36. *The Substance of Two Reports of the Faculty of Amherst College to the Board of Trustees* (Amherst, Mass., Carter and Adams, 1827).
37. G. H. Bode, "Universities," *North American Review,* Vol. 27, July, 1828, p. 71; Henry Johnson, *The Other Side of Main Street* (New York, Columbia University Press, 1943), pp. 109–110.
38. For a good historical account of the problem, see Merle L. Borrowman, *The Liberal and Technical in Teacher Education* (New York, Teachers College, Columbia University, 1956).
39. Albert A. Sutton, *Education for Journalism in the United States from Its Beginning* (Evanston, Ill., Northwestern University Press, 1940), Chap. 2.
40. Lawrence Cremin *et al., A History of Teachers College, Columbia University* (New York, Columbia University Press, 1954).
41. Arthur C. Weatherhead, *History of Collegiate Education in Architecture in the United States* (Los Angeles, published by the author, 1941), pp. 250–251.
42. Melvin T. Copeland, *And Mark an Era* (Boston, Little, Brown, 1958).
43. *Ibid.,* pp. 7, 148–150.
44. *Ibid.,* Chap. 9.
45. Charles R. Mann, *A Study of Engineering Education* (Carnegie Foundation, Bulletin No. 11, 1918).
46. Carnegie Foundation for the Advancement of Teaching, *The Professional Preparation of Teachers for American Public Schools* (Carnegie Foundation, Bulletin No. 14, 1920).
47. Algo D. Henderson, "Innovations in Educating for the Professions," *Educational Record,* Vol. 49, Spring, 1968, p. 196.
48. Edgar H. Schein, *op. cit.,* p. 67.
49. Lewis B. Mayhew, *The Carnegie Commission on Higher Education* (San Francisco, Jossey-Bass, 1973), p. 325.

50. See pp. 84–88.
51. Charles W. Eliot, "The History of American Teaching," *Educational Review,* Vol. 42, November, 1911, p. 360.
52. See Chapter 9.
53. William James, "The Ph.D. Octopus," *Harvard Monthly,* March, 1903, reprinted in *Educational Review,* Vol. 55, February, 1918, pp. 149–157; Walter A. Jessup, "Faculty Selection and Advancement," Carnegie Foundation, *Annual Report,* 1935, p. 12.
54. W. O. Thompson, "The Care of Freshmen," *Proceedings of the National Educational Association,* 1907, p. 727.
55. David S. Jordan, "University Tendencies in America," *Popular Science Monthly,* Vol. 63, June, 1903, p. 146, and "Perplexities of a College President," *Atlantic Monthly,* Vol. 85, April, 1900, pp. 490–491.
56. William R. Harper, *The Trend in Higher Education* (Chicago, University of Chicago Press, 1905), pp. 97–98.
57. Andrew F. West, *Short Papers on American Liberal Education* (New York, Scribner, 1907), pp. 52–56; Association of American Universities, *Sixth Annual Conference,* 1905, pp. 65–66. For a much later complaint to the same effect see Jacques Barzun, *Teacher in America* (Boston, Little, Brown, 1945), Chap. 14.
58. Charles W. Eliot, "Inaugural Address," quoted in Richard Hofstadter and Wilson Smith (eds.), *American Higher Education: A Documentary History* (Chicago, University of Chicago Press, 1961), pp. 603–604.
59. George Santayana, "Spirit and Ideals of Harvard University," *Educational Review,* Vol. 7, April, 1894, p. 215; Woodrow Wilson, in Clark S. Northrop, William C. Lane, and John C. Shwab (eds.), *Representative Phi Beta Kappa Orations* (Boston, Houghton Mifflin, 1915), pp. 467–471; Henry S. Canby, *Alma Mater* (New York, Farrar, Straus & Giroux, 1936), Chap. 8; Henry S. Pritchett, "The Organization of Higher Education," *Atlantic Monthly,* Vol. 102, December, 1908, pp. 788–789.
60. Dexter M. Keezer, *The Light That Flickers* (New York, Harper & Row, 1947), Chap. 4.
61. Edmund E. Day, *Education for Freedom and Responsibility* (Ithaca, N.Y., Cornell University Press, 1952), pp. 103–106; Werrett W. Charters, "Sizing Up the Faculty," *Journal of Higher Education,* Vol. 11, December, 1940, pp. 457–461; William B. Munro, "A Self-Study of College Training," *ibid.,* Vol. 3, December, 1932, pp. 459–463. For a method of evaluating, see American Association of University Professors, *The Evaluation of Faculty Services* (Ann Arbor, n.p., 1939).
62. Max McConn, *College or Kindergarten* (New York, New Republic, 1928), pp. 3–4.
63. Jay W. Hudson, *The College and New America* (Englewood Cliffs, N.J., Prentice-Hall, 1920), Chaps. 2–3, 6; Henry S. Canby, *College Sons and College Fathers* (New York, Harper & Row, 1915), pp. 48–55.
64. Ernest P. Earnest, *Academic Procession* (Indianapolis, Bobbs-Merrill, 1953), p. 300.
65. American Association of University Professors, *Report of the Committee on College and University Teaching* (published by the Association, 1933). For other surveys, see Fred J. Kelly, *Toward Better College Teaching* (U.S. Office of Education, Bulletin No. 13, 1950); Institute for Administrative Officers of Higher Institutions, *Training of College Teachers,* 1930; A. J. Klein, "Administrative Procedures for Improving College Teaching," in Earl Hudelson (ed.), *Problems of College Education* (Minneapolis, University of Minnesota Press, 1928).
66. *American Association of Colleges, Bulletin,* Vol. 12, 1926, p. 41.
67. *Ibid.,* Vol. 15, 1929, pp. 40–43.
68. Henry Suzzalo, "The Intellectual Life in the Colleges," *Ibid.,* Vol. 16, 1930, pp. 53–54.
69. Santayana, *op. cit.*
70. National Education Association, Association for Higher Education, *College and University Bulletin,* Vol. 10, November 15, 1957, pp. 1–3.
71. Howard Mumford Jones, *Education and World Tragedy* (Cambridge, Mass., Harvard University Press, 1946), p. 136.
72. Bernard Berelson, *Graduate Education in the United States* (New York, McGraw-Hill, 1960).
73. Everett Walters, "The Immutable Ph.D.," *Saturday Review,* January 15, 1966, p. 75.
74. Perry Miller, "The Master of Philosophy," *Ventures,* Vol. 6, Spring, 1966, pp. 1–4.
75. *New York Times,* April 9, 1967.
76. Norman Foerster, *The American State University* (Chapel Hill, University of North Carolina Press, 1937), pp. 112–114; Theodore C. Blegen and Russell M. Cooper, *Conference on the*

Preparation of College Teachers (Washington, D.C., American Council on Education, 1950).

77. American Association of University Professors, *op. cit.*, Part 2; for a collection of such lectures, see Bernice B. Cronkhite (ed.), *A Handbook for Teachers* (Cambridge, Mass., Harvard University Press, 1950).

78. Robert M. Hutchins, *The University of Utopia* (Chicago, University of Chicago Press, 1953), p. 44.

79. Luther P. Eisenhardt, *The Educational Process* (Princeton, N.J., Princeton University Press, 1945); Raymond M. Hughes, "A Study of the Graduate Schools of America," *Bulletin of the Association of American Colleges*, Vol. II, 1925; President's Commission on Higher Education, *Higher Education in American Democracy* (New York, Harper & Row, 1948), Vol. I.

80. *The Chronicle of Higher Education*, March 18, 1974. The Hazen Foundation helped finance the publication of this report together with the magazine *Change*.

81. See such books as Kenneth Eble, *Professors as Teachers* (San Francisco, Jossey-Bass, 1972); Joseph Axelrod, *The University Teacher as Artist* (San Francisco, Jossey-Bass, 1973); Walter H. Mais, *College Teaching: Its Practice and Its Potential* (New York, Harper & Row, 1956); and William McKeachie, *Tips for Teaching* (Ann Arbor, Mich., G. Wahr Publishing, 1956).

82. H. F. Fisk, "The Importance of Pedagogical Training for College Professors," *Proceedings of the National Education Association, 1891*, pp. 701–708; Herman H. Horne, "The Study of Education by Prospective College Instructors; the Views of Some College Presidents," *School Review*, Vol. 16, March, 1908, pp. 162–170; W. B. Pitkin, "Training College Teachers," *Popular Science Monthly*, Vol. 74, June, 1909, pp. 588–595.

83. William H. Cowley, "The Higher Learning versus the Higher Education," *Journal of Higher Education*, Vol. 25, November, 1954, pp. 404–405. See also, James E. Rogers, "Higher Education as a Field of Study at the Doctoral Level," Association for Higher Education, 1969.

84. Archie M. Palmer, "Professional Study of Higher Education," *Bulletin of the Association of American Colleges*, Vol. 16, 1930, pp. 283–285. See also Theodore C. Blegen and Russell M. Cooper, *The Preparation of College Teachers* (Washington, D.C., American Council on Education, 1950), p. 108; and *The Chronicle of Higher Education*, March 25, 1974.

85. *The Chronicle of Higher Education*, March 25, 1974.

86. E. g., *Education at Berkeley* (Berkeley, University of California Printing Department, 1966) and *Crisis at Columbia* (New York, Vintage Books, 1968), often referred to as the Muscatine and Cox reports, respectively.

87. For a list of the theses put forward by this Assembly, see *The Chronicle of Higher Education*, January 18, 1971.

88. *Report on Higher Education* (Washington, D.C., U.S. Office of Education, 1971), Chap. 13.

89. For a summary of findings, see *The Chronicle of Higher Education*, October 9, 1973, pp. 4–18. For further comment on the undertaking as a whole, see Lewis B. Mayhew, *The Carnegie Commission on Higher Education* (San Francisco, Jossey-Bass, 1974).

90. Donald McDonald, "A Six Million Dollar Misunderstanding," *The Center Magazine*, Vol. 6, September-October, 1973, pp. 32–52.

91. Paul Klapper, *College Teaching* (Yonkers, N.Y., World Book, 1920); Raymond A. Kent (ed.), *Higher Education in America* (Lexington, Mass., Ginn, 1930); Ernest E. Lindsay and Ernest O. Holland, *College and University Administration* (New York, Macmillan, 1930). Perhaps the earliest theoretic treatise on higher education was Francis Wayland's *Thoughts on the Present Collegiate System in the United States* (Boston, Gould, Kendall, and Lincoln, 1842) which seems to have had some reverberations from Sir William Hamilton's "On Patronage and Superintendence of Universities," *Edinburgh Review*, Vol. 59, April, 1834, pp. 196–227.

92. Other notable volumes were Nevitt Sanford (ed.), *The American College* (New York, Wiley, 1962); Algo D. Henderson, *Policies and Practices in Higher Education* (New York, Harper & Row, 1960); Joseph Justman and Walter H. Mais, *College Teaching: Its Practice and Its Potential* (New York, Harper & Row, 1956); and two histories of higher education, Frederick Rudolph, *The American College and University* (New York, Knopf, 1962); and John S. Brubacher and Willis Rudy, *Higher Education in Transition* (New York, Harper & Row, 1976).

93. Samuel Baskin, *Higher Education: Some Newer Developments* (New York, McGraw-Hill, 1965), pp. 213–218.

94. Robert M. Hutchins, *The Higher Learning in America* (New Haven, Conn., Yale University Press, 1936), pp. 39, 45–48.

95. Abraham Flexner, "The Graduate School in the United States," *Proceedings of the Association of American Universities,* 1931, p. 117; Thorstein Veblen, *The Higher Learning in America* (New York, B. W. Huebsch, 1918), p. 27; Abraham Flexner, *Universities: American, English, German* (New York, Oxford University Press, 1930), pp. 27–33, 162–177.
96. Veblen, *op. cit.,* p. 31; Robert M. Hutchins, "The Organization of a University," *Journal of Higher Education,* Vol. 5, October, 1934, pp. 349–354. Similarly, see below, pp. 259, 260.
97. Robert M. Hutchins, *Morals, Religion, and Higher Education* (Chicago, University of Chicago Press, 1950).
98. Veblen, *op. cit.,* p. 28.
99. Robert M. Hutchins, *The Higher Learning in America* (New Haven, Conn., Yale University Press, 1936), p. 52; Roscoe Pound, in Kent, *op. cit.,* Chap. 9.
100. Woodrow Wilson, "Should an Antecedent Liberal Education Be Required of Students in Law, Medicine, and Theology?" *Proceedings of the National Education Association,* 1893, pp. 112–117.
101. Alfred N. Whitehead, "Universities and Their Function," *Atlantic Monthly,* Vol. 141, May, 1928, pp. 638–639; Edmund J. James, "Function of the State University," *Science,* Vol. 22, November, 1905, p. 615. For a further discussion of the role of theory and practice in the philosophy of higher education, see Chap. 14.

Chapter 11. The Federal Government and Higher Education

1. Carl Brent Swisher, *The Growth of Constitutional Power in the United States* (Chicago, University of Chicago Press, 1946), pp. 44–45.
2. Richard G. Axt, *The Federal Government and the Financing of Higher Education* (New York, Columbia University Press, 1952), pp. 272–273.
3. Benjamin Rush, "An Address to the People of the United States," *American Museum,* January, 1787. One Samuel Blodget, Jr., later claimed to have broached the subject of a national university to General Washington as early as October, 1775, but several students of the subject doubt this assertion.
4. Joel Barlow, *Prospectus of a National Institution* (Washington, D.C., 1806). Barlow emphasized: "No rudiment of knowledge should be below its attention, no height of improvement above its ambition, no corner of our empire beyond its vigilant activity for collecting and diffusing information."
5. Max Farrand (ed.), *The Records of the Federal Convention of 1787* (New Haven, Conn., Yale University Press, 1911), Vol. II, pp. 321, 616; Vol. III, p. 122.
6. James D. Richardson, *A Compilation of the Messages and Papers of the Presidents, 1789–1897* (Washington, D.C., U.S. Congress, 1899), Vol. I, pp. 66, 202, 410, 485, 568, 576; Vol. II, p. 312. There was some difference of opinion among these Presidents as to whether a constitutional amendment might be necessary to establish the university. Jefferson and Monroe, for example, seem to have doubted that the power to take this action was implied in the Constitution.
7. Edgar B. Wesley, *Proposed: The University of the United States* (Minneapolis, University of Minnesota Press, 1936), pp. 4–8; Carl W. Tvedt, "A Brief History of the National University," *School and Society,* Vol. 33, January 10, 1931, pp. 46–47; Albert Castel, "The Founding Fathers and the Vision of a National University," *History of Education Quarterly,* Vol. 4, December, 1964, pp. 280–298.
8. *Ibid.,* p. 294.
9. Edward Everett, "University Education," *North American Review,* Vol. 10, January, 1820, p. 137; Philip Lindsley, *Educational Discourses* (Philadelphia, Lippincott, 1859), pp. 354–355; Benjamin A. Gould, "An American University," *Barnard's American Journal of Education,* Vol. 2, 1856, pp. 273–277.
10. We find President Timothy Dwight telling the Yale students in 1814 that if Europeans were encouraged to come over and teach at such a national university, "they would not be Christians; but Edinburgh Reviewers—men who would throw religion out of the world with one stroke. . . . There would be danger that such sentiments would be encouraged at our seat of government, for there is much irreligion there." Theodore Dwight, Jr., *President Dwight's Decisions of Questions in Yale College, in 1813 and 1814* (New York, Jonathan Leavitt, 1833), pp. 228–229. After the middle of the nineteenth century, this denominational opposition to

the proposed national university was strengthened when the Roman Catholic church adopted a policy of active opposition to the project.

11. John W. Hoyt, *Memorial in Regard to a National University* (Washington, D.C., Government Printing Office, 1892); Wesley, *op. cit.,* pp. 14–15.

12. *Proceedings of the National Educational Association,* 1873, pp. 110–120.

13. *Ibid.,* 1901, pp. 459–471; Edmund J. James, "The Constitutionality of a National University," *Educational Review,* Vol. 18, December, 1899, pp. 451–466.

14. Richardson, *op. cit.,* Vol. VII, p. 479.

15. Charles W. Eliot to Daniel C. Gilman, October 12, 1873, Gilman Papers, Johns Hopkins University (courtesy of Professor Thomas LeDuc); Henry James, *Charles W. Eliot* (Boston, Houghton Mifflin, 1936), Vol. I, pp. 324–329.

16. Wesley, *op. cit.,* pp. 17–24.

17. Charles Van Hise, "A National University a National Asset," National Education Association, *Proceedings, 1912,* pp. 210–220; Jacob G. Schurman to John W. Hoyt, October 22, 1894, Schurman Papers, Cornell University (courtesy of Professor LeDuc).

18. Richard Hofstadter and C. De Witt Hardy, *Development and Scope of Higher Education in the United States* (New York, Columbia University Press, 1952), pp. 116–117.

19. In 1925, the U.S. Military Academy was accepted as an approved technological institution by the Association of American Universities. Two years later it was admitted to membership in the Association of American Colleges. Not until 1933 did an act of Congress authorize it to award the bachelor of science degree.

20. R. Ernest Dupuy, *Men of West Point* (New York, William Sloane Associates, 1951), pp. 7–8, 445–446.

21. See pp. 198–200.

22. *Letter from the Acting Secretary of War, Transmitting a Statement of the Probable Annual Expense of the Military Academy from the Year 1801 to 1816* (Washington, D.C., William A. Davis, 1817); Board of Visitors, *Report on the U.S. Military Academy at West Point for 1826;* Board of Visitors, *Report on the U.S. Military Academy, June 20, 1839* (Washington, D.C., A. B. Claxton, 1839); *Regulations of the U.S. Military Academy at West Point, New York, 1832* (New York, Harper & Row, 1832); *Letter from the Secretary of War Transmitting a Copy of the Rules and Regulations for the Government of the Military Academy at West Point,* February 25, 1820 (Washington, D.C., Gales and Seaton, 1820). Thayer had been purposely sent by the War Department to France, rather than to England or Germany. It was felt that French technical and military training would be more congenial to the spirit of the young American Republic than the drillmaster methods of Prussia or the aristocratic system of Great Britain.

23. Sidney Forman, *West Point* (New York, Columbia University Press, 1950), pp. 74–89, 214–215; William Baumer, *West Point, Moulder of Men* (Englewood Cliffs, N.J., Prentice-Hall, 1942), pp. 7–9, 14–16; *Regulations Established for the Organization and Government of the Military Academy at West Point, 1839* (New York, Wiley & Putnam, 1839); *A Catalogue of the Graduates of the U.S. Military Academy . . . Together with the Regulations for the Admission of Cadets* (New York, Graham, 1847).

24. Baumer, *op. cit.,* pp. 16–43; Forman, *op. cit.,* pp. 167–168, 216–217; Dupuy, *op. cit.,* pp. 445–448.

25. U.S. Naval Academy, *Guide to the Naval Academy* (New York, Devin-Adair, 1941), pp. 25–31; William D. Puleston, *Annapolis* (Englewood Cliffs, N.J., Prentice-Hall, 1942), pp. 2–3; Kendall Banning, *Annapolis Today* (New York, Funk & Wagnalls, 1945), pp. 75–78; John Crane and James Kieley, *U.S. Naval Academy* (New York, McGraw-Hill, 1945), p. 42.

26. *Regulations for the Government of the Naval Academy at Annapolis, Md. Prepared by a Board of Navy Officers, 1851* (Washington, D.C., C. Alexander, 1851); *Regulations of the U.S. Naval Academy at Annapolis, Md., 1855* (Washington, D.C., A. O. Nicholson, 1855); U.S. Naval School, *Report of the Board of Visitors to the Secretary of the Navy for 1864* (New York, Van Nostrand Reinhold, 1864); *Regulations of the United States Naval Academy as Approved by the Secretary of the Navy, Jan. 1, 1876* (Washington, D.C., Government Printing Office, 1876); Puleston, *op. cit.,* pp. 112–120, 157–158, 213–214; Board of Visitors to the U.S. Naval Academy, *Reports,* 1919–39 (Washington, D.C., Government Printing Office, 1919–39).

27. Mary Irwin (ed.), *American Universities and Colleges* (Washington, D.C., American Council on Education, 1956), p. 88; U.S. Merchant Marine Academy, *Catalogue, 1949; U.S. Air Force,*

The Aviation Cadet, The Official Indoctrinal Book for the United States Air Force Cadet, 1950.

28. David McClure and Elijah Parish, *Memoirs of the Reverend Eleazar Wheelock* (Newburyport, Mass., Edward Little, 1811), p. 133; James Madison to Ezra Stiles, June 18, 1782, in Isabel M. Calder (ed.), *Letters and Papers of Ezra Stiles* (New Haven, Conn., Yale University Library, 1933), pp. 50–51; Joel T. Headley, "Our Colleges in the Revolution," *Knickerbocker Magazine,* Vol. 57, April, 1861, pp. 353–362; Howard H. Peckham, *"Collegia Ante Bellum:* Attitudes of College Professors and Students Toward the American Revolution," *Pennsylvania Magazine of History and Biography,* Vol. 95, January, 1971, pp. 70–72.

29. John N. Waddel, *Academic Memorials* (Richmond, Va., Presbyterian Committee of Publication, 1891), pp. 362–363; Earl Swem, *Kentuckians at William and Mary Before 1861* (Filson Club, 1949), p. 22; Samuel Eliot Morison, *Three Centuries of Harvard* (Cambridge, Mass., Harvard University Press, 1936), p. 303; Merle E. Curti, *Growth of American Thought* (New York, Harper & Row, 1943), pp. 459–468.

30. John O. Gross, "The College and World War I," *Bulletin of the Association of American Colleges,* Vol. 28, May, 1942; John A. Widstoe, "The Four Quarter Plan of University Operation during the War and After," *NEA Proceedings,* 1917, pp. 299–304; Charles F. Thwing, *American Colleges and Universities in the Great War* (New York, Macmillan, 1920), pp. 246–247; Parke R. Kolbe, *The Colleges in War Time and After* (Englewood Cliffs, N.J., Prentice-Hall, 1919).

31. I. L. Kandel, *The Impact of the War upon American Education* (Chapel Hill, University of North Carolina Press, 1948), pp. 123–134, 151–153, 160–161; John W. Nason, "What Have We Learned," *Journal of Higher Education,* Vol. 15, June, 1944, pp. 287–298.

32. Paul S. Bond (ed.), *Military Science and Tactics* (Washington, D.C., P. S. Bond Publishing, 1941); Charles W. Dabney, "Land-Grant and Other Colleges and The National Defense," *Proceedings of the Association of Land-Grant Colleges,* Vol. 12, 1898, pp. 67–68.

33. Seymour M. Lipset and Gerald M. Schaflander, *Passion and Politics: Student Activism in America* (Boston, Little, Brown, 1972) p. 138; Bond, *op. cit.;* Merritt M. Chambers, *Every Man a Brick* (Bloomington, Ill., Public School Publishing, 1927), pp. 13–15. Here again we have an example of a specialized, "programatic" federal activity in higher education. The objective of the program was not to help the colleges financially, but to provide trained man power for the armed services.

34. Chambers, *op. cit.* Beginning in 1924, the Navy Department began to develop its own Naval R.O.T.C. units at various colleges, "miniature naval academies." Puleston, *op. cit.,* pp. 120–129.

35. William W. Folwell, *Letters and Autobiography* (Minneapolis, University of Minnesota Press, 1933), p. 204; Merle Curti and Vernon Carstensen, *History of the University of Wisconsin* (Madison, University of Wisconsin Press, 1949), Vol. I, pp. 412–418; Earl D. Ross, *Democracy's College* (Ames, Iowa State College Press, 1942), pp. 122–127; Robin Myers, *America Arms the Schools* (Chicago, Young People's Socialist League, 1937); Winthrop Lane, *Military Training in Schools and Colleges of the U.S.* (New York, Committee on Military Training, 1926); Ralph Bishop, *Educational Value of Military Instruction in Universities and Colleges* (Washington, D.C., Government Printing Office, 1932); James Gray, *University of Minnesota, 1851–1951* (Minneapolis, University of Minnesota Press, 1951), pp. 367–371.

36. Lloyd E. Blauch, "Higher Education and the Federal Government," *Higher Education,* Vol. 13, December 15, 1956, p. 55.

37. Gordon Canfield Lee, *The Struggle for Federal Aid* (New York, Teachers College, Columbia University, 1949).

38. Carl Brent Swisher, *American Constitutional Development* (Boston, Houghton Mifflin, 1943), pp. 1017–1018.

39. This policy was based, for its constitutional authority, on the "general welfare" clause of the Constitution and the right of the federal government to dispose of its own property as it saw fit.

40. Edward H. Reisner, "Antecedents of the Federal Acts concerning Education," *Educational Record,* Vol. 11, July, 1930, p. 202; John L. Seaton, "The Federal Government and Higher Education," *Bulletin of the Association of American Colleges,* Vol. 25, May, 1939, pp. 245–246.

41. George N. Rainsford, *Congress and Higher Education in the Nineteenth Century* (Knoxville, University of Tennessee Press, 1972), pp. 129–130.

42. These later federal subsidies took the form of monetary grants rather than lands.

43. David S. Hill, *Control of Tax-Supported Higher Education in the United States* (New York, Carnegie Foundation, 1934), pp. 19–20.

44. Swisher, *op. cit.,* pp. 372–375; Axt, *op. cit.,* pp. 60–61.

45. Wilfred E. Binkley and Malcolm C. Moos, *A Grammar of American Politics* (New York, Knopf, 1952), pp. 81–82; Swisher, *op. cit.,* pp. 384–385; Rainsford, *op. cit.,* p. 131.

46. Rainsford, *op. cit.,* p. 132; A. C. True, "History of the Hatch Experiment Station Act of 1887," *Proceedings of the Association of Land-Grant Colleges,* Vol. 40, 1926, pp. 100–104.

47. The whole trend set in motion by federal legislation after 1862 had the effect of stimulating utilitarian and technological studies. No federal funds were available for general or humanistic education. Yet the uncommitted federal land grants before 1862 had mainly gone for the support of general liberal-arts training. Thus the more recent federal policies represented a revolutionary about-face in more ways than one. On this, see William Lowe Bryan, "Educational Policies of the United States Government," *Educational Record.* Vol. 11, April, 1930, p. 56; Swisher, *op. cit.,* pp. 384–388.

48. Hill, *op. cit.;* Davidson, *op. cit.,* pp. 112–113; C. A. Prosser, "The Smith-Hughes Act and the Land Grant Colleges," *Proceedings of the Association of Land-Grant Colleges,* Vol. 31, 1917, pp. 79–83.

49. National Youth Administration, *Final Report for 1936–1943* (Washington, D.C., Government Printing Office, 1944), pp. 46–48; Aubrey Williams, *Administration and Program Operation of the N.Y.A., 1935–37* (Washington, D.C., National Youth Administration, 1937).

50. Director of War Mobilization, *The Veteran and Higher Education* (Washington, D.C., Government Printing Office, 1946), pp. 30–32; Axt, *op. cit.,* p. 122; Davidson, *op. cit.,* pp. 114–115.

51. This amount constituted more than 70 per cent of all the research being carried on in those institutions. This federal program also involved the granting of predoctoral and postdoctoral fellowships through the National Science Foundation.

52. H. P. Allen, *The Federal Government and Education* (New York, McGraw-Hill, 1950); Homer D. Babbidge, Jr., and Robert M. Rosenzweig, *The Federal Interest in Higher Education* (New York, McGraw-Hill, 1962), p. 30.

53. Robert H. Knapp and Joseph H. Greenbaum, *The Younger American Scholar* (Chicago, University of Chicago Press, 1953), pp. 93–94.

54. Harold Orlans, *The Effects of Federal Programs on Higher Education* (Washington, D.C., Brookings Institution, 1962), pp. 293–294.

55. Amendments to the act in 1955 increased the funds available for loans and broadened the scope of the program to include various types of noninstructional college buildings. Irwin, *op. cit.,* p. 87; Arnold H. Diamond, "The College Housing Program: Its History and Operations," *Educational Record,* Vol. 38, July, 1957, pp. 204–208.

56. Babbidge and Rosenzweig, *op. cit.,* pp. 62–64.

57. Davidson, *op. cit.,* p. 115; "Higher Education Act of 1965," *Saturday Review,* Vol. 48, November 20, 1965, p. 82.

58. A notable example of a federally operated civilian school of this type was the graduate school of the Department of Agriculture. James Russell, *Federal Activities in Higher Education After the Second World War* (New York, King's Crown Press, 1951), pp. 11–12, 15–16.

59. Blauch, *op. cit.,* pp. 54–56; Irwin, *op. cit.,* pp. 85–89.

60. Russell, *op. cit.,* pp. 3, 13, 217–219. This total, by the way, was *four* times the combined income of all institutions of higher education in the United States in 1939.

61. For a comprehensive survey of federal activities in higher education as of June, 1956, see Charles A. Quattlebaum, *Federal Aid to Students for Higher Education: A Report Prepared in the Legislative Reference Service of the Library of Congress* (Washington, D.C., Government Printing Office, 1956); the quotation is from Babbidge and Rosenzweig, *op. cit.,* p. 30.

62. The President's commission found that the growth of expenditures on higher education was not keeping pace with the growth of gross national income in the 1940s. Not enough was going to endowment from private gifts. More and more was going for current operating expenses. Thus the colleges had no alternative but to keep raising their tuition fees. U.S. President's Commission, *Higher Education for American Democracy: A Report* (New York, Harper & Row, 1948), Vol. I, p. 27.

63. A nationwide survey of the scholarship records of NYA students showed that there was relatively little relationship between students' financial inability to attend college and their

scholastic ability. National Youth Administration, *op. cit.,* p. 76.

64. The NEA made a survey in 1949 which revealed that 83 per cent of the heads of private colleges and 80 per cent of those representing public institutions approved of a federal aid program, provided it was divorced from federal control. On this problem, see American Association of Universities, *Proceedings,* 41st Annual Conference, 1939; James B. Conant, "Education Beyond the High School," *Bulletin of the Association of American Colleges,* March, 1947, pp. 15–16; William S. Gray, *Needed Readjustments in Higher Education* (Chicago, University of Chicago Press, 1933), p. 17.

65. The commission had representatives from both public and private institutions, from women's colleges, and from three religious faiths.

66. President's Commission, *op. cit.,* Vol. I, p. 101.

67. *Ibid.,* Vol. I, p. 41. This estimate was based on the results of the Army General Classification Test, a test of verbal, arithmetical, and mechanical ability given to almost 10,000,000 men during World War II. These were then equated to the results of other widely used tests, such as the American Council on Education Psychological Examination, 1942 College Edition.

68. The commission had in mind granting 10,000 such scholarships at once to be administered by the states, 20,000 to be awarded in 1949–1950, and 30,000 by 1950–1951.

69. President's Commission, *op. cit.,* Vol. V, pp. 56–61. Under the proposed capital outlay program the federal grant would cover one-third of the cost, to be matched by a contribution of two-thirds by the states.

70. *Ibid.,* Vol. II, p. 29; Vol. V, pp. 65–68.

71. For a good summation of this debate, together with pertinent extracts, see Gail Kennedy (ed.), *Education for Democracy, The Debate over the Report of the President's Commission on Higher Education* (Lexington, Mass., Heath, 1952); also see James G. Harlow, "Five Years of Discussion," *Journal of Higher Education,* Vol. 24, January, 1953.

72. For many years, educators had been warning of the dangers of "federalization" of educational policy in Washington by means of a centralized dictatorship over educational institutions effected by making them dependent on the federal government for support. See American Association of Universities, *Proceedings,* 41st Annual Conference, 1939, pp. 83–85, 90–91; American Council on Education and N.E.A. Educational Policies Commission, *Federal-State Relations in Education* (Washington, D.C., 1945), pp. 45–47.

73. John K. Norton, "The Need for Federal Aid for Education," *School and Society,* March 17, 1956, pp. 87–88.

74. "Higher Education Act of 1965," *Saturday Review,* Vol. 48, November 20, 1965, p. 83.

75. *New York Times,* February 28, 1971, IV, p. 9; June 24, 1972, p. 1; June 27, 1972, p. 40.

Chapter 12. Articulation of Secondary and Higher Education

1. Merle Curti and Vernon Carstensen, *The University of Wisconsin, a History 1848–1925* (Madison, University of Wisconsin Press, 1949), Vol. I, p. 187.

2. For a fuller description of early requirements, see pp. 11, 12.

3. Edwin C. Broome, *A Historical and Critical Discussion of College Admission Requirements* (New York, Macmillan, 1903), Chap. 3.

4. Claude M. Fuess, *The College Board, Its First Fifty Years* (New York, Columbia University Press, 1950), pp. 6–7, 17–18.

5. R. R. Browker, "The College of Today," *Princeton Review,* January, 1884, pp. 105–106.

6. Curti and Carstensen, *op. cit.,* p. 293.

7. University of Michigan, *Annual Report of the President,* 1878, pp. 7–8; Charles W. Eliot, *Educational Reform* (Englewood Cliffs, N.J., Prentice-Hall, 1898), pp. 200–201. For a fuller treatment of this practice, see pp. 104, 106, 108.

8. National Education Association, *Report of the Committee on College Entrance Requirements,* 1899, pp. 27–45.

9. William W. Ferrier, *Origin and Development of the University of California* (Berkeley, Calif., Sather Gate Book Shop, 1930), pp. 374–382.

10. Willard K. Clement, "The Northwestern State University and Its Preparatory School," *Educational Review,* Vol. 17, February, 1899, pp. 154–163; Willis F. Dunbar, "The University and its Branches," *Michigan Alumnus Quarterly Review,* Vol. 46, July, 1940, pp. 313–315.

11. *The American College* (New York, Holt, Rinehart & Winston, 1915), pp. 180–192.

12. Clarence King, "Artium Magister," *North American Review,* Vol. 147, October, 1888, p. 375.

13. Earl D. Ross, *History of Iowa State College* (Ames, Iowa State College Press, 1942), pp. 22, 69.

14. Francis Wayland, *Thoughts on the Present College System* (Boston, Gould, Kendall, and Lincoln, 1842), pp. 105–107.

15. Charles F. Smith, "Southern Colleges and Schools," *Atlantic Monthly,* Vol. 54, October, 1884, pp. 543–544.

16. Henry S. Pritchett, Carnegie Foundation for the Advancement of Teaching, *Annual Report, 1921,* pp. 73–74.

17. George W. Pierson, *Yale College, An Educational History, 1871–1921* (New Haven, Conn., Yale University Press, 1952), p. 390.

18. James B. Angell, *Reminiscences* (New York, McKay, 1912), pp. 236–239. See also William F. Galpin, *Syracuse University: The Pioneer Days* (Syracuse, N.Y., Syracuse University Press, 1952), p. 40.

19. For an early comparison of course marks with marks on entrance examinations as measures for college admissions, see Clyde M. Furst, "Tests of College Efficiency," *School Review,* Vol. 20, May, 1919, pp. 323–325.

20. Broome, *op. cit.,* Chap. 4.

21. Calvin O. Davis, *A History of the North Central Association of Colleges and Secondary Schools, 1895–1945* (Ann Arbor, Mich., the Association, 1945).

22. Isaac L. Kandel, *Examinations and Their Substitutes in the United States* (New York, Carnegie Foundation, Bulletin No. 28, 1936), pp. 37–38.

23. Eliot, *op. cit.,* pp. 206–219.

24. Fuess, *op. cit.,* pp. 23–39.

25. Wilson Farrand, "Five Years of the College Entrance Examination Board," *Educational Review,* Vol. 30, October, 1905, pp. 217–230.

26. Fuess, *op. cit.,* pp. 49–53.

27. *Ibid.,* pp. 107–111.

28. James Gray, *The University of Minnesota, 1851–1951* (Minneapolis, University of Minnesota Press, 1951), pp. 198–199. The expanding use of tests found notable expression by mid-century in the formation of the Educational Testing Service, which combined the former services of the College Entrance Examination Board, the Cooperative Test Service of the American Council on Education, and the General Record Examination of the Carnegie Foundation for the Advancement of Teaching. Howard Savage, *Fruit of an Impulse* (New York, Harcourt Brace Jovanovich, 1953), pp. 301–302.

29. Ernest H. Wilkins, *The Changing College* (Chicago, University of Chicago Press, 1927), pp. 75–77.

30. William S. Learned and Ben D. Wood, *The Student and His Knowledge* (New York, Carnegie Foundation, Bulletin No. 29, 1938), pp. 60–61.

31. Elmo Roper, *Factors Affecting the Admission of High School Seniors to College* (Washington, D.C., American Council on Education, 1949), pp. 79–84; Andrew C. Ivy and Irwin Ross, *Religion and Race; Barriers to College?* (New York, Public Affairs Committee, 1949); Richard J. Roche, *Catholic Colleges and the Negro Student* (Washington, D.C., Catholic University Press, 1948), p. 79.

32. Lawrence A. Cremin, "The Revolution in American Secondary Education, 1893–1918," *Teachers College Record,* Vol. 56, March, 1955, pp. 295–308.

33. National Education Association, National Council of Education, *Report of the Committee of Ten on Secondary School Studies,* 1893, pp. 51–52.

34. *Ibid.,* p. 17.

35. *Ibid.,* pp. 51–52.

36. *Ibid.* For further exposition of this theory, see pp. 290–294.

37. G. Stanley Hall, *Adolescence* (Englewood Cliffs, N.J., Prentice-Hall, 1904), Vol. II, p. 513.

38. In defense of the committee, see Eliot, *op. cit.,* pp. 303–339.

39. Hall, *op. cit.;* Charles T. Burnett, *Hyde of Bowdoin* (Boston, Houghton Mifflin, 1931), pp. 189–191. In defense of the committee again see Charles W. Eliot, "The Fundamental Assumptions in the Report of the Committee of Ten," *Educational Review,* Vol. 30, November, 1905, pp. 333–335.

40. National Education Association, *Report of the Committee on College Entrance Requirements,* 1899, pp. 38–45.

41. National Education Association, *Report of the Committee of Nine on the Articulation of High School and College,* 1911, pp. 564–565.

42. National Education Association, Report of the Commission on the Reorganization of Secondary Education, *The Cardinal Principles of Secondary Education,* 1918, p. 20.

43. William M. Aiken, *The Story of the Eight Year Study* (New York, Harper & Row, 1942), Chaps. 1, 6–7.

44. Robert L. Duffus, *Democracy Enters College* (New York, Scribner, 1936), Chap. 6. See also p. 385.

45. *The Carnegie Unit, Its Origin, Status, and Trends* (U.S. Department of Health, Education and Welfare, Bulletin No. 7, 1954). In *The American College* (New York, Holt Rinehart & Winston, 1915), p. 111, John H. Finley parodied the "Carnegie unit" thus:

45 minutes make an hour	15 units make a matriculant	
5 hours make a week	5 matriculant hours (for one year)	
36 hours make a unit	make a point or count	
	60 points or counts make a degree	

46. Dael Woefle, *American Resources of Specialized Talent* (New York, Harper & Row, 1958), p. 8.

47. *Bridging the Gap Between School and College* (New York, Fund for the Advancement of Education, 1953). See also *General Education in School and College* (Cambridge, Mass., Harvard University Press, 1952).

48. Samuel Baskin, *Higher Education: Some Newer Developments* (New York, McGraw-Hill, 1965), pp. 107, 110–113.

49. *College Entrance Examination Board—A Guide to the Advanced Placement Program* (New York, College Entrance Examination Board, 1965), p. 7.

50. Samuel P. Capen, "The Dual Obligation of University and College," in Henry P. Fairchild (ed.), *The Obligation of Universities to the Social Order* (New York, New York University Press, 1933), pp. 59–61.

51. Jurgen Herbst, "Liberal Education and the Graduate Schools: An Historical Review of College Reform," *History of Education Quarterly,* Vol. 2, December, 1962, pp. 244–258.

52. John W. Burgess, *Reminiscences of an American Scholar* (New York, Columbia University Press, 1934), pp. 349–368; Andrew D. White, "The Future of American Universities," *North American Review,* Vol. 151, October, 1890, pp. 446–550.

53. Jacques Barzun, "College to University—and After," *American Scholar,* Vol. 33, Spring, 1964, pp. 212–220. Cf. David Boroff, "A Plea to Save the Liberal Arts," *New York Times Magazine,* May 10, 1964.

54. Henry P. Bowditch, *Remarks Made at a Meeting of the Harvard Academic Council* (Boston, David Clapp & Son, 1887), pp. 13–14, 17.

55. Earl McGrath, *The Graduate School and the Decline of Liberal Education* (New York, Teachers College, Columbia University, 1959).

56. Christopher Jencks and David Riesman, *The Academic Revolution* (Cambridge, Mass., Harvard University Press, 1968), p. 13.

57. Charles W. Eliot, *Educational Reform* (Englewood Cliffs, N.J., Prentice-Hall, 1898), pp. 151–176.

58. Nicholas M. Butler, "The American College," *Educational Review,* Vol. 25, January, 1903, pp. 10–20.

59. National Education Association, "Length of the Baccalaureate Course and Preparation for the Professional Schools," *Proceedings,* 1903, pp. 496–500. For later developments, see Ernest L. Boyer, "How Much Time for Education?" *Educational Record,* Vol. 53, Fall, 1972, pp. 271–280.

60. John A. Sexson and John W. Harbeson, *The New American College* (New York, Harper & Row, 1946), pp. 14–15. Yale played with the idea, but finally rejected the three-year degree because it thwarted a strongly entrenched four-year social system. Pierson, *op. cit.,* p. 210.

61. Monroe Smith, "The Combined Course for the Collegiate and Professional Degrees," *Educational Review,* Vol. 26, October, 1903, pp. 254–265.

62. U.S. Bureau of Education, Bulletin No. 18 (Washington, D.C., 1913), p. 18.

63. Cf. W. Scott Thomas, "Changes in the Age of School Graduation," *Popular Science Monthly,* Vol. 63, June, 1903, pp. 159–171.

64. William R. Harper, "The Length of the College Course," *Educational Review,* Vol. 26, September, 1903, pp. 134–140.
65. National Education Association, *Proceedings,* 1903, pp. 500–504.
66. Harper, *op. cit.*
67. Association of American Universities, *Fifth Annual Conference,* 1904, pp. 40–41.
68. William R. Harper, *The Trend in Higher Education* (Chicago, University of Chicago Press, 1905), p. 382.
69. H. G. Noffsinger, "One Third of a Century of Progress," *Junior College Journal,* Vol. 5, May, 1935, p. 395.
70. William H. Cowley, "The War on the College," *Atlantic Monthly,* Vol. 169, June, 1942, p. 721.
71. Edward R. Beauchamp, "An American Gymnasium: The Round Hill School, 1823–1834," *Educational Record,* Vol. 37, January, 1973, pp. 159–167.
72. Walter C. Eells, "Abolition of the Lower Division: Early History," *Junior College Journal,* Vol. 6, January, 1936, pp. 194–195.
73. Edmund J. James, "Function of the State University," *Science,* Vol. 22, November, 1905, p. 616; University of Michigan, *Annual Report of the President,* 1883, p. 12; Orrin L. Elliott, *Stanford University: The First Twenty-five Years* (Stanford, Calif., Stanford University Press, 1937), pp. 518–533. For a later revival of the same idea, see Robert M. Hutchins, *No Friendly Voice* (Chicago, University of Chicago Press, 1936), pp. 78–80.
74. University of Chicago, *Annual Report of the President,* 1898–99, pp. xx–xxi.
75. William W. Folwell, *University Addresses* (Bronx, N.Y., H. W. Wilson, 1909), pp. 100–112.
76. Lewis W. Smith, "Early Junior College—Harper's Influence," *Junior College Journal,* Vol. 11, May, 1941, p. 516.
77. In 1898 the University of Chicago commenced awarding the title of "Associate" for completion of lower-division or junior-college work. Walter C. Eells, "The Bachelor's Degree," *Bulletin of the Association of American Colleges,* Vol. 28, October, 1942, pp. 594–595. President Conant of Harvard lent some support to granting the bachelor's degree at the end of junior college. See *Education and Liberty* (Cambridge, Mass., Harvard University Press, 1953), pp. 57–58.
78. Walter C. Eells, "The Bachelor's Degree at the Sophomore Level," *AAUP Bulletin,* Vol. 28, June, 1942, pp. 327–351.
79. Edward C. Elliott, *Rise of a University* (New York, Columbia University Press, 1937), Vol. II, pp. 211–212.
80. Charles K. Adams, "The Next Step in Education," *Forum,* Vol. 10, February, 1891, pp. 629–630.
81. Cowley, *op. cit.,* pp. 722–726; A. Lawrence Lowell, "Universities, Graduate Schools, and Colleges," *Atlantic Monthly,* Vol. 150, August, 1932, pp. 219–221. George H. Palmer, "The Junior College," *Atlantic Monthly,* Vol. 139, April, 1927, pp. 498–501.
82. Walter C. Eells, *The Junior College* (Boston, Houghton Mifflin, 1931), Chap. 3; Smith, *op. cit.,* pp. 517–518; Robert M. Hutchins, "Significance to the University of Educational Developments on the Junior College Level," *Proceedings of the Association of American Universities,* 1937, pp. 106–108.
83. Elbert K. Fretwell, *Founding Public Junior Colleges* (New York, Teachers College, Columbia University, 1954), Chap. 2.
84. Leland L. Medsker and Dale Tillery, *Breaking the Access Barriers* (New York, McGraw-Hill, 1971), p. 18.
85. Jesse P. Bogue, *The Community College* (New York, McGraw-Hill, 1950).
86. Clyde M. Hill, "The University's Responsibility to the Junior College," *Proceedings of the Association of American Universities,* 1937, pp. 111–112; A. Monroe Stowe, *Modernizing the College* (New York, Knopf, 1926), pp. 55–56.
87. Anan Raymond, "The New University," *Educational Review,* Vol. 48, September, 1914, p. 153.
88. Daniel Bell, *The Reforming of General Education* (New York, Columbia University Press, 1966), p. 104.
89. John M. Thomas, "Report of the Commission on the Distribution of Colleges," *Bulletin of the Association of American Colleges,* No. 7, May, 1921, p. 8; John B. Johnston, *Proceedings of the Association of American Universities,* Vol. 26, May, 1924, pp. 76–77; George F. Zook, "The Emergency in Higher Education," *Proceedings of the National Education Association,* 1920, p. 233.

90. John D. Millett, "The Impending Crisis in Higher Education," *School and Society,* Vol. 81, June, 1955, p. 195; Francis H. Horn, "Problems Facing Higher Education," *Teachers College Record,* Vol. 57, March, 1956, pp. 360–361.

91. Daniel Bell, *op. cit.*

92. See pp. 62–64.

93. Hutchins, *No Friendly Voice,* p. 74.

94. L. J. Elias, "Democracy Hands Colleges a Dilemma," *Bulletin of the Association of American Colleges,* No. 34, December, 1948, p. 486.

95. *Middlebury College* v. *Chandler* (16 Vt. 683).

96. *Esteb* v. *Esteb* (138 Wash. 174).

97. Lotus D. Coffman, *The State University* (Minneapolis, University of Minnesota Press, 1934), pp. 76–79; Robert J. Havighurst, "Social Foundation of General Education," National Society for the Study of Education, Fifty-first Yearbook, *General Education* (Chicago, University of Chicago Press, 1952), pp. 71–73.

98. President's Commission on Higher Education, *op. cit.,* Vol. I, p. 37.

99. Johnston, *op. cit.,* pp. 78–79.

100. Coffman, *op. cit.,* p. 90; cf., at a much earlier time, Charles W. Eliot, in David A. Weaver (ed.), *Builders of American Universities* (Alton, Ill., Shurtleff College Press, 1950), Vol. I, pp. 21–22.

101. Frederick C. Kintzer, *Middleman in Higher Education* (San Francisco, Jossey-Bass, 1973).

102. Cf. W. B. Derall, "Community Colleges: Dissenting Views," *Educational Record,* Vol. 49, Spring, 1968, pp. 168–172.

103. Alvin C. Eurich, "A Renewed Emphasis upon General Education," National Society for the Study of Education, Thirty-Eighth Yearbook, *General Education in the American College* (Bloomfield, Ill., Public School Publishing, 1939), pp. 6–7.

104. See pp. 271–276.

105. Earl J. McGrath, "The General Education Movement," *Journal of General Education,* Vol. 1, October, 1946, pp. 3–8; President's Commission on Higher Education, *op. cit.,* Vol. I, p. 49. See also Russell Thomas, *The Search for a Common Learning* (New York, McGraw-Hill, 1963); and Hoyt Trowbridge, "Forty Years of General Education," *Journal of General Education,* Vol. 11, July, 1958, pp. 161–169.

106. Thomas R. McConnell, in *Association for General and Liberal Education* (Washington, D.C., 1945), pp. 38–39. Cf. also William S. Gray (ed.), *The Junior College Curriculum* (Chicago, University of Chicago Press, 1929), pp. 16–18; Ruth Eckert, *Outcomes of General Education* (Minneapolis, University of Minnesota Press, 1943), pp. 40–43; Ernest H. Wilkins, "Society and the College," *Bulletin of the Association of American Colleges,* No. 18, March, 1932, pp. 15–17. For various ways to organize these categories for instructional purposes, see pp. 280–281; also Werrett W. Charters, "Patterns of Courses in General Education," *Journal of General Education,* Vol. I, October, 1946, pp. 58–63. But "when colleges speak, as they do, of 'having general education' and point to an 'interdepartmental' course as the sole evidence (a course which might be an elective among a long list of electives) it is fair to ask whether they have really considered the fundamental conceptual problem which historically has always been at the heart of the meaning of general education." See Russell Thomas, *The Search for a Common Learning* (New York, McGraw-Hill, 1962), p. 75.

107. Gray, *op. cit.,* pp. 308–323; Malcolm MacLean, "A College of 1934," *Journal of Higher Education,* Vol. 5, June, 1934, pp. 240–252; Eckert, *op. cit.,* Chap. 12.

108. Cornelia T. Williams, *These We Teach* (Minneapolis, University of Minnesota Press, 1943).

109. Ivol Spafford *et al., Building a Curriculum for General Education* (Minneapolis, University of Minnesota Press, 1943).

110. Gray, *op. cit.,* p. 321.

111. Cf. *General Education in a Free Society* (Cambridge, Mass., Harvard University Press, 1945).

112. Cf. *Association for General and Liberal Education.*

113. Carnegie Commission on Higher Education, *Open Door Colleges* (New York, McGraw-Hill, 1970) and Leland Medsker and Dale Tillery, *op. cit.* See also Clyde E. Blocker *et al., The Two-Year College* (Englewood Cliffs, N.J., Prentice-Hall, 1965) and Samuel B. Gould and K. Patricia Gross, *Explorations in Non-Traditional Study* (San Francisco, Jossey-Bass, 1972).

114. Cyril Houle, *The External Degree* (San Francisco, Jossey-Bass, 1973).

115. Friedrich Schönemann, "A German Looks at American Higher Education," in Paul Schilpp (ed.), *Higher Education Faces the Future* (New York, Liveright, 1930), p. 120; William

McDougall, "Functions of the Endowed Universities in America," *ibid.,* p. 233; Gilbert Highet, "The American Student as I See Him," *American Scholar,* Vol. 10, Autumn, 1941, pp. 422–423.

116. *The Chronicle of Higher Education,* April 20, 1970. See also Daniel P. Moynihan, "On Universal Higher Education," *Educational Record,* Vol. 52, Winter, 1971, pp. 5–11.

117. Paul Taubman and Terrence Wales, *Mental Ability and Higher Educational Attainment in the Twentieth Century* (New York, National Bureau of Economic Research, 1972), pp. 19, 22–23. See also Jencks and Riesman, *op. cit.,* p. 95.

118. Martin Trow, "The Transition from Mass to Universal Higher Education," *Daedalus,* Vol. 99, Winter, 1970, pp. 24–27.

119. Roy Lucas, "The Right to Higher Education," *Journal of Higher Education,* Vol. 41, January, 1970, pp. 55–64. See also *post* pp. 76–79, 351, where higher education as a right or privilege is approached from the angle of due process.

120. Fritz Machlup, *The Chronicle of Higher Education,* November 16, 1970; Robert M. Hutchins, "Second Edition/The Idea of a College," *Center Magazine,* Vol. 5, May-June, 1972; pp. 45–49; and James J. Zigerell, "The Community College in Search of an Identity," *Journal of Higher Education,* Vol. 41, pp. 701–712.

121. Cf. Buell Gallagher, *Campus in Crisis* (New York, Harper & Row, 1974), pp. 204–205, where the author opposes "tracking" because in some places like New York City it has led to all-black colleges.

122. Jencks and Riesman, *op. cit.,* p. 150. Some critics from the counterculture of the 1960s, while they seemed to prefer an egalitarian society, also seemed inclined to treat inequalities of social and educational status by ignoring rather than reducing them. *Ibid.,* p. 153.

123. Thomas V. Smith, *The American Philosophy of Equality* (Chicago, University of Chicago Press, 1927), pp. 308–309.

124. Jerome Karabel, "Perspectives on Open Admissions," *Educational Record,* Vol. 53, Winter, 1972, pp. 35–36.

125. Kenneth H. Ashworth, *Scholars and Statesmen* (New York, McGraw-Hill, 1972), pp. 71–76, 88–89. See also, Gerald Grant and David Riesman, "An Ecology of Academic Reform" in *Daedalus,* Vol. 104, Winter, 1975, pp. 176–182.

126. Philip Jacob, *Changing Values in College* (New York, Harper & Row, 1957).

127. Stephen B. Withey *et al., A Degree and What Else?* (New York, McGraw-Hill, 1972), pp. 128–130.

128. Lewis B. Mayhew, *College Graduates and Jobs* (New York, McGraw-Hill, 1973), p. 131.

Chapter 13. Innovations in Curriculum and Methods

1. Chapter 5.
2. Chapter 6.
3. The average number of courses offered in liberal arts in ten representative institutions rose from 217 in 1900 to 338 in 1910, to 445 in 1920, and to 605 in 1930. Charles H. Judd, "The Improvement of Teaching," *Journal of Higher Education,* Vol. 3, December, 1932, p. 471.
4. William J. Tucker, "Administrative Problems of the Historic College," *Educational Review,* Vol. 43, May, 1912, p. 444.
5. Chapter 13.
6. Clark S. Northrup, William C. Lane, and John C. Schwab (eds.), *Representative Phi Beta Kappa Orations* (Boston, Houghton Mifflin, 1915), pp. 470–471; Nicholas M. Butler, "A New Method of Admission to College," *Educational Review,* Vol. 38, September, 1909, pp. 170–171.
7. Clarence F. Birdseye, *Individual Training in Our Colleges* (New York, Macmillan, 1907), pp. 195–196.
8. Northrup *et. al., op. cit.,* p. 472.
9. Cf. Robert M. Hutchins, *No Friendly Voice* (Chicago, University of Chicago Press, 1936), p. 30; Henry M. Wriston, in *Educational Yearbook* (Bureau of Publications, Teachers College, Columbia University, 1943), pp. 200–201.
10. Henry B. Mitchell, "A New System of Honor Courses in Columbia," *Educational Review,* Vol. 40, October, 1910, pp. 217–228; C. Wright Mills, *White Collar: The American Middle Classes* (New York, Oxford University Press, 1951), pp. 266–267. Max McConn suggested that some

colleges specialize in being "super-kindergartens" where adolescents could be tended in aesthetic surroundings and amused with healthful games while being given a modicum of instruction. *College or Kindergarten* (New York, New Republic, 1928), p. 21.

11. Northrup *et al., op. cit.,* p. 475; Robert M. Hutchins, *The Higher Learning in America* (New Haven, Conn., Yale University Press, 1936), Chap. I.

12. Thomas LeDuc, *Piety and Intellect at Amherst College, 1865–1912* (New York, Columbia University Press, 1946).

13. Edward L. Thorndike, "The Selective Influence of the College," *Educational Review,* Vol. 30, June, 1905, pp. 1–11. Cf. Samuel Eliot Morison, *Development of Harvard University Since the Inauguration of President Eliot, 1869–1929* (Cambridge, Mass., Harvard University Press, 1930), p. lxxx; George W. Pierson, *Yale College, 1871–1921* (New Haven, Conn., Yale University Press, 1952), Chap. 13.

14. R. T. Crane, *The Futility of All Kinds of Higher Schooling* (Chicago, H. O. Shepherd, 1909). See also Irvin C. Wyllie, "The Businessman Looks at the Higher Learning," *Journal of Higher Education,* Vol. 23, June, 1952, pp. 295–300. Wyllie notes that though tycoons like Carnegie, Rockefeller, and Vanderbilt were not college graduates, they did send their sons and daughters to college.

15. Frank Aydelotte, "Honors Courses in American Colleges and Universities," *Bulletin of the National Research Council,* Vol. 7, Part 4, January, 1924, pp. 1–18.

16. Henry S. Canby, *Alma Mater* (New York, Farrar, Straus & Giroux, 1936), pp. 85–88. For another account of college teaching at the time, cf. Bliss Perry, *And Gladly Teach* (Boston, Houghton Mifflin, 1935), Chaps. 3, 4, 6, 7, 10.

17. Aydelotte, *op. cit.,* pp. 1–18; Norman Foerster, *The American State University* (Chapel Hill, University of North Carolina Press, 1937), p. 187.

18. See pp. 212–215.

19. Canby, *op. cit.,* 84–87.

20. For a bundle of student criticism of the college, see *The Students Speak Out* (New York, New Republic, 1929).

21. Willis Rudy, *The Evolving Liberal Arts Curriculum: A Historical Review of Basic Themes* (New York, Teachers College, Columbia University, 1960). See also, Mowat G. Fraser, *The College of the Future* (New York, Columbia University Press, 1937), Chap. 9; Louis T. Benezet, *General Education in the Progressive College* (New York, Teachers College, Columbia University, 1943), pp. 33–48.

22. For a quick rundown of the main points of these plans, see R. H. Eliassen, "Survey of New College Plans," *Journal of Higher Education,* Vol. 10, May, 1939, pp. 256–262.

23. A. Lawrence Lowell, "Self-Education in College," *Journal of Higher Education,* Vol. 1, February, 1930, pp. 65–72.

24. Leon B. Richardson, *A Study of the Liberal College* (Hanover, N. H., n. p., 1924), pp. 237–240.

25. Woodrow Wilson, "The Preceptorial System at Princeton," *Educational Review,* Vol. 39, April, 1910, pp. 385–390; Andrew F. West, "The Tutorial System in College," *Educational Review,* Vol. 32, December, 1906, pp. 500–514. See also Henry W. Bragdon, *Woodrow Wilson: The Academic Years* (Cambridge, Mass., Belknap Press, 1967), pp. 304–308.

26. A. Lawrence Lowell, *At War with Academic Traditions* (Cambridge, Mass., Harvard University Press, 1934), pp. 302–306.

27. A. Lawrence Lowell, "General Examinations and Tutors at Harvard College," *Educational Record,* Vol. 8, April, 1927, pp. 64–67.

28. Frank Aydelotte, *Breaking the Academic Lockstep* (New York, Harper & Row, 1944), pp. 40–41; Raymond Walters, "A College Majors in Scholars," *American Scholar,* Vol. 1, pp. 473–477. See also Burton R. Clark, *The Distinctive College* (Chicago, Aldine, 1970), Chaps. 7–9, and Frances Blanchard, *Frank Aydelotte of Swarthmore* (Middletown, Conn., Wesleyan University Press, 1970), pp. 158–159.

29. Joseph W. Cohen, *The Superior Student in American Higher Education* (New York, McGraw-Hill, 1966), pp. 14–15, 25–27, 40. See also, Frank Aydelotte, *An Adventure in Education* (New York, Macmillan, 1941), p. 224.

30. Paul L. Dressel and Mary M. Thompson, *Independent Study: A New Interpretation of Concepts* (San Francisco, Jossey-Bass, 1973).

31. James Morgan Hart, *German Universities: A Narrative of Personal Experience,* quoted in Richard Hofstadter and Wilson Smith, *American Higher Education: A Documentary History*

(Chicago, University of Chicago Press, 1961), p. 577.

32. Robert Bonthius *et al.*, *Independent Study Programs in the United States* (New York, Columbia University Press, 1957), p. 199.

33. Beardsley Ruml, *Memo to a College Trustee* (New York, McGraw-Hill, 1959).

34. Norman F. Coleman, "How We Teach at Reed College," *Bulletin of the Association of American Colleges,* Vol. 14, November, 1928, pp. 407–408. Hutchins acted similarly toward the extracurriculum at Chicago.

35. Burton R. Clark, *op. cit.,* Chaps. 4–6.

36. *Ibid.,* Chaps. 1–3. See also, Algo D. Henderson and Dorothy Hall, *Antioch College: Its Design for Liberal Education* (New York, Harper & Row, 1946); Algo D. Henderson, in William S. Gray (ed.), *Provision for the Individual in College Education* (Chicago, University of Chicago Press, 1932), Chap. 8. Students at Bennington College often used their abnormally long winter vacation to seek employment as a recognized part of their college studies. See also James W. Wilson and Edward H. Lyons, *Work-Study College Programs* (New York, Harper & Row, 1961), pp. 1–7. For use of the community as part of the curriculum, see Baker Brownell, *The College and the Community* (New York, Harper & Row, 1952).

37. Ralph L. Ketcham, "Moral Philosophy," *Journal of Higher Education,* Vol. 24, October, 1953, pp. 363–369. See also Wilson Smith, *Professors and Public Ethics* (Ithaca, N.Y., Cornell University Press, 1956).

38. Edmund S. Morgan, *The Gentle Puritan* (New Haven, Conn., Yale University Press, 1962), pp. 381–382.

39. Russell Thomas, *The Search for a Common Learning* (New York, McGraw-Hill, 1963). See also Trowbridge Hoyt, "Forty Years of General Education," *Journal of General Education,* Vol. 11, July, 1958, pp. 161–169.

40. See p. 260.

41. Thomas, *op. cit.,* pp. 52–53.

42. *Ibid.,* pp. 73, 82.

43. Alexander Meiklejohn, *The Experimental College* (New York, Harper & Row, 1932), and *Freedom and the College* (Englewood Cliffs, N.J., Prentice-Hall, 1923), pp. 201–202. It is interesting to note that, with much more practical ends in view, the Civil Affairs Training School at the time of the Second World War took over this idea in its "area" training programs. In planning for service in a foreign country men combined with the study of the language of that country a study of its customs, history, geography, politics, and even religion. Lawrence G. Thomas, "Can the Social Sciences Learn from the Army Program?" *Journal of Higher Education,* Vol. 17, January, 1946, pp. 17–25.

44. Lawrence Veysey, "Stability and Experiment in American Undergraduate Curriculum," in Carl Kaysen (ed.), *Content and Context* (New York, McGraw-Hill, 1973), pp. 56–57. An attempt was made to revive Meiklejohn's idea to meet student criticism of higher education at the University of California in the sixties but again it failed for lack of faculty support. See Joseph Tussman, "The Experimental College at Berkeley," in W. Hamlin and L. Porter (eds.), *Dimensions of Change in Higher Education* (Yellow Springs, Ohio, Union for Research and Experimentation in Higher Education, 1967).

45. Jacques Barzun, in *Association for General and Liberal Education,* Bulletin No. 1 (Washington, D.C., n.p., 1945).

46. "Let us show him [the student] the whole first," wrote Preserved Smith, "let us lead him into the universe and turn all the lights on at once, rather than bring him into it in the dark and then throwing a flash-light now into this corner, now into that . . . at the very outset of the college course, set before him, in panorama infinitely reduced in scale but true to proportion, the whole scheme of things entire as we know them." "The Unity of Knowledge and the Curriculum," *Education Review,* Vol. 45, April, 1913, p. 340.

47. Cf. John G. Fowlkes (ed.), *Higher Education for American Democracy* (Madison, University of Wisconsin Press, 1949), Chap. 8.

48. See pp. 256, 259, 260.

49. Robert M. Hutchins, *The Idea and Practice of General Education* (Chicago, University of Chicago Press, 1950), Chap. 1; Floyd W. Reeves, Wesley E. Peik, and John D. Russell, *Instructional Problems in the University* (Chicago, University of Chicago Press, 1933), pp. 109–116; Robert M. Hutchins, "The Chicago Plan and Graduate Study," *Proceedings of the Association of American Universities,* 1931, pp. 137–139; *Five College Plans* (New York, Columbia University Press, 1931), pp. 95–98.

50. Hutchins, *The Higher Learning in America*, Chap. 4.

51. John Erskine, *My Life as a Teacher* (Philadelphia, Lippincott, 1948), Chap. 12.

52. Stringfellow Barr, "A College in Secession," *Atlantic Monthly*, Vol. 168, July, 1941, pp. 41–49.

53. Jacques Barzun, *Teacher in America* (Boston, Little, Brown, 1945), pp. 156–159.

54. Hutchins, *The Higher Learning in America*, p. 78.

55. Sidney Hook, *Education for Modern Man* (New York, Dial Press, 1946), pp. 204–205.

56. *General Education in a Free Society* (Cambridge, Mass., Harvard University Press, 1945).

57. Daniel Bell, *The Reforming of General Education* (New York, Columbia University Press, 1966).

58. *Ibid.*, pp. 155–159. For the underlying psychology of this view of the curriculum, see Jerome Brunner, *The Process of Education* (Cambridge, Mass., Harvard University Press, 1960), pp. 6–9. Bell seems also to be familiar with materials on the structure of knowledge, such as G. W. Word and Lawrence Pugno (eds.), *The Structure of Knowledge and the Curriculum* (Skokie, Ill., Rand McNally, 1964). For a further extrapolation of these views, see Charles Muscatine, "What Direction for Higher Education?" *Think*, Vol. 32, November-December, 1966, pp. 24–28.

59. Roy I. Johnson, *Explorations in General Education* (New York, Harper & Row, 1947), pp. 6–11; Werrett W. Charters, "Four Convergent Trends in General Education," *Journal of Higher Education*, Vol. 15, June, 1944, pp. 307–314.

60. Not unlike the University of Chicago, Bennington recognized four main areas or divisions— science, social studies, humanities, and art.

61. Conference on Science Philosophy and Religion, *Goals for American Education* (New York, the Conference, 1950), Vol. IX, p. 444.

62. Barbara Jones, *Bennington College* (New York, Harper & Row, 1946); Constance Warren, *A New Design for Women's Education* (Philadelphia, Lippincott, 1940); C. Harold Gray, "Progressive Teaching vs. General Education," in *Association for General and Liberal Education*, Bulletin No. I, pp. 42–45; Benezet, *General Education in the Progressive College*, pp. 79–80, 137–140; Hubert Herring, "Education at Bennington," *Harper's Magazine*, Vol. 181, September, 1940, pp. 408–413.

63. Cf. Dexter M. Keezer, *The Light That Flickers* (New York, Harper & Row, 1947), pp. 46–48.

64. Robert M. Hutchins, "The College and the Needs of Society," *Journal of General Education*, Vol. 3, April, 1949, p. 179. For a critique of the "life adjustment" curriculum, see Lawrence Cremin, *The Transformation of the School* (New York, Knopf, 1961), pp. 308–318, 332–338.

65. Cf. Herring, *op. cit.*, pp. 416–417.

66. Alexander Meiklejohn, "Required Education for Freedom," *American Scholar*, Vol. 13, Autumn, 1944, p. 395.

67. Foerster, *op. cit.*, pp. 158–159.

68. Gerald Grant and David Riesman, "An Ecology of Academic Reform", *Daedalus*, Vol. 104, Winter, 1975, pp. 166–191.

69. *New York Times*, January 16, 1971.

70. Axelrod *et al.*, *op. cit.*, p. 66. See also W. David Maxwell, "Some Dimensions of Relevance," *AAUP Bulletin*, Vol. 55, Autumn, 1969, pp. 337–340.

71. *New York Times*, December 20, 1971; December 25, 1973; December 30, 1973; and *Chronicle of Higher Education*, February 4, 1974. The International Council on the Future of the University looked on this trend as a "vulgarization" of higher education. See *New York Times*, March 19, 1974. See also Logan Wilson, *The Abuses of the University*, Commencement address at Michigan State University, 1968.

72. Dwight R. Ladd, *Change in Educational Policy* (New York, McGraw-Hill, 1970), Chap. 9. See also Arthur E. Levine and John R. Weingart, *Reform of Undergraduate Education* (San Francisco, Jossey-Bass, 1973). The authors of this volume were involved as undergraduates in educational reform and after graduation made this study.

73. Michael Brick and Earl McGrath, *Innovation in the Liberal Arts Colleges* (New York, Teachers College Press, 1969), p. 83. For a directory of these "free universities" see *FUD* (Washington, D.C., American Association for Higher Education, 1972). See also Steven E. Deutsch and Joseph Fashing, "Experimental Colleges and Their Impact on the Curriculum," *Educational Record*, Vol. 53, Fall, 1972, p. 329.

74. Paul Goodman, *The Community of Scholars* (New York, Random House, 1962). The author's predeliction for freedom no doubt stems from a remark in his preface that the book is an essay in anarchism. Goodman was not opposed to order but he thought order should be spontane-

ously chosen. See his chapter in Samuel Gorovitz (ed.), *Freedom and Order in the University* (Cleveland, Ohio, Press of Western Reserve University, 1967).

75. John W. Blassingame, "Black Studies: An Intellectual Crisis," *American Scholar,* Vol. 38, Autumn, 1969, pp. 548–561; Andrew F. Brimmer, "The Black Revolution and the Economic Future of Negroes in the United States," *op. cit.,* pp. 629–643; Wilson Record, "Some Implications of the Black Studies Movement for Higher Education in the '70's," *Journal of Higher Education,* Vol. 43, March, 1973, pp. 191–216; and Clifton R. Wharton, "Reflections on Black Intellectual Power," *Educational Record,* Vol. 53, Fall, 1972, pp. 284–286.

76. Ann Heiss, *An Inventory of Academic Reform* (New York, McGraw-Hill, 1970). For an earlier inventory see Samuel Baskin, *Higher Education: Some Newer Developments* (New York, McGraw-Hill, 1965) and Carnegie Commission on Higher Education, *Reform on the Campus* (New York, McGraw-Hill, 1972). For vignettes of what actually was happening on various campuses, see Verne Stadtman and David Riesman, *Academic Transformation* (New York, McGraw-Hill, 1973).

77. J. B. Lon Hefferlin, *Dynamics of Academic Reform* (San Francisco, Jossey-Bass, 1971), p. 57. Cf. Laurence Veysey, "Stability and Experiment in the American Undergraduate Curriculum," in Carl Kaysen (ed.), *Content and Context* (New York, McGraw-Hill, 1973), pp. 45–49.

78. Carnegie Commission on Higher Education, *Less Time, More Options* (New York, McGraw-Hill, 1971).

79. *Columbia Reports,* April, 1973, pp. 3–6.

80. E.g., Amitai Etzioni, *Columbia Reports.*

81. Michael Brick and Earl McGrath, *op. cit.,* pp. 119–124. See also Richard L. Desmond, "The Enigmatic Trimester Calendar," *Educational Record,* Vol. 52, Fall, 1971, pp. 371–376.

82. *New York Times,* March 10, 1974.

83. Clark H. Bouman, "De-Schooling the Semester," *Liberal Education,* Vol. 57, December, 1971, pp. 488–499.

84. Elliott, *op. cit.,* p. 169; Mortimer J. Adler, "Liberal Education, Theory and Practice," *Association for General and Liberal Education,* Bulletin No. I, 1945.

85. Joseph Axelrod, "The Technique of 'Group Discussion' in the College Class," *Journal of General Education,* Vol. 2, April, 1948, pp. 227–237.

86. LeDuc, *op. cit.,* Chap. 8.

87. William L. Phelps, *Autobiography with Letters* (New York, Oxford University Press, 1939), pp. 287–288.

88. McConn, *op. cit.,* pp. 188–189.

89. Meiklejohn, *The Experimental College,* pp. 121–126.

90. A. Lawrence Lowell, "Self-Education in Harvard College," *Journal of Higher Education,* Vol. 1, February, 1930, p. 67.

91. Hutchins, *The Higher Learning in America,* pp. 37–38.

92. Meiklejohn, *The Experimental College,* pp. 121–126.

93. "It seems to me ridiculous," Phelps further commented on his own teaching career, that in most colleges today lectures and recitations are regarded as a penalty for the dull and lazy; all the students are trying to get on the 'dean's list' which means that if they are sufficiently intelligent or industrious, they will not have to attend classes regularly. The implication is that they are more brilliant than their teachers; and should not have to be forced to listen to the stupidity of specialists." *Op. cit.,* p. 98.

94. That academic success in college had high predictive value for success after college should have been a primary motivation for most undergraduates. See A. Lawrence Lowell, "College Rank and Distinction in Life," *Atlantic Monthly,* Vol. 156, October, 1903, pp. 513–517; Walter S. Gifford, "Does Business Want Scholars?" *Harper's Magazine,* Vol. 156, April, 1928, pp. 671–673.

95. Ordway Tead, *Trustees, Teachers, Students—Their Role in Higher Education* (Salt Lake City, University of Utah Press, 1951), p. 81.

96. Meiklejohn, *op. cit.,* Chap. 8; Tead, *op. cit.,* pp. 77–79; Robert J. Havighurst, "Emotional Outcomes of General Education," *Journal of General Education,* Vol. 1, October, 1946, pp. 39–44.

97. John Dewey, *Democracy and Education* (New York, Macmillan, 1916), pp. 151–152.

98. Alexander Smith, "Rehabilitation of the American College," *Science,* Vol. 30, October, 1909,

pp. 459–460; Elizabeth K. Adams, "The Psychological Gains and Losses of the College Woman," *Educational Review,* Vol. 39, March, 1910, pp. 248–249.

99. Lowell, *At War with Academic Traditions,* pp. 292–297.
100. *New York Times,* May 15, 1966.
101. John Dewey, *How We Think* (Lexington, Mass., Heath, 1910), Chap. 6.
102. Edward C. Elliott, *The Rise of a University* (New York, Columbia University Press, 1937), Vol. II, pp. 331–334. See also Meiklejohn, *The Experimental College,* pp. 49–52; John D. Millett, *Financing Higher Education in the United States* (New York, Columbia University Press, 1952), p. 18.
103. Havighurst, *loc. cit.*
104. Alfred N. Whitehead, *Essays in Science and Philosophy* (New York, Philosophical Library, 1947), p. 218; Dewey, *Democracy and Education,* pp. 321–322.
105. Hutchins, *The Higher Learning in America,* p. 74.
106. Frederick C. Hicks, "Library Problems in American Universities," *Educational Review,* Vol. 49, April, 1915, pp. 325–326; Harvie Branscomb, *Teaching with Books* (Chicago, Association of American Colleges—American Library Association, 1949).
107. Raymond P. Whitfield, "Ills of College Teaching: Diagnosis and Prescription," *Journal of Higher Education,* Vol. 44, January, 1973, pp. 1–14.
108. Joseph Axelrod *et al., op. cit.,* p. 77; Harold Taylor, *How to Change Colleges: Notes on Radical Reform* (New York, Holt, Rinehart & Winston, 1971); and Harold Taylor, *Students Without Teachers: Crisis in the University* (New York, McGraw-Hill, 1969), Chaps. 8–9, 11–12. See also *The Chronicle of Higher Education,* March 18, 1974; *New York Times,* June 2, 1974. There is still further support in Samuel B. Gould and K. Patricia Cross, *Explorations in Non-Traditional Study* (San Francisco, Jossey-Bass, 1972), pp. 3–9, and Lewis B. Mayhew, *Colleges Today and Tomorrow* (San Francisco, Jossey-Bass, 1969), pp. 79–81.
109. Lewis B. Mayhew, *The Carnegie Commission on Higher Education* (San Francisco, Jossey-Bass, 1973), pp. 64–65.
110. Michael Brick and Earl McGrath, *op. cit.,* pp. 64–65.
111. *Ibid.*
112. Kenneth Eble, *Professors as Teachers* (San Francisco, Jossey-Bass, 1972), Chaps. 1–2.
113. Ann Heiss, *op. cit.*
114. Paul L. Dressel, *College and University Curriculum* (Berkeley, Calif., McCutcheon Publishing, 1971), pp. x–xi. Nevitt Sanford wrote his *The American College* (New York, Wiley, 1962) in order to make research in the social sciences available for college teachers. Cf. Ohmer Milton, *Alternatives to the Traditional: How Professors Teach and How Students Learn* (San Francisco, Jossey-Bass, 1972), p. 106.
115. Benjamin S. Bloom, "Twenty-five Years of Educational Research," *American Educational Research Journal,* Vol. 3, May, 1966, p. 217. See also earlier studies, Earl Hudelson, *Class Size at the College Level* (Minneapolis, University of Minnesota Press, 1928) and Albert E. Brown, *The Effectiveness of Large Classes at the College Level* (Iowa City, University of Iowa Studies in Education, 1932), Vol. 8, No. 3.
116. Robert Glaser, "Ten Untenable Assumptions of College Instruction," *Educational Record,* Vol. 52, Spring, 1971, pp. 154–159.
117. Jay L. Chronister, "Institutional Accountability in Higher Education," *Educational Record,* Vol. 52, Spring, 1971, pp. 171–175. See also John Harris, "Baccalaureate Requirements, Attainments or Exposure," *Educational Record,* Vol. 53, Winter, 1972, pp. 62–63.
118. Alexander Astin, "Challenge to the Credentialing Process," *Liberal Education,* Vol. 58, May, 1972, pp. 183–188, and Harold Taylor, *How to Change Colleges: Notes on Radical Reform* (New York, Holt, Rinehart & Winston, 1971), p. 73.
119. Leon B. Richardson, *History of Dartmouth College* (Hanover, N.H., Dartmouth College Publications, 1932), Vol. I, pp. 434–435.
120. Morison, *Development of Harvard University,* p. lxiii.
121. Hutchins, *The Idea and Practice of General Education,* p. 95.
122. *Report on Higher Education* (Washington, D.C., U.S. Office of Education, 1971), pp. 69–70.
123. Jencks and Riesman, *op. cit.,* pp. 61–64.
124. Ben D. Wood, "Structure and Content of the Comprehensive Examination for the College Sophomore," in William S. Gray (ed.), *Recent Trends in American College Education* (Chicago, University of Chicago Press, 1931), Chap. 20; Ralph W. Tyler, "Development of

Examinations at Ohio State University," *ibid.,* Chap. 23; Melvin E. Haggerty, in Raymond A. Kent (ed.), *Higher Education in America* (Lexington, Mass., Ginn, 1930).

125. *The Chronicle of Higher Education,* September 16, 1974.
126. For a definition of "excellence," see Rubin Gotesky, "The Pursuit of Excellence," *Educational Theory,* Vol. 20, Fall, 1970, pp. 406–416.
127. Nathan Glazer, "Are Academic Standards Obsolete?" *Change,* November-December, 1970; Louis G. Geiger and Helen M. Geiger, "The Revolt Against Excellence," *AAUP Bulletin,* Vol. 56, September, 1970, pp. 297–301; and *The Chronicle of Higher Education,* February 20, 1973.

Chapter 14. The Philosophy of Higher Education

1. See pp. 61, 62, 147–153.
2. "Original Papers in Relation to a Course of Liberal Education," *American Journal of Science,* Vol. 15, January, 1829, p. 7. For an even earlier statement to the same effect, see Philip Lindsley, "Improvement of Time," in *Educational Discourses* (Philadelphia, Lippincott, 1866), Vol. I, p. 15. For a similar contemporary statement at the University of Pennsylvania, see Saul Sack, "Liberal Education: What Was It? What Is It?" *History of Education Quarterly,* Vol. 2, December, 1962, p. 215.
3. Charles Francis Adams enunciated this doctrine in a Phi Beta Kappa address as late as the turn of the nineteenth century. "Some Present Collegiate Tendencies," *Educational Review,* Vol. 32, September, 1906, p. 152.
4. James McCosh, *The New Departure in College Education* (New York, Scribner, 1885), p. 809. See also P. N. Garber, *John Carlisle Kilgo* (Durham, N.C., Duke University Press, 1937), p. 127.
5. David A. Weaver, *Builders of American Universities* (Alton, Ill., Shurtleff Press, 1950), Vol. I, pp. 142–154. Later in the century S. N. Fellows tried to prove this point by showing the large percentage of public offices held by college-bred men. "The Practical Value of a College Education," *Proceedings of the National Education Association,* 1885.
6. Thomas LeDuc, *Piety and Intellect at Amherst College* (New York, Columbia University Press, 1946), Chaps. 2–4.
7. For an American Catholic view of higher education, see John Spalding, *Opportunity and Other Essays* (Chicago, A. C. McClurg, 1900), pp. 72, 140.
8. Noah Porter, *The American College and the American Public* (New Haven, Conn., C. C. Chatfield, 1870), pp. 262–268.
9. George E. Peterson, *The New England College in the Age of the University* (Amherst, Mass., Amherst College Press, 1964), pp. 28–39.
10. Quoted in Samuel Eliot Morison, *Three Centuries of Harvard* (Cambridge, Mass., Harvard University Press, 1936), p. 287.
11. Sack, *loc. cit.*
12. Cited in Richard Hofstadter and Wilson Smith (eds.), *American Higher Education: A Documentary History* (Chicago, University of Chicago Press, 1961), p. 584; Russell H. Chittenden, *History of the Sheffield Scientific School of Yale University* (New Haven, Conn., Yale University Press, 1928), Vol. I, pp. 136–139. A similar struggle over the issue of utility occurred in the universities as well as the colleges. See Laurence R. Veysey, *The Emergence of the American University* (Chicago, University of Chicago Press, 1965), Chap. 2. See also Ralph Waldo Emerson who cut an even wider swath in his *American Scholar* by attacking the notion that the scholar is a recluse and defending the notion that thought must mate with action. Howard Mumford Jones, *Emerson on Education* (New York, Teachers College, Columbia University, 1966), pp. 86–90.
13. W. P. Atkinson, "Liberal Education of the Nineteenth Century," *Proceedings of the National Education Association,* 1873.
14. Russell Thomas, *The Search for a Common Learning* (New York, McGraw-Hill, 1962), p. 22.
15. *Ibid.,* p. 28.
16. Frederick Rudolph, *The American College and University* (New York, Knopf, 1962), pp. 279–280.
17. So too had William James and Charles W. Eliot. See Lloyd G. Humphreys, "Transfer of Training in General Education," *Journal of General Education,* Vol. 5, April, 1951, pp. 210–216.

18. The pioneer in these studies was E. L. Thorndike and R. S. Woodworth's "The Influence of Improvement in one Mental Function upon the Efficiency of Other Functions," *Psychological Review,* Vol. 8, May, July, November, 1901, pp. 247–261, 384–395, 553–564.

19. While 75 per cent of the statements of college aims from 1842–76 included mental discipline, only 25 per cent did in the period 1909–21. See C. C. Crawford and L. V. Koos, "College Aims Past and Present," *School and Society,* Vol. 14, December, 1921, pp. 499–509.

20. Walter B. Kolesnick, *Mental Discipline in Modern Education* (Madison, University of Wisconsin Press, 1958).

21. Eric M. Rogers, "The Good Name of Science: a Discussion of Science Courses for General Education," *Science,* Vol. 110, December, 1949, pp. 600–601.

22. Curt J. Ducasse, "Liberal Education and the College Curriculum," *Journal of Higher Education,* Vol. 15, January, 1944, pp. 1–10; Alexander Meiklejohn, *The Experimental College* (New York, Harper & Row, 1932), pp. 46–48; Henry M. Wriston, "Nature, Scope, and Essential Elements in General Education," in W. S. Gray (ed.), *General Education* (Chicago, University of Chicago Press, 1932), Chap. 1; John E. Wise, *The Nature of the Liberal Arts* (Milwaukee, Wisc., Bruce Publishing, 1947), Chap. 10; Max Black, "What Is General Education?" *Journal of Higher Education,* Vol. 15, March, 1944, pp. 117–121.

23. Jerome Bruner, *The Process of Education* (Cambridge, Mass., Harvard University Press, 1960), pp. 6–9. See also Calvin B. T. Lee (ed.), *Improving College Teaching* (Washington, D.C., American Council on Education, 1967), pp. 392–394.

24. Daniel Bell, *Reforming General Education* (New York, Columbia University Press, 1966), pp. 157–159, 166.

25. See pp. 276, 277.

26. See p. 260.

27. W. R. Harris, *Five Counter-Revolutions in Higher Education* (Corvallis, Oregon State University Press, 1970).

28. Theodore M. Greene, *Liberal Education Reexamined* (New York, Harper & Row, 1943), p. 10; Allan P. Farrell, *The Jesuit Code of Liberal Education* (Milwaukee, Wisc., Bruce Publishing, 1938), pp. 423–424.

29. Irving Babbitt, *Literature and the American College* (Boston, Houghton Mifflin, 1908), pp. 8–11, 78–81; "President Eliot and American Education," *Forum,* Vol. 81, January, 1929, pp. 1–10.

30. Norman Foerster, in *Educational Yearbook of the International Institute* (New York, Teachers College, Columbia University, 1939), pp. 333–337.

31. Even as Foerster wrote, the term "general education" was just beginning to win the popular usage he had in mind. For further consideration of "general education," see pp. 271–275.

32. Babbitt, *Literature and the American College,* pp. 8–11, 78–81; "President Eliot and American Education," *op. cit.*

33. Paul Shorey, *The Assault on Humanism* (Boston, Atlantic Monthly, 1917), pp. 73–74.

34. Harold Taylor, "The Philosophical Foundations of General Education," in *Fifty-First Yearbook of the National Society for the Study of Education,* Part II (Chicago, University of Chicago Press, 1952), pp. 33–35. An instance of the line humanists drew between thinking and acting is seen in their neglect of the performing arts by consigning them to the extracurriculum and including in the academic curriculum only such intellectual subjects as history and appreciation of art, music, and the like.

35. Robert M. Hutchins, *The Higher Learning in America* (New Haven, Conn., Yale University Press, 1936).

36. See Mortimer J. Adler, "God and the Professors," in *Conference on Science, Philosophy and Religion* (New York, Harper & Row, 1941), Chap. 7.

37. See the article by Hastings Rashdall in Powicke and Emben (eds.), *The Universities of Europe in the Middle Ages* (London, Oxford University Press, 1936), Vol. III, pp. 441–442.

38. Taylor, *op. cit.,* pp. 27–30. As still preferring theology, see William A. Brown, *The Case for Theology in the University* (Chicago, University of Chicago Press, 1938); John J. Ryan, *The Idea of a Catholic College* (New York, Sheed & Ward, 1945). Opposed to theological, metaphysical, or any other kind of unity in the university is Harvey Cox, *The Secular City* (New York, Macmillan, 1966), Chap. 10.

39. Hutchins, *op. cit.,* pp. 66–67. For a more complete statement, see Robert M. Hutchins, "The Philosophy of Education," in R. N. Montgomery (ed.), *The William Rainey Harper Memorial Conference* (Chicago, University of Chicago Press, 1938). See also his *The University of Utopia* (Chicago, University of Chicago Press, 1953), Chap. 3. It is interesting to compare Hutchins'

theory of higher education with that of educators in Germany, which had so profound an impact on America. For a comparison of Hutchins's philosophy of higher education with that of Alfred North Whitehead, see Albert W. Levi, "The Problem of Higher Education: White-head v. Hutchins," *Harvard Educational Review,* Vol. 7, October, 1937, pp. 451–465.

40. Robert M. Hutchins, *Conflict in Education in Democracy* (New York, Harper & Row, 1953), pp. 82–83.

41. Robert M. Hutchins, "Morals, Religion, and Higher Education" (address delivered at Western Michigan State College of Education, Kalamazoo, Mich., October 25, 1949).

42. Adler, *op. cit.,* pp. 128–129; Robert M. Hutchins, *No Friendly Voice* (Chicago, University of Chicago Press, 1936), p. 33. But especially see Mortimer J. Adler and Milton Mayer, *The Revolution in Education* (Chicago, University of Chicago Press, 1958), p. 167.

43. Norman Foerster, *The American State University* (Chapel Hill, University of North Carolina Press, 1937), pp. 216–220, 245–247.

44. Also emphasizing the importance of taste and appreciation in liberal education were Jacques Maritain, "Thomist Views on Education," in Fifty-Fourth Yearbook of the National Society for the Study of Education, *Modern Philosophies and Education* (Chicago, University of Chicago Press, 1955); Theodore M. Greene, "The Realities of Our Common Life," *Journal of Higher Education,* Vol. 13, October, 1942, p. 344; F. B. Millett, *The Rebirth of Liberal Education* (New York, Harcourt Brace Jovanovich, 1945), pp. v–vi; H. Chidsey, "Culture in Education," *Journal of Higher Education,* Vol. 8, April, 1937, pp. 175–184.

45. Mortimer J. Adler, "Labor, Leisure, and Liberal Education," *Journal of General Education,* Vol. 6, October, 1951, pp. 35–45.

46. Hutchins, *The Higher Learning in America,* p. 70, and "The College and the Needs of Society," *Journal of General Education,* Vol. 3, April, 1949, pp. 175–181; John Wild, "Education and Human Society: A Realistic View," in Fifty-Fourth Yearbook of the National Society for the Study of Education, *Modern Philosophies and Education* (Chicago, University of Chicago Press, 1955), pp. 28–34.

47. See pp. 217, 218.

48. Albert Nock, *Theory of Education in the United States* (New York, Harcourt Brace Jovanovich, 1932), pp. 118–119.

49. Robert M. Hutchins, "Second Edition/The Idea of a College," *Center Magazine,* Vol. 5, May-June, 1972, p. 547.

50. Adler, "God and the Professors," p. 44; Mark Van Doren, *Liberal Education* (New York, Holt, Rinehart & Winston, 1943), pp. 31–32, 166; Scott Buchanan, "Liberal Education and Politics," *American Scholar,* Vol. 13, Autumn, 1944, p. 397.

51. The naturalism considered here may be variously called "pragmatic," "instrumental" or "experimental."

52. See pp. 274, 275.

53. *The Daily Maroon* (University of Chicago undergraduate newspaper), November 14, 1940.

54. John Dewey, *Democracy and Education* (New York, Macmillan, 1916).

55. John Dewey, "President Hutchins' Proposals to Remake Higher Education," *Social Frontier,* Vol. 3, January, 1937, pp. 103–104. See also Charles E. Clark, "The Higher Learning in a Democracy," *International Journal of Ethics,* Vol. 47, April, 1937, pp. 317–319; Horace M. Kallen, "Education and its Modifiers," *Philosophy and Phenomenological Research,* Vol. 7, December, 1946, pp. 249–250.

56. Sidney Hook, *Education for Modern Man* (New York, Dial Press, 1946), Chap. 2.

57. Harold Taylor, "Philosophical Aspects of the Harvard Report," *Philosophy and Phenomenological Research,* Vol. 7, December, 1946, p. 234.

58. Charner Perry, "Education: Ideas or Knowledge," *Journal of International Ethics,* Vol. 47, April, 1937, pp. 355–357.

59. Donald A. Piatt, in *The Authoritarian Attempt to Capture Education* (New York, King's Crown Press, 1945), p. 112; Clark, *loc cit.,* Dewey, *op. cit.,* p. 104; Harry W. Chase, "Hutchins' 'Higher Learning' Grounded," *American Scholar,* Vol. 6, Spring, 1937, pp. 242–244.

60. Frederick Jackson Turner, *The Frontier in American History* (New York, Holt, Rinehart & Winston, 1920); Earl J. McGrath and Charles H. Russell, *Are Liberal Arts Colleges Becoming Professional Schools?* (New York, Teachers College, Columbia University, 1958).

61. Lotus D. Coffman, *The State University* (Minneapolis, University of Minnesota Press, 1934), pp. 159–160; Algo D. Henderson, in *The Authoritarian Attempt to Capture Education* (New

York, Kings' Crown Press, 1943), pp. 100–101; Ernest Earnest, "Even A.B.'s Must Eat," *American Scholar,* Vol. 13, Autumn, 1944, p. 405; William F. Cunningham, *General Education and the Liberal College* (St. Louis, Herder, 1953), p. 28. According to Alexander Meiklejohn, the principal distinction to keep in mind was not that between cultural and vocational but "general" and "special" education. *The Experimental College* (New York, Harper & Row, 1932), p. 17.

62. See p. 111.

63. John Dewey, "The Problems of the Liberal Arts College," *American Scholar,* Vol. 13, October, 1944, pp. 391–392.

64. See p. 247.

65. Algo D. Henderson, *Revitalizing Liberal Education* (New York, Harper & Row, 1944).

66. Principally active in applying Dewey's philosophy to the problems of higher education was Harold Taylor, president of one of the experimental colleges, Sarah Lawrence, and a former professor of philosophy. See his "Education as Experiment," in *Conference of Science, Philosophy and Religion* (New York, Harper & Row, 1950), Chap. 18; *Essays in Teaching* (New York, Harper & Row, 1950), Chap. 1; "Philosophical Foundations of General Education," *op. cit.,* pp. 35–44. Cf. Alfred N. Whitehead, "Universities and Their Function," *Atlantic Monthly,* Vol. 141, May, 1928, p. 641, and "Harvard, the Future," *ibid.,* Vol. 158, September, 1936, pp. 267–268.

67. Richard Hofstadter, *Anti-Intellectualism in American Life* (New York, Knopf, 1963), Part 4.

68. Merle Curti, "Intellectuals and Other People," *American Historical Review,* Vol. 60, January, 1955, p. 274.

69. Baker Brownell, *The College and the Community* (New York, Harper & Row, 1952), Chap. 1.

70. Dewey, "The Problems of the Liberal Arts College," p. 393 (italics in original); *Democracy and Education,* pp. 366–372. Cf. Howard M. Jones, *Education and World Tragedy* (Cambridge, Mass., Harvard University Press, 1946), p. 113.

71. Huston Smith, The Purposes of Higher Education (New York, Harper & Row, 1955), Chaps. 2–3.

72. Courtney Murray, "The Making of a Pluralistic Society: A Catholic View," in Erich A. Walter (ed.), *Religion and the State University* (Ann Arbor, University of Michigan Press, 1958), Chap. 1.

73. *General Education in a Free Society* (Cambridge, Mass., Harvard University Press, 1945). A less well known but promising attempt at synthesis was undertaken by the faculty of the University of Washington. See Smith, *op. cit.* For a symposium on the goals of higher education, see *Conference on Science, Philosophy and Religion,* Vol. 9.

74. *General Education in a Free Society,* p. 50.

75. Raphael Demos, "Philosophical Aspects of the Recent Harvard Report," *Philosophy and Phenomenological Research,* Vol. 7, December, 1946, pp. 187–263. See particularly his "Reply" to critics, *ibid.,* p. 265. For a different synthesis, see Malcolm M. Marsden, "General Education: Compromise between Transcendentalism and Pragmatism," *Journal of General Education,* Vol. 7, July, 1953, pp. 228–239.

76. Sidney Hook, "Synthesis or Eclecticism," *Philosophy and Phenomenological Research,* Vol. 7, December, 1946, pp. 214–225; Harold Taylor, "Philosophical Aspects of the Harvard Report," *Philosophy and Phenomenological Research,* Vol. 7, December, 1946, pp. 226–239; Boyd Bode, "The Harvard Report Once More," *Journal of Higher Education,* Vol. 17, April, 1946, p. 203.

77. Babbitt, *op. cit.,* pp. 9–10; Bernard E. Meland, *Higher Education and the Human Spirit* (Chicago, University of Chicago Press, 1953), p. 136.

78. Adler and Mayer, *op. cit.* Perhaps, anyhow, as Sidney Hook wrote, the formulation of a viable philosophy of higher education did not require the precondition of agreement on first principles. See also Horace T. Morse (ed.), *General Education in Transition* (Minneapolis, University of Minnesota Press, 1951), p. 69 and Cox, *op. cit.,* p. 228.

79. Edward J. Shoben, "The Liberal Arts and Contemporary Society: The 1970's," *Liberal Education,* Vol. 56, March, 1970, pp. 29–31. Cf. David Bakan, "Youth, the Future, and Liberal Education," *Liberal Education,* Vol. 58, May, 1972, pp. 189–198.

80. Edward J. Bloustein, "The New Student and His Role in American Colleges," in Walter P. Metzger (ed.), *Dimensions of Academic Freedom* (Urbana, University of Illinois Press, 1969), pp. 101–103. But the contemporary knowledge explosion rendered obsolete the traditional

notion that the liberally educated man should be broadly educated. See Edward W. Weidner, "Problem Focused Education: the Environment," *Educational Record,* Vol. 52, Fall, 1971, pp. 314–320.

81. Edward Shils, "Dreams of Plenitude, Nightmares of Scarcity," in Seymour M. Lipset and Philip G. Altbach (eds.), *Students in Revolt* (Boston, Houghton Mifflin, 1968).

82. *Ibid.* pp. 33–35. For other authors reasserting the traditional relevance of liberal education, see Nevitt Sanford, *Where Colleges Fail* (San Francisco, Jossey-Bass, 1967), pp. 4–6; Theodore D. Lockwood, *The Chronicle of Higher Education,* March 25, 1974.

83. James Morgan Hart, *German Universities: A Narrative of Personal Experience,* 1873, quoted in Hofstadter and Smith (eds.), *American Higher Education: A Documentary History* (Chicago, University of Chicago Press, 1961), p. 573.

84. Robert Nisbet, *Degradation of the Academic Dogma* (New York, Basic Books, 1971), p. 34. See also Nisbet, "The Academic Community: Conflicting Loyalties," in Calvin B. Y. Lee (ed.), *op. cit.,* pp. 16–19. For the evolution of one department see Robert L. Church, "Economists as Experts," in Lawrence Stone (ed.), *The University in Society* (Princeton, N.J., Princeton Universtiy Press, 1974), Vol. 2.

85. John D. Millett, "The Ethics of Higher Education," *Educational Record,* Vol. 48, Winter, 1967, p. 17.

86. Walter Lippmann, "The University," *New Republic,* Vol. 154, May, 1966, pp. 17–20. Cf. Eric Ashby, *The Structure of Higher Education* (New York, McGraw-Hill, 1973).

87. Robert P. Wolff, *The Ideal of the University* (Boston, Beacon Press, 1969), pp. 48–53, 59–76. See also Kalman Goldberg and Robin C. Linstromberg, "The University as an Anachronism," *Journal of Higher Education,* Vol. 40, March, 1969, pp. 193–204.

88. John R. Searle, in Samuel Gorovitz (ed.), *Freedom and Order in the University* (Cleveland, Ohio, Press of Western Reserve University, 1967), pp. 96–97.

89. Cf. Sidney Hook, *Academic Freedom and Academic Anarchy* (New York, Cowles Book, 1969), pp. 36–46.

90. Daniel Yankelovitch, *Changing Values on Campus: Political and Personal Attitudes of Today's College Students* (New York, Simon & Schuster, 1972), p. 170, and Samuel B. Gould, *Today's Academic Condition* (Hamilton, N.Y., Colgate University Press, 1970), p. 19.

91. Buell Gallagher, *Campus in Crisis* (New York, Harper & Row, 1974), pp. 130–131, 134. Cf. Kenneth B. Minogue, *The Concept of a University* (Berkeley, University of California Press, 1973), Chap. 8.

92. John R. Silber, "The Pollution of Time," *Boston University Alumni Magazine,* September, 1971.

93. Buell Gallagher, *op. cit.* p. 168. See Lewis B. Mayhew, *Colleges Today and Tomorrow* (San Francisco, Jossey-Bass, 1969), p. 74, where the author criticizes the student view of the university.

94. Harland G. and Sue M. Boland, *American Learned Societies in Transition* (New York, McGraw-Hill, 1974).

95. Kingman Brewster, "If Not Reason, What?" *American Scholar,* Vol. 39, Spring, 1970, pp. 243–252.

96. W. John Minter and Ian M. Thompson (eds.), *Colleges and Universities as Agents of Social Change* (Boulder, Colo., Western Interstate Commission for Higher Education, 1968); W. Allen Wallis, "Institutional Coherence and Priorities," in Charles G. Dobbins (ed.), *Whose Goals for American Higher Education?* (Washington, D.C., American Council on Education 1967); Robert Nesbit, *op. cit.,* Chaps. 5, 10; and John F. A. Taylor, "Politics and the Neutrality of the University," *AAUP Bulletin,* Vol. 59, Winter, 1973, pp. 389–401.

97. C. Vann Woodward, "The Erosion of Academic Privileges and Immunities," *Daedalus,* Vol. 1, Fall, 1974, (American Education: Toward an Uncertain Future), p. 36.

98. Frederick J. Kelly, *The American Arts College* (New York, Macmillan, 1925), p. 17; Jay W. Hudson, *The College and New America* (Englewood Cliffs, N.J., Prentice-Hall, 1920), pp. 57–58.

99. Edward Gross and Paul V. Grambsch, *Changes in University Organization 1964–1971* (New York, McGraw-Hill, 1974), Chap. 1.

100. Carnegie Commission on Higher Education, *Reform on the Campus* (New York, McGraw-Hill, 1972), p. 32, Chap. 6.

101. Sidney Hook, "The Campus Peace Plan that President Nixon Endorsed," *The Chronicle of Higher Education,* September 28, 1970; and Robert M. Hutchins, "United States Universities

Don't Know What They Are Doing or Why," *ibid.*, March 9, 1970. See also Harold Taylor, *How to Change Colleges: Notes on Radical Reform* (New York, Holt, Rinehart & Winston, 1971), pp. 67–68. Cf. Warren B. Martin, *Conformity, Standards, and Change in Higher Education* (San Francisco, Jossey-Bass, 1969), Chaps 4, 8. For a modest attempt at such a philosophy of higher education, see John S. Brubacher, *The University: Its Identity Crisis* (New Britain, Central Connecticut State College, 1972).

Chapter 15. Academic Freedom

1. Samuel Eliot Morison, *Harvard College in the Seventeenth Century* (Cambridge, Mass., Harvard University Press, 1936), pp. 308–309.
2. Richard Hofstadter and Walter P. Metzger, *The Development of Academic Freedom in the United States* (New York, Columbia University Press, 1955), p. 161.
3. *Ibid.*, pp. 163–177.
4. Charles F. Thwing, *History of Higher Education in America* (Englewood Cliffs, N.J., Prentice-Hall, 1906), p. 60.
5. Thomas J. Wertenbaker, *Princeton, 1746–1896* (Princeton, N.J., Princeton University Press, 1946), pp. 121–123.
6. Hofstadter and Metzger, *op. cit.*
7. Ralph H. Lutz, "The History of the Concept of Freedom," *Bulletin of the American Association of University Professors,* Vol. 36, Spring, 1950, pp. 27–28; Henry W. Tyler and Edward O. Cheyney, "Academic Freedom," *Annals of the American Academy of Political Science,* Vol. 200, November, 1938, pp. 102–107. See also, Sherman B. Barnes, "Learning and Piety in Ohio Colleges, 1865–1900 and 1900–1930," *Ohio Historical Quarterly,* Vol. 69, October, 1960, pp. 327–352 and Vol. 70, July, 1961, pp. 214–243.
8. Clement Eaton, *Freedom of Thought in the Old South* (Durham, N.C., Duke University Press, 1940), Chap. 8.
9. Leon B. Richardson, *History of Dartmouth College* (Hanover, N.H., Dartmouth College Publications, 1932), Vol. II, pp. 508–513. For an instance at the University of Michigan, see I. N. Demmon (ed.), *University of Michigan Regents' Proceedings, 1837–1864,* pp. 501–503.
10. Allen P. Tankersley, *College Life at Old Oglethorpe* (Athens, University of Georgia Press, 1951), pp. 38–40. Woodrow Wilson's uncle, James Woodrow, had the same trouble. See Clement Eaton, "Professor James Woodrow and the Freedom of Teaching in the South," *Journal of Southern History,* Vol. 28, February, 1962, pp. 3–17.
11. Samuel Eliot Morison, *Three Centuries of Harvard* (Cambridge, Mass., Harvard University Press, 1936), p. 308.
12. Harris E. Starr, *William Graham Sumner* (New York, Holt, Rinehart & Winston, 1925), pp. 346–347.
13. See Chapter 5.
14. Richardson, *op. cit.,* Vol. I, p. 120.
15. Edward P. Cheyney, *History of the University of Pennsylvania, 1740–1940* (Philadelphia, University of Pennsylvania Press, 1940), pp. 120–125.
16. Francis Wayland, *The Dependence of Science on Religion* (Providence, Marshall, Brown, 1835), p. 40.
17. See pp. 147–153.
18. Nathaniel F. Cabell, *Early History of the University of Virginia as Contained in the Letters of Thomas Jefferson and Joseph C. Cabell* (Richmond, Va., J. W. Randolph, 1856), pp. 436, 442.
19. Roy J. Honeywell, *Educational Works of Thomas Jefferson* (Cambridge, Mass., Harvard University Press, 1931), p. 99.
20. Cabell, *op. cit.,* p. 339. See also Samuel Eliot Morison, *Freedom and Contemporary Society* (Boston, Little, Brown, 1956) and Gordon E. Hooker, "Thomas Jefferson on Academic Freedom," *AAUP Bulletin,* Vol. 39, Autumn, 1953, pp. 377–387.
21. Hofstadter and Metzger, *op. cit.,* p. 144.
22. Morison, *Three Centuries of Harvard,* pp. 254–255. See also Morison, *Freedom and Contemporary Society,* p. 119.
23. For a longer but still incomplete list of cases, see Howard C. Warren, "Academic Freedom," *Atlantic Monthly,* Vol. 114, November, 1914, pp. 693–694; and Thomas E. Will, "A Menace to Freedom: the College Trust," *Arena,* Vol. 26, December, 1901, p. 244.

24. Elizabeth Donnan, "A Nineteenth Century Academic Cause Celebre," *New England Quarterly,* Vol. 25, March, 1952, pp. 23–46; Walter C. Bronson, *History of Brown University, 1764–1914* (Providence, R.I., Brown University, 1914), pp. 462–466.

25. Orwin L. Elliott, *Stanford University: the First Twenty-five Years* (Stanford, Calif., Stanford University Press, 1937), pp. 326–378; Edward A. Ross, *Seventy Years of It* (Englewood Cliffs, N.J., Prentice-Hall, 1936), pp. 94–95. It is interesting that seven faculty members resigned in protest against Ross's ouster while thirty-four signed a statement supporting President Jordon. See Laurence R. Veysey, *The Emergence of the American University* (Chicago, University of Chicago Press, 1965), p. 414.

26. Harold E. Bergquist, "The Edward Bemis Controversy at the University of Chicago," *AAUP Bulletin,* Vol. 58, December, 1972, pp. 384–393.

27. Merle Curti and Vernon R. Carstensen, *The University of Wisconsin, a History* (Madison, University of Wisconsin Press, 1949), Vol. I, pp. 508–527; Richard T. Ely, *The Ground Under Our Feet, an Autobiography* (New York, Macmillan, 1938), pp. 218–219, 233.

28. Cheyney, *op. cit.,* pp. 367–371.

29. For a further discussion of this problem, see pp. 28–30, 373.

30. To be exact, it should be noted that *akademische Freiheit* had two aspects, *Lernfreiheit* and *Lehrfreiheit.* See Walter P. Metzger, in Samuel Gorovitz (ed.), *Freedom and Order in the University* (Cleveland, Ohio, Press of Western Reserve University, 1967), pp. 62–68. The former concerned the freedom of the student to sample academic wares, determine the sequence of studying them, attend courses as he saw fit, and be exempt from all examinations save the final one. This aspect of academic freedom had its impact on the United States in the form of Eliot's "elective" system. Indeed, Dean Andrew West of Princeton, writing under the title of "What is Academic Freedom?" *North American Review,* Vol. 140, May, 1885, pp. 432–444, mentioned only this aspect.

    The latter, *Lehrfreiheit,* the freedom of the professor to determine the content of his courses and his method of instruction, examine evidence, and report the results of inquiry, is our chief concern here. See Walter P. Metzger, "The German Contribution to the American Theory of Academic Freedom," *AAUP Bulletin,* Vol. 41, Summer, 1955, pp. 214–230; Leo L. Rockwell, "Academic Freedom—German Origins and American Development," *ibid.,* Vol. 36, Summer, 1950, pp. 225–236.

    But note that in the 1960s there was a concern for the academic freedom (*Lehrfreiheit* variety) and civil liberties of students. See American Civil Liberties Union, *Academic Freedom and Civil Liberties of Students in Colleges and Universities* (New York, American Civil Liberties Union, 1962); *AAUP Bulletin,* Vol. 50, Autumn, 1964, pp. 254–257; "Student Rights and Campus Rules," *California Law Review,* Vol. 54, March, 1966, pp. 1–175.

31. Marguerite Clapp (ed.), *Nineteenth Century Ideas of the University in Continental Europe* (Ithaca, N.Y., Cornell University Press, 1950), pp. 20–21; For a similar view, see Metzger, *op. cit.,* p. 129. For a somewhat opposite view, see Fritz Machlup, "On Some Misconceptions Concerning Academic Freedom," *AAUP Bulletin,* Vol. 41, Winter, 1955, pp. 753–784.

32. Walter P. Metzger, *Academic Freedom in the Age of the University* (New York, Columbia University Press, 1955), pp. 130–131, 141–185.

33. Alton B. Parker, "Rights of Donors," *Educational Review,* Vol. 23, January, 1902, pp. 19–21; Nicholas M. Butler, *Scholarship and Service* (New York, Scribner, 1921), pp. 171–172; Arthur Twining Hadley, "Academic Freedom in Theory and in Practice," *Atlantic Monthly,* Vol. 91, February, 1903, pp. 152–160. A poll of the governing boards of Chicago, Columbia, Hopkins, Pennsylvania, Princeton, and Yale by a Northwestern trustee showed almost unanimous support for this position. Metzger, *Academic Freedom in the Age of the University,* p. 185. Some equated the cherished liberties of a democratic society with free enterprise in economic life. Reinhold Niebuhr, "Higher Education in America," *Confluence,* Vol. 6, Spring, 1957, p. 6; Richard H. Shryock, "The Academic Profession in the United States," *Bulletin of the American Association of University Professors,* Vol. 38, Spring, 1952, pp. 54–55. For a latter-day iteration of this point, see William F. Buckley, *God and Man at Yale* (Chicago, Regnery, 1951); and a latter-day rebuttal, Russell Kirk, *Academic Freedom* (Chicago, Regnery, 1955), p. 118–130.

34. W. Carson Ryan, *Studies in Early Graduate Education* (New York, Carnegie Foundation, 1939), pp. 127–128.

35. Charles W. Eliot, "Academic Freedom," Phi Beta Kappa address at Cornell, May 29, 1907.

36. Edward C. Elliott, *The Rise of a University* (New York, Columbia University Press, 1937), Vol. II, p. 40.

37. Metzger, *op. cit.* pp. 130–131.

38. Cf. Walter P. Metzger, "The German Contribution to the American Theory of Academic Freedom," *AAUP Bulletin,* Vol. 41, Summer, 1955, p. 228.

39. Henry Wriston, "Academic Tenure," *American Scholar,* Vol. 9, Summer, 1940, pp. 339, 344; Fritz Machlup, "In Defense of Academic Tenure," *AAUP Bulletin,* Vol. 50, Summer, 1964, pp. 112–124.

40. Curti and Carstensen, *op. cit.,* Vol. II, pp. 54–56. See also above.

41. Quoted in Norman Foerster, *The American State University* (Chapel Hill, University of North Carolina Press, 1937), pp. 164–165.

42. Paul N. Garber, *John C. Kilgo, President of Trinity College, 1894–1910* (Durham, N.C., Duke University Press, 1937), Chap. 4.

43. A. Lawrence Lowell, *At War with Academic Traditions in America* (Cambridge, Mass., Harvard University Press, 1934), pp. 267–272.

44. Curti and Carstensen, *op. cit.,* Vol. I, p. 262.

45. Fritz Machlup, "On Some Misconceptions Concerning Academic Freedom," *AAUP Bulletin,* Vol. 41, Winter, 1955, pp. 768–771. But note the case of Bertrand Russell, just before the outbreak of the Second World War, who was prevented from occupying a chair of philosophy at the City College of New York because religious groups took exception to his moral opinions and were sustained in the New York courts. Said Robert M. MacIver of this case, "The decision in the Russell Case highlighted issues of the greatest significance. One is the right of a court of law to void an appointment in an institution of learning because of its objection to the opinions of the appointee. On this basis the judge in question overrode the faculty that recommended and the constituted authority that approved the appointment. . . . The judge voided the decision of the properly constituted administrative body, essentially not because that authority had exceeded the bounds of its competence but because he disapproved the course it took. It has been pointed out many times that this kind of judicial intervention is calculated to destroy the basis of all civil liberties." *Academic Freedom in Our Time* (New York, Columbia University Press, 1955), pp. 155–156.

46. William R. Harper, *Decennial Report,* 1892–1902, p. xiii. Thus Harper reprimanded Professor Bemis before his dismissal from the University of Chicago.

47. Metzger, *Academic Freedom in the Age of the University,* pp. 115–117.

48. Lowell, *op. cit.,* pp. 267–271.

49. Note how at the opening of the twentieth century President Van Hise of the University of Wisconsin had said ". . . it is our aim to take out the knowledge, whether the people ask for it or not. . . . Therefore we are not going to wait for the people to come to us: we are going to take our goods to them." *National Association of State Universities, Transactions and Proceedings,* 1908, p. 131.

50. Walter Lippmann, "The University," *New Republic,* Vol. 154, May 28, 1966, pp. 17–20. Cf. Richard J. Storr, "The Public Conscience of the University, 1775–1956," *Harvard Educational Review,* Vol. 26, Winter, 1956, pp. 71–83; Harvey Cox, *The Secular City* (New York, Macmillan, 1966), p. 228.

51. George S. Counts, *Dare the Schools Build a New Social Order?* (New York, John Day, 1932).

52. John Dewey, "Academic Freedom," *Educational Review,* Vol. 23, January, 1902, pp. 1–14.

53. David A. Weaver, *Builders of American Universities* (Alton, Ill., Shurtleff College Press, 1950), pp. 18–19.

54. *Ibid.,* pp. 19–20. See also Charles W. Eliot, *University Administration* (Boston, Houghton Mifflin, 1908), p. 176. See also Andrew D. White, *Annual Report,* Cornell University, 1884, pp. 64–65. Yet President Gates at Amherst showed open hostility to Professor Garman, who was famous for his ability to make students think. Alfred E. Stearns, *An Amherst Boyhood* (Amherst, Mass., Amherst College, 1946), pp. 106–109.

55. Andrew D. White, *Autobiography of Andrew Dickson White* (London, Macmillan, 1905), pp. 380–381. Alexander Meiklejohn was ambivalent on this issue, agreeing with White in "Teachers and Controversial Issues," *Harper's Magazine,* Vol. 177, June, 1938, pp. 17, 21–22, and yet preferring to pick his faculty for professional competence rather than the opinions it held. *The Liberal College* (Boston, Marshall Jones, 1920), pp. 84–96.

56. Noah Porter, *The American College and the American Public* (New Haven, Conn., C. C. Chatfield, 1870), pp. 228–229.
57. Curti and Carstensen, *op. cit.*, Vol. I, p. 58.
58. Comment, "Academic Freedom and the Law," *Yale Law Journal*, Vol. 46, February, 1937, p. 671.
59. John M. Mecklin, *My Quest for Freedom* (New York, Scribner, 1945), Chap. 5.
60. Twenty years later the membership was 11,500 and in another twenty years it was 43,615.
61. John Dewey, *Introductory Address*, American Association of University Professors, 1915, pp. 3–4. For a later discussion of professionalism vs. trade-unionism as the policy for the association, see A. O. Lovejoy, "Professional Association or Trade Union," *AAUP Bulletin*, Vol. 24, May, 1938, pp. 409–417; Earl E. Cummings and Harold A. Larrabee, "Individual vs. College Bargaining for Professors," *ibid.*, Vol. 24, October, 1938, pp. 487–496; and Logan Wilson, *The Academic Man* (New York, Oxford University Press, 1942), pp. 220–221.
62. Quoted in *School and Society*, Vol. 3, January, 1916, p. 175.
63. Hofstadter and Metzger, *op. cit.*, pp. 482–483.
64. For a fuller statement of the breach, see pp. 368–372.
65. There was some complaint against this practice. See Samuel P. Capen, "Privileges and Immunities," *AAUP Bulletin*, Vol. 23, March, 1937, pp. 190–201.
66. For an extended account of the theory and development of academic freedom, see Ralph F. Fuchs, "Academic Freedom—Its Basic Philosophy, Function, and History," *AAUP Bulletin*, Vol. 52, September, 1966, pp. 290–291.
67. "General Declaration of Principles," *AAUP Bulletin*, Vol. 1, 1915, pp. 20–39. Universities indoctrinating a particular point of view the Declaration classified as proprietary. Without committing itself as to their desirability, the Declaration excepted them from the application of its principles. For another rationalization of academic freedom, see Thomas Emerson and David Haber, "Academic Freedom of the Faculty Member as Citizen," *Law and Contemporary Problems*, Vol. 28, Summer, 1963, p. 545. For a rebuttal of misconceptions of academic freedom, see Machlup, "On Some Misconceptions Concerning Academic Freedom," pp. 753–784.
68. *Ibid.*, p. 32.
69. The American Association of University Professors has had difficulty defining what "responsibly" means. See the Koch Case at the University of Illinois reported in *AAUP Bulletin*, Vol. 49, Spring, 1963, pp. 25–43.
70. For a statement of professional ethics, see *AAUP Bulletin*, Vol. 52, September, 1966, pp. 290–291.
71. Figures compiled from annual reports of Committee A and published in the association's *Bulletin* from time to time indicated:

	1928	1930	1935	1940	1945	1950	1954
Cases pending Jan. 1	10	10	11	50	74	61	96
New cases since Jan. 1	19	27	56	54	43	40	66
Old cases revised	—	1	7	4	5	2	3
Total	29	38	74	108	122	103	165

72. Metzger, *Academic Freedom in the Age of the University*, p. 217.
73. *Ibid.*, p. 220.
74. In at least one case, St. John's University, Brooklyn, professors employed the strike in an endeavor to redress what they regarded as an infringement of their academic freedom. *New York Times*, December 18, 1965.
75. Metzger, *Academic Freedom in the Age of the University*, pp. 215–216.
76. "Report of Self-Survey Committee of the American Association of University Professors," *AAUP Bulletin*, Vol. 51, May, 1965, pp. 110, 116–117.
77. Carol S. Gruber, "Academic Freedom at Columbia University, 1917–1918: the Case of James McKeen Cattell," *AAUP Bulletin*, Vol. 58, September, 1972, pp. 297–305.
78. Hofstadter and Metzger, *op. cit.*, p. 499.
79. James Gray, *The University of Minnesota, 1851–1951* (Minneapolis, University of Minnesota Press, 1951), pp. 246–258, 386–389; Philip A. Bruce, *A History of the University of Virginia* (New York, Macmillan, 1920), Vol. V, p. 366. Happily Schaper was rehabilitated after the war hysteria had subsided.

80. Morison, *Three Centuries of Harvard,* pp. 454–456. In another case involving social security, the Boston police strike, Lowell threatened to resign if the Harvard Corporation discharged Harold Laski, who defended the strikers. *Ibid.,* pp. 436–466.

81. Lowell, *op. cit.,* pp. 267–271. It is interesting that the Civil Liberties Union came to take an interest in academic freedom. "Academic Freedom and Academic Responsibility," *AAUP Bulletin,* Vol. 42, Autumn, 1956, pp. 517–529.

82. *AAUP Bulletin,* Vol. 4, February-March, 1919, p. 30.

83. For this and other clarifications of the 1915 declaration, see Louis Joughin (ed.), *Academic Freedom and Tenure* (Madison, University of Wisconsin Press, 1967).

84. James H. Morgan, *Dickinson College, 1783–1933* (Carlisle, Pa., Dickinson College, 1933), p. 16.

85. "Statement of Committee B of the American Association of University Professors," *AAUP Bulletin,* Vol. 23, January, 1937, pp. 26–32.

86. *Wieman* v. *Updegraff,* 344 U.S. 183 (1952).

87. *Baggett* v. *Bullitt,* 377 U.S. 360 (1964).

88. *Tolman* v. *Underhill* (39 *California* [2nd Series] 708). For a detailed account of all the facts leading up to the decision, see David P. Gardner, *The California Oath Controversy* (Berkeley, University of California Press, 1967).

89. MacIver, *op. cit.,* p. 186.

90. E.g., in New York see the Rapp-Coudert Committee's investigation of the City College of New York. Willis Rudy, *The College of the City of New York, a History, 1847–1947* (New York, City College Press, 1949), pp. 450–452.

91. Calvin Coolidge, "Enemies of the Republic," *Delineator,* June, July, 1921. See also Henry C. Black, *Socialism in American Colleges, Bulletin of the National Association for Constitutional Government,* No. 4, December, 1920, pp. 31–32.

92. Elliott, *op. cit.,* pp. 28–29.

93. For the first notable case at the University of Washington, see Charles M. Gates, *The First Century at the University of Washington* (Seattle, University of Washington Press, 1961), Chap. 13. For discussion of principles involved, see Ernest Van den Haag, "Academic Freedom and Its Defense," *Phi Delta Kappan,* Vol. 36, December, 1954, pp. 113–118; Sidney Hook, *Heresy, Yes: Conspiracy, No* (New York, John Day, 1953).

94. For more details of this difficult period see Paul F. Lazarsfield and Wagner Thielens, *The Academic Mind* (New York, Free Press, 1958). See also Robert K. Carr, "Academic Freedom, the A.A.U.P., and the U.S. Supreme Court," *AAUP Bulletin,* Vol. 45, March, 1959, pp. 5–24.

95. "Academic Freedom and National Security," *AAUP Bulletin,* Vol. 42, Spring, 1956, p. 99.

96. *Ibid.,* p. 100. See also Clark Byse, "Teachers and the Fifth Amendment," *ibid.,* Vol. 41, Autumn, 1955, pp. 465–466; and the Slochower case, *New York Times,* April 10, 1956.

97. Ralph B. Perry, letter to the *New York Times,* April 28, 1953. See also Robert E. Summers, *Freedom and Loyalty in Our Colleges* (New York, H. W. Wilson, 1954).

98. Kirk, *op. cit.,* pp. 18–31, 115.

99. See p. 318.

100. William P. Murphy, "Academic Freedom—An Emerging Constitutional Right," *Law and Contemporary Problems,* Vol. 28, Summer, 1963, pp. 447–486.

101. *Ibid.,* p. 457.

102. Louis Joughin, "Academic Due Process," *Law and Contemporary Problems,* Vol. 28, Summer, 1963, pp. 573–601.

103. 354 U.S. 234. See also Robert M. Hutchins, *The University of Utopia* (Chicago, University of Chicago Press, 1953), Chap. 4.

104. Louis Joughin, *loc. cit.* See also Clark Byse and Louis Joughin, *Tenure in American Higher Education* (Ithaca, N.Y., Cornell University Press, 1959), pp. 132–147.

105. Walter P. Metzger, "Academic Tenure in America: A Historical Essay," in *Commission on Academic Tenure in Higher Education,* pp. 93–158.

106. R. S. Morison, "Some Aspects of Policy Making in the American University," *Daedalus,* Vol. 99, Summer, 1970, pp. 609–644.

107. In one controversial case a scholar at Harvard not only claimed freedom to publish the results of his scholarship but also the privilege to keep his sources secret. A lower court denied the privilege. See *Joseph* v. *Julian,* letter to the editor, *The Chronicle of Higher Education,*

January 29, 1972. See also Samuel Hendel and Robert Bard, "Should There Be a Researcher's Privilege?," *AAUP Bulletin*, Vol. 59, Winter, 1973, pp. 398–401.

109. Arthur W. Galston, "The Scientist as Socially Responsible Citizen," *Key Reporter*, Autumn, 1973. See also *New York Times*, November 18 and 21, 1973.

109. Sidney Hook, *Academic Freedom and Academic Anarchy* (New York, Cowles, 1969), pp. 159–160, 169.

110. Sidney Hook, "Freedom to Learn But Not Freedom to Riot," *New York Times Magazine*, January 3, 1965; Fred M. Hechinger, "Academic Freedom in America," *Change*, November–December, 1970, pp. 32–36; and Henry Steele Commager in Sidney Hook, (ed.), *In Defense of Academic Freedom* (New York, Pegasus, 1971), Chap. 9.

111. Professor Herbert Marcuse even advocated intolerance of tolerance. See his "Repressive Tolerance" in a *A Critique of Pure Intolerance* with Robert P. Wolff and Barrington Moore (Boston, Beacon Press, 1969). For a critique of this critique, see Sidney Hook, *Academic Freedom and Academic Anarchy*, pp. 36–46.

112. *Report of the Committee on Freedom of Expression at Yale* (Yale University, 1975).

113. Edward Manier and John Houck (eds.), *Academic Freedom and the Catholic University* (Notre Dame, Ind., Fides Publishers, 1967). See also John W. Donohue, "Catholic Universities Define Themselves: A Progress Report," *America*, Vol. 128, April, 1973, pp. 354–358, and Andrew M. Greeley, *From Backwater to Mainstream: a Profile of Catholic Higher Education* (New York, McGraw-Hill, 1969).

Chapter 16. Reintegration of Curriculum and Extracurriculum

1. Howard E. Wilson, "The Problem of Intellectualism and the Bifurcated College," Note No. 2, September 13, 1954 (Washington, D.C., Educational Policies Commission, mimeographed report, 1954).

2. See pp. 120–121.

3. Frank C. Abbott (ed.), *Student Life in the United States*, American Council on Education Studies, Series I, No. 57 (Washington, D.C., American Council on Education, 1953), pp. 4–5.

4. George W. Pierson, *Yale: The University College, 1921–1937* (New Haven, Conn., Yale University Press, 1955), p. 221.

5. Eugenie Andruss Leonard, *Origins of Personnel Services in American Higher Education* (Minneapolis, University of Minnesota Press, 1955). For an example of this early type of program, see William S. Tyler, *History of Amherst College During the Administration of its First Five Presidents* (New York, Frederick H. Hitchcock, 1895), p. 98.

6. Note the experience of Gilman at Johns Hopkins and Hall at Clark. See Chap. 9.

7. "The term 'behavioral sciences,' to include all the sciences concerned with the study of human behavior, both biological and social, has become current only since World War II." Ralph W. Tyler, Director, Center for Advanced Study in the Behavioral Sciences, Stanford, California, to the authors, January 22, 1957.

8. Louis Wirth, "The Social Sciences," in Merle E. Curti (ed.), *American Scholarship in the Twentieth Century* (Cambridge, Mass., Harvard University Press, 1953); Zoe E. Leatherman, *A Further Study of the Maladjusted College Student* (Columbus, Ohio, H. L. Hedrick, 1928), pp. 7–14; William H. Cowley, "Some History and a Venture in Prophecy," in Edmund G. Williamson, *Trends in Student Personnel Work* (Minneapolis, University of Minnesota Press, 1949).

9. Jack Edward Walters (ed.), *College Personnel Procedures: The Purdue-Wabash Conference*, October 28–29, 1929, Bulletin No. 21, Engineering Extension Department (Lafayette, Ind., Purdue University, 1930), p. 10.

10. Archibald MacIntosh, *Behind the Academic Curtain* (New York, Harper & Row, 1948).

11. A study of student attitudes at Syracuse University in 1926 revealed that nearly half the undergraduates were dissatisfied with the lack of pertinence of their formal studies to their needs, academic, vocational, or personal. Daniel Katz and Floyd H. Allport, *Students' Attitudes: A Report of the Syracuse University Reaction Study* (Syracuse, N.Y., Craftsman Press, 1931), pp. 319–322.

12. Hugh M. Bell, "Counseling and Guidance," in P. F. Valentine (ed.), *The American College* (New York, Philosophical Library, 1949); *New York Times*, October 29, 1964.

13. C. Gilbert Wrenn and Reginald Bell, *Student Personnel Problems* (New York, Farrar, Straus & Giroux, 1942), pp. 2–6.

14. See p. 260.

15. J. J. Coss (ed.), *Five College Plans* (New York, Columbia University Press, 1931), p. 4.

16. William H. Cowley, "Intelligence Is Not Enough," *Journal of Higher Education*, Vol. 8, December, 1937, pp. 469–477.

17. Personnel workers pointed out that the period of college residence coincided with a crucial stage of adolescence, involving significant physiological and psychological changes. Life was "never more intensely felt nor more furiously lived than by the boy or girl between eighteen and twenty-two." William H. Cowley, "The College Guarantees Satisfaction," *Educational Record*, Vol. 16, January, 1935, pp. 42–43.

18. Prominent in advocating this approach among the college presidents of the 1920s were E. H. Wilkins of Oberlin and Lotus D. Coffman of Minnesota. For discussions of this point of view, see Coss, *op. cit.;* Esther M. Lloyd-Jones and Margaret R. Smith, *A Student Personnel Program for Higher Education* (New York, McGraw-Hill, 1938); Leatherman, *op. cit.;* Helen Q. Stewart, *Some Social Aspects of Residence Halls for College Women* (New York, Professional and Technical Press, 1942); Hugh Hartshorne (ed.), *From School to College* (New Haven, Conn., Yale University Press, 1939); William S. Gray, *Provision for the Individual in College Education* (Chicago, University of Chicago Press, 1932), pp. 6–11.

19. Cowley, "The College Guarantees Satisfaction," pp. 47–48.

20. Wrenn and Bell, *op. cit.*, p. 8.

21. See pp. 268, 269.

22. William H. Cowley, "European Influences on American Higher Education," *Educational Record*, Vol. 20, April, 1939, p. 190.

23. Edmund G. Williamson, *How to Counsel Students: A Manual of Techniques for Clinical Counselors* (New York, McGraw-Hill, 1939), pp. 1–3.

24. Kenneth Keniston, "Faces in the Lecture Room," *Yale Alumni Magazine*, April, 1966, p. 25.

25. Daniel C. Gilman, *Launching of a University* (New York, Dodd, Mead, 1906), p. 53. Gilman later insisted that the introduction of the "preceptorial system" at Princeton by Woodrow Wilson was related, at least in part, to the latter's residence in Baltimore as a graduate student.

26. William Rainey Harper, *The Trend in Higher Education* (Chicago, University of Chicago Press, 1905), pp. 94–95, 320–325.

27. Rollo Walter Brown, *Dean Briggs* (New York, Harper & Row, 1926); Samuel Eliot Morison (ed.), *Development of Harvard University Since the Inauguration of President Eliot, 1869–1929* (Cambridge, Mass., Harvard University Press, 1930), pp. xxiii–li; James P. Findlay, "Origin and Development of the Work of the Dean of Men," *Bulletin of the Association of American Colleges*, Vol. 25, May, 1939, pp. 279–280. For a statement of Briggs's philosophy of "deaning," see LeBaron Russell Briggs, *Routine and Ideals* (Boston, Houghton Mifflin, 1904), pp. 42–62.

28. According to one study, the median year for the establishment of the office of dean of men in a select group of colleges was 1911; of that of dean of women, 1905. Findlay, *op. cit.;* William H. Cowley, "Preface to the Principles of Student Counseling," *Educational Record*, Vol. 18, April, 1937, pp. 224–225.

29. For representative discussions, see Robert J. Aley, "Care of Freshmen in Large Universities," *NEA Proceedings*, 1908, pp. 680–689; Stephen B. L. Penrose, "The Organization of a Standard College," *Educational Review*, Vol. 43, September, 1912, p. 121; James H. Baker, *American University Progress* (New York, McKay, 1916), p. 64; Edwin E. Slosson, *Great American Universities* (New York, Macmillan, 1910). Slosson, for example, found the great weakness of American higher education to be the lack of close personal contact between student and professor. This was not due to mere numbers alone, he argued, but to faulty organization and philosophy.

30. A. Lawrence Lowell, *At War With Academic Traditions in America* (Cambridge, Mass., Harvard University Press, 1934), pp. 32–45.

31. Professor Edmund G. Williamson, University of Minnesota, to the authors, December 19, 1956.

32. Malcolm M. Willey, "The University and Personnel Work," in Williamson, *Trends in Student Personnel Work*, pp. 8–9.

33. Findlay, *op. cit.*, pp. 280–281; Leatherman, *op. cit.*, pp. 14–15.

34. James Gray, *The University of Minnesota, 1851–1951* (Minneapolis, University of Minnesota Press, 1951), pp. 348–360; Williamson, *Trends in Student Personnel Work*, pp. 3–6, 131–132; Lloyd-Jones and Smith, *op. cit.*, pp. 1–3. There were also notable personnel programs in the 1920s at the University of Chicago and Northwestern University. See Gray, *op. cit.*, pp.

57–59, and Esther M. Lloyd-Jones, *Student Personnel Work at Northwestern University* (New York, Harper & Row, 1929).

35. David A. Robertson, "A Cooperative Experiment in Personnel Procedure," *School and Society,* Vol. 26, August 27, 1927, pp. 1–6; Robert L. Duffus, *Democracy Enters College* (New York, Scribner, 1936), pp. 84–85; Willard W. Blaesser, "The Contributions of the American Council on Education to Student Personnel Work in Higher Education" (unpublished doctoral dissertation, George Washington University, 1954).

36. Cowley estimates that by 1956 there were at least 7,500 persons in the United States devoting all of their working time to student personnel activities. This amounted to an average of at least four such officials in each of the nation's 1,900 colleges and universities. William H. Cowley, "Student Personnel Services in Retrospect and Prospect," *School and Society,* Vol. 85, January 19, 1957, p. 21. See also the detailed discussion in Howard E. Wilson's *American College Life as Education in World Outlook* (Washington, D.C., American Council on Education, 1956), pp. 7–33, 46–53, 106–131, 168–186. To update this field, see Charles F. Warnath, *New Myths and Old Realities: College Counseling in Transition* (San Francisco, Jossey-Bass, 1971).

37. Gray, *op. cit.;* Ernest T. Walker, *Relation of Housing of Students to Success in a University* (Chicago, University of Chicago Libraries, 1935).

38. Housing and Home Finance Agency, *The College Housing Program—The What, and the Why of Title IV, Housing Act of 1950* (Washington, D.C., Government Printing Office, 1952).

39. Harper built four dormitories in the first group of buildings at Chicago, and by 1900 had erected three more.

40. President's Report, *Decennial Publications of the University of Chicago,* First Series, Vol. I (Chicago, University of Chicago Press, 1903), pp. 387–390; Joseph E. Gould, "William Rainey Harper and the University of Chicago" (unpublished doctoral dissertation, Syracuse University, 1951), pp. 218–220, 227–228, 245–250.

41. See p. 130; Stephen C. Swett, "Princeton: Changing Underclass Years," *Harvard Crimson,* November 6, 1954, p. 3.

42. William H. Cowley, "European Influences upon American Higher Education," *Educational Record,* Vol. 20, April, 1939, p. 187.

43. Stewart, *op. cit.*

44. Robert C. Angell, *The Campus* (Englewood Cliffs, N.J., Prentice-Hall, 1928), pp. 163–164.

45. See Chapter 13; Alexander Meiklejohn, *The Experimental College* (New York, Harper & Row, 1932).

46. James B. Conant *et al., History and Traditions of Harvard College* (Cambridge, Mass., Harvard Crimson, 1936), pp. 70–73.

47. He was contemplating such plans as early as 1907. Lowell, *op. cit.,* pp. 27–31.

48. James Rowland Angell, *American Education* (New Haven, Conn., Yale University Press, 1937), pp. 260–261, 277–282.

49. For these purposes Harkness ultimately donated $11,392,000 to Harvard and $15,725,000 to Yale. Pierson, *op. cit.,* pp. 211–212, 225–227, 240–252. The first Harvard "houses" were open by 1932; the first Yale "colleges," however, did not get under way until September, 1933.

50. *Ibid.,* pp. 214–215, 407, 423.

51. *Ibid.,* p. 220; *Harvard Crimson,* December 6, 1956, p. 2.

52. One study points out that it would be necessary, in order to realize the full educational value of the student quadrangles, not only to have resident faculty members, but to make their work there as tutors and counselors a definite part of their academic careers. In other words, such work would have to be officially recognized and rewarded for purposes of promotion and tenure. Of course, without independent endowments, such a system would be difficult, if not impossible, to establish. Robert M. Strozier *et al., The Housing of Students,* American Council on Education Studies, Series VI, No. 14 (Washington, D.C., 1950), pp. 4–5, 38–39.

53. Pierson, *op. cit.;* William Mather Lewis, "The College and Leisure," *Bulletin of the Association of American Colleges,* Vol. 9, April, 1923, pp. 166–167. On this point, see Stephen Vincent Benét, *The Beginning of Wisdom* (New York, Holt, Rinehart & Winston, 1921), pp. 64–65. A walk across the venerable "Old Campus" at Yale brought "such happiness as is not given twice . . . it always brought with it peace and that sense of fed accomplishment that comes like sleep after hours of annihilating toil."

54. Edward C. Elliott (ed.), *Rise of a University* (New York, Columbia University Press, 1937), Vol.

II, pp. 231–233. These views on student housing perhaps embodied more closely the "genteel tradition" as it had been taking shape in America than they did the Oxford and Cambridge educational tradition.

55. Strozier *et al., op. cit.,* pp. 4, 38–39; Stewart, *op. cit.,* pp. 54–57; William H. Cowley, "History of Student Residential Housing," *School and Society,* Vol. 40, December 8, 1934, pp. 758–764.
56. George Santayana, "Persons and Places," *Atlantic Monthly,* Vol. 171, May, 1943, p. 85.
57. Strozier *et al., op. cit.,* pp. 48–49.
58. Stewart, *op. cit.,* p. 23.
59. William McDougall, "Functions of the Endowed Universities of America," in Paul A. Schilpp (ed.), *Higher Education Faces the Future* (New York, Liveright, 1930), pp. 242–243. This view should be contrasted with that expressed by Professor Ernest R. Holme, a visitor from Australia, in 1920. Holme praised the American college dormitory system as the source of the "wonderful life-long enthusiasm of the American University man for his University" and suggested that it was "fit to serve all the British Dominions as a model." *The American University, An Australian View* (Sydney, Angus and Robertson, 1920), pp. 148–149, 213–214.
60. Charles W. Eliot, *University Administration* (Boston, Houghton Mifflin, 1908), pp. 248–250.
61. Gray, *op. cit.,* Chap. 17; Fred J. Kelly and Ella B. Ratcliffe, *College Projects for Aiding Students,* U.S. Office of Education Bulletin, 1938, No. 9 (Washington, D.C., Government Printing Office, 1938); Samuel C. Newman and Ross L. Mooney, "Effects of Self-help," *Journal of Higher Education,* Vol. 11, November, 1940, pp. 435–442; Walter Greenleaf, *Self-help for College Students,* U.S. Bureau of Education Bulletin, 1929, No. 2 (Washington, D.C., Government Printing Office, 1929).
62. Newman and Mooney, *op. cit.*
63. Algo D. Henderson and Dorothy Hall, *Antioch College: Its Design for Liberal Education* (New York, Harper & Row, 1946), pp. 4–5, 114–115, 126; see Chapter 13.
64. Richard G. Axt, *Federal Government and Financing Higher Education* (New York, Columbia University Press, 1952), pp. 216–217.
65. Walter Van Dyke Bingham, *Placement Service in American Colleges and Universities* (New York, Personnel Research Federation, 1926).
66. This group had organized itself originally under the name of Associated College Employment Officers. Within a year the name was changed to its present form. Helen MacMurtrie Voorhees, *History of Eastern College Personnel Officers* (Boston, Thomas Todd, 1952).
67. Ruth E. Boynton, "Medical Services for Students," in Williamson, *Trends in Student Personnel Work;* Gray, *op. cit.;* Harold S. Diehl and Charles Shepard, *Health of College Students* (Washington, D.C., American Council on Education, 1939), p. 11.
68. Diehl and Shepard, *op. cit.,* pp. 11–12; Gray, *op. cit.*
69. Boynton, *op. cit.* An important index of the progress of the movement is furnished by the holding of National Conferences on College Hygiene. The first of these was held in 1931. They worked consistently for a broader view of student health and the extension of health work in colleges. For an example, see Proceedings, Second National Conference on College Hygiene, *Health in Colleges* (New York, National Tuberculosis Association, 1937).
70. Diehl and Shepard, *op. cit.,* pp. 13–16.
71. Dana L. Farnsworth, "College Health Comes of Age," *Journal-Lancet,* Vol. 74, October, 1954, pp. 397–398.
72. R. W. Bradshaw, "Research in Student Health," *American Journal of Public Health,* Vol. XIX, November, 1929, pp. 1229–1234.
73. Dana L. Farnsworth and Augustus Thorndike, "Health in Colleges and Universities," *New England Journal of Medicine,* Vol. 255, November 15 and 22, 1956, pp. 949–955, 992–996.
74. The American mental health movement may be said to have begun formally in 1908 with the organization of a society for which Adolf Meyer coined the term "mental hygiene." Robert G. Hinckley, "A Social Movement and a Clinical Service," in Williamson, *Trends in Student Personnel Work,* pp. 136–137.
75. Ernest R. Groves, "Mental Hygiene in the College and the University," *Social Forces,* Vol. VIII, September, 1929, pp. 37–50; Clements Fry and Edna Rostow, *Mental Health in College* (New York, Commonwealth Fund, 1942), pp. 17–18; William L. Hughes, *The Administration of Health and Physical Education for Men in Colleges and Universities* (New York, Teachers College, Columbia University, 1932).
76. Lloyd-Jones and Smith, *op. cit.,* pp. 2–3.

77. Fry and Rostow, *op. cit.,* pp. 3–4; Robert C. Angell, *A Study in Undergraduate Adjustment* (Chicago, University of Chicago Press, 1930).

78. Victor V. Anderson, *Psychiatry in Education* (New York, Harper & Row, 1932), pp. 21–22; Leatherman, *op. cit.,* pp. 20–23. G. Stanley Hall, at Clark, and Stewart Paton, at Princeton, had proposed psychiatric service for students before the First World War.

79. Fry and Rostow, *op. cit.,* pp. xi–xvii.

80. Farnsworth, *op. cit.,* p. 400.

81. "Freshman Week" as a full-fledged institution was launched at the University of Maine in 1923 and attracted national attention. Jay Carroll Knode, *Orienting the Student in College* (New York, Teachers College, Columbia University, 1930); Ernest H. Wilkins, *The Changing College* (Chicago, University of Chicago Press, 1927), Chap. 6; Albert B. Crawford, *Incentives to Study* (New Haven, Conn., Yale University Press, 1929), p. 125.

82. Charles T. Fitts and Fletcher H. Swift, *The Construction of Orientation Courses for Freshman, 1888–1926* (Berkeley, University of California Press, 1928); Earle Edward Emme, *The Adjustment Problems of College Freshmen* (Nashville, Cokesbury Press, 1933). A closely related phenomenon was the publication of an increasing number of books designed to help orient the young person who was planning to enter college. See publications such as Christian Gauss, *Life in College* (New York, Scribner, 1930); Samuel L. Hamilton, *What It Takes to Make Good in College* (New York, Public Affairs Committee, 1941); Bernard C. Ewer, *College Study and College Life* (Boston, Richard G. Badger, 1917); J. Franklin Messenger, *The Art of Going to College* (New York, Crowell, 1937).

83. Maurice S. Sheehy, *Problems of Student Guidance* (Baltimore, Md., Dolphin Press, 1929). This work indicates the increasingly wide scope of the counseling movement in American colleges.

84. Ruth Strang, "Democracy in the College," *Journal of Higher Education,* Vol. 11, January, 1940, pp. 33–37; Chauncey Samuel Boucher, "Current Changes and Experiments in Liberal Arts Colleges," *Bulletin of the Association of American Colleges,* Vol. 17, May, 1931, pp. 182–183.

85. Allan C. Lemon, *Experimental Study of Guidance and Placement of Freshmen in Lowest Decile of the Iowa Qualifying Examination* (Iowa City, University of Iowa, 1925); Katz and Allport, *op. cit.,* pp. 321–323.

86. Gray, *op. cit.,* pp. 61–62; Boucher, *op. cit.,* pp. 185–187.

87. William H. Cowley, "Preface to the Principles of Student Counseling," *Educational Record,* Vol. 18, April, 1937, pp. 228–229; Lloyd-Jones and Smith, *op. cit.;* Boucher, *op. cit.,* p. 186; Williamson, *Trends in Student Personnel Work,* p. 4; William S. Gray, *The Junior College Curriculum* (Chicago, University of Chicago Press, 1929).

88. William H. Matlock, "Instruction in Religion in State Universities," *Educational Review,* Vol. 40, October, 1910, pp. 256–265; Charles F. Kent, *Undergraduate Courses in Religion at Tax-Supported Universities* (New York, National Council on Religion in Higher Education, 1923); M. M. Cunningim, *The College Seeks Religion,* pp. 222–225; Willard L. Sperry, *Religion in America* (Cambridge, Eng., Cambridge University Press, 1946), pp. 167–168; Sherman B. Barnes, "Learning and Piety in Ohio Colleges, 1900–1930," *Ohio Historical Quarterly,* July, 1961, pp. 214–238. See also the notable case of *Calvary Bible Presbyterian Church* v. *Regents of the University of Washington,* 71 Wash. 912; 436 P. 2nd. 189 (1967).

89. Hugh Hartshorne and Quinter Miller, *Community Organization and Religious Education* (New Haven, Conn., Yale University Press, 1932), pp. 147, 153, 164–167, 176, 186–188, 196–200; Theron C. McGee, *Religious Education in Certain Evangelical Colleges* (Philadelphia, University of Pennsylvania, 1928); Council of Church Boards of Education, *What, Why, How, Who* (New York, 1925).

90. Gould Wickey, "A National Survey of the Religious Preferences of Students in American Colleges and Universities, 1936–1937," *Christian Education,* Vol. XXI, October, 1937, pp. 49–55.

91. Ordway Tead, *Character Building and Higher Education* (New York, Macmillan, 1953), p. 100.

92. Richard H. Edwards and Ernest R. Hilgard, *Student Counseling* (New York, National Council on Religion in Higher Education, 1928); Cunningim, *op. cit.,* pp. 222–225; Charles E. McAllister, *Inside the Campus* (Old Tappan, N.J., Revell, 1948); Russell A. Beam, *The Religious Attitudes and Habits of College Freshmen* (Chicago, University of Chicago Libraries, 1937). Evidence of this sort casts serious doubt on the charges of "godlessness" in the colleges contained in works such as Dan Gilbert, *Crucifying Christ in Our Colleges* (Los Angeles, Calif., Dan Gilbert, 1933).

93. Preston W. Slosson, *The Great Crusade and After* (New York, Macmillan, 1931), pp. 274–275;

Foster R. Dulles, *America Learns to Play* (Englewood Cliffs, N.J., Prentice-Hall, 1940), pp. 348–352; Frank G. Menke, *The Encyclopedia of Sports* (Cranbury, N.J., A. S. Barnes, 1953); Roger Kahn, "Halfbacks Carry the Mortgage," *Nation,* December 22, 1956, pp. 539–541.

94. Little, *op. cit.,* p. 211; William S. Gray, *Needed Readjustments in Higher Education* (Chicago, University of Chicago Press, 1933), Chap. 12.

95. *The Chronicle of Higher Education,* September 24, 1973, and October 1, 1973. See also *New York Times,* March 10 and 12, 1974.

96. The term "intramural" is taken to mean "competitive and recreative sport which takes place within the walls of a particular school." Elmer D. Mitchell, *Intramural Sports* (Cranbury, N.J., A. S. Barnes, 1939), pp. 1–2.

97. *Ibid.,* pp. 4–6; Howard J. Savage, *American College Athletics* (New York, Carnegie Foundation, 1929), pp. 30–31; Claude Fuess, *Amherst* (Boston, Little, Brown, 1935), p. 296. The intramural movement seems to have made the most rapid progress in the West and Middle West. It also quickly attained a place of prominence at women's colleges, where there were usually no established programs of intercollegiate athletics.

98. Mitchell, *op. cit.,* pp. 7–10; Carl L. Nordly, *The Administration of Intramural Athletics for Men in Colleges and Universities* (New York, Teachers College, Columbia University, 1937), pp. 1–36; U.S. Navy, Aviation Training Division, *Intramural Programs* (Annapolis, Md., U.S. Naval Institute, 1950), p. 5.

99. Angell, *The Campus,* pp. 102–103.

100. *Harvard Crimson,* December 6, 1956, p. 5.

101. W. Henry Johnston, "The Harvard Athletic Program," *North Central Association Quarterly,* Vol. 27, April, 1953.

102. Brumbaugh, *op. cit.,* p. 10.

103. Abraham Flexner, *Universities, American, English, German* (New York, Oxford University Press, 1930), p. 68. In this connection, it is interesting that in England, supposedly the leading exemplar of the "collegiate way of life," American visitors after the First World War were apt to find professors at the urban and provincial universities highly critical of the Oxford and Cambridge tutorial system as "spoon feeding." Pierson, *op. cit.,* p. 219.

104. Cowley, "Intelligence Is Not Enough."

105. Willey, *op. cit.,* pp. 10–11.

106. Cowley, "Preface to the Principles of Student Counseling," pp. 230–231.

107. Cowley, "Student Personnel Services in Retrospect and Prospect," p. 20.

108. Boucher, *op. cit.,* p. 184.

109. Brumbaugh, *loc. cit.*

110. Ernest H. Wilkins, "Assumptions Underlying the Individualization of College Education," in Gray, *Provision for the Individual in the College,* p. 11; Hartshorne, *op. cit.,* pp. 306–307.

111. Robert M. Strozier, "The Student in the United States and His University," in Abbott, *op. cit.,* p. 31.

112. Tead, *Education for Character, A Neglected Objective.*

113. Keniston, *loc. cit.*

114. *New York Times,* April 30, 1966, p. 49; Jonathan Randal, "Relaxed Campus Rules," April 25, 1966, pp. 1, 28. For more general statistics, see Buell Gallagher, *Campus in Crisis* (New York, Harper & Row, 1974), p. 193.

115. Gail Kennedy (ed.), *Education at Amherst* (New York, Harper & Row, 1955), pp. 290–292.

116. James P. O'Brien, "The Development of the New Left," in *The Annals of the American Academy of Political and Social Science,* Vol. 395, May, 1971, pp. 15–25.

117. For an excellent exposition of the moral limits of student civil disobedience, see Charles Frankel, "Rights and Responsibilities in the Student-College Relationship," in Lawrence Dennis and Joseph Kauffman (eds), *The College and the Student* (Washington, D.C., American Council on Education, 1966). See also Edward Bloomberg, *Student Violence* (Washington, D.C., Public Affairs Press, 1970) and John R. Silber, "Respect for the Law on the Campus," *Educational Record,* Vol. 51, Spring, 1970, pp. 130–133.

118. Donald T. Williams, "The Awesome Effectiveness of Confrontation," *Educational Record,* Vol. 51, Spring, 1970, pp. 130–133.

119. *Ibid.* See also Robert M. O'Neil *et al., No Heroes, No Villains: New Perspectives on Kent State and Jackson State* (San Francisco, Jossey-Bass, 1972) and Carnegie Commission on Higher Education, *Dissent and Disruption* (New York, McGraw-Hill, 1971), pp. 78–89.

120. Philip C. Altbach and Patti Peterson, "Before Berkeley: Historical Perspectives on Student Activism," *The Annals of the American Academy of Political and Social Science,* Vol. 395, May, 1971, pp. 1–14. See also K. Sale, *SDS* (New York, Random House, 1973).

121. For an extended compilation, see Altbach and Peterson, *loc. cit.* For a comparison of the old left and the new left, see *The Chronicle of Higher Education,* March 11, 1974.

122. Brumbaugh, *op. cit.,* pp. 12–13; Tully C. Knoles, "American Education—Whence and Whither?" in Schilpp (ed.), *op. cit.,* p. 69; American Civil Liberties Union, *What Freedom for American Students?* (Committee on Academic Freedom, 1941); Robert M. MacIver, *Academic Freedom in Our Time* (New York, Columbia University Press, 1955).

123. Altbach and Peterson, *op. cit.*

124. "Congress Looks at the Campus: The Brock Report on Student Unrest," *AAUP Bulletin,* Vol. 55, Autumn, 1969, pp. 327–336.

125. "Student Protest," *AAUP Bulletin,* Vol. 55, Autumn, 1969, pp. 309–326. There are excellent bibliographical materials in the Commission's report.

126. President's Commission on Campus Unrest (Washington, D.C., Government Printing Office, 1970); see also *Chronicle of Higher Education,* Vol. 5, October, 1970. The Carnegie Commission on Higher Education in its volume *Dissent and Disruption* (New York, McGraw-Hill, 1971) took this same view.

127. Sidney Hook, in *Chronicle of Higher Education,* September 28, 1970.

128. See *Gott* v. *Berea,* 156 Ky. 376 (161 S.E.204) 1913.

129. Warren Seavy, "Dismissal of Students," *Harvard Law Review,* Vol. 70, June, 1957, p. 1406.

130. Charles A. Wright, "The Constitution and the Campus," *Vanderbilt Law Review,* Vol. 22, October, 1969, pp. 1027–1088. See also John S. Brubacher, *The Courts and Higher Education* (San Francisco, Jossey-Bass, 1971), pp. 8–34. For a suggested Model Bill of Rights, see *The Chronicle of Higher Education,* March, 1971, and United States District Court for Western Missouri, *Educational Record,* Vol. 50, Winter, 1969, pp. 12–20.

131. See *Dickey* v. *Alabama State Board of Education,* 273 Fed.Supp. 613 (1967) and *Antonelli* v. *Hammond,* 308 Fed.Supp. 1329 (1970). See also Lawrence Dennis and Joseph Kaufmann (eds.), *The College and the Student* (Washington, D.C., American Council on Education, 1966), pp. 252–292; William W. Van Alstyne, "Student Academic Freedom and the Rule Making Powers of Public Universities: Some Constitutional Considerations," *Law in Transition Quarterly,* Vol. 2, Winter, 1965, pp. 1–34. See also Sanford Kadish in Samuel Gorovitz, (ed.), *Freedom and Order in the University* (Cleveland, Ohio, Press of Western Reserve University, 1967), pp. 134–136; Pamphlet of the American Civil Liberties Union, *Academic Freedom and Civil Liberties of Students in Colleges and Universities,* 1970; and "Joint Statement of the Rights and Freedoms of Students," in *College and University Business,* September, 1967, pp. 78–81, adopted by the Association of American Colleges, American Association of University Professors, and the National Student Association.

132. *Hammond* v. *South Carolina State College,* 281 Fed.Supp. 280 (1968).

133. *Dixon* v. *Alabama State Board of Education,* 294 Fed.2nd 150 (1961) See also Dennis and Kaufmann, *op. cit.* pp. 305–332.

134. E.g., *Soglin* v. *Kaufmann,* 295 Fed.Supp. 978 (1968). Cf. *Estaban* v. *Central Missouri State College,* 415 Fed.2nd 1077 (1969).

135. James A. Perkins, *The University and Due Process* (Washington, D.C., Chronicle of the American Council on Education, 1967). But Clark Byse, a professor of law and a past president of the American Association of University Professors, took issue in "The University and Due Process: a Somewhat Different View," *AAUP Bulletin,* Vol. 54, Summer, 1968, pp. 143–148.

136. Irving L. Horowitz and William Friedland, *The Knowledge Factory* (Chicago, Aldine, 1970), p. 175. For further statistics on disturbances, see Alane Boyer and Alexander Astin, "Campus Unrest: Was It Really All That Quiet?" *Educational Record,* Vol. 52, Fall, 1971, pp. 301–313.

137. Christopher Jencks and David Riesman, *The Academic Revolution* (Garden City, N.Y., Doubleday, 1968).

138. For further treatment of the impact of student demands on administration, see *post* pp. 375, 376.

139. Edward J. Bloustein, "The New Student and His Role in American Colleges," in Walter P. Metzger *et al., Dimensions of Academic Freedom* (Urbana, University of Illinois Press, 1969) and Floyd Turner, "The Student Movement as a Force for Educational Change," *Liberal Education,* Vol. 56, March, 1970, pp. 39–50.

140. There is a vast literature analyzing the college population from which but three items are mentioned here: Kenneth Kenniston, *Youth and Dissent in the Rise of a New Opposition* (New York, Harcourt Brace Jovanovich, 1971); Jencks and Riesman, *op. cit.;* and Joseph Schwab, *The College Curriculum and Student Protest* (Chicago, University of Chicago Press, 1969), Chap. 1.

141. One of the most thorough treatments is Lewis F. Feuer's *The Conflict of Generations* (New York, Basic Books, 1969).

142. The most popular exposition is Theodore Roszak's *The Making of a Counter Culture* (Garden City, N.Y., Doubleday, 1969). See also John R. Searle, *The Campus War: a Sympathetic Look at the University in Agony* (New York, World, 1971), Chap. 5.

143. Nihilism gave some point to George Kennan's "Rebels Without a Program," *New York Times Magazine,* January 21, 1968. See also Louis Halle, "The Student Drive to Destruction," in William P. Gerberding and Duane E. Smith (eds.), *The Radical Left: The Abuse of Discontent* (Boston, Houghton Mifflin, 1970), pp. 185–192.

144. Cf. the "free university movement," *ante* p. 279.

145. Kenneth Kenniston, *op. cit.,* p. 181.

146. Irving L. Horowitz and William Friedland, *op. cit.,* p. 105.

147. Daniel Yankelovich, "The New Naturalism," *Saturday Review,* April 1, 1972. See also Kenneth Benne, "Contemporary Irrationalism and the Idea of Rationalism," and Henry D. Aiken, "Rationalism, Education and the Good Society," *Studies in Philosophy and Education,* Vol. 6, Spring, 1969, pp. 249–282, 317–340.

148. *New York Times,* April 23, 1973, and December 13, 1970. See also, C. Vann Woodward, "What Became of the 1960s?" *New Republic,* Vol. 171, November 9, 1974, pp. 18–25.

149. Kingman Brewster, *Chronicle of Higher Education,* January 5, 1970.

150. Lewis Mayhew, "The Steady Seventies," *Journal of Higher Education,* Vol. 45, March, 1974, pp. 163–173; and *Youth: Transition to Adulthood,* Report of the Panel on Youth of the President's Science Advisory Committee (Chicago, University of Chicago Press, 1974).

151. Kenneth Kenniston, "The Agony of the Counter-Culture," *Educational Record,* Vol. 52, Summer, 1971, pp. 205–211. See also Harold Taylor, *How to Change Colleges: Notes on Radical Reform* (New York, Holt, Rinehart & Winston, 1971), pp. ix–xi, 2–11.

152. Daniel Yankelovich in *The Chronicle of Higher Education,* May 28, 1974.

Chapter 17. Enlarging Scope of the Administration of Higher Education

1. See pp. 30–31.

2. Fred W. Hicks, "The Constitutional Autonomy of the University of Michigan and Its Significance in the Development of a State University" (unpublished doctoral dissertation, University of Michigan, 1963).

3. *Drake* v. *University of Michigan* (4 Mich. 98).

4. James Gray, *The University of Minnesota, 1851–1951* (Minneapolis, University of Minnesota Press, 1951), pp. 298–307. For decisions similar to Michigan's in other states, see *State* v. *Chase,* 175 Minnesota 259 (1928); *State* v. *State Board of Education,* 33 Idaho 415 (1921); and *Trapp* v. *Cooke Construction Co.,* 24 Oklahoma 850 (1909).

5. Edward C. Elliott and Merritt M. Chambers, *The Colleges and the Courts* (New York, Carnegie Foundation, 1936), pp. 146–149. Malcolm Moos and Francis E. Rourke, *The Campus and the State* (Baltimore, Md., Johns Hopkins Press, 1959).

6. See p. 71.

7. John H. McNeely, *Supervision Exercised by States over Privately Controlled Institutions of Higher Education,* U.S. Office of Education, Bulletin No. 8, 1934; Fred J. Kelly and John H. McNeely, *The State and Higher Education* (New York, Carnegie Foundation, 1933).

8. Frank C. Abbott, *Government Policy and Higher Education: A Study of the Regents of the University of the State of New York, 1784–1949* (Ithaca, N.Y., Cornell University Press, 1958), pp. 24–28, 31. The author also notes how the Regents came to exercise control over higher education through an annual Convocation which in its early days was a real work session to discuss such questions as degree and entrance requirements.

9. *Ibid.,* p. 71. See also Harlan H. Horner, "Coordination in New York State," *Journal of Higher Education,* Vol. 4, March, 1933, pp. 135–138.

10. Walter J. Ziemba, "Changes in Policies and Procedures of the Accrediting Process of the

Commission on Colleges and Universities of the North Central Association of Colleges and Secondary Schools, 1909–1958" (unpublished doctoral dissertation, University of Michigan, 1966), pp. 94–95.

11. McNeely, *op. cit.*

12. G. W. Knight, "The State and the Private College," *Educational Review,* Vol. 10, June, 1895, pp. 57–70.

13. John H. McNeely, "Degrees Conferred by Private Institutions," *Journal of Higher Education,* Vol. 5, November, 1934, pp. 433–442. Some states relied on judicial proceedings *in quo warranto* to eliminate fraudulent institutions. Edward C. Elliott and Merritt M. Chambers, *The Colleges and the Courts* (New York, Carnegie Foundation, 1936), pp. 205–206.

14. William K. Selden, *Accreditation* (New York, Harper & Row, 1960), pp. 47–50; *New York Times,* July 27, 1972, pp. 1, 28.

15. Andrew S. Draper, "Shall the State Restrict the Use of the Terms College and University?" *Educational Review,* Vol. 24, June, 1902, pp. 10–22; Henry S. Pritchett, "Sham Universities," Carnegie Foundation for the Advancement of Teaching, *Annual Report,* 1912, pp. 158–162.

16. See pp. 242–245.

17. Henry S. Pritchett, "The Organization of Higher Education," Carnegie Foundation for the Advancement of Teaching, *Annual Report,* 1908, pp. 150–151.

18. American Association of Universities, *Journal of Proceedings and Addresses,* January, 1908, p. 76.

19. Fred J. Kelly *et al., College Accreditation,* U.S. Office of Education Bulletin, 1940, pp. 16–17.

20. George F. Zook and Melvin E. Haggerty, *Principles of Accrediting Higher Institutions* (Chicago, University of Chicago Press, 1936), pp. 19–22. For various ratings of top universities in the United States in rank order of excellence, see *Report of the Committee on Graduate Instruction* (Washington, D.C., American Council on Education, 1934); Walter C. Eells, "Another Rating of American Graduate Schools," *School and Society,* Vol. 46, August, 1937, pp. 282–284; *Time,* Vol. 87, No. 21, May 27, 1966, p. 55.

21. Henry S. Pritchett, "The Place of the College in American Education," Carnegie Foundation for the Advancement of Teaching, *Annual Report,* 1907, pp. 79–80.

22. Cornell's president, Jacob Gould Schurman, a trustee of the Foundation, thought the foundation's influence excessive. See Howard Savage, *Fruit of an Impulse* (New York, Harcourt Brace Jovanovich, 1953), pp. 90–92.

23. Zook and Haggerty, *op. cit.,* pp. 26–28.

24. Alfred M. Meyer, "History of the Southern Association of Colleges and Secondary Schools" (unpublished dissertation, George Peabody College for Teachers, 1936), pp. 5–6.

25. Zook and Haggerty, *op. cit.,* pp. 25–26.

26. *Ibid.,* p. 35.

27. The fear that voluntary accrediting agencies might be an infringement on state sovereignty was laid at rest by *Langer* v. *North Central Association,* 23 Fed.Supp. 694 (1938).

28. Paul M. Limbert, *Denominational Policies in the Support of Higher Education* (New York, Teachers College, Columbia University, 1929), pp. 91–92, 106.

29. Charles S. Johnson, *The Negro College Graduate* (Chapel Hill, University of North Carolina Press, 1938), pp. 292–296.

30. Kelly *et al., op. cit.,* pp. 108–109, 183–184.

31. Robert L. Duffus, *Democracy Enters College* (New York, Scribner, 1936), pp. 69–71.

32. George F. Zook, "The President's Annual Report," *Educational Record,* Vol. 30, July, 1949, pp. 278–280; Walter A. Jessup, "Facing Actualities in American Higher Education," Carnegie Foundation for the Advancement of Teaching, *Annual Report,* 1934, pp. 3–4.

33. John D. Russell, *The Outlook for Higher Education* (Chicago, University of Chicago Press, 1939), Chap. 14.

34. Samuel P. Capen, *The Management of Universities* (Buffalo, Foster and Stewart, 1953), pp. 261–263.

35. Fred O. Pinkham, "The Accrediting Problem," *Annals of the American Academy of Political Science,* Vol. 103, September, 1955, pp. 67–71.

36. William A. Kaplin and J. Philip Hunter, "The Legal Status of the Educational Accrediting Agency: Problems in Judicial Supervision and Governmental Regulation," *Cornell Law Quarterly,* Vol. 52, 1966, pp. 104–107; *New York Times,* July 27, 1972, p. 1.

37. See pp. 11–12, 22–23.

38. Philip A. Bruce, *A History of the University of Virginia* (New York, Macmillan, 1920), Vol. I, p. 365.

39. Charles M. Perry, *Henry Philip Tappan, Philosopher and University President* (Ann Arbor, University of Michigan Press, 1933), p. 281. Cf. Donald Tewksbury, *The Founding of American Colleges and Universities before the Civil War* (New York, Teachers College, Columbia University, 1932), pp. 188–189, 201, 206–207.

40. See pp. 69–74.

41. Francis P. Cassidy, *Catholic College Foundations and Their Development in the United States, 1767–1860* (Washington, D.C., Catholic University of America Press, 1924), pp. 85–86; John T. Ellis, *The Formative Years of the Catholic University of America* (Washington, D.C., Catholic University of America Press, 1940), pp. 312–315.

42. Sebastian A. Erbacher, *Catholic Higher Education for Men in the United States, 1850–1866* (Washington, D.C., Catholic University of America Press, 1931), pp. 70–73; Roy DeFarrari, *College Organization and Administration* (Washington, D.C., Catholic University of America Press, 1947), p. 62–63.

43. Henry S. Pritchett, "The Relations of Christian Denominations to Colleges," *Educational Review*, Vol. 36, October, 1908, pp. 217–241.

44. *Horace Mann League et al.* v. *Board of Public Works*, 220 Atl. 51 (1966). The United States Supreme Court refused a review. For a different rule in the federal cours, see Tilton *v.* Finch, 312 Fed. Supp. 1191 (1970).

45. Noah Porter, *The American College and the American Public* (New Haven, Conn., C. C. Chatfield, 1870), pp. 233–237, Chap. 12.

46. Morris Hadley, *Arthur Twining Hadley* (New Haven, Conn., Yale University Press, 1948), p. 229.

47. William J. Tucker, *My Generation: An Autobiographical Interpretation* (Boston, Houghton Mifflin, 1919), pp. 262–264.

48. See pp. 28–29.

49. Walter P. Metzger, "College Professors and Big Business Men" (unpublished doctoral dissertation, University of Iowa, 1950), pp. 135–136.

50. Earl J. McGrath, "The Control of Higher Education in America," *Educational Record*, Vol. 17, April, 1936, pp. 163–164.

51. Hubert P. Beck, *Men Who Control Our Universities* (New York, King's Crown Press, 1947).

52. Scott Nearing, "Who's Who Among College Trustees?" *School and Society*, Vol. 6, September, 1917, pp. 298–299.

53. Howard J. Savage, "Do Trustees Need Informing?" Carnegie Foundation for the Advancement of Teaching, *Annual Report*, 1935.

54. For an attempt to make up this deficiency, see Raymond M. Hughes, *A Manual for Trustees of Colleges and Universities* (Ames, Iowa, Collegiate Press, 1945).

55. John F. Budd, Jr., "Are College Trustees Obsolete?" *Saturday Review/World*, Vol. 1, March 9, 1974, pp. 48–49.

56. Thorstein Veblen, *The Higher Learning in America* (New York, B. W. Huebsch, 1918), pp. 67–68.

57. Frederick Rudolph, *Mark Hopkins and the Log* (New Haven, Conn., Yale University Press, 1956), pp. 201–202.

58. Laura H. Moseley, *Diary of James Hadley, 1843–1852* (New Haven, Conn., Yale University Press, 1951), p. 308.

59. Webster S. Stover, *Alumni Stimulation* (New York, Teachers College, Columbia University, 1930), pp. 13–15.

60. E. D. Duryea, "Evolution of University Organization," in James A. Perkins (ed.), *The University as an Organization* (New York, McGraw-Hill, 1973), p. 33.

61. Percy Marks, "The Pestiferous Alumni," *Harper's Magazine*, Vol. 153, July, 1926, pp. 144–149; Henry S. Prichett, "The Influence of Alumni on Their Colleges," Carnegie Foundation for the Advancement of Teaching, *Annual Report*, 1923, pp. 38–39, 115–117.

62. For an attempt to improve alumni work as well as that of trustees, see Robert W. Sailor, *A Primer for Alumni Work* (Ithaca, N.Y., American Alumni Council, 1944).

63. Walter Schenkel, "Who Has Been in Power?" in Harold L. Hodgkinson and L. Richard Meeth (eds.), *Power and Authority* (San Francisco, Jossey-Bass, 1971), p. 15.

64. W. A. Asbrook, "The Board of Trustees," *Journal of Higher Education,* Vol. 3, January, 1932, pp. 8–10.
65. Henry S. Pritchett, "Development of an Effective Board of Government," Carnegie Foundation for the Advancement of Teaching, *Annual Report,* 1911, pp. 112–113; Charles E. McAllister, *Inside the Campus* (Old Tappan, N.J., Revell, 1948), Chap. 2.
66. Merritt M. Chambers, "The Tenure of State University Trustees," *Educational Record,* Vol. 18, January, 1937, pp. 126–136.
67. George P. Schmidt, *The Old Time College President* (New York, Columbia University Press, 1930), pp. 184–187.
68. Homer P. Rainey, "Some Facts about College Presidents," *School and Society,* Vol. 30, October, 1929, pp. 581–582; John A. and Margaret H. Perkins, "From These Leadership Must Come," *School and Society,* Vol. 70, September, 1949, pp. 162–164.
69. Earl D. Ross, *Democracy's College* (Ames, Iowa State College Press, 1942), pp. 105–106.
70. James B. Angell, *Reminiscences* (New York, McKay, 1912), pp. 242–243.
71. Hadley, *op. cit.,* pp. 122–132.
72. William Lyon Phelps, *Autobiography with Letters* (New York, Oxford University Press, 1939), p. 161.
73. Josiah Quincy, *The History of Harvard University* (Cambridge, Mass., Harvard University Press, 1840), Vol. II, pp. 344–353.
74. Charles W. Eliot, *University Administration* (Boston, Houghton Mifflin, 1908), pp. 228–229, 235.
75. Bruce, *op. cit.,* Vol. V, pp. 1–38.
76. Laurence R. Veysey says that university administrators came in two waves, the first composed of men like Eliot, White, and Angell and the second of men like Harper and Butler. The former had a worldly sophistication which seemed old fashioned alongside the latter. *The Emergence of the University, 1865–1915* (Chicago, University of Chicago Press, 1966), pp. 305–310.
77. William J. Tucker, *op. cit.,* thought it an "infelicity" that there was no academic way to prepare for the college presidency. For a prescription of his training, see Robert M. Hutchins, "The Administrator," *Journal of Higher Education,* Vol. 17, November, 1946, p. 406.
78. Earl J. McGrath, "Evolution of Administrative Offices in Institutions of Higher Education, 1860–1933" (unpublished doctoral dissertation, University of Chicago, 1933), p. 47.
79. Public relations had been an early concern of colleges and universities. Especially new ones like Cornell and Chicago used dignified and sophisticated advertising to call attention to their wares. Eliot deliberately resorted to publicity to discourage the notion that Harvard was a rich man's college. Veysey, *op. cit.,* p. 336.
80. David S. Jordan, *Days of a Man* (Yonkers, N.Y., World Book, 1922), Vol. I, pp. 207–208.
81. Gray, *op. cit.,* pp. 577–579.
82. Merle S. Kuder, *Trends in Professional Opportunities in the Liberal Arts College* (New York, Teachers College, Columbia University, 1937), Chap. 11.
83. Merle Curti and Vernon R. Carstensen, *The University of Wisconsin, a History, 1848–1925* (Madison, University of Wisconsin Press, 1949), Vol. I, pp. 609–615.
84. Quincy, *op. cit.,* Vol. II, p. 336; Bruce, *op. cit.,* Vol. I, pp. 325–326.
85. E. D. Duryea, *op. cit.,* pp. 30–31.
86. Paul L. Dressel and Donald J. Reichard, "The University Department: Retrospect and Prospect," *Journal of Higher Education,* Vol. 41, May, 1970.
87. Paul L. Dressel, F. Craig Johnson, and Philip M. Marcus, *The Confidence Crisis* (San Francisco, Jossey-Bass, 1971), p. 8.
88. Stanley O. Ikenberry and Reness C. Friedman, *Beyond Academic Departments* (San Francisco, Jossey-Bass, 1972).
89. Samuel Eliot Morison, *The Development of Harvard University Since the Inauguration of President Eliot, 1869–1929* (Cambridge, Mass., Harvard University Press, 1930), p. xxxvi; Henry M. Wriston, in Isaac L. Kandel (ed.), *Educational Yearbook* (New York, International Institute, Teachers College, 1943), pp. 198–199.
90. "University Administration in the United States," *Educational Review,* Vol. 41, April, 1911, pp. 342–343; *Five College Plans* (New York, Columbia University Press, 1931), pp. 19–21.
91. Capen, *op. cit.,* pp. 1–21. See also Upton Sinclair, *The Goose-Step* (Pasadena, Calif., the author, 1923).

92. For an elaboration of the academic freedom facet of this crisis, see pp. 312–313.
93. G. Stanley Hall admits this fault in his *Confessions of a Psychologist* (Englewood Cliffs, N.J., Prentice-Hall, 1919), pp. 345–347. David Starr Jordan actually took a stand for a strong presidency in which he advised against faculty meetings, a faculty role in making new appointments, even tenure for faculty. Veysey, *op. cit.*, p. 398.
94. James P. Munroe, "Closer Relations between Trustees and Faculty," *Science*, new series, Vol. 22, December 29, 1905, pp. 849–854. James H. Baker, *American University Progress and College Reform Relative to School and Society* (New York, McKay, 1916), pp. 131–132. See also David B. Tyack, *The One Best System; A History of American Urban Education* (Cambridge, Mass., Harvard University Press, 1974), pp. 133–135.
95. Harold J. Laski, "The American College President," *Harper's Magazine*, Vol. 164, February, 1932, pp. 313–316.
96. John E. Kirkpatrick, *Academic Organization and Control* (Yellow Springs, Ohio, n.p., 1931), Chap. 5.
97. Perry, *op. cit.*, Chap. 13; Jasper Adams, "On the Relation Subsisting Between the Board of Trustees and the Faculty of a University," *American Institute of Instruction*, 1837, pp. 147–149.
98. Curti and Carstensen, *op. cit.*, Vol. I, pp. 25–27; Nicholas M. Butler, *Across the Busy Years* (New York, Scribner, 1939), Vol. I, p. 79.
99. Andrew S. Draper, "Government in American Universities," *Educational Review*, Vol. 28, October, 1904, pp. 228–239.
100. E.g., see H. W. Widener, "The College in a Pecuniary Culture," *Educational Record*, Vol. 16, April, 1935, pp. 188–202.
101. Nicholas M. Butler, *Scholarship and Service* (New York, Scribner, 1921), pp. 168–169.
102. *Bracken v. William and Mary*, 3 Call (Va.) 587 (1790).
103. William P. Murphy, "Academic Freedom—An Emerging Constitutional Right," *Law and Contemporary Problems*, Vol. 28, Summer, 1963, pp. 447–486; Richard Hofstadter and Walter P. Metzger, *The Development of Academic Freedom in the United States* (New York, Columbia University Press, 1955), pp. 460–465; Merritt M. Chambers, "The Legal Status of Professors," *Journal of Higher Education*, Vol. 2, December, 1931, pp. 481–486.
104. William R. Keast and John W. Macy, Jr., *Faculty Tenure* (San Francisco, Jossey-Bass, 1973), pp. 1–8.
105. Richard Chait and Andrew Ford, "Can a College Have Tenure . . . and Affirmative Action, Too?" *The Chronicle of Higher Education*, Vol. 7, October 1, 1973, p. 16.
106. William Van Alstyne, "Tenure: A Summary, Explanation, and Defense," *AAUP Bulletin*, Vol. 57, Autumn, 1971, pp. 328–333; Bardwell L. Smith *et al.*, *The Tenure Debate* (San Francisco, Jossey-Bass, 1973), pp. 205–214; and *Commission on Academic Tenure in Higher Education*, pp. ix–x. Frederick H. Jackson and Robin S. Wilson in their article, "Toward a New System of Academic Tenure," *Educational Record*, Vol. 52, Fall, 1971, pp. 338–342, proposed a system of renewable term contracts in place of tenure to avoid abuses and still insure continuity. It is notable that nontenured junior faculty were preparing to make tenure a major negotiable issue when unionism and collective bargaining arrived on their campuses. See William F. McHugh, "Faculty Unionism and Tenure," in *Commission on Academic Tenure in Higher Education*, Chap. 7.
107. *The Chronicle of Higher Education*, Vol. 8, July 8, 1974, p. 2.
108. Thorstein Veblen, *The Higher Learning in America* (New York, B. W. Huebsch, 1918), pp. 48–49. Veblen was not far off the mark at the University of Chicago, because William R. Harper had deliberately designed its administrative organization on corporate lines. *University of Chicago Official Bulletin* #1.
109. A. Lawrence Lowell, *At War with Academic Traditions* (Cambridge, Mass., Harvard University Press, 1934), pp. 281–291.
110. Ordway Tead, *Trustees, Teachers, and Students; Their Role in Higher Education* (Salt Lake City, University of Utah Press, 1951), p. 6.
111. J. McKeen Cattell, "University Control," *Science*, Vol. 23, March, 1906, pp. 476–477.
112. J. McKeen Cattell, *University Control* (New York, Science Press, 1913). Even student representation on the board was suggested in some quarters. William H. Cowley, "The Government and Administration of Higher Education: Whence and Whither," *Journal of the American Association of College Registrars*, Vol. 22, July, 1947, p. 483.

113. Walter P. Metzger, *Academic Freedom in the Age of the University* (New York, Columbia University Press, 1955), pp. 198–199.

114. Catherine Beecher, *Educational Reminiscences* (New York, J. B. Ford, 1874), p. 184.

115. Lowell, *op. cit.,* pp. 50–51. See also a joint "Statement on Government of Colleges and Universities" by the American Association of University Professors, the American Council on Education, and the Association of Governing Boards of Universities and Colleges in the *Bulletin of the American Association of University Professors,* Vol. 52, December, 1966, pp. 375–379. Also here for the first time on high authority is a recommendation for responsible student participation in the government of higher education.

116. Butler, *Scholarship and Service,* pp. 163–168.

117. *Five College Plans* (New York, Columbia University Press, 1931), pp. 7–28.

118. David S. Jordan, "Perplexities of a College President," *Atlantic Monthly,* Vol. 85, April, 1900, pp. 488–489.

119. William A. Neilsen (ed.), *Charles William Eliot and His Beliefs* (New York, Harper & Row, 1926), pp. 217–239.

120. Kirkpatrick, *op. cit.,* pp. 66–73.

121. George W. Pierson, *Yale College, an Educational History, 1871–1921* (New Haven, Conn., Yale University Press, 1955), Chap. 7. Later Yale found some of its democracy cumbersome. See George W. Pierson, *Yale: the University College, 1921–1937* (New Haven, Conn., Yale University Press, 1955), Chap. 13.

122. George G. Bogert, "Historical Survey of Faculty Participation in University Government in the United States," in John Dale Russell and Donald M. Mackenzie (eds.), *Emergent Responsibilities in Higher Education* (Chicago, University of Chicago Press, 1946), pp. 115–117.

123. "Report on Role of Faculties in College and University Government," *Bulletin of the American Association of University Professors,* Vol. 22, March, 1936, pp. 183–190; and Vol. 34, Spring, 1946, pp. 55–66.

124. Charles P. Dennison, *Faculty Rights and Obligations in Eight Independent Liberal Arts Colleges* (New York, Teachers College, Columbia University, 1955), pp. 14–18.

125. "Place and Function of Faculties in College and University Government," *AAUP Bulletin,* Vol. 26, April, 1940, pp. 171–185.

126. T. R. McConnell and Kenneth Mortimer, *The Faculty in University Governance* (Berkeley, University of California, 1971), pp. 1–3.

127. Budd, *op. cit.,* p. 49.

128. Schenkel, *op. cit.,* pp. 18–19.

129. Duryea, *op. cit.,* p. 32.

130. Earl J. McGrath, *Should Students Share the Power?* (Philadelphia, Temple University Press, 1970), p. 21.

131. *The Chronicle of Higher Education,* Vol. 4, April 27, 1970, p. 3.

132. Guenter Lewy and Stanley Rothman, "On Student Power," *AAUP Bulletin,* Vol. 56, September, 1970, pp. 279–282.

133. Gottfried Dietze, *Youth, University, and Democracy* (Baltimore, Md., Johns Hopkins Press, 1970), p. 87.

134. McGrath, *op. cit.,* pp. 38–50.

135. *New York Times,* November 28, 1972.

136. Michael Brick and Earl J. McGrath, *Innovation in Liberal Arts Colleges* (New York, Teachers College Press, 1969), pp. 83–111.

137. Lewy and Rothman, *op. cit.,* p. 280; Brick and McGrath, *op. cit.,* pp. 84–86; Frederic W. Ness, "Campus Governance and Fiscal Stability," in William W. Jellema (ed.), *Efficient College Management* (San Francisco, Jossey-Bass, 1972), pp. 45–46.

138. At the turn of the century most college presidents took unabashed delight in the increasing number of students attending their institutions. Veysey, *op. cit.,* p. 356. Later in the twentieth century, however, they were almost frightened at the mounting numbers.

139. John S. Brubacher, *A History of the Problems of Education* (New York, McGraw-Hill, 1966), pp. 410–411.

140. Charles F. Thwing, *A History of Higher Education in America* (Englewood Cliffs, N.J., Prentice-Hall, 1906), Chap. 14.

141. Darrel G. Harmon, "Some Trends in Financing Higher Education," *Social Science,* Vol. 6, April, 1931, pp. 97–109.

142. Richard Hofstadter and C. DeWitt Hardy, *The Development and Scope of Higher Education in*

the United States (New York, Columbia University Press, 1952), pp. 31–32.

143. In 1866 President F. A. P. Barnard of Columbia stated as his opinion that universities could not spring into existence in a single financial bound but needed to grow by gradual financial accretions over many years. But the founding of Hopkins, Clark, Stanford, and Chicago contradicted him. See Merle Curti and Roderick Nash, *Philanthrophy in the Shaping of American Higher Education* (New Brunswick, N.J., Rutgers University Press, 1965), p. 112. See also Seymour E. Harris, *The Economics of Harvard* (New York, McGraw-Hill, 1970), Chaps. 34–48.

144. Ernest V. Hollis, *Philanthropic Foundations and Higher Education* (New York, Columbia University Press, 1938), Chap. 3, and pp. 201–204.

145. Curti and Nash, *op. cit.;* George L. Omwake, "Sources of Financial Support for the Liberal Arts College," *Educational Record,* Vol. 12, July, 1931, pp. 283–285; Lotus D. Coffman, *AAUP Bulletin,* Vol. 17, May, 1931, p. 378.

146. Curti and Carstensen, *op. cit.,* Vol. II, pp. 223–232.

147. For a criticism of the impact of foundations on research, see Harold Laski, "Foundations, Universities, and Research," *Harper's Magazine,* Vol. 157, August, 1928, pp. 296–302.

148. Irene H. Gerlinger, "College and University Financing," *Bulletin of the Association of American Colleges,* Vol. 25, November, 1939, pp. 426–427.

149. In addition to annual fund drives alumni used a variety of other devices, one of which in particular has a long history. In 1839 a donor made the University of Vermont a gift on condition that the university pay him an annual income from it during his life after which the principal would revert to the university. During the depression a hundred years later, when this form of giving had become quite popular, many institutions found themselves paying out more than they were taking in. After the Second World War the scheme had such renewed popularity as a means of dodging income taxes that the federal government had to discourage it. Richard L. Desmond, *Higher Education and Tax Motivated Giving* (Washington, D.C., American College Public Relations Association, 1967).

150. Harmon, *op. cit.,* p. 109.

151. Arthur J. Klein, *Survey of Land Grant Colleges and Universities* (Washington, D.C., U.S. Office of Education, 1930), pp. 13–15.

152. Angell, *op. cit.,* pp. 243–244.

153. Curti and Carstensen, *op. cit.,* Vol. I, p. 592; Gray, *op. cit.,* pp. 563–576.

154. Trevor Arnett, *Trends in Tuition Fees* (New York, General Education Board, Occasional Papers, No. 11, 1939), p. 60. See also Harris, *op. cit.,* Chaps. 5–8.

155. John D. Russell, "Student Fees as a Source of Support for Higher Education," in William S. Gray (ed.), *Needed Readjustments in Higher Education* (Chicago, University of Chicago Press, 1933).

156. Earl McGrath (ed.), *Universal Higher Education* (New York, McGraw-Hill, 1966), p. 202.

157. Ernest H. Wilkins, *The Changing College* (Chicago, University of Chicago Press, 1927), pp. 81–82. Cf. Report of Commission on Financing Higher Education, *Nature and Needs of Higher Education* (New York, General Education Board, 1952), p. 120; Walter J. Greenleaf, "Financial Support of Colleges," *Journal of Higher Education,* Vol. 1, May, 1930, p. 257.

158. Barbara Jones, *Bennington College* (New York, Harper & Row, 1946), p. xii; Hamilton Holt, "The Unit Cost Plan of College Finance," *Journal of Higher Education,* Vol. 4, October, 1933, pp. 355–357. For a theory that higher education should be priced at cost, see André Danière, *Higher Education in the American Economy* (New York, Random House, 1964).

159. Henry O. Severance, *Richard Henry Jesse* (Columbia, Mo., published by the author, 1937), pp. 56–57.

160. Orrin L. Elliott, *Stanford University: The First Twenty-five Years* (Stanford, Calif., Stanford University Press, 1937).

161. McGrath, *op. cit.,* p. 216.

162. Trevor Arnett, *Recent Trends in Higher Education* (New York, General Education Board, 1940), Chap. 2.

163. Report of the Commission on Financing Higher Education, *op. cit.,* pp. 59–87; Robert J. Havighurst, "The Governing of the University," *School and Society,* Vol. 79, March, 1954, pp. 86–87.

164. John P. Jones, "Factors Affecting Incomes," *Journal of Higher Education,* Vol. 8, April, 1937, pp. 185–190.

165. John D. Russell (ed.), *The Outlook for Higher Education* (Chicago, University of Chicago Press, 1939), Chap. 7.

166. Edward C. Elliott, *Rise of a University* (New York, Columbia University Press, 1937), Vol. II, pp. 450–459.

167. American Academy of Political and Social Science, *Methods of Financing Higher Education* (Philadelphia, the Academy, 1955).

168. Richard R. Price, *The Financial Support of State Universities* (Cambridge, Mass., Harvard University Press, 1924).

169. See pp. 232–237. *President's Advisory Commission on Higher Education,* 1947, Vol. V, pp. 4–6.

170. J. Harold Goldthorpe, "Tax Exemptions," *Journal of Higher Education,* Vol. 15, November, 1944, pp. 421–427.

171. In *Smith* v. *Barlow,* 13 N.J. 145 (1953), the court affirmed the right of a private business corporation to make a gift to Princeton.

172. Curti and Nash, *op. cit.,* Chap. 11; Edward Hodnett, *Industry-College Relations* (Cleveland, Ohio, World Publishing, 1955); John W. Hill and Albert L. Ayars, "More Money for our Colleges," *Saturday Review,* July 30, 1955, pp. 7–9.

173. Floyd Reeves and John D. Russell, "The Management of Endowment Funds," in Gray, *op. cit.,* Chap. 13.

174. Stanley King, *A History of the Endowment of Amherst College* (Amherst, Mass., Amherst College, 1950), p. 166. Cf. Thad L. Hungate, *Financing the Future of Higher Education* (New York, Teachers College, Columbia University, 1946); Harold T. Smith, "Endowment and Security," *Journal of Higher Education,* Vol. 4, February, 1933, p. 74. See also Harris, *op. cit.,* Chaps. 49–50.

175. *New York Times,* September 24, 1972, III, p. 1. But see "Rethinking the Endowment," *The Chronicle of Higher Education,* November 18, 1974.

176. *Ibid.,* April 4, 1971, p. 1; John G. Simon, *The Ethical Investor* (New Haven, Conn., Yale University Press, 1972), pp. 2–7, 107–108; "Morality of Investment," *Radcliffe Quarterly,* December, 1972, pp. 41–42.

177. *New York Times,* December 18, 1970, p. 1; July 16, 1972, p. 1; July 23, 1972, p. 1; March 31, 1974, p. 1; *The Chronicle of Higher Education,* Vol. 8, October 1, 1973, p. 1; *Time,* May 24, 1971, pp. 49–50.

178. Earl F. Cheit, *The New Depression in Higher Education* (New York, McGraw-Hill, 1971), pp. 137–138; William G. Bowen, *The Economics of the Major Private Universities* (Berkeley, Calif., Carnegie Commission on Higher Education, 1968), pp. 4–5.

179. Cheit, *op. cit.,* pp. viii–xi.

180. *The Chronicle of Higher Education,* Vol. 7, April 16, 1973, p. 4.

181. *New York Times,* January 11, 1971, p. 17; July 7, 1971, p. 30; *The Chronicle of Higher Education,* Vol. 8, May 20, 1974, p. 5.

182. *New York Times,* May 3, 1973, p. 1; September 7, 1974, p. 1; *The Chronicle of Higher Education,* Vol. 8, January 28, 1974, p. 5; February 4, 1974, p. 1.

183. *New York Times,* December 18, 1970, p. 9; February 22, 1971, p. 1; April 30, 1972, p. 1.

184. *Yale Alumni Magazine,* Vol. 37, February 1974, pp. 28–30; J. Anthony Lukas, "Historians' Conference: The Radical Need for Jobs," *New York Times Magazine,* March 12, 1972, pp. 38–47; *AHA Newsletter,* Vol. 7, February, 1970; Vol. 9, March, November, 1971; Vol. 11, November, 1973.

185. *New York Times,* January 31, 1971, p. 28; *The Chronicle of Higher Education,* Vol. 8, August 5, 1974, pp. 4–5.

186. *New York Times,* June 19, 1972, p. 39.

187. G. Stanley Hall, *Adolescence* (Englewood Cliffs, N.J., Prentice-Hall, 1904), Vol. II, p. 520.

188. Oberlin College, *Annual Report of the President,* 1908–09. Cf. Clyde Furst, "Tests of College Efficiency," *School Review,* Vol. 20, May, 1912, pp. 327–334.

189. Walter C. Eells, *Surveys of American Higher Education* (New York, Carnegie Foundation, 1937).

190. William H. Cowley, "Two and a Half Centuries of Institutional Research" in Richard Axt *et al., College Self-Study* (Boulder, Colo., WICHE, 1960).

191. Francis Rourke and Glenn Brooks, *The Managerial Revolution* (Baltimore, Md., Johns Hopkins Press, 1966), p. 45.

192. Horace Coon, *Money to Burn* (New York, McKay, 1938), pp. 136–139. For discussions of cost

accounting in higher education, see Arthur T. Hadley, "Methods of Ascertaining and Apportioning Cost of Instruction in Universities," *Educational Review,* Vol. 45, January, 1913, pp. 58–69; B. R. Buckingham, "Critical Present-Day Issues in the Administration of State Higher Education," National Education Association, *Proceedings,* 1917, pp. 305–313. See also Harris, *op. cit.,* Chap. 63.

193. Morris L. Cooke, *Academic and Industrial Efficiency* (New York, Carnegie Foundation, 1910).

194. Abbott, *op. cit.,* pp. 4–5.

195. Moos and Rourke, *op. cit.,* Chap. 3.

196. James L. Miller, "The Two Dimensions of State-Wide Higher Education Coordination," *Educational Record,* Vol. 43, April, 1962, p. 163; see also M. W. Ertell, *Interinstitutional Cooperation in Higher Education* (New York State Education Department, 1959), Chap. 3.

197. *Ibid.,* pp. 163–164. Perhaps it might be said that New York was the first to have a master coordinating board when it established the Regents of the University of the State of New York. This university, modeled on French lines, it will be remembered, was an administrative rather than a teaching agency. It notably included private as well as public institutions of higher education. See also, Edward C. Elliott and Merritt M. Chambers, *The Colleges and the Courts* (New York, Carnegie Foundation, 1936), pp. 155–156.

198. Thomas D. Richardson, *The New Jersey Master Plan for Higher Education: Phase II* (Montclair, N.J., Montclair State College, 1971).

199. Keith L. Scott, "Voluntary Coordination of State Higher Education in Colorado: A Case Study" (unpublished doctoral dissertation, University of Colorado, 1964).

200. Protestant denominations supporting colleges set up similar denominational boards to coordinate their activities in higher education. See Paul M. Limbert, *Denominational Policies in Support and Supervision of Higher Education* (New York, Teachers College, Columbia University, 1929). Catholic colleges did not take similar action. See Fred J. Kelly, *Privately Controlled Higher Education in the United States,* U.S. Office of Education, Bulletin No. 12, 1934, p. 51; Daniel S. Sanford, Jr., *Inter-Institutional Agreements in Higher Education* (New York, Teachers College, Columbia University, 1934), pp. 2–4, 28–29; and Lotus D. Coffman, "The New Situation in Education," *Journal of Higher Education,* Vol. 5, March, 1935, pp. 118–119.

201. Millett, *op. cit.,* pp. 236–244.

202. E. Wilson Lyon, "English Precedents in the Associated Colleges at Claremont," *Bulletin of the Association of American Colleges,* Vol. 34, October, 1948, pp. 270–275.

203. Charles Mosmann, *Academic Computers in Service* (San Francisco, Jossey-Bass, 1973), pp. 5–8.

204. Samuel Baskin, *Higher Education: Some Newer Developments* (New York, McGraw-Hill, 1965), Chap. 10.

205. T. R. McConnell, "Accountability and Autonomy," *Journal of Higher Education,* Vol. 42, June, 1971, pp. 445–451.

206. June O'Neill, *Resource Use in Higher Education* (Berkeley, Calif., Carnegie Foundation, 1971), p. 49.

207. Frank Newman, "Autonomy, Authority, and Accountability," *Liberal Education,* Vol. 59, March, 1973, p. 19; Christopher Jencks and David Riesman, *The Academic Revolution* (Garden City, N.Y., Doubleday, 1968), p. 266.

208. David D. Henry, "Accountability: To Whom, For What, By What Means?" *Educational Record,* Vol. 53, Fall, 1972, p. 291.

209. William H. Danforth, "Management and Accountability in Higher Education," *AAUP Bulletin,* Vol. 59, Summer, 1973, p. 135.

210. *New York Times,* July 6, 1974, p. 20; John E. Shay, Jr., "Coming to Grips with Faculty Workload," *Educational Record,* Vol. 55, Winter, 1974, p. 57.

211. Danforth, *op. cit.,* p. 135.

212. John J. Corson, "Institutional Governance Within a System," *Educational Record,* Vol. 54, Spring, 1973, pp. 107–114; *Report of the Board of Regents-AAUP Workload Study Committee, University of Rhode Island* (Kingston, R.I.), March 20, 1974, p. 5.

213. Paul L. Dressel and William H. Faricy, *Return to Responsibility* (San Francisco, Jossey-Bass, 1972), p. 194.

214. Beardsley Ruml and Sidney G. Tickton, *Teaching Salaries Then and Now* (New York, Fund for the Advancement of Education, Bulletin No. 1, 1955), pp. 29–47. See also Harris, *op. cit.,* Chaps. 16–19; and Viva Boothe, *The Cost of Living in Twenty-Seven State Universities and*

Colleges (Columbus, Ohio State University Press, 1932); and *AAUP Bulletin,* Vol. 44, March, 1958, p. 256, where Committee Z of the association, reporting on the economic status of the profession between 1939 and 1956, compiled the following figures for median salaries in five state universities:

	1939–40	1949–50	1955–56
Professor	$4,877	$7,296	$9,024
Assoc. Prof.	3,570	5,568	6,696
Ass't. Prof.	2,927	4,545	5,528
Instructor	2,134	3,519	4,465

215. Malcolm M. Willey, *Depression, Recovery, and Higher Education* (New York, McGraw-Hill, 1937); Sumner Slichter, "A Survey of the Economic Condition of the Academic Profession," Association of American Universities, *Proceedings,* 1934, pp. 98–99.

216. Yandell Henderson, *Incomes and Living Costs of a University Faculty* (New Haven, Conn., Yale University Press, 1928), Chap. 13.

217. Arthur T. Hadley, "The College and the Nation," *Harper's Magazine,* Vol. 139, June, 1919, p. 106. While supply continued to exceed demand as late as 1940 (Edgar S. Furniss, Association of American Universities, *Annual Conference,* 1940, p. 103), demand was expected far to outrun supply by the 1960s. W. T. Laprade, "As One Teacher Sees It," *AAUP Bulletin,* Vol. 34, Spring, 1948, pp. 39–49.

218. William G. Sumner, "Ways and Means for Our Colleges," *Nation,* Vol. 11, September, 1870, p. 153.

219. Francis Wayland, *The Present College System* (Boston, Gould, Kendall and Lincoln, 1842), pp. 69–70; Russell, *op. cit.,* Vol. I, pp. 200–203.

220. Richard H. Shryock, "The Academic Profession in the United States," *AAUP Bulletin,* Vol. 38, Spring, 1952, p. 51. And, as Claude C. Bowman said, if the professor's shelter was humble, his food plain, his life monotonous, it was the wife who suffered the real effacement, the silent deprivation, the painful economy. *The College Professor in America* (Philadelphia, published by the author, 1938), pp. 49–52.

221. Walter C. Eells, "Origin and Early History of Sabbatical Leave," *School and Society,* Vol. 48, September, 1962; pp. 253–256.

222. Fritz Machlup, "Grading of Academic Salary Scales," *AAUP Bulletin,* Vol. 44, Spring, 1958, pp. 219–236. When Committee Z reported, in 1960, the following was the scale of average salaries. The double AA rating was an ideal to aim at.

	AA	A	B	C	D	E	F
Professor	$17,500	$14,300	$11,650	$10,000	$8,400	$6,850	$5,700
Assoc. Prof.	11,750	10,100	8,750	7,500	6,600	5,700	4,850
Ass't Prof.	8,750	7,500	6,600	5,700	5,100	4,550	4,000
Instructor	6,600	5,450	4,825	4,300	4,000	3,725	3,450

For actual average salaries 1974–1975, see the *Chronicle of Higher Education,* February 10, 1975.

223. "Unions Woo the College Faculties," *Business Week,* May 1, 1971, p. 69; "Unionizing College Faculties," *Saturday Review,* June 19, 1971, p. 52; *New York Times,* January 1, 1971, pp. 1, 31.

224. Robert K. Carr and Daniel K. Van Eyck, *Collective Bargaining Comes to the Campus* (Washington, D.C., American Council on Education, 1973), pp. 20–28.

225. Everett Carll Ladd, Jr., and Seymour M. Lipset, *Professors, Unions, and American Higher Education* (Washington, D.C., Carnegie Foundation, 1973), pp. 5–9.

226. Carr and Van Eyck, *op. cit.,* pp. 180–181; John H. Bunzel, "The Faculty Strike at San Francisco State College," *AAUP Bulletin,* Autumn, 1971, pp. 341–350.

227. *The Chronicle of Higher Education,* Vol. 8, May 20, 1974, p. 1; June 10, 1974, p. 24.

228. Carr and Van Eyck, *op. cit.* pp. 292–293; Dressel and Faricy, *op. cit.* pp. 108–109.

229. Henry S. Pritchett, "History of Professors' Pensions," Carnegie Foundation for the Advancement of Teaching, *Annual Report,* 1906, pp. 31–32.

230. Henry S. Pritchett, "The Policy of the Carnegie Corporation for the Advancement of Teaching," *Educational Review,* Vol. 32, June, 1906, pp. 83–93.

231. By 1950 the foundation had paid out $57,492,000 in benefits to 4,797 beneficiaries, of whom 2,089 were still living. Howard Savage, *Fruit of an Impulse* (New York, Harcourt Brace Jovanovich, 1953), p. 39.

232. "Report on Academic Retirement," *AAUP Bulletin,* Vol. 36, Spring, 1950, pp. 99–100.

233. Sherman A. Flanagan, *Insurance and Annuity Plans for College Staffs,* U.S. Office of Education Bulletin, 1937, pp. 6–13; Coon, *op. cit.,* Chap. 9.

234. Flanagan, *op. cit.,* pp. 6–13.

235. Coon, *op. cit.,* Chap. 9.

236. Savage, *op. cit.,* pp. 115–117.

237. John D. Russell, *The Outlook for Higher Education* (Chicago, University of Chicago Press, 1939), Chap. 11.

238. Alan Pifer, "Fifty Years of TIAA: Its Past and Promise," *Educational Record,* Vol. 49, Fall, 1968, p. 413.

Chapter 18. Distinguishing Features of American Higher Education

1. This, indeed, has also been true of all other major aspects of American culture. See Ralph B. Perry, *Characteristically American* (New York, Knopf, 1949).

2. James B. Conant, "America Remakes the University," *Atlantic Monthly,* Vol. 177, May, 1946, p. 42.

3. Laurence R. Veysey, *The Emergence of the American University* (Chicago, University of Chicago Press, 1965), pp. 439–444.

4. Merritt M. Chambers, "University Student Population in the World," *Bulletin of the Association of American Colleges,* October, 1948, pp. 265–266; Oliver C. Carmichael, *The Changing Role of Higher Education* (New York, Macmillan, 1952); Raymond Walters, "Statistics of Attendance in American Universities and Colleges, 1949," *School and Society,* Vol. 70, December, 1949, p. 392; Ernest Barker, "Universities in Great Britain," in Walter M. Kotschnig (ed.), *The University in a Changing World* (London, Oxford University Press, 1932), pp. 103–104; Educational Policies Commission, *Higher Education in a Decade of Decision* (Washington, D.C., National Education Association, 1957), pp. 4–5, 31–32.

5. Ralph E. Turner, "U.S. Higher Education and the World," *Bulletin of the Association of American Colleges,* Vol. 30, March, 1944, pp. 92–94.

6. Francis M. Rogers, *Higher Education in the United States* (Cambridge, Mass., Harvard University Press, 1952), pp. 1–2; *New York Times,* December 16, 1949.

7. *New York Times,* March 17, 1949.

8. Fred McCuiston, *Graduate Instruction for Negroes in the United States* (Nashville, Tenn., George Peabody College for Teachers, 1939), pp. 101–104; Edward C. Elliott and Merritt M. Chambers, *The Colleges and the Courts* (New York, Carnegie Foundation, 1936), pp. 12–13; Felix C. Robb and J. W. Tyler, "The Law and Segregation in Southern Education," *Educational Forum,* Vol. 16, May, 1952, pp. 475–480; Mathew J. Whitehead, "Significant Achievements of Negroes in Education, 1907–1947," *Quarterly Review of Higher Education Among Negroes,* Vol. 16, January, 1948, pp. 4–7.

9. Merle E. Curti, "Intellectuals and Other People," *American Historical Review,* Vol. 60, January, 1955, p. 278.

10. Conant, *op. cit.,* pp. 42–43.

11. Willis Rudy, *The Evolving Liberal Arts Curriculum: A Historical Review of Basic Themes* (New York, Teachers College, Columbia University, 1960), pp. 39–47; see discussion of this point by the German scholar Hugo Münsterberg, *The Americans* (New York, McClure, Phillips, 1905), pp. 395–396.

12. Educational Policies Commission, *op. cit.,* p. 8.

13. Edmund J. James, *Address Before The Convention of the American Bankers Association* (New York, American Bankers Association, 1882), pp. 27–28.

14. Nicholas Murray Butler, *Across the Busy Years* (New York, Scribner, 1935), Vol. I, pp. 176–177.

15. Abraham Flexner, *Universities, American, English, German* (New York, Oxford University Press, 1930), pp. 152–153, 172–179.

16. Charles W. Eliot, "Resemblances and Differences among American Universities," *Science,* Vol. 22, December 15, 1905, pp. 779–780; William R. Harper, *The Trend in Higher Education* (Chicago, University of Chicago Press, 1905), pp. 12–19, 156–157.

17. Daniel C. Gilman, *University Problems* (Englewood Cliffs, N.J., Prentice-Hall, 1898), pp. 309–310; Educational Policies Commission, *op. cit.,* p. 8.

18. In Australia, however, a similarly close relationship developed between the state universities and the sustaining society. James R. Angell, "The University Today," in Henry P. Fairchild (ed.),

Obligation of Universities to the Social Order (New York, New York University Press, 1933), pp. 36–38.

19. Josiah Royce, "Present Ideals of American University Life," *Scribner's Magazine,* Vol. 10, September, 1891, pp. 387–388.

20. Frank J. Woerdehoff, "Dr. Charles McCarthy: Planner of the Wisconsin System of Vocational and Adult Education," *Wisconsin Magazine of History,* Summer, 1958, pp. 270–274.

21. Educational Policies Commission, *op. cit.,* pp. 8–10.

22. Cecil W. Creel, "Land-Grant Colleges and Their Contribution to American Life," *Proceedings of the Association of Land-Grant Colleges,* Vol. 52, 1938, pp. 25–28; Andrew Soule, "Contributions of the Land-Grant Colleges to our Social and Economic Progress," *ibid.,* Vol. 44, 1930, pp. 28–38; F. B. Mumford, "The Land-Grant Colleges and the National Welfare," *ibid.,* Vol. 51, 1941, pp. 25–29; A. C. True, "Report of the Bibliographer," *ibid.,* Vol. 29, 1915, pp. 32–35; Edward D. Eddy, Jr., *Colleges for Our Land and Time: The Land-Grant Idea in American Education* (New York, Harper & Row, 1956); Stephen Stephan, "Backgrounds and Beginnings of University Extension in America, 1826–1915," *Harvard Educational Review,* Vol. 18, Spring, 1948, pp. 99–108.

23. Ernest E. Schwartztrauber, *Workers' Education, A Wisconsin Experiment* (Madison, University of Wisconsin Press, 1942); Caroline F. Ware, *Labor Education in Universities* (New York, American Labor Education Service, 1946); Irvine L. H. Kerrison, *Workers Education at the University Level* (New Brunswick, N.J., Rutgers University Press, 1951); Carroll D. Clark, "Non-Academic Higher Education," *Journal of Higher Education,* Vol. 3, November, 1932, pp. 401–406.

24. James S. Coleman, "The University and Society's New Demands Upon It," in Carl Kaysen, *Content and Context* (New York, McGraw-Hill, 1973), pp. 361–364.

25. For representative nineteenth-century criticisms, see Andrew D. White, *Some Important Questions in Higher Education* (Ithaca, N.Y., Andrus and Church, 1885); and Charles E. Norton, "Harvard University," in *Four American Universities* (New York, Harper & Row, 1895), pp. 7–8.

26. Gilman, *op. cit.,* pp. 290–293.

27. William R. Harper, *The Prospects of the Small College* (Chicago, University of Chicago Press, 1900), pp. 17–18, 45–46.

28. John D. Millett, *Financing Higher Education in the United States* (New York, Columbia University Press, 1952), pp. 92–95.

29. Educational Policies Commission, *op. cit.,* pp. 111–112.

30. Ernest V. Hollis, *Philanthropic Foundations and Higher Education* (New York, Columbia University Press, 1938); Guy Stanton Ford, *On and Off the Campus* (Minneapolis, University of Minnesota Press, 1938), pp. 143–145.

31. Mary B. Pierson, *Graduate Work in the South* (Chapel Hill, University of North Carolina Press, 1947), pp. 74–75; Association of American Universities, *Proceedings,* 14th Annual Conference, 1912, p. 14; 15th Annual Conference, 1913, pp. 58–60.

32. Educational Policies Commission, *op. cit.,* pp. 110–114.

33. Aaron John Brumbaugh and S. Sugg Redding, Jr., "Recent Developments in State and Regional Planning of Higher Education," *Annals of the American Academy of Political and Social Science,* Vol. 301, September, 1955, pp. 32–40; Veysey, *op. cit.,* pp. 312–317.

34. Joseph Ben-David, *American Higher Education* (New York, McGraw-Hill, 1972), p. 7.

35. Harold H. Punke, "Public, Private, and Church Control in Higher Education," *School and Society,* Vol. 70, November 19, 1949, pp. 323–325.

36. Peter Sammartino and Willis Rudy, *The Private Urban University, A Colloquium* (Rutherford, N.J., Fairleigh Dickinson University Press, 1966); Henry S. Pritchett, "State Aid without State Control," Carnegie Foundation for the Advancement of Teaching, *7th Annual Report,* 1912, pp. 152–153.

37. James Bryce, *The American Commonwealth* (London, Macmillan, 1888), Vol. II, pp. 547–548; Harold J. Laski, "The American College President," *Harper's Magazine,* Vol. 164, February, 1932, pp. 311–320; Ernest R. Holmes, *The American University, An Australian View* (Sydney, Angus and Robertson, 1920), pp. 45–46.

38. Henry S. Pritchett, "Shall the University Become a Corporation?" *Atlantic Monthly,* Vol. 96, September, 1905, pp. 295–299.

39. Richard H. Shryock, "The Academic Profession in the United States," *AAUP Bulletin,* Vol. 38, Spring, 1952, pp. 33–36.

40. Lewis B. Mayhew, "Higher Education—Toward 1984," *Educational Record,* Vol. 53, Summer, 1972.
41. Percy Marks, *Which Way Parnassus?* (New York, Harcourt Brace Jovanovich, 1926); Charles Cestre, "L'Université Harvard," *Revue Internationale de L'Enseignement,* May 15, 1898, p. 402.
42. Daniel W. Brogan, *The American Character* (New York, Knopf, 1944), pp. 141–142.
43. Howard E. Wilson, "The Problem of Intellectualism and the Bifurcated College, Note No. 2, September 13, 1954" (Washington, D.C., Educational Policies Commission, mimeographed report, 1954).
44. Talcott Parsons and Gerald M. Platt, *The American University* (Cambridge, Mass., Harvard University Press, 1973).
45. Barnabas Binney, *Oration Delivered on the Late Public Commencement at Rhode-Island College in Providence: September, 1774* (Boston, John Kneeland, 1774).
46. William T. Harris, "The Use of Higher Education," *Educational Review,* Vol. 15, September, 1898, p. 155.
47. Flexner, *op. cit.,* pp. 221–222.
48. *Ibid.;* Norman Foerster, *The American State University* (Chapel Hill, University of North Carolina Press, 1937), pp. 57–61, 80–82; Robert M. Hutchins, *The Higher Learning in America* (New Haven, Conn., Yale University Press, 1936).
49. Pierre DeCoubertin, "L'Amerique Universitaire," *Cosmopolis,* Vol. 5, March, 1897, pp. 786–794; Gabriel Compayre, *L'Enseignement Superieur aux États-Unis* (Paris, Librairie Hachette, 1896); Maurice Caullery, *Universities and Scientific Life in the United States* (Cambridge, Mass., Harvard University Press, 1922); Otto Gross, "Amerikanisches Universitatsleben," *Die Gegenwart,* Vol. 16, September 20, 1879, pp. 188–190; Bruno Gebhardt, "Amerikanische und Englische Universitaten," *ibid.,* Vol. 35, April 6, 1889, pp. 211–212; Bryce, *op. cit.,* Vol. II; H. G. Wells, *The Future in America* (New York, Harper & Row, 1906); Robert Risk, *America at College* (London, Archibald Constable, 1908); John A. Benn, *Columbus, Undergraduate* (Philadelphia, Lippincott, 1928); Harold J. Laski, "English and American Universities," *Harvard Alumni Bulletin,* Vol. 22, March 4, 1920, pp. 539–540; Eugen Kuehnemann, *Charles W. Eliot, President of Harvard University* (Boston, Houghton Mifflin, 1909); Holme, *op. cit.*
50. Friedrich Schoenemann, "A German Looks at American Higher Education," in Paul Schilpp (ed.), *Higher Education Faces the Future* (New York, Liveright, 1930), pp. 118–119; McDougall, *op. cit.,* pp. 237–247; Edward Fiddes, *American Universities* (Manchester, Eng., Manchester University Press, 1930), pp. 16–17; Risk, *op. cit.,* pp. 209–210; Wells, *op. cit.,* pp. 211–212.
51. Laski, *op. cit.,* pp. 538–540.
52. Karl Lamprecht, *Americana: Reiseeindrucke, Betrachtungen, Geschichtliche Gesamtansicht* (Freiburg, Hermann Heyfelder, 1906), pp. 86–91; Wells, *op. cit.*
53. Barbara B. Burn, *Higher Education in Nine Countries* (New York, McGraw-Hill, 1971), pp. 2–10.
54. Hugo Münsterberg, *American Traits from the Point of View of a German* (Boston, Houghton Mifflin, 1901), pp. 89–90, 96–97, 104–107, 112–118, 126–129; Charles F. Thwing, *The American and the German University* (New York, Macmillan, 1928), pp. 174–175, 220–221.
55. As quoted in Veysey, *op. cit.,* pp. 428–429.
56. Abraham Flexner, "The Usefulness of Useless Knowledge," *Harper's Magazine,* Vol. 179, October, 1939, pp. 550–551; Dael Wolfle, *The Home of Science: The Role of the University* (New York, McGraw-Hill, 1972), pp. 1–4, 85–94.
57. Berelson, *op. cit.,* pp. 190–195.
58. Frank Tannenbaum (ed.), *A Community of Scholars, The University Seminars at Columbia* (New York, Praeger, 1965).
59. James S. Coleman, "The University and Society's New Demands upon It," *op. cit.,* pp. 362–363, 377–379.
60. Robert S. Schwantes, "Results of Study Abroad: Japanese Students in America, 1865–1885," *School and Society,* Vol. 72, December 9, 1950, pp. 375–376; Hideo Aoki, "The Effect of American Ideas upon Japanese Higher Education," *Dissertation Abstracts,* Vol. 17, July, 1957, p. 1506.
61. John Barrow, "American Institutions of Higher Learning in China," *Higher Education,* Vol. 4, February 1, 1948, pp. 121–124.

62. Abul H. K. Sassani, "American Institutions of Higher Learning in the Near East," *Higher Education,* Vol. 6, September 15, 1949, pp. 13–18.
63. *New York Times,* June 25, 1972, pp. 1, 43.
64. *Ibid.,* April 14, 1966.
65. William W. Brickman, "John Dewey's Foreign Reputation as an Educator," *School and Society,* Vol. 70, October 22, 1949, pp. 257–265.
66. Theodore Stanton, "University Reform in France," *Open Court,* Vol. 12, June, 1898, pp. 376–377.
67. Augustus Trowbridge, "The New Ph.D. in Great Britain and France," Association of American Universities, *Proceedings,* 1931, pp. 101–103; Lord Elton, *The First Fifty Years of the Rhodes Trust and the Rhodes Scholarships, 1903–1953* (Oxford, Eng., Basil Blackwell, 1955), pp. 113–114, 152–153.
68. Stephen Duggan, *Observations on Higher Education in Europe,* Bulletin No. 3 (New York, Institute of International Education, 1920), pp. 380–381; C. K. Allen, *Forty Years of Rhodes Scholarships* (Oxford, Eng., Oxford University Press, 1944). Despite these changes, it was noted that Rhodes scholars from Australia and New Zealand continued to fare more successfully than those from the United States, apparently because their local systems of preparatory schools were more akin to the British than were the American ones. Lord Elton, *op. cit.,* pp. 186–187.
69. David Starr Jordan, *The Voice of the Scholar* (San Francisco, Paul Elder, 1903), p. 26.

A Bibliography of American College and University Histories

Academy of the New Church
Members of faculty, *The Academy of the New Church, 1876–1926* (1926).

Akron, University of
George W. Knepper, *New Lamps for Old: One Hundred Years of Urban Higher Education at the University of Akron* (1970).

Alabama, University of
James B. Sellers, *History of the University of Alabama, 1818–1902* (1953).

Allegheny College
Ashton Ernest Smith, *Allegheny—A Century of Education, 1815–1915* (1916).

Amherst College
George R. Cutting, *Student Life at Amherst College* (1871).
Thomas LeDuc, *Piety and Intellect at Amherst College, 1865–1912* (1946).
Claude Moore Fuess, *Amherst: The Story of a New England College* (1935).

Antioch College
Burton R. Clark, *The Distinctive College: Antioch, Reed, and Swarthmore* (1970).
Algo D. Henderson and Dorothy Hall, *Antioch College: Its Design for Liberal Education* (1946).

Arkansas, University of
John Hugh Reynolds and David Yancey Thomas, *History of the University of Arkansas* (1910).

Asbury–De Pauw University
William Warren Sweet, *Indiana Asbury–De Pauw University, 1837–1937: A Hundred Years of Higher Education in the Middle West* (1937).

Barnard College
Annie Nathan Meyer, *Barnard Beginnings* (1935).
Marian Churchill White, *A History of Barnard College* (1954).

Bates College
Alfred Williams Anthony, *Bates College and Its Background: A Review of Origins and Causes* (1935).

Beloit College
Edward Dwight Eaton, *Historical Sketches of Beloit College* (1928).

Bennington College
Barbara Jones, *Bennington College: The Development of an Educational Idea* (1946).

Berea College
John A. R. Rogers, *Birth of Berea College: A Story of Providence* (1903).

Black Mountain College
Martin Duberman, *Black Mountain: An Experiment in Community* (1973).

Boston College
David R. Dunigan, *A History of Boston College* (1947).

Boston University
Edward R. Speare, *Interesting Happenings in Boston University's History* (1957).

Bowdoin College
Louis C. Hatch, *The History of Bowdoin College* (1927).

Brockport College, New York State University
W. Wayne Dedham, *Cherishing This Heritage: The Centennial History of the State University College at Brockport, New York* (1969).

Brooklyn College
Thomas Evans Coulton, *A City College in Action: Struggle and Achievement at Brooklyn College, 1930–1955* (1955).

Brown University
Walter C. Bronson, *The History of Brown University, 1764–1914* (1914).
Donald Fleming, *Science and Technology in Providence, 1860–1914: An Essay on the History of Brown University in the Metropolitan Community* (1952).

Bryn Mawr College
Cornelia Lynde Meigs, *What Makes a College? A History of Bryn Mawr* (1956).

Bucknell University
J. Orin Oliphant, *The Rise of Bucknell University* (1965).

Buena Vista College
William H. Cumberland, *The History of Buena Vista College* (1966).

California, University of
William Warren Ferrier, *Origin and Development of the University of California* (1930).
Robert Sibley, *The Romance of the University of California* (1928).
Albert G. Pickerell and May Dorkin, *University of California 1868–1968: A Pictorial History* (1970).

California College
Samuel H. Willey, *A History of the College of California* (1887).

Carleton College
Delavan L. Leonard, *The History of Carleton College* (1966).

Catawaba College
Jacob Calvin Leonard, *History of Catawaba College* (1927).

Catholic University of America
Patrick Henry Ahern, *The Catholic University of America, 1887–1896: The Rectorship of John J. Kearne* (1948).
Colman J. Barry, *The Catholic University of America, 1903–1909: The Rectorship of Denis J. O'Connell* (1950).
John Tracy Ellis, *The Formative Years of the Catholic University of America* (1946).
Peter E. Hogan, *The Catholic University of America 1896–1903: The Rectorship of Thomas Conaty* (1949).

Charleston, University of
James Harold Easterby, *A History of the College of Charleston, Founded 1770* (1935).

Chicago, University of
Thomas Wakefield Goodspeed, *A History of the University of Chicago Founded by John D. Rockefeller: The First Quarter-Century* (1916).
Richard J. Storr, *Harper's University: The Beginnings. A History of the University of Chicago* (1966).

Cincinnati, University of
Reginald C. McGrane, *The University of Cincinnati: A Success Story in Urban Higher Education* (1963).

Claremont Colleges, The
William W. Clary, *The Claremont Colleges: A History of the Development of the Claremont Group Plan* (1970).

Clark University
Wallace W. Atwood, *The First Fifty Years: An Administrative Report* (1937).
Edmund C. Sanford, *A Sketch of the History of Clark University* (1923).

Colby College
Edwin Carey Whittemore, *Colby College, 1820–1925: An Account of Its Beginnings, Progress and Service* (1927).

College of the City of New York
S. Willis Rudy, *The College of the City of New York: A History, 1847–1947* (1949).
Mario Emilio Cosenza, *The Establishment of the College of the City of New York as the Free Academy in 1847* (1925).

Columbia College
Dwight C. Miner (ed.), *A History of Columbia College on Morningside* (1954), one of the vols. in *The Bicentennial History of Columbia University* (1954–1957).

Columbia University
John Howard Van Amringe *et al.*, *A History of Columbia University, 1754–1904* (1904).
Jacques Barzun (ed.), *A History of the Faculty of Philosophy, Columbia University* (1957).
R. Gordon Hoxie *et al.*, *A History of the Faculty of Political Science, Columbia University* (1955).
Frederick Paul Keppel, *Columbia* (1914).

Concordia College
Das Concordia—College zu Fort Wayne Indiana in Wort und Bild (1909).

Connecticut Agricultural College
Walter Stemmons, *Connecticut Agricultural College—A History* (1931).

Cornell University
Carl L. Becker, *Cornell University: Founders and the Founding* (1943).
Morris Bishop, *A History of Cornell* (1962).
Malcolm Carron, *The Contract Colleges of Cornell University: A Co-operative Educational Enterprise* (1958).
Waterman Thomas Hewett, *Cornell University: A History* (1905).
Kermit C. Parsons, *The Cornell Campus: A History of Its Planning and Development* (1968).
Walter P. Rogers, *Andrew D. White and the Modern University* (1942).

Cumberland University
Winsted Paine Bone, *A History of Cumberland University, 1842–1935* (1935).

Davidson College
Walter Lee Lingle, *Memories of Davidson College* (1947).
Cornelia Rebekah Shaw, *Davidson College, Intimate Facts* (1924).

Denison University
G. Wallace Chessman, *Denison: The Story of an Ohio College* (1957).

Dickinson College
James Henry Morgan, *Dickinson College: The History of One Hundred and Fifty Years, 1783–1933* (1933).
Charles C. Sellers, *Dickinson College: A History* (1973).

Douglass College
George P. Schmidt, *Douglass College* (1968).

Drexel Institute of Technology
Edward D. McDonald and Edward M. Hinton, *Drexel Institute of Technology, 1891–1941* (1942).

Duke University
Nora Campbell Chaffin, *Trinity College, 1839–1892: The Beginnings of Duke University* (1950).

Elmira College
W. Charles Barker, *Elmira College: The First Hundred Years* (1955).
Gilbert Meltzer, *The Beginnings of Elmira College, 1851–1868* (1941).

Emory University
Henry Morton Bullock, *A History of Emory University* (1936).

Fordham University
Robert I. Gannon, *Up to the Present: The Story of Fordham* (1967).

Franklin and Marshall College
Joseph H. Dubbs, *History of Franklin and Marshall College* (1903).

General Theological Seminary
Powel Mills Dawley, *The Story of the General Theological Seminary: A Sesquicentennial History, 1817–1967* (1969).

Georgetown College (Georgetown, Kentucky)
Leland Wenfield Meyer, *Georgetown College* (1929).

Georgetown University
John M. Daley, *Georgetown University: Origin and Early Years* (1957).
John R. Friant, *Glimpses of Old Georgetown* (1939).

Georgia, University of
Robert Preston Brooks, *The University of Georgia Under Sixteen Administrations, 1785–1955* (1956).
E. Merton Coulter, *College Life in the Old South,* 2nd ed. (1951).

Georgia Institute of Technology
Marion Luther Brittain, *The Story of Georgia Tech* (1948).

Gonzaga University
Wilfred P. Schoenberg, *Gonzaga University; Seventy-five Years, 1887–1962* (1963).

Goucher College
Anna Heubeck Knipp and Thaddeus P. Thomas, *The History of Goucher College* (1938).

Grinnell College
John Scholte Nollen, *Grinnell College* (1953).

Hamilton College
Charles Elmer Allison, *A Historical Sketch of Hamilton College, Clinton, New York* (1889).
Joseph D. Ibbotson and S. N. D. North, *Documentary History of Hamilton College* (1922).

Hampden-Sidney College
Alfred J. Morrison (ed.), *The College of Hampden-Sidney: Calendar of Board Minutes, 1776–1876* (1912).

Hanover College
William Alfred Millis, *The History of Hanover College from 1827 to 1927* (1927).

Harvard University
Seymour M. Lipset and David Riesman, *Education and Politics at Harvard* (1975).
Samuel Eliot Morison (ed.), *The Development of Harvard University Since the Inauguration of President Eliot, 1869–1929* (1930).

Samuel Eliot Morison, *The Founding of Harvard College* (1935).
Samuel Eliot Morison, *Harvard College in the Seventeenth Century*, 2 vols. (1936).
Samuel Eliot Morison, *Three Centuries of Harvard, 1636–1936* (1936).

Haverford College
Rufus M. Jones, *Haverford College: A History and an Interpretation* (1933).

Hobart College
Haight Milton Turk, *Hobart: The Story of a Hundred Years, 1822–1922* (1921).

Howard University
Walter Dyson, *Howard University: The Capstone of Negro Education* (1941).

Illinois, University of
Richard A. Hatch, *Some Founding Papers* (1967).
Allan Nevins, *Illinois* (1917).
Winton U. Solberg, *The University of Illinois 1867–1894: An Intellectual and Cultural History* (1968).

Illinois College
Charles Henry Rammelkamp, *Illinois College: A Centennial History, 1829–1929* (1928).

Indiana University
Burton Dorr Myers, *History of Indiana University, 1902–1937* (1952).
James Albert Woodburn, *History of Indiana University, 1820–1902* (1940).
T. A. Wylie, *Indiana University, Its History from 1830* (1890).

Iowa State College
Earl D. Ross, *A History of the Iowa State College of Agriculture and Mechanic Arts* (1942).

Iowa Wesleyan College
Herbert N. Jeffrey, *Historical Sketch and Alumni Record of Iowa Wesleyan College* (1917).

Johns Hopkins University
John C. French, *A History of the University Founded by Johns Hopkins* (1946).
Hugh Hawkins, *Pioneer: A History of the Johns Hopkins University, 1874–1889* (1960).

Kansas, University of
Clifford S. Griffin, *The University of Kansas, A History* (1974).

Kansas State College of Agriculture and Applied Science
Julius Terrass Willard, *History of the Kansas State College of Agriculture and Applied Science* (1940).

Kentucky, University of
James F. Hopkins, *The University of Kentucky: Origins and Early Years* (1951).
Helen D. Irvin, *Hail Kentucky! A Pictorial History of the University of Kentucky* (1965).
Charles G. Talbert, *The University of Kentucky: The Maturing Years* (1965).

Knox College
Ernest Elmo Calkins, *They Broke the Prairie* (1937).

Lafayette College
Selden J. Coffin, *The Men of Lafayette* (1891).
David Bishop Skillman, *The Biography of a College: Being the History of the First Century of the Life of Lafayette College*, 2 vols. (1932).

La Salle College
Thomas J. Donaghy, F.S.C., *Conceived in Crisis, A History of La Salle College* (1965).

Lehigh University
Catherine Drinker Bowen, *A History of Lehigh University* (1924).

Louisiana State University
Walter L. Fleming, *Louisiana State University, 1860–1896* (1936).

Macalester College
Daniel Henry Funk, *A History of Macalester College: Its Origin, Struggle, and Growth* (1910).

Maine State College and the University of Maine
Merritt Caldwell Fernald, *History of the Maine State College and the University of Maine* (1916).

Marietta College
Arthur G. Beach, *A Pioneer College: The Story of Marietta* (1935).

Marquette University
Raphael N. Hamilton, *The Story of Marquette University: An Object Lesson in the Development of Catholic Higher Education* (1953).

Maryland, University of
George H. Callcott, *A History of the University of Maryland* (1966).
Eugene Fauntleroy Cordell, *University of Maryland, 1807–1907*, 2 vols. (1909).

Maryville College
Samuel Tyndale Wilson, *A Century of Maryville College, 1819–1919: A Story of Altruism* (1916).

Massachusetts, University of
Harold Whiting Cary, *The University of Massachusetts: A History of One Hundred Years* (1962).

Massachusetts Institute of Technology
Samuel C. Prescott, *When M.I.T. Was "Boston Tech," 1861–1916* (1954).

Miami University
Walter Havighurst, *The Miami Years, 1809–1959* (1958).

Michigan, University of
Elizabeth M. Farrand, *History of the University of Michigan* (1885).
Burke A. Hinsdale, *History of the University of Michigan* (1906).
Howard H. Peckham, *The Making of the University of Michigan, 1817–1967* (1967).
Kent Sagendorph, *Michigan: The Story of the University* (1948).

Michigan State University
Madison Kuhn, *Michigan State: The First Hundred Years* (1955).

Middlebury College
William Storrs Lee, *Father Went to College: The Story of Middlebury* (1936).

Minnesota, University of
James Gray, *The University of Minnesota, 1851–1951* (1951).
C. W. Hall, *The University of Minnesota; An Historical Sketch* (1896).

Mississippi, University of
Allen Cabaniss, *The University of Mississippi: Its First Hundred Years* (1971).

Missouri, University of
Jonas Viles *et al., The University of Missouri: A Centennial History* (1939).

Montgomery College
William Lloyd Fox, *Montgomery College: Maryland's First Community College, 1946–1970* (1970).

Morehouse College
Griffith Benjamin Brawley, *History of Morehouse College* (1917).

Mount Holyoke College
Arthur C. Cole, *A Hundred Years of Mount Holyoke College: The Evolution of an Educational Ideal* (1940).

Nebraska, University of
Robert Platt Crawford, *A History of the College of Agriculture of the University of Nebraska* (1925).

Nevada, University of
Samuel Bradford Doten, *An Illustrated History of the University of Nevada* (1924).

New Hampshire, University of
Philip M. Marston (ed.), *History of the University of New Hampshire, 1866–1941* (1941).

New Mexico State University
Simon F. Kropp, *That All May Learn: New Mexico State University, 1888–1964* (1972).

New York University
Henry M. MacCracken *et al., New York University* (1901).
Theodore F. Jones (ed.), *New York University, 1832–1932* (1933).

North Carolina, University of
Kemp Plummer Battle, *History of the University of North Carolina,* 2 vols. (1907–1912).
David A. Lockmiller, *History of the North Carolina State College of Agriculture and Engineering of the University of North Carolina, 1889–1939* (1939).
William S. Powell, *The First State University: A Pictorial History of the University of North Carolina* (1972).
Louis R. Wilson, *The University of North Carolina, 1900–1930: The Making of a Modern University* (1957).

North Dakota, University of
Louis G. Geiger, *University of the Northern Plains: A History of the University of North Dakota, 1883–1958* (1958).

Northeast Missouri State Teachers College
Lucy Simmons, *History of Northeast Missouri State Teachers College* (1927).

Northwestern University
Estelle Frances Ward, *The Story of Northwestern University* (1924).

Notre Dame, University of
Arthur J. Hope, *Notre Dame: One Hundred Years* (1943).

Oberlin College
John Barnard, *From Evangelicalism to Progressivism at Oberlin College, 1866–1917* (1969).
Robert Samuel Fletcher, *A History of Oberlin College from Its Foundation Through the Civil War,* 2 vols. (1943).

Occidental College
Robert Glass Cleland, *The History of Occidental College, 1887–1937* (1937).

Oglethorpe College
Allen P. Tankersley, *College Life at Old Oglethorpe* (1951).

Ohio State University
James E. Pollard, *History of the Ohio State University: The Story of its First Seventy-Five Years, 1873–1948* (1952).

Ohio University
Thomas N. Hoover, *The History of Ohio University* (1954).

Oklahoma, University of
Roy Gittinger, *The University of Oklahoma, 1892–1942* (1942).

Oregon, University of
Henry D. Sheldon, *History of the University of Oregon* (1940).

Ottawa University
Samuel M. Le Page, *A Short History of Ottawa University* (1929).

Pembroke College
Grace E. Hawk, *Pembroke College in Brown University* (1967).

Pennsylvania, University of
Edward Potts Cheyney, *History of the University of Pennsylvania, 1740–1940* (1940).

Pennsylvania State College
Wayland Fuller Dunaway, *History of the Pennsylvania State College* (1946).

Philadelphia College of Pharmacy and Science
Joseph W. England (ed.), *The First Century of the Philadelphia College of Pharmacy, 1821–1921* (1922).

Pittsburgh, University of
Agnes L. Starrett, *Through One Hundred and Fifty Years* (1937).

Pomona College
Frank P. Brackett, *Granite and Sagebrush: Reminiscences of the First Fifty Years of Pomona College* (1944).
Edith Parker Hinckley and Katharine Norton Benner, *The Dean Speaks Again: Edwin Clarence Norton, Pioneer Dean of Pomona College* (1955).
Charles Burt Summer, *The Story of Pomona College* (1914).

Princeton University
Varnum Lansing Collins, *Princeton* (1914).
George P. Schmidt, *Princeton and Rutgers: The Two Colonial Colleges of New Jersey* (1964).
Thomas Jefferson Wertenbaker, *Princeton, 1746–1896* (1946).

Principia College
Edwin S. Leonard, Jr., *As the Sowing: The First Fifty Years of Principia* (1951).

Purdue University
William Murry Hepburn and Louis Martin Sears, *Purdue University: Fifty Years of Progress* (1943).

Randolph-Macon Woman's College
Roberta D. Cornelius, *The History of Randolph-Macon Woman's College: From the Founding in 1891 Through the Year of 1949–1950* (1951).

Rensselaer Polytechnic Institute
Palmer Chamberlain Ricketts, *History of Rensselaer Polytechnic Institute, 1824–1914* (1932).

Rhode Island, University of
Herman F. Eschenbacher, *The University of Rhode Island* (1967).

Rochester, University of
Jesse Leonard Rosenberger, *Rochester, the Making of a University* (1927).

Rollins College
Alfred J. Hanna, *The Founding of Rollins College* (1935).

Rutgers State University
William H. S. Demarest, *A History of Rutgers College, 1766–1924* (1924).
George P. Schmidt, *Princeton and Rutgers: The Two Colonial Colleges of New Jersey* (1964).

St. Joseph's College
Francis X. Talbot, *Jesuit Education in Philadelphia; St. Joseph's College, 1851–1926* (1927).

St. Louis University
William H. W. Fanning, *Historical Sketch of the St. Louis University* (1908).

San Jose State College
Mrs. Estelle Greathead, *The Story of an Inspiring Past: Historical Sketch of San Jose State Teachers College from 1862 to 1928* (1928).

Smith College
Elizabeth Deering Hanscom and Helen French Green, *Sophia Smith and the Beginnings of Smith College* (1925).

South Carolina, University of
Daniel Walker Hollis, *University of South Carolina,* 2 vols. (1951–1956).

South Dakota State University
William H. Powers (ed.), *A History of South Dakota State College* (1931).

Southern California, University of
Manuel P. Servin and Iris Higbie Wilson, *Southern California and Its University: A History of USC, 1880–1964* (1969).

Stanford University
Orrin Leslie Elliot, *Stanford University: The First Twenty-Five Years* (1937).

Syracuse University
William Freeman Galpin, *Syracuse University, The Pioneer Days* (1952).

Texas A. & M. University
George Sessions Perry, *The Story of Texas A. & M.* (1951).

Trinity College
Glenn Weaver, *History of Trinity College* (1967).

Tufts College
Russell E. Miller, *Light on the Hill: A History of Tufts College, 1852–1952* (1966).

Tulane University
John P. Dyer, *Tulane: The Biography of a University, 1834–1965* (1966).

Tusculum College
Allen E. Ragan, *A History of Tusculum College, 1794–1944* (1945).

Union College
Dixon Ryan Fox, *Union College: An Unfinished History* (1945).
Andrew Van Vranken Raymond (ed.), *Union University: Its History, Influence, Characteristics, and Equipment* (1907).

United States Military Academy
Sidney Forman, *West Point: A History of the U.S. Military Academy* (1950).

United States Naval Academy
Leland P. Lovette, *School of the Sea* (1941).

Valparaiso University
John Strietelmeier, *Valparaiso's First Century: A Centennial History* (1959).

Vanderbilt University
Edwin Mins, *History of Vanderbilt University* (1946).

Vassar College
James Monroe Taylor and Elizabeth Hazelton Haight, *Vassar* (1915).

Vermont, University and State Agricultural College of
Julian Ira Lindsay, *Tradition Looks Forward: The University of Vermont, A History, 1791–1904* (1954).

Virginia, University of
Philip Alexander Bruce, *History of the University of Virginia, 1819–1919* (1920–1922).

Virginia Military Institute
Francis H. Smith, *The Virginia Military Institute, Its Building and Rebuilding* (1912).

Virginia Polytechnic Institute
Duncan Lyle Kinnear, *The First 100 Years: A History of Virginia Polytechnic Institute and State University* (1972).

Wabash College
James I. Osborne and Theodore G. Gronert, *Wabash College: The First Hundred Years, 1832–1932* (1932).

Washington, University of
Charles M. Gates, *The First Century at the University of Washington* (1961).

Washington and Lee University
Ollinger Crenshaw, *General Lee's College: The Rise and Growth of Washington and Lee University* (1969).

Washington State College
Enoch Albert Bryan, *Historical Sketch of the State College of Washington, 1890–1925* (1928).

Wellesley College
Florence Converse, *The Story of Wellesley* (1915).
Florence Converse, *Wellesley College: A Chronicle of the Years, 1875–1939* (1939).
Alice Payne Hackett, *Wellesley: Part of the American Story* (1949).

Wesleyan University
George Matthew Dutcher, *An Historical and Critical Survey of the Curriculum of Wesleyan University and Related Subjects* (1948).
Carl F. Price, *Wesleyan's First Century* (1932).

Western Reserve University
Frederick Clayton Waite, *Western Reserve University: The Hudson Era* (1943).

Westminster College
M. M. Fisher and John J. Rice, *History of Westminster College, 1851–1903* (1903).

Whittier College
Helen W. Ludlow, *Evolution of the Whittier School* (1902).

William & Mary, The College of
Lyon Gardiner Tyler, *The College of William & Mary in Virginia, 1693–1907* (1907).

William Penn College
S. Arthur Watson, *Penn College: A Product and a Producer* (1971).

Williams College
Frederick Rudolph, *Mark Hopkins and the Log: Williams College, 1836–1872* (1956).
Leverett Wilson Spring, *A History of Williams College* (1917).

Winona State College (Minnesota)
Orval Clyde Ruggles, *Winona State Normal School, 1860–1910* (1910).

Wisconsin, University of
Merle Curti and Vernon Carstensen, *The University of Wisconsin: A History, 1848–1925*, 2 vols. (1949).
Wilbur H. Glover, *Farm and College: The College of Agriculture of the University of Wisconsin: A History* (1952).
James F. A. Pyre, *Wisconsin* (1920).

Wisconsin, University of (Milwaukee)
J. Martin Klotsche, *The University of Wisconsin—Milwaukee: An Urban University* (1972).

Wisconsin State University (Whitewater)
Mary Bohi, *A History of Wisconsin State University* (1967).

Wofford College
David Duncan Wallace, *History of Wofford College* (1951).

Wooster, College of
Lucy Lilian Notestein, *Wooster of the Middle West* (1937).

Wyoming, University of
Wilson O. Clough, *A History of the University of Wyoming, 1887–1937* (1937).

Yale University
Russell H. Chittenden, *History of the Sheffield Scientific School of Yale University, 1846–1922*, 2 vols. (1928).
Edgar S. Furniss, *The Graduate School of Yale: A Brief History* (1965).
Ralph Henry Gabriel, *Religion and Learning at Yale: The Church of Christ in the College and University, 1757–1957* (1958).
Brooks M. Kelley, *Yale: A History* (1974).
William Lathrop Kingsley (ed.), *Yale College: A Sketch of Its History*, 2 vols. (1879).
Edwin Oviatt, *The Beginnings of Yale, 1701–1726* (1916).
George Wilson Pierson, *Yale: College and University 1871–1937*, 2 vols. (1952–1955).
Richard Warch, *School of the Prophets: Yale College, 1701–1740* (1973).

Index